£19.50

WOMEN IN THE PRIESTHOOD?

A Systematic Analysis in the Light
Of the Order of Creation and Redemption

MANFRED HAUKE

Women in the Priesthood?

A Systematic Analysis in the Light of
the Order of Creation and Redemption

Translated by
David Kipp

IGNATIUS PRESS   SAN FRANCISCO

Title of the German original:
Die Problematik um das Frauenpriestertum
vor dem Hintergrund der
Schöpfungs- und Erlösungsordnung
© 1986 Verlag Bonifatius-Druckerei, Paderborn

Cover by Roxanne Mei Lum

With ecclesiastical approval
© 1988 Ignatius Press, San Francisco
All rights reserved
ISBN 0–89870–165–1
Library of Congress catalogue number 87–80794
Printed in the United States of America

MATRI BONI CONSILII

GENERAL CONTENTS

PART ONE

The Relevance of the Created Order
To the Question of Female Priests

The Question of Women in the Priesthood
Against the Background of the Order of Redemption

ANALYTICAL CONTENTS

9

PART TWO

The Question of Women in the Priesthood
Against the Background of the Order of Redemption

PREFACE TO
THE AMERICAN EDITION

The position of women in the Church is a vigorously disputed subject today. In particular, the fact that the sacramental priesthood in the Catholic Church is conferred only upon men has aroused strong protest. Is this fact an outdated discrimination or is it an essential matter of faith?

The present work was accepted as a doctoral dissertation by the Theological Faculty of the Ludwig Maximilian University of Munich in 1981. Thanks are owed first of all to Professor Leo Scheffczyk, who supervised the doctoral research with great understanding.

For the encouragement to take up the topic at all, fraught as it is with problems, I must thank Professor Peter Bläser, the former director of the Johann Adam Möhler Institute for Ecumenism in Paderborn.

The work was thus accompanied by an ecumenical concern from the very start, to which I am indebted insofar as I have tried to take due account of the international debate on my topic, including the part played by non-Catholic Christian communities. I have, therefore, placed special value on the biblical foundations of the larger structure of the Catholic Faith, and have proceeded from there in connection with Tradition.

The thesis was first published in Germany in 1982, and the second edition appeared in 1986. This work has met with an extremely lively reception. "Undoubtedly, supporters will celebrate it enthusiastically and opponents will find it a source of irritation"—this was rightly predicted by one of the first reviewers, Dr. Helmut Moll (*Pastoralblatt*, March 1983).

Perhaps the work's most important single contribution, as things turned out, was the analysis of the "command of the Lord" in the First Letter of Paul to the Corinthians (pp. 358ff.) The breadth of the perspective from which the central topic was approached also met with special approval. At issue was not only the isolated question of "Women in the Priesthood?", but also the more general problem of the position of men and women within Christianity. The aim, of course, was not to produce a comprehensive encyclopedia, but rather a summary review of all the relevant aspects of the problem.

Such a summary review seems particularly important given the rise of feminist theology, which advocates the most far-reaching changes in our conceptions of God and man (the ideal goal being "androgyny"; see pp. 39–42, 65–66). Critical confrontation with this theology, which was developed largely in the United States, is a central and recurrent aspect of the work, extending far beyond the chapter on feminist theology itself.

I am very glad that an English edition will now be published in the United States, for here the topic of "women in the Church" is discussed with special fervor. On quite a number of pages, the reader will find references to the American situation and citations from American literature.

The present edition in English corresponds to the second edition published in Germany; some more footnotes and an index have been added.

I am especially thankful to all who have made this extensive publication possible: the staff of Ignatius Press and its editor, Fr. Joseph Fessio, S.J., and the translator, Dr. David Kipp. May this volume contribute to the discovery of the God-given richness of being a man or a woman!

> Dr. Manfred Hauke
> Augsburg, October 15, 1987
> (Feast of Saint Teresa of Avila)

INTRODUCTION

Women in the priesthood is a particularly hotly disputed topic in contemporary theological debate. As a subject of inquiry, it cannot be considered in isolation, since it involves a multitude of factors that make it an exemplary focal point of theological contention. In the course of this work, I will have to show that the topic is connected in many ways with the organic totality of the religious life of the Church.

These interconnections, unfortunately, are seldom given their due in writings about the problem; often, authors content themselves with cursory allusions to changed sociocultural conditions, to which the Church must supposedly adapt. This sort of attitude is especially marked in Protestant circles, from which numerous influences have found their way into Catholic theology:

> "When it comes to practical aspects of service in the church, we do not think much of theological justifications"—these words do not occur in some newspaper article, but in a commentary by a church directorate on the draft of a legislative bill in Hanover about the legal position of female pastors.[1]

With reference to the situation in her hometown, Berlin, the Protestant theologian Eva Senghaas-Knobloch states: "Theological justifications play no role in the supporting arguments [for the ordination of women]. This could be an indication that, in general, exegetic and dogmatic lines of thought lead only to restrictive, or totally negative, results."[2]

This situation is also reflected in the literature of the ecumenical movement. At a conference of the World Council of Churches in 1971, the

[1] Wolfgang Trillhaas (On the subject "the ordination of women" ["Frauenordination"]; untitled), *Lutherische Monatshefte* 1 (1962): 201. In the Danish Lutheran church, ordination of women was introduced even though no ecclesiastical or theological commission had conducted prior inquiry into the matter: Regin Prenter, *Die Ordination der Frauen zu dem überlieferten Pfarramt der lutherischen Kirche* [The ordination of women to the traditional ministry of the Lutheran church], Luthertum 28 (Berlin and Hamburg, 1967), p. 16.

[2] Eva Senghaas-Knobloch, *Die Theologin im Beruf. Zumutung—Selbstverständnis—Praxis* [Women in the theological profession: demands—self-understanding—practice] (Munich, 1969), p. 89.

Presbyterian Ian M. Frazer complained: "What seems lacking to some is a positive theological case for ordaining women. It is agreed that the negative work has been done well, but . . . this . . . is insufficient." Frazer then expressed the opinion that there could not be any theological case for ordaining women and made reference to the ministry of all God's people, which suffices to resolve the matter.[3]

Relevant publications in the Catholic sphere show a predominance of the same sociocultural pattern of thought. Haye van der Meer, in line with his methodology, puts a question mark after all the classical arguments against female priests yet does not attempt to make a positive case for the opposing position: "Perhaps theology should be content to place its trust in the results of secular psychosocial developments."[4]

Thus Karl Rahner, the supervisor of van der Meer's doctoral research, feels able to write in this connection: "The behavior of Jesus and his apostles can be adequately explained by the cultural and social environment of their day, in which they not only acted but could not have acted otherwise than they did."[5]

In Ida Raming's book, the second Catholic monograph on our topic in the German-speaking world, this position emerges even more clearly.[6] Hans Küng formulates it as follows: "The resolution of the problem depends on the general sociological conditions at the time and place concerned. It is fully and wholly a question of the existing cultural circumstances."[7]

There is no need here to criticize these authors' attempts to account for the exclusion of women from the priesthood in terms of restrictive social factors. Such factors certainly deserve extended attention, and the

---

[3] Brigalia Bam, ed., *What Is Ordination Coming to? Report of a Consultation on the Ordination of Women Held in Cardigny, Geneva, Switzerland, 21st–26th September, 1970* (Geneva, 1971), p. 19.

[4] Haye van der Meer, *Priestertum der Frau? Eine theologiegeschichtliche Untersuchung* [Women in the priesthood? A theological-historical study], QD 42 (Freiburg, Basel and Vienna, 1969), p. 176.

[5] Karl Rahner, "Priestertum der Frau?" [Women in the priesthood?], *Stimmen der Zeit* 195 (1977): 299.

[6] Ida Raming, *Der Ausschluss der Frau vom priesterlichen Amt. Gottgewollte Tradition oder Diskriminierung? Eine rechtshistorisch-dogmatische Untersuchung der Grundlagen von Kanon 968 § 1 des Codex Iuris Canonici* [The exclusion of women from priestly office—divinely willed tradition or discrimination? A legal-historical and dogmatic study of the foundations of Canon 968 § 1 of the *Codex iuris canonici*] (Cologne, 1973), pp. 222ff.

[7] In the (unpublished) "Progress Report to the House of Bishops" by the "Community to Study the Proper Place of Women in the Church's Ministry" (1966): Mary Daly, *Kirche, Frau und Sexus* [trans. of: *The Church and the Second Sex*] (Olten, 1970), p. 208. Cf. Hans Küng, "Thesen zur Stellung der Frau in Kirche und Gesellschaft" [Theses on the position of women in church and society], *ThQ* 156 (1976): 132; Hans Küng and Gerhard Lohfink, "Keine Ordination der Frau?" [No ordination of women?], *ThQ* 157 (1977): 144–146.

relevance of their influence will have to be critically examined. What appears questionable is only the reduction of the terms of inquiry to the social situation. Through such reduction, theology basically renounces the use of its own proper cognitive methodology and runs the risk of turning into (amateurishly practiced) sociology.[8]

That sort of approach is, moreover, self-contradictory. Philipp Potter, then secretary-general of the World Council of Churches, stated the following in an address to a meeting: "The Church has certainly perpetuated an image of woman that derives from the myths, customs, stereotypes and prejudices of society."[9]

If it is assumed that the Church's position on women and the priesthood is grounded in socially conditioned prejudices of the past, then present-day theology will have to submit itself to the same sort of critical scrutiny. Might not many modern authors also be caught up in mere stereotyped notions of the day, destined to be rendered obsolete, possibly very soon, by historical change?[10]

On this point, Professor Scheffczyk makes reference to the sociologist P. L. Berger, who, "with a certain drollness", observes: "One . . . redeeming feature of sociological perspective is that relativizing analysis, in being pushed to its final consequence, bends back on itself. The relativizers are relativized; the debunkers are debunked."[11]

Recently, the advocates of so-called feminist theology, which originated mainly in the United States, have tried to develop a positive case for female priests against a more comprehensive background than that of restrictive social factors. This is based on the assumption that the traditional Christian image of God needs to be purged of patriarchal influences, then invested with traits that are either neutral or equally balanced between masculine and feminine. The next step is to derive from this parity in the image of God an argument for parity in the priesthood. In what is to follow, this sort of theology will be taken into account insofar as

[8] Cf. Leo Scheffczyk, "Das Wesen des Priestertums—auf dem Hintergrund der Nicht-ordination der Frau" [The nature of the priesthood—against the background of the non-ordination of women], *Klerusblatt* 58 (1978): 37f.

[9] Philipp Potter, "Address at the Public Meeting", in *Sexism in the 1970s. Discrimination against Women. A Report of a World Council of Churches Consultation*, West Berlin, 1974 (Geneva, 1975), p. 31.

[10] This critical question is raised by the Protestant theologian Peter Brunner in "Das Hirtenamt und die Frau" [The pastorate and woman], *Lutherische Rundschau* 9 (1959/60): 307, and by G. A. Danell, "Die Bibelkommission und die Zulassung der Frau zum Pastorenamt" [The Bible commission and the admission of women to the ministry] in E. Wagner, ed., De Fundamentis Ecclesiae. *Gedenkschrift für Pastor Dr. theol. H. Lieberg* [De Fundamentis Ecclesiae. Commemorative volume for the Reverend H. Lieberg, D.D.] (Brunswick, West Germany, 1973), pp. 156–75.

[11] Cf. P. L. Berger, *Auf den Spuren der Engel* [trans. of: *A Rumour of Angels*] (Frankfurt, 1970), p. 67; Scheffczyk, "Wesen", p. 37.

the general problem of "sexual" traits in the image of God and in the understanding of the Church will be examined.

In a certain sense, the concerns of feminist theology overlap with the objectives of the Roman declaration "On the Question of Admitting Women to the Priesthood".[12] In this document by the Sacred Congregation, the aim is not solely to present arguments based on Scripture and Tradition against the notion of female priests; the positive concern is to take a broad view and to show how the traditional attitude of the Church fits into the total structure of Christian belief. It argues for a connection between exclusion of women from the priesthood, on the one hand, and the mystery of Christ and the Church, on the other. Thus it appeals to all Christians, against the backdrop of the debate about the ordination of women, "to inquire more deeply into the nature and significance of the offices of bishop and priest, and to rediscover the authentic position of the priest in the community of the baptized, to which he himself belongs as a member, yet from which he is also set apart".[13]

The lines of inquiry suggested by the Sacred Congregation will be pursued in this work. In particular, it is very much my hope that thoroughgoing inquiry into the *ratio theologica* will shed additional light not only on the nature of the office of priest but also on the image of God and the meaning of the Church.

This approach effectively meets the requirements set by Haye van der Meer, who was the first in the Catholic sphere to have extensively questioned the classical arguments, although without approaching the problem systematically. In his view, a proper theological solution would require:

1. undertaking a thorough inquiry into the nature of the *sacramentum ordinis* and the office of the bishop;
2. into the Church and the figure of Mary;
3. into the proper use of Scripture and the Church fathers in theology; and
4. taking account of the whole metaphysics, psychology and sociology of man and woman.[14]

An attempt to carry out this demanding program will be made in this book, bearing in mind, however, that the task must be limited here to providing a *summary review* of relevant points from the above-listed areas

---

[12] "Erklärung der Kongregation für die Glaubenslehre zur Frage der Zulassung der Frauen zum Priesteramt" (Verlautbarungen des Apostolischen Stuhls 3) [Declaration of the Sacred Congregation for the Doctrine of the Faith on the question of admitting women to the priesthood (Promulgations of the Apostolic See, 3)], issued by the Sekretariat der Deutschen Bischofskonferenz, 53 Bonn, Kaiserstr. 163; *AAS* 69 (1977): 98–116.

[13] Erklärung Nr. 5 [Declaration no. 5], p. 18; *AAS* 69 (1977): 113.

[14] Meer, *Priesturtum*, p. 13.

(every component of which could, in principle, be expanded to near-encyclopedic dimensions). The aim will be to interrelate all the essential aspects in such a way as to open up a theological "vista" through which, in an exemplary manner, the organic totality of the world of present-day Catholic Faith may be viewed.

Throughout the work, *ratio theologica* will be kept tied as closely as possible to relevant historical material such as we meet with, above all, in Holy Scripture and in early Tradition. Especially in the exegesis of Saint Paul and in the reconstruction of the second century of Church history, facts emerge that are not dealt with in the standard treatises, but that nevertheless possess a considerable—in my opinion, even decisive—relevance.

The scope of the work is restricted to the topic of the possible ordination of women as *priests*. The question of admitting women to the diaconate can only be touched on in an excursus, since it would require a detailed study of its own. As the office of priest (and bishop) is essentially different from that of deacon, however, treating it separately can be justified.[15]

---

[15] Meanwhile, I have also published an article about this subject: Manfred Hauke, "Überlegungen zum Weihediakonat der Frau", *ThGl* 77 (1987), 708–727. English translation: "Observations on the Ordination of Women to the Diaconate" in *The Church and Women*: a compendium in preparation by Ignatius Press.

PART ONE

The Relevance of the Created Order to
The Question of Female Priests

CHAPTER ONE

The Question of the "Emancipation of Women" as a Background to the Theological Debate

I. THE INCREASING PARTICIPATION OF WOMEN IN PUBLIC AFFAIRS

The vehement controversy about the subject of this book would seem to be connected not so much with advances in theological knowledge as with changes in the social sphere. In the wake of developments decisively influenced by the ideals of the French Revolution ("liberty, *equality*, fraternity") and by industrialization, women in the modern world have assumed an increasingly large role in public affairs.[1] More and more areas have been opened up to female endeavor: higher education, politics (the right to vote and to run for office) and numerous new occupations and careers. Much of what we readily take for granted today would have been regarded as monstrous by even our great-grandfathers (for example, a woman as a professor, lawyer or head of government).

In all areas of life, the roles of men and women seem to be becoming more and more similar, while sociological studies such as those by Margaret Mead (about whom more will be said later) have given currency to the view that the vast majority of differences between the sexes are but products of social conditioning.

[1] On the historical development, see Josef Mörsdorf, *Gestaltwandel des Frauenbildes und Frauenberufs in der Neuzeit* [The changing forms of the image and occupation of women in modern times], Münchener Theologische Studien II, 16 (Munich, 1958). The present situation is described in Evelyne Sullerot, *Die Frau in der modernen Gesellschaft* [Women in modern society] (Munich, 1971); Evelyne Sullerot, ed., *Die Wirklichkeit der Frau* [The reality of woman] (Munich, 1979), pp. 594–629; René König, "Die Stellung der Frau in der modernen Gesellschaft" [The position of women in modern society], in *Materialien zur Soziologie der Familie* [Studies in the sociology of the family], 2nd ed. (Cologne, 1974), pp. 253–319.

29

Within the context of trends and assumptions such as these, any and every restriction of women's scope of activity tends to be seen as an instance of unjust "discrimination" and thus as running directly counter to the demand for "equal rights" and "emancipation".

2. "TREND SETTERS" OF "EMANCIPATION"

This climate of opinion is also supported by certain philosophical and political movements, which tend to enter into the theological debate as well, if only below the surface. Two of the most important of these would seem to be socialism and liberalism, whose respective positions on the "question of women" may be roughly outlined as follows.

Socialism

Orthodox Marxism

According to Karl Marx, the main task is not to interpret the world but to change it.[2] This activity of change is effected primarily through "working to transform the material world".[3] Once all unjust power structures have been overthrown, productive labor will supposedly bring society to its culminating state of "communism", in which all forms of "alienation" will have ceased to exist.

In order to achieve this goal, a "new man" must be created who will live for nothing but the social collective and who, as far as possible, will possess exactly the same qualities as all the others. By such means, the "domination of man by man" will supposedly be brought to an end. Any biological and psychological obstacles can be overcome along the way, since a man is nothing more than an "ensemble of social relationships".[4]

Actually, existing structures in man or in the world are not to be taken as guides and standards for action, but as mere material for potentially unlimited transformation.

[2] "Thesen über Feuerbach" [Theses on Feuerbach], in Karl Marx, *Frühe Schriften II* [Early writings II] (Stuttgart, 1971), p. 4.

[3] "Zur Kritik der Nationalökonomie" [Critique of the national economy], in Karl Marx, *Frühe Schriften I* [Early writings I] (Stuttgart, 1962), p. 568.

[4] Marx, "Feuerbach", p. 3.

Such transformation must extend to the relations between men and women. The family and its role structures only reflect the oppression of the proletariat by the capitalist class: "Modern society is grounded on a blatant or concealed domestic enslavement of women, and modern society is a material mass consisting of molecules of numerous individual families. The husband is the *bourgeois* of the family, and the wife represents the proletariat."[5]

Women must be liberated from the constraints of raising children and doing housework, which effectively relegate them to the level of animals, or of "nature". Since man becomes truly human only through socially productive labor, the role of women must be made equivalent to that of men: "the liberation of women" has "as its main precondition . . . the reintegration of the whole female sex into the public industrial sector".[6] According to Engels, private households must, as far as possible, be broken up and children raised by the state.[7]

The first comprehensive treatise on these matters was August Bebel's *Women and Socialism* (1879), which publicized views similar to those just noted, although more moderate in certain points of practical detail.[8] This popular work was regarded by many women of its time as "nearly gospel".[9]

The official teachings of historical materialism are faithfully echoed by the East German writer Helga Hörz: the question of women is a "social question". "Private property in general provides the basis on which the oppression of women is founded."

> Differences in behavior between the sexes are determined not by nature, but by social conditions. There is no eternally fixed female nature, and no scientific justification for any of the specific characteristics attributed to it. The latest research permits only continued adherence to the view that such characteristics are acquired through education and social conditioning.[10]

Attempts at concrete implementation of these ideas and aims have been energetically pursued in Soviet Russia, although certain practical

[5] Friedrich Engels, *Der Ursprung der Familie, des Privateigentums und des Staates* [The origin of the family, private property and the state], 17th ed. (Stuttgart, 1919), p. 62.

[6] Engels, *Ursprung*, p. 62.

[7] Engels, *Ursprung*, p. 64.

[8] August Bebel, *Die Frau und der Sozialismus*, edited with commentary by Monika Seifert (Hannover, 1974).

[9] Marielouise Janssen-Jurreit, *Sexismus. Über die Abtreibung der Frauenfrage* [Sexism: on the aborting of the question of women], 2nd ed. (Munich and Vienna, 1977), p. 213.

[10] Helga Hörz, *Die Frau als Persönlichkeit. Philosophische Probleme einer Geschlechterpsychologie* [Woman as personality: philosophical problems of a psychology of the sexes] (Berlin, 1968), p. 119.

difficulties arose, especially in relation to the family, and certain reversals of policy proved necessary.[11]

"Revisionist" directions

The "revisionist" socialist or social-democratic parties in the Western world, which have come strongly under the sway of the "New Left" since the late sixties, do not consider themselves beholden to the Marxist "church fathers" in the way that their Eastern cousins do, but their views on society take similar directions. The differences between the sexes, and especially any one-sided association of women with the domestic sphere, are seen as undesirable; every human being should be guaranteed equal opportunity in every sociopolitical respect.

A typical example of this attitude is an opinion expressed in 1973 by Swedish Prime Minister Olaf Palme: "No one should be forced into any preconceived role because of his or her sex; rather, all should be afforded better opportunities to develop their personal capabilities."[12]

It is in Sweden, perhaps even more than in the countries of the Eastern bloc, that the policy of "equal rights" for men and women has been taken the furthest. During Olaf Palme's period of office, an "Equal Opportunity Commission", with massive public funds at its disposal, was set up in order to eradicate all instances of unequal treatment. The sociopolitical aim is to make the roles of men and women exactly the same in all areas of work and life. All women should be brought into the work force, and, when necessary, husbands should receive child-support benefits and maternity leave rather than their wives.[13]

A deep-rooted antipathy to conventional social roles is also evident in the [West] German Social Democratic party's study papers on the politics of the family (1975); for example: "Families are relatively permanent communities made up of one adult or more living together with one child or more"[14] and "The raising of children is a task for society as a whole. . . . Responsibility for this task is transferred in our society to families and to extrafamilial institutions."[15]

[11] Sullerot, *Frau*, pp. 81ff.

[12] Una Kroll, *Besondere Kennzeichen: Frau. Sinn und Unsinn einer Frage* [Distinguishing marks: woman. Sense and nonsense of a question] (Aschaffenburg, 1976), p. 130.

[13] Nina Grunenberg, "Was vom Glück bleibt. Beobachtungen in Schweden" [What remains of happiness. Observations in Sweden], *Evangelische Kommentare* 7 (1974): 100–101.

[14] Ursula Erler, *Zerstörung und Selbstzerstörung der Frau. Emanzipationskampf der Geschlechter auf Kosten des Kindes* [Destruction and self-destruction of women: the struggle for emancipation of the sexes at the expense of children] (Stuttgart, 1977), p. 150.

[15] Thus comments a commission of experts appointed by the (West German) federal government in the so-called "Zweiten Familienbericht" [Second report on the family] of

That women should participate in the work force and be self-sufficient is an "unalterable prerequisite . . . to changing society in the direction of democratic socialism".[16]

Liberalism

General characteristics

Alongside the Marxist or quasi-Marxist interpretation of the differences between the sexes, there is one that derives its inspiration from liberalism. Like socialism, this one also tends to aim at achieving equality of the sexes in the social sphere. Although often close to Marxist ways of thinking ("abolition of power structures"), it usually rejects violent imposition of collectivist ideals and relies less heavily on economic models. Its rise coincided with the French Revolution, in the course of which a *"Déclaration des droits de la femme"* (1791) was formulated.[17] Liberal thought characteristically concerns itself with enabling autonomous, self-governing individuals to have the widest possible range of choices when planning their lives.

Simone de Beauvoir

An extraordinary version of this liberalism was developed by Simone de Beauvoir, the longtime companion of the existentialist philosopher Jean-Paul Sartre. Central to Sartre's thought is the notion of "freedom", which is understood as a pure "project": "human beings are nothing but what they make of themselves".[18]

1975: Gottfried Eisermann, "Krise der Familie oder Krise der Gesellschaft?" [Crisis in the family or crisis in society?], in Gerd-Klaus Kaltenbrunner, ed., *Verweiblichung als Schicksal? Verwirrung im Rollenspiel der Geschlechter* [Feminization as destiny? Confusion in the roles of the sexes] (Freiburg, Basel and Vienna, 1978), p. 131. This passage was amended in the following Report on the Family because of strong public criticism. However, it remains symptomatic.

[16] Arbeitsgemeinschaft Sozialdemokratischer Frauen 1975 [Working party of Social Democratic women, 1975], in Erler, *Zerstörung*, p. 139.

[17] The author was Olympe de Gouges, whose ideas were supported by people including Condorcet, sometime president of the National Assembly. Her theses were not, however, successful at the time; for the French revolutionaries, "human rights" were largely "male rights". It was not until the age of industrialization that the "égalité" idea began to be applied more strongly to women. Cf. Hannelore Schröder, ed., *Die Frau ist frei geboren. Texte zur Frauenemanzipation I: 1789–1870* [Women are born free. Texts on the emancipation of women I: 1789–1870] (Munich, 1979), pp. 36–49.

[18] J.-P. Sartre, *Ist der Existentialismus ein Humanismus?* [Is existentialism a humanism?] (Zurich, 1947), p. 14.

For the sake of this freedom, Sartre postulates atheism. If God exists, then there would also be values that exist independently of human "self-making" and that demand concrete realization; there is "no human nature because there is no God to conceive of one".[19]

Obstacles to freedom are posed not only by God but also by other *men*: "With the appearance of the Other's look my state of being an object reveals itself to me."[20]

By means of the presence of "Others", each person also becomes an "Other", an "object" of other persons' wishes and desires. Nevertheless, a hostile attitude to the world around one is necessary if personal self-realization is to occur: ". . . human beings [are] constantly objects for human beings . . . , but conversely, an object cannot be grasped as such apart from a subject that realizes itself as such."[21] This dialectic, then, has markedly tragic implications.

Not only God and the "Other" but also one's own *body* stand in the way of Sartrean "freedom": "It [the body] is the in-itself as surpassed by the for-itself, in the course of which the for-itself, by the very act of surpassing the in-itself, first annihilates and then recomprehends itself."[22] In other words, the body is of value only to the extent that its qualities lose their value for the sake of "freedom". It serves to remind the for-itself—or that human subjectivity that is basically the only valuable thing—that it, as for-itself, is "not its own ground".[23] The body, as mere material for the project of oneself, is a "tool-among-tools-being".[24]

Simone de Beauvoir applies this existentialism to the situation of women. In her book *Le deuxième sexe*,[25] she declares: "One does not arrive in the world as a woman, but one becomes a woman. No biological, mental or economic fate determines the form that a female human being takes on in the womb of society."[26]

The way that she develops Sartre's ideas about the "Other" is typical of de Beauvoir. She says that the tension between one's own subjectivity and the "Other" exists everywhere people live together. While such tension normally implies a relationship of reciprocity, this reciprocity is absent from the relationship between the sexes: "She [the woman] is defined and

[19] Sartre, *Existentialismus*, p. 14.

[20] J.-P. Sartre, *Das Sein und das Nichts. Versuch einer phänomenologischen Ontologie* [Being and nothingness. An essay in phenomenological ontology] (Hamburg, 1962), p. 454.

[21] Sartre, *Existentialismus*, p. 95.

[22] Sartre, *Sein*, p. 405.

[23] Sartre, *Sein*, p. 405.

[24] Sartre, *Sein*, p. 456.

[25] German: "The Other Sex"; literally: "The Second Sex".

[26] Simone de Beauvoir, *Das andere Geschlecht. Sitte und Sexus der Frau* [The other sex: morality and sexuality of women] (Hamburg, 1952), p. 285.

differentiated with reference to the man, but not the man with reference to her; she is the accidental as opposed to the essential. He is the subject, he is the absolute; she is the other."[27]

This self-alienation is felt by the woman not only in the social context but also in her bodily constitution. She is bound to the interests of the species—to the process of pregnancy, birth and child raising—and is therefore a less self-sufficient individual than the man: "of all female mammals, woman is the one that is most subject to self-alienation and that feels this alienation most passionately; in no other case does the procreative function subjugate the body so strongly, nor is it undergone with such difficulty."[28] "From puberty until menopause, she is the staging place for a series of events that take place within her, but have nothing to do with her."[29] "If we compare her lot with a man's, a man seems infinitely more advantaged."[30]

This degrading situation needs to be overcome. De Beauvoir therefore appeals to every human being (and especially every woman) "to rise above all differences of sex and to pride oneself on the difficult glory of one's free existence".[31]

Contrary to what these words suggest, however, her actual ideal is not to become a "human being", but to become a "man". For her, even ten- to 12-year-old girls are "thwarted boys, that is, children that are not permitted to be boys".[32] Consequently, her depiction of female puberty is a veritable horror painting.[33] Logically enough, she goes on to represent the adult woman as an "abortive man".

Like Marx, she bases her understanding of man on the notion of *"homo faber"*:[34] "Because he [the husband] is productively employed, he passes beyond the interests of the family toward those of society and gives the family a future by contributing to building a future for the social whole. He is an embodiment of transcendence. The wife is left with responsibility for preserving the species and managing the household, which means nothing but immanence."[35]

Simone de Beauvoir's position ultimately implies that women can achieve emancipation only by emancipating themselves from their femininity, . . .

[27] Beauvoir, *andere Geschlecht*, p. 10.
[28] Beauvoir, *andere Geschlecht*, p. 47.
[29] Beauvoir, *andere Geschlecht*, p. 44.
[30] Beauvoir, *andere Geschlecht*, p. 47.
[31] Beauvoir, *andere Geschlecht*, p. 712.
[32] Beauvoir, *andere Geschlecht*, p. 310.
[33] Beauvoir, *andere Geschlecht*, pp. 310ff.
[34] Beauvoir, *andere Geschlecht*, p. 86.
[35] Beauvoir, *andere Geschlecht*, p. 432.

which requires that they divest themselves of precisely those characteristics that previously constituted their being as women. . . . Femininity [stands] in the way of becoming a human being . . . , rather than bestowing formative directions for its achievement.[36]

It is difficult to overestimate the influence of de Beauvoir's ideas. The entire women's movement in Europe, and perhaps even more so in the United States, has come under the sway of this "bible of feminism",[37] as has theology itself. The first major publication by Mary Daly, one of the founders of feminist theology, is based largely on de Beauvoir's ideas, which are adopted almost to the letter.[38]

3. CONTEMPORARY FEMINISM

Developments in the United States

The "new" women's movement originated in the United States. Other countries in the Western world have seen parallel developments, often influenced by American "women's liberation", but nowhere equaling its scope and intensity.

At first sight, it seems astonishing that neofeminism[39] should have arisen precisely in a country where women's influence in public affairs has, for decades, been so large as to evoke references to a "matriarchy".[40] The movement for the granting of voting rights to women ("suffragettes"), which was particularly widespread and vocal in the United States, had attained its goals by the end of World War I, and "equal rights" had been largely secured. Throughout the fifties, therefore, "feminism" was regarded as something that lay in the past. Nevertheless, it was not long before general disquiet broke out again, coinciding with the appearance, in 1963, of Betty Friedan's best-seller *The Feminine Mystique*. "The feminine

---

[36] Karen Böhme, *Zum Selbstverständnis der Frau. Philosophische Aspekte der Frauenemanzipation* [On the self-understanding of women. Philosophical aspects of the emancipation of women], Monographien zur philosophischen Forschung 105 (Meisenheim am Glan, 1973), pp. 15, 16.

[37] Alice Schwarzer, in Erler, *Zerstörung*, p. 69.

[38] Cf. especially Daly, *Kirche*, pp. 11ff., 39, 239.

[39] In the United States, the groups referred to here describe their movement as "feminism".

[40] Heinz-Horst Schrey, "Ist Gott ein Mann? Zur Forderung einer feministischen Theologie" [Is God a man? On the question of a feminist theology], *Theologische Rundschau* 44 (1979): 227f.

mystique says that the highest value and the only commitment for women is the fulfilment of their own femininity . . . the new image this mystique gives to American women is the old image: 'Occupation: housewife'."[41]

In Friedan's opinion, being a housewife is synonymous with suppression of one's capacities as a woman, since she proceeds from the assumption "that both sexes have the same innate abilities, even if some of these are destroyed by society".[42] Thus she demands that the roles of men and women be made equivalent: "Women, as well as men, can only find their identity in work that uses their full capacities."[43] Child rearing and housework should be shared equally by husband and wife, so that women are not deterred from having jobs or careers and need not fear being doubly burdened by household duties.[44]

The "old" feminism aimed to achieve "equal rights" as compared with those of men, yet more or less allowed itself to be guided by characteristically "male" standards. This is also (tacitly) the case with the "new" feminism, as evidenced, for example, by Friedan's comments on the "housewife trap".[45] The actual intention, however, is not to conform to any preexisting stereotypes but to set up new ideals and social structures. This goal was elaborated with reference to the economic sphere by Caroline Bird,[46] and in 1966 Betty Friedan herself founded the influential National Organization of Women, whose "Bill of Rights", which provides for the abolition of "discrimination against women", has met with far-reaching success in legal circles.

The rise of the more radical women's liberation movement itself is usually dated at 1968 and is seen as closely linked to the anti-Vietnam demonstrations and student riots of that time, in which neo-Marxist and "antihierarchical" tendencies were connected with a general dissatisfaction with "society".[47] The best-known female protagonist of this movement is Kate Millet, who caused a sensation in 1970 with her work *Sexual Politics*. Taking Marxism as her point of departure, she attempts to radicalize it. She says that the most deep-seated oppressive structure in human society is not domination by the capitalist class but rather by the privileged social position of men. Capitalism is generated by patriarchalism, not vice versa. Apart from the most basic biogenital characteristics, there

---

[41] Betty Friedan, *Der Weiblichkeitswahn oder die Mystifizierung der Frau* [The feminine mystique] (Hamburg, 1966), p. 33.

[42] Friedan, *Weiblichkeitswahn*, p. 92.

[43] Friedan, *Weiblichkeitswahn*, p. 227.

[44] Cf. Friedan, *Weiblichkeitswahn*, pp. 243f.

[45] Friedan, *Weiblichkeitswahn*, p. 227.

[46] "The High Cost of Keeping Women Down", 1968.

[47] Cf. Jutta Menschik, *Feminismus. Geschichte, Theorie, Praxis* [Feminism: history, theory, practice] (Cologne, 1977), pp. 83ff.

are no differences between men and women.[48] In the interest of enabling
the free development of women, Millet (like Engels) calls for the abolition
of the family, for this is the "fundamental instrument and the foundation
unit of patriarchal society".[49]

The claim that sexual differences provide the primary means of oppressing
women is made more strongly still by Shulamith Firestone. In *The
Dialectic of Sex* (1970)—probably the most radical book among the "classics"
of American feminism—she demands the elimination of even the genital
sexual characteristics, because she sees that, even among animals, a certain
subordination of the female results from these differences. The "reproduction of the species"[50] enslaves women, and is "barbaric": "Pregnancy
is the temporary deformation of the body of the individual for the sake of
the species."[51]

Firestone looks to modern biology to provide the means for realizing
her utopia: "Choice of sex of the fetus, test–tube fertilization . . . are just
around the corner."[52]

This hostility toward sexuality manifests itself in certain women's
liberation fringe groups as a radical hatred of men. Valerie Solanas, in her
"Manifesto" of the Society for Cutting Up Men (SCUM), calls for the
creation of a fully automated society in which all money has been
abolished. This would provide the basic conditions for procreation
without any need for men.[53]

For Betsy Warrior, the "stronger sex" is as superfluous as dinosaurs
once were. In the atomic age, the bellicose aggressiveness of men threatens
life itself and has become ecologically intolerable. If the male sex were
exterminated and children produced in laboratories, these dangers, as well
as the evils of the population explosion, would be removed.[54]

A particularly extreme, but now commonly accepted, development of
feminism focuses on concrete sexual behavior. In (excessive) reaction to
certain one-sided theories of Sigmund Freud, which have won many
enthusiastic followers especially in the United States,[55] demands are made

---

[48] Kate Millet, *Sexus und Herrschaft. Die Tyrannei des Mannes in unserer Gesellschaft* [Sexual
politics. The tyranny of men in our society] (Munich, Vienna and Basel, 1971), p. 37.

[49] Millet, *Sexus*, p. 42.

[50] Shulamith Firestone, *Frauenbefreiung und sexuelle Revolution* [The dialectic of sex]
(Frankfurt, 1975), p. 19.

[51] Firestone, *Frauenbefreiung*, p. 185.

[52] Firestone, *Frauenbefreiung*, p. 184.

[53] Menschik, *Feminismus*, p. 53.

[54] Menschik, *Feminismus*, pp. 54f.

[55] Sigmund Freud holds that it is a typical trait of the female sex to envy the characteristics
of males ("penis envy"). His student Helene Deutsch, who has done systematic research into
the "psychology of women", tones down many of her master's theories, but, like him,
characterizes the female soul in terms of three essential traits: narcissism, passivity and

that the male and female roles should be equivalent even in the area of sexual relations. The "traditional" conjugal union of husband and wife is put on a level with "rape", something that has actually spread to a frightening extent in the United States.[56]

As this example shows, "our ability to continue thinking in terms of the male-female couple is obviously decreasing today".[57] A logical consequence of the "anti-Freud campaign" is the massive increase in both male and female homosexuality in the United States. Lesbian women often see themselves as nothing less than the very spearheads of the feminist movement: "feminism in theory and lesbianism in practice".[58]

Social trends toward "androgyny"

The extreme developments of feminism in the United States did not originate in anyone's study but are concrete manifestations of a general increase in "role insecurity" and "role equivalence" in the Western world. In a prosperous and highly technologized society, biological differences seem, at least on the surface, to play a smaller role than ever before. This state of affairs is reinforced by a consciously generated "equality craze", whose results may be seen even in the erotic sphere:

Fashion today dictates that young girls should wear, as their usual form of dress, straight-legged blue jeans and corduroy trousers, skintight and narrow hipped, thus imitating as far as possible the bodily forms of young males.[59]

More and more, we find that the models appearing in women's fashion magazines look young and even "childish", and that aesthetic preference is widely given to . . . a somewhat boyish female type, with small breasts, relatively broad shoulders, slim hips and long legs.[60]

Inasmuch as the biological nature of women cannot adapt to such ideals—for there is no such thing as inheritance of acquired characteristics— "the chubby little daughters of modern prosperity, by the age of fourteen

---

masochism; cf. Helene Deutsch, *Psychologie der Frau I* [Psychology of woman I] (Bern, 1948), p. 5.

[56] On this see Menschik, *Feminismus*, pp. 210ff., and the critical position taken by Richard Huber, "Emanzipation oder Feminismus? Biologische Überlegungen zur Mann-Frau-Beziehung" [Emancipation or feminism? Biological reflections on the man-woman relationship], in Kaltenbrunner, *Verweiblichung*, pp. 68ff.

[57] Erler, *Zerstörung*, p. 102.

[58] This is a familiar slogan of American lesbianism. Cf. Menschik, *Feminismus*, p. 55.

[59] Christa Meves, *Freiheit will gelernt sein* [Freedom has to be learned], 7th ed. (Freiburg, Basel and Vienna, 1978), p. 87.

[60] Huber, "Emanzipation", p. 66.

at the latest, come in for a paralyzing shock: the realization that they cannot fulfill the unwritten ideal".[61] Drawing on her professional experience as an educational psychologist and counselor, Christa Meves describes some heartrending examples of this plight.[62]

When the differences between the sexes are obscured to such an extent, erotic tension tends to be focused, solely and exaggeratedly, on genital sexuality, as Margaret Mead suggests with an example from ethnology.[63] At the same time, the erotic instinct itself becomes less sure, and there is a veritable "boom" in homosexuality.

Developments of this sort, which can only be hinted at here, seem to be converging more and more clearly of late on an androgynous, or "man-woman", ideal. The notion of an "androgynous utopia"[64] may be understood either as a purely imagined goal or as a biological postulate.

In his own day, the psychoanalyst C. G. Jung put forward the theory that modern society suffers from repression of the feminine aspects of the human soul. Masculine and feminine qualities are common to both sexes and need to be integrated into a harmonious totality in everyone. To be sure, Jung occasionally stresses that this totality would need to be differently accentuated in each sex,[65] but, in practice, his ideas have been largely interpreted as supporting the ideal of androgynous equivalence.[66]

At the close of an international colloquium on "The Reality of Woman" in 1978, Evelyne Sullerot called attention to the generally widespread wish "to overcome traditional dualisms, a wish in which the search for the unity of the human being expresses itself".[67]

This sort of postulate is perfectly compatible with an emphasis on feminine characteristics, but these are then understood as general human characteristics. In the United States, meanwhile, numerous publications have sprung up that elaborate this androgynous ideal in greater detail.[68] Often enough, preference is given to the feminine qualities, as, for example, in so-called ecofeminism, which aims to protect the earth with

[61] Meves, Freiheit, p. 87.

[62] Meves, Freiheit, pp. 86ff.

[63] Margaret Mead, Mann und Weib. Das Verhältnis der Geschlechter in einer sich wandelnden Welt [Male and female. A study of the sexes in a changing world] (Hamburg, 1977), p. 81.

[64] As described in Huber, "Emanzipation", p. 67.

[65] For example, "Die Frau in Europa" [Women in Europe], in C. G. Jung, Gesammelte Werke X [Collected works X], (Olten and Freiburg, 1974), p. 140: "in men . . . the feminine [exists] in the background, as does the masculine in women. . . . A man ought to live as a man, and a woman as a woman."

[66] On Jung, cf. pp. 128–133 below.

[67] Sullerot, Wirklichkeit, p. 636.

[68] Cf. Barbara Haber, Women in America. A Guide to Books, 1963–1975 (Boston, 1978), pp. 33, 117, 147.

"motherly" care from technological pillage and extols a consciously "antimasculine" counterculture.[69]

A special contribution to androgynous thought is made by Ernest Bornemann, whose book *Patriarchy* is intended to do for the women's movement what Marx' *Capital* did for the workers' movement.[70] According to Bornemann, the "classless society of the future" will have to go hand in hand with the "sexless future of our species". "The one is unattainable without the other."[71]

Not long ago, in German feminist circles, a work called *The Nature of Woman in the Male State and the Nature of Man in the Female State* by Mathias and Mathilde Vaerting (1921) was "rediscovered and triumphantly celebrated".[72] According to the Vaertings' "reversal, or pendulum, theory",[73] even the biological differences between the sexes, with the exception of the female's childbearing capacity, are but products of social conditioning. Throughout history, there has been a constant oscillation between female and male rule, and sexual characteristics have been attributed according to the given power structure. "It is always the subordinate sex that is charged with managing the household and caring for the family . . . , with feeding and minding the babies . . . ; it possesses the more voluptuous bodily forms . . . and the greater sense of sexual modesty."[74]

An especially zealous champion of these ideas is Alice Schwarzer, according to whom "the childbearing capacity . . . [is] the sole remaining difference between men and women. Everything else is artificially acquired, a matter of how one's personal identity is formed".[75]

The effects of "androgynous" thought on the Church

The trends discussed above have not been without their effects on the Church. Haye van der Meer thinks that "it has not yet been clearly

---

[69] Günter Bartsch, "Achsenverlagerung. Von den Suffragetten zum Öko-Feminismus" [Shift of the axis: from the suffragettes to ecofeminism], in Kaltenbrunner, *Verweiblichung*, pp. 102f.

[70] Ernest Bornemann, *Das Patriarchat. Ursprung und Zukunft unseres Gesellschaftssystems* [Patriarchy: origin and future of our social system] (Frankfurt, 1975), p. 7.

[71] Bornemann, *Patriarchat*, p. 21.

[72] Menschik, *Feminismus*, p. 120.

[73] Mörsdorf, *Gestaltwandel*, p. 142.

[74] Mörsdorf, *Gestaltwandel*, pp. 142f.; also gives precise sources and references pertaining to the reception that the fanciful theories published by Vaerting met with in the scientific community.

[75] Alice Schwarzer, *Der kleine Unterschied und seine grossen Folgen* [The small difference and its great consequences], 2nd ed. (Frankfurt, 1977), p. 193.

decided just what characteristics make up timelessly valid types of the masculine and the feminine".[76] Masculine qualities can be definitive of women, and feminine of men. Along with C. G. Jung, he interprets the increasing equivalence of sexual roles as a secular event marking the historical progress of the Church toward the "fullness of eschatological time", after which all differences between human beings will become irrelevant.[77]

Ida Raming's anthropological conclusions are based on a writing by Mathilde Vaerting containing ideas similar to those noted above. Vaerting is cited by Raming so frequently—and always with approval—that she might be regarded as nothing less than an "auctor probatus". In a similar spirit, Raming also cites the following by S. Hunke: "What we label as 'masculine' or 'feminine' is a product of our culture and can no more claim universal validity than can the dogma of a polar opposition between the sexes."[78]

At the level of the so-called basis, even more drastic pronouncements are occasionally made. During an interview with Karl Rahner, the Catholic writer Anita Röper declared: "Until the time when human beings are produced in laboratories, instead of having to be brought into the world by women, men will have an essential advantage over women, and they will exploit it. Until that time, then, the notion of 'equal rights' will remain an unrealizable dream."[79]

In 1979, a conference was held at the Catholic Academy of Munich on the topic "The Emancipation of Women: Between Biology and Ideology". In the course of his contribution, one biologist made the cautiously formulated suggestion "that it might, perhaps, be the case that the female sex is naturally endowed with an emotional orientation toward 'caring for the brood' in connection with the raising of children". This conjecture met with such violent debate that the astonished biologist was moved to comment: "The reaction could not have been worse if I had said that women all have the itch."[80]

[76] Meer, Priesturtum, p. 168.

[77] Meer, Priesturtum, p. 196.

[78] S. Hunke, Am Anfang waren Mann und Frau [In the beginning were man and woman] (Hamm, 1955), p. 261; Raming, Ausschluss, pp. 223f., n. 5.

[79] Anita Röper, Ist gott ein Mann? Ein Gespräch mit Karl Rahner [Is God a man? A conversation with Karl Rahner] (Düsseldorf, 1979), p. 51.

[80] Erika Weinzierl, ed., Emanzipation der Frau. Zwischen Biologie und Ideologie [Emancipation of women: between biology and ideology] (Düsseldorf, 1980), p. 93.

4. "ROLE THINKING" AND ITS BEARING ON THE QUESTION OF WOMEN PRIESTS

The contemporary debate about the bases of the relationship between men and women thus tends to proceed on the assumption that the differences between the sexes are rooted solely in sociological circumstances, that is, in changeable, and largely exchangeable, social "roles". This tendency to "role thinking" goes along with a demand for equivalence in the tasks and duties of men and women, for a more-or-less thoroughgoing "androgynous utopia".

Whether, or to what extent, the Church can reconcile herself to this sort of outlook will be examined later. If, however, the theological response to the question of women in the priesthood depends ultimately on the currently dominant stream of ideas in the world—as the authors surveyed above and widespread opinion in theological circles would both suggest— the solution to the problem would be of a purely pragmatic sort. Any continued refusal to allow women to serve as priests would be seen as a rigid clinging to outmoded cultural traditions, as well as an effective blocking of the "openness to the world" that was encouraged by the Second Vatican Council. Moreover, it would involve the risk—reminiscent of what occurred once before when the labor question was ignored—of depriving the Church of important avenues of influence. Many committed women could become alienated from the Church, and, at a time when there is a catastrophic shortage of priests, such rigidity would only leave numberless Catholics bereft of spiritual care and support.[81]

[81] Cf. J.-M. Aubert, *La femme. Antiféminisme et christianisme* [Woman: antifeminism and Christianity] (Paris, 1975), p. 177.

CHAPTER TWO

The Controversy about Ordination of Women in the Non-Catholic Sphere

Since the Second Vatican Council, contemporary Catholic theology has become involved in a process of close interchange with non-Catholic influences, especially from the Protestant sphere. Indeed, it is in Protestant circles that the question of the admissibility of women to religious office was first raised for debate. Experience shows that the more "Protestant" a church community is, the more quickly and clearly it will assent to the ordination of women. In many sects and independent churches in the United States, women have participated in "offices", including that of preacher, since the nineteenth century, and additional areas were opened to them in the fifties and sixties of this century.

1. THE LUTHERAN CHURCH IN SWEDEN AS "TREND SETTER"[1]

The general trend for developments throughout the world was set by the Lutheran church in Sweden. Members of the clergy there are employees of the state, and the Swedish government thus found itself faced with the embarrassing fact that it was permitting discrimination against women within its own administrative ranks, although the abolition of such

---

[1] On the points discussed here, compare especially: Bo Reicke, "Schwedische Diskussion über die Zulassung von Frauen zum Pfarramt" [The Swedish debate on the admission of women to the ministry], *Theologische Literaturzeitung* 77 (1952): 184–188; Sten Rodhe, "Schwedische Meinungsverschiedenheiten über die Ordination von Frauen zum Pfarramt" [Differences of opinion in Sweden about the ordination of women to the ministry], *Lutherische Rundschau* 7 (1957/58): 421–36 and 8 (1958/59): 470–78; F. R. Refoulé, "Le problème des 'femmes-prêtres' en Suède", *Lumière et Vie*, 43 (1959): 65–99; Bo Giertz "Die Heilige Schrift, die Frau und das Amt des Pfarrers" [Holy Scripture, woman and the office of minister], *Informationsblatt für die Gemeinden in den Niederdeutschen Lutherischen Landeskirchen* 10/13 (1961): 205–9; Bo Giertz, "Treue, Freiheit und Einmütigkeit" [Fidelity, freedom and

discrimination was called for by the United Nations "Charter on Human Rights" of 1948. Sweden, of course, likes to see itself as leading the way toward a society fully characterized by the ideals of "liberty, equality and fraternity".

After an unsuccessful proposal to remedy the situation was made by a governmental commission in 1923, the entire public was mobilized to resolve the question of the ordination of women. All the women's organizations, from the Socialists to the ladies of the conservative Farmers' party, agitated in favor of female pastors. The clergy, on the other hand, adopted a rather reserved attitude. Many, especially younger, clergymen even came out in strong opposition to the ordination of women. This opposition drew much of its strength from a "new" theology, influenced by the Anglican High church, whose adherents produced numerous studies—particularly of an exegetical nature—with "Catholic" tendencies that effectively shocked some sections of the public.

As early as the fifties, then, Sweden was already a virtual "exercise ground" for arguments pro and contra women in the priesthood. In my opinion, there can hardly be a single line of thought, including specifically Catholic ones, that has not already been discussed through and through there.

By 1958, the general synod was finally forced to make a decision on the matter. A majority of the strongly politically motivated lay members voted for introducing ordination of women, as did—after initial hesitation—a majority of the bishops, while a large portion of the ministers rejected the proposal.

Thus the conditions were created for the first ordinations of women, which took place on Palm Sunday in 1960. "Conservative" resistance from within the clergy was still so strong, however, that these ordinations

---

unanimity], in H.-F. Richter, ed., *Die kommende Ökumene* [The coming church unity] (Wuppertal, 1972), pp. 127–36; Danell, "Bibelkommission"; Kerstin Berglund [The witness and experience of] "The Swedish Lutheran Church", in Michael Hamilton and Nancy Montgomery, eds., *The Ordination of Women: Pro and Con* (New York, 1975), pp. 102–10; H.-L. Hass, "Bericht von der Synode der schwedischen Kirche" [Report on the synod of the Swedish church], in *Brüdern. Rundbrief für Christen Augsburgischen Bekenntnisses* 30 (5/1979), Sonderbeilage; Ulf Inge Löfström, "Frauen auf der Kanzel. Probleme der schwedischen Kirche" [Women in the pulpit: problems of the Swedish church], *Evangelische Kommentare* 12 (1979): 28, 33–34; KNA-Informationsdienst Nr. 5, 1. 2. 79, 309; *Swedish writings on the ordination of women that have come to our attention*, in Bertil Gärtner, *Das Amt, der Mann und die Frau im Neuen Testament* [Office, man and woman in the New Testament] (Bad Windsheim, 1963); Nils Johansson, *Women and the Church's Ministry. An Exegetical Study of 1 Corinthians 11–14* (Ottawa, 1972); Krister Stendahl, "Die biblische Auffassung von Mann und Frau" [The biblical conception of man and woman], in Elisabeth Moltmann-Wendell, ed., *Menschenrechte für die Frau, Christliche Initiativen zur Frauenbefreiung* [Human rights for women: Christian initiatives for the liberation of women] (Munich, 1974), pp. 147–61.

brought the Lutheran church to the very brink of schism. Up to the present, this situation remains unchanged and may even have worsened. Many younger theologians refuse to be ordained together with women or to work together with them in the ministry. When the decision in favor of ordaining women was taken in 1958, numerous ministers resigned, and theology students abandoned their studies. Swedish exegesis—about which more will be said later[2]—is largely responsible for this development. Thus, in 1972, a sympathizer with these (by liberals so-called) woman-haters was moved to write about them: "Their morale is unbroken; they have the confidence of the faithful. In spite of constant pressure, they appear to be the victors!"[3]

The conflicts over this issue in Sweden, then, are far from having reached an end, and future developments in the Lutheran church there may well contain some surprises.

2. DEVELOPMENTS IN OTHER PROTESTANT DENOMINATIONS

The debate in the Protestant churches of the German-speaking region, where resistance to the ordination of women is less strong, has unfolded rather differently. Dialectical theology, and in particular Karl Barth, served to prepare the way. Although Barth himself adheres to the principle of a "subordinate" role for women, his student Charlotte von Kirschbaum— whose writings her mentor describes as continuing the line of his own thought—adds to this a call for female ministers, claiming that they are needed under present-day conditions if the church is to reverse its declines in membership. This sort of consideration has made the decision for change easier for many "conservatives".[4] An even more important factor than the theological developments was, of course, that of praxis: because numerous clergymen were absent from their parishes during the Second World War, pastoral duties were often taken over by women. What was first seen as a provisional necessity was later to be made official practice.

Widely noted reservations about the ordination of women were ex-pressed by Peter Brunner, who joined the idea of the "cephalo-structure" of the relationship between the sexes to the argument from "represen-tation" (a minister acts in place of Christ),[5] and by the bishop of Bavaria,

[2] Cf. pp. 364, 474f. below.

[3] Johansson, *Women*, p. 10.

[4] Eva Beyse-Jentschura, "Pfarrerin—ein attraktiver Frauenberuf?" [Minister—an attrac-tive profession for women?], *Deutsches Pfarrerblatt* 77 (1977): 635. On Barth and Kirschbaum, cf. pp. 75–80 below.

[5] Brunner, "Hirtenamt".

Hermann Dietzfelbinger, who succeeded in preventing the ordination of women in Bavaria as long as he was in office.[6]

Since then, almost all the regional branches of the German Evangelical church have accepted the ordination of women,[7] and the opponents of this practice—as seen from the perspective of a Lutheran supreme consistory —are engaged in a rearguard action.[8]

With regard to the Lutheran church in the United States, the situation is similar, even if the rearguard fighters (Missouri Synod) are more formidable there.

The Evangelical theologian Erika Reichle comments as follows on developments in the Protestant sphere:

> The admission of female theologians to the ministry became possible only after two decisions had been taken that signified a break with centuries-old conceptions of order in church and society: the binding force of the orthodox image of woman was renounced, and all Catholic-like tendencies in the understanding of clerical office were rejected. One might even . . . say [that the] . . . admission of women to the ministry . . . ensures that the self-understanding implicit in the Reformation's foundations is also expressed, more than before, in its organizational structures.[9]

What seems to be meant here by the Reformation's self-understanding is particularly the rejection of a special priesthood in the Catholic sense.[10]

---

[6] Hermann Dietzfelbinger, "Vom Dienst der Frau in der Kirche" [On women's service in the Church], in *Christus praesens. Vorträge, Aufsätze, Predigten* [*Christus praesens*. Lectures, essays, sermons] (Munich, 1968), pp. 156–75.

[7] The sole exception is the tiny Schaumburg-Lippe regional church; cf. *Amtsblatt der EKD* 31 (1977), Statistische Beilage Nr. 53.

[8] From a letter to Prof. Peter Bläser.

[9] Erika Reichle, *Die Theologin in Württemberg. Geschichte-Bild-Wirklichkeit eines neuen Frauenberufes* [The female theologian in Württemberg. History, form and actuality of a new profession for women], Europäische Hochschulschriften XXIII 35 (Bern and Frankfurt, 1975), p. 359.

[10] In this section I have limited myself mainly to developments in the German Evangelical church. On the historical background and "taking stock", see especially: Peter Bläser, "Liturgische Dienste und die Ordination von Frauen in nichtkatholischen Kirchen" [Liturgical services and the ordination of women in non-Catholic churches], *Liturgisches Jahrbuch* 28 (1978): 155–69; Maria Hermann, "Theologinnen der älteren Generation" [Female theologians of the older generation], *Deutsches Pfarrerblatt* 74 (1974): 660–62; Senghaas-Knobloch, *Theologin*, pp. 27–39; Reichle, *Theologin*; Reichle, "Die Theologin im Pfarramt in der BRD" [The female theologian in the ministry in the Federal Republic of Germany], *Lutherische Rundschau* 25 (1975): 62–68; Beyse-Jentschura, "Pfarrinen"; *Die Frau in Familie, Kirche und Gesellschaft* [Woman in family, church and society], issued by a committee of the German Evangelical church, 2nd ed. (Gütersloh, 1980), pp. 138–45; Susanne Kahl, "Die Situation der Pfarrerin. 'Eine Frau als Pastor kann nicht väterlich sein, aber Gott ist Vater' " [The situation of the female minister. "A woman as pastor cannot be fatherly, but God is the Father"], in Susanne Kahl, ed., *Die Zeit des Schweigens ist vorbei. Zur Lage der Frau in der Kirche*

3. ANGLICANISM

Some interesting perspectives are also provided by developments in the Anglican church, which sees itself, in the ecumenical sphere, as a mediator between Protestantism and Catholicism. When, in 1944, the bishop of Hong Kong ordained a woman for Macao, where no "priest" was otherwise available, this led, in 1948, to condemnation of the decision by the Lambeth Conference, on the grounds that it ran counter to Tradition and also prejudiced ecumenical relations. The ordained woman herself, meanwhile, had resigned voluntarily two years before.[11]

Another chapter unfolded at the Lambeth Conference in 1968, where a

---

[The time for silence is past. On the situation of women in the Church] (Gütersloh, 1979), pp. 90–99.

A summary of the situation at the world level is given by: J. E. Lynch, "The Ordination of Women: Protestant Experience in Ecumenical Perspective", *JEcSt* 12 (1975): 173–97. On the situation in the United States, see Elsie Gibson, *Femmes et ministères dans l'Église* (Tournai, 1971); J. H. Smylie, [The witness and experience of] "The Protestant Churches", in Hamilton and Montgomery, *Ordination*, pp. 82–99.

A selection of Protestant statements on the ordination of women:

Pro: Ernst Wolf, "Das Frauenamt in Amt der Kirche" [The office of women in the office of the Church], in *Peregrinatio II* (Munich, 1965), pp. 179–90 (Referat von 1942 [Paper from 1942]); Charlotte von Kirschbaum, *Die wirkliche Frau* [The real woman] (Zollikon and Zurich, 1949), pp. 51ff.; Charlotte von Kirschbaum, *Der Dienst der Frau in der Wortverkündigung* [The part of women in preaching God's word], Theologische Studien 31 (Zollikon and Zurich, 1951); Gerhard Heintze, "Das Amt der Pastorin" [The office of the female pastor], *EvTh* 22 (1962): 509–35; Helmut Thielicke, "Exkurs: Die Frau im Verkündigungsamt der Kirche" [Excursus: women in the office of church preacher], in *Theologische Ethik III* (Tübingen, 1964), pp. 689–95; Walter Rupprecht, *Der Dienst der Theologin–eine ungelöste Frage in der evangelischen Kirche* [The role of the female theologian—an unsolved problem in the Protestant church], Arbeiten zur Theologie I 19 (Stuttgart, 1965); Ilse Bertinetti, *Frauen im geistlichen Amt. Die theologische Problematik in evangelisch-lutherischer Sicht* [Women in spiritual office. The theological problem from the Protestant and Lutheran viewpoint], Theologische Arbeiten 21 (Berlin, 1965); Stendahl, "Auffassung", pp. 147–61; W. H. Ritter, " 'Das Weib schweige in der Gemeinde . . .'? Bermerkungen zu einem umstrittenen Thema" ["Women should keep silence in the churches . . ."? Remarks on a controversial topic], *Deutsches Pfarrerblatt* 77 (1977): 501–6; Reinhard Frieling, "Rom gegen die Frauenordination. Belastung für die Ökumene?" [Roman opposition to the ordination of women—difficulty for the ecumene?], *Lutherische Monatshefte* 16 (1977): 130–31.

Contra: Giertz, "Schrift"; Gärtner, *Amt*; Dietzfelbinger, "Dienst"; Brunner, "Hirtenamt"; J.-J. von Allmen, "Est-il légitime de consacrer des femmes au ministère pastoral?" in *Prophétisme sacramental* (Neuchâtel, 1964), pp. 247–83; G. G. Blum, "Das Amt der Frau im Neuen Testament" [The office of woman in the New Testament], *Novum Testamentum* 7 (1964/65): 142–61; Prenter, *Ordination*; Johansson, *Women*; Walter Reissinger, "Die Frau und das Amt in der Kirche" [Women and office in the Church], in H.-F. Richter, ed., *Die kommende Ökumene* [The coming church unity] (Wuppertal, 1972), pp. 147–62.

[11] Christian Howard, "'Ordination of Women in the Anglican Communion and the Ecumenical Debate", *The Ecumenical Review* 29 (1977): 234f.

relevant commission of inquiry decided that it could find no conclusive reasons against the ordination of women. This formulation of the commission's findings was revised by the plenary session along the lines that, so far, there were no conclusive reasons either for or against the ordination of women, and thus that further studies would have to be carried out.[12]

The following years were characterized by an attitude of "anticipatory obedience". In 1971, the bishop of Hong Kong ordained two women, and this step was sanctioned in the same year by the Anglican Consultative Council, albeit by a very small majority. This was confirmed by the Lambeth Conference in 1978, which gave general assent to the ordination of women.[13] As in Sweden, resistance to the decision came mainly from the ranks of the ministry, whereas the majority of bishops and laymen were in favor of it. At the English general synod in 1978, the blocking minority of "priests" was even so strong that, for the time being, there are no "lady priests" in the country where Anglicanism originated.[14] The crucial factors behind the English position were not only considerations of principle, but also, and especially, a concern for ecumenical relations with the Catholic and Orthodox churches, which no one wanted to prejudice unnecessarily.

Also noteworthy here is the situation in the United States, where, in 1974, eleven illegal ordinations took place that were subsequently sanctioned, in 1976, by the relevant synod. This occasioned a split within the church, and the opponents of the ordination of women established their own community.[15]

[12] Howard, "Ordination", p. 235.

[13] *HK* 32 (1978): 494f.

[14] *HK* 32 (1978): 645; 40 (1986): 367f.; 41 (1987): 12f.

[15] On the historical development, see, in addition to the cited article by Howard, especially Hugh McCullum, "The Experience in Anglicanism": Hamilton and Montgomery, *Ordination*, pp. 136–51, and Michael Perry, "Why Not Now?" in Hugh Montefiore, ed., *Yes to Women Priests* (Great Wakering, 1978), pp. 73–88.

The first extensive debates already took place during the period between the two World Wars. The way to ordaining female priests began to be prepared in 1920 with the official introduction of deaconesses; in 1968, the Lambeth Conference, in line with a controversial study paper from 1920 (!), decided to include deaconesses in the "Holy Orders" on a par with male deacons. An important forward-pushing role seems to have been played by the frequent use of women as altar assistants, lectors and acolytes as well as by the training of the two sexes in common at theological seminaries: Emily Hewitt and Suzanne R. Hiatt, *Women Priests: Yes or No?* (New York, 1973), p. 15; Daniel Corrigan, "Why I Ordained a Woman in Philadelphia", in Hamilton and Montgomery, *Ordination*, p. 58. A good insight into the Anglican *debate*, which, in many respects, is as similar to the Catholic as one egg to another, is provided by: *Report of the Archbishops' Commission on Women and Holy Orders* (London, 1966); Hamilton and Montgomery, *Ordination*.

Besides the contributions in those collections, I would also like to mention:

Pro (ordination of women): M. E. Thrall, *The Ordination of Women to the Priesthood. A*

4. ORTHODOXY

An almost unanimous rejection of the ordination of women may be found in the Orthodox churches. Their attitude is given characteristic expression by the archbishop of Great Britain, Athenagoras of Thyateira, saying that the demand for female priests is a "contemporary fashion which over-throws the evangelical order and the experience of the Church".[16]

The explanation for this attitude seems to lie, to a singular extent, with the fervent and unchangingly timeless liturgy of the Orthodox church:

> In offering the unbloody sacrifice . . . , the bishop (or the priest . . .) becomes . . . the icon of the Word incarnate. It is this iconic character of the figure of the priest in Orthodox worship that, it seems to me, embodies the strongest argument against the admission of women to the . . . sacramental priesthood.[17]

On the other hand, it is precisely any hint of the sacred in the priesthood that often causes advocates of the ordination of women to "shudder".[18]

Study of the Biblical Evidence (London, 1958); Hewitt and Hiatt, *Women Priests*; Report of the Working Party set up jointly by the Ministry Committee of the Advisory Council for the Church's Ministry and the Council for Women's Ministry in the Church, in *Women in Ministry* (London, 1968); Alan Richardson, "Women and the Priesthood", in *Lambeth Essays on Ministry* (London, 1969), pp. 75–78; Montefiore, *Yes*.

Contra: C. S. Lewis, "Priestesses in the Church?" in *Undeceptions. Essays on Theology and Ethics* (London, 1971), pp. 191–96; E. L. Mascall, *Women Priests?* (Westminster, 1972); Michael Bruce and G. E. Duffield, eds., *Why Not? Priesthood and the Ministry of Women* (Appleford Abington Berkshire, 1972); also worthy of attention is the well-documented article by the Old Catholic Kurt Pursch, "Frauen als Priester" [Women as priests], *Internationale Kirchliche Zeitschrift* 63 (1973): 129–67.

[16] Howard, "Ordination", p. 246. Cf. the strongly committed "Orthodox Statement on the Ordination of Women from the Orthodox-Anglican Consultation", in Hamilton and Montgomery, *Ordination*, pp. 175f.; and, similarly, the contribution by John Meyendorff [The witness and experience of] "The Orthodox Churches", in Hamilton and Montgomery, *Ordination*, pp. 128–34, which also includes additional American material. Also noteworthy are the contributions by N. Chitescu and G. Khodre to the WCC collection *Zur Frage der Ordination der Frau* [On the question of the ordination of women], Studien des Ökumenisichen Rates der Kirchen 1 (Geneva, 1964), pp. 67–71, 72–75.

[17] Elisabeth Behr-Sigel, "The Participation of Women in the Life of the Church", in Ion Bria, ed., *Martyria/Mission. The Witness of the Orthodox Churches Today* (Geneva, 1980), p. 59. Cf. also Paul Evdokimov, *Die Frau und das Heil der Welt* [Woman and the salvation of the world] (Munich, 1960), pp. 237f.: to involve woman in the priesthood—"that would be to betray her very nature". For Evdokimov, *Christ* and *Mary* are, so to speak, "icons" that indicate symbolically the positions of man and woman in the Church.

[18] So says the Dutch Catholic theologian Tine Govaart-Halkes, "Die Frau in Kirche und Pfarrdienst" [Woman in Church and ministry], in *Kirche in Freiheit. Gründe und Hintergründe des Aufbruchs in Holland* [Church in freedom. Reasons and deeper reasons for the upheaval in Holland] (Freiburg, Basel and Vienna, 1970), p. 111.

Two Anglican theologians, Emily C. Hewitt and Suzanne R. Hiatt, take a defensive attitude toward the unconscious structures of the soul to which the liturgy appeals. "Christ has freed us . . . from the 'powers and principalities', the evil forces beyond our control."[19]

5. THE WORLD COUNCIL OF CHURCHES

During the past few decades, the World Council of Churches (WCC) in Geneva has proven itself an especially effective instrument for furthering the debate.[20] Its guidelines on the "question of women" were drawn up as early as its inaugural session in Amsterdam in 1948: "The Church consists of both men and women, and both have the same degree of personal worth, even if this fact is often disregarded in practice."[21]

Since then, the question of the ordination of women has been pursued especially strongly by two bodies within the WCC: the "Commission for Faith and Order" and (as it is called at present) the "Department on Cooperation of Men and Women in Church, Family and Society". An initial large-scale study by both appeared in 1964. Apart from the authors of two Orthodox contributions, all those involved spoke out more-or-less clearly in favor of the ordination of women.[22] The "Department on Cooperation of Men and Women", in particular, subsequently became very active in pursuit of this cause.[23] A characteristic example was the conference in 1970 on "What Is Ordination Coming To?" held in res-

[19] Hewitt and Hiatt, *Women Priests*, p. 100. More will be said about this problem in my treatment of the symbolism of priestly representation; cf. pp. 193–94 below.

[20] More and more, the Orthodox church takes up the topic systematically. A prominent example: Thomas Hopko, ed., *Women and the Priesthood* (Crestwood, New York), 1983. A very strong rejection of female priesthood appears in the "Declaration of Athens" in 1978, the official report of a special session of the Common Anglican-Orthodox Theological Commission. The orthodox theologians state that the "foundation of Christian faith" is at stake; the ordination of women priests is "a violation of the apostolic faith and of the apostolical order in the church". Women priests in Anglicanism are a "disastrous rollback" for the ecumenical dialogue: *Dokumente* wachsender Übereinstimmung. Sämtliche Berichte und Konsenstexte interkonfessioneller Gespräche auf Weltebene, 1931–1982, ed. by H. Meyer et al. (Paderborn, 1983), pp. 91–93 (Documents of increasing agreement. All reports and texts of consensus of inter-denominational talks on world-wide level.)

[21] "The assembly at Amsterdam stated . . . that the Church as the Body of Christ consists of men and women, 'created as responsible persons to glorify God and to do his will', and went on to admit that 'this truth, accepted in theory, is too often ignored in practice' ": Philipp Potter, "Address at the Public Meeting", in *Sexism*, p. 28.

[22] Hamilton and Montgomery, *Ordination*.

[23] Cf. Potter, "Address", p. 29.

ponse to stimulus from the World Churches conference at Uppsala in 1968.[24]

At the conference on "Faith and Order" in Akkra in 1974, a consensus paper was issued in which attention was drawn to the "positive experiences" that many churches had accumulated with regard to women in office. Other churches, too, were urged to "think seriously about their attitude to this matter". On the other hand, the point was made that the long tradition of opposition to the ordination of women should "not be dismissed as a simple lack of respect for the role of women in the Church".[25] It was also noted that theology's position on the matter was "perhaps . . . negatively influenced . . . by the predominance of masculine ideas and concepts in the modern sociocultural environment".[26]

This concern was taken up more comprehensively at the conference on "Sexism in the 1970s" held in Berlin in 1974.[27] The whole problem of the ordination of women was deepened to the extent that—in parallel with secular feminism in America—emphasis was now placed not on the need to take over preexisting "masculine" structures but on the need to change them.[28] Pauline Webb, a member of the Central Committee of the WCC, provided this semiofficial definition of the concept of sexism: "By sexism, we mean any kind of subordination or devaluation of a person or group solely on the ground of sex."[29]

This effectively brands every form of social precedence for males that is

---

[24] Bam, Ordination. Another typical example is "The Community of Women and Men in the Church. A Study by the World Council of Churches", in The Ecumenical Review 27 (1975): 386–93; this contains a list of relevant questions for discussion in the General Assembly. The newest publication (commissioned under "Faith and Order") is C. F. Parvey, ed., Ordination of Women in Ecumenical Perspective. Workbook for the Church's Future, Faith and Order Papers 105 (Geneva, 1980), which already shows strong influences from feminist theology (to be mentioned shortly here).

[25] Geiko Müller-Fahrenholz, ed., Eine Taufe—eine Eucharistie—ein Amt. Drei Erklärungen, erarbeitet und autorisiert von der Kommission für Glauben und Kirchenverfassung [One baptism—one Eucharist—one office. Three explanations, drafted and authorized by the Commission for Faith and Order], 3rd ed. (Frankfurt, 1977), p. 37.

[26] Müller-Fahrenholz, Taufe, p. 38. Cf. the essentially more progressive formulation of the draft: "Das ordinierte Amt in ökumenischer Perspektive. Dokument der Kommission für Glauben und Kirchenverfassung" [Ordained office in ecumenical perspective. A document of the Commission for Faith and Order], Ökumenische Rundschau 22 (1973): 244f.

[27] Sexism. Cf. Elisabeth Moltmann(-Wendel), "Sexismus in den siebziger Jahren. Ökumenischer Frauenkongress in Berlin" [Sexism in the seventies. Ecumenical women's congress in Berlin], Evangelische Kommentare 7 (1974): 484–85; Nelle Morton, "Auf dem Weg zu einer ganzheitlichen Theologie" [On the way to a holistic theology], Lutherische Rundschau 25 (1975): 16–26.

[28] This radical turn of thought is outlined by Philipp Potter, "Address", pp. 27–33, especially p. 29.

[29] Pauline Webb, "Address at the Public Meeting", in Sexism, p. 10.

connected with a certain subordination of women as "heresy",[30] or, as suggested by Philipp Potter, as "demonic".[31]

Particular satisfaction is taken in portraying any subordination of women as comparable to the oppression of Blacks (racism) and of workers (capitalism).[32] The struggle against sexism is seen as an integral part of liberation theology, whose influence has become dominant in most WCC bodies since the World Churches conference at Uppsala in 1968.[33] Consequently, the Christian message is often identified with a commitment to social liberation. A Madagascan delegate at the "Sexism" conference all but glorified the developments brought about by "scientific socialism" in the countries of the Eastern bloc and held up, as the specifically Christian goal, alliance with the Socialist cause, so that a world will be created from which, in accordance with Galatians 3:28, all discrimination will be banished.[34] In a programmatic article for "International Women's Year" in 1975, Paul D. Hanson equates the (obviously Marxist-oriented) struggle against power structures[35] with Divine Reality itself, saying that we regard

the Bible as an historical record . . . which draws attention . . . to a liberating dynamic within the historical process which is variously called Yahweh, Elohim or Adonai. The various parts of that scriptural record must be interpreted in relation to that liberating dynamic.[36]

In this vein, Hanson represents the Old Testament image of God, with its predominantly masculine traits, as a mechanism of oppression, which has to be done away with in the interest of the liberation that is the Old Testament's actual aim. Similar arguments are made by Marianne Katappo, who calls for a reconstruction of the image of God in Hindu, and other, directions.[37]

The activity of the WCC in this area is closely linked to corresponding

[30] Webb, "Address", p. 9.

[31] Potter, "Address", p. 31.

[32] Sexism, pp. 10, 27, 81.

[33] Potter, "Address", p. 32. Cf. Gottfried Hoffman, Der Ökumenismus heute. Geschichte—Kritik—Wegweisung [Ecumenism today. History—criticism—future directions] (Stein am Rhein, 1978), pp. 63ff.

[34] R. R. Andriamanjato, "Economic-Political Factors and the Status of Woman in Asia, Africa and Latin America in the Seventies", in Sexism, pp. 66–83, especially 77–82. Cf. also the contribution by the East German theologian Christa Lewek, "The Role of Women in a Socialist Society", in Sexism, pp. 84–93.

[35] P. D. Hanson, "Masculine Metaphors for God and Sex—discrimination in the Old Testament", The Ecumenical Review 27 (1975): 318.

[36] Hanson, "Metaphors", p. 316.

[37] Marianne Katappo, Compassionate and Free. An Asian Woman's Theology (Geneva, 1979), especially pp. 78f. Cf. Parvey, Ordination, pp. 46f.

measures taken by the United Nations, and this gives rise to a certain division of labor.[38] While the United Nations plays the stronger role in combating concrete discrimination in the secular world, the WCC seems to occupy itself more with the "patriarchal" spiritual and psychological structures that serve as the most deeply rooted sources of the differences between the sexes in the secular realm.[39]

Thus, the World Council of Churches has obviously become one of the most important transshipment ports for feminist theology, about which more will be said later.[40] However, the tendencies discussed above, in relation to relevant WCC bodies, are not necessarily representative of the entire institutional membership of the WCC. In 1970, women were ordained in only seventy-two out of 239 communities, although it must be noted that this number was considerably smaller prior to the developments in Sweden.[41]

---

[38] Cf., for example, *Sexism*, pp. 10, 32.

[39] Gisèle Halimi, "A World Divided in Two", in *Sexism*, p. 19: "We will never be able to achieve complete equality between the sexes until we have brought about a fundamental change in every aspect of our lives—in the economical and political structures. This cultural revolution, which consists in attacking the mental structures, . . . should take priority over all other revolutions."

[40] Cf. pp. 65–72 below.

[41] Lynch, "Ordination", p. 192. In 1975, 295 (?) members of the WCC, on being asked whether they ordained women, responded as follows: 104 yes, 57 no. Among the remainder, it is assumed that 17 churches practiced ordination of women, while 117 did not; cf. Parvey, *Ordination*, p. 9, n. 3. On the number of members of the WCC: Philipp Potter, in 1974, set this at 267, out of which 75 practiced the ordination of women: "Address", p. 29. It should be noted that, besides the Catholic Church, quite a few smaller, but fairly active, Protestant communities are *not* members of the WCC, and this often goes together with a conservative, antiliberal outlook. These groups reject any ordination or ministry of women.

In recent years the developments sketched have continued. The "paper of Lima", the newest document by the commission of "Faith and Order" from 1982, briefly outlines the controversial positions: *Dokumente*, p. 573 (n. 18). The "Department on Cooperation of Men and Women" produced a text in 1981: Constance Parvey, ed., The Community of Women and Men in the Church, The Sheffield Report, Geneva 1981.

CHAPTER THREE

The Problem of Women in the Priesthood as a Consequence of the "Conciliar Upheaval"

I. KEY STATEMENTS FROM "PACEM IN TERRIS" AND "GAUDIUM ET SPES" ON THE MODERN "QUESTION OF WOMEN"

In the encyclical *Pacem in terris* of 1963, Pope John XXIII includes the entrance of women into public life—along with the rise of the working class and the steadily increasing liberation of peoples from foreign domination—in the three "signs of the times" that characterize today's world to a notable degree. The new role of women seems to be regarded by the Pope as a natural consequence of Christian culture. What underlies all three signs is the disappearance of traditional "ways of thought . . . , on the basis of which certain human groups regarded themselves as subordinate, while others imagined themselves superior, whether because of their economic or social position, or because of their sex or their standing in society."[1]

In 1965, in the pastoral constitution "The Church in the Modern World" (*Gaudium et spes*), the Second Vatican Council called for the overcoming of all "forms of social or cultural discrimination in basic personal rights", including unjust treatment "on the grounds of sex".[2]

---

[1] No. 43: Bundesverband der Katholischen Arbeitnehmerbewegung (KAB) Deutschlands, ed., *Texte zur katholischen Soziallehre. Die sozialen Rundschreiben der Päpste und andere kirchliche Dokumente* [Texts on Catholic social doctrine. The social encyclicals of the Popes and other church documents], 4th ed. (Kevelaer, 1977), p. 282; *AAS* 55 (1963): 268.

[2] Art. 29: Karl Rahner and Herbert Vorgrimler, *Kleines Konzilskompendium* [Short conciliar handbook] (Freiburg, Basel and Vienna, 1966), p. 476; *AAS* 58 (1966): 1048f. Cf. also Art. 9, where the demands of "humanity" are represented: "Women demand for themselves legal and factual equality with men in all areas where they have still not been granted these"; in Rahner and Vorgrimler, *Konzilskompendium*, p. 456; *AAS* 58 (1966): 1031.

Both of these statements are significant for the course of the debate on the "question of women" during the past twenty to twenty-five years. However, not enough attention seems to have been paid to the way that the texts are tied in with the totality of Church doctrine. The *aggiornamento* of John XXIII cannot be understood, insofar as it relates to our topic here, in isolation from the earlier guiding statements by Pius XI and Pius XII, which are referred to again and again in *Pacem in terris* and *Gaudium et spes*.

2. THE EMBEDDEDNESS OF THE STATEMENTS IN TRADITION

In the encyclical on marriage, *Casti connubii* of 1930, Pius XI stresses the "equality of rights" of husband and wife "in those rights that belong to the dignity of the human soul and that are proper to the marriage contract and inseparably bound up with wedlock". At the same time, however, the Pope remarks that "in other things there must be a certain inequality and due accommodation, which is demanded by the good of the family and the right ordering and unity and stability of home life".[3]

Pius XI speaks in sharp terms against the false notions of emancipation associated with both individualistic liberalism and socialistic collectivism.[4] He stresses the value of the "hierarchical" structure of marriage, which by no means implies any degradation of women: "For if the man is the head, the woman is the heart, and as he occupies the chief place in ruling, so she may and ought to claim for herself the chief place in love."[5]

This arrangement does not imply conservative adherence to past, "patriarchal" social structures, but is thoroughly flexible:

> Again, this subjection of wife to husband in its degree and manner may vary according to the different conditions of persons, place and time. In fact, if the husband neglects his duty, it falls to the wife to take his place in directing the family. But the structure of the family and its fundamental law, established and confirmed by God, must always and everywhere be maintained intact.[6]

Pius XII comments to similar effect. He refers forcibly to the new social circumstances that demand stronger participation by women in public

---

[3] No. 77. This text, and the following one, are cited from Joseph Mausbach and Gustav Ermecke, *Katholische Moraltheologie III* [Catholic moral theology III], 10th ed. (Münster, 1961), p. 66; cf. *AAS* 22 (1930): 549f., 568.

[4] No. 78.

[5] No. 27f.

[6] No. 27f.

affairs.[7] At the same time, however, he underlines that the sexes each have special characteristics that must be taken into consideration, particularly the social leadership role (more exactly, responsibility) of men[8] and the maternal qualities of women (which are not to be understood as solely biological):[9] "The particular traits that differentiate the two sexes present themselves so clearly to the eyes of all that their value to the social order could be misunderstood, or even overlooked, only through blindness or fatally unworldly stubbornness."[10]

3. CURRENT MISUNDERSTANDINGS

Pope John obviously presumes the existence of such "clarity", and he places less importance on distinguishing it from error than did his predecessors.

[7] Especially in the address of October 21, 1945: Michael Chinigo, *Der Papst sagt. Lehren Pius' XII* [The Pope says. Teachings of Pius XII] (Frankfurt, 1955), pp. 58ff.; *AAS* 37 (1945): 284–95.

[8] Cf. Chinigo, *Der Papst*, p. 45.

[9] Chinigo, *Der Papst*, p. 54; *AAS* 37 (1945): 286.

[10] Chinigo, *Der Papst*, p. 53; *AAS* 37 (1945): 285. The statements by the last two Popes Pius suffice only to indicate the more immediate background to the conciliar statements. Other Popes have, of course, concerned themselves with the modern question of women from a much earlier time:

Leo XIII, in his encyclical *Quod apostolici muneris*, takes a strong stand against the equivalence of the sexes in the communist-socialist system of thought; his encyclical on marriage, *Arcanum*, stresses the equal worth of husband and wife in marriage while also upholding the notions of the social precedence of men and the chiefly maternal responsibility of women that are under attack by contemporary feminism.

Pius X was the first to have treated the question of women as an independent problem. In opposition to excessive conservatism, he points out that the duties of women must not be restricted solely to the domestic sphere. Especially important is the social apostolate of women in bringing up children, educating girls and caring for the sick and needy.

Benedict XV also expressly recognizes the fact that there must be a change in roles in modern society. However, he warns against abandoning the notion that it is the *family* that forms the *center* of the sphere of female activity. Women are by no means excluded from participation in public affairs; as a rule, however, this is not their proper, central area of activity. Benedict's views are unusually extensively reflected in the book by Augustin Rösler on the question of women, which was highly commended by the Pope: Augustin Rösler, *Die Frauenfrage vom Standpunkte der Natur, der Geschichte und der Offenbarung* [The question of women from the standpoint of nature, history and revelation], 2nd ed. (Freiburg, 1907). On all this, cf. J. A. Wahl, *The Exclusion of Woman from Holy Orders*, Catholic University of America, Studies in Sacred Theology, Second Series, no. 110 [dissertation] (Washington, 1959), pp. 20–22; also gives detailed documentation.

This good-natured attitude seems, however, not to have been understood when someone like Mary Daly writes about *Pacem in terris*: "Missing
is the usual disparagement of feminine emancipation. . . ." The "reference
to 'equal rights and duties for man and woman' " is "unaccompanied by
any nullifying statement about the need for 'a certain inequality' ".[11]

Daly therefore accuses Pope Paul VI, who spelled out the differences
between the sexes more clearly again,[12] of not having been "specific about
the implications of this 'equality' [in rights between the sexes]".[13]

A similar fate has befallen the pastoral constitution "The Church in the
Modern World". Again and again, in writings on the subject, mention is
made of the passage opposing "discrimination" against women, but I
know of no instance in which the relevant Article 29 is quoted in context.
Yet, just two sentences after the passage in question, the point is stressed
that "there are rightful differences between people".[14]

Roughly the same situation exists regarding the other statements by the
Council on the "question of women". A passage often favored for citation
is the thoroughly traditional remark from *Lumen gentium* that: "In Christ
and in the Church there is . . . no inequality arising from race or nationality,
social condition or sex."[15] The same article clearly emphasizes, however,
that "this very diversity of graces, of ministries and of works"—thus,
variety—"bear[s] witness to the wonderful unity in the Body of Christ".[16]
Galatians 3:28 (unity) is placed side by side with 1 Corinthians 12 (variety).

In particular similarity to Pius XII, the "Decree on the Lay Apostolate"
calls for a "developing participation" by women "in the various sectors of
the Church's apostolate", because "in our days women are taking an
increasingly active share in the whole life of society".[17] That this does not
mean equal participation in activities proper to men should be obvious
from the context as presented here.

The "Declaration on Christian Education" stresses the differing natures
of the sexes with unusual clarity and urges that those differences be
consciously accepted and developed. Parents and teachers should, "in the

---

[11] Daly, *Kirche*, p. 96.

[12] Especially necessary in the "International Women's Year"; on this, cf. *Declaration*,
Introduction, p. 3; *AAS* 69 (1977): 98.

[13] Daly, *Kirche*, p. 100.

[14] Rahner and Vorgrimler, *Konzilskompendium*, p. 476; *AAS* 58 (1966): 1049.

[15] *Lumen gentium*, 32, with reference to Galatians 3:28 and Colossians 3:11, in Rahner and
Vorgrimler, *Konzilskompendium*, p. 162; *AAS* 57 (1965): 38.

[16] *Lumen gentium*, 32, in Rahner and Vorgrimler, *Konzilskompendium*, p. 163; *AAS* 57
(1965): 38.

[17] *Apostolicam actuositatem*, 9, in Rahner and Vorgrimler, *Konzilskompendium*, p. 400;
AAS 58 (1966): 846.

entire educational program . . . make full allowance for the difference of sex and for the particular role that Providence has appointed to each sex in the family and in society".[18]

Thus, the difference between the sexes is seen, not within the framework of an "equality eschatology", as a troublesome role model that has to be overcome, but rather as something firmly anchored in Divine Providence. Along with this—as shown particularly by the express reference to the encyclical on education of Pius XI—a certain gibe at coeducation is evident.[19]

Formal references to the subordination of women—a term of provocation these days—are largely avoided in postconciliar Church documents, even if it cannot be said that the thought content behind the term has been abandoned. Some translations of the original Latin texts into the vernacular have tended to suggest the contrary, but, on closer inspection, they turn out to be misleading. For instance, according to the episcopally approved German translation, the passage cited earlier from *Pacem in terris* is directed against (among other things) subordination of the female sex. Yet the Latin text—which, moreover, does not describe the Church's position but rather trends outside the Church—uses the word inferior, taken in contradistinction to the notion *"prima pars"*. Inferior, however, along with its basic sense of the lower, often conveys associations of subjugation and inadequacy,[20] which are, in fact, *not* identified with, but distinguished from, the notion of subordination in the well-defined statements by Pius XI and Pius XII.

Something similar occurred in the German translation of the declaration by the Sacred Congregation for the Doctrine of the Faith on the question of women in the priesthood, which contains a subordinate clause expressing opposition to "a supposed natural authority of man over woman".[21] The

---

[18] *Gravissimum educationis*, 8, in Rahner and Vorgrimler, *Konzilskompendium*, p. 344; cf. Art. 1, in Rahner and Vorgrimler, *Konzilskompendium*, p. 336; *AAS* 58 (1966): 729, 735.

[19] Rahner and Vorgrimler, *Konzilskompendium*, p. 336, n. 6; p. 344, n. 27; *AAS* 58 (1966): 729, n. 6; p. 735, n. 27. This concludes what I take to be a listing of the most important relevant conciliar statements. For more detailed information that goes beyond the scope of the present inquiry, see: Barbara Albrecht, "Die Aussagen des II. Vatikanischen Konzils in ihrer Bedeutung für die berufliche Mitarbeit der Frau in der Kirche" [The statements of the Second Vatican Council in their significance for the professional participation of women in the Church's work], in Otto Semmelroth, ed., *Martyria, Leiturgia, Diakonia. Fs Hermann Volk* [*Martyria, Leiturgia, Diakonia*: essays for Hermann Volk] (Mainz, 1968), pp. 431–50; Wilhelm Wiesen, *Die Frau in der Seelsorge* [Women as pastoral workers] (Würzburg, 1973).

[20] *Der kleine Stowasser, Lateinisch-deutsches Schulwörterbuch* [The short Stowasser: Latin-German school dictionary], ed. by Michael Petschenig (Munich, 1970).

[21] *Declaration*, no. 5, p. 15.

original text, however, is directed against a "superiority" (*excellentia*)[22] of the male sex, which is also opposed, for example, by Pius XI, as witness the encyclical *Casti connubii*.[23]

The corresponding English translation, moreover, leads Wijngaards to conclude that the Roman declaration abandons support for the position of the husband as head of the family.[24] That would be correct only in the sense that the declaration stresses the existence of *differences* between the sexes without, however, going into detail about their specific nature. It does, of course, also stress that Christ's relation to the Church is that of "head", and regards this as a natural analogy to a male priesthood.[25]

4. THE DEVELOPMENT OF THE DEBATE ABOUT FEMALE PRIESTS

The question of the ordination of women was already being occasionally discussed in the Catholic Church at the time of the rise of the secular women's movement. In 1934, Oda Schneider thought that the "cry for the priesthood" had already "ebbed away"; there were, of course, "still petitions being sent from here and there to the highest authorities . . . , demanding admission of women to the priesthood".[26]

Very early on, attempts had already been made to establish stronger connections between the historical material and reflections on the symbolism of the sexes, such as those by Engelbert Krebs (1922),[27] Oda Schneider (1934),[28] and, above all, Gertrud von le Fort, whose book *The Eternal Woman* (1934)[29] was accorded both admiration and hostility on a worldwide scale.

At the time of the Council, however, there was a resurgence of interest

[22] *AAS* 69 (1977): 110.

[23] This should not be taken as forestalling my discussion of the meaning of the "subordination" of women in the context of this book's topic. On this, cf. pp. 202–4 and 351–57 below.

[24] J. N. M. Wijngaards, *Did Christ Rule out Women Priests?* (Great Wakering, 1977), pp. 19f.

[25] *Declaration*, No. 5, pp. 17f.; *AAS* 69 (1977): 112f.

[26] Oda Schneider, *Vom Priestertum der Frau* [On priesthood for women] (Vienna, 1934), p. 8. Cf. Ida F. Görres, "Über die Weihe von Frauen zu Priesterinnen" [On the consecration of women as priests], in *Der christliche Sonntag* 25 (1965): 197.

[27] Engelbert Krebs, "Vom 'Priestertum der Frau' " [On "Priesthood for women"], in *Hochland* 19 (1922): 196–215.

[28] O. Schneider, *Priestertum*.

[29] Gertrud von le Fort, *Die ewige Frau* [The eternal woman] (Munich, 1963).

in the question, and a group of German women drew up a now well-known submission to the Preparatory Commission.[30] The earlier-mentioned dissertation by the Rahner student Haye van der Meer,[31] which was completed in 1962, soon became a key resource document for those in favor of women in the priesthood, although it did not appear as a book until 1969 and its influence in the United States was restricted until the English translation appeared in 1973.[32] In 1963, a large Catholic women's organization, the "St. Joan's International Alliance", which originated as an offshoot of the English suffragist movement, voted in favor of women in the priesthood. Women are "more than ready and willing . . . to devote themselves to the priesthood if the Church in its wisdom should decide that it is time to extend this honor to women".[33]

In the wake of the generally widespread readiness for change that existed after the Council, the exclusion of women from the sacramental priesthood was more and more called into question. The editors of the magazine *Concilium*, which has become one of the main organs for furthering the cause of women in the priesthood,[34] have portrayed developments against a fourfold backdrop:

1. a change in the understanding of what it means to hold office, which is now seen as something more strongly tied to a call from the community
2. the new recognition of the worth of women, in view of which unequal treatment of the sexes appears contradictory to the spirit of the gospel
3. the unmasking of the theological arguments, especially the arguments

---

[30] Gertrud Heinzelmann, ed., *Wir schweigen nicht länger! Frauen äussern sich zum Zweiten Vatikanischen Konzil* [We will stay silent no longer! Women express their views on the Second Vatican Council] (Zurich, 1964).

[31] Meer, *Priestertum*. Cf. Gertrud Heinzelmann, *Die getrennten Schwestern. Frauen nach dem Konzil* [The divided sisters. Women after the Council] (Zurich, 1967), p. 21, n. 20.

[32] Among others, the following works are worth mentioning here: José Idigoras, *La femme dans l'ordre sacré?* (Lima, 1963); summarized in *Informations catholiques internationales*, no. 204, Nov. 15, 1963, pp. 32–34; José Idigoras, *La misión directiva de la mujer en la historia de la salvación* (Lima, 1965); summarized in *Informations catholiques internationales*, no. 245, Aug. 1965, pp. 29–31; V. E. Hannon, *The Question of Women and the Priesthood. Can Women be Admitted to Holy Orders?* (London, Dublin and Melbourne, 1967); R. J. A. van Eyden, "Die Frau im Kirchenamt. Plädoyer für die Revision einer traditionellen Haltung" [Woman in Church office. A plea for the revision of a traditional attitude], in *Wort und Wahrheit* 22 (1967): 350–62; René van Eyden, "Das liturgische Amt der Frau" [The liturgical office of women], in *Conc* 8 (1972): 107–15; Raming, *Ausschluss*, A. M. Gardiner, ed., *Women and Catholic Priesthood: An Expanded Vision* (New York, Paramus and Toronto, 1976).

Against women in the priesthood is the first, preconciliar dissertation on the topic: Wahl, *Exclusion*.

[33] Heinzelmann, *Schweigen*, p. 78.

[34] Cf. especially *Conc* 4 (1968): 288–319; 8 (1972): 107–15; 12 (1976): 1–73; 14 (1978): 287–94; 16 (1980): 229–306.

from symbolism, which serve only to legitimize the power positions of men

4. ecumenical considerations[35]

For those who think that the theological arguments against the ordination of women have been unmasked, the problem remains a real one only at the "pastoral level. The question facing us today is: What should we do?"[36]

Since it is obvious that not all goals can be achieved at once, a step-by-step advancement is indicated. A modest starting point, for example, would be girl acolytes and female pastoral assistants with clerical duties, while female deacons would appear to be regarded as an especially promising entrance door. Hanna-Renate Laurien, former vice-president of the Würzburg synod, remarks in this connection that it "is fatal to fix one's sights on step 10 before step 3 or 4 has been taken".[37]

In 1970, the Dutch Pastoral Council came out in favor of ordaining women as priests,[38] and the Canadian bishops also supported this at the episcopal synod in 1971.[39] The problem is particularly hotly debated in the United States, with a large number of nuns taking part. "They are more numerous than priests or monks, and their influence as teachers, especially in the United States with its network of parochial schools, boarding schools and colleges, is great."[40]

The process of postconciliar change was particularly extensive in the female religious orders. The "new nuns" frequently decided not to wear religious habit and set about trying to liberate themselves from the constraints of existing structures so that they could participate more actively in efforts to change society and in apostleship. The number of women who withdrew altogether from religious orders in the United

[35] Dokumentation Concilium, "Der Platz der Frau im Amt der nichtkatholischen Kirchen" [The place of women in the office of non-Catholic churches], Conc 4 (1968): 309f.

[36] These are the words of a Dutch theologian to Mrs. Halkes: Halkes, Frau, p. 105.

[37] Andreas Heinz, "Die liturgischen Dienste der Frau. Studeintagung 1978 der Arbeitsgemeinschaft Katholischer Liturgiker im deutschen Sprachgebiet" [The liturgical services of women. 1978 study conference of the working party of Catholic liturgists from German-speaking areas]: LJ 28 (1978): 131; cf. also Manuel Alcalà, "Die Frauenemanzipation: Ihre Herausforderung an die Theologie und an die Reform der Kirche" [The emancipation of women: its challenge to theology and to Church reform], Conc 16 (1980): 287; Johannes Neumann, "Die Stellung der Frau in der Sicht der katholischen Kirche heute" [The position of women in the view of the Catholic Church today], ThQ 156 (1976): 121; Küng, "Thesen", p. 132.

[38] HK 24 (1970): 57.

[39] HK 25 (1971): 534.

[40] Daly, Kirche, p. 118. In 1965, there were roughly 180,000 (!) women in religious orders in the United States: Heinzelmann, Schwestern, p. 29.

States was disproportionately high, and this attests to the intensity of the upheaval. Barbara Haber even takes the view that the "new nuns" were trendsetters for the women's liberation movement, which began somewhat later than theirs.[41] The nature of their activities brought them closer and closer to the sorts of responsibility properly reserved for clergymen, especially as the pastoral situation, marked by an increasing scarcity of priests, made it more urgent for the religious orders to participate in community work. Women in religious orders also made up the overwhelming majority of the roughly two thousand participants at the first "Women's Ordination Conference", which took place in Detroit in 1975. The addresses delivered at this widely influential function[42] left nothing to be desired in the sharpness of their language and of their demands. This event, together with the developments in the Anglican church, seems to have served as the immediate occasion for the relevant declaration by the Sacred Congregation for the Doctrine of the Faith.[43] A further conference

[41] Haber, *Women in America*, p. 155.

[42] Gardiner, *Expanded Vision*.

[43] *Negative reactions* to the Roman document: Peter Hünermann, "Roma locuta—causa finita? Zur Argumentation der vatikanischen Erklärung über die Frauenordination" [*Roma locuta—causa finita?* On the arguments in the Vatican declaration on the ordination of women], in *HK* 31 (1977): 206–9; Küng and Lohfink, "Keine Ordination"; K. Rahner, "Priestertum"; Leonard and Arlene Swidler, eds., *Women Priests. A Catholic Commentary on the Vatican Declaration* (New York, 1977); Wijngaards, *Did Christ? Église et Théologie* 9 (1978): 1–235 (with contributions by, among others, W. Vogels, J.-P. Michaud, J. K. Coyle, A. Guindon, A. Peelman, N. Provencher; cf. the index).

In the period following the appearance of the document, the reaction that took place would seem not to have been *"Roma locuta—causa finita"*, but rather *"Roma locuta—causa stimulata!"* (Swidler, *Women Priests*, p. 3). The same thing is true, but in a differing sense, of the *positive responses*, which are concerned above all with the symbolic significance of the sexual polarity in ecclesiology, Mariology, and Christology. Cf. especially Scheffczyk, "Wesen"; H. U. von Balthasar, "Welches Gewicht hat die ununterbrochene Tradition der Kirche bezüglich der Zuordnung des Priestertums an den Mann?" [What weight does the unbroken Tradition of the Church have in respect of the reservation of the priesthood for men?], in *Die Sendung der Frau in der Kirche. Die Erklärung "Inter insigniores" der Kongregation für die Glaubenslehre mit Kommentar und theologischen Studien* [The mission of women in the Church. The declaration *"inter insigniores"* of the Sacred Congregation for the Doctrine of the Faith, with commentary and theological studies], ed. by the German-speaking editorial staff of the *Osservatore Romano* (Kevelaer, 1978), pp. 54–57; Joseph Cardinal Ratzinger, "Das Priestertum des Mannes—ein Verstoss gegen die Rechte der Frau?" [The male priesthood—an offense against the rights of women?], in *Sendung*, pp. 78–82; Barbara Albrecht, *Vom Dienst der Frau in der Kirche. Aktuelle Fragen und Biblisch-spirituelle Grundlegung* [The service of woman in the Church. Topical issues and biblical-spiritual foundations] (Vallendar and Schönstatt, 1980); Theophora Schneider, "Kirche und Frau" [Church and woman], *Quatember* 41 (1977): 204–12.

The cited authors (see also the other titles cited in the bibliography) take up the concern of *Inter insigniores* to show how the not merely functionally, but symbolically-sacramentally understood role of the priest as representative of Christ is bound up with the larger totality of

followed in 1978, in Baltimore, where the participants protested against the Roman position by marching through the city in symbolic chains.[44]

In recent years, the branch of feminist theology that regards the demand for women in the priesthood as just part of the general struggle against "patriarchalism" and "clericalism" has become more prominent even in Catholic circles.[45]

---

the Faith. Also relevant in this context is a study by Louis Bouyer that appeared shortly before *Inter insigniores*: *Frau und Kirche*, Kriterien 42 (Einsiedeln, 1977). English translation: Woman in the Church (San Francisco: Ignatius Press, 1979).

[44] Joan Morris, "Ordination der Frau" [Ordination of women], *Informationen zu Amt-Diakonat der Frau* 1 (1979): 3–4 (issued by the Sekretariat des Internationalen Diakonatszentrums [IDZ], Postfach 420, D-7800 Freiburg).

[45] Cf. especially *Conc* 12 (1976): 1–73; 14 (1978): 287–94; 16 (1980): 229–306; *US* 32 (1977): 261–307; 35 (1980): 291–95, 325–51; *Conc* 17 (1981): 209–62; 18 (1982): 135–44; 19 (1983): 632–40, 646–53; 20 (1984): 31–38; 21 (1985): 387–98, 443–48.

CHAPTER FOUR

Characteristics of Feminist Theology

1. THE "ANDROGYNOUS UTOPIA" AS STARTING POINT

Feminist theology proceeds from the basic assumption that all "forms of domination and oppression of man by man are social expressions of that dualism that is rooted more deeply than any others: the elevation of the male sex above the female".[1]

Every form of subordination of the female sex to the male contradicts the "gospel's demand for the full equality of all human beings".[2] The axiom of equality also demands that the differences between men and women be narrowed. Feminist theology does not deny, in general, the existence of "male" and "female" characteristics, but is opposed to the development of such traits in differently emphasized ways by men and by women: "It is not a matter of denying the existence of the polarities, but one of abandoning their attribution to one or the other of the biological sexes; for polarities are alive in everyone, and the trick is to learn to deal with them in such a way that they are brought into productive interrelation with one another."[3]

From its base in feminism outside the Church, the notion of an "androgynous utopia" is being pushed more and more to the forefront: "Both sexes have the potential ability . . . to integrate [the polarities] within themselves, and thus to become autonomous individuals, deve-

[1] Catharina J. M. Halkes, *Gott hat nicht nur starke Söhne. Grundzüge einer feministischen Theologie* [God does not only have strong sons. Fundamentals of a feminist theology] (Gütersloh, 1980), p. 30.

[2] L. M. Russell, "Sprachveränderung und Kirchenreform" [Linguistic change and Church reform], in L. M. Russell, ed., *Als Mann und Frau ruft er uns. Vom nicht-sexistischen Gebrauch der Bibel* [trans. of: The liberating word. A guide to nonsexist interpretation of the Bible] (Munich, 1979), p. 73.

[3] Halkes, *Söhne*, p. 25.

loping toward wholeness and androgyny [man-womanness]."[4] This ideal would seem to be the jumping-off point for feminist theology.[5]

The androgynous goal is best summed up in the concept of wholeness, which Catharina Halkes defines as "the tension-filled unity of a multiplicity of characteristics and values that have, until today, been separately distributed between the two sexes and also between the Eastern and Western cultures".[6] The counterconcept to wholeness is dualism, especially if this implies a relationship of ascendancy and subordination.[7]

2. THE STRUGGLE AGAINST "BODY–SOUL DUALISM"

The dualism of man and woman is reflected, at another level, in the distinction between consciousness and the unconscious,[8] and especially in the distinction between body and soul. The mind must not make the body subordinate, as Greek-influenced traditional theology maintains, but must rank it equally with itself. Otherwise, the "hierarchical precedence of mind over body" will serve only to legitimize all other sorts of relationship between ruler and ruled.[9]

The body-soul diastasis is also operative in the separation of understanding from feeling, of abstraction from intuition. The feminist theologians are opposed to "the overvaluing of Greek logic and abstract thought" that have become embodied in an excessively objectivized and technologized civilization. Catharina Halkes registers a passionate protest against her own "progressive" Church environment, which scorns the Marian piety of the people and suffers from rationalistic aridity. This sort of thinking is perhaps well enough suited to filing aspects of living reality

---

[4] Halkes, *Söhne*, p. 26.

[5] Cf. Halkes, *Söhne*, pp. 47f.

[6] Halkes, *Söhne*, pp. 43f.

[7] Cf. Halkes, "Feministische Theologie. Eine Zwischenbilanz" [Feminist theology. An interim account], *Conc* 16 (1980): 295; R. R. Ruether, *Frauen für eine neue Gesellschaft. Frauenbewegung und menschliche Befreiung* [trans. of: New woman—new earth. Sexist ideologies and human liberation] (Munich, 1979), p. 16. In a later publication, C. Halkes dismisses the word "androgyny" in order to avoid the misunderstanding of hermaphroditism; but the characterized ideal is not changed: *Zoekend naar wat verloren ging* (Baarn 1984). An even stronger point about "androgyny" and against the duality of sexes is made by R. R. Ruether, *Sexismus und die Rede von Gott* (Sexism and God-Talk) (Gütersloh 1985), p. 138f.

[8] So says Ruether (*Frauen*, p. 172), together with Erich Neumann.

[9] Ruether, *Frauen*, p. 203. Cf. Halkes, "Theologie", p. 295; Morton, "Weg", p. 18; Moltmann(-Wendel), "Sexismus", p. 485.

away in this or that little drawer, "but the heart, the mystery and the symbol, with its many levels, escape it".[10]

Along with this criticism of rationalism goes a fervent antipathy to any and every form of objectively valid, timeless truth. The decisive source of theological knowledge is lived experience, which is constantly changing: "Life . . . would have to be . . . accepted just as it is lived. For there would then be no more dichotomy of the sort that is presupposed when the mind . . . sets up . . . its absolutely valid dogmas about matters of the body."[11]

Theology is "a dialectical process of action and reflection",[12] which requires "a less linear and less logically consistent type of thought" than did the "old theology", as well as "a shift toward inventive, improvisational action, less objectivity, greater ambiguity".[13]

3. THE REJECTION OF "HIERARCHY"

As with the relationship between understanding and feeling, there is to be no element of "one above the other" in the organizational structures of society and the Church, but only that of "one next to the other": if the Church wants to support justice, "she must transform herself from a power pyramid into a 'circular' community, in which the greatest possible degree of responsibility and power is transferred to the oppressed and, in particular, to women."[14]

More recently, this "circle ideal" seems to have become a standard formula in the thinking of progressive and feminist theologians.[15] The enemy, on the other hand, is identified as clericalism, which Rosemary Ruether describes as "second-level sexism". "After all, it is from the community itself, and not from its 'administrators', that the Church derives its direction and effective power. . . . Those who hold office are only the self-articulation of the life of the community."[16]

[10] Halkes, *Söhne*, p. 114.

[11] Morton, "Weg", p. 18.

[12] Halkes, *Söhne*, p. 36.

[13] Halkes, *Söhne*, pp. 36, 73.

[14] M. L. Tobin, "Die Haltung der katholischen Kirche zu der Frauenbewegung in den Vereinigten Staaten" [The Catholic Church's attitude to the women's movement in the United States], *Conc* 12 (1976): 71.

[15] Cf. Halkes, *Söhne*, pp. 84, 90; Maria Agudelo, "Die Aufgabe der Kirche bei der Emanzipation der Frau" [The Church's task in the emancipation of women], *Conc* 16 (1980): 301–6.

[16] Ruether, *Frauen*, pp. 96f. Ruether is a Catholic theologian. Cf. Elisabeth Schüssler

"From this point of view, it is understandable that radical feminists hardly feel the need to worry themselves to any great extent about the question of women in office. For they regard the existing official positions, constituted within present-day Church structures, as not even worth occupying."[17]

4. THE RELATIONSHIP TO RELIGIOUS TRUTH

The policy of giving priority to experience sets itself not only against the administrative structures of the Church but also against the religious teachings that those structures support. This state of affairs is most immediately obvious in the approach taken to Holy Scripture. Elisabeth Schüssler thinks "that revelation and truth are contained only in those traditions and texts in which the influence of patriarchal culture and male-centered religion is critically evaluated and transcended".[18]

In other words, a selection has to be made.[19] Sharon Ringe justifies this method on the grounds that the "authority" of the biblical texts rests "on their power and ability . . . to take up and illuminate the most basic questions of life".[20] These most basic questions, furthermore, are to be identified with whatever most corresponds to the self-experience of feminists.[21]

The Irish theologian Mary Condren is therefore consistent in saying: "The claim that the process of revelation came to an end with Christ's

Fiorenza, "Women Apostles: The Testament of Scripture", in Gardiner, *Expanded Vision*, p. 97; "The Twelve", in Swidler, *Women Priests*, pp. 114–22; Ida Raming, "Von der Freiheit des Evangeliums zur versteinerten Männerkirche. Zur Entstehung und Entwicklung der Männerherrschaft in der Kirche" [From the freedom of the gospel to the petrified male Church. On the origin and development of male domination in the Church], *Conc* 16 (1980): 231.

[17] Halkes, *Söhne*, p. 45.

[18] Elisabeth Schüssler Fiorenza, "Für eine befreite und befreiende Theologie: Frauen in der Theologie und feministischen Theologie in den USA" [For a liberated and liberating theology: women in theology and feminist theology in the United States], *Conc* 14 (1978): 202; cf. her "Interpretation patriarchalischer Traditionen" [Interpretation of Patriarchal Traditions]: Russell, p. 51; *In memory of her. A Feminist Theological Reconstruction of Christian Origins* (New York, 1983).

[19] Halkes, "Theologie", p. 298.

[20] S. H. Ringe, "Autorität der Bibel und Bibelinterpretation" [Authority of the Bible and biblical interpretation], in Russell, *Als Mann*, p. 20.

[21] L. M. Russell, "Einführung: Die befreiende Macht des Wortes Gottes" [Introduction: the liberating power of the word of God], in Russell, *Als Mann*, p. 11.

death, and that the only task left for theology is to deduce 'eternal truth' from what was then revealed, is made in the interest of the Church's power structures."[22]

5. THE LINK WITH ECOFEMINISM AND SOCIALISM

In conjunction with the earlier-mentioned ecofeminism, calls are made for the establishment of a new relationship with nature. The feminist theologians point to the negative consequences of technological plundering of the earth, which they trace back to the traditional understanding of an account of creation written by priests. Since man is called on, in that account, to subdue the earth, this implies a certain subordination of the earth to man's activities. But in and through such subordination—according to Rosemary Ruether—nature automatically comes to be regarded as "bad".[23] However, subspiritual natural realities are "no longer . . . objects that we want to control, but rather . . . cosubjects with which we are interconnected".[24]

Ideas like these go together with a strong emphasis on the interpersonal community that derives its strength from the self-experience of the "sisterly" groups: "Sisters, awake! Our time has come! . . . So sisters, let us enjoy ourselves and be free."[25]

Here, feminism begins to merge with socialism, for which the female theologians concerned feel strong sympathies, although no detailed description is given. Catharina Halkes, for instance, dreams, along with Herbert Marcuse, of a "feminist socialism", in which (here on earth) the performance principle no longer plays a part.[26]

---

[22] Mary Condren, "Für die verbannten Kinder Evas. Eine Einführung in die feministische Theologie" [For the banished children of Eve. An introduction to feminist theology], US 32 (1977): 307. Halkes says something similar: Söhne, p. 60.

[23] Ruether, Frauen, p. 200; cf. p. 100. See also Mary Daly, Jenseits von Gottvater Sohn & Co. Aufbruch zu einer Philosophie der Frauenbefreiung [trans. of: Beyond God the Father: toward a philosophy of women's liberation] (Munich, 1980), pp. 196–200; Mary Daly, Gyn/Ecology. The Metaethics of Radical Feminism (Boston, 1978).

[24] Halkes, Söhne, pp. 82f.

[25] This slogan was formulated at the "sexism" conference of the WCC in 1974 and was modeled, in particular, on the liturgy: Sexism, p. 11.

[26] Halkes, Söhne, p. 29; cf. pp. 28, 89, 117. See also Ruether, Frauen, pp. 193f., 224; in Ruether, Frauen, p. 180, the relevant book by Friedrich Engels (cf. p. 31 above) is seen as a "basic text" of feminism.

Along with the ecological concern and the experience of "sisterhood" goes a "new spirituality", which is linked to a cult of "mother earth", "our authentic ground of being".[27] Thus God is seen in terms of motherly images that effectively push his world-transcending authority into the background. With Leslie Dewart, Mary Daly stands opposed to an "all-powerful, all-just God who evidently wills or, at least, permits oppressive conditions to exist".[28] Rosemary Ruether repudiates a creation of the world "from above", which implies a contrast between God as a "transcendent spiritual principle" and a "subordinated material reality".[29] Here, God's immanence is accorded priority over his transcendence.[30] The origin of this "choice", within the history of ideas, is to be sought primarily in Paul Tillich's theology,[31] whose image of God has been received with increasing sympathy in the United States.[32] God may be seen as the "energy source of all being", whose "earthly ground" is "the community".[33] Or the divine may appear "as the nodal point, rather than the authoritarian peak, of all reality".[34]

When God is viewed as bound up with the world to this extent, it becomes difficult to grasp God's reality as something self-sufficient and independent of the world: "They [feminist theologians] are therefore fearful of being all too quick to characterize God as a person."[35]

Consequently, preference is given to using transpersonal descriptions of God, such as "the source of being", or at least to using locutions devoid of male connotations, such as "Elohim" or "Yahweh".[36] In cases where male traits nevertheless still find their way into our image of God, they

[27] Ruether, *Frauen*, p. 229.

[28] Daly, *Kirche*, p. 181.

[29] Ruether, *Frauen*, p. 28. Cf. R. R. Ruether, *Mary—the Feminine Face of the Church* (Philadelphia, 1977), pp. 14f., 77f.

[30] So says Halkes, "Theologie", p. 296.

[31] Halkes, *Söhne*, p. 86; J. A. Romero, "The Protestant Principle: A Woman's-Eye View of Barth and Tillich", in R. R. Ruether, ed., *Religion and Sexism. Images of Woman in the Jewish and Christian Tradition* (New York, 1974), pp. 319–40; Ruether, *Mary*, p. 11; Daly, *Vater*, pp. 19f.

[32] Elisabeth Moltmann-Wendel, "Christentum und Frauenbewegung in Deutschland" [Christianity and the women's movement in Germany], in Elisabeth Moltmann-Wendel, ed., *Frauenbefreiung. Biblische und theologische Argumente* [Women's liberation. Biblical and theological arguments], 2nd ed. (Munich, 1978), p. 72. On Tillich, cf. pp. 271, 311f. below.

[33] Halkes, *Söhne*, p. 37.

[34] Halkes, *Söhne*, p. 37.

[35] Halkes, *Söhne*, p. 38.

[36] Halkes, *Söhne*, pp. 36, 58; L. M. Russell, "Sprachveränderung und Kirchenreform" [Linguistic change and Church reform], in Russell, *Als Mann*, p. 78.

have to be counterbalanced with female ones. "We have to learn to speak of God as father and mother, as son and daughter, as he and she."[37] According to Letty Russell, the "expression 'our Father' should be avoided unless it can be supplemented with other metaphors".[38] In this connection, Mary Daly talks of a "castration" of God.[39]

The less God is seen as a person, the more his attributes of eternality and immutability also tend to evaporate. The "feminist God" is "dynamic", so it is appropriate that he "should no longer be designated by a concrete noun, but rather by a verb".[40] Such a God cannot keep anyone, and especially not any woman, tied down "to a certain body or to static concepts".[41] An eternal God might serve as a model for an "eternal woman", which Mary Daly sees as a "demon" that needs to be "exorcised".[42] "If this God is actually unchanging, then mankind stands helpless and hopeless before him."[43]

7. THE SIGNIFICANCE OF FEMINIST THEOLOGY

At this point, one might well ask whether certain aspects of feminist theology do not amount to an offense against the most basic truths of the Faith. The just-mentioned Mary Daly, a former nun, has answered this question affirmatively insofar as she has added to the second edition of the book referred to above a new "Post-Christian Preface" (1975), and, in her "standard text" of feminism, *Beyond God the Father*, has constructed a new, "feminist" religion.[44]

---

[37] Schüssler, "Theologie", p. 292.

[38] L. M. Russell, "Sprachveränderung", p. 78.

[39] Daly, *Vater*, pp. 24, 33. *Daly* does not want any "equalization" but rather the creation of a "matriarchal" religion from which the male element is excluded: "*God* represents the necrophilia of patriarchy, whereas *Goddess* affirms the life-loving being of women and nature": Daly, *Gyn/Ecology*, p. xi; cf. p. 76. A background factor in this case is lesbianism (Daly, *Vater*, pp. 9, 145f.), which is connected with the "androgynous utopia" but is not supported by all feminist theologians (on this see Halkes, *Söhne*, pp. 39f.).

[40] Halkes, *Söhne*, p. 37. Cf. Daly, *Vater*, p. 49: God appears there as a verb that is asserted of *man* (as substantive). In this connection, Daly refers to various pantheistic or panentheistic [*Tr.*: this term seems to have been coined by the German philosopher K. C. F. Krause and means "all in God", as distinct from pantheistic "God in all"] philosophers: Daly, *Vater*, pp. 52, 210.

[41] Halkes, *Söhne*, p. 87.

[42] Daly, *Kirche*, p. 165.

[43] Daly, *Kirche*, p. 181.

[44] Cf. Haber, *Women in America*, pp. 155f.; Daly, *Vater*, p. 5; Daly, *Gyn/Ecology*, p. xi. The Unitarian Carol Ochs describes her system explicitly as "monism": *Behind the Sex of*

However, it should be noted that feminist theology is still in the midst of its development and is anything but a unified movement. A number of common basic tendencies can, nevertheless, be discerned within it, and my aim in this chapter was to describe the most prominent aspects of those tendencies. Denominational differences play practically no role in this theology, so there seemed to be no point in drawing more precise distinctions between Catholic and non-Catholic authors, although the Catholic group was favored in the selection of passages for quotation.

Basically, feminist theology must be understood as calling into question the male cast of both the image of God and the office of priest, and this will be critically evaluated, within a systematic framework of inquiry, in what follows: ". . . test everything; hold fast what is good".[45]

God. Toward a New Consciousness. Transcending Matriarchy and Patriarchy (Boston, 1977), pp. 132, 137.

[45] 1 Th 5:21. On this place, the description of feminist theology cannot be but rather sketchy. Nevertheless, the essential questions that arise from this thinking are broadly taken up as a background of the following sections. More biographical references can be found in the latest works of the Dutch theologian Catharina Halkes (especially: Zoekend naar wat verloren ging [Baarn, 1984]) and in the second German edition of my thesis. Critical remarks on the feminist theology can be found, for example, in the German writings of Barbara Albrecht's Jesus-Frau-Kirche [Jesus-Woman-Church] (Vallendar-Schönstatt, 1983), Helmut Moll's "Feministische Theologie"—eine Herausforderung ["Feminist theology"—a challenge], MThZ 34, (1983): 118–28; Ingeborg Hauschildt's Gott eine Frau? Weg und Irrweg der feministischen Theologie [God as a woman? Way and wrong way of feminist theology] (Wuppertal, 1983), Frauen im theologischen Aufstand. Eine Orientierungshilfe zur "Feministischen Theologie" edited by Peter Beyerhaus [Women in a theological rebellion. A help for orientation about the "feminist theology"], Wort und Wissen 14, Stuttgart, 1983, Lutz von Padberg's Feminismus—eine ideologische und theologische Herausforderung [Feminism—an ideological and theological challenge], Evangelium und Gesellschaft 5, Wuppertal 1985, Jutta Burggraf's Die Mutter der Kirche und die Frau in der Kirche. Ein kritischer Beitrag zum Thema 'feministische Theologie' [The mother of the Church and woman in the Church. A critical contribution about 'feminist theology'], Kleine Schriften des Internationalen Mariologischen Arbeitskreises Kevalaer, Kevelaer 1986.

CHAPTER FIVE

The Creation-Theological Approach
to a Resolution of the Problem

I. THE RELATION OF THE SOCIOLOGICAL COMPONENTS
TO THE CATHOLIC DOCTRINE OF CREATION

The tendency to "role thinking" that was discussed earlier, and that is predominant in the world today, needs to be seen within the framework of the Catholic doctrine of creation. Undoubtedly, the problem of the specific natures of the two sexes cannot be resolved without taking account of its sociological components, even if merely reducing it to social factors will have to be called into question. For the social dimension is an essential part of the nature of man, and that nature, with all its predispositions, has been created by God. The divine order of creation, however, is closely bound up with the order of redemption, for God does not call man into his community without, at the same time, taking into service both man himself and the worldly reality in which man is bound up. Thus, for example, the water used in baptism or the material forms of bread and wine in the Eucharist become efficacious signs of divine self-communication. *Gratia supponit naturam* ("grace presupposes nature")—this basic axiom is an indispensable structural underpinning of the Catholic Faith.[1]

[1] Cf. Leo Scheffczyk, *Katholische Glaubenswelt* [The world of Catholic Faith], 2nd ed. (Aschaffenburg, 1978), pp. 295–99.

73

2. NOMINALIST–ORIENTED CRITICISM OF RECOURSE
TO THE ORDER OF CREATION

Nominalism in the late Middle Ages

Things are rather different for Protestant thought. There, almost as if coursing from subterranean canals, the influence of the nominalism of the late Middle Ages continues to exert itself even today. Nominalism holds, of course, that our concepts can signify absolutely nothing of the essence of things, but are only stuck-on, interchangeable "names" (nomina).[2] This philosophical doctrine was then also taken over as a basis for thought by theology. Nominalistic theologians maintained that God's redemptive actions were not inherently intelligible and illumined by divine reason but were, rather, mere emanations of a sovereign divine will. Whereas the classical position of Saint Thomas Aquinas holds that divine actions arise equally from reason and will (= love), here, the light of reason in God's nature is extinguished. The omnipotence and freedom of God's actions are misrepresented as mere arbitrariness. Thus, the view was sometimes taken that, since there was absolutely no reasonable explanation for the fact that the Second Divine Person was incarnated as a man, Christ might just as well have assumed the form of a donkey.[3]

Nominalist influences on Martin Luther

Many of the features of this arbitrary God that were soon dispelled from orthodox Catholic thought found their way into Reformation Christianity through Luther's teacher, Gabriel Biel. Martin Luther rails against the "whore of reason", which he sees as incapable of reaching knowledge of God through the works of creation.[4] In his numerous writings on the Eucharist, Luther puts so much emphasis on the sacramental words and pays so little attention to the symbolism of bread and wine that the Protestant theologian K. G. Steck was once led to remark: "According to

---

[2] Josef Lortz, Geschichte der Kirche in ideengeschichtlicher Betrachtung I [History of the Church in relation to history of ideas I], 22nd/23rd ed. (Münster, 1962), pp. 455f.

[3] In connection with William of Ockham; cf. Johannes Hirschberger, Geschichte der Philosophie I [History of philosophy I], 9th ed. (Basel, Freiburg and Vienna, 1974), p. 566.

[4] Hartmann Grisar, Luther III (Freiburg im Breisgau, 1912), pp. 836f. Cf. Josef Lortz, Die Reformation in Deutschland I [The reformation in Germany I], 4th ed. (Freiburg im Breisgau, 1962), pp. 172ff.; Georg Koepgen, Wilhelm von Ockham. Anfang und Ende de Reformation [William of Ockham. Beginning and end of the Reformation], (Regensburg, [1973?]).

Luther, the eucharistic offerings, instead of being bread and wine, might just as well be crab-apples."[5] The world and man are so corrupted by sin that they are totally unable to provide any indication of God's nature. "Grace alone" (*sola gratia*) leads man to God.[6]

Nominalist influences in modern Protestant theology

Description of Karl Barth's position

What may be called this "anticreation passion" recurs, with especially crass emphasis, in Karl Barth's dialectical theology. The *analogia entis*, or correspondence in being between Creator and created, is Barth's main reason for not becoming a Catholic.[7] In particular, he is critical of the analogies of symbolic thought: "It does not follow as a matter of course from the symbolical that we call God 'Father' or Christ 'the Light'. Christ could also have called himself 'the Darkness'."[8]

The same, markedly Protestant approach also sets the direction for Barth's writings on the relations between the sexes, which have exerted a far-reaching influence. With reference to the biblical account of creation, Barth states that "a human being . . . never and nowhere [exists] as a human being pure and simple, but always and everywhere as a human *man* or as a human *woman*".[9] This difference is the "first and, at the same time, the exemplary dimension of human social interrelatedness".[10]

He is opposed to certain developments in the "modern women's movement", which he sees as containing a "vestige of theoretical and emotional pathos . . . in the direction of a confusion between what pertains to oneself and what to others".[11]

Also, he is strongly critical of the above-mentioned "androgynous

[5] K. G. Steck, "Symbol", in *Evangelisches Kirchenlexikon III* [Encyclopedia of the Protestant church III], 2nd ed. (Göttingen, 1962), p. 1238.

[6] Josef Lortz, *Geschichte der Kirche in ideengeschichtlicher Betrachtung II* [History of the Church in relation to history of ideas II], 22nd/23rd ed. (Münster, 1964), pp. 96f.

[7] Karl Barth, *Kirchliche Dogmatik I, 1* [Church dogmatics I, 1], 7th ed. (Zollikon and Zurich, 1955), pp. viiif.

[8] This quote is based on oral information and reflects only the general sense of what was said; cf. Erwin Iserloh, "Bildfeindlichkeit des Nominalismus und Bildersturm im 16. Jht." [Nominalistic antipathy to imagery and iconoclasm in the sixteenth century], in Wilhelm Heinen, ed., *Bild—Wort—Symbol in der Theologie* [Image—word—symbol in theology] (Würzburg, 1969), p. 127.

[9] Karl Barth, *Kirchliche Dogmatik III, 4* [Church dogmatics III, 4], 2nd ed. (Zollikon and Zurich, 1957), p. 130.

[10] Barth, *KD III, 4*, p. 128.

[11] Barth, *KD III, 4*, p. 172.

utopia", whose origins he traces back mainly to Schleiermacher, the secret "Church father" of the secular women's movement.[12] In fact, he himself expresses great sympathy for this sort of solution,[13] but finds no way of reconciling it with "God's law"; thus, he effectively places human thought in unmediated opposition to divine revelation.[14] Only for this reason is he able to describe the "androgyne" as "a boldly and freely invented mythical being . . . upon which, as with all beings of this sort, we can only decisively turn our backs".[15]

In Barth's view, a hidden atheism is the deepest root of androgynous thought: "*God is for them* (man and woman) *a oneness*: by virtue of this, they are spared having to *become one* among themselves, and dissuaded from wanting to *become one*."[16]

Schleiermacher thus succumbed to the temptation of intermixing the divine with the human. Barth levels the same accusation at the Catholic teaching on marriage, which includes the notion of a sacramentally grounded participation in the Divine Life.[17]

God created man, although not only as "man *or* woman", but also, and primarily, as "man *and* woman".[18] The sexes are constituted as naturally correlative. This correlation is grounded in God himself: "What is meant by man's having been made in the image of God, in Genesis 1:27f., is: that God created them, a man and a woman, in this relationship so as to reflect the fact that God himself is also in relationship, is not alone within himself."[19]

Just as it is only through their interrelations that the three Divine Persons are constituted as such, something similar obtains with respect to the interpersonal relations between man and woman: "The you, the not-I that, precisely as such, is constitutive of the I, is woman."[20] Thus we find in Barth an "identification of the *essences* of the two sexes with this *relationship*".[21]

The mutual relationship between man and woman cannot be reversed

---

[12] Cf. Elisabeth Moltmann(-Wendel), "Letztes Glied in der Kette der Befreiten. Theologie und Emanzipation der Frau" [The last link in the chain of the liberated. Theology and the emancipation of women], in *Evangelische Kommentare* 8 (1975): 672; Moltmann-Wendel, "Christentum", p. 20.

[13] Barth, *KD III, 4*, p. 174.

[14] Barth, *KD III, 4*, p. 174f.

[15] Barth, *KD III, 4*, p. 178.

[16] Barth, *KD III, 4*, p. 175.

[17] Barth, *KD III, 4*, p. 137.

[18] Barth, *KD III, 4*, p. 165.

[19] Barth, *KD III, 4*, p. 128.

[20] Barth, *KD III, 4*, p. 165.

[21] Barth, *KD III, 4*, p. 182.

at will, since man is "A" and woman is "B": "in matters of precedence, belonging and devotion", man "takes priority over woman", which means "that, in all their being and acting together, he is the stimulator, leader, arouser, who always takes the initiative. . . . Order implies an ordered *ranking* of *before* and *after*, *above* and *below*."[22]

In liberal Protestantism, a "canon within a canon" was (and is) often set up. Leopold Zscharnack (1902), for instance, plays off Galatians 3:28 ("there is neither male nor female; for you are all one in Christ Jesus") against 1 Corinthians 11 and similar passages that speak of the subordination of women.[23] Zscharnack obviously takes as his "measuring stick" the Enlightenment "ideas of the equality and fraternity of all mankind",[24] and not the biblical message in its entirety.

Similarly, Protestant theologians often do not regard the subordination of women as part of the order of creation, but rather explain it as a consequence of the Fall, which has, in principle, been overcome through the order of grace. Exactly this position is expressed today, most notably by Elisabeth Moltmann-Wendel.[25]

Barth opposes such views and takes a very positive attitude toward the encyclical *Casti connubii* of Pius XI.[26] With reference to Ephesians 5, he sees the subordination of women as a "particular form of the obedience that the Christian community owes to Jesus Christ".[27] Behind this, he also sees in the Old Testament a clear symbolism of man and woman as an "emblem of the Covenant".[28]

Logical contradictions in Karl Barth's thought

Barth's last-mentioned view is obviously incompatible with his usual aversion to symbolical thought, which—as evident, for example, in the Catholic teaching on marriage—establishes a connection between God and man that precludes any dialectical opposition of the two. This anti-symbolical tendency shows itself as well in his call "to refrain from

---

[22] Barth, *KD III, 4*, p. 189.

[23] Leopold Zscharnack, *Der Dienst der Frau in den ersten Jahrhunderten der christlichen Kirche* [The service of women in the early centuries of the Christian Church] (Göttingen, 1902), pp. 15f.

[24] Zscharnack, *Dienst*, p. 13.

[25] Moltmann(-Wendel), "Letztes Glied", p. 673. Elisabeth Moltmann-Wendel, *Freiheit, Gleichheit, Schwesterlichkeit. Zur Emanzipation der Frau in Kirche und Gesellschaft* [Liberty, equality, sisterhood. On the emancipation of women in Church and society] (Munich, 1977), p. 71.

[26] Barth, *KD III, 4*, p. 217; cf. p. 56 above.

[27] Barth, *KD III, 4*, p. 192.

[28] Barth, *KD III, 4*, pp. 165f.

phenomenological or *typological* approaches to the problem of the sexes".[29]
Barth caricatures any juxtaposition of complementary traits by pointing
out that, for example, no woman is merely "person oriented" and no man
merely "thing oriented". He ignores the fact that the writers he criticizes
are obviously concerned with polar relations between characteristics that
may be found in everyone, yet that are differently accentuated from
person to person. This nominalist-influenced scepticism hardly sits well
with his own attempt to see man as the "arouser" and woman as the
"recipient" within their mutual relationship. Here, he falls victim to his
own claim that those who attempt to formulate a typology would
"presume to *know* in advance . . . the content of God's law".[30] In view of
this sort of criticism, trying to uphold the relationship of ascendancy and
subordination or to oppose the interchanging of roles (which roles?) could
only appear highly arbitrary.

A similar inconsistency is evident in Barth's thought on the nature of
relationship in this context. That man must be an essentially relational
being because God is in relationship with himself cannot be derived in this
way from the biblical text.[31] The claim presupposes a certain natural
analogy between God and man. Moreover, Barth seems to assume that
relationship defines the essence of man in the same way that it grounds
the three Persons of the Trinity. Since the Divine Persons are pure
relationship, their common nature is preserved; but if Barth equates the
relationship of man and woman with their essences, as he seems to do in at
least the above-cited passages, then the independent natures of each are
dissolved. For there is no relationship if it is not sustained by particular
things in relation.[32] Thus, Barth has here ignored the very distinction
between God and man that he elsewhere more than clearly stresses.

Further development of Barth's thought
by Charlotte von Kirschbaum

Similar tensions are evident in the writings of Barth's student Charlotte
von Kirschbaum, who aims to develop her mentor's thought consistently
with its established directions.[33] She describes in great detail the symbolical
nature of the sexes, calling attention to the "bond between man and
woman as an emblem" for "Yahweh's love and faithfulness to Israel".[34]

[29] Barth, *KD III, 4*, p. 168.
[30] Barth, *KD III, 4*, p. 167.
[31] Cf. p. 199 below.
[32] On the concept of relation, cf. p. 178 below.
[33] Cf. Barth, *KD III, 4*, p. 192.
[34] Kirschbaum, *Frau*, p. 12.

With reference to Ephesians 5, Kirschbaum finds that the wives mentioned there "reflect, in their natural position as wives vis-à-vis their husbands, the position of the Christians, which is that of the community, vis-à-vis their Lord. . . . A man is always faced with having to find his way . . . to this position . . . , whereas a woman can see it as prefigured in her own natural position."[35]

Regarding the "*mulier-taceat* verses" from 1 Corinthians 14,[36] she even says: "The women who keep silent represent the listening Church, which is something that the teaching Church must become over and over again."[37] Thus she accepts the subordination of women called for by Paul as a matter of course; but, in view of the present-day need to build up the religious community, she nevertheless supports the ordination of women.[38]

In contrast to the arguments based on symbolism just noted, and in agreement with Simone de Beauvoir (!), Kirschbaum points out that "Scripture" recognizes "no universal images and programs".[39] Thus, she also writes critically of Gertrud von le Fort's *The Eternal Woman*, which confronts "man not with a reality, but with a symbol that has become a character, with . . . a—*myth*".[40] To the "eternal" woman she opposes the "real" woman or, more precisely, the real *human being*.[41]

The radicalization of the Protestant critique of Karl Barth and its background

The above-noted contradictions are pointed out by Ilse Bertinetti, who accuses Kirschbaum (and thus also Barth) of "interpreting aspects of natural life as providing evidence about the sacred realm (if . . . only in the sense of symbolic representations)".[42] Any reasoning about "the male nature of the ministry" or even about "the 'sex' of God" is, therefore, "pagan speculation".[43]

Furthermore, Bertinetti bases her case on the absolution of sinners, which must apply equally to all.[44] Kirschbaum's "equality of pardons"

[35] Kirschbaum, *Frau*, p. 13.
[36] Cf. pp. 363ff. below.
[37] Kirschbaum, *Frau*, p. 51.
[38] Kirschbaum, *Frau*, pp. 52f.; Kirschbaum, *Dienst*.
[39] Kirschbaum, *Frau*, p. 94.
[40] Kirschbaum, *Frau*, p. 84.
[41] Kirschbaum, *Frau*, pp. 85, 87.
[42] Bertinetti, *Frauen*, p. 148.
[43] Said at a conference by Marga Bührig, with whom Bertinetti agrees: Bertinetti, *Frauen*, pp. 150, 152.
[44] Bertinetti, *Frauen*, p. 124.

must also be carried over into an "equality of rights" in the secular world. Therefore, to assume that there is "an 'essential' difference between man and woman" would be to contradict the biblical message.[45] In particular, the subordination of women has been, "in view of Galatians 3:28, . . . already potentially overcome".[46]

In classical Protestantism, as is well known, absolution is widely regarded as a purely external judicial act, corresponding to no transformation in one's actual being: *"simul justus et peccator"*.[47] The important thing is to grasp salvation through belief; the works are only fruits of this belief and not themselves grounds of merit.[48] Consequently, there is no difference in kind or degree of holiness, for grace is equal for everyone, as is blessedness in heaven.[49] The rejection of Purgatory[50] or of the appeal to saints,[51] to name just two typical examples, can be understood only if seen against this backdrop.

It would appear that the spread of modern "equality thinking", which bears the stamp of the Enlightenment, was encouraged by Protestant views such as these. Especially in the United States, this sort of connection would seem to apply. If, moreover, under the influence of Barth, any typology of the sexes is played off against an inaccessibility of "God's law", one can easily be led into seeking the constantly changing content of that law[52] in the particular views that happen to be dominant in the world at any given time. The sole efficacy of God can then be turned dialectically into the self-determination of his creatures. The Protestant theologian Walter Reissinger thus states rather sarcastically that "in the total process of *turning the Church into the world* . . . the diabolical spirits of the whole inhabited earth (. . . Eph 6:12) . . . have been remarkably quick to make themselves at home" in his church.[53]

---

[45] Bertinetti, *Frauen*, p. 148.

[46] Bertinetti, *Frauen*, p. 124.

[47] Cf., among others, the Schmalkaldian Articles: Martin Luther, *Der grosse Katechismus. Die Schmalkaldischen Artikel* [The major catechism. The Schmalkaldian articles], Calwer Luther-Ausgabe 1, 2nd ed. (Gütersloh, 1977), pp. 205f.

[48] Confessio Augustana 6, in *Das Augsburger Bekenntnis*, ed. by Heinrich Bornkamm (Gütersloh, 1978), p. 19.

[49] The Council of Trent opposes this view in Canon 32 of the Decree on Absolution: *DS*, 1582.

[50] Schmalkaldische Artikel, in Luther, *Katechismus*, pp. 184f.

[51] Schmalkaldische Artikel, in Luther, *Katechismus*, p. 188.

[52] Cf. Barth, *KD III, 4*, pp. 171, 173.

[53] Reissinger, "Frau", p. 151.

"Conservative" and "progressive" nominalism

In our times, marked as they are by philosophical empiricism and positivism, it is not unusual to find certain parallels to "nominalist" tendencies in theological treatises. Underlying this, two main directions can be distinguished, one "conservative" and the other "progressive".

As a conservative representative of this general trend, one might well cite the Lutheran bishop Bo Giertz, who is an energetic opponent of the ordination of women in Sweden. Although Giertz recognizes a difference between men and women that is rooted in the order of creation, he is of the opinion that this distinction has different implications in the religious sphere from those that apply in the secular sphere. The subordination of women is valid only "in marriage and in the religious community", but "not . . . in general social relationships".[54]

Here, Church and civil society are not only justifiably distinguished, but the two appear to be totally separated. In order, then, to justify the exclusion of women from religious office, one can appeal, basically, only to an isolated and almost arbitrary seeming notion of "God's law".[55]

If there is a tendency in Protestant circles to refer exclusively to Scripture, without bringing any additional viewpoints to bear on the matter, there is a similar tendency in Catholic circles with regard to Tradition. The task of weighing up this Tradition in its contemporary context and in its relevance to the totality of the Faith is something with which most seem all too happy to dispense. A typical example, among many, would be the following.

In 1973, a working party of American bishops published a paper consisting of "theological reflections", which were intended to outline a position on the constantly increasing demands for the ordination of women. The statements from Scripture, and especially the passages from the letters of Saint Paul that are full of "provocative words", are dismissed without much ceremony as "sociohistorically conditioned": "these Pauline texts should not be cited as arguing against the ordination of women".[56]

Arguing a specifically theological case against the ordination of women was not even attempted, but instead, reference was made to the traditional structures of the Church and to the possibly forthcoming pronouncement on the matter by the Magisterium.[57]

[54] Giertz, "Schrift", p. 208.
[55] Giertz, "Schrift", p. 206.
[56] Bishops' Committee on Pastoral Research and Practices, "Theological Reflections on the Ordination of Women", *JEcSt* 10 (1973): 697.
[57] "Reflections", p. 698.

The previously described[58] progressive direction is often willing to admit that the established practices of the Church are based on the example of Jesus' own behavior but regards that behavior itself as socio-historically conditioned. Given the context of "Judaic-Palestinian thought", Jesus was either unwilling or unable to plan beyond his own times.[59] Today, he would act quite differently.

While conservative nominalism thus withdraws into reliance on the arbitrary-seeming behavior of Christ or of the Church, nominalism's progressive representatives base their decisions on constantly changing sociocultural circumstances.

Both of these directions are positivist in orientation, because they break off a few isolated fragments from the whole complex of realities that should be considered and then base their decisions on those alone. A positivism of Scripture (or of Tradition) differs from a positivism of social facts, which may well distance itself even further from the center of Faith, only in respect of their differing lines of sight; their "blinders" are common to both.

3. INDISPENSABLE ANTHROPOLOGICAL PRESUPPOSITIONS
   OF THE THEOLOGY OF CREATION

Consideration of all lines of inquiry relevant to the topic

When progressive nominalism, which is probably the leading influence today, allows itself to be impressed by the process of social change, it overlooks the structures that are rooted in creation itself and that persist unchanged throughout all time. These structures inhere not only in the area of reality studied by sociology, but also, and above all, in those studied by biology, psychology and philosophy.

The inadequacy of currently fashionable theological approaches

Since all such elements are so little changeable, they are held in great suspicion by modern man, programmed as he is for progress, and they

---

[58] Cf. pp. 21f., 61–64 above.
[59] Thus, for example, Stendahl, "Auffassung", p. 148.

also enter only relatively rarely into the theological debate. Although present-day theology places great emphasis on the need for dialogue with the human and natural sciences, the results of such talk frequently appear quite meager. Often, there is a lack of even the simplest and most basic knowledge of the natural sciences, despite the fact that such knowledge is indispensable to attaining the highest levels of thought in philosophy and theology.

The discipline of biology is usually totally avoided, and even when it is occasionally touched on, this is almost always in conjunction with sociological data that impart an appearance of relativity to the biological facts.

Things seem slightly better regarding the discipline of psychology, although its biological foundations are frequently overlooked, with the result that characteristics of mind and soul appear capable of being formed in almost limitless directions and of being shared indifferently by either men or women. Una Kroll, for example, regards as possible a culture in which "all the children—assuming that they were raised as individuals, without having sexist roles forced on them—would have the possibility of developing into complete human beings, differing from one another solely in their biological functions".[60]

Philosophical deliberations are often regarded as of little significance and are caricatured with words like: "The eternal feminine appears to us today as little more than an eternally changing notion of the feminine."[61]

Structure and scope of the material in the following chapters

If, however, one wishes to inquire into the relations between the order of creation and the order of redemption, which are considered important in Catholic thought, it is necessary first of all to take account of as much of the entire range of created reality as is relevant to the topic. For this, it is not sufficient, in line with current fashion, to limit the inquiry to the findings of sociology, which—if taken in isolation—just relativize all timeless connections. My starting point, then, will be the physical bases of being human, as studied in the discipline of biology. Next, the effects of these will be pursued into the area of psychology, after which consideration will be given to the formative influences exerted by differing social conditions. The results of all this will, in turn, lead to considerations

[60] Kroll, Kennzeichen, p. 83. Reference has already been made to comments by Meer (Priesturtum) and Raming (Ausschluss) that tend in the same direction: cf. pp. 41–42 above.

[61] Oliver Brachfeld, "Das Bild der Frau im Wandel der Zeit" [The image of woman and historical change], in Michael Schmaus and Elisabeth Gössmann, eds., Die Frau im Aufbruch der Kirche [Women and the upheaval in the Church] (Munich, 1964), p. 9.

of a philosophical sort, which can be combined with the findings of religious phenomenology. At this highest level of reflective thought, philosophy, the significance of the symbol will be of special interest, as it represents an important *praeambulum fidei* to understanding the sacrament of the ordination of priests.

Of course, given the complex variety of the relevant findings of biology, psychology, sociology, religious phenomenology and philosophy, little more can be attempted here than to open up a broad vista. Since, however, such a synthesis is indispensable to any study based on the theology of creation, and since it has been treated in a rather stepmotherly way in previous writings on our topic, it will have to be pursued at somewhat greater length than might normally be expected in a systematic theological work.

CHAPTER SIX

Anthropological Foundations

I. BASIC BIOLOGICAL FACTS

The significance of hereditary factors

Hereditary factors determine that every human being is either a male or a female. There is no single cell in the human body (the gametes being a special case) that is not sexually imprinted. All vital processes are controlled by chromosomes that reside in the nucleus as complex, threadlike structures of nucleic acids. Certain segments of nucleic acid in a chromosome constitute a gene, a hereditary factor.

Man normally possesses forty-six chromosomes in each cell; the genes in two chromosomes determine membership of one of the two sexes and corresponding sexual development. For males, these are two different chromosomes, termed X and Y, while, for females, the two are the same, XX. The gametes, which result from a process of division, contain only half of these chromosome pairs, thus having either an X or a Y chromosome. In accordance with the kinds of gametes that happen to come together at fertilization, a male or a female cell will be created, a new human being.

Genetic membership of one of the sexes, determined by the chromosomes, then serves as the basis for further differentiations. Between the fifth and eighth weeks of pregnancy, the rudimentary reproductive gland develops into ovaries, in the case of XX cells, or testes, in the case of XY cells ("gonadal sexual differentiation"). Certain hormones that are brought into play by the genes contribute to this process. Between the twelfth and sixteenth weeks, under the continuing influence of hormones, the external genital organs take shape ("genital sexual differentiation") and, in connection with this, after birth, "general somatic sexual differentiation" occurs, which also includes the secondary sexual characteristics. Finally, as "the highest level of integration of genetic, gonadal, genital and somatic sexual differentiation . . . psychosocial sexual differentiation" is formed under the influence of environment and education.[1]

The genetically based sexual differences can be influenced by hormones, which are produced mainly by the gonads. Female and male sex hormones are found "side by side in the male and the female organism", even though there is a "decided sexual polarization and specialization".[2] Due to differences in the distribution of these hormones, the sex characteristics of men and women can be more or less strongly developed, with the result that women who strike one as masculine and men who appear feminine can occur.[3]

The physical appearance of men and women

The differences in physical appearance can be divided into primary and secondary sex characteristics. Included in the first group are the internal and external sex organs, and in the second, the other characteristic differences in bodily form.

The primary sex characteristics serve the interest of coitus, which, in turn, ensures the preservation of life. In the act of coitus, the female naturally has the role of receiving and assimilating, which corresponds to the male role of effecting and imparting. "If what occurs regarding the female is a *centripetal* process, directed from the outside inward toward the center of life, what occurs regarding the male is a *centrifugal* one, directed from the center of life outward."[4]

---

[1] H. Höhn, "Genetische Aspekte der Geschlechtsdifferenzierung beim Menschen" [Genetic aspects of sexual differentiation in man], in H. Autrum and U. Wolf, eds., *Humanbiologie* [Human biology] (Berlin, Heidelberg and New York, 1973), p. 123. Exceptions can occur in this developmental series. In quite rare instances, there can be defects "in the interaction between the hormones and the areas they normally influence" (Höhn, "Aspekte", p. 128), so that, for example, a masculinizing hormone cannot exert its proper effects, and the person developed is, to all appearances, feminine. Somewhat more frequent are cases in which more than one sex chromosome is present in one of the parental gametes. If there is an extra X or Y chromosome, the corresponding male or female qualities are developed in a particularly one-sided way. On the basis of genetic factors, there are no true hermaphrodites, since the decisive element in sexual determination is the presence or absence of a male Y chromosome. Individuals of indeterminate sex in the wider sense number 1 to 2 per 1,000 in the general population.

[2] S. M. Rapoport, *Medizinische Biochemie* [Medical biochemistry] (Berlin, 1975), p. 769.

[3] On the subject of sex chromosomes and hormones, cf. also the relevant biological contributions in Sullerot, *Wirklichkeit*, especially pp. 64–84 (Ohno, Royer, Jost, Sullerot) and 100–108 (Jost). On the theory mentioned there about a "female proto-sex" (for example, pp. 70, 104), something will be said later; cf. pp. 188f. below.

[4] Philipp Lersch, *Vom Wesen der Geschlechter* [On the nature of the sexes], 4th ed. (Munich and Basel, 1968), p. 25.

Because of the nature of the female reproductive organs, women are, to a greater extent than men, "sexual beings".[5] The very fact that their sex organs are situated largely inside the body points to a closer connection with other bodily processes. Much more strongly than is the case with men, "disorders of the sex organs, on the one hand, [affect] other organs", while "other sorts of disorder, on the other hand, [involve] the sex organs".[6]

The monthly periods, which are regulated by the activity of the ovaries, influence women (mentally as well as physically) so strongly that, "in a certain respect, the life of the female body" is "constantly under the sway of the menstrual law".[7]

The periods, in turn, subserve the possibility of conception and motherhood, during which a woman's being is centered for nine months on the new life that is developing in her body.

The secondary sex characteristics are closely bound up with the primary ones. The body's bone structure (*skeleton*) tends, on the average, to be weaker in women than in men. Given the function of the skeleton, this means that men are better suited than women to overcoming physical resistance. "Men's bone structure gives them more *steadfastness*, a firm attacking stance as well as greater powers of resistance and endurance in relation to their surroundings."[8] The more powerful male hand, for example, is obviously "intended . . . for practical-technical and constructive mastery of the environment, while the slighter, more delicately structured female hand is more suited to taking the environment in hand, carefully tending to it and providing for it".[9]

The male and female physical structures differ not only quantitatively, that is, in respect to sheer mass, but also qualitatively, in respect to form. The bodily forms of the male are "more sharp edged, angular, rugged and broken", while even the skeleton of the female exhibits "rounder and less extreme contours and more obtuse angles".[10] Here, it should be noted that angular bodily forms are more suited than round ones to making outward, attacking thrusts against sources of resistance.

The softer, smoother forms of the female are defined not only by the skeleton, but also by the *musculature*. The striated muscles, which are capable of sudden, strong contraction, are more strongly developed in

[5] Theoderich Kampmann, *Anthropologische Grundlagen ganzheitlicher Frauenbildung I* [Anthropological foundations for comprehensive education of women I] (Paderborn, 1946), p. 151.

[6] Kampmann, *Grundlagen I*, p. 151.

[7] Kampmann, *Grundlagen I*, p. 131.

[8] Lersch, *Wesen*, p. 31.

[9] Lersch, *Wesen*, p. 31.

[10] Lersch, *Wesen*, p. 31.

men. Their more powerful arm muscles, for example, enable them to take, literally, a more solid "grip" on the world. This "difference in musculature" is "no . . . product of culture . . . , but a concrete expression of the physiological distinctiveness of the sexes".[11]

Corresponding to the more strongly developed musculature of men, the bodies of women contain a larger proportion of fatty tissue. The ratio of fat to muscle, relative to body mass, is 28 percent to 39 percent in the adult woman and 18 percent to 42 percent in the adult man.[12]

A woman's *skin* is softer, smoother and less hairy. This, along with a larger number of nerve endings in the skin, results in a greater sensitivity to tactile stimuli and thus in a special attunement to the "things encountered in the immediately surrounding areas of the environment".[13] For such matters, women have, in the truest sense of the word, their own "special touch".[14] In men, the skin is more strongly involved in mediating a sense of direction to the organs of activity, especially the hands.

Along with those differences that apply to the body as a whole, the *relationships of the individual parts of the body to one another* are also significant. Arms and legs are organs "that serve, above all, the acts of reaching out into the world and of overcoming and conquering space".[15] These are, in relation to the entire body, longer in men and shorter in women. The female figure appears to converge more toward the center of the trunk and the male figure, to spread out more away from that point. The center of the female body is also emphasized by the fact that the abdominal area, in the interest of carrying children, is longer and fuller than it is in the male.

Also noteworthy is the relationship between shoulder and pelvis widths. In men, the shoulders are broader and the hips narrower, while in women the reverse applies. The male, accordingly, is more strongly directed toward the "outside", and the female, toward the "inside".

The dynamics of the body

The general *style of movement* of the sexes differs in three respects: in the *direction*, in the *execution* and in the *degree of integration* of the movements. The "origin and goal of movements by women is their own body—as axis —to a larger degree than is the case with males, whose way of moving also

[11] Kampmann, *Grundlagen I*, p. 164.
[12] Lersch, *Wesen*, p. 32.
[13] Lersch, *Wesen*, p. 33.
[14] Lersch, *Wesen*, p. 34.
[15] Lersch, *Wesen*, p. 35.

shows them to be more strongly oriented toward, and bound up with, the external environment."[16]

These differences in *direction* of movement are not primarily results of conditioning, but manifest themselves in babies, even during the first year of life. A student of Buytendijk, for example, conducted extensive observations of the movements of babies in a maternity hospital and found that, even at this early age, those of females are more strongly related to their own body and to their immediate surroundings, while those of males are directed more toward distant aspects of the environment.[17]

The *execution* of the movements of women is more even and more flowing, whereas men move more "smartly". When walking, for instance, men emphasize more strongly the concluding phase of each step, while the steps of women are less accentuated. The "movements of males consist of countless *endings*; the movements of females are *endlessly continuous*."[18] More characteristic of women is a rhythmical form of movement—"rhythm" comes from the Greek word *rhein*, which means "to flow"—and of men, a beatlike form: "The [German] word *Takt* comes from *tangere* ('to beat') and signifies the beat that constantly recurs at equal temporal intervals, punctuating the rhythmical flux and underlining its variability with an invariable series of ups and downs."[19]

One could illustrate the distinction in question by the following diagram:

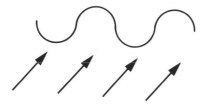

Rhythm
(more characteristic
of the female)

Beat
(more characteristic
of the male)[20]

Also significant is the *degree of integration* of the movements, through which the movements of the individual parts are combined into one whole. The movements of females "are much more integrated than those

[16] Lersch, *Wesen*, p. 38.

[17] F. J. J. Buytendijk, *Die Frau. Natur—Erscheinung—Wesen* [Woman. Nature—appearance—essence] (Cologne, 1953), p. 246, n. 1.

[18] Buytendijk, *Frau*, p. 231.

[19] Kampmann, *Grundlagen I*, pp. 209 f., based on a formulation by Ludwig Klages. The American writer John Steinbeck expresses this state of affairs in his own way as follows: "Man, he lives in jerks. . . . Woman, it's all flow, like a stream, little eddies, little waterfalls, but the stream it goes right on." Cf. Buytendijk, *Frau*, p. 225.

[20] A similar diagram occurs in Lersch, *Wesen*, p. 44, with reference to the ways that men and women speak.

of males, which are broken up into movements of particular members and are, as such, specialized for performing particular functions".[21] Thus women also tend to react as organic wholes ("expression movement"), whereas the movements of men can be concentrated more strongly on particular areas.[22]

In view of all this, the following seems to apply regarding the direction, execution and degree of integration of movements:

The dynamics of the male are expansive, outer directed and aimed at overcoming particular sorts of resistance. The dynamics of the female are more adaptive in nature, that is, more strongly adjusted to the demands of the existing situation.

2. THE DEVELOPMENT OF BIOLOGICAL SEX DIFFERENCES AT THE PSYCHOLOGICAL LEVEL

The intimate interconnection between body and soul

Psychologists often attempt to gain evidence about the psychological differences between the sexes by conducting tests and experiments. The results of these tend to be dismissed by adherents of role thinking with comments about limited frames of reference and sociocultural relativity. Evelyne Sullerot seeks to come to grips with this model of inquiry in terms of her own sociological categories.[23]

There is, however, a simpler method, which has been applied with much success for centuries: that of observation. This method proceeds on the assumption that man's mind and soul do not lead isolated lives of their own but are intimately bound up with bodily states and feelings. In life as we know it, there would seem to be no mental function whose actual employment does not presuppose, in one way or another, some biological foundation.

The body is not something external to the human person, but is—in Thomistic terminology—one of its "incomplete substances", as is the soul. The human soul, to be sure, cannot simply be reduced to the incomplete material substance and is, by virtue of its spiritual oneness,

---

[21] Lersch, *Wesen*, p. 39.

[22] Lersch, *Wesen*, p. 39.

[23] In, among other places, the Colloquium on the Psychological Differences of the Sexes: Sullerot, *Wirklichkeit*, pp. 333ff; cf. also pp. 527f.

immortal; but it is, as "formal principle", predisposed to the body and retains this *desiderium naturale* even after death.[24]

It should, therefore, be possible to move from a precise analysis of how things stand with the body to conclusions about the life of the soul. In this area, special distinction has been achieved by *phenomenologically* oriented psychology, which, by virtue of its characteristic method, enjoys the advantage of "ideology-free" objectivity. Particular reliance will be placed here on these studies, which have met with widespread recognition in professional circles; whereas any evaluation of the more controversial psychoanalytic movement, which is fragmented into numerous "confessions", will be largely dispensed with in the present context.[25] Among works of the relevant sort, those by Lersch and Buytendijk seem, by virtue of their unusual precision, especially valuable. Their findings have recently received interesting confirmation from research in cerebral physiology, although that work is, admittedly, only in its early stages.[26]

Reason and will as basic faculties of the soul

The basic faculties of man's soul are his intellectual capacities of knowledge and active desire, or reason and will.[27]

[24] On this, cf. the recent study drawing on the phenomenological method by Josef Seifert, *Leib und Seele* [Body and soul] (Salzburg and Munich, 1973). Also: Josef Seifert, *Das Leib-Seele-Problem in der gegenwärtigen philosophischen Diskussion* [The body-soul problem in contemporary philosophical debate], *Erträge der Forschung* 117 (Darmstadt, 1979).

[25] Later on, however, something will be said about *Jung's* psychology, certain basic assumptions of which have spread so widely outside psychological circles that they are almost common knowledge: cf. pp. 128–33 below.

[26] In the relevant literature, reference is made particularly to differences in the structure and function of the two sides of the brain in men and women. Cf. Sullerot, *Wirklichkeit*, pp. 341–68; Huber, "Emanzipation", p. 62; Beatrice Flad-Schnorrenberg, *Der wahre Unterschied. Frau sein—angeboren oder angelernt?* [The true difference. Being a woman—innate or acquired?] (Freiburg, Basel and Vienna, 1978), pp. 36–39. According to these findings, women have a greater facility for linguistic expression, while men's sense of spatial orientation and, in connection with this, capability for logical abstraction are more strongly developed.

A brilliant survey of the anthropological research can be found in the important work of Stephen B. Clark, *Man and Woman in Christ: An Examination of the Roles of Men and Women in Light of Scripture and the Social Sciences* (Ann Arbor, 1980).

[27] Empirical psychology calls these "cognition" and "conation". Cf. James Drever and W. D. Fröhlich, *Wörterbuch zur Psychologie* [Dictionary of psychology], 9th ed. (Munich, 1975).

Reason (abstraction and intuition)

Reason, in the broader sense, embraces two different areas, namely, "reason" (in the narrower sense) and "understanding".[28] Both contribute to the intellectual grasp of reality, but in different ways. Reason (*Verstand*, from German for "to understand", "to be well versed in"; Latin, *ratio*) extracts from the manifold contents of experience the things that it takes for essential and imposes order on them, whether with a view to effecting practical change or simply to gain a systematic perspective. The main means through which understanding works is the concept.

Understanding, on the other hand (*Vernunft*, from German for "to perceive"; Latin, *intellectus*), is not so much concerned with putting the world at its disposal, but more with allowing things, to a certain extent, to impress themselves on it. The means for this intellectual seeing (intuition) is the image.

Now, reason and understanding may be seen as exhibiting certain parallels with the two differing dynamics of the sexes. Whereas the outwardly thrusting tendency of reason corresponds to the expansive dynamics, understanding's greater tendency to dwell contemplatively on things aligns it with the adaptive dynamics.

These differing sorts of intellectual orientation manifest themselves even at the biological level. It is well known that the activity of the intelligence depends on the apprehension of sense data, especially through the sense of sight. While the female gaze tends more strongly toward "*resting* on things and *taking them in*", thereby evidencing a state of "being with" the things it sees, the male eye is more inclined to focus sharply on the environment and to view things as "objects" in front of it.[29]

Along with reason goes abstraction, which utilizes concepts to effect its generalizations from the fullness of concrete reality. It is less oriented toward people than toward complex states of affairs.

With understanding, the case is different. It thinks in images and has a deeper affinity with individual realities, a special proportion of which are persons. Accordingly, women possess a greater sensitivity to the values inherent in things around them and to interpersonal relations, while men tend more to see the world in terms of obstacles and means to ends. Women's horizon of experience lies more in the direction of subjective, personal impressions, while men are more able to discount the concrete details of a situation and to try to resolve it in terms of objectively valid, general principles.

[28] Cf. on this Josef de Vries, "Vernunft" [Reason], in Walter Brugger, ed., *Philosophisches Wörterbuch* [Philosophical dictionary], 14th ed. (Freiburg, Basel and Vienna, 1976), pp. 433f.

[29] Buytendijk, *Frau*, p. 183.

Will ("aggressive" and "affective")

The importance of reason to the life of the mind is equalled by that of will. The capacity of active desire points reason in this or that particular direction and guides the processing of the impressions received through cognition. Insofar as the will actively directs itself toward some goal, it is accompanied and supported by tension in the striated muscles, which are more highly developed in men. Along with this goes, as well, a higher degree of aggressiveness.[30]

The capacity of active desire in women, on the other hand, is more reactive in nature. As "feeling", it allows itself to be formed by the various impressions received, which explains why the female sex has been called *le sexe affectif*.[31] A stronger "certainty of feeling"[32] does not, of course, mean simply passivity, since every feeling carries an impulse toward some sort of behavior (which would, naturally, have a different character than would be the case for a man).

"Symmetry" and religious experience

The fact that women are guided more strongly by intuition and feeling also means that they are more open to concrete experience, whereas men always behave more critically. A reserved attitude is often accompanied by an asymmetrical bodily posture, whereas a symmetrical posture is expressive of an unreserved "being present".[33] In all cultures, for example, the posture of prayer is symmetrical, as is the posture adopted when contemplating a beautiful landscape, appearing before a superior and so forth.

An asymmetrical appearance occurs more frequently in men. In the standardized postures of everyday life, to be sure, there are no great differences. But when those constraints are absent, it becomes clear, for instance, that "a woman's face [is] less asymmetrical than a man's".[34]

Given all this, it seems probable that women display a greater readiness for devotedness in respect of God as well. Their faculties of mind and soul are more cohesively integrated, whereas men are more inclined to dissociate certain areas and, in extreme cases, to make absolutes of them,

[30] Buytendijk, *Frau*, p. 120.

[31] Auguste Comte, in Lersch, *Wesen*, p. 59.

[32] Buytendijk, *Frau*, p. 189.

[33] Lersch, *Wesen*, p. 60.

[34] Buytendijk, *Frau*, p. 186. Buytendijk also refers in this connection to the portraits in the history of painting that provide exemplary evidence for this state of affairs. I might note here the possibility that the greater asymmetry of males could derive from their asymmetrical set of XY chromosomes, which contributes to the forming of their total bodily being.

as, for example, of *ratio*. "From the fact that a woman's nature is more an interbalanced whole, one can also understand why a woman who is untrue to her inner being errs more gravely than a man."[35] Accordingly, the piety of women has a crucial, if not all-determining, significance in human life.

Women's readiness for devotedness is indicated not only by their just-discussed tendency to favor symmetrical postures, but also, as mentioned earlier, by the greater openness of their glance,[36] and both of these facts are expressive of deeper aspects of the life of the soul. It might be noted that, in a certain respect, this quality of receptivity is shared by women with children, who, as is well known, display a heightened readiness for devotedness.[37] Whereas, however, a child's ability to bring "inwardness" under the control of its own thought processes is still only weakly developed, a woman can take a conscious attitude toward what is experienced.

In the sense that women possess a greater, less-divided readiness for devotedness, they are, it would seem, more religious than men. Nevertheless, responsiveness alone is not ultimately decisive. What matters much more is having a clear goal before one's eyes and constantly directing the various sides of human nature toward it, even if doing so clashes with some current mood or feeling. In respect to this, primacy must go to men. Even in the area of religion, then, men and women are counterparts who must complement each other.

The experience of men and women

Reason and will, as constituted in the two sexes, lead to differences in the experiencing of one's own person. A man, with his abstractive reason, is able to distance himself rather far from the concrete things around him, and he often adopts the same attitude toward his own body (and himself). Max Scheler comments on this as follows: "In comparison with the way that a woman constitutively experiences her body—the way that she feels and knows herself as in it—a man walks his around at such a distance from himself that it might well be a dog on a leash."[38]

[35] Robert and Alice Scherer, "Vom Wesen der Frau" [On the essence of woman], in Alice Scherer, ed., *Die Frau. Wesen und Aufgaben* [Woman. Essence and challenges], Wörterbuch der Politik VI (Freiburg im Breisgau, 1951), p. 9.

[36] Cf. p. 92 above.

[37] Additional details can be found in Buytendijk, *Frau*, pp. 179–84. This special receptivity of children was taken up by Jesus and used as an example for his disciples: Matthew 18:3 and other passages.

[38] Buytendijk, *Frau*, p. 271.

This is expressed, for example, in Saint Francis' attitude and behavior toward his body: "Brother Ass". To my knowledge, no statement as drastic as this has ever been made by a female saint.

The differing "world horizons"

"Near world" and "far world"

These same behavioral dispositions carry over into the area of the "world horizons"[39] of the two sexes. Whereas women live more in a state of symbiosis with their environment and are more concerned with the "*near world*", men are more strongly oriented toward the "*far world*". They often overlook the things that are (literally) nearest to them and tend to worry more than women about unsolved problems that lie beyond the near world.[40]

Nature and "history"

The categories near and far also refer to the dimensions of time. Women, with their special relationship to rhythmically recurring processes, tend to remain subject to the cycles of *nature* (= the present), while men more readily break out of these cycles in the direction of the open horizon of the future. "It is men who make *history*"—this sentence may be rather pointed, but, in the sense intended, it is correct.

"Species" and "individual"

Insofar as men, by virtue of their biological-psychological constitution, tend to take a more detached attitude toward things, they are more deeply representative of the *individual*. Women are more bound to their own bodies, whose functions are directed in a variety of respects toward motherhood, and their greater settledness in the near world serves the interests of their relationship to children. Motherliness in a broader sense can, of course, also be realized independently of raising children. Women, then, by virtue of their strong natural ties to reproduction and child raising, are more strongly representative of the interests of the *species*.[41]

---

[39] Lersch, *Wesen*, p. 61.

[40] Thus, according to Buytendijk, the creative genius who breaks out of everything near and familiar, is found much more often among men. Women, on the other hand, who are much less free of ties, therefore have a stronger sense of duty. Cf. Buytendijk, *Frau*, p. 262, n. 1.

[41] Thus it is not sufficient for a child to be cared for by just any person whose role might be played equally well by the father. A child needs a mother, who, by virtue of her entire

This situation may well mean that half of mankind is disadvantaged in relation to participation in public affairs—something that disturbs many ideologues of emancipation—but it also means that the other half, in turn, is denied the gift of something whose worth is truly not to be underestimated, namely, motherhood.

3. "CENTRALITY" AND "ECCENTRICITY" AS SUMMARY FORMS OF THE DIFFERENCES BETWEEN THE SEXES

The foregoing biological-psychological outline may be concluded with a diagram:[42]

The *"eccentricity"* of men and their tendency toward history-oriented activity can be represented by the "symbol of a line originating at the center of the subject and thrusting outward into the world":[43]

To express the *"centrality"* of women and their position of stronger involvement in the rhythms of nature, what suggests itself is "the image of a circle encompassing its center point":[44]

These basic principles of eccentricity and centrality are found in the animal world as well, especially among birds and mammals. This parallel is a clear sign that the outlined differences between men and women are firmly rooted in biological nature.

Because of all this, there exists a certain polarity between men and women: masculine and feminine qualities seem to diverge in tending toward two different poles, and the special character of man's existence is defined by the tension and interplay between them. The structures underlying this polarity are genetically determined in men and women, but,

---

biological and psychological makeup, is much more suited to this sort of task than is the male parent. Cf. the article by Christa Meves, "Waisenknaben. Warum die Mutter nicht Mutter und die Hausfrau nur Hausmann heissen darf" [Orphan boys. Why the mother must not be called mother and the housewife must be called only househusband], *Rheinischer Merkur* 52 (Dec. 29, 1978): 27.

[42] Based on Lersch, *Wesen*, pp. 62f.

[43] Lersch, *Wesen*, p. 62.

[44] Lersch, *Wesen*, p. 63.

given that basis, there is still considerable scope for movement and variation, especially in respect to mental and spiritual qualities. No man, for example, is moved solely by sheer objectively calculating, abstracting reason, and no woman lives solely under the guidance of intuition. The above-mentioned interplay of masculine and feminine traits is present to a certain extent in every individual. According to C. G. Jung, each person's soul carries within itself, so to speak, a "shadow image" of the opposite sex, the so-called animus or anima. These images have to be integrated into one's personality as a whole.[45]

It would be a mistake, however, to conclude from this that only hermaphrodites, masculine women, feminine men and neuters (in short, androgynous beings) would be complete human beings. In a healthy man, the animus is clearly predominant, and in a woman, the image of the anima.

4. THE RELEVANCE OF SOCIOLOGY

The biological "framework" of social roles

The same "law of polarity"[46] also influences the relationships between the sexes in the social sphere, where, as a rule, it applies even more strongly.

In this connection, to be sure, a basic rule operates that is true of all hereditary factors: an innate range of potentials for actualization is subject to variable environmental and educational influences. What is concretely actualized can thus take many and varied forms yet must always remain within the limits of a predetermined biological framework.

Now, it is possible to imagine social situations in which masculine traits are emphasized to an equal degree for both men and women, others in which feminine qualities are given preeminence, and still others in which it is expected that men will show almost exclusively masculine characteristics and women, only feminine ones. A society would even be possible in which it was the lot of women to play an emphatically masculine role and the lot of men, a feminine one. In no way, however, would the relevant hereditary predispositions be changed.

---

[45] Cf. p. 130 below.
[46] Lersch, *Wesen*, p. 117.

Examples of social influence on the positions of men and women, with critical evaluation

For all of these imagined possibilities, there are actual examples. Many theologians who like to bolster their arguments in favor of the ordination of women with references to "constantly changing social conditions" rely heavily on the remarkable studies by Margaret Mead. During the twenties and thirties, this anthropologist and sociologist conducted research into socially conditioned sex differences among half a dozen native peoples of the Pacific region. Here are some sample excerpts:

Among the Tchambuli in New Guinea, the men wear strings of ornaments, do the shopping, carve wood and paint. The women "go with shaven heads, unadorned, determinedly busy about their affairs".[47] Since the women are busy with agricultural work all day long, their husbands take over a portion of the maternal duties: " 'We could milk the goats and feed the babies', they said. 'The women are busy and have other things to do.' "[48]

In this case, the roles of husband and wife are, to a certain extent, exchanged, but a neighboring tribe of headhunters, the Mundugumor, shows a strong masculine emphasis. Although hunting, for example, is reserved for men, an aggressive attitude is instilled in both sexes from youth onward. A newborn baby "is kept sharply hungry, so as to suck vigorously on a woman's breast until milk comes in. . . . The Mundugumor women actively dislike childbearing, and they dislike children."[49] Because there is almost no polarity between male and female in so many areas, the contrast between the sexes is concentrated into an exaggerated concern with genital sexuality.[50]

Again, quite a different situation exists among the Arapesh, where both sexes seem to live, to the same degree, for the ideal of "motherliness". They help each other with the work, and "the greatest interest of both men and women is in growing things—children, pigs, coconut trees. . . ."[51]

There is no reason to misuse findings such as these in an attempt to justify unbridled emancipation, for every one-sided development of a biologically given predisposition ultimately exacts its revenge, and that applies even to an "abolition of all distinctive characteristics".[52]

[47] Mead, *Mann und Weib*, p. 79.
[48] Mead, *Mann und Weib*, pp. 181f.
[49] Mead, *Mann und Weib*, p. 57.
[50] Mead, *Mann und Weib*, p. 81.
[51] Mead, *Mann und Weib*, p. 45.
[52] This interpretation of certain notions of emancipation was reached by Erler: *Zerstörung*, pp. 10f.

Margaret Mead herself condemns any such one-sidedness: "But where the Tchambuli system crumbled under a reversal in the ethos of men and women and the Mundugumor system was invaded and disintegrated by an emphasis on a common hostile ethos that lacked counterpoint or any complementary character beyond the bare facts of sexual anatomy, the Arapesh system is rendered innocuous by an emphasis on the maternal, parental aspects of both men and women."[53]

On the hypothesis of the "matriarchate"

The theories of Bachofen, Morgan and Engels

In 1861, Johann Jakob Bachofen published a work of far-reaching influence: *Maternal Law. An Inquiry into the Gynaecocracy of the Ancient World in Its Religious and Legal Aspects*. Drawing on Egyptian and Greek myths that tell of a victorious struggle waged by gods against goddesses,[54] he postulates the occurrence of a historical transition from "matriarchy" to "patriarchy". That women were once dominant is attested to, according to Bachofen, by certain ancient writers, who make reference to a "gynaeco-cracy", or "rule by women", in Lycia, and to similar tendencies in Egypt.[55] From the fact that succession was matrilineal in Lycia and that children there were named after the mother, he concludes that women generally held the positions of power in the society.

This (later so named) "matriarchate" represents, as Bachofen interprets the myths, the material principle, which is supplanted in the "patriarchate" by the psychical principle, naturally embodied in men. The matriarchate appears as the first, most general stage of man's development, from which, fortunately, the male spirit ultimately freed itself.[56]

In 1877, a book called *Ancient Society*, by the American Henry Morgan, was published that seemed to offer confirmation of Bachofen's thesis about a prehistorical matriarchate. Morgan based his work mainly on evidence about the Iroquois tribe of Indians, which he took as exemplifying a general type of man's development. To him, the Iroquois provided a perfect model of liberty, equality and fraternity and thus a shining ideal for American democracy.[57]

[53] Mead, *Mann und Weib*, p. 82.

[54] Uwe Wesel, *Der Mythos vom Matriarchat. Über Bachofens Mutterrecht und die Stellung von Frauen in frühen Gesellschaften vor der Entstehung staatlicher Herrschaft* [The myth of the matriarchate. On Bachofen's maternal law and the position of women in ancient societies before the rise of state rule] (Frankfurt, 1980), pp. 12f., 58f.

[55] Wesel, *Matriarchat*, pp. 13f.

[56] Wesel, *Matriarchat*, pp. 13, 18.

[57] Wesel, *Matriarchat*, pp. 19ff.

These writings had momentous consequences when, in 1884, Friedrich Engels published his *The Origin of the Family, Private Property, and the State*. This work, which is essentially an excerpt from *Ancient Society*, traces a line of development from the matriarchate through the (reprehensible) patriarchate to the fraternal state of society under ultimate communism. Even today, Engels' theories continue to form an integral part of the official doctrine of historical materialism.

General evaluation

The hypothesis of a prehistorical matriarchate may well have been pretty well pulled to pieces by historical and ethnological research during the past one hundred years, but large sections of the new women's movement continue to guard it like a precious treasure. In theological circles, too, slogans like "from matriarchy through patriarchy to fraternity" seem to have been received with a certain sympathy, whose tacit influence can be detected behind many writings on the question of women in the priesthood. Thus, it seems appropriate here to take a summary look at the problem of the matriarchate.

First, it is necessary to keep certain concepts clearly distinguished. Matriarchate, as opposed to patriarchate, means "rule by mothers" or, more precisely, "the predominance of women in the family and in society".[58] The German term *Mutterrecht* has a rather variable meaning. It can serve, firstly, as a synonym for matriarchate; it can signify, secondly, legal succession through women or mothers; or it can have, thirdly, a mixture of the two preceding meanings. Bachofen's thesis trades on these ambiguities. He identifies certain legal arrangements with a social predominance of women.

When children are regarded as being related only to the family of their mother or to that of their father, one speaks of matrilineality or patrilineality. In addition, there are numerous mixed systems. The point of these kinship systems is probably the classification of children.[59] Matrilineal arrangements exist only in certain agriculture-based societies, while they have not yet been found in the more ancient, hunting-based societies.[60] In any case, matrilineality that was brought to light by Bachofen can in no way be equated with a matriarchate. For in both patrilineal and matrilineal societies, things are, as a rule, directed by men.[61]

A similar situation exists regarding matrilocality and patrilocality,

---

[58] Wesel, *Matriarchat*, p. 33.
[59] Wesel, *Matriarchat*, pp. 34, 99, 149.
[60] Wesel, *Matriarchat*, pp. 77, 127.
[61] Wesel, *Matriarchat*, pp. 71, 126.

which refer to the place of residence of a new family. Matrilocality occurs only in matrilineal societies, while matrilineality can coexist with patrilocal arrangements. Patrilineal societies are, as a rule, patrilocal.[62] Whereas matrilineal societies can evolve into patrilineal ones, the reverse of that process is unknown.[63]

In societies that are simultaneously matrilineal and matrilocal, "the social position of women can be unusually good, yet not be such as to justify references to rule by women". If, in addition, women possess a certain predominance in the family, and sometimes also outside the family, one may speak of a "matristic" society, or of "matrifocality", which means that women stand "at the center, or focal point, of social relationships".[64]

Some typical examples

After these general points, some revealing concrete examples will be useful. Henry Morgan based his theory largely on the *Iroquois*, whose social structures are, in fact, very interesting. "Among the more than one hundred [matrilineal] societies known at present, they are perhaps . . . the only one that can, with some justification, be regarded as matriarchal."[65] At any event, they are "the one that most closely approximates to the idea of a matriarchate".[66]

In the eighteenth century, the Iroquois, a group of only fifteen thousand people, inhabited a huge area "that was ten times the size of Oregon, stretching from southern Canada to northern Virginia, from eastern Tennessee to the New England states".[67] The Iroquois were farmers and hunters. While the women tended the fields, the men went hunting or were on the warpath, often traveling many miles and staying away from their families for weeks or months on end. These circumstances resulted in a sharp separation of the world of men from that of women: "Men lived and conversed with men, and women, with women. Even at daily meals in the longhouse, they ate in separate groups."[68]

Since the women were left to themselves at home, they themselves had to settle the problems of the village and regulate the distribution of the food that they produced, without any help from the men. An older woman was, therefore, the highest authority in the village, with respon-

---

62 Wesel, *Matriarchat*, p. 34.
63 Wesel, *Matriarchat*, p. 77.
64 Wesel, *Matriarchat*, p. 35.
65 Wesel, *Matriarchat*, p. 25.
66 Wesel, *Matriarchat*, p. 114.
67 Wesel, *Matriarchat*, p. 107.
68 Wesel, *Matriarchat*, p. 100.

sibility for coordinating the economic and social matters there. The mothers arranged the marriages and even determined political affairs: they, and not the men, elected the representatives for the various governing bodies.

However, they elected only men. In the tribal councils, and especially in the council of the central league, where the really important political decisions were made, not a single woman ever participated as a full member. Women were allowed to attend only the open meetings and only as observers, although they were able to exert a certain influence on the voting there.

When pressure from the white settlers forced the Iroquois into living on a reservation, their whole system of social order broke down. For the men were now at home, and, although the matrilineal structure was retained, a typical patriarchate was developed. Thus, one could say rather pointedly: "The power of the women was the absence of the men. It was an exceptional situation."[69]

Bachofen focused his attention above all on *Lycia*, about which there are "the most definite and also most substantial sorts of evidence" for the existence of "maternal law".[70] In fact, matrilineality and matrilocality were to be found there—something that struck the Greeks as scandalous—as well as a certain influence in the domestic sphere because of the frequent absence of the men (piracy), but never political and social rule by women.[71]

In *Egypt*, women were fully entitled to act in business matters and had the same legal rights as men—which Herodotus regarded as "turning the world upside down"—but the most important positions at court, in administration and in handicraft were occupied by men.[72]

A similar picture emerges in respect to *Crete*, where the ancestors of the Lycians probably lived, and which had close cultural ties with Egypt. Female deities play a dominant role in the Cretan religion, and worship is almost totally in the hands of women. Men, apparently, can participate in ceremonies only if dressed as women, and in public life the female sex seems more prominent than the male.[73] This does not, however, involve the women in masculine roles, as Vaerting thinks.[74] Rather, the whole culture is decidedly feminine in character, as evidenced particularly by Cretan art "in its fragrance and musicality, delicate softness and dreamy

[69] Wesel, *Matriarchat*, p. 117.

[70] Wesel, *Matriarchat*, p. 40. This was Bachofen's opinion.

[71] Wesel, *Matriarchat*, pp. 36–40.

[72] Wesel, *Matriarchat*, pp. 41–46.

[73] Friedrich Heiler, *Die Frau in den Religionen der Menschheit* [Women in the world religions] (Berlin and New York, 1977), p. 7; Wesel, *Matriarchat*, p. 48.

[74] Cf. p. 41 above.

grace, tasteful love of colors and shallow 'decorativeness', along with its avoidance of all logical and architectural discipline and any themes of 'virile' life".[75]

Nevertheless, Crete also possesses "a tightly structured system of government, headed by a king, rather than a queen, and a large number of administrative officials. All the evidence suggests that these, too, were men. Any references to a 'matriarchate' here are totally out of place."[76]

A possible explanation for the domination of women in Cretan public affairs could be the fact that seafaring activities on this island state, the "England of the ancient world", had developed to an unusual degree, with the result that a large proportion of the men were constantly away on voyages. As was the case with the Iroquois, the women were then left to themselves and were in a position to create a culture in which they could play a leading social role as well. Once Cretan seafaring began to decline, this situation also changed.[77]

Summary and conclusions

Thus, there never was any such thing as a matriarchate. Wesel is probably right when he dismisses this idea as a modern myth. Even semiofficial Soviet and East German publications have recently begun to distance themselves from Bachofen's hypothesis.[78] The well-known sociologist René König thus observes that "remnants" of this theory are found "now only . . . in political journalism and vulgar Marxism".[79] A close study of the historical facts discloses not the relativity of man's biology and psychology but rather their essential constancy even under the most widely varying social conditions.

---

[75] Egon Friedell, *Kulturgeschichte Ägyptens und des Alten Orients. Leben und Legende der vorchristlichen Seele* [Cultural history of Egypt and the ancient East. Life and legends of the pre-Christian soul], 3rd ed. (Munich, 1951), p. 494.

[76] Wesel, *Matriarchat*, p. 51.

[77] Johannes Leipoldt, *Die Frau in der antiken Welt und im Urchristentum* [Women in the ancient world and in early Christianity], 2nd ed. (Leipzig, 1955), pp. 11f.

[78] Wesel, *Matriarchat*, p. 30.

[79] René König, *Die Familie der Gegenwart. Ein interkultureller Vergleich* [The family today. A cross-cultural comparison], 3rd ed. (Munich, 1978), p. 149, n. 43. The thesis of a matriarchate was also unanimously rejected by the international colloquium of scientists on the "Reality of Woman": Sullerot, *Wirklichkeit*, pp. 484f.

Women in social leadership positions in the secular and religious spheres

The secular sphere

Against the background of the material just surveyed here, it is certainly no coincidence that the overwhelming majority of human societies so far known, whatever their geographical and historical positions, evidence a clear preponderance of the male sex in positions of social leadership. This fact stands out with particular clarity when the great, highly developed cultures of the Near East, India, China and Europe are taken into account. Surely fifteen thousand Iroquois or five hundred Tchambuli natives of New Guinea cannot simply be placed on the same level with a civilization such as China's, as theologians and some sociologists, following Margaret Mead, like to try to do. Of course, the social leadership role of men can, as a result of human sinfulness, sometimes degenerate into an oppression of women, but *abusus non tollit usum*.[80]

It is also not foreseeable that this situation will ever change. For, as has been shown earlier, the differences between the sexes are not limited to the merely anatomical sphere, as with the difference between muscle power and softness, but also carry over into qualities of mind and soul. Consequently, these differences will not be eliminated even in a highly technologized and automated society. This is evident precisely in those institutions that are striving to move in the opposite direction.

The United Nations, which has issued numerous declarations against any sort of discrimination between the sexes, seems to have attained its goal, at least insofar as women make up 50 percent of its personnel. Nevertheless, 80 percent of its higher positions are filled by males. "Among the top thirty-five officials, there was only one woman, and, at the next-highest level, eight women found themselves facing 292 men."[81]

A similar situation exists in the Soviet Union, although it is precisely there that a conscious struggle is waged against social differentiations between the sexes. Three-quarters of the teachers, for example, are women, but three-quarters of the administrators are men.[82] The situation in the higher ranks of the party and state is well-known.

---

[80] Cf. pp. 202–4, 351–57 below.

[81] Agudelo, "Aufgabe", p. 301.

[82] H.-R. Laurien, "Der andere Mensch, nicht der schlechtere Mann—Emanzipation konkret" [The other sort of person, not the inferior version of the male—concrete emancipation], in Weinzierl, *Emanzipation*, p. 79.

Protestant communities

This small proportion of women in leading positions is also characteristic of the religious sphere. In the American Methodist church, for example, the ordination of women was introduced as early as 1956 and did not meet with energetic resistance of the kind that occurred later in Sweden. Nevertheless, in 1970, only 0.7 percent of the clergy were women.[83]

The situation in other American churches, where the proportion of female officeholders seems to have averaged out at 3 percent, is slightly less striking.[84] In the German Evangelical church, the proportion of female pastors has even reached 4 percent,[85] but there seems little likelihood that a parity of 50 percent will be reached in the foreseeable future.

Also, there are constantly recurring complaints within Protestant communities that females in the clergy are forced into marginal positions by the male competition, having to accept subordinate roles or smaller parishes.[86] Most of the female clergy are assigned to special areas of church work, such as, in particular, caring for women and children. The situation in Württemburg is characteristic, of which it could be said in 1975 that "only two out of thirty-eight female theologians 'are in the parish ministry', both working as subordinates and only one enjoying contractually regulated conditions".[87]

Thus the introduction of female pastors into the ministry has obviously not (yet?) sufficed to bring about equal rights. Instead, what has often happened is that the inequalities have become more glaringly apparent.

Sects

A particularly interesting subject for study is the sects, insofar as the term "sect" is understood in the religious-sociological sense, namely, as referring to a smaller religious community, relatively easily perceptible as such by its individual members, that has broken away from some larger grouping and developed its own spiritual outlook, often described as "subjectivist" by outside observers.[88]

[83] Smylie, "Protestant Churches", p. 87. In absolute terms, the largest number of female clergy in the United States is to be found in these churches. Recent developments would seem to indicate that, in the longer term, the 0.7 percent figure might rise to 5 percent.

[84] Cf. Hewitt and Hiatt, *Women Priests*, p. 124, n. 3.

[85] *Frau in Familie*, p. 142; cf. also p. 133.

[86] Cf., among others, Lynch, "Ordination", pp. 180, 194f.; Bam, *Ordination*, pp. 10f.; Smylie, "Protestant Churches", pp. 91f.

[87] Reichle, *Theologin*, p. 310.

[88] On the concept of a sect, cf. Kurt Keinath, "Sekten und Freikirchen" [Sects and independent churches], in Konrad Algermissen, *Konfessionskunde* [Study of religious confessions], 8th ed. (Paderborn, 1969), pp. 672–75.

Friedrich Wiechert[89] presents a whole showcase of sects that, time and again throughout the entire history of the Church, have called on females to hold office. This "ancestral gallery" of the ordination of women stretches from Gnosticism and Montanism to the "Brothers of the Free Spirit" in the Middle Ages and numerous Protestant groups since the eighteenth century. In recent times, more detailed studies have been conducted into the history of the Catharists and the Waldenses. Both of these groups utilized female preachers, who also administered the Eucharist, which the Waldenses even understood in the orthodox sense as the Sacrifice of the Mass. Nevertheless, as the leadership structure of these sects developed and expanded, this sort of activity by women became less and less frequent, even though express measures forbidding it were never imposed.[90]

Against this background, it is easy to see why many advocates of the ordination of women accompany their arguments with demands for "base communities" and less clerical structuring of official positions.[91] Admitting women to the priesthood does, in fact, seem to be an effective means of loosening up the hierarchy and of turning the pyramid into a circle of equals. For the particular strengths of women, in which they hold an advantage over men, do not allow them to take a leadership role in the same way that is typical of their "opposite number". Their specific, if not therefore exclusive, "area of activity . . . is not organization, but the personal sphere".[92] That this does not imply inferiority of any sort hardly needs to be pointed out here.

The significance of social differentiations between the sexes

In contrast to animals, whose roles are inherently fixed, man is faced with the important task of exerting conscious control over the formation of his system of social differentiation. This formation, as has been shown above, can vary greatly between societies, but it is always a present and significant

[89] Friedrich Wiechert, "Der Dienst der Frau ausserhalb der Grosskirche" [The service of women outside the main Church], Eine heilige Kirche 21 (1939): 129–39.

[90] Gottfried Koch, Frauenfrage und Ketzertum im Mittelalter. Die Frauenbewegung im Rahmen des Katharismus und des Waldensertums und ihre sozialen Wurzeln (12.–14. Jh.) [The question of women and heresy in the Middle Ages. The women's movement in context of Catharism and Waldensianism and its social roots (twelfth to fourteenth centuries)] (Berlin, 1962), pp. 38, 52, 129f., 158f., 168f., 173f., 182.

[91] Elisabeth Gössmann, "Die Frau als Priester?" [Women as priests?], Conc 4 (1968): 297; van Eyden, "Amt", p. 114; Agudelo, "Aufgabe", pp. 305f.

[92] Scherer, "Wesen der Frau", p. 12.

factor. According to the French sociologist Evelyne Sullerot,[93] the social "signs, roles and attitudes" that differentiate the sexes "show no evidence of a tendency toward conformity among mankind as a whole".[94] An excessive lack of social differentiation between the sexes is not the mark of a higher stage in man's development ("evolution"), but rather a fall back into primitive conditions:

> As a rule, it is in the earliest stages of a civilization that the differences between the social positions of men and women are relatively small. The more a civilization consolidates and refines itself, the wider the gap between the social roles of women and men becomes.[95]

This statement does not imply, of course, that there is never any justification for doing away with outdated inequalities. For it is surely unjust if the gap between the social roles becomes too wide, and if, for example, women in a culturally advanced society are denied voting rights or equal payment for equal work. When, however, demands are made that half of the number of parliamentary seats (or, as in Lutheran Sweden, half of the number of bishop's seats) must be occupied by women, then it is a matter of having strayed beyond the realities of human existence into a mere utopia.

The relation between biology and sociology from the standpoint of theology of creation

Man's created nature consists not only of the body but also of the mind, which—in contrast to the situation of the animals—can consciously give formal direction to biological predispositions and anchor these in ordered social relationships. From this, the conclusion is sometimes drawn that man's nature is his culture, and that biological realities are mere material that can be formed and reformed as desired. Perhaps it would even be possible, in the future, to breed sexless or hermaphroditic beings.

It is also "possible", of course, to blow up our planet with atomic bombs. Not all that is possible is permissible. The fact that man's nature is biologically based clearly expresses how closely it is bound to preexisting norms. Whereas the mind can reach out to embrace a potentially endless horizon of being, the body is much more confined. Once man becomes

[93] Mme Sullerot holds a chair in the sociology of women at the Sorbonne (Paris), the only chair of this sort in France.

[94] Sullerot, *Frau*, p. 8.

[95] Sullerot, *Frau*, p. 18.

conscious of the possibilities of his mind, he often feels himself restricted by his body, and this can even go so far that he regards everything pertaining to the body as evil. This was the case, for example, among the Gnostics and Manichaeans.

Anyone who wants to be nothing but a mind, and to bring everything biological under the control of his own will, is secretly striving to raise himself to the level of God. For the fact of having been determined in being by the Divine Creator expresses itself concretely more through bodily finitude than in the realm of the mind. The atheist Sartre senses this relationship to God quite clearly when he writes that the body "is . . . the fact that the for-itself [the mind] is not its own ground".[96]

A woman's relationship to her body is usually more intimate than a man's relationship to his.[97] Therefore, when women such as Simone de Beauvoir rebel against their bodily natures, such an attitude must seem especially radical and fateful. If it is true, as Ursula Erler thinks, that this sort of rebellion is the norm today,[98] this would suggest the existence of a hidden, large-scale atheism that is far from being adequately dealt with by the Church's pastoral efforts.

Those who believe in God the Creator will develop a different kind of relationship to their bodies (and to biology in general) than will agnostics or atheists, for whom "transformation", in the Marxist sense, is often the measure of all things.[99] Whereas a Sartre can feel "disgust" at the body,[100] believers in God are called on to accept their corporeality and to develop it in the direction that the Creator has implanted, at least as a seedlike predisposition, within it.

To be sure, whether sexual differentiation is an inalienable aspect of that predisposition, or whether realization of an "androgynous utopia" is permissible, cannot be answered with absolute clarity from within the perspective of an (isolated) set of beliefs about creation. It is only through supernatural revelation that a final resolution of this question would seem possible, even though many of the results of natural reflection also indicate that the complementarity of the sexes is a valuable component of human existence. More will be said about this problem later, in the context of an examination of the biblical account of creation.[101]

---

[96] Sartre, *Sein*, p. 405.

[97] Cf. p. 94 above.

[98] Erler, *Zerstörung*, p. 88.

[99] "A conviction of the changeability of all things is the criterion by which one assesses whether or not a view is progressive": Bornemann, *Patriarchat*, p. 534.

[100] J.-P. Sartre, *La nausée* (Paris, 1948).

[101] Cf. pp. 198ff. below.

5. PHILOSOPHICAL ANTHROPOLOGY

The need for philosophical integration of the findings of the special sciences, and the main problems involved

The enumeration of a variety of specific findings from biology, psychology and sociology can lead to a certain sense of unease, inasmuch as all these statements, at first sight, may seem to be just strung together, rather than interrelated in any orderly way. Still, some of the findings met with so far here result from tracing a multitude of singly observed facts back to a common basic principle; in particular, the polar opposition of eccentricity to centrality goes beyond the strictly empirical realm, even if it has been crystallized out of precise, detailed investigation of scientifically verifiable material.

Examining the reality that is perceived by the senses with a view to discovering its ultimate structural constituents and principles is the task of philosophy. Since the subject matter of philosophy extends beyond the tangible and the scientifically verifiable and pushes into the realm of the ideal, it has met with considerable scepticism in our empiricist and positivist, or, in short, nominalist times. In part, this scepticism is justified. For the higher the level of reality, the less easily man, bound as he is to his senses, can attain knowledge of it. What is most clearly knowable for God—namely, ideal reality—is least clearly knowable for man. Correspondingly, even today, the discipline of philosophy is beset with more contradictions than is, for example, that of geography.

It would not do, then, to assume that all the philosophical issues surrounding the problem of the duality of the sexes can be solved with a snap of the fingers. Serious thinking about these matters is still in its early stages, partly because of the scope and variety of the empirical material and partly because of a certain shyness about the subject of sexuality. Even textbooks on biology and psychology often deal solely with "man" in general, and the Western philosophical tradition defines man as the *animal rationale*. This definition is certainly applicable, but it needs to be supplemented by a perspective enabling clearer recognition of the basic dichotomy of the sexes.

Taking a philosophical view can often open up horizons that remain closed to more cursory observation; indeed, Kant "spoke of a 'vista on the infinite' that 'opens' itself here; in this can be . . . intimated that we are drawing near to a primordial phenomenon".[102]

---

[102] Erwin Metzke, "Anthropologie der Geschlechter. Philosophische Bemerkungen zum

In the presence of associations such as these, however, there is no need for total intellectual capitulation. For philosophy, as such, is not some ideological contrivance that projects the "intellectual spiderweb" of its own prejudices on reality, but basically means nothing more than a deepened receptiveness to the effects of that reality. According to Saint Thomas, man's understanding is not only a faculty that "posits" things, but also—and first of all—one that "registers" them.[103] This basic assumption by the *doctor angelicus* corresponds to the phenomenological viewpoint, as anticipated, for example, in Philipp Lersch's above-mentioned pair of contrasting concepts. Philosophy is inescapably referred back to the reality that is graspable by the senses: *Nihil est in intellectu, quod non prius fuerit in sensu.*

Polar oppositions like Lersch's are found, usually in prescientific form, in most ages and cultures. In general, they seem to reveal a convergence of philosophical thought in the direction of identifying the masculine more with a creatively assertive principle, and the feminine, more with a receptively formative one. "This notion (of a polar opposition) is as old as human thought itself."[104]

Josef Burri locates the origins of the "polarity theory" in "romanticism", and regards it as marking a transition from a "subordination thesis" to an "emancipation thesis", for which he feels special sympathy.[105] According to Burri, the development of history progresses from "subordination" through "dissimilarity" to "equality".[106] Romanticism means, for him, that "man's historicity", or, more precisely, his sociology,[107] has "not been taken seriously enough".[108]

Use of the word polarity in connection with the duality of the sexes seems, in fact, to have occurred for the first time in the work of Wilhelm von Humboldt, whose allocation to the age of romanticism might well be questioned. In any case, the word did not originate in speculations of an aesthetic-literary sort but was a product of von Humboldt's many years of research in the natural sciences. The subordination of women was, in fact,

---

Stand der Diskussion" [Anthropology of the sexes. Philosophical observations on the present state of debate], *Theologische Rundschau* 22 (1954): 211.

[103] Cf. Josef de Vries, "Abstraktion" [Abstraction]: Brugger, *Wörterbuch*, pp. 2–5.

[104] Buytendijk, *Frau*, p. 43.

[105] Josef Burri, *"als Mann und Frau schuf er sie"*. *Differenz der Geschlechter aus moral- und praktisch-theologischer Sicht* ["male and female he created them". The difference between the sexes from the moral and practical-theological viewpoint] (Zurich, Einsiedeln and Cologne, 1977), pp. 32, 61, 93, 170.

[106] The equality axiom emerges with particular clarity in the commentary on the latest Council: Burri, *Differenz*, pp. 177–83.

[107] Burri, *Differenz*, p. 40.

[108] Burri, *Differenz*, p. 197.

seen from a special perspective—which led, especially in romanticism, to greater esteem for the nature of woman[109]—but it did not disappear altogether, as Burri suggests.[110]

The factual realities that underlie the polarity are, of course, as old as man himself, as will become particularly evident when material from the study of religion is discussed later on.[111]

It should be noted here that there is *no* question of *identifying* concrete women and concrete men with the corresponding polar principles. As a rule, both principles can be seen to be active in members of each sex. Nevertheless, men and women tend, in a quite specific way, to fall under *one* of these dual concepts.

Anthropological and cosmological interpretation of the polarity of the sexes in Aristotelian hylomorphism

At first, there is a tendency to interpret the polarity of the sexes as an elemental *human* phenomenon. Fairly soon, however, the discovery is made that this duality is also characteristic, in a similar way, of nonhuman reality. Then the world no longer appears as a reflection of man, but vice versa: the active powers of the cosmos interpenetrate, in differing ways, all the regions of being, including the microcosm that is man. An anthropologically focused outlook thus expands into a cosmological one.

The earliest, and even today most influential, examples of concern with such matters in the Western philosophical tradition are provided by Plato and, above all, Aristotle. Already in Plato, a determining principle, that of the ideas, is opposed to a determinable one, and these two elemental powers are linked to the notions of male and female. The father exemplifies the impressing principle, while the mother resembles "matter", lying ready, "like a mass of formable material", to let herself "be moved and formed under the impress of that which enters into her".[112] The receptive principle is "the assistant and, in a certain sense, the nurse of all coming to be".[113]

This line of thought is developed further by Aristotle, who compresses it into the polar opposition "matter = form" ("hylomorphism").[114] As

---

[109] Cf. Mörsdorf, *Gestaltwandel*, pp. 122ff.

[110] Burri, *Differenz*, p. 194.

[111] Cf. pp. 133ff. below.

[112] *Timaeus*, 49e–50, in Plato[n], *Spätdialoge II* [Late dialogues II], Artemis-Paperback-ausgabe VI (Zürich–München, 1974), p. 238.

[113] *Timaeus*, 48d–49b, p. 236.

[114] On what follows, cf. C. v. Bormann, W. Franzen, A. Krapiec and L. Oeing-Han-

opposed to both the conservatism of Parmenides, who recognizes only unchanging being, and the progressivism of Heraclitus, for whom there is only constant change, or a flux of becoming, he adopts the position that there is a balanced interrelationship between the changeable and the unchangeable in the structural elements of reality. The configurative determination of a thing through its form corresponds to the eternal Platonic idea. There are, however, processes of change from one form to another, and these cannot be accounted for in terms of the nature of the forms themselves, but only through a third thing that underlies the formal structure, thus enabling a transition to occur from one sort of form to its opposite. This constant, underlying "material", which, "together with the form, enables things to come into being, is like a mother".[115]

In contrast to Plato's theory of ideas, which places the eternal ideas in unmediated opposition to the changeable material world and is thus unable to solve the problem of becoming, Aristotle holds that form and matter do not exist in separation but are mutually dependent principles of being. Their relationship is like that of actuality to potentiality, or of determination to determinability.

The concrete application of this matter-form duality in the human sphere is linked to scientific assumptions that have, in part, been disproved today. Because the female egg cells and their part in reproduction were unknown, the father was regarded as the real transmitter of hereditary factors. The mother's function was simply to allow the rudimentary human being that was already present in the male sperm to grow within her womb. Thus, she can be compared to a field in which seeds are sown; the woman's role in conception is passive, and the man's, active.

Since the effect resembles the cause, the male seeks to produce something like himself, in other words, a son. If a daughter is born, this is attributable to negative external influences or to a failure on the part of the mother.[116]

Modern observers often find these assumptions so shocking that they decidedly reject any and every connection between the metaphysics of matter-form and the duality of the sexes. This sort of reaction seems to go too far. For it is not because Aristotle proceeds from certain false scientific assumptions that he sees a connection between his hylomorphism and the

---

hoff, "Form" [Form], in Joachim Ritter, ed., *Historisches Wörterbuch der Philosophie II* [Historical dictionary of philosophy II] (Basel, 1972), pp. 977–1030.

[115] Aristotle, *Physics* I, 9: 192a, in Aristoteles, *Physikalische Vorlesung* [Lecture of physics], ed. by Paul Gohlke (Paderborn, 1956), p. 56.

[116] Erna Lesky, *Die Zeugungs- und Vererbungslehren der Antike und ihr Nachwirken* [Teachings on procreation and heredity in antiquity and their historical influence], Abhandlungen der geistes- und sozialwissenschaftlichen Klasse 1950, no. 19 (Mainz, 1951), pp. 126ff.

polar opposition male–female. The Philosopher was a very exact student of nature, and of biology in particular. His writings on natural science have been generally admired right up to modern times and long remained unsurpassed. It was in nature that Aristotle was able to discover the same sort of thing that, in our time, Philipp Lersch has described: namely, that female creatures, including the human female, behave differently from their male counterparts. He recognized that the behavior of men was more strongly formative, while that of women was more strongly receptive, and that there was an analogy here to his contrasting concepts matter–form. Aristotle did not derive this analogy from false (metaempirical) theories about reproduction. Rather, it was the theories that were erroneously inferred from indubitable (empirical) observation of nature. Without such prior observation, the theories would never have been formulated.

Even today, the metaphysics of matter and form would seem, despite the varying ways in which it can be concretely developed, to have lost none of its relevance. In particular, precisely along the lines developed by Aristotle and Saint Thomas, it may provide a very good explanation of even the most recent findings in microphysics.[117] For present purposes, of course, there is no absolute necessity to favor any one particular school of philosophy. The main point is that the characteristic natures of man and woman are rooted in structural aspects of reality that extend beyond the merely human sphere of being.

The analogia entis *as a hermeneutic key to the application of hylomorphism*

The analogies of attribution and proportionality

Regarding the application of philosophical categories to the topic in hand, the principle of the analogy of being (*analogia entis*) merits special attention.[118]

Beings, of whatever sort, are neither totally different from one another nor totally identical; rather, what obtains is a state of diversity within unity, a correspondence with one another, that extends at least to a common participation in being. All beings are similar to one another. This similarity can assume quite different forms:

---

[117] Josef de Vries, "Zur Sachproblematik von Materie und Form" [On the material problems of matter and form], *Scholastik* 33 (1958): 481–505.

[118] J. B. Lotz, "Analogie" [Analogy], in Brugger, *Wörterbuch*, pp. 11–13.

In the *analogy of attribution*, some characteristic of one being is attributed (*attribuere*) to another. What they have in common analogically (the analogue) is carried over to the second term of the analogy, but dependently on the first. An oft-cited example of this is the predicate healthy: the "first term of the analogy is the human body, in which the state of being healthy manifests itself; second terms of the analogy might, then, be the facial complexion or the diet, which can be called 'healthy' because of their relationship to the health of the body".[119] Whereas what is involved in this case is an external attribution, there are also internal analogies of attribution involving an internal connection between the two terms; the most important example of this is the relation between God, the absolute Being, and the beings of his creation.

By an *analogy of proportionality* is meant the correspondence of two relationships to one another: *a* is related to *b* as *c* is related to *d* ($a:b::c:d$). When the polar opposition man-woman is brought into relation with that of matter-form, this sort of analogy is involved.

Proper understanding of the subordination of women

It should be noted here that the polar opposition matter-form is not always concretely instanced in precisely the same way. If the terms involved in the relation are two different levels of being, then the form is always the one that possesses the greater potency of being: for example, the body, as a part of a human being that is subject to formation through and through, occupies a lower level of being than does the soul. The soul is not only predominant over the body but also has a higher value.

This analogy of body and soul is often used to characterize the relationship between men and women, and there is a certain justification in this: the man appears more as the leading, predominant one, and the woman, more as the subordinate one. This comparison should not, however, be taken too far, because the polarity of the sexes is not one between different levels, but rather, one *within the same level of being*. Men *and* women have a spiritual soul, which impresses itself on their corporeality. The intellectual (and physical) qualities of men possess no higher value than do those of women. Women are as superior to men in many areas as men are to women in other areas. These different sorts of superiority seem to be fairly evenly balanced.

Also, superiority and inferiority have nothing to do with subordination. In managing relationships that involve a strong personal element and in acting effectively within a small, relatively closed sphere, for example,

[119] Lotz, "Analogie", p. 12.

women would seem to be superior to men. Nevertheless, in those areas of social life that extend beyond the personal sphere, men are the leaders and are thus predominant over women in respect to functioning within the larger society.[120]

This hierarchical principle is found in all realms of human life, as could easily be shown by drawing here on the anthropological findings discussed earlier. Women are always dependent, in one way or another, on the leadership of men; but men, without the intuition and assistance of women, are only half human.

This mutual interdependence forms a link between the hierarchical principle and the recently much-stressed concept known in German as *Partnerschaft*. The German word stems from "partnership", "which is widely used in business and economics, and means, more or less, participation, or involvement, as a partner".[121] "Involvement as a partner", furthermore, usually implies having an *equal* part in some relationship, in this case, the marriage relationship.

Insofar as the matter concerned is, in fact, one involving equal rights and duties, as is the marriage relationship in the narrower sense,[122] it is permissible to speak of a partnership. However, in some respects, marriage is not an association of two equals, but rather, of two whose positions are different. Partnership is only *one* category of social life among many, and it should be applied to marriage only within certain limits.[123]

The superiorities of men, to express things pointedly, lead to a position of authority, but the superiorities of women, to a position of subordination. Here, authority and subordination do not represent differences in value at the levels of being, but are related to one another in the context of the two sexes, as two poles in tension. Thus, there are an upper pole and a lower pole, but not a good pole and a less good pole.

It should also be remembered that, even in the realm of natural ethics, the position of authority is not to be understood as dominance in a *negative*, oppressive sense but must rather be seen as implying a relation of care and service toward the subordinated.

Thus, with regard to all analogies of proportionality whose terms are not on the same level of being,[124] it is necessary to pay precise attention to the analogue, or the common third element, so that any confusion is

[120] On this, cf. pp. 87, 91ff., 95–97, 106–7 above.

[121] Hildegard Harmsen, *Die Frau heute. Fragen an die Kirche* [Women today. Questions for the Church] (Bergen and Enkheim, 1967), p. 13.

[122] Cf. p. 56–57 above.

[123] Cf. Mausbach-Ermecke, *Theologie III*, pp. 323ff., especially 326.

[124] Such as body-soul, on the one hand, and woman-man, on the other.

avoided. Only if this hermeneutic premise is observed can the matter-form structure, with its manifold potential complexities, be carried over into the core of the relationship between the sexes.

Discussion of typical philosophical models for a solution

The duality of existence and essence as a model for the relationship between the sexes?

The metaphysical duality of possibility and actuality is present in every created being; only God is *actus purus*, pure actuality, containing in himself all perfections, in the highest degree and undividedly unified. Possibility (passive potency) originates as soon as the first being is created by God: as a being, it is real only to the extent that it *receives* its being from God.

At the heart of the matter here is the first, fundamental dichotomy between being and beings. This corresponds to the relationship between existence and essence: the essence is logically (and, for Saint Thomas, also really) distinct, and only by virtue of existence can it move from the realm of possibility to that of actuality. Potentially infinite existence is delimited through essence.

The relationship between act and potency, which is a precondition for the opposition of being to beings and existence to essence, finds expression in the physical realm (according to Saint Thomas) in the relationship between matter and form.

Throughout the philosophical tradition, this relationship is applied again and again to the polarity of the sexes, because it is more directly relevant to that polarity than is the metaphysically more remote dichotomy between existence and essence. Still, an approach based on this more fundamental relationship would be quite conceivable. To my knowledge, there was no detailed attempt at this until, in modern times, the book *The Rhythmics of Being* by Angelika Walter (1932). Contrary to what one might expect, Walter does not associate existence with men and essence with women, but rather vice versa. She understands existence as the enduring foundation of beings, out of and against which essence has to differentiate itself. One of the ways in which she tries to illustrate the "unity in tension" of "(being-)so" [= essence] and "(being-)there" [= existence] is through the image of a pyramid:

> I saw it at first as something in space that was both resting inertly and raising itself up. The main impression was one of rest, the sign of (being-)there. Then, in the position of (being-)there, existence appeared as the all-pervasive fundament of the figure, and essence, as its omnifaceted peak.
>
> (Being-)there assumes its founding and constituting role, and (being-)so,

the direction and representation: the necessity of the fundament extends all the way up to the tip, and the efficacy of the principle, all the way down to the base: a total interpenetration of one with the other, unity from duality.[125]

This illustration strongly recalls Lersch's polar opposition, discussed earlier, in which an outward-thrusting principle is contrasted with one at rest within itself (eccentricity and centrality). It might well be asked, however, whether the relationship between existence and essence is the most appropriate designation for this. For, according to the above, what is decisive in the relationship between existence and essence is the fact that essence *receives* existence and that existence is the active principle.

Walter's theories, with all their metaphysical implications, need not be discussed in detail here; in my opinion, it is, nevertheless, more philosophically productive to consider the opposition existence-essence against the backdrop of the dualities potentiality-actuality or matter-form.[126]

On the oppositions "acting-being" and "activity-passivity"

In one of his essays, the Spanish philosopher Ortega y Gasset associates men with "acting" and women with "being" or "essence". He says it is

> not through their action, but through their essence, that women attract men. Thus, the fundamental contribution of women to world history need not . . . consist . . . in deeds. . . . Just as light . . . , without any effort or intention, illumines things and elicits the song of their colors, so women achieve what they achieve, entirely and by chance and solely because they are there, are present and send out rays.[127]

This seems correct insofar as the activity of men is directed more strongly outward. However, it is necessary to avoid the misunderstanding that would result from assuming that women behave totally passively. Women are involved in activity to the same degree as men—the "sending out rays" that Gasset mentions is also an activity, even if it tends to remain in the background.

A particularly popular characterization of the polarity of the sexes is the opposition between active and passive. This is derived from the duality of either form and matter or actuality and potentiality, in which there is a contrast between an efficacious (active) principle and a receptive (passive) one. Throughout the material world, there is, of course, no instance of

[125] T. A. Walter, *Seinsrhythmik. Studie zur Begründung einer Metaphysik der Geschlechter* [The rhythmics of being. Study on the foundations for a metaphysics of the sexes] (Freiburg im Breisgau, 1932), pp. 66, 72f.

[126] On this, cf. also Edith Stein, *Die Frau. Ihre Aufgabe nach Natur und Gnade* [Woman. Her task according to nature and grace], Werke V (Louvain, 1959), pp. 132f., n. 21.

[127] José Ortega y Gasset, *Vom Einfluss der Frau auf die Geschichte* [On the influence of women on history] (Stuttgart, n.d.), pp. 30f.

pure form or pure matter, just as, in the realm of creation, there can be no actuality apart from some potentiality. There is no matter that is not already formed matter, which means that the nature of the relation between form and matter can vary significantly according to the levels of being involved. Since it is particularly necessary to avoid misunderstanding in respect to the relationship between men and women, the female role should not be designated as passive but rather as receptive. For receptive behavior is not devoid of movement, but is rather thoroughly and strongly efficacious.[128]

Polar oppositions in philosophy as expressions of emphasis and structural principles

The polar opposition eccentricity-centrality could also be characterized by linking it to the contrast creative-receptive. At this point, it is important to stress explicitly something that has already been implied more than once in the course of the discussion so far:

There is *no* question here of an *exclusive identification* of men or women with one of these two poles, but only of an *accentuation*. In the case of men, creativity and activity come to the fore *more strongly* than does receptivity, while the reverse applies in the case of women. Their formula would be: *receptivity* plus (co-)activity; that of men: *activity* plus receptivity.

Creativity and receptivity are found in both sexes, yet in differing degrees. Such a schematization makes good sense because the many differences between the sexes tend to assume a unified direction, and can, therefore, be regarded from a unified perspective.

The polarity approach is open to misunderstanding inasmuch as it presents the relationship between the sexes chiefly from the viewpoint of dissimilarity. Counter to this, Josef Burri thus rightly emphasizes "the aspect of the overarching equality of all human beings".[129]

It is certainly correct that, by virtue of their biological inheritance, men and women have more in common than they have that differentiates them. Out of forty-six chromosomes, only two are sexually determinative. Still, one cannot just separate the common traits and the differences into two adjacent piles, treating all equally, like so many bricks, and then count up the numbers in each pile. Rather, the common and the different aspects are so intimately bound up with each other that, even at the level of bodily cells and organs, there are only male *or* female structures. Humanity

---

[128] Lersch takes a similar view, introducing here the concept of "pathy" [Pathik]: Lersch, *Wesen*, pp. 26f.
[129] Burri, *Differenz*, p. 23.

bears, all the way down to the body's most deep-seated bases, an inherent sexual stamp.

Masculinity and femininity are, then, *structural principles*, which always operate to steer the human in a particular direction. To put it in an image: an ellipse has two poles, to which every point in the mathematical figure can be related. The area between the poles is very wide, and the points at the middle can be aligned with both extremities. The points in each of the two halves are paralleled by points in the other (= "common traits"), but they are always related to *their* pole. While not being identical with that pole, they are still oriented toward it.

Diether Wendland objects to the polarity model because it does not allow for the need to regard one pole as subordinate to the other.[130] This objection vanishes if one introduces the distinction between an upper pole and a lower one. That this does not imply any devaluation of the being of women has already been explained above.

Those who scorn any such philosophical summarization that aligns masculinity and femininity with distinct poles just abandon themselves to the random play of sociological processes and to mindless conformity with those processes. Moreover, they renounce the possibility of seeing the human sexual polarity as part of a wider horizon whose significance extends—as will be seen later here—all the way up to the image of God.

Characterization of the polarity of the sexes as "immanence" and "transcendence"

In conclusion, an attempt may be made to add another specific dimension to Lersch's polar opposition between eccentricity and centrality. To represent this opposition, Lersch employed two symbols: the line originating at the center of the subject and *thrusting outward* into the world, and the circle *encompassing its center point*.[131]

Simone de Beauvoir seems to have had some awareness of this state of affairs when she associated women with "immanence" and men with "transcendence".[132] Immanent signifies remaining within a certain area, and transcendent means going beyond the limits of given reality. The

---

[130] Diether Wendland, *Der Mensch. Mann und Frau* [The human being. Man and woman], Der Christ in der Welt I, 3 (Aschaffenburg, 1957), p. 30.

[131] Cf. p. 96 above.

[132] Cf. p. 35 above. This classificatory contrast is drawn in a similar, but positively intended, way by Buytendijk; *Frau*, pp. 206ff.: "The Mystery of Immanence".

immanence of women refers to their being more strongly bound up with their bodies, with caring for their children and husbands and with the near world. De Beauvoir passionately rejects this order of things. In doing so, she would appear to be misunderstanding the specific values of women, which are realized precisely in and through their immanence. Women recognize their stronger ties to the concrete things and personal relations of their immediate environment, and it is easier for them than for men to control and influence these realities from within. Women are, in a specific sense, relational beings, and tend to recede into the background as opposed to their children and husbands. Yet it is precisely this situation that gives women their strength, for men are more strongly inclined to take a detached, classifying approach that separates things instead of relating them to one another within a comprehensive point of view. Angelika Walter rather pointedly summarizes this previously described state of affairs[133] as follows: "While the feminine seeks a place for all, the masculine puts each in *his* place."[134]

Immanence and transcendence are thus complementary concepts here, which correspond quite well to the phenomenological contrast between eccentricity and centrality. Both sets of opposites refer to a particular manifestation, in the area of the polarity of the sexes, of the dualities potentiality-actuality and matter-form. Anthropology and metaphysics come together here.

---

[133] Cf. p. 92 above.
[134] Walter, *Seinsrhythmik*, p. 182.

CHAPTER SEVEN

Sexuality and the Image of God:
Inquiries Based on the Study of Religion

I. THE COMBINATION OF ABSTRACT AND PERSONAL DIMENSIONS IN THE RELATIONSHIP BETWEEN GOD AND MAN

In the course of the preceding philosophical considerations, it has become evident that the difference between the sexes is not a purely anthropological problem, but has implications that extend beyond itself into the realm of metaphysics. At the next-higher level of reflection, where attention will be focused on the relation between God and man, the philosophical method will continue to apply. Yet metaphysical statements lose their purely matter-of-fact character when it is persons that are their subjects. In what follows, not abstract philosophical connections but the personal relationship between God and man will emerge as the reality to which the difference between the sexes ultimately refers us.

2. THE MEANINGFULNESS OF SYMBOLS IN PHILOSOPHY OF RELIGION

Definition of a symbol

In the context of my characterization of the analogy of being, it was established that two or more realities can agree with each other in some particular respect. This sort of similarity finds its special expression in the *symbol*, where two realities enter into sensibly apprehensible interconnection. The very etymology of the word conveys this idea: συμβάλλειν = "throw together", "compare".

121

A symbol is something more than an arbitrarily defined sign, such as the use of "red" for "stop" in the regulation of street traffic. As an emblem [German: *Sinnbild* = "meaning-image"], it is suited in advance, by virtue of its inner structure, to entering into certain relationships; for example, "sun" and "light" in relation to intellectual clarity. H. R. Schlette therefore defines a symbol as "any being . . . that implicitly refers to another being in and through some inherent similarity".[1]

Man's dependence on the senses as the anthropological basis of symbolic thought

As a creature tied to the senses, man is naturally predisposed to symbolically mediated meanings. The human soul does not, as it were, circle around itself, but rather has constant contact with the external world. It derives intelligible structures—according to the realistic epistemology of Saint Thomas—solely from the images that are presented to it by the five senses: *nihil est in intellectu, quod non prius fuerit in sensu.*

On the other hand, the intellectual soul finds so much of its expression in the sensible realm (*anima forma corporis*) that one can call the human body the "symbol" of the soul. Man's biological dimension is thus no objectlike material for technological manipulation, but is correlated to the core of personhood and is a mirror image of mental and spiritual life.

The human body as symbol: obstacles to this conception in Western intellectual history

If all creation is a symbol, an emblem, of the Creator, then this applies in special measure to man, including his sexually differentiated bodily nature. In our times, however, there is much that prevents us from seeing the symbolical nature of created things:

According to the nominalism of the late Middle Ages, our concepts are only arbitrarily defined names (*nomina*), which convey nothing of the essences of things and which thus cannot provide any indications about higher realities. God's existence and essence are unknowable to man apart from special revelation.[2]

Descartes draws so sharp a distinction between man's body and soul that

---

[1] H. R. Schlette, "Symbol", in Heinrich Fries, ed., *Handbuch theologischer Grundbegriffe 4* [Handbook of basic theological concepts 4], 2nd ed. (Munich, 1974), p. 169.

[2] Cf. above, pp. 74ff.

the *res cogitans* and the *res extensa* are regarded as only externally connected to each other. "The human body thus resembles a machine with a highly refined operating program. A body understood in this way, however, as only loosely connected with mind and soul, loses all powers of symbolic expressiveness."[3]

In taking this view of the body as a manipulatable machine, Descartes shows himself to be a forerunner of present-day ways of thinking. What passes for truth, in the final analysis, is not the reality that confronts man as given, but rather, whatever he himself has made and whatever, in the future, he may yet be able to make (*Marxism*).

An important proponent of this constructivism in modern times is certainly Immanuel *Kant*, for whom the thing in itself is regarded as unknowable. The human mind casts a spider web of thought, made up of its own ideas, over the chaotic data of the senses; that is, it imposes reality.

Symbol and mystery

This one-dimensional understanding of reality has a particularly significant effect on religious thought, since symbolism subserves the mysteries, and especially the inexhaustible Mystery of God. A symbol often serves to reflect complex intellectual and spiritual contents that can be only inadequately broken down into single concepts. What Gertrud von le Fort asserts of the metaphysical realm in general is especially valid for natural theology:

Symbols are "signs or images in which ultimate metaphysical realities and principles are not abstractly known, but emblematically presented to intuition; symbols are thus the language that is spoken in the seeable by the unseeable."[4]

Comprehension by means of concepts retains its full relevance even in the religious sphere, for both concept and image are related to intellectual knowledge. Symbols involve a comprehension of the same sorts of reality, although not discursively and analytically, but intuitively and at a glance.

Thus, concept and image cannot be played off against one another in the area of natural theology. In particular, one cannot drive a wedge between a religious reality, supposedly knowable only through symbols, and a

[3] Anton Ziegenaus, " 'Als Mann und Frau erschuf er sie' (Gen 1:27). Zum sakramentalen Verständnis der geschlechtlichen Differenzierung des Menschen" ["Male and female he created them" (Gen 1:27). On the sacramental understanding of the sexual differentiation of man], *MThZ* 31 (1980): 210.

[4] Fort, *Frau*, p. 7.

profane world, where things are treated predominantly in terms of rational concepts.[5] Like mystery, symbols are suprarational, but not irrational.

Comprehension of symbols as an integral process

Whereas concepts are rather detached from sensory connections, symbols remain closely tied to these and can provide special sorts of goals at which sensory striving, or "feeling", can aim. Thus, symbolic language presents a direct contrast to rationalism, which largely ignores sensory experience and allows the values of feeling to wither away. Inasmuch as symbols are directed at both head *and* heart, they take hold of man more strongly in his *entirety*, while a purely conceptual thought world exerts its claim solely on man's head.

The concreteness and historical nature of symbolic thought

In dealing with symbolic thought, it is necessary to avoid two dangers: (1) neglecting the concrete and the individual in favor of the general and (2) overlooking the historical component of human existence.

Plato's doctrine of ideas, in my opinion, falls victim to both of these dangers, since it leaves the intelligible and the material worlds standing side by side in a more-or-less unconnected way. To be sure, it was Plato who aroused a keen appreciation of the symbolic nature of being, which points beyond itself to the metaempirical realm. However, the trans-individual and transhistorical reality to which this symbolism points tends to eclipse the individual character of the symbol itself. With reference to the present topic, one might, then, join Sally Cunneen in lodging the following protest: "It is impossible to live out an archetypal pattern every minute of one's life. Real women are just not like that."[6]

However, this very widespread objection to symbolic thought, especially when applied to the area of the differences between the sexes, goes somewhat too far. For one could then claim that a definition such as "Man is endowed with reason and free will" is an unrealistic idea, since "real"

---

[5] This remark is directed mainly against Paul Tillich, for whom the religious can be expressed *only* in symbols. Cf. Peter Lengsfeld, "Symbol und Wirklichkeit: die Macht der Symbole nach Paul Tillich" [Symbol and reality: the power of symbols according to Paul Tillich], in Heinen, *Bild*, p. 215.

[6] Sally Cunneen, *Geschlecht: weiblich, Religion: katholisch. Ein Sozialreport über die Frau* [Sex: female, religion: Catholic. A social report on women] (Munich, 1971), p. 48.

men often behave quite differently. Yet it would occur to no one to declare such a definition meaningless in view of empirical reality.

Both the general idea and the symbol do not, so to speak, hover *above* the particular realities, but are, instead, realized *in* them. Man's nature is not exhausted in reason and free will, but he *possesses* these faculties, which he can develop in varying ways or allow to atrophy. Regarding symbolic thought, then, I take my bearings less by Plato than by Aristotle, who establishes the transempirical, which can be grasped in general concepts, firmly in the worldly realm, as the formative principle of individual empirical realities. Accordingly, the "real" woman cannot, then, be played off against the "eternal" woman.

A designated meaning is thus not part of the concept of a symbol, for a symbol, as such, in my definition, is characterized precisely by its naturally inherent referential meaningfulness.[7]

Of course, the symbolic aspects of our world are so multitudinous that a selection—in some cases one-sided—is always made from among them. Although a symbol cannot be designated in its meaning, it can be given prominence in some special way. Furthermore, the same basic image can be used to express differing intellectual contents: the symbol of a mother can signify a mother goddess in a pagan context, but the Mother of God, a created being, in the Christian context.

Historical codifications of symbolism in revealed religion

Historical thought recognizes that the usage of symbols can change. Designation of meaning does not belong to the concept of a symbol, but it does belong to a symbol's practical application. A historical choice of symbols is to be expected particularly in the context of a philosophy of religion that regards supernatural revelation by God as possible. God is able to shape man's structures of religious symbolism in a special way. For example, it is possible to prescribe bread and grape wine for the celebration of the Eucharist and, at the same time, to exclude other sorts of food or drink. In this way, man is referred back to a revelation by God in *history*, which, as such, nevertheless transcends all historical changes brought about by *man*. A revelation that occurred only once can thus be kept in presence throughout the entirety of subsequent human history.

A historical determination of this kind is also to be expected regarding

---

[7] Contrary to Franz Mitzka, who brings the notion of a construction into the definition of a symbol itself: Franz Mitzka, "Symbolismus als theologische Methode" [Symbolism as a theological method], *ZkTh* 67 (1943): 24.

the symbolism of the sexes, especially in view of the anthropological centrality of matters in that area. Whether any such singling out in fact occurred will have to be investigated later on in the framework of the theology of revelation.

To exclude in advance any determination of symbolic meanings through revelation would be, for a theologian who accepts divine self-communication, highly contradictory at best. Paul Tillich, the most important figure behind the rise of feminist theology, rejected any emphasis on particular symbols within the Christian sphere. This attitude was, at the time, behind his break with the Protestant, liturgically oriented Berneuchen Circle; for, in the liturgy, there is always an emphasis on sacred symbols that are elevated above the profane realm.[8] In Christianity, however, the essential content of sacred symbols derives ultimately from the revelation of Christ (water in baptism, bread and wine in the Eucharist and so forth).

The "transformational nature" of symbols

Symbols do not coincide completely with experienced reality, but point beyond it. If, in so doing, they appear as goals for which to strive, they tend to assume the nature of *ideals*. Then they serve not merely to reflect the all-too-often ethically mediocre world of everyday existence or even to lend it ideological justification, but rather, to ennoble it. Symbols are—to use an expression of C. G. Jung in a new sense—symbols of transformation, which should assist in man's ascent to God.

A symbol, then, cannot just be played off against experience, as, for example, sometimes happens in the Catholic sphere with respect to the Mother of God: "for us girls and women, there was only one model: that of the humble and pure Virgin Mary. . . . This . . . no longer fit in with our experience."[9] Mary is seen "as raised up on a pedestal that no mere woman could ever attain to".[10] For Rosemary Ruether, the notion of the Virgin Birth is too "exalted", so she makes Mary into "a normal married woman".[11]

This attitude is not limited to the figure of Mary. For the feminist

---

[8] Cf. Lengsfeld, "Symbol", pp. 210f.

[9] Halkes, *Söhne*, p. 93.

[10] Condren, "Kinder", p. 303.

[11] Ruether, *Mary*, p. 36; cf. Ruether, *Frauen*, p. 64. According to the Protestant Alicia Faxon, Mary was "an average woman, just as we are all average people. . . . She did not regard herself as anything special": A. C. Faxon, *Frauen im Neuen Testament. Vom Umgang Jesu mit Frauen* [trans. of: Women and Jesus] (Munich, 1979), pp. 19f.

theologian Letty Russell, the masculine and feminine symbols in the image of God should, quite generally, "give expression to our own changing human experience".[12]

Certainly, symbols are addressed to experience, not, however, in order to remain with experience but rather to call it into question and to transform it.

The reduction of symbols to mere expressions of everyday experience also occurs, in a certain sense, with the psychologist C. G. Jung, according to whom good and evil manifest themselves in symbols in equivalent ways and must both be integrated into the life of the soul. Evil is regarded as an independent entity and is even attributed, as an equally valuable aspect alongside of the good, to God.[13]

This metaphysical dualism, which was already advocated in a similar way by the Manichaeans, finds concrete expression in, for example, the accusation that the figure of Mary is seen as too one-sidedly positive by the Catholic Church. The negative traits, which would make Mary a witch, should supposedly be integrated in the interests of psycho-hygiene.[14]

This attitude is surely connected with Jung's agnosticism, which places the existence of God in brackets. The symbols of transformation, then, are not means of assistance on the way to God but subserve the process of individuation that supposedly helps man to achieve psychic wholeness.[15] In all this, good is not integrated with good (the Catholic *et–et*), but rather, *et Deus et diabolus*.

Symbols as expressive of the sacred

The ideal nature of symbols in the ethical sphere is connected with their use in the liturgy, in which man's relationship with God finds particularly intense expression. According to Mircea Eliade, "religious experience" presupposes "a bifurcation of the world into the sacred and the profane".[16]

---

[12] Russell, "Einführung", p. 11.

[13] Jung, *GW XI*, p. 670; cf. pp. 130f. below.

[14] Herbert Unterste, *Theologische Aspekte der Tiefenpsychologie von C. G. Jung* [Theological aspects of the psychoanalytic psychology of C. G. Jung] (Düsseldorf, 1977), p. 131; also contains documentation.

[15] Raymond Hostie, *C. G. Jung und die Religion* [C. G. Jung and religion] (Freiburg im Breisgau, 1957), p. 188.

[16] Mircea Eliade, "Prolegomenon zu eimen religiösen Dualismus: Dyaden und Polaritäten" [Prolegomenon to religious dualism: dyads and polarities], in *Die Sehnsucht nach dem Ursprung. Von der Quellen der Humanität* [The quest: history and meaning in religion] (Frankfurt, 1976), p. 179.

This bifurcation corresponds to the distinction between God and man: God alone is sacred, in contrast to whom man repeatedly falls into sin. Divine reality, in contrast to the purely worldly one, appears as the *mysterium tremendum et fascinosum*; the encounter with the Mystery of God takes place through symbols, by means of which a *setting apart* of the divine, as opposed to the profane, must also be made sensorily accessible. If this elevated display of the sacred through living symbols is neglected, the sense of reverence for God wanes; God and man are placed alongside each other as partners with equal rights, and each, as it were, becomes the other.

This fundamental religious-phenomenological finding loses none of its significance when, as Christians, we accept that God became man. The divine and the human realities are, to be sure, unseparatedly bound up with one another in the God–man, Christ, and, analogically, in the baptized, but, at the same time, they remain unmixed.[17] The setting apart of divine reality is at least as necessary for Christians in this world as it is for heathens; it is effected primarily through private and liturgical prayer, in which specific times, places and persons are separated and brought into connection with symbolic meaning structures.[18]

3. SYMBOLS IN C. G. JUNG'S PSYCHOANALYTIC PSYCHOLOGY

The significance of symbols for the study of religion impresses itself even more strongly on our awareness if we observe the human soul. The special achievement of psychoanalytic psychology, founded by Sigmund Freud, was to direct attention to the unconscious dimensions of the soul. The mind's cognitions and strivings are often under the direction of unconscious psychic structures more deep-seated than waking consciousness.

Whereas Sigmund Freud attempted to research the development of the unconscious in the life history of the individual person, C. G. Jung broadened this line of inquiry by looking for aspects of the unconscious that were common to all mankind. In the matter of a more precise description of this collective unconscious, Jung may well have left some questions unanswered, but certain of his basic assumptions have been

---

[17] According to the dogma of Chalcedon: DS, 302.

[18] These prolegomena to the significance of the liturgy are supplemented below: pp. 193–94.

adopted by a large number of psychologists. At the same time, central Jungian ideas have met with broad reception in other disciplines. The topic of the collective unconscious was introduced by Jung "into that area . . . in which theology, the study of religion and psychoanalysis cut across one another".[19]

The point of departure for Jungian psychology is the "libido", or psychic energy, which is formed and directed in the most different ways by conscious and, above all, unconscious structures. A fundamental role, as "form principle of driving [psychic] energy",[20] is played in this by the archetype, which Jung's student Erich Neumann defines as "an inner image active within the human psyche".[21] Jung occasionally compares the archetypes to a riverbed, through which the "water" of psychic energy streams before us.[22] They are, "in a certain sense, the deeply hidden foundations of the conscious soul, or . . . its roots", which it has sunk into the soil of the unconscious.[23]

The notion that there are preexistent forms, which might be parts of an inheritable collective unconscious,[24] or may, in the course of man's history, even have left "groovelike traces" on the brain,[25] need not be endorsed in accepting Jung's basic thesis. It is important, however, that the archetypes, graspable by the senses and comprising various individual components, appear as *symbols*. Symbols combine the conscious and the unconscious, the rational and the emotional, and are therefore an expression of psychic wholeness, which, at the same time, is also the goal for self-development.[26] A symbol, in contrast to a sign, cannot be artificially produced by consciousness, but is a form in which especially the unconscious manifests itself.[27] It has an elemental nature, insofar as it reflects something present, and, at the same time, a transformational nature, which points toward some goal.[28]

[19] Ulrich Mann, "Symbole und tiefenpsychologische Gestaltungsfaktoren der Religion" [Symbols and formative factors from the unconscious in religion], in C. Hörgl and F. Rauh, eds., *Grenzfragen des Glaubens. Theologische Grundfragen als Grenzprobleme* [Borderline questions of belief. Basic theological questions as borderline problems] (Einsiedeln, Zurich and Cologne, 1967), p. 156.

[20] Jung, *GW VIII*, p. 39.

[21] Erich Neumann, *Die Grosse Mutter. Eine Phänomenologie der weiblichen Gestaltungen des Unbewussten* [The great mother. A phenomenology of the feminine formations of the unconscious], 2nd ed. (Olten and Freiburg, 1974), p. 19.

[22] Hostie, *Jung*, p. 79.

[23] Jung, *GW X*, p. 45.

[24] Jung, *GW IX*, 1, pp. 55ff.

[25] On this see Hostie, *Jung*, pp. 79–82.

[26] Hostie, *Jung*, p. 52.

[27] Cf. Hostie, *Jung*, p. 55.

[28] Unterste, *Aspekte*, pp. 116f.

4. THE SIGNIFICANCE OF C. G. JUNG'S MASCULINE AND FEMININE ARCHETYPES

Animus and anima

According to C. G. Jung, there is an interplay in the human soul between elements of masculine and feminine symbolism, between the archetype of the animus and that of the anima. These notions refer to images of the opposite sex that all of us carry within ourselves: for men the anima, and for women, the animus. These images of the opposite must not be suppressed but need to be consciously integrated into the total psychic structure.[29]

Father and mother archetypes

The beginning of the development of the individual is marked by the presence of the feminine archetype: the child feels itself secure in the tender care of its mother. This experience of psychic unity is reflected in the unconscious life of the soul, to which conscious contents are only gradually added later on.

The more the child learns to perceive and to modify its environment consciously, the more it opposes itself to the external world and develops its own personality. Now, in the course of this development, the father plays a special role. As the main bearer of authority in the family, he serves to further the child's perception of those structures of order through which life and the individual personality are consciously formed.

The roles of father and mother, then, correspond roughly to a dichotomy between transpersonal and personal elements, on the one hand, and between the unconscious and consciousness, on the other.[30]

[29] Cf. among others Jung, *GW X*, pp. 43–65 ("Seele und Erde" [Soul and earth]); pp. 135–56 ("Die Frau in Europa" [Women in Europe]). See also Jolande Jacobi, *Die Psychologie von C. G. Jung. Eine Einführung in das Gesamtwerk* [The psychology of C. G. Jung. An introduction to his work as a whole], 4th ed. (Zurich, 1959), pp. 173–87.

[30] Unterste, *Aspekte*, pp. 122f. These basic assumptions of C. G. Jung have been developed and systematized by Erich Neumann, especially in *Ursprungsgeschichte des Bewusstseins* [History of the origins of consciousness] (Munich, 1968); *Zur Psychologie des Weiblichen* [On the psychology of the feminine] (Munich, 1969); and *Mutter*. Matriarchate and patriarchate (and fraternity?) are seen as psychic stages in the development of both the individual and universal mankind. With respect to ontogenesis, the first two stages seem to

For Jung, the mother plays a larger role than is the case for Freud,[31] whose thought circles almost entirely around the significance of the father, seen all but exclusively as an order-creating legislator. The tender, motherly qualities hardly feature at all in his parental image. "With this exclusion of the mother figure, Freud does for psychology what Luther did for religion. Freud is, so to speak, the psychologist of Protestantism."[32]

"Equality of rights" of masculine and feminine symbols against the background of philosophical anthropology

Thus, Jung's psychology is a reaction against an overemphasis on certain traits found in the father figure, but also against an exclusive emphasis on God's transcendence at the cost of his immanence.[33] To be sure, certain reservations might already be raised about the equivalence of fatherly and motherly archetypes that is involved in Jung's position. Consciousness and the unconscious, or more pointedly, mind and instinct, have equality of rights for Jung.[34] This position is obviously based on regarding the human soul as lacking any substantial character by virtue of which it would exert authority over the body and sensual impulses. Rather, the soul is more a personification of unconscious contents,[35] which thus have effective primacy. The unconscious, to be sure, is to be made conscious, but this transformation does not occur as a result of confronting the unconscious with anything *new*. Instead, consciousness is just a sort of differential emergence, or formal manifestation, of the underlying, formless unconscious.

---

have a certain probability, while the evolutionary extension of the theory to phylogenesis would seem to encounter difficulties similar to those found in the above-described notions of Bachofen about a social matriarchate. Cf. p. 147 below.

[31] "C. G. Jung's psychology can, in my opinion, be characterized as a psychology of the mother symbol": Antoine Vergote, *Religionspsychologie* [Psychology of religion] (Olten, 1970), p. 210.

[32] Erich Fromm, *Der moderne Mensch und die Zukunft*, 2nd ed. (Frankfurt, 1967), p. 43; Unterste, *Aspekte*, p. 118.

[33] On these two concepts, cf. pp. 141f. below.

[34] Unterste, *Aspekte*, p. 122.

[35] Unterste, *Aspekte*, p. 135.

The "transpersonal" image of God

Description

In Jung's philosophical anthropology, if one can speak of such a thing, there are basically no persons, but only transpersonal structures. Just as the soul is made up of a bundle of images, so, for Jung, God is seen as a psychodynamic state, that is, a personification of unconscious contents.[36] To be sure, Jung does not want to give any answer to the question of God's existence, and he employs the notion of a soul's "God-imago", which might also be an illusion.[37] However, with respect to this "portrait of God", the conception of God's personality is, to put it cautiously, not particularly clear.[38]

Criticism

If we accept the terms transpersonal and personal as pointedly characteristic of the difference between the sexes[39] and consider their applicability to the doctrine of God, then a theistic understanding of God will require that preference be given to his personal aspects. Although God includes in himself—as we can say from our limited point of view—all "transpersonal" traits such as truth, goodness and beauty, these are nevertheless combined from the start into a personlike unity. C. G. Jung's ideas tend more in the direction of a genealogy of the gods, in which a figuratively personal god emerges in self-differentiation from a transpersonal chaos. This conception would fit in with ideas from Oriental religions and Gnosticism that will be discussed later on and are known to have exerted a strong influence on Jung. According to Gilles Quispel, C. G. Jung developed "the most important Gnosticism of our century".[40]

Thus, in the matter of the equivalence of masculine and feminine traits in the image of God, Jung, on closer inspection, gives primacy to the feminine elements. It is not surprising, then, that this psychologist, despite his extravagant praise of the dogma on the Assumption of Mary of 1950,[41] allocates to the figure of Mary nothing but a place-holding function for a mother goddess, or, more exactly, for an image of God (or,

---

[36] Jung, GW VI, p. 265.

[37] Unterste, Aspekte, p. 134.

[38] Unterste, Aspekte, p. 240; cf. also Vergote, Religionspsychologie, p. 213.

[39] Although only with some reservations; cf. on this pp. 114–16 above.

[40] Gilles Quispel, Gnosis als Weltreligion [Gnosticism as a world religion] (Zurich, 1951), p. 46.

[41] On this, cf. Unterste, Aspekte, pp. 139ff.

once man's religious neurosis[42] has been overcome, an image of man) in which masculine and feminine traits are combined in *one* figure, *pari cum pari*:[43] "The mother symbolizes God at least [!] as much as does the father."[44]

Historical influence

C. G. Jung is the most important psychologist to have prepared the way for feminist theology, and his influence can also be seen in areas outside this movement. The Catholic religious educator Paul Schmidt, for example, thinks that one should begin by telling small children about "God as mother", since that notion would be closer to their own experience. The concept of the fatherhood of God should "preferably be introduced only to older children".[45] The masculine image of God needs to be changed into a human one, so the following form of prayer is recommended when making the sign of the Cross: "In the name of the Father and the Mother and the Brother. Amen."[46]

5. CENTRAL NATURAL SYMBOLS AND THEIR RESPECTIVE "SEXUAL" ASSOCIATIONS

The relative significance of natural symbols and their interpretation in context of the philosophy of religion

With respect to the interpretation of symbols, C. G. Jung rendered the service of establishing a bridge between psychoanalytic psychology and the phenomenology of religion. In the dreams of his patients, where the unconscious manifested itself particularly strongly, he discovered symbolic images similar to those that appear in the myths and religions of peoples throughout the world. Allowing for a certain variability that is often traceable to geographical and sociological factors, there is, in fact, a large degree of constancy, which can be accounted for psychologically and

[42] Unterste, *Aspekte*, p. 139.

[43] Unterste, *Aspekte*, p. 141.

[44] Vergote, *Religionspsychologie*, p. 212, on Jung's position.

[45] Paul Schmidt, *Vater–Kind–Bruder. Biblische Begriffe in anthropologischer Sicht* [Father–child–brother. Biblical concepts in anthropological perspective] (Düsseldorf, 1978), p. 133.

[46] P. Schmidt, *Vater*, p. 135. Tendencies of this sort are discussed in greater detail below.

philosophically in the way that certain natural symbols are associated with qualities of the sexes. Especially if the philosophical background of a symbolic system is known, it is possible to proceed in the reverse direction, inferring a corresponding philosophy from the use of certain "imprinted" symbolic images.

In what follows, I will limit myself to consideration of a few central symbols that are interpreted in the same ways throughout the most differing sorts of culture. Many of these symbolic images, of course, admit of a certain ambiguity; the moon, for example, can be regarded as masculine in some respects, and as feminine in others. It must be noted, however, that, in the same sort of context, the same aspect of a symbol never contains both masculine and feminine qualities. The kinds of sexual feature that are rediscovered in the natural realm seem to be fairly uniform: procreation, conception, authority, loving care and so forth. By contrast, the *selection* of the symbols that are associated with these unvarying qualities has a certain margin of variability, which, in the course of history, can be put to use in different ways. The contrast between heaven and earth, for example, seems to have penetrated man's consciousness in a specially accentuated way only after the development of agriculture. Life then became dependent on the fruits of the earth, whose thriving was guaranteed by the rains from heaven.

Natural symbols, then, are simultaneously expressive of anthropological dimensions and cosmic powers, of which man is the mirror image. When symbolic images have once been consciously perceived as such, they soon become "active symbols": they serve to interpret and reinforce the human relationships with which they are associated, so that there is a process of reciprocal influence between man and symbol.

Heaven and earth as bearers of symbolic meaning

"The sacred duality heaven–earth . . . is one of the central motifs of general mythology."[47] When these two powers are opposed to one another, then heaven is always representative of the masculine, while earth is invested with feminine qualities.[48]

[47] Mircea Eliade, *Die Religionen und das Heilige. Elemente der Religionsgeschichte* [Religions and the sacred. Elements of the history of religion] (Salzburg, 1954), p. 273.

[48] An exception is Egyptian mythology, in which the earth divinity is male and the heaven divinity female. Here, however, the whole symbolic context must be taken into account. The feminine heaven is seen as a mother who repeatedly gives birth to the sun. The sun-god (Ra) who is produced in this way then assumes the sovereign role that is elsewhere given to heaven, in whose center he is enthroned. Cf. Jean Chevalier and Alain Gheerbrant, *Dictionnaire des symboles* (Paris, 1969), pp. 204ff.

Heaven opens up an endless horizon. It is, at the same time, a symbol of majestic power, endlessly exalted above everything earthly. People on earth are wholly dependent on influences from "above", and especially on life-giving rain, which, like heaven, is regarded as masculinely procreative.

Earth, by contrast, appears as feminine. It receives the rain that falls from heaven, combines it with maternal powers, and gives birth to the whole abundance of the plant world. It is not only a symbol of birth but also of death, since it takes all life back, like a grave, into its womb. Earth offers man security and is a symbolic image of the life-forces that arise from within, out of the depths, to shelter and sustain him.

Heaven, on the other hand, as the power of the heights, is a symbol of all that is imposed on man from the outside and over which he has no control. It embodies the creative force of God, and is thus also a symbolic image of human *sovereignty*, which is grounded in the transcendent. The series of concepts heaven, Creator God and ruler comprises a virtually "classic totality".[49]

In natural religions, there is often found a "belief in . . . a personal, highest god . . . , who stands as independent above all things, especially above other beings and powers, and has existed from the beginning of the world". As a rule, this highest being is then seen as connected with heaven: the highest god is also the heaven god.[50]

Sun and moon

Along with the duality of heaven–earth goes that of sun and moon. The rays of the sun are a symbol of the influence of heaven, at whose center the sun is found. In a sense, sun is short for heaven. The light of the sun, in which things appear clearly and distinctly in their various forms and colors, is a symbolic image of the ordering and distinguishing human intellect and of consciousness that is "as clear as day".

Perhaps even more so than heaven, the sun is a full-fledged symbol of sovereignty, to be associated with the king but also with the father.[51]

Thus, the sun is seen as typically masculine, and the moon, as feminine. Admittedly, there are more exceptions in this case than with the duality heaven–earth,[52] and in certain contexts the moon, in particular, can serve

[49] Chevalier and Gheerbrant, *Dictionnaire*, p. 204.

[50] Ferdinand Herrmann, *Symbolik in den Religionen der Naturvölker* [Symbolism in the religions of primitive peoples], Symbolik der Religionen IX (Stuttgart, 1961), p. 65.

[51] Chevalier and Gheerbrant, *Dictionnaire*, p. 713.

[52] Cf. especially F. Herrmann, *Symbolik*, p. 81.

as a bearer of masculine symbolism. Then it can stand, for example, for the cooly reflecting function of abstract thought, derived from the "sun" of intuition; in that case, it is associated with the brain, and the sun, with the heart.[53]

Still, the classification of the two heavenly bodies in terms of sex types is significant. *When*, namely, sun and moon are seen expressly in respect to *their relationship to one another*, then the sun is regularly masculine and the moon, feminine.[54] This is shown quite unequivocally in all astral mythologies, which have been especially receptive to the symbolism of the stars and planets.[55]

In them, it is clearly seen that the moon does not generate its own light but *receives* it from the sun. As luminary of the night, it bathes the world in a soft light, which reveals the outlines of things less distinctly than is the case with the stronger rays of the sun. The moon's light may well have only derivative significance, but in it, the sun's influence is modified in a special way so that a totally new quality of light results. It becomes emblematic of the all-caring powers of the mother and of security within the depths of the unconscious, which manifests itself particularly in nighttime dreams. In psychoanalytic psychology, sun and moon are regarded as symbols par excellence of consciousness and the unconscious. As ruler over the unconscious, the moon is seen by many peoples as "the goddess of love, awakener of those mysterious forces, beyond human understanding, that drive certain people irresistibly together or, just as unaccountably, drive them apart".[56]

In connection with lunar symbolism, adherents of the Jungian school like to regard woman as the principle of *eros*, which binds things gently together. The masculine sun, by contrast, appears as the principle of *logos*, which consciously distinguishes and separates.[57]

In some mythologies, the moon appears as "the heavenly counterpart of the motherly earth"[58] and acts as a mediator between sun and earth. Receiving the light of the sun is the moon's first basic symbolic aspect. In second place is the fact that the moon, in contrast to the sun, goes through different phases during the month, changing its form as it does.[59] In this connection, the receptivity of the moon simultaneously appears as instability or—seen negatively—as waywardness.

[53] Chevalier and Gheerbrant, *Dictionnaire*, pp. 711f.

[54] Chevalier and Gheerbrant, *Dictionnaire*, p. 475.

[55] Chevalier and Gheerbrant, *Dictionnaire*, p. 713.

[56] Esther Harding, *Frauen-Mysterien einst und jetzt* [Female mysteries, past and present] (Zurich, 1949), p. 261.

[57] Jung, *GW X*, pp. 145f.; Harding, *Mysterien*, pp. 29, 261.

[58] Manfred Lurker, ed., *Wörterbuch der Symbolik* [Dictionary of symbolism] (Stuttgart, 1979), p. 390.

[59] Chevalier and Gheerbrant, *Dictionnaire*, p. 474.

These changes are brought into relation with the female menstrual cycle, whose periods are of roughly corresponding lengths. The cycle, in turn, is related to fertility, whose active principle is also often identified with the moon. At the same time, there is an association with water, which represents the source of life and whose ebb and flow are determined by the phases of the moon.

The feminine character of water symbolism

Water symbolism must be numbered among the most interesting areas of psychoanalytic psychology and the phenomenology of religion. The rain that falls from heaven is regarded as masculine, and so, too, are rivers, inasmuch as they—like the Nile in Egypt—are seen as fertilizers of the earth. Nevertheless, one must agree with C. G. Jung when he says that it is the feminine characteristics of water that come especially clearly to the forefront: "The maternal significance of water . . . is one of the clearest symbolic meanings in the whole area of mythology."[60]

This maternal symbolism applies to water as ocean, as wellspring and as still water.[61] The ocean symbolizes the still unformed origins, the "primal mass" or *materia prima*, out of which life in its various particular forms arises. In numberless myths, it is, like the mass of the earth, a symbol of primordial chaos, out of which life, and often even the gods, only later arise.[62]

In contrast to fire, which naturally rises up toward heaven, water is frequently seen as having a kinship with earth.[63] Similarly to earth, it embodies the depths of being, especially if the unfathomable chasms of the major oceans are borne in mind. "In dreams and fantasies, the ocean and other larger bodies of water signify the unconscious", which, together with maternal care, is present at the beginning of the development of the individual person.[64] "It must be of some consequence that the childish word ma-ma (mother's breast) crops up repeatedly in every possible language" and, at the same time, is used extraordinarily often, in connection with the basic syllable m(a), to designate the ocean.[65] Mother and ocean are often virtually synonymous concepts.

In particular, the ocean is seen as a medium for birth, often in connec-

[60] Jung, *GW V*, p. 276.

[61] Jung, *GW IX*, pp. 1, 96.

[62] Chevalier and Gheerbrant, *Dictionnaire*, pp. 303ff.

[63] Lurker, *Wörterbuch*, p. 355.

[64] Jung, *GW V*, p. 278; cf. *GW IX*, pp. 1, 28.

[65] Jung, *GW V*, p. 322; for more precise documentation, see especially Gertrude Jobes, *Dictionary of Mythology, Folklore and Symbols II* (New York, 1961), p. 1030.

tion with the myth of the "cosmic egg". This symbol probably originates in the experience of the sunrise: "At dawn, when at first only a small segment of the sun is visible, its reflection in the ocean can resemble the form of an egg, so that one might well come to the conclusion that it rises up out of this egg."[66]

The bases for water as a symbol of birth may also lie in the early developmental stages of the child: the embryo in the mother's womb is suspended in amniotic fluid, which protects it from external influences and makes possible its first unconscious experience of security. The myth of the primal egg has its place in cosmology: out of an egg laid by a bird or a snake arises the sun-god or the sun in the form of a bird. "At the same time, however, there is associated with the egg the idea that its breaking open resulted in two separate halves: the bottom half fell down to form the earth, while the top shell rose up to become heaven."[67]

When—as in the just-mentioned, widely distributed conception—heaven is interpreted as masculine, and earth, as feminine, then both arise from an "androgynous" origin that contains both masculine and feminine undifferentiatedly within itself. Paradoxically, however, the androgynous symbol is endowed with feminine traits, since the egg, like water, is a birth symbol. This paradox will crop up more than once in what follows here.

Water, like earth, is not only a symbol of birth but also of death: just as the sun, so to speak, rises up out of the waters in the morning, so it sinks back into the depths again at evening. The ocean "gives birth to" life and "devours" it again.[68]

The symbolism of vessels, wellsprings and trees

Related to the symbolism of water is that of *vessels*. Everything concave, rounded or hollow, especially when it can contain a fluid, is seen as feminine. The same applies to cavernous recesses in the earth, whose symbolic content is intensified if springs issue from them. "The cave is the entrance and womb of the earth."[69]

Well-springs are connected, in special measure, with the earth, from whose womb they flow forth, bringing to light the forces of the depths. If water in general is seen as a purifying element anyway, then this is even more notably true of wellsprings. They combine the senses of maternal

[66] F. Herrmann, *Symbolik*, p. 84.
[67] F. Herrmann, *Symbolik*, p. 82.
[68] Jung, *GW V*, pp. 276f.
[69] Lurker, *Wörterbuch*, p. 139.

origins and virginal purity;[70] both of these qualities are also attributed to unspoilt regions of the earth.

The art historian Friedrich Muthmann published an extensive inquiry into the worship of wellsprings under the title *Mother and Wellspring*; time and again, he ran across the most different sorts of variation on a theme that endures from ancient mythology up to the modern adoration of Mary: the "notion of the earth as the divine mother of the wellsprings that issue from her womb".[71] Mother and wellspring are seen as mutually related.

The symbolisms of water and earth come together in the emblematic image of the *tree*, which sinks its roots into the watery soil of the earth and, from this foundation, strives upward toward heaven. The idea of a tree can be associated with a wide variety of symbolic meanings, but when attention is directed to its rootedness and deep-foundedness, it begins to take on feminine qualities. In many areas of Asia, trees are seen as the abodes of local spirits, and this, according to Chevalier, is because of their rootedness and their ties to the subterranean realm, which is seen here as more important than their connection with heaven.[72] Oda Schneider points out the related fact that, in ancient Greece, the "placebound spirits of trees and wellsprings" were regarded as female, while "the soul of the swiftly flowing river" was seen as male.[73] Feminine traits were connected more with the unchangeably localized, the near world; and masculine traits, more with the inconstantly sweeping, the surging into the far world. Schneider regards "this need to tie the 'mother' to one definite place" as a primal human longing that must ultimately be understood as religious: "We speak of our Lady of Czestochowa, of Lourdes, of Fatima, of Schönstatt, of Mariazell. . . . There is no parallel to this in the area of the worship of male saints."[74]

Circle symbolism

The line of a circle is without beginning or end; in it there is no separation or partition. It appears as a symbol of unchangingness and perfection—in short, of eternity. Frequently, the circle, as emblematic of God and

[70] Chevalier and Gheerbrant, *Dictionnaire*, p. 720.

[71] Friedrich Muthmann, *Mutter und Quelle. Studien zur Quellenverehrung im Altertum und im Mittelalter* [Mother and wellspring. Studies on the worship of wellsprings in antiquity and the Middle Ages] (Basel, 1975), p. xi.

[72] Chevalier and Gheerbrant, *Dictionnaire*, p. 60.

[73] Oda Schneider, *Die Macht der Frau* [The power of women] (Salzburg, 1938), p. 184.

[74] O. Schneider, *Macht*, pp. 184f.

heaven, is opposed to the square or rectangle, taken as emblematic of creation and earth.[75] "Le carré est une figure antidynamique, ancrée sur quatre côtes. Il symbolize l'arrêt, ou l'instant de solidification."[76] The square occurs as the basic plan of cities, which thus become, in a special way, symbolic of mankind as opposed to, and created by, God. Temples, too, which are most often constructed with four corners, appear as emblems of creation that are able to accommodate the presence of God.[77]

Insofar as the circle does not signify something unchangeable but rather a constantly recurring process, a "circulation", it then becomes a symbol of time. Thus, it appears among, for example, the Babylonians as a rolling wheel, which in India is seen as the "wheel of rebirths".[78]

The circle takes on a special meaning when it is considered, to a certain extent, as a "dynamic figure" that originates from a continually expanding point. The basic theme behind the Oriental *mandala*[79] "is the sensing of a personality center, a central point, so to speak, within the soul, toward which everything tends, through which everything is ordered and which, at the same time, represents a source of energy".[80]

This personality center, which acts from within, "out of the depths", appears as the experiential locus for a corresponding activity on the part of the Divinity. The symbol of the mandala shows God—to borrow an expression from feminist theology[81]—as "the energy source of all being", which supports and interpenetrates the world from within. Here, the distance between God and the world is almost removed: "Although the center represents, on the one hand, an inner point, it also has, on the other hand, a periphery or circumference, which contains in it everything that belongs to the self."[82] Between center and periphery (peripheries), between God and world, there is no sharp distinction but rather a confluent transition.

Understandably, the mandala, as a symbol of God's relationship to the world, is an important means of expression for mysticism, which often begins with an experience of oneness and, in Oriental and Neoplatonic thought, usually remains with this starting point. As Plotinus had done earlier,[83] Pseudo-Dionysius sees the creation that flows forth from God in

---

[75] Chevalier and Gheerbrant, *Dictionnaire*, pp. 158ff.
[76] Chevalier and Gheerbrant, *Dictionnaire*, p. 138.
[77] Chevalier and Gheerbrant, *Dictionnaire*, p. 130.
[78] Chevalier and Gheerbrant, *Dictionnaire*, p. 159.
[79] Sanskrit for "circle": Jung, *GW IX*, 1, p. 375.
[80] Jung, *GW IX*, 1, p. 37.
[81] Cf. p. 70 above.
[82] Jung, *GW IX*, 1, p. 377.
[83] Cf. pp. 166f. below.

terms of concentric circles that—like those created when a stone is thrown into water—keep expanding ever more widely.[84] In thought of this type, emanation from God plays a large role, but also, at the same time, the return to the One, the reintegration of the circle into the point.

The mandala symbol is connected in a special way with the feminine thematics of being. In order to express the centrality of women, as well as their stronger involvement with the rhythms of nature, Philipp Lersch chose the image of a circle that gathers itself around a central point, moving outward from it, yet turning inward again toward it. Whenever we meet with a symbol structured in this way, we must, then, expect a feminine image of God. In such cases, the femininity need not be explicitly described, but can also be intimated parenthetically and subconsciously.

6. GOD'S TRANSCENDENCE AND IMMANENCE AS PROTOTYPES OF THE POLARITY OF MAN AND WOMAN

Women and the mystery of immanence

With the concluding remark on mandala symbolism, an important bridge has now been established: between philosophical anthropology and the image of God there is a direct connection. Lersch's concept of centrality has already been described as immanence. Women are more strongly embedded in the near world, on which they exert a formative influence from within. The immanence of women is thus emblematic of God's indwelling the world, of nature's dependence on its divine primal ground. God appears here, so to speak, as the depths, which can be represented through the symbols of earth, roots, wellsprings and ocean.

A distinction can be drawn between the immanence of the Creator that is active in and through the world, which is mainly under discussion here, and intradivine immanence, that is, the life of God that rests within itself and remains hidden from man. In the latter, God appears as an impenetrable Mystery, who has not yet transcended himself through an act of externalization. Since the dynamics of women is less expansive than that of men, women's essence is more strongly self-contained and appears more as an inscrutable mystery. So, too, there have been "numberless more-or-less scientific treatises written about women—and hardly a single

[84] Chevalier and Gheerbrant, *Dictionnaire*, p. 158.

one about men".[85] The mystery of immanence, then, is attributable in special measure to women,[86] and one might well say, in a somewhat paradoxical way: through her immanence, woman transcends herself in the direction of the Mystery of God.

Transcendence and the masculine thematics of being

The transcendence of God means going beyond all worldly realities. God's function does not exhaust itself in being the foundation of creation but is elevated infinitely above this. To be sure, the world is bound most intimately to God, and its Creator remains more intimate to the world than the world to itself. Still, creation is not to be understood as an overflowing or an emanation of the essence of God, but as a free, determinative act.[87] God did not have to create the world (or *this* world), since he, as absolute Being, lacks no perfection whatever. Those who regard creation as a necessity thereby attribute a deficiency, an imperfection, to God. The unconditioned would become the conditioned, and the Creator, the created; the boundaries between God, which is basically not God, and world, which is deprived of its unique status as such, would disappear. If the distinction between God and spiritual creation is removed, there are also, of course, no relevant personal relationships, as these presuppose independent, substantial entities that enter into relation: God and world become interfluent, a neutral it.

Thus, God's transcendence consists in rising above and beyond the world and remaining opposed to it in an infinitely elevated way. God is seen here not in his foundational unity with creation but precisely in his independent reality. In contrast to immanence, transcendence presupposes that God, in the act of creation, does not remain, so to speak, locked in his inwardness but is rather able to bring about something new outside of what is contained in his own nature. In creation, God directs himself, so to speak, powerfully outward.

In all this, God's transcendence has been seen in twofold perspective: God goes beyond the reality of the world because he has first, through an act of free determination, gone beyond himself.

Now, going beyond given realities corresponds to the essence of the masculine qualities, which Lersch has described as "eccentricity". His related "symbol of a line originating at the center of the subject and thrusting outward into the world"[88] is a clear emblem of God's tran-

---

[85] Buytendijk, *Frau*, p. 29.

[86] Buytendijk, *Frau*, p. 210.

[87] Cf. especially DS, 3024.

[88] Cf. p. 96 above.

scendence. As natural symbols of this, there are, above all, the heaven that rises endlessly above the earth, and the sun as the all-dominating source of light.

The interconnectedness of immanence and transcendence and the priority of transcendence

Immanence and transcendence are not properties of God in the strict sense. They do not refer to God's essence but to his relation to the world, and so presuppose the perspective of the creature. In God's perspective "transcendence" and "immanence" are one.

Man should always understand transcendence and immanence together. At the origin of both philosophical knowledge and mystical experience of God lies the perception of God's work in the world, his immanence. In a second stage, it is understood that God's being is not exhausted in being the efficient and final cause of creation, but surpasses even its fundamental mode of being. The unity of both perspectives is expressed in Augustine's well known formula: "God is above what is highest in me and more deeply within than my inmost self."[89]

Immanence and transcendence are not of equal rank. Rather, transcendence, with respect to the image of God, possesses the greater significance. Immanence circumscribes only a tiny fraction of all that God can bring about. In his transcendence, God towers endlessly above and beyond being in the world. Immanence and transcendence are related to each other almost as are zero and infinity, or as a grain of sand is to the shores of the sea.

In transcendence, the immanence of God is always implicit anyway, since transcendence is a concept that is first formed on the basis of God's *relationship* to the world. The concept of immanence is thus, in a certain sense, included in that of transcendence, but the reverse does not apply. Pantheism holds that God and the world are identical, and thus it remains at the level of immanence. Determining the relationship between transcendence and immanence and its metaphysical background will be undertaken in more detail later on. At this point, however, a set of conceptual tools has been provided that will prove helpful in the following inquiries into various concrete manifestations of religion. Without an awareness of the relationship between transcendence and immanence, no meaningful interpretation of the "sexual" aspects in the image of God is possible.

[89] Cf. Leo Scheffczyk, *Der eine und dreifaltige Gott*, Unser Glaube 3 (Mainz, 1968), p. 129; Helmut Ogiermann, *Sein zu Gott. Die philosophische Gottesfrage* (Munich and Salzburg, 1974), p. 186.

7. THE SIGNIFICANCE OF FEMININE TRAITS IN THE IMAGE OF GOD: AN INQUIRY INTO REPRESENTATIVE PHILOSOPHIES, RELIGIONS AND MYTHOLOGIES

Method and goal of the inquiry

Symbols have a power to bring together the most different sorts of cultural worlds. Masculine and feminine traits are expressed over and over again in particular images, such as sun and moon, heaven and earth. The remarkable constancy of these associations derives from the depths of man's unconscious, over which conscious aspects of the soul often only "ripple", like waves over the abysses of the ocean. The most basic psychic processes are only insignificantly modified under the influence of sociological factors. The meanings of father and mother, as well as of the symbolisms associated with these, exhibit far more similarities than differences across all cultures. It is not necessary, therefore, to run through all the philosophical and religious thought systems known to human history. Rather, it will be sufficient to examine relatively few, although central and typical, structures. In selecting these, I have given preference to examples in which feminine components of the image of God play a special role. They will serve, at the same time, as background information that can be drawn on when evaluating feminist theology (especially, here, Indian religion) and attempting a Christian assessment of the modern postulate "God is also mother".

The "maternal" nature of ancient Greek mythology

In the pantheon of the Greek gods, the most important role is played by the father figure, Zeus. This commonplace needs to be supplemented by an awareness that, in the most ancient cosmological myths, the greater importance was apparently attached to the mother, although this does not imply any corresponding position as ruler.

According to Mensching, the world of the ancient Greek gods was, in general, characterized by a basic maternal orientation: ". . . the pre-Homeric gods are essentially maternal powers of the earth, dark, mysterious and of unimaginable form. The Homeric gods are masculine figures, bright and clear in their various characteristic shapes."[90]

In Hesiod's *Theogony*, chaos is seen as the unformed, primal principle,

[90] Gustav Mensching, "Das Ewig-Weibliche in der Religionsgeschichte" [The eternal feminine in the history of religion], in *Gott und Mensch* [God and man] (Goslar, 1948), p. 39.

out of which everything else, including the worlds of gods and men, only later differentiated itself. In many mythologies, however, chaos is linked to the earth or a primal ocean, which means that it is associated with feminine qualities. The same is the case in Hesiod: it gives birth to the earth, which (analogously to its origins) brings forth, without any male participation, the starry heavens. In Greek mythology, the earth is always the province of mothers or is identified with them.[91]

Within the history of ideas, there is, perhaps, a cross-connection here with the cult of the Near Eastern earth mother, which had its center in Phrygia. The mother of the gods, Cybele, plays a role there that stands out above the entire world of the gods, being connected with the importance of the earth, and thus with a fertility religion. At the same time, Cybele possesses androgynous traits, because she brings forth, without any male participation, Dionysus (or Agditis, Mise), who also possesses bisexual qualities.[92] Therefore, it can probably be assumed that chaos, or the earth, in Hesiod's *Theogony* also possessed an androgynous nature, with the female qualities predominating.[93]

In an ancient prayer, handed down to us by Aeschylus, these words occur: "Mother Earth, Mother Earth, ward off the terrible cries. O Father, Son of the Earth, Zeus."[94]

While in this case the father of the gods arises from the earth, in Orphic cosmology he originates from the cosmic ocean, or, more exactly, from a cosmic egg generated out of a shapeless mass. Perhaps Oriental ideas, which are evident particularly in the Orphic doctrine of metempsychosis, played some role here. In the beginning, there is nothing but eternal chaos, neither dark nor light, neither cold nor warm, diverse yet locked up in boundless unity within this primordial state. After an infinite period of time, chaos delivers itself of a gigantic egg, which is described as androgynous because masculine and feminine traits are combined in it. When this cosmic egg breaks open, it gives rise to earth and heaven. Here we meet with the peculiar paradox that the primordial state is, on the one hand, male-female in nature, yet, on the other hand, exhibits mainly female traits, for giving birth is attributed to both chaos and the egg.[95]

According to Aristophanes, night also produces an egg, from which Eros arises, and Eros is regarded as bisexual by Greeks of all periods.[96] A similar myth is carried over to the Phoenix, an androgynous bird figure.

---

[91] Marie Delcourt, *Hermaphrodite. Mythes et rites de la Bisexualité dans l'Antiquité classique* (Paris, 1958), pp. 28f.

[92] Delcourt, *Hermaphrodite*, p. 48.

[93] Mircea Eliade, *Méphistophélès et l'Androgyne* (Paris, 1962), p. 134.

[94] Heiler, *Frau*, p. 9.

[95] Delcourt, *Hermaphrodite*, pp. 105–7.

[96] Delcourt, *Hermaphrodite*, p. 106.

The androgynous ideal, which was widespread in antiquity and can already be clearly discerned in the notions just outlined, will be discussed in more detail later in connection with Gnosticism.

A vestige of these myths about the origin of things has, perhaps, been preserved in the notion of the mass of earth, or the maternal *materia prima*, which was regarded as uncreated even by Plato and Aristotle. According to this, there was no creation of the world out of nothing, but only a modeling of it in previously existing material, which was effected by a "demiurge". Here, there is no securing of the absolute transcendence of God.

The Olympic gods already appear largely as personifications of intra-worldly powers and as bearers of human qualities, which means that they are caught up from the start in previously existing processes. In particular, fate is something that they, too, cannot escape. As the goddess Moira, however, the power of fate is endowed with feminine traits. In the *governance* of the world, she seems to have a significance similarly comprehensive to that of the earth, or birth-giving chaos, in the *generation* of the world.[97]

The cult of the great mother in Near Eastern fertility religion

The religious-historical context

In the early stages of man's history, there obviously existed cult worship of a fertility goddess, who was seen as "the mother of all living things, of man as well as of the animals".[98] This worship was already present during the period when man sustained himself mainly by hunting and gathering. It acquired special importance when man's existence became more settled and his interest more centered on agriculture.

The cycles of nature, which, so to speak, brought forth from themselves, in ever-recurrent rhythms, the fruits of the fields, were associated with female qualities. Women produce, in a similar way, almost year by year a child, and their entire physical existence is more strongly bound up with corporeality and the powers that mysteriously govern nature.

They embody the stability of nature that persists throughout all change and are credited with having a special nearness, of a mystical sort, to the

---

[97] August Vetter calls attention to Moira's precedence over the Olympic gods: "Zur Symbolik der Geschlechter" [On the symbolism of the sexes], in Johannes Tenzler, ed., *Urbild und Abglanz* [Original image and its reflections], Festgabe für H. Doms [In honor of H. Doms] (Regensburg, 1972), p. 260.

[98] Neumann, *Mutter*, p. 101.

earth. Consequently, the divinity, too, is seen through the image of the "Great Mother". Most noteworthy here is the idea of an equivalence between earth/nature and body/woman.[99]

Many scholars of religion, following Bachofen, assume that there was a "religious matriarchate". Man's early history was, supposedly, totally under the sway of worship of the "Great Mother", which was only later supplanted by a "father religion". Erich Neumann draws a parallel between this development and the maturation stages of the individual person: after an infantile "oneness of being" with the mother comes the impressing of structures of order by the father, during which the ties to both mother and father must be brought into harmonious interrelation;[100] there is a correspondence between ontogenesis and phylogenesis.

The last-mentioned idea is close to Ernst Haeckel's "biogenetic law", according to which man, while still in the womb, passes through all the developmental stages of life in general, from reptiles through apes to man. According to more recent biological research, however, this theory is a typical fabrication of misdirected evolutionism.[101] Against the assumption of a matriarchate that was supplanted, in the history of religion, by a patriarchate, basically the same arguments apply that were worked out for the sociological sphere.[102] In particular, in the forms of culture that preceded fixed settlement—remnants of which have been preserved up to the present in various primitive social groups—there was no exclusive worship of a mother goddess. Rather, precisely in those groups, there is frequently belief in a father divinity, which is symbolized as heaven and often strongly suggests monotheism, although without, of course, reaching that full height.[103]

The ethnological material on these matters provides a richer source for historical reconstruction than do the meager archaeological findings relied on by Erich Neumann and others.[104] In the Eurasian region, several dozen female figurines have been found that stem from the Old Stone Age and that seem to offer evidence of worship of a mystical ancestor mother.[105] Figures of females have been discovered more frequently than those of males, but of course, in view of the fragmentary nature of this material, no

[99] Neumann, *Mutter*, p. 65.

[100] Cf. above, p. 130, n. 30.

[101] A detailed refutation, whose basic aspects have been generally accepted, is provided by the embryologist Erich Blechschmidt, *Wie beginnt das menschliche Leben* [How does human life begin?], 4th ed. (Stein am Rhein, 1976), pp. 55ff.

[102] Cf. pp. 99–103 above.

[103] Cf. F. Herrmann, *Symbolik*, p. 66.

[104] Neumann, *Mutter*, p. 99.

[105] Mircea Eliade, *Geschichte der religiösen Ideen I* [History of religious ideas I] (Freiburg, Basel and Vienna, 1978), p. 30.

conclusions can yet be drawn about a possible predominance of "mother worship". A more recent discovery, in Siberia, may well be representative, where, on the site of a Paleolithic settlement, religiously interpretable statues of both women and men were found, and in almost equal numbers.[106]

Bachofen's theory rests heavily on material from agrarian cultures, in which a development of a certain kind may have occurred. The so-called Neolithic revolution (New Stone Age) refers to the introduction of systematic cultivation of useful crops. This discovery was, at first, entrusted to the guardianship of women and was tied to the religious structures noted earlier here.[107] Concentration of interest on the growing of crops can correspond to religious focus on a mother figure, but this need not imply sociological developments of a similar sort.

Many scholars assume that there was an eventual overthrow of this (religious) matriarchate: the more man strives toward active transformation of nature, and the more it becomes necessary to take a strong "grip" on the world, the more the activity of males comes to the fore. In this, the introduction of the plow (phallic symbol) might well play a certain role. The highest Divinity is then seen less as a guarding and protecting "Great Mother", and more as a "Father" who actively influences and shapes natural processes.[108] This new understanding of God did not regard itself as an absolute, but assigned the "Great Mother" to second place within the context of an extensive heaven of deities.

Whether such a development actually occurred is, to be sure, uncertain, for, in the mythologies of ancient peoples, many traits can exist alongside one another that would appear contradictory to our modern ways of thinking. In the Canaanite religion, for instance, the fertility goddess, Astarte, is equally the mother and the wife of Baal. Again, Baal, on the one hand, is king over gods and men, possessing in part the traits of the supreme God, El, yet, on the other hand, is defeated year after year in his struggle with the cosmic powers (= autumn) and undergoes resurrection every spring.[109]

[106] Eliade, *Geschichte*, pp. 30f.

[107] Eliade, *Geschichte*, pp. 44ff.

[108] The "great mother appears as an originally independent deity; the male god associated with her occupies a subordinate position as her son or lover. . . . It is only under the influence of patriarchal culture that the great mother acquires, and is subordinated to, a male husband": Heiler, *Frau*, p. 8.

This hypothesis refers above all to the Mediterranean region. Cf. also E. O. James, *The Cult of the Mother Goddess. An Archaeological and Documentary Study* (London, 1959), pp. 10f., 228.

[109] Cf. the contribution by J. Pedersen on "Kanaanäische Religion" [Canaanite religion], in J. P. Asmussen et al., eds., *Handbuch der Religionsgeschichte II* [Handbook of the history of religion II] (Göttingen, 1972), pp. 33–59.

The Canaanite religion

The Canaanite religion is the exemplary instance of a fertility cult. I have chosen it here also in order to make clear, at an early stage, the antithetical background of the Old Testament image of God.

The two divine parents are El (Bull El, Father Schunem) and Ashera (Elat), whose traits often merge with those of their children, Baal and Astarte.[110]

This younger, more dynamic pair play the most important roles in the fertility cult, which has strong sexual undertones. The whole annual cycle is seen as a "holy wedding" (Hieros Gamos): The "sperm" of the rain (= activity of the heaven god, Baal) fertilizes the fecund earth (Astarte). This coupling is carried out ritually in the form of temple prostitution.

Here, the image of God blatantly reflects natural processes in which the male and female principles participate, so to say, *pari cum pari*. Precisely behind the Canaanite pantheon of gods, there is a tendency to hypostatize the forces at work in the world into divine beings.[111] Interest is thus clearly centered on God's immanence.

The Chinese universe

General characterization

The Chinese religion contains what is probably the most precisely worked out symbolism of the sexes in the world's history. An early formulation of this way of thinking is found in the *I Ching*, the *Book of Changes*. The course of nature appears as a cyclical process of interaction between "yin" and "yang", the feminine and masculine principles. The difference between the sexes is regarded not as something merely anthropological, but rather—as is more or less the case in all cultures[112]—as a concrete manifestation of a more comprehensive, cosmic polarity. "Yin, in its original sense, is the cloudy, the dreary; yang strictly means: banner fluttering in the sunlight—that is, something illuminated, bright."[113]

Along with the contrast bright-dark go other sorts of opposition, in which the feminine element is always subordinated to the masculine, but

---

[110] Raphael Patai, *The Hebrew Goddess* (Ktav, 1967), pp. 55ff.; Eliade, *Geschichte*, p. 146.

[111] Michael Schmaus points out that, for this reason, all polytheisms are ultimately pantheisms, "personalistic concentrations" of [aspects of] an " 'it' world": *Der Glaube der Kirche II* [The Faith of the Church II], 2nd ed. (Munich, 1979), p. 14.

[112] Eliade, "Prolegomenon", p. 179.

[113] Richard Wilhelm, *I Ging. Das Buch der Wandlungen* [I Ching. The Book of Changes], translated with commentary by Richard Wilhelm (Düsseldorf and Cologne, 1972), p. 16.

without thereby acquiring connotations of inferiority: "The creative is the strongest thing in the world. . . . The receptive is the most devoted thing in the world."[114]

The polarity of heaven and earth appears especially significant: "The creative is heaven, and thus it is called father. But the receptive is the earth, and thus it is called mother."[115]

The social structure is a reflection of the cosmos: "The proper place of women is inside; the proper place of men is outside. That men and women have their proper places is the greatest concept in nature."[116] "Heaven and earth form an opposition, but their activity is effected in common. Men and women form an opposition, but their strivings tend toward unification."[117]

The opposition yin-yang is later systematized more strongly, especially in Taoism: "Yang is the male, active, procreative, creative, bright principle; yin, the female, passive, receptive, devoted, shadowy." These are "the two sides of the universally one, constantly changing being".[118]

This universal One, embracing both yin and yang, is known as Tao, which may be translated (among other possibilities) as "life", "meaning", "way" or "law".[119] It is represented graphically as a circle with two halves:

Yin   Yang

"Chinese universism"[120] recognizes no unique events, but basically only an eternal cyclical process. Yin and yang always work together, but in certain phases. The still interval between two world epochs is seen as a formless state, containing everything in potentiality, which is reminiscent of the state of primordial chaos that is a feature in many other mythologies. It is represented as a simple circle, which only subsequently shapes itself into yin and yang.

---

[114] Wilhelm, *I Ging*, p. 325.

[115] Wilhelm, *I Ging*, p. 254.

[116] Wilhelm, *I Ging*, p. 509.

[117] Wilhelm, *I Ging*, p. 513.

[118] Helmuth von Glasenapp, *Die fünf grossen Weltreligionen I* [The five major world religions I] (Düsseldorf and Cologne, 1952), p. 155.

[119] Wilhelm, *I Ging*, p. 16.

[120] This term is applied to Chinese thought by Glasenapp in order to indicate its cosmic references.

Maternal symbolism in the Tao Te Ching

At the origins of Taoism, and thus particularly of Chinese mysticism, stands Lao-tzu, whose maxims (*Tao Te Ching*) are characterized by highly memorable, intuitive comparisons. His sayings were regarded in ancient China as holy writ, to which a similar importance should be ascribed as to the Koran in Islam or the Bible in Christianity.[121]

The sage's mystical experience of oneness serves as the starting point for his philosophy: "*One* was he with everything, and everything was *universal One*."[122] On the one hand, Tao contains the masculine and feminine principles inseparately within itself; it is "the origin of heaven and earth".[123] On the other hand, it is described again and again, in the most varying symbolic terms, as a maternal (and not as a paternal) primal ground: "The empty abyss of Tao is the mother of all beings. Whoever recognizes the mother knows himself a child of the divine."[124]

Tao is the "root" of all things,[125] the "primal ground of self",[126] the "depths of the universe",[127] an "eternally flowing wellspring". It is "unmoved and dark, like the bottom of the sea".[128] As "hidden birth giver . . . it gives birth without end. Inexhaustibly, it brings forth fullness."[129] The "primal womb of the world" is "formless" and "without qualities. I call it: the boundless, the circle that turns back into itself."[130]

Tao is a circle not only insofar as a certain process is continually repeated within it. It also appears as a central point bound up in a seamless way with the "peripheries": it is "the primal womb and midpoint of all beings".[131]

In the symbol of the circle, the maternal images of the Tao seem to find their center. A circle is, on the one hand, an emblem of the activity of the divine in nature, which continually repeats itself, and, on the other hand, a sign of the immanence that exerts itself from the inside of things, including the human soul. Lao-tzu is representative of a pronounced "immanence-mysticism". No historical effects of Tao, and no transcendence bound up

---

[121] K. O. Schmidt: *Lao-Tse, Tao-Teh-King. Weg-Weisung zur wirklichkeit* [Lao-tzu, Tao Te Ching. Pointing the way to reality], edited with commentary by K. O. Schmidt (Engelberg [Switzerland] and Munich, 1977), p. 17.

[122] K. O. Schmidt, *Lao-Tse*, p. 12.

[123] K. O. Schmidt, *Lao-Tse*, p. 31, maxim 1.

[124] K. O. Schmidt, *Lao-Tse*, p. 159, maxim 52.

[125] K. O. Schmidt, *Lao-Tse*, p. 72, maxim 16.

[126] K. O. Schmidt, *Lao-Tse*, p. 72, maxim 16.

[127] K. O. Schmidt, *Lao-Tse*, p. 45, maxim 6.

[128] K. O. Schmidt, *Lao-Tse*, p. 83, maxim 20.

[129] K. O. Schmidt, *Lao-Tse*, p. 45, maxim 6.

[130] K. O. Schmidt, *Lao-Tse*, p. 94, maxim 25.

[131] K. O. Schmidt, *Lao-Tse*, p. 39, maxim 4.

with the creation of the world, are expressed in the symbols of the *Tao Te Ching*.

The significance of feminine symbolism in the world of the Hindu gods

Relative position within the history of ideas

Within Indian religion and philosophy, ideas similar to the Chinese conceptions just covered can be found. In India, the maternal characteristics of the divine receive particularly abundant expression, more so than in any other culture: "The Hindu tradition . . . developed the ritual, devotion and theology of female divinity more profusely, and perhaps more profoundly, than any other major religious tradition."[132]

Thus, the sympathy that feminist theologians feel for Hindulike conceptions of God is understandable.[133]

Brahman and Brahma: Indian pan(en)theism

In Indian thought, the "source, ground and goal of all things" is Brahman. Since the "highest quintessence of the universe" has no personal characteristics, "the generation of the world from it involves no unique act of will on the part of a creator god".[134] The personal god, Brahma, is thus but a secondary "personification of the neutral Brahman concept".[135] In the *Bhagavad-Gita*, Brahman is depicted as fertile topsoil (matrix) in which a seed is sown.[136] Elsewhere, the substance of the universe appears as a golden egg, out of which the personal god is born,[137] or it is embodied in the primal seas.[138] Willibald Kirfel regards the relation Brahman-Brahma as the reflection of a pre-Aryan myth: the relationship world mother–god-son, resembling that of the pairs Cybele-Attis (Asia Minor) and Isis-Horus (Egypt). In any case, primal seas (ocean) and egg are elements of maternal symbolism.[139]

---

[132] C. M. Brown, *God as Mother: A Feminine Theology in India. An Historical and Theological Study of the Brahmavaivarta Purana* (Hartford, 1974), p. 115.

[133] Especially strong in Katappo, *Free*, pp. 72ff.

[134] Jan Gonda, *Die Religionen Indiens I* [The religions of India I], Die Religionen der Menschheit 11, 2nd ed. (Stuttgart, 1978), p. 265.

[135] Gonda, *Indiens*, p. 263.

[136] Chevalier and Gheerbrant, *Dictionnaire*, p. 499.

[137] F. Herrmann, *Symbolik*, p. 83.

[138] Gonda, *Indiens*, p. 262; Jobes, *Mythology*, p. 1193.

[139] Willibald Kirfel, *Symbolik des Hinduismus und des Jainismus* [Symbolism of Hinduism and Jainism], Symbolik der Religionen IV (Stuttgart, 1959), p. 14.

In comparison with Brahman, Brahma has a subordinate role. Indian piety centers more strongly on later emanations that have acquired personal forms.[140]

What we find here is the classical instance of a pantheistic emanation doctrine: God is not only the efficient, but also the material cause (*causa materialis*) of the world, allowing, like a wellspring, all things to flow forth from himself.[141] Consequently, the world has no beginning in time and no real history; the cosmic process takes place through constantly recurring cycles.[142]

Even when the image of the Divinity has strong theistic traits and is linked to a personally toned piety, things never go beyond so-called panentheism, according to which God is, in fact, more than the world, yet is, at the same time, identical with it.[143]

Theological and anthropological apersonalism

This monism is expressed quite clearly in the Brahman-Atman doctrine. "Atman" means "life breath, soul", and can also mean "person, ego, self".[144] Particularly since the time of the *Upanishads*, Brahman and Atman are identified with one another:[145] Atman is an expression of the impersonal power of Brahman, into which it longs to return. Just as Brahman is seen as the deep center of being, so the human soul is obviously seen as the deep center of man, which discloses itself in breathing (in German, to breathe = *atmen!*). To the recurrent course of events in the world correspond the process of metempsychosis and the "cycle of existences" (*samsara*).[146] The goal of this movement is the dissolution of personal identity in the ocean of Brahman. The idea that the "notion of God is a 'thou' or an 'I' presupposes an anthropological personalism" is illustrated here in terms of a counterexample.[147]

---

[140] Ernst Dammann, *Grundriss der Religionsgeschichte* [Outline of the history of religion], 2nd ed. (Stuttgart, 1972), p. 28.

[141] Glasenapp, *Weltreligionen I*, p. 58.

[142] Dammann, *Religionsgeschichte*, p. 29.

[143] Glasenapp, *Weltreligionen I*, p. 40; *Weltreligionen II*, p. 476.

[144] Dammann, *Religionsgeschichte*, p. 28.

[145] Gonda, *Indiens*, p. 265; Dammann, *Religionsgeschichte*, p. 28.

[146] Dammann, *Religionsgeschichte*, p. 29.

[147] Piet Schoonenberg, "Gott als Person und Gott als das unpersönlich Göttliche. Bhakti und Juana" [God as Person and God as the impersonal divine. Bhakti and Juana], in Gerhard Oberhammer, ed., *Transzendenzerfahrung, Vollzugshorizont des Heils. Das Problem in indischer und christlicher Tradition* [Experience of transcendence, salvation's horizon of fulfillment. The problem in the Indian and Christian traditions], Publications of the De Nobili research Library V (Vienna, 1978), p. 211.

Apersonalism and female divinities

A male divinity in India is almost always associated with a female one. "Shakti" represents the power of God as it works in the world,[148] and her importance for devotion is often greater than that of her male partner.[149] It is significant that Shakti always appears as a *later* personification of the worldly aspect of a male god.[150] Also, Brahman, the impersonal Absolute, manifests itself—as will emerge even more clearly shortly—chiefly through feminine traits. Probably the individual Shaktis are to be seen as aspects of what was originally one mother goddess.[151]

The individual characteristics of the various goddesses, as of Brahman, are seldom very prominent; they usually serve as female copies of male attributes.[152] The Shaktis appear less as entities with independent natures than as relational beings. Male divinities, by contrast, are automatically endowed with personal characteristics, which is already evident in Brahma as the first emanation of the cosmic substance. Nevertheless, the image of God is by no means male, and Shakti is often given preference in actual worship. Thus, the more personal nature of male deities can hardly be due to repressive religious structures that might operate against the female *divinum*.

The androgynous image of God

The male-female doubling in the forms of the Indian deities results from a basically androgynous outlook: "The divinity (Brahman) and its power (Shakti) are not two things, but rather, one divine principle in the two forms of male and female."[153]

A doctrine of emanation is always connected with androgynous notions, as is shown particularly clearly here.[154] The masculine aspect of the androgynous is also overshadowed by the feminine.

The androgynous image of God is paralleled in a certain way by an androgynous image of man. For example, the goal of the Tantra mysticism

---

[148] Thomas Schipflinger, "Der fraulich-mütterlich Aspekt im Göttlichen. Eine religionswissenschaftliche Studie" [The womanly-motherly aspect of the divine. A study in religious scholarship], *Kairos* 9 (1967): 281.

[149] Dammann, *Religionsgeschichte*, p. 36.

[150] Cf. the development in Buddhism: Schipflinger, "Aspekt", p. 281.

[151] Kirfel, *Hinduismus*, p. 45.

[152] Kirfel, *Hinduismus*, p. 45.

[153] Ramakrishna: Schipflinger, "Aspekt", p. 287.

[154] Cf. Kirfel, *Hinduismus*, p. 27. In Buddhism, too, male and female deities emanate from androgynous "Dhyani-Buddhas": Willibald Kirfel, *Symbolik des Buddhismus* [Symbolism of Buddhism], Symbolik der Religionen V (Stuttgart, 1959), pp. 63f., 80.

of the yogis is attainment of the divine primal state, that is, an "andro-gynization".[155]

Given the fundamental bisexuality of the divine, the individual figures in the pantheon may also be thought of, at one and the same time, in terms of masculine and feminine qualities, as is the mother of the gods, Aditi: "Aditi is the heaven, Aditi the air, Aditi the mother; she is father and son."[156]

Hinduism as an immanence religion

Since God is identical with the world in Indian religion, all the characteristics of nature can be attributed to God in the same sense in which they show themselves there. Willibald Kirfel, therefore, correctly regards the Hindu deities as "personifications of potencies that are naturally at work within the world".[157]

Because of this, the reference to divine immanence is as centrally influential as it is in the Near Eastern fertility cults. From the Indian perspective, there is no reason not to apply the titles father and mother, which are used with equal frequency in the worldly realm, in that same measure, *pari cum pari*, to God.

Syncretism and ethical ambivalence

This concern with blurring all dualities is found not only in relation to the androgynous nature of the divinities. If there is no absolute, transcendent God, then the claims of *truth* are also not absolute. Truth and error, being and appearance, melt into one another, as do God and world: "The Hindu does not pose the question of truth, but sees in all appearances particular expressions of the One, the Absolute."[158] From this perspective, all religions are equal; the Hindu is "tolerant".

To this indifference toward the transcendentalism of truth corresponds a deficient sense of the *good*, that is, of the very thing at which all man's strivings aim. It is surely no coincidence that in India there is no excessive readiness to carry out plans for reforming the world. Not only error (which actually does not exist) and truth but also evil and good are

---

[155] Eliade, *Androgyne*, p. 146. Similar psychotechniques are found in Chinese Taoism: Eliade, *Androgyne*, p. 149, n. 83.

[156] Alfred Bertholet, *Das Geschlecht der Gottheit* [The sex of the Divinity], Sammlung gemeinverständlicher Vorträge und Schriften aus dem Gebiet der Theologie und Religionsgeschichte 173 (Tübingen, 1934), p. 19.

[157] Kirfel, *Hinduismus*, p. 54.

[158] Dammann, *Religionsgeschichte*, p. 32; cf. p. 39.

frequently viewed as equivalents. The Indian divinities are almost always "two-faced", that is, cruel and frightening as well as loving to the point of "blind infatuation".[159] According to the Vedas, the gods (devas) and demons (asuras) are engaged in a bitter war that is, however, just an illusory battle. For they both share the same origin; they are equally worthy, mutually complementary modes of appearance of the same divine power.[160]

From all this, despite high flights of asceticism in certain areas, what results is a virtually permissive, tolerant morality: *et Deus et diabolus*. On the one hand, then, Ramakrishna can describe the "heart of the pure virgin" as the greatest manifestation of the divine mother.[161] On the other hand, he can say in the "harlots on the streets . . . I discern . . . as well the divine mother, who amuses herself in a different way".[162] The Hindu "missionary", Vivekananda, once called it "a sin to describe any person as a sinner".[163]

The significance of Vishnu and Shiva and their female companions

The Indian "trinity of gods" consists of Brahma, Vishnu and Shiva.[164] Whereas the "creator god" (better: demiurge), Brahma, plays no special role in popular piety, Vishnu is regarded "in practical Hinduism . . . as the Divinity itself".[165] The cosmos emanates from him and flows back again into him, as the "point of contraction"; it is he who sustains the eternal cycles.[166] At the same time, he appears, in and through the most different sorts of "descent to earth" (avatars), as a savior incarnate. One of the best-known avatars is Krishna, upon whom an especially fervent and personally toned piety (bhakti) is centered.[167]

Krishna's female companion is his Shakti, Radha, who exists on the human plane as well as on the divine. On the one hand, Radha is of "equal rank" to Krishna, "in fact, out of love and in love, she stands above him.

---

[159] Eliade, *Androgyne*, p. 111.

[160] Eliade, *Androgyne*, p. 115.

[161] *Sri Ramakrishnas ewige Botschaft* [Sri Ramakrishna's eternal message] (Zurich, 1955), p. 195.

[162] Ramakrishna, *Leben und Gleichnis. Die Botschaft des grössten indischen Heiligen* [Life and emblem. The message of the greatest Indian saint], selected and translated by Ursula von Mangoldt (Bern, Munich and Vienna, 1975), p. 135.

[163] Dammann, *Religionsgeschichte*, p. 38.

[164] Cf. Kirfel, *Hinduismus*.

[165] Kirfel, *Hinduismus*, p. 34.

[166] Kirfel, *Hinduismus*, p. 34.

[167] Dammann, *Religionsgeschichte*, pp. 30f.

She is the highest divinity."[168] On the other hand, she is "the symbol of the God-loving soul", by virtue of embodying the receptive openness and devotional powers of the pious.[169] Here, divine and human are not differentiated into masculine and feminine poles but are mixed together in equal proportions.

The next-most-important divinity, after Vishnu, is Shiva, who, in a particularly drastic way, is described as androgynous and linked to a process of emanation.[170] His wife (and Shakti), Kali, is the most important mother figure among the Indian deities and an "equal, perhaps even greater, partner" to Shiva.[171]

Ramakrishna's maternal symbolism as a typical expression of the Hindu image of God

Kali, the divine mother, assumes a role within Ramakrishnan piety that eclipses all others. This nineteenth-century mystic has been chosen here as a typical example of Hindu religion because, in his highly pictorial language, Indian religiosity and its symbols are presented with special vividness. His image of God, which "impartially" binds together masculine and feminine traits, is sometimes held out as a shining example for the "opening up" of "patriarchal" Western spirituality:[172] the pious "love and worship him (the personal god) as servant or friend, as mother or father, as wife or beloved".[173]

The divine mother is identical with the cosmos: "My dear child, nothing exists in the world except me."[174] As well, Kali is seen in one and the same perspective with Brahman: "My Divine Mother is the personal aspect of the impersonal universal One."[175] Ramakrishna therefore has moving words for a personal, loving and trusting relationship with God. But this personal exchange is not for him the ultimate: "Only when I (Kali) extinguish everything differentiated and personal can the universally one, transpersonal primal essence be experienced."[176]

An image of Brahman that constantly recurs in Ramakrishna's thought (and also elsewhere in Hinduism) is the shoreless, immeasurable ocean, in

---

[168] Schipflinger, "Aspekt", p. 292.
[169] Schipflinger, "Aspekt", p. 292.
[170] Kirfel, *Hinduismus*, p. 27.
[171] Kirfel, *Hinduismus*, p. 45.
[172] Schipflinger, "Aspekt", p. 287.
[173] *Botschaft*, p. 159.
[174] Ramakrishna, *Leben*, p. 101.
[175] *Botschaft*, p. 75.
[176] *Botschaft*, p. 75.

which all personal differences are dissolved.[177] "Just as the ice (in the world's oceans) . . . persists for a while in the water, but then melts away in it, so the personal god stands in relation to the impersonal. He arises out of the impersonal, endures for a time, then returns at last from whence he came and vanishes."[178]

Now, the ocean is a classical example of maternal symbolism. This connection becomes particularly clear in Ramakrishna when he describes Kali as "the mother and destroyer of the universe. . . . All things are born of her and are taken up into her again."[179] Kali is loving as well as cruel and bloodthirsty: *et Deus et diabolus*.

Ramakrishna is as tolerant of a personal as of an impersonal image of God. But his ice-floe comparisons show[180] that this tolerance is only an appearance, since ultimate reality takes the form of an impersonal "it".

To this theological apersonalism corresponds an anthropological one: for him, the ideal man is like a doll made of salt that lets itself be annihilated in the waters of the Absolute, or like an onion whose skins (the "I") can be continuously peeled away until nothing more of it exists.[181]

In Ramakrishna, then, we can see, in virtually three-dimensional fullness, how pantheism (or "panentheism") leads to apersonalism. That the intermixing of the divine and the human leads to an ambivalent attitude toward moral norms has already been shown above. Naturally enough, we also find in him an attitude of indifference toward truth, for knowledge of truth subserves a striving for the good: "Just as one can get to the roof of a house with the aid of a bamboo pole or of a ladder or in various other ways, such, too, is the case regarding the ways and means that lead to God. Every religion is one way in the world of drawing near to him."[182]

Gnosticism

Emanationism and androgyny

Many of the traits characteristic of Indian religion can also be found in Gnosticism, which needs to be covered briefly here because of its historical influence and various intellectual parallels to modern theologies.

[177] *Botschaft*, pp. 75f.

[178] Ramakrishna, *Leben*, p. 125.

[179] Ramakrishna, *Leben*, p. 11.

[180] Similarly, the image of the waves of the relative that well up in the divine seas of the Absolute: *Botschaft*, p. 261.

[181] Ramakrishna, *Leben*, pp. 131, 142.

[182] Ramakrishna, *Leben*, p. 110.

The differing systems of thought that are brought together under the heading "gnosis" agree with one another in assuming that man's salvation is attained essentially through knowledge (γνῶσις), which is reserved for an initiated elite. By the term "Gnosticism", what is meant are the Gnostic systems of the second century A.D.[183] According to Hans Jonas, two main groups of Gnosticism can be distinguished: the Iranian and the Syrian-Egyptian types.[184] The first group regards good and evil as two basic primordial powers that wage war with each other: metaphysical dualism. Along with this go the following associations: spirit = good; matter = evil.

In the second group, too—under which most of the surviving texts fall—there is a devaluing of the material world, but the fundamental structure is provided by a doctrine of emanation: the corporeal realm is a darkened level of being, within the divine world of light, that fell away from the original state of things by virtue of a naturally pre-indicated crisis. The task of the Gnostic, therefore, is to discover the divine spark of light within himself and to work at gradually freeing it from all bondage to the realm of the body and of matter. The falling away from the light must be followed by a re-ascent to divine fullness, to the "pleroma".

That the divine origins combine maleness and femaleness is a typical expression of the thought of Gnosticism (and of gnosis): alongside of the "divine father there is usually a divine mother, the feminine aspect of the Divinity; the Divinity has, after all, a polar nature, and comprehends all opposites".[185]

A text from the *Megale Apophasis*, handed down to us by Hippolytus, is characteristic: There is "*one* power, divided into upper and lower, self-engendering, self-propagating, . . . its own mother, its own father, its own sister, its own consort, its own daughter, its own son, mother, father, one, root of the universe".[186]

To the androgyny of God corresponds an androgyny of the primal man, who appears as a likeness of God;[187] he is "male-female, engendered by a male-female father".[188] The difference between the sexes is thus seen as the result of a failing and is overcome in the pleroma.

---

[183] This usage has been adopted in gnosis research since 1966: Walther Eltester, ed., *Christentum und Gnosis* [Christianity and gnosis] (Berlin, 1969), pp. 129f.

[184] Cf. Kurt Rudolph, *Die Gnosis. Wesen und Geschichte einer spätantiken Religion* [Gnosis. Essence and history of a religion of late antiquity] (Göttingen, 1978), pp. 73f.

[185] Quispel, *Gnosis*, p. 34.

[186] Hippolyt[us], *Refutatio omnium haeresium VI,17,3*, in Carl Andresen, ed., *Die Gnosis I* [Gnosis I] (Zurich and Stuttgart, 1969), p. 333; GCS 26, p. 143.

[187] Rudolph, *Gnosis*, p. 100.

[188] Corpus Hermeticum I, 12–15, in Rudolph, *Gnosis*, p. 125.

Origin and significance of the ancient androgyne myth

Before drawing on a few prominent examples to illustrate Gnosticism in greater detail, I would like to take a look at the history and significance of the ancient androgyne myth. Two sorts of influence seem to have been involved in a particular way:

1. A misinterpretation of the biblical account of creation, in which Adam is taken as a man-woman. More about this will be said later.[189]
2. An allegory from Plato's *Symposium*, in which a generally widespread human longing finds expression.[190] There, Aristophanes, describing the nature of love (*eros*), tells the following story:

   In earliest times, there existed a race that combined "the forms and names of the male and female sexes into a single being". These people had four hands, four feet and so forth, with the result that they took the form of a sphere. "Their strength was great and superhuman; their spirits were bold, to the extent that they even tried challenging the gods."

   In order to dampen their arrogance, Zeus cut these blasphemers into two halves. "From that day on, my friends, Eros has been born into all men, so that he can lead them to recover their former nature by coming together in pairs, thereby healing their wounded being."[191]

In interpreting this myth here, two points need to be given special emphasis:[192]

1. The difference between the sexes appears as a limitation.
2. Man strives to be like God and to overcome his own creaturely limits. An expression of this wish is the quasi-divine power that is attributed to the man-woman.

As a rule, this striving is not to be understood so realistically as to imply that hermaphrodites are emulated as examples of ideal human beings. In antiquity, hermaphroditic children were ordinarily rejected and often

---

[189] Cf. p. 199 below.

[190] In this, as I see it, only the main axis of the historical development is indicated; it is reflected especially clearly in later forms of thought; cf. Ernst Benz, *Adam. Der Mythus vom Urmenschen* [Adam. The myth of the primal man] (Munich and Planegg, 1955), p. 15. Mircea Eliade describes the sources of gnosis as follows: "à côté de la gnose juive, des spéculations sur l'adam primordial et sur la Sophie, on y retrouve l'apport des doctrines néo-platoniennes et néo-pythagoréennes, et des influences orientales, surtout iraniennes": *Androgyne*, p. 132. Similarly, Eltester, *Gnosis*, p. 131.

[191] *Symposion*, 189d–191e, in Plato, *Gastmahl. Phaidros. Phaidon* [Symposium, Phaedrus, Phaedo] (Wiesbaden, 1978), pp. 28–30.

[192] Cf. Eliade, *Androgyne*, p. 152.

exposed.[193] On the other hand, however, the myth does reflect a desire to be rid of sexually determined limitations. The overcoming of opposites seems not only to relate to the purely mental sphere but also to the bodily sphere. Numerous divinities in antiquity are endowed with androgynous features. In addition to the aforementioned earth goddess Cybele,[194] who is depicted as also having male characteristics, there are, for example, a six-breasted Zeus, a bearded Aphrodite and particularly the effeminate wine god Dionysus.[195] Even the warlike Heracles repeatedly appears as a transvestite.[196] The androgynous aspects of the world of the gods are paralleled by a variety of customs involving exchanges of dress between the sexes. All in all, androgyny is a widespread ideal goal.

Many folk customs can be explained as means of warding off demons or as rites of passage. Thus, initiation ceremonies occasionally place emphasis on the young male's feminine traits, which will be less in evidence from that time onward.[197] In addition, various frivolous elements can be found in ancient art that betray a certain homosexual influence.[198]

With all these explanations, however, justice has still not been fully done to the broad, total stream of what has come down to us. The essential idea seems, rather, to be the same as the salient point of the Platonic allegory. Marie Delcourt sees there a striving for unity and superhuman power, a dream of rebirth and eternal life,[199] as expressed in a concentrated form in the symbol of the androgynous bird, Phoenix, which promises immortality.[200]

Creaturely restrictedness and submergence in the world-historical process are relegated to the background by every form of man-woman ideal.[201] The goal to be striven for, according to Mircea Eliade, is a regression to an unformed, primordial state, the maternal womb of chaos, out of which a rebirth is then hoped for.[202]

Particular variant forms of gnosis

Barbelo gnosis is "one of the largest groupings" within Gnosticism. "Barbelo represents the feminine side of the Father and is a kind of Gnostic

---

[193] Delcourt, *Hermaphrodite*, p. 66.
[194] Cf. p. 145 above.
[195] Delcourt, *Hermaphrodite*, pp. 29, 43.
[196] Delcourt, *Hermaphrodite*, p. 33.
[197] Delcourt, *Hermaphrodite*, pp. 11f.
[198] Delcourt, *Hermaphrodite*, pp. 102f.
[199] Delcourt, *Hermaphrodite*, pp. 107–27.
[200] Delcourt, *Hermaphrodite*, pp. 63f.
[201] Eliade, *Androgyne*, pp. 140f., 152.
[202] Eliade, *Androgyne*, p. 141.

mother divinity." At the same time, this figure has bisexual traits, thus embodying, in a special way, the androgynous ideal of the Gnostics.[203] In connection with Barbelo, the process of emanation unfolds through male-female eons.[204] The Holy Spirit is regarded as "the mother of all".[205]

Similar ideas recur in the so-called three-principle systems,[206] as, for example, with the Naassenes. The previously existent, the self-generated (= the male-female Adamas) and the effused chaos comprise the system's triadic point of departure. The Naassenes got their name from the snake (Hebrew, *nachasch*; Grecized, *naas*),[207] which represents "an everlasting interplay . . . from up to down and from down to up".[208]

In the beginning, there was chaos, or more precisely, a formless cosmic ocean: "when the ocean subsides, that means the coming of men, but when it rises . . . , that means the coming of gods".[209]

Thus the basis of the system, as in Hinduism, is an eternal cyclical process,[210] which is described with the help of maternal symbolism: ocean.

A maternal-androgynous primal ground is also apparent in the image of the earth, from out of which Geryones, the male-female primal man, "flowed forth".[211] Like the original man, the "new man", too, should be androgynous.[212]

The image of God corresponds to the image of man. The original unity of the three principles is referred to in the same way as "father and mother".[213] A noted hymn from the Naassene liturgy ran as follows: "From you, Father, and through you, Mother, the two immortal names, the parents of the eons, you resident of heaven, you man with the exalted name."[214]

Valentinian gnosis was a source of powerful competition to Christianity.

[203] Rudolph, *Gnosis*, p. 89.

[204] Andresen, *Gnosis I*, p. 145.

[205] Andresen, *Gnosis I*, p. 149.

[206] Andresen, *Gnosis I*, p. 336.

[207] Rudolph, *Gnosis*, p. 93.

[208] Andresen, *Gnosis I*, p. 315.

[209] Hippolyt[us], *Refutatio omnium haeresium V, 7, 38*, in Andresen, *Gnosis I*, p. 347; *GCS* 26, p. 88.

[210] Andresen, *Gnosis I*, p. 338.

[211] Hippolyt[us], *Refutatio omnium haeresium V, 8, 4*, in Andresen, *Gnosis I*, pp. 348f.; *GCS* 26, p. 89.

[212] Hippolyt[us], *Refutatio omnium haeresium V, 7, 14*, in Andresen, *Gnosis I*, p. 342; *GCS* 26, p. 82.

[213] Andresen, *Gnosis I*, p. 316.

[214] Hippolyt[us], *Refutatio omnium haeresium, V, 6, 5*, in Andresen, *Gnosis I*, p. 339; *GCS* 26, p. 78.

There, too, the typical doctrine of emanation is to be found. The primal ground and the silence form the starting point of becoming, after which follow the pair *nous* and truth. The principles of the "upper quaternity" are "in each case counted, and also treated, as two", yet are simultaneously "*one* male-female being".[215] From this quaternity issue the eons, the last and youngest being "Sophia", which gives birth to the Holy Spirit. The second principle, "sige" (silence), serves to introduce the pleroma, which "leads down into the depths of the primal ground".[216] Again, depths and primal ground tend to be maternal images; the first principle of the Father, to which they are applied, is thus regarded by some Valentinians as "male-female".[217]

Maternal symbolism also seems to be preferred for describing the entire upper quaternity: "man, too, who has been created in the image of the upper power, contains within himself the power of the one source. . . . From there, the powers flow toward the image of the upper quaternity."[218]

In some respects, the Valentinians anticipated, and even outdid, the plans of the feminist theologians, for one of their baptismal invocations reads: "In the name of the unknown father of the universe, of the truth, mother of all things, and of him, who in Jesus came down to earth for the unification, for the salvation and for the communion of the powers."[219]

Praise of "God as mother" in the divine service was by no means an isolated phenomenon in Gnostic circles. Mother epicleses, which were probably sung even at the Eucharist, are found especially in Bardesanean gnosis[220] and in Manichaeanism. The *Acts of Thomas*, which originated in Syria in the first half of the third century, are a connecting link between these two movements.[221] The mother of life in the ancient Eastern fertility religion forms a remoter backdrop to the relevant hymns.[222]

In a Gnostic epiclesis, the following invocations, among others, are found:

> "(Come, gift of the highest . . .)
> Come, consummate charity;
> Come, communion with the masculine;

[215] Andresen, *Gnosis I*, p. 165.

[216] Irenaeus, *Adversus haereses I, 21, 2*, in Andresen, *Gnosis I*, p. 283; *PG* 7, p. 657.

[217] Irenaeus, *Adversus haereses I, 11, 5*, in Andresen, *Gnosis I*, p. 256; *PG* 7, p. 569.

[218] Irenaeus, *Adversus haereses I, 18, 1*, in Andresen, *Gnosis I*, pp. 227f.; *PG* 7, p. 644.

[219] Irenaeus, *Adversus haereses I, 21, 3*, in Andresen, *Gnosis I*, pp. 283f.; *PG* 7, p. 658.

[220] Günther Bornkamm, "Thomas-Akten" [Acts of Thomas], in Edgar Hennecke and Wilhelm Schneemelcher, eds., *Neutestamentliche Apokryphen in deutscher Übersetzung II* [New Testament Apocrypha in German translation II], 3rd ed. (Tübingen, 1964), p. 307.

[221] G. Bornkamm, "Thomas-Akten", pp. 307f.

[222] G. Bornkamm, "Thomas-Akten", p. 306.

(Come, Holy Spirit . . .);
Come, she who knows the secrets of the elect; . . .
Come, rest (silence), . . .
Holy Dove, . . .
Come, concealed mother . . .
. . . rest for all who are bound to you;
Come and partake with us of this Eucharist,
Which we celebrate in your name,
And partake of this love feast,
To which we are gathered at your behest."[223]

Particularly close parallels to the hymns in the *Acts of Thomas* crop up in early Mandaean psalms and, not least, in *Manichaeanism*, in which the "mother of life" is invoked at "sacramental meals".[224] In the Turfan texts, this doxology, among other things, is preserved:

"Praised be the pure wholeness of the holy religion
Through the father's (. . .) power
Through the mother's (. . .) blessing
And the son's [Jesus'] goodness."[225]

Manichaeanism designates the sun as Jesus and the moon as virgin of light, with the virgin of light often being ranked equally with Jesus. The basis for this identification is the androgynous nature of the virgin, which recurs later in the Iranian notion of the hermaphroditic world god.[226]

Immanentism and anthropocentrism

The Gnostic images of God and man are related to each other through the notion of the androgynous utopia. On the basis of an emanation that takes place without being breached by an act of creation, the characteristics of God and those of the world become the same. A typical example is the statement in the *Corpus Hermeticum* that God is, from the start, always immanent in his works, identical with that which he produces.[227]

---

[223] Cap. 50: G. Bornkamm, "Thomas-Akten", p. 329.

[224] G. Bornkamm, "Thomas-Akten", p. 307.

[225] W. Bousset, "Manichäisches in den Thomasakten" [Manichaean elements in the *Acts of Thomas*], *ZNW* 18 (1917/18): 11.

[226] Günther Bornkamm, *Mythos und Legende in den apokryphen Thomas-akten. Beiträge zur Geschichte der Gnosis und zur Vorgeschichte des Manichäismus* [Contributions to the history of gnosis and to the prehistory of Manichaeanism] (Göttingen, 1933), pp. 104f.

[227] *Corpus Hermeticum I, 11, 13*, in Delcourt, *Hermaphrodite*, p. 120.

Thus God is seen here only in his immanence, not in his transcendence.[228] Accordingly, it is no wonder that maternal symbolism predominates in the myths of origin cited.

Worldly, especially human, qualities such as fatherhood and motherhood can be applied equally to God. Quispel thus describes Gnosticism as a "mythical projection of [man's] self-experience".[229] God becomes shorthand for an illusory sort of psychohygiene based on the *fata morgana* of the androgyne. In all this, of course, the equality of the masculine and feminine turns out to be deceptive, since feminine traits are more strongly definitive of the Gnostic immanence religion than are masculine ones, even if they are often only cryptically encoded in symbols such as ocean, earth or cyclical process.

For immanentism, not God but *man* is the beginning and end of all thought.[230] According to Hans Jonas, *anthropos* is here elevated "to an inner-worldly god", who "puts" the Creator "in his place".[231]

> The position of man as equal to God, by virtue of the origins of his nature, is very clearly formulated in places: "God created man, and men created God. So it is, too, in the world, since men create gods and worship them as their creations." The earliest palpable Gnostics, such as Simon Magus, Menander and Epiphanes, put this idea into practice, allowing themselves—or at least so say the Church fathers—to be worshipped as gods.[232]

Gnosticism is, in part, to be seen as a heretical, anthropological turn within Christianity, whose historical influence will be taken up later here.[233] In it, man's self-idolization is bound together with pantheism, which finds expression in the axiom "God is also [or, rather, *above all*] mother."

The axiom "God is also mother" in ancient philosophy

Whereas Gnosticism has a strongly mythical coloring, most of the other systems of philosophical thought in antiquity contain a more rational, "more enlightened" strain. That many divinities are seen, even at the level of folk religion, as bisexual has already been shown.[234] Androgynous

---

[228] Cf. Quispel, *Gnosis*, p. 34.
[229] Quispel, *Gnosis*, p. 17.
[230] Quispel, *Gnosis*, p. 18.
[231] Hans Jonas, *Gnosis und spätantiker Geist I* [Gnosis and the spirit of late antiquity I] FRLANT 51, 2nd ed. (Göttingen, 1957), p. 383.
[232] Rudolph, *Gnosis*, p. 101.
[233] Cf. pp. 267–70 below.
[234] Cf. p. 161 above.

connotations may also be presumed to underlie the expression that often serves as a "placeholder" for unknown divinities: *sive mas sive femina*.[235]

Orphism, whose androgynous cosmology was mentioned earlier,[236] occasionally describes Zeus as the one who is simultaneously father and mother.[237] According to Jamblich, the *Pythagoreans*, who have connections with Orphism, see the numinous as simultaneously containing masculine and feminine traits. God is, in a certain sense, the germ, the matrix, out of which male and female arise. Echoes of Hesiod are heard when the divine is depicted as the vessel of primordial chaos, that is, in terms of primarily feminine symbolism.[238]

The *Stoics* regard Zeus as a synthesis of the fertilizing heaven god and the receptive earth, of sun (*Helios*) and moon (*Selene*). Symbols for the creator (heaven, sun) and for creation (earth, moon) are thus made equivalent within one divine figure, which is probably connected with Stoic monism (pantheism): Zeus (Jupiter) and cosmos (*universum*) are interchangeable concepts.[239]

Theology becomes liturgy, as, for example, in the following prayer by the Stoic poet Valerius Soranus: "Mighty Jupiter, father of kings, things and gods, at the same time mother of gods, you the only, and each and every, god."

> He [the Stoic Varro] says . . . about this that, since we take for male what emits the seed and for female what receives the seed, and since Jupiter, as the world, both emits the seed from himself and receives it into himself, Soranus had "good reason for writing: at once both father and mother."[240]

Pantheistically inclined ideas are also characteristic of *Neoplatonism*, the doctrine of emanation par excellence. According to Plotinus, there is no creation in time, since the imperfect follows from the perfect with correlative necessity.[241] The founder of Neoplatonism, to be sure, does not speak of a divine mother, but only of the father as the universal One. Nevertheless, he makes use of an abundant symbolism that tends more in a feminine, as opposed to a masculine, direction. To express the relationship of the Absolute to the relative, he draws on the following images: an overflowing of a wellspring, an unfolding out of a seed or a root.[242] Even

---

[235] Delcourt, *Hermaphrodite*, p. 45; also Bertholet, *Gottheit*, p. 3, which also contains a reference to Babylonian parallels to this formula involving androgynous images.

[236] Cf. p. 145 above.

[237] Delcourt, *Hermaphrodite*, p. 72.

[238] Jamblich, *Theologumena arithemeticae 4, 17*, in Delcourt, *Hermaphrodite*, pp. 116f.

[239] Delcourt, *Hermaphrodite*, p. 109.

[240] Augustine, *De civitate Dei, VII, 9*: BKV 1, p. 349; CCL 47, p. 194.

[241] Hirschberger, *Geschichte I*, p. 305.

[242] Venanz Schubert, *Plotin. Einführung in sein Philosophieren* [Plotinus. An introduction to his philosophy] (Munich, 1973), p. 21.

the symbol of the sun, on the basis of his doctrine of emanation, is endowed with feminine traits: "It [being] surrounds That [the One], is a brightness radiating out of That all around, out of That, and yet It persists; just like the brightness of the sun, which, so to speak, dances around it, is ceaselessly born out of it and yet persists."[243]

Sun symbolism is integrated into mandala symbolism: a central point and the peripheries that arise from it, spreading outward like rays, are seen in a single perspective. Thus, Plotinus expressly refers to the primal ground of all being as the "center point of a circle", to which different radii are linked: ". . . through such a point [on a radius] in ourselves we come into contact with it as well, are united with and linked to it, indeed, find in it our foundation."[244]

The symbol of the foundation alludes to the mystical experience of the "depths", which tie the ground of one's own soul to the divine primal Source of being: the soul completes a "circular movement" around an absolute center point.[245]

All these symbols point to an intellectual kinship with Indian philosophy. Here, too, maternal images of the Absolute stand for the dissolution of the human self in an apersonal, divine "It".[246] Endre von Ivánka therefore characterizes the Neoplatonic thought world through the formula "secularized God–deified world";[247] divine and human are intermixed.

The basic maternal temper of Neoplatonism remains concealed in Plotinus' thought insofar as he refers to the One only as father. But, in later periods, the relevant symbols tend again and again toward an androgynous image of God, with the maternal characteristics also being consciously stated. This applies especially to the history of the influences exerted by this philosophical mysticism on Christianity—which will be discussed later—but probably also even to its original impact in heathen circles. For instance, the Neoplatonist Porphyry handed down to us the following prayer, directed to Zeus: "You are father and, at the same time, endearing mother, just as much a delicate flower garland of children, you idea of ideas, soul and breath, you harmony and number."[248]

[243] *Enneaden V, 1, 6: Plotins Schriften Ia* [Enneads V,1,6: Plotinus' writings Ia], translated by R. Harder (Hamburg, 1956), p. 223.

[244] *Enneaden V, 1, 11: Plotin*, p. 237.

[245] *Enneaden VI, 9, 8: Plotin*, p. 195.

[246] Schubert, *Plotin*, pp. 76f.

[247] Endre von Ivánka, *Plato Christianus. Übernahme und Umgestaltung des Platonismus durch die Väter* [Plato Christianus. The continuation and redirection of Platonism by the Church Fathers] (Einsiedeln, 1964), p. 89.

[248] Porphyrius, *De philosophia ex oraculis haurienda*, translated from Delcourt, *Hermaphrodite*, p. 110.

The Cabala as "feminist theology" in Judaism

Its basic concern

The Jewish Cabala is a decidedly feminist theology, if feminist implies here an emphasis on the immanent, feminine aspects of God. The word cabala means " 'receiving from', 'handing down' and, indeed, in an indirect way, as opposed to the direct one of the 'Torah' ". What is involved is a "secret teaching",[249] an "esoteric tradition",[250] whose deeper understanding is reserved for the initiated. Nonetheless, the Cabala has met with great popularity in Judaism[251] and was, for a time, "a veritable mass religion",[252] regarded as the deepest fulfillment of Torah piety.

Its special concern is to bind together the element of sacred history with the *cosmic* references of the law, which had become lost to purely historical thought. As opposed to abstract, legalistic formalism, it cultivates an imagistic, symbolic approach and draws on past mythological contents. Thus, strongly bound up in this way with the sense world, it appeals to the emotions and feelings and is naturally suited to awakening popular interest.[253]

The Cabala is a mysticism that begins with experience of God's immanence and, indeed, largely remains at that level.[254] Its typical mark is emphasis on a maternal aspect of God, which acquires a certain independence, and often comes to the fore as the main object of worship.[255] In large part, the Cabala is a natural human reaction against the overmasculinized religiosity of rabbinic Judaism, whose exclusively transcendent image of God has various parallels with classical Protestantism.[256]

---

[249] Ernst Bischoff, *Die Kabbalah. Einführung in die jüdische Mystik und Geheimwissenschaft* [The Cabala. An introduction to Jewish mysticism and occult science], 4th ed. (Leipzig, 1930), p. 1.

[250] Gershom Scholem, *Zur Kabbala und ihrer Symbolik* [On Cabala and its symbolism] (Zurich, 1960), p. 120.

[251] Scholem, *Kabbala*, p. 142.

[252] Patai, *Goddess*, p. 159.

[253] Scholem, *Kabbala*, p. 127.

[254] Scholem, *Kabbala*, p. 167.

[255] Patai, *Goddess*, p. 186.

[256] Ernst Benz, *Die christliche Kabbala. Ein Stiefkind der Theologie* [Christian Cabala. A stepchild of theology], Albae Vigiliae, Neue Folge XVIII (Zurich, 1958), p. 7.

"Maternal" and pantheistic traits in the sephiroth doctrine

"Mythology's revenge on its conquerors"[257] began in southern France in the twelfth century, "in the middle of the golden age of medieval Jewish enlightenment".[258] The first, and even now still influential, expression of this is the little book *Bahir*, written in Nîmes in 1180 by Rabbi Isaac the Blind.[259] In it, the so-called sephiroth doctrine, which represents the main feature of Cabalist metaphysics, appears for the first time.[260]

The ten sephiroth (singular, sephirah) are the "basic powers of all being"; the word derives from "saphar" = "to number", and consequently designates the "ten archetypal numbers".[261] The sephiroth usually appear in the symbol of a tree, which is described in the *Bahir* as follows: "All the powers of God are arranged one atop the other [in layers], thus resembling a tree: just as it is through *water* that the tree produces its *fruits*, so, too, it is through *water* that God increases the powers of the '*tree*'. And what is *God's water*? That is [female] *khokmah* [wisdom], and that [namely, the *fruit* of the *tree*] is the soul of the righteous, which [all] flow from the '*wellspring*' to the 'great channel', and it rises up and hangs on the *tree*. And what is it through which the tree blooms? Through Israel: if they are good and righteous, then the [female] *shekina* dwells among them, and through their works they abide in *God's womb*."[262]

Regarding this classical text, the following three features can be emphasized for purposes of example:

1. The biblical point of departure is the doctrine of wisdom, which is described as feminine.[263]
2. Contrary to the Old Testament, something created (Israel) is identified with something divine (the shekina). This idea is also expressed in the fact that the world tree is not planted by God, but rather, itself represents "the mythical structure of God's creative powers".[264] As always in the Cabala, the sephiroth are the "self-unfolding divine unity, which contains within itself the archetypes of all being". This world is "a world of intradivine being"; it "overflows, however, without interruption and with no new beginnings, into the secret and visible worlds of creation, all of which, in their inner structure, repeat

---

[257] Scholem, *Kabbala*, p. 132.
[258] Scholem, *Kabbala*, pp. 131f.
[259] Scholem, *Kabbala*, p. 121; Bischoff, *Kabbalah*, p. 61.
[260] Bischoff, *Kabbalah*, p. 61.
[261] Scholem, *Kabbala*, p. 135.
[262] *Bahir* § 85, in Scholem, *Kabbala*, p. 123. (Emphases are mine.)
[263] Cf. here pp. 279–81 below.
[264] Scholem, *Kabbala*, p. 123.

that intradivine structure and reflect it in themselves".[265] With this, any notion of a divine creation out of nothing is "liquidated".[266] If, in the later Cabala, the creation concept is grafted onto the relevant symbolism, this occurs only in consequence of profound speculation.[267]

The Cabala is a typical emanation theory, reminiscent of various aspects of Neoplatonism.[268] Interest is concentrated, in a pantheistic way, on the divine immanence that sustains the world.[269]

3. The immanence mysticism is reflected in feminine symbols: water that works its way upward out of the earth, fruits of a tree, wellspring, cloud (associated with the shekina),[270] womb.

A feminine thematics of being thus forms the background of Cabalist speculation. The tree of God and the world in its entirety, the En Sof ("the Endless"), is described, in respect of its origin, as the "hidden root"[271] or the "root of all roots".[272] The all-important thing is mystical experience of the "depths", which loses itself in the divine abyss. The abyss and the depths are seen as "nothingness", as a "transbeing in God himself".[273] The philosophical concept of nothingness, which, as the absence of being, possesses no independent ontological status, has its function mythically redefined here and appears as primordial, formless chaos: "In the beginning . . . [a dim flame] sprang up, in the most hidden of all regions, out of the mystery of the Endless, like a fog that takes shape in the formless. . . . In the deepest center of the flame, a wellspring opened, out of which colors flowed down on everything lower, hidden in the mysterious concealments of the Endless."[274]

This last quotation comes from the book Zohar, the main classic of the Cabalists. Originating in thirteenth-century Spain, and containing more than a million words, it is a "kind of bible", which enjoyed "virtually canonical esteem" in Judaism for centuries.[275] In it, the doctrine of the world tree that was outlined in the Bahir is developed in much greater detail.

Along with the symbol of the tree of life, and recalling Plotinus' sun

---

[265] Scholem, Kabbala, pp. 135f.
[266] Scholem, Kabbala, p. 136.
[267] Scholem, Kabbala, pp. 138f.
[268] Scholem, Kabbala, p. 61; Bischoff, Kabbalah, pp. 38f., 67.
[269] Scholem, Kabbala, p. 165.
[270] Cf. p. 280 below.
[271] Scholem, Kabbala, p. 53.
[272] Scholem, Kabbala, p. 138.
[273] Scholem, Kabbala, pp. 137f.
[274] Zohar I,15a, in Scholem, Kabbala, p. 138.
[275] Scholem, Kabbala, pp. 7, 121.

mysticism, there also occurs the symbolic image of a shining star, with the star and its rays of light being seen as an intrafluent unity.[276] Mandala symbolism can be detected, among other places, in an interpretation of Psalms 150:1, described in the first sephirah as: "immeasurable periphery of the outward expansion of his [God's] innermost point";[277] correspondingly, the sephiroth as a whole are seen through the image of concentric circles.[278]

The first three sephiroth, which issue from the divine primal Source,[279] are regarded in the late Cabala as "the triune essence of the Divinity".[280] A Christian trinitarian doctrine is not meant by this, of course, for what is in question are emanations, which continue to effuse themselves until the fullness of the "tenfold unity" is reached.[281] The third sephirah is called the "upper mother" or "primal mother of all being"; it is the "demiurgic potency", associated in a special way with the world, that releases the seven additional emanations from itself. Six of these sephiroth are regarded as masculine, while the seventh—or, in relation to the whole structure, the tenth—is feminine, the "lower mother".[282]

Historical and structural connections with ancient Gnosticism

The world tree of sephiroth strongly recalls the Gnostic doctrine of eons,[283] which is also based on emanation. The book *Bahir* originated in southern France at a time when, precisely in that region, Neo-Manichaeanism was celebrating its triumphs in Catharism and Albigensianism. That there were certain "threads . . . that bind the oldest Cabalist tradition also historically to the Gnostic heritage" may thus be regarded as "certain". Nevertheless, it is probably more a matter of "parallel psychological and structural developments" that "were independently generated" within the Cabala.[284] Precisely in this independence, the close connections between symbolism and philosophy express themselves.

[276] Bischoff, *Kabbalah*, pp. 100, 97.

[277] The passage from the psalm reads literally, in German: "Lobet ihn in der Ausbreitung seiner Stärke" ["Praise him in the extension of his might"; English biblical version: "Praise him in his mighty firmament"!], in Benz, *Kabbala*, p. 49.

[278] Bischoff, *Kabbalah*, pp. 100, 67.

[279] Benz, *Kabbala*, p. 54: "God's essence" is "ultimately" a "source of movement".

[280] Bischoff, *Kabbalah*, p. 103.

[281] Benz, *Kabbala*, pp. 52–54.

[282] Scholem, *Kabbala*, pp. 141–44.

[283] Scholem, *Kabbala*, p. 135.

[284] Scholem, *Kabbala*, p. 131.

Shekina as a central figure in Cabalist piety

In terms of her numbered position, the "lower mother" may well be regarded as the last sephirah, but not in terms of her significance. In connection with the tetragrammaton (YHWH, Yahweh), the Cabala worships the four figures of father, mother, son and daughter.[285] The tenth sephirah, the "daughter", is then endowed with the Latin borrowing *Matronita*,[286] which suffices to indicate that she represents the feminine in general, and is thus "mother, wife and daughter all at once".[287] Within the Cabalist tetrad, she assumes the most important role; like the Greek Moira, she is regarded as the ruler of human destiny. As early as in the *Bahir*, she is designated as the "shekina" and "seen as an aspect of God that is understood as a feminine element in him and is given a quasi-independent status".[288] She is the "most powerful expression" of the idea of a "Hebrew goddess".[289]

"Shekina" derives from the verb *"shaken"* = "to dwell in".[290] The concept does not yet appear in the Bible but is later linked to the notion of a cloud, which renders emblematically visible the glory of God as well as his indwelling tabernacle and temple.[291] In the Cabala, this *immanence* is extended to God's presence "in the world and especially in Israel". The shekina is God's "countenance".[292]

The beginnings of these notions can already be found in the *Talmud*.[293] Something new, however, is that, in the *Bahir*, the divine figure is identified "with the mystical ecclesia of Israel, on the one hand, and with the soul . . . , on the other".[294] Feminine symbolism was already alive in the *Talmud* and *Midrash*, especially in the allegorical interpretation of the "Song of Songs".[295] Its accent, however, lay not on description of God's

---

[285] Patai, *Goddess*, p. 162. A similar Cabalism crops up again recently in modern authors. Mario Bachiega (*Dio Padre o Dea Madre?* [Florence, 1976]) interprets the first letter of the tetragrammaton, Y or J, as implying a feminine principle of God, and the remaining letters, HWH, a masculine principle of God: Schrey, "Gott", p. 229. Feminist theologians (male and female) claim that the biblical name Elohim is androgynous: R. T. Barnhouse, "An Examination of the Ordination of Women to the Priesthood in Terms of the Symbolism of the Eucharist", *Anglican Theological Review* 56 (1974): 284; Morton, "Weg", p. 20; Leonard Swidler, "Goddess Worship and Women Priests", in Swidler, *Women Priests*, p. 174, n. 12.

[286] Patai, *Goddess*, p. 186.

[287] Scholem, *Kabbala*, p. 141.

[288] Scholem, *Kabbala*, p. 141.

[289] She is "the most poignant . . . expression of the idea of a goddess": Patai, *Goddess*, p. 186.

[290] Patai, *Goddess*, p. 140.

[291] Ex 40:35; 1 Kings 8:10–11; cf. Patai, *Goddess*, pp. 136ff.

[292] Scholem, *Kabbala*, p. 140.

[293] Patai, *Goddess*, p. 141.

[294] Scholem, *Kabbala*, p. 142.

[295] On this, see Wilhelm Riedel, *Die Auslegung des Hohenliedes in der jüdischen Gemeinde*

shekina, but on characterization of the *people's* receptive attitude and readiness for devotion. While the community Israel here stands opposite God within a personal relationship, it appears in the Cabala as an emanation of the divine. Thus, the strongly emphasized femininity and materiality of God here are a consequence of pantheism: God and the world are identical.

Since the divine and the human spheres are intermixed, the Cabala attributes human qualities to God in their literal sense. The notion of the shekina's "exile" can already be found in the *Talmud*. "This, however, meant nothing more than that God's presence constantly accompanied Israel during its exiles. But in the Cabala, this idea implies: something of God himself is exiled from God himself."[296]

This notion corresponds to the Gnostic idea of a "falling away", of the soul's exile from its origins.[297] In Cabala of Safed, the shekina's exile is seen as the great fall into sin; salvation consists in bringing God and his shekina back together again. The formula "for the sake of the unification of God and his shekina" was found "in all liturgical texts and books of later Judaism. . . , before it . . . was removed . . . in horror from the [Western] prayer books . . . by the enlightened Judaism of the nineteenth century".[298]

Apersonalistic "practical Cabala" and metaphysical dualism

If God himself has to be redeemed from a "separation", then he is no longer a self-directing Person, but rather, an impersonal force. Such an impersonal "It", however, is subject to human manipulation—and magic can be practiced on it. In the *Zohar*, there is an image of the descending chain of beings, in which "all things" are "shifted, in a magical way, one into the other"; also, a nut[299] is seen as a unity of "shell-like layers all contained one in the other" and is "used as a cosmic symbol".[300] In the liturgy, to be sure, the traditional ritual is retained but is reinterpreted. It now contains the "idea of a magical nexus that . . . is realized in and through the sacred proceedings".[301] Magical activity is so significant that it takes its place, as practical Cabala, alongside the fundamental speculations of the theoretical Cabala, and is also described as such.[302]

---

und der griechischen Kirche [The interpretation of the "Song of Songs" in the Jewish community and the Greek church] (Leipzig, 1898), pp. 1–46.

[296] Scholem, *Kabbala*, p. 144.
[297] Scholem, *Kabbala*, p. 144.
[298] Scholem, *Kabbala*, pp. 145f.
[299] Similarly to Ramakrishna's "onion"; cf. p. 158 above.
[300] Scholem, *Kabbala*, pp. 164f.
[301] Scholem, *Kabbala*, p. 173.
[302] Bischoff, *Kabbalah*, pp. 1, 115, 120ff.

This magic is based, however, not only in theological apersonalism but also in metaphysical dualism. Even the *Bahir* claims that "there is a principle in God that is called 'evil' ".[303] God says: "I love the gates of Zion. . . . Why? Because they are the flanks of evil."[304] Similar thoughts can be found in contemporary "Christian" Neo-Manichaeanism.

Therefore, the following reaction by a rabbi from southern France is understandable: "God preserve us from any inclination to such heretical talk."[305] Precisely because of the dualistic cast of the Cabala, which surfaces over and over again, this doctrine has never been quite acceptable to Jewish orthodoxy. Still, this mistrust did not prevent "Gnostic and quasi-Gnostic systems" from becoming, "for pious orthodox Cabalists, the deepest expression of the world of their Jewish faith".[306] A consequence of this dualism is an exaggerated fear or even a virtual worship of demons. "Demonization of life" is thus described even by sympathetic interpreters of the Cabala as "one of the most effective and, at the same time, most dangerous factors" in its development, giving rise to a definite element of "disunity".[307]

The dualism is also reflected in a certain two-facedness on the part of shekina, who appears, at one and at the same time, as charitable and as cruel, similar to the Indian goddess Kali. Scholem speaks of "quasi-demonic aspects".[308] The ethical ambivalence is rooted in an ontological one: on the one hand, the demoness Lilith, originally a figure in Babylonian mythology, is regarded as the adversary of Matronita; on the other hand, this struggle—similar to the one in Vedic mythology between the devas (gods) and the asuras (demons)[309]—is not a real one, for both figures embody the same numen and are emanations of God.[310] After the destruction of the temple of Jerusalem, God is forced (!) to replace Matronita, as his wife, with Lilith,[311] who from that time onward is enthroned as queen at his side.[312]

Androgyny as "principle of the system"

Divine immanence comes so strongly to the fore in the Cabala that the concepts of God and man seem all but interchangeable. The signs of the

---

[303] *Bahir* § 109, in Scholem, *Kabbala*, p. 124.
[304] *Bahir* § 26, in Scholem, *Kabbala*, p. 124.
[305] Scholem, *Kabbala*, p. 122.
[306] Scholem, *Kabbala*, p. 132.
[307] Scholem, *Kabbala*, p. 134.
[308] Scholem, *Kabbala*, p. 143.
[309] Cf. p. 156 above.
[310] Patai, *Goddess*, p. 243.
[311] Patai, *Goddess*, p. 239.
[312] Patai, *Goddess*, p. 207.

tree of life "are also depicted as bodily members of the metaphysical 'primal man' (Adâm kadmōn . . .), so that they can be explained in terms of the living organism".[313] The members of Adam are equated with the "body of the Divinity", which is sometimes to be understood quite literally.[314]

The primal man, in turn, is seen as androgynous, just as was the case in the Jewish gnosis of antiquity. "Everything that the holy God created, he created as masculine and feminine [androgynous]"—this oft-quoted formula appears, especially "in the later Cabala", as a veritable "principle of the system".[315] Even souls, which are thought of as preexistent, are imagined as androgynous, either on the sense of being still sexually indeterminate or in the literal sense.[316] Against this backdrop, it is noteworthy that the divine world tree also appears as a soul tree.[317]

Given an androgynous image of man, the androgynous image of God, as described here, is not surprising (and vice versa). Masculine and feminine emanations are interwoven with one another; the Father is closely tied to the shekina. Still, within this bisexual unity—even if somewhat covertly—feminine traits take priority: root, abyss, depths, wellspring, mandala. The desire to create a balance between masculine and feminine symbols in the image of God thus seems to be deceptive, just as it was in the Oriental religions and in Gnosticism. A pari cum pari has led here to pantheism.

8. THE PRIMACY OF MASCULINE SYMBOLISM IN THE IMAGE OF GOD

The basic thesis: transcendence as the precondition for immanence

In the image of God, as we have seen earlier here,[318] transcendence possesses greater significance than immanence. Still more: transcendence logically presupposes immanence, whereas pantheistic systems remain at the level of immanence. As the one who goes beyond the world, God is, at the same time, the inner ground of creation, which would sink back into

---

[313] Bischoff, Kabbalah, p. 103.

[314] Scholem, Kabbala, p. 173.

[315] Bischoff, Kabbalah, p. 38, n. 2.

[316] Bischoff, Kabbalah, p. 108. In Cabala, this is also connected with a doctrine of metempsychosis: Bischoff, Kabbalah, p. 110.

[317] Scholem, Kabbala, p. 123.

[318] Cf. p. 143 above.

nothingness without his constant sustaining influence. Thus, in a certain sense, transcendence contains immanence within itself, yet without this implying that the two dimensions could be placed, as equals, on the same level. For just as God is infinitely elevated above his creation, which for him is as much as nothing, so, too, transcendence has an incomparable priority over immanence.

Man, of course, experiences God first of all as the one who grounds his personal existence and the being of the cosmos. This experience of immanence is thus given to him in and through his very origins. Any attempt to conceive of "pure" transcendence apart from immanence would fail to take seriously man's created nature. Nevertheless, theocentric thinking, if it postulates God as the absolute measure of truth and ultimate end of all striving, must move at once beyond immanence in the direction of transcendence. As soon as this fundamental step has been taken, immanence and transcendence will, to be sure, still be kept in view together, yet, in respect of God's relation to the world, the unequivocal accent will always fall on transcendence.

A "democratic image of God"?

If the bodily nature of men is a symbol of transcendence, then the masculine traits in the image of God must also be given priority. Any attempt to introduce equal rights here would place transcendence on a level with immanence and idolize the created as an equally worthy partner of the Creator. The examples surveyed above—especially the Oriental religions, Gnosticism and the Cabala—have adequately demonstrated that projection of masculine and feminine qualities on God in equal degrees leads, almost of necessity, to a pantheism in which the divine and the human are indiscriminately thrown together: "secularized God—deified world".[319]

This kind of attempt at equalization, however, not only endangers the purity of the image of God but also is self-contradictory from the very start. If, in the sphere of the symbolic, immanence is put on a plane with transcendence, then transcendence has, in fact, disappeared. Even Indian panentheism, which still admits a little bit of transcendence, is nothing but disguised pantheism. For God's transcendence means precisely that he is

---

[319] This conclusion was also reached earlier by the Protestant theologian W. Schulze: *Das androgyne Ideal und der christliche Glaube* [The androgynous ideal and the Christian Faith] (Lahr and Dinglingen, 1940) (extract from a dissertation, Heidelberg, 1939), p. 38: "In almost every case, a conception of creation as emanation provides the foundation for claims that God is androgynous."

elevated above worldly immanence not only a little, but *infinitely*. Transcendence made equal is no longer transcendence. It is, therefore, only logically consistent to regard immanence and its symbols as the solely valid things. In fact, we have also seen that relevant symbolic images, such as wellspring, ocean, earth and so forth, set the tone in pantheistic systems, even if what appears on the surface is an interplay between heaven and earth as equally ranked elements.

All the perfections of creation find their highest fulfillment in God. As well, all opposites are fulfilled in him. It is to this *coincidentia oppositorum* (Nicholas of Cusa) that Andrew Greeley appeals when, in line with feminist theology, he postulates: "In God . . . *feminine and masculine traits are blended in equal proportions.*[320]

Here, however, what requires proof is presupposed in advance (*petitio principii*). For whether or not opposites can, in each case, both be attributed to God in the *same* way must always be determined separately for each particular case. With respect to the opposition heaven-earth, for example, what is found in the history of religion is the polarization: representation of the Divine-symbolization of creation.[321] As with the polarity man-woman, it is here a question of perfections whose ways of representing God must first be examined in their concrete individuality. In the Old Testament, God is compared, among other things, to a "moth", a "king", a "lion" and a "canker".[322] These images, too, are all equally applicable to God, but not all in the same way.

Transcendence and personality

Divine and human personality as transcendence

A transcendent image of God automatically takes on personal characteristics, whereas an immanence religion ultimately recognizes only a divine "It". Given theological apersonalism, man, too, becomes objectified. Being a person means having a spiritually grounded self-identity.[323] A

---

[320] Andrew Greeley, *Maria—Über die weibliche Dimension Gottes* [trans. of: The Mary myth—on the femininity of God] (Graz, Vienna and Cologne, 1979), p. 147; cf. pp. 71, 74f. On Greeley, see pp. 309–12 below.

[321] Cf. pp. 134f. above and pp. 219f., 241f. below. The *petitio principii* is even clearer with an opposition such as light-dark: darkness represents no independently existing entity but refers only to the absence of light. It is certainly for that reason that Christ did not say: "I am the darkness and the light", but rather: "I am the light."

[322] Hos 5:12; Ps 97; Hos 11:10.

[323] Boethius: Persona est rationalis naturae individua substantia. Cf. here Schmaus, *Glaube II*, pp. 55–59.

person's relationships are not constitutive of his essence but are additional to the traits that define him as such. A person realizes himself in and through relationships but is not the sum of these. Without (at least two) substantial terms in relation, moreover, one can only speak in a qualified sense of a relationship, which by definition means the particular way that one being stands with regard to another.[324] In the human sphere, personality is thus tied to the assumption of a substantial spirituality.

To be sure, it is only in the more primitive systems of thought that the existence of the soul is denied, yet in the higher pantheisms as well, man's spiritual individuality is ultimately submerged in the boundless ocean of an impersonal Absolute. The substantial transcendence of the soul over the body and the transcendence of God over the world are mutually conditioned; between anthropology and theology there is reciprocal interaction.[325]

Personality and the symbolism of the sexes

If the experience of a personal God presupposes the transcendence of the soul and of God himself, then it aligns itself with masculine symbolism. Women, of course, are persons just as much as are men, but their personhood is lived out more strongly through relationships; they are, to a special degree, relational beings.[326] Their individuality stands out less sharply from the near world, while men—in their greater directedness toward the far world—appear more in their self-reality and eccentricity. Even at the physical level, men's contours are more strongly pronounced, while the softer forms of women are more suited to coalescing with their environment, as is clear particularly in their relationship with children. Religious scholars sometimes speak, in this context, of a "figurative-personal image of God".[327] Women are no less persons than are men, but the individual, self-dependent reality of the personal is just symbolized to a lesser degree in women.

A personal image of God is always bound up with sexual references. Anthropology serves, to a certain extent, as preparatory to theological understanding, and, in the human sphere, it is a fact that persons appear as

---

[324] J. B. Lotz, "Beziehung" [Relation], in Brugger, *Wörterbuch*, p. 48. Logically, of course, the *esse ad aliquid*, as the specific of the relation, is distinct from the *esse in aliquo*, and this is important for the doctrine of the Trinity: Franz Diekamp and Klaudius Jüssen, *Katholische Dogmatik nach den Grundsätzen des heiligen Thomas I* [Catholic dogma according to the principles of Saint Thomas I] (Münster, 1958), p. 340.

[325] Cf. the "counterexample" of feminist theology: pp. 66, 69f. above.

[326] Cf. p. 120 above.

[327] Alfred Bertholet, "Göttin" [Goddess], in Alfred Bertholet and Hans Freiherr von Campenhausen, *Wörterbuch der Religionen* [Dictionary of religions], 2nd ed. (Stuttgart, 1962), p. 196.

men *or* as women. Only the subpersonal realm of things is generally thought of under the sexually neutral little word it. The personal name of a human being always has a masculine or a feminine context. The religious scholar Alfred Bertholet thus observes that it like names correspond to a dynamistic, apersonal image of God. Not until numen becomes nomen can the "question of the sex of the Divinity properly arise".[328] In the history of religion, there are various examples of a sex change occurring in one and the same deity,[329] which indicates that the very presence of sexual characteristics suggests personality.[330]

Nevertheless, masculine symbolism is more closely apposite to a personal image of God than is its feminine counterpart. My examples from the study of religion have shown that an apersonal Absolute, which is in oneness with its worldly surroundings, is invariably referred to through feminine symbols. The mother embodies divine immanence, a multirelational embeddedness in the world. God's personality, however, is bound up in a special way with transcendence. Bertholet thus observes that goddesses play their main role "before the formation of a figurative-personal image of God. . . . Only in monotheism does the goddess give way once and for all to the fatherly name of God."[331]

The mother symbol as a "component" of the father symbol

The relations between transcendence-immanence and omnipotence-benevolence/justice-mercy

Thus, it is clear that, given a theistic image of God, at least the *accent* must be placed on masculine symbolism. Furthermore, however, one could also totally exclude feminine symbolism. For immanence is, in a certain sense, a component of transcendence, and, in the same way, masculine symbolism also seems to enframe feminine symbolism.

As will be shown more precisely in connection with the biblical image of God,[332] the "concept 'father' partly" includes "the emotional qualities . . . that are bound up, for us, with the word 'mother' ".[333] Fatherhood embodies, in particular, the qualities of benevolence and mercy, as well as those of power and justice with the accent here being on justice. Regarding

---

[328] Bertholet, *Gottheit*, pp. 4f.

[329] Bertholet, *Gottheit*, p. 15.

[330] Bertholet, *Gottheit*, p. 22.

[331] Bertholet, "Göttin", p. 196.

[332] Cf. pp. 223–25 below.

[333] Kurt Leese, *Die Mutter als religiöses Symbol* [The mother as a religious symbol], Sammlung gemeinverständlicher Vorträge und Schriften aus dem Gebiet der Theologie und Religionsgeschichte 174 (Tübingen, 1934), p. 35.

motherhood, matters are weighted the other way around: authority is, to be sure, also pertinent here, but to a lesser extent than for fatherhood. What comes to the fore is maternal caring, mercy. "The father acts with power; the mother is simply powerful."[334]

The pair of concepts just-merciful is to be understood as a concretization of the duality of power and goodness, inasmuch as those concepts bear on the area of human sinfulness. The omnipotence of God is of greater significance than is his condescending goodness toward the world. As with transcendence and immanence, both qualities must always be kept together but cannot be rendered equivalent. In his mercy, God—to speak figuratively—steps down from his infinitely exalted throne in order, in a special way, to give support to man. Mercy is thus linked to the experience of immanence. The infinite buttress, however, without which mercy cannot be understood, is omnipotence and the justice that is grounded in this: the stepping down presupposes greatness; transcendence thus means a *powerful* superiority of God vis-à-vis the world. A merely immanent God cannot be kind, since he is not in a position to intervene in the world in a helping and merciful way.

Maternal authority is related to divine omnipotence to a lesser extent, because that is not a matter involving the special capacities of a mother. The notion of a father, by contrast, is often all but identical with the concept of authority.[335] Fatherhood includes within itself, in large part, motherly mercy, just as motherhood includes fatherly authority. But since authority has the greater significance, one might well agree, with respect to the image of God, with Kurt Leese's pointed formulation that the "mother symbol [inheres] in the father symbol".[336]

Notes from empirical psychology

The conclusion, reached on the basis of speculative reasoning, that the father symbol has richer application to the image of God than does the mother symbol can also be supported through empirical psychology. The psychologist of religion Antoine Vergote, using representative material from profane and religious literature, drew up two lists consisting of paternal and maternal qualities. As a second step, 178 students—boys and girls—were asked

> to correlate these different categories with the [ideal] images of mother, father and God. . . . The statistical data led to the following conclusions:

[334] Gerardus van der Leeuw, *Phänomenologie der Religion* [Phenomenology of religion], 2nd ed. (Tübingen, 1956), p. 99.
[335] Bertholet, *Gottheit*, p. 24.
[336] Leese, *Mutter*, p. 35. On pp. 224f. below, this idea is made more precise.

the two parental images were distinguished from each other more clearly through paternal qualities than through maternal ones. Thus, the father image is more complexly multiform; it encompasses a large portion of the maternal qualities yet is also defined by certain specific qualities that set it clearly apart from the mother image.

Although qualities such as intimacy and tenderness were attributed to the mother, the general result was: "The gap between God and the father is noticeably smaller than that between God and the mother. All these qualities, as such, are more readily linked to the father and God than to the mother and God."[337]

The sex chromosomes as the basis
of masculine and feminine symbolism

Vergote thus thinks that the father image is inherently "richer in content . . . than the merely symmetrical and contrastingly opposed figure of the mother".[338] The opposition between symmetry and asymmetry that is intended here is reminiscent of the psychological studies outlined earlier in this book that attest to a strong tendency toward symmetrical bodily postures on the part of women, whereas men incline more toward asymmetry. This peculiarity may, perhaps, have deeper bases at the genetic level.[339] The male set of chromosomes, as we know, is asymmetrical (XY), the female set, symmetrical (XX). Furthermore, the sex chromosomes not only play a role in man's formative development but also serve, in the biochemical sphere, as functional regulators whose influence pervades all aspects of bodily life.

Asymmetry means breaking apart a relationship of mutual correspondence. An asymmetrical bodily posture gives emphasis to the individuality of one's being, as opposed to symmetry, which expresses an experience of unity. Symmetry and asymmetry are thus a manifestation of centrality and eccentricity, yet, at the same time, are also a symbol of immanence and transcendence.

Just as with immanence in transcendence, but regarding the case of the sex chromosomes, the female is, in a sense, contained in the male (X in XY). From the male hereditary factor, it would be theoretically possible, by doubling the X chromosome, to produce a female chromosomal set, but not vice versa. Woman is, in a sense, taken "out" of man. The Y chromosome almost appears to be a symbol of transcendence.

If so, woman would originate out of man yet would nevertheless be

---

[337] Vergote, *Religionspsychologie*, pp. 233f.
[338] Vergote, *Religionspsychologie*, p. 235.
[339] Cf. p. 93, n. 34 above.

something more than a poor copy. For, precisely through the doubling of the X chromosome, women acquire qualities that men do not possess in the same intensity. Thus, on the basis of biological-psychological findings alone, I have postulated a parity in value between men and women.

However, since transcendence and immanence precisely do not have parity with each other, the biological facts constitute a merely broken symbolism, beyond which, in any case, one cannot go when making assertions about God. Nevertheless, they retain their nature as symbolic indicators, so that the relationship transcendence-immanence can be said to manifest itself even at the biochemical level.[340]

Masculine symbolism as an expression of God's revelation in history

A transcendent image of God is bound up with the notion of a *creation* of the world out of nothing, with a sovereign determination based on freely active love. The idea of a creation can be arrived at, at least theoretically, even through philosophy, drawing on the principle of causality.[341] If an initial divine determination was made that laid the foundations for perpetual ontological dependency of the world on God, then further determinations of a similar kind would seem possible as well. Those religions that accept the reality of divine *revelation* (Christianity, Judaism, Islam) take such a determination as their starting point: they recognize an intervention by God in history, through which man is confronted with words and deeds that lay claim to him. In addition to this, Christianity assumes that, by virtue of the historical self-revelation of God through Christ and through the radical new enactment of *grace*, man himself can participate in the life of God.

A historical revelation is thus grounded in the supramundane transcendence of God. Pantheistic Hinduism, by contrast—in order to cite but one marked example—characteristically recognizes no religious founder. Thus, the contents of faith do not confront man as a claim that originates outside of him but rather arise from the depths of his own being. The criterion is not any preexistent revelation but the human experience of each individual.

God's action in history, like his preceding act of creation, is described in terms of primarily masculine symbolism. In it, the new historical deter-

---

[340] On the relative methodological position of the biological statements, cf. pp. 188f. below.

[341] Cf. DS, 3026, 3538.

mination from the outside is a counterconcept to the sustainment of nature from the inside that was there from the start. Divine immanence is related to a rhythm that constantly repeats itself, to the cyclical process of nature. This continually recurring circular process is the dominant theme in the fertility cults, in the Oriental images of world and God and in Gnosticism— or, in short, in all immanence religions. The unrepeatably unique course of world history was first brought to human consciousness through the idea of a divine revelation in history.

Nature's cyclical process, however, is associated in a special way with the feminine thematics of being, as is shown, in particular, by the basic maternal aspect of pantheistic systems, in which God is equated with the cyclical process of change in the world. Mandala symbolism, which corresponds to centrality, resembles the symbol of the circle as a rhythmically recurring process, with which the deeply rooted physical nature of women manifests a close kinship.[342]

The predominance of masculine symbolism in the image of God: a mechanism of patriarchal oppression?

It is thus certainly anything but a coincidence that precisely Christianity, Judaism and Islam are characterized by an image of God that is decidedly masculine in nature. Precisely there, one recognizes very clearly that God is not a sexual being, but an infinitely elevated, personal spirit. God contains in himself, in an analogical way, all creaturely perfections, which he thereby also transcends: *Deus semper major*. Occasionally, as we will see with respect to the Old and New Testaments, feminine traits, too, are ascribed to God. But masculine traits outweigh these—for example, "king", "judge", "savior", "master", "father".

Very often, this fact is traced back to the patriarchal society in which these religions apparently arose. The insistence with which one makes such a claim, however, usually stands in inverse relation to the degree of one's knowledge of the history of religions. For, in thoroughly patriarchal societies, such as India or China, the feminine element in the Divine takes on great significance, often far more than that of the masculine. Gnosticism devalued everything bodily as a product of darkness, and, for that reason, did not esteem women, who are linked in a special way to the body, particularly highly. Yet, precisely here, mother figures assume an important role. Popular sociologism can be reduced even more clearly ad absurdum if one takes account of the Cabala. Arising from, and embedded

[342] Cf. pp. 87, 96, 139–41 above.

in, the decidedly father-centered familial and social structures of Judaism, it was centrally characterized by worship of the shekina, the feminine aspect of God.

Thus, the what and how of the sexual cast of the image of God cannot be explained primarily in sociological terms but ultimately requires philosophical and theological interpretation. For immanence religions, God is not only father but also, or even still more, mother; for a personal, transcendent image of God, by contrast, it is the masculine traits that occupy the foreground. In all this, consciously determined symbolism plays only a minor role, since philosophical and religious world views are psychologically rooted in the depths of the unconscious. Sociological factors may play a certain role, but only in an accidental way; psychology is so strongly embedded in innate biological predispositions that essential understanding of man's most basic symbols (father, mother) is, apart from pathological instances, merely scratched by sociology. The central structures of the image of God are ultimately independent of any processes of social evolution.

"Democratism" as a background to the feminist slogan "God is also mother"

The ideological accusation thus ultimately falls back on sociologism itself, for precisely feminist theology is a virtual showcase for a socioideological current that Alfons Rosenberg terms "democratism": the "tension between higher and lower, between sacred and profane. . . , between masculine and feminine has given way, at least since the turn of the century, even if the change was being prepared much earlier, to a tensionless equivalence of such opposites. . . . The stratification of culture has been replaced by a serialization, an endless ribbonlike succession of one next to the other." Rosenberg sees the origin of this ideology as lying in the slogan "liberty, equality, fraternity" of the French Revolution.[343]

Of course, there are also some inequalities that result not from a naturally given tension but rather from unjust structures. Any justified demand for equality is thus but a special instance of justice as such, which demands that each be given his own. Equal things are to be treated equally, and unequal things, unequally.

---

[343] Alfons Rosenberg, *Die Erhebung des Weiblichen. Ordnung und Aufstand der Frau in unserer Zeit* [The rise of the feminine. Position and rebellion of women in our times] (Olten and Freiburg im Breisgau, 1959), pp. 55f.

In large part, feminist theology is the perfect example of a false understanding of democracy, extending its demand for equality even to the image of God. Every structure that involves any kind of subordination appears as the very incarnation of evil, which has to be driven out with the exorcistic chant of "liberty, equality, sisterhood": the subordination of the body to the soul gives way to equal rights, and the regulatory power of truth, to the inconstancies of experience. The duties of leadership in society and Church are seen as second-level sexism, even though it is quite clearly recognized that a certain hierarchy in the human realm has its basis in the sovereign transcendence of God.

The Lord, Father, or—even worse—King is, so to speak, brought down from heaven and transferred, as the energy source of all being, to the earthly realm. God is then no longer the authoritarian peak, but the world-immanent nexus of all reality. These images show quite clearly, by the way, that the equal rights called for in respect of the image of God are a mere appearance, since pantheisticlike maternal symbolism is plainly centrally determinative in feminist theology.

The positive aspect of feminist theology, of course, is to have thrown open, on a broad front, the question of sexual traits in the image of God. That God is above all the Father was so self-evident to earlier Christian generations that this time-honored assumption never needed reflective justification. What formerly had entered into piety in a more strongly intuitive way should now also come under the scrutiny of rationally analytic theology, so that it will shine forth again as new, for the living relationship to God. If, in the conveyance of the image of God, the switch rails are falsely positioned, more catastrophic consequences result than from the denial of single, explicitly defined truths of faith. If transcendence and immanence are made equivalent by way of introducing masculine and feminine symbolism as equally ranked into the image of God, then this ultimately results in an equivalence between Creator and created, between God and man. It may well accord with a certain human wish if God is seen both as father and mother, as is manifest clearly in polytheism. But a "God that is prayed to by many people as the fulfillment of their strivings, their needs and their wishes is too human to be truly a wholly Other. . . . God does, indeed, attract human wishes to himself, but he also contradicts them."[344] The axiom God is also mother, understood in the feminist sense, thus ultimately leads to an equal ranking of God and man, or to a *self-idolization of the creature*.[345]

---

[344] Vergote, *Religionspsychologie*, p. 387.
[345] Cf. on this Leeuw, *Phänomenologie*, p. 195.

9. THE PRIMACY OF FEMININE SYMBOLISM IN THE DEPICTION OF CREATION

Prefatory note

The preceding section may have given rise, especially for some female readers, to a certain feeling of unease. For, if men are particularly well suited to symbolizing God, while women are so only to a lesser degree, does this not imply attributing a lesser value to the feminine?

If what was said were taken in isolation, it could, indeed, create such an impression. In what follows, however, I will provide some necessary supplementation by examining in more detail the unique nature of feminine symbolism. In the end, it will emerge that each sex enjoys, to the same extent, its own inexchangeable *and* equally ranked place in the symbolic sphere.

Woman as a likeness of creation

That women are symbolic, in a special way, of God's intradivine and world-sustaining immanence has already been demonstrated here. The *accent* of feminine symbolism falls, however, not on the representation of God but on the depiction of creation. In the first instance, man, as creature, does not have a relation of active transaction with, or ready disposal over, God, but rather is a recipient of God's gifts. Receptivity, openness, readiness are the appropriate attitudes in the presence of the Creator. As we have seen, however, this receptivity is, to a higher degree, a characteristic of women. Consequently, the female human being is more likely to be suitably representative of the state of creaturely being before God. Woman is, in a sense, a *likeness of creation*.

However, owing to the passive attitude of readiness (which, in its own way, of course, demands the highest activity), this representative function is carried out not so much in the resistant public sphere, but more through the inconspicuous and the hidden. "Seen in cosmic perspective, men stand at the forefront of power; women encamp in its depths."[346]

The natural symbols that are emblematic of God's immanence are, to an even greater degree, emblems of creation: the earth, as recipient of the sun's rays and the rain, which comes from heaven; the moon, which

[346] Fort, *Frau*, p. 20.

reflects the light of the sun; the wellspring, which bubbles up out of the depths of the earth; the tree, which, from its roots upward, reaches toward heaven and so forth.

Thus, he who believes in a personal and transcendent God is not deprived of a single natural symbol, yet he imparts to the images of creation a different direction than does the pantheist.

Woman as a representative of mankind

As the favored representatives of worldly being, women are simultaneously *representatives of mankind*, in which all of creation can bestir itself in the direction of God and be brought to speak in praise before him. Women, namely, without any detriment to their personal worth, more strongly represent the interest of the species, mankind, than that of the individual who values his own independence.[347]

Regarding the matter of representing man's position vis-à-vis God, women thus have an incomparable advantage over men. In relationship to God, man certainly remains a person, but even all-surrendering love can in no way, through its own power, place God at its disposal. Incommunicable personal identity must allow itself to enter into a relationship. The eccentric symbolism of men, oriented toward sovereignty and power, is thus not suited to representing adequately this attitude of open receptivity. It is, therefore, surely no coincidence that, in monotheistic mysticism, man's soul never appears in relation to God as masculine, but rather always as feminine.[348]

As symbolic of human *receptivity*, women are simultaneously emblems of deep-rooted, personal *devotion* to God, for, precisely in receiving, the soul simultaneously engages in a state of highest activity.

The (feminine) mandala is an image of the vital forces that well up from man's innermost being, the core of the person. The psychic dynamics of women seem to be more strongly gathered around an inner midpoint (centrality), so that they can orient themselves more completely toward God, while men are more inclined, in a certain sense, to split up their souls.

The *heart* is the most important symbol of this devotion that comes from the center and constitutes the essence of love. Pius XI therefore designates the husband as the head, and the wife as the heart, of the family:

[347] Cf. pp. 95f., 120 above.
[348] Ruether, *Mary*, p. 47.

"as he occupies the chief place in ruling, so she may and ought to claim for herself the chief place in love".[349] This devotion of the heart "is the sole absolute power that a created being possesses".[350]

Excursus: woman as typal of mankind from the biological viewpoint

Women's capacity for representing mankind's position before God perhaps rests, in a specific way, on biological predisposition, and this may be a more far-reaching consideration than the anthropological data already mentioned, convincing though those may be in themselves. Since what immediately follows—like the earlier remarks on the sex chromosomes— is merely hypothetical in nature, I said nothing about it in the anthropological section.

Female mammals, including the human female, could be described, in a certain sense, as the basic sex. If, namely, the production of the specific sex hormones is blocked in male embryos, this leads to the development of female sex organs. An analogous development in the case of female fetuses does not seem to be possible.[351]

Ashley Montagu regards women, from a biological standpoint, as the "stronger sex".[352] This hypothesis—just like its opposite extreme—has not been undisputedly accepted by biologists; however, its core of truth would seem to lie in the fact that the list of sex-typical illnesses for men is twice as long as that for women,[353] something Montagu traces back to the female chromosomes. X chromosomes are, namely, larger than Y chromosomes,[354] and may well produce more disease-resisting substances.[355] Possibly also significant is the fact that very many more boys (20 to 50 percent) than girls are conceived. Nevertheless, their high death rate leads

---

[349] Cf. p. 56 above.

[350] Fort, *Frau*, p. 27.

[351] Flad-Schnorrenberg, *Unterschied*, p. 25; Alfred Jost, "Die pränatale geschlechtliche Entwicklung" [Prenatal sexual development], in Sullerot, *Wirklichkeit*, pp. 103ff.; Etienne Baulieu and France Haour, "Die physiologischen und pathologischen Unterschiede zwischen Mann und Frau" [The physiological and pathological differences between men and women], in Sullerot, *Wirklichkeit*, pp. 170f.

[352] Ashley Montagu, *The Natural Superiority of Women*, 2nd ed. (New York and London, 1968), p. 83.

[353] Montagu, *Women*, pp. 82f.

[354] Montagu, *Women*, pp. 70–84.

[355] Cf. on this also Léon Eisenberg, "Die differentielle Verteilung der psychiatrischen Störungen auf die Geschlechter" [The differential distribution of psychiatric disturbances between the sexes], in Sullerot, *Wirklichkeit*, pp. 383ff.

to something like an equalization in the overall number of children that survive.[356]

Thus, in the biological development of mankind as such, women seem, perhaps, to be especially characteristic, and this is not unimportant for the symbolism of the sexes, in which women appear as representative of mankind (before God). This superiority of biological type is thoroughly compatible with the thesis presented earlier, also based on considerations of chromosomal set, that woman originates out of man, to whom primacy of origin is therefore attributable. Both of these theses are presented here expressly as mere *hypotheses*; the remaining anthropological, philosophical and theological statements in no way depend on them but could, as the case may be, derive from them a certain support.

The priority of feminine symbolism over masculine

Now, if we briefly sum up the symbolism of the sexes as man = symbol of God, woman = symbol of creation—does that not still imply that women are inferior?

Here it is necessary to observe that, although men represent the transcendence of God, they do not themselves embody it. A man is simply not God. Women, however, are not only emblematic of creation, but themselves belong to it. They embody the symbolized values in their own persons. Thus, there is a special density proper to feminine symbolism, whereas a greater brokenness is found in its masculine counterpart. This inauthenticity is ultimately to be explained by God's transcendence, which, despite all symbolic expressibility, can be represented in the created realm only as a very weak reflection, as a shadow image.

Women, then, are bearers of symbolic meaning in a more comprehensive way than men, since, in them, symbol and reality are in agreement.[357]

---

[356] Odette Thibault, "Die Frage der Geschlechtsbestimmung" [The question of sex determination], in Sullerot, *Wirklichkeit*, p. 87.

[357] This idea is stressed in a similar way by, in particular, Louis Bouyer: *Woman in the Church*, p. 49. With reference to this, Hans Urs von Balthasar ("Welches Gewicht", p. 57) finds: women "do not . . . represent . . . but are; while men do have to represent, and are thereby both more and less than they are. They are more insofar as they are the 'heads' in relation to women and, in the Christian context, mediators of God's goodnesses; they are less, however, insofar as they depend on women as their sheltering homeplaces and exemplary realizations."

Bouyer relates the representation idea to what is implied by *fatherhood* and *motherhood* or, as the case may be, maidenhood (*Woman in the Church*, pp. 33–35, 49, 51). My inquiries, however, were intended to have a wider scope, inasmuch as their initial focus is being a *man* or a *woman*. Fatherhood and motherhood are, then, the completest forms of realization of

Naturally, this does not imply any romantic idealization of women, for the symbol is not only an indicative but also an imperative: become what you are.

Also, the bearer of the symbolism can resist, even quite energetically, being such a symbol, but in this case the striking words of Gertrud von le Fort are apposite: "The symbol says . . . nothing, in any particular instance, about its bearer's empirical character or state, but only about its bearer's metaphysical significance. The bearer of the symbol can fall away from the symbol, but the symbol does not fall as a result."[358]

10. THE RELATIONSHIP BETWEEN THE IMAGE OF GOD AND THE PRIESTHOOD

The two basic structures of priestly representation

A "priest", in the broadest sense of the word, is a mediator between God and man. Accordingly, two basic structures are decisive for his activity:

1. The representation of the Divinity in relation to man. When the emphasis is on transcendence and the active workings of God, particularly in history, it seems appropriate to reserve the priesthood for men, whose relation to the environment is more distanced and more powerfully efficacious.

2. The public representation of man in relation to the Divinity. For this, too, men tend to be more suitable. As the representative of his community, a man steps, so to speak, "outward" into the presence of God, and, by virtue of his more strongly developed capacities for abstract thought and energetic will, is more likely to be able, in an

---

those more comprehensive categories. Certainly both being a father and being a mother have equally great importance for the development of the child; thus Bouyer's theories need supplementation in many respects. Still, it remains true that the woman, for reasons that begin with her biological constitution, is more closely tied to the child and is so on the basis of its very developmental origins: not the father but rather the mother carries the infant beneath her heart for nine months. A woman is more strongly claimed by being a mother than is a man by his task as a father (cf. p. 306 below). Men function more strongly as *representatives* of divine Fatherhood, whereas women not only represent motherly conception and gestation of the child but realize this in themselves. From this perspective, it seems no coincidence that Christ had a *human mother* but no human, and only a *divine*, *Father*.

[358] Fort, *Frau*, p. 8.

objective and not subjective-emotive way, to represent the common interest and lead the religious group.[359]

Priestesses and their significance for the study of religion

Particularly the second basic structure of priestly symbolism is in line with general considerations from sociology, which, even in this age of emancipation, sees social leadership roles as being, for reasons of biological constitution, largely the province of men.[360] As will be explained in more detail shortly, these social foundations are further strengthened, in the religious sphere, by the symbolic structure, whose effects operate mainly at the subconscious level. In almost all religions, "women play a minor role, or none at all, in the cult, at least in its most sacred and most important ceremonies".[361]

The fact that women assume no official function in public worship is not to be mistrusted indiscriminately as hatred of women. For in other, nonofficial religious contexts women are seen as superior to men, namely, with respect to ecstatic visions and divination. These areas depend in a special way on "inspiration from above", which—if at all—can be officially regulated only in a secondary way. Such an institutionalization of prophecy has occurred more frequently in the history of religion: "There seems to be a positive correlation between feminine physiological and psychic qualities and the special cult functions that are allocated to women, such, for instance, as prophecy."[362] "The function of priestesses was, in most cases, the mantic one: ecstatic prophecy, such as we are familiar with through Pythia and Sibyl."[363]

Nevertheless, emancipated women have always known how to make their way into the official ranks of even those cults dedicated to male deities. Where there was no explicit divine prohibition—and such seems

[359] This is true particularly with respect to larger groups, whereas, in smaller communities, termed sects in the language of sociology of religion, the subjective element comes more strongly to the fore and women are given decisive leading roles more frequently; cf. pp. 105f. above. This phenomenon is also intimated in the ecstatic mystery religions and Gnostic conventicles of antiquity; cf. pp. 343f., 404–8 below.

[360] Cf. p. 104 above.

[361] Joachim Wach, *Religionssoziologie* [Sociology of religion] (Tübingen, 1951), p. 244.

[362] Wach, *Religionssoziologie*, p. 244.

[363] Alfred Bertholet and Edvard Lehmann, eds., *Lehrbuch der Religionsgeschichte I* [Textbook on the history of religion I], originated by Chantepie de la Saussaye, 4th ed. (Tübingen, 1924), p. 50; cf. Asmussen, *Handbuch I*, p. 268. On the meaning of the mantic, see especially Heiler, *Frau*, pp. 9ff.

not to have been laid down in any pre-Christian form of religion—male indulgence could quite readily oblige these passions for emancipation. In Egypt and Greece, for instance, women stood *pari cum pari* with their professional colleagues of the opposite sex in the service of male deities.[364]

Naturally, priestesses play a special role in the service of female deities, and particularly of mother goddesses. The first basic priestly structure, which, especially in the monotheistic religions, is directed toward the representation of transcendence, now assumes the function of symbolizing God's immanence. Such a representation of the great mother is found in Egypt, Japan and elsewhere;[365] it is particularly well developed in the matriarchally inclined Cretan religion, in which men are allowed to participate in the divine service only in a subordinate capacity.[366] Something similar can be seen in the maternal religion of the Khasi in Assam (northeastern India): "to be sure, a priest officiates alongside of her [the priestess]; but it is unmistakable that he is only her agent and she is the central figure, so that, without her activity, the sacrifice cannot be offered at all."[367]

Between the image of God and that of the priest there is thus an intimate connection. If the sexual composition of the priesthood undergoes a change, then it can be assumed that, at least in the longer term, effects on the image of God will follow. A woman in the role of official representative of God could, perhaps even very soon, institute the prayer: "Our Mother, who art in heaven. . . ." The Protestant communities in the United States that ordain women can be taken as trend setters here; as reports have it, liturgical experts are, in fact, already diligently pursuing experimentations.[368]

From the religious-philosophical standpoint alone—which is my only subject of concern at the moment—any such incursion of feminist theology into the liturgy is more than suspect: "If we really wanted to take all that seriously,[369] then we would have to become involved with some other religion.[370] . . . The religious life of a child that had been taught to

[364] Hans Bonnet, *Reallexikon der ägyptischen Religionsgeschichte* [Encyclopedia of the history of Egyptian religion] (Berlin, 1952), pp. 607f.; E. R. Hardy, "The Priestess in the Greco-Roman World", in Bruce and Duffield, *Why Not?* pp. 56–62; Heiler, *Frau*, pp. 25f.

[365] Heiler, *Frau*, pp. 21f.

[366] Cf. pp. 102–3 above.

[367] Alfred Bertholet, "Weibliches Priestertum" [Female priesthood], in *Fs. R. Thurnwald, Beiträge zur Gesellungs- und Völkerwissenschaft* [Essays for R. Thurnwald, contributions to sociology and anthropology] (Berlin, 1950), p. 43.

[368] What can possibly be expected here is shown by L. M. Russell, in "Sprachveränderung", pp. 70–84. A "ritual-book" of feminist liturgy has been published by R. R. Ruether, *Women-Church: Theology and Practice of Feminist Liturgical Communities* (San Francisco, 1985).

[369] Which has, I note, already happened in the meanwhile.

[370] Namely, I note, with a pantheistic-tending immanentism.

pray to a Mother in heaven would be radically different from that of a Christian child."[371] "One must belong completely to the earth in order, with Lichtenberg, to pray in the following way: 'Our Mother, who art in heaven'."[372]

11. PRIESTLY REPRESENTATION AND LITURGY

The arguments from the study of religion against the admission of women to priestly office go beyond any mere pragmatism and functionalism. For the various aspects of world and man are not just means that can be employed for this or that practical activity. Rather, as created realities, they are, in addition, emblems of God, who brought them into being as a mirror image of his own nature, as symbols.

In the area of the symbolism of the sexes, the preceding inquiries have revealed a clear association of women with divine immanence and, above all, with creation. Symbols of this sort are deeply embedded in man's being, all the way down to the hidden abysses of the unconscious. The Anglican lay theologian C. S. Lewis therefore states: "We have no authority to take the living and sensitive figures that God has painted on the canvas of our nature and shift them about as if they were mere geometrical figures."[373]

If archetypal structures of this sort are blurred or effaced, this can bring about unforeseen consequences for the spiritual well-being of mankind. That applies in particular to the religious sphere, in which man gives over his innermost being to God; and there, in turn, it applies preeminently to the liturgy, which, as we know, avails itself quite strongly of the language of symbolism.

It is certainly no coincidence that many advocates of female priesthood are often instinctively overcome by sheer horror precisely when they experience the liturgy in its full form.[374] Orthodoxy, which is stamped in a special way by its unbrokenly traditional, heavily symbolic liturgy, has remained until the present day a bulwark in the defense of the male priesthood.[375]

[371] Lewis, "Priestesses", pp. 193f.
[372] Leeuw, *Phänomenologie*, p. 99; cf. G. C. Lichtenberg, *Aphorismen und Schriften. Sein Werk ausgewählt und eingeleitet von E. Vincent* [Aphorisms and writings. His work selected and introduced by E. Vincent], 2nd ed. (Leipzig, 1935), p. 189.
[373] Lewis, "Priestesses", p. 195.
[374] Cf. p. 50 above.
[375] Cf. the evaluation by Behr-Sigel: p. 50 above.

To the sphere of liturgical symbolism also, surely, belongs the priest as representative of the community before God and of God vis-à-vis the community. The objection (with reference here to the Christian realm) "who would maintain that the representation of Christ must be carried over to the biological-physical level?"[376] fails to recognize that unity of body and soul, founded in the deepest aspects of man's being, in and through which all the ramifications of biological life, including membership of one of the sexes, operate to influence the life of the soul and, in addition, to make the whole person a self-transcending symbol.

This symbolic dimension is of much greater significance in the religious sphere, and especially in ceremonial worship, than in the secular world. For, in normal everyday life, it is often necessary only that certain functions are performed as appropriately as possible. Here, man is a component within a means-ends mechanism. If a priest, too, were but a little cog within a sociological apparatus that required only to be run with the fewest possible disturbances, that is, if he were only a functionary, then, in the present-day cultural situation, the strict exclusion of women from priestly office would not be justifiable. Then, indeed, one could, like the American nun Mary Daly,[377] call for a priority of "professional competence" and a movement "away from symbolic roles . . . and toward functional roles freely chosen in accordance with personal inclinations and capabilities".[378]

In the religious sphere, however, as I have tried to show above, interrelations of a pragmatic nature are not of primary importance. Man's self-surrender to God and the representation, in response to this, of God's gracious self-affirmation shatters all inner-worldly interrelationships and, even more so, all means-ends thinking. This living and meaningful supraempirical reality, to be sure, runs directly counter to a historical current strongly saturated with scientific-sociological positivism and nominalism. But, precisely in our industrial civilization, many people hunger most deeply for transcendence, for the life of God. If the traditional churches, under the pretense of a false *aggiornamento*, fail to recognize these signs of the times and allow themselves to be taken in by the modern movement for emancipation, then they will only succeed, even if unconsciously and unintentionally, in driving many religiously questing people into the arms of false prophets. The new youth religions are surely a sign that the churches are not living out their orientation toward God with sufficient intensity.

---

[376] Meer, *Priesturtum*, p. 196.
[377] Cf. pp. 71f. above.
[378] Daly, *Kirche*, p. 218.

CHAPTER EIGHT

The Relevance of the Material from Anthropology and Religious Studies to the Discussion of the Order of Redemption

I. SUBSTANTIAL CONCLUSIONS

Now, what significance do the findings from anthropology and religious studies, as presented so far here, have for our theology inquiry?

As I see it, they serve to clarify the following:

1. The *sociological findings*, which derive from biological and psychological bases, show that men are better suited than women to the duties of a holder of spiritual office that must be performed in the resistant public sphere. This conclusion, taken by itself, is not enough to justify excluding women from priestly service. For, especially under present-day social conditions, numerous women can be found who would be more capable than most men of filling an educational and administrative office of this sort. There are even some aspects of pastoral care for which women possess a special aptitude. Often cited in this connection is the area of personal conversation between individuals, which demands one's whole-hearted engagement.[1] Of course, it must also be remembered here that the apostolate does not consist solely of the activities of the clergy.[2]

One thing alone is undeniably clear: *if* God, in and through his historical actions, reserves the public priesthood for one of the two sexes only, *then* it is not just arbitrary to choose the male sex.

The sociological findings are strengthened, in the religious sphere, by the symbolic references, which clearly align men with the officeholder's eccentric self-surrender to God as represented in public worship.

---

[1] Corona Bamberg, "Die Aufgabe der Frau in der Liturgie" [The role of women in the liturgy], *Anima* 19 (1964): 315; Gibson, *Femmes*, pp. 62ff.; Montefiore, *Yes*, p. 59.

[2] On this, see Wiesen, *Frau*.

2. At the same time, the *material from the study of religions* provides an explanation of why the image of God in the theistic religions of revelation has more masculine than feminine traits, and, along with this, why men are chosen as his priestly representatives.

Conversely, the accent of feminine symbolism is on the representation of the values of creation. Since women not only represent creation but also belong to it themselves, the symbolism in them is more strongly realized. Men, by contrast, represent something that, in the end, they themselves are not.

The *basic axis of the symbolism of the sexes* can thus be equated with the relationships *man = God, woman = creation*, without—because of the differences in density of the symbolisms—this implying a lesser evaluation of women.[3]

Just as with God and creation, so men and women are different from one another, yet, precisely in and through this difference, are essentially referred to one another. An androgynous image of man, on the other hand, leads to the death of the human relationships, and the androgynous image of God derived from it annihilates the personal interchange between God and man: secularized God—deified world.

2. THE STRUCTURES OF THE ORDER OF CREATION AS ARGUMENTS OF CONVENIENCE

The argument that has been developed so far rests on the fact that man's nature, as given from the time of creation, is taken into service through the order of redemption. Since redemption, however, constitutes something radically new, the what and how of its mediation cannot be derived *more geometrico* $(2 + 2 = 4)$ from preexisting realities, which have been brought into disorder through sin. On the basis of the order of creation, only rough indications can be arrived at, that is, *arguments of convenience*. These are not to be dismissed as inconclusive, but rather—as I will have to show in what follows—give rise, in conjunction with the redemptive structures created by revelation, to a multileveled succession of argumentational grounds that reaches its peak in the activity of Jesus. Since, however, that activity cannot simply be stuck onto man's nature and sacred history, the enumeration of such arguments of convenience is intended, so to speak, as a way of gradually raising it up out of the

[3] Cf. pp. 189f. above.

darkness of tradition-based positivism into the light of reason as illumined by faith.

The first level of argumentation is intended, together with the immediately following exposition of the biblical account of creation, to elucidate the order of creation. As the second level, then, the outline of the Old Testament order of salvation will follow, and finally, serving to conclude the chain of argumentation, the activity of Jesus, as attested to and carried on by the Church, will be considered.

CHAPTER NINE

The Statements about the Relation between Man and Woman in the Biblical Account of Primal History

1. RELATIVE SIGNIFICANCE AND LITERARY GENRE

The relation between man and woman is a central object of interest in the first three chapters of the biblical account of primal history. Nowhere else in the Old Testament is this theme dealt with in such detail and so fundamentally.

The biblical authors, especially the Yahwist, make use here of pictorial language whose elements are, in part, mythic in origin. Whereas, however, a myth is only the imaginative depiction of a basically timeless occurrence in the cycles of nature, the Bible is concerned at this point with history, with the beginning of things as freely and sovereignly determined by God and with man's behavior in response to the gifts entrusted to him.[1]

2. THE CREATION OF MAN ACCORDING TO THE PRIESTLY TEXT

In both accounts of creation, that of the priestly text[2] and that of the Yahwist,[3] the sexual differentiation of mankind is willed by God.

[1] On the question of the "historicity" of the statements, cf. especially the survey of the results of biblical scholarship in Leo Scheffczyk, *Einführung in die Schöpfungslehre* [Introduction to the doctrine of creation] (Darmstadt, 1975), pp. 10–16. See also the commentaries on biblical primal history that are listed in the bibliography, especially those by Claus Westermann, Gerhard von Rad, Theodor Schwegler and Henricus Renckens.

[2] Gen 1:1–2:4a.

[3] Gen 2:4b–25.

As presented by the priestly text,[4] God does not call into being a double-sexed primal man, as later Gnostic speculation tries to read into the text,[5] but rather "male and female he created them".[6]

Both sexes are formed, in equal measure, "in the image of God", and there is no mention of any evaluative gradation, in the sense, for example, that woman would be any less in the image of God than is man.

The meaning of being in the image of God is not, itself, defined, but its consequences are indicated: at God's behest, man is to have dominion over the earth. "Just as the great worldly kings erect a likeness of themselves, in provinces of their realm where they do not personally come and go, as a sign of their claim to sovereignty—so man, placed on earth in his likeness to God, . . . is enjoined to preserve and enforce God's claim to sovereignty on earth."[7]

Whether man is a likeness of God "also through the polarity of the sexes"[8] cannot be decided solely on the basis of the biblical text. The concept of the likeness probably includes reference to bodily form,[9] even if it cannot be limited to that.[10] Still, the most obvious preconditions for carrying out the mandate of creation are, in the first instance, the intellectual capacities of reason and will, which distinguish man from all other inhabitants of the earth.[11]

Through his spiritual endowments, man is "created for kinship with

---

[4] Gen 1:26–27.

[5] The same applies for Genesis 2. Cf. Jacob Jervell, *Imago Dei. Gen 1,26f. im Spätjudentum, in der Gnosis und in den paulinischen Briefen* [Image of God. Gen 1:26f. in late Judaism, gnosis and the Pauline letters] FRLANT 76 (Göttingen, 1960), p. 161; F.-X. Arnold, *Mann und Frau in Welt und Kirche* [Man and woman in world and Church], 2nd ed. (Nuremberg, 1959), pp. 39f. See also p. 160 above.

[6] Cf. Gerhard von Rad, *Das erste Buch Mose* [The first book of Moses], ATD 2/4 (Göttingen, 1972), p. 39.

[7] Rad, *Mose*, p. 39.

[8] So says F.-X. Arnold, *Mann und Frau*, p. 19. Cf. Barth, *KD III,4*, p. 128. See also pp. 76f. above. That Barth has taken the meaning of the text too far in formulating his thesis may be regarded as exegetically certain; cf. on this J. J. Stamm, "Die Imago-Lehre von Karl Barth und die alttestamentliche Wissenschaft" [The Imago doctrine of Karl Barth and Old Testament scholarship], in Leo Scheffczyk, ed., *Der Mensch als Bild Gottes*, [Man as image of God], Wege der Forschung 124 (Darmstadt, 1969), pp. 49–68, especially 62.

[9] Rad, *Mose*, p. 37.

[10] W. H. Schmidt, *Die Schöpfungsgeschichte der Priesterschrift* [The story of creation in the priestly text], WMANT 17 (Neukirchen and Vluyn, 1964): p. 133, n. 1. The Hebrew word ṣelem signifies "by no means necessarily a 'plastic figure', but basically just an 'image' ".

[11] Cf. the name giving in Genesis 2:20, which, in biblical understanding, presupposes a knowledge of the essence of that named: P. van Imschoot, "Name" [Name], in Herbert Haag, ed., *Bibellexikon* [Encyclopedia of the Bible], 2nd ed. (Einsiedeln, Zurich and Cologne, 1968), pp. 1215–16.

God, the infinite Thou".[12] The likeness to God shows itself as well in the personal "being-an-answering . . . in respect to God",[13] which is fulfilled most purely in the act of turning toward God in prayer on the Sabbath.[14]

Being a likeness of God means that men and women are fundamentally equal before God, but not the same. For the difference between the sexes appears in Genesis 1:27 as a relationship between human beings that precedes all other social realities and is anchored in the will of God.

Although the mandate of creation does not expressly distinguish between the tasks of men and women, that these will take different forms is still parenthetically assumed. For every action is grounded in a certain sort of being (man or woman) and is correlative to that (*agere sequitur esse*).[15]

The masculine nature, in particular, is more strongly directed toward mastery of the external world than is that of women. But this task of mastery appears as a specific consequence of being a likeness of God.[16] In my remarks in the area of philosophy of religion, I linked the concepts power (mastery), eccentricity and transcendence with one another and arrived at the position that, just as women represent creation, so, in a special way, men represent God. Now, man's symbolic dimension is related to his being a likeness of God,[17] so that men might well possess a certain advantage in the *representation* of that likeness, without this, of course, in any way prejudicing the *essential* equality in rank of the sexes.[18]

This idea, which goes beyond mere exegesis, may perhaps receive a certain degree of support in the second account of creation, which will be discussed next: the eccentric, outward-directed sort of action appears in connection with the man, who gives the woman her name.[19]

---

[12] Ziegenaus, "Menschen", p. 213.

[13] Scheffczyk, *Schöpfungslehre*, p. 83.

[14] Gen 2:2–3; cf. Ziegenaus, "Menschen", p. 213. The extensive problems surrounding the issue of man's likeness to God can, in the present context, only just be hinted at. For further information, cf. Scheffczyk, *Mensch* and *Schöpfungslehre*, pp. 79–84.

[15] As opposed to Thrall, *Ordination*, p. 36, who attributes equal authority to both sexes indifferently. Similarly: Marie de Merode-de-Croy, "Die Rolle der Frauen im Alten Testament" [The role of women in the Old Testament], *Conc* 16 (1980): 273. This viewpoint was represented as early as the nineties of the last century by Elizabeth Cady Stanton in *The Woman's Bible*; this book has been rediscovered by the neofeminist movement of recent years: Elizabeth Clark and Herbert Richardson, *Women and Religion. A Feminist Sourcebook of Christian Thought* (New York, 1977), p. 218. Men and women exercise authority in an equal way over nonhuman aspects of creation, but whether they do so in the same way is precisely the question.

[16] Gen 1:28; cf. Ps 8:6–9; Sir 17:2–4.

[17] Cf. Scheffczyk, *Mensch*, p. xli.

[18] For more on this, see pp. 348f. below.

[19] Gen 2:23. Cf. also the name giving in Genesis 2:20 and the terms of punishment in

3. THE CREATION OF WOMAN ACCORDING TO THE YAHWIST

A more developed statement of the relation between the sexes is given by the Yahwist, whose account seems to supplement what was said in the priestly text and concentrates wholly on the creation of man.[20]

Initially, it is only the man who appears as the representative of being human, but God then frees him from his loneliness through "a helper fit for him", or—as the Hebrew expression means literally—"a helper as his counterpart".[21]

The notion of a helper is not restricted to the spheres of work or sexuality but signifies "support in the broader sense".[22] Among the nineteen occurrences of the word in the Old Testament, fifteen are applied to God, so it can hardly imply any devaluation of the woman.[23]

In the expression "as his counterpart", there are connotations of being the same in kind as well as of being supplementary,[24] which presupposes a certain degree of being different.

After announcing the helper, God makes the woman out of one of Adam's "ribs". Prior to this, it becomes clear that nonpersonal creatures (animals) cannot be genuine partners to man.[25] The formation out of the rib, as well as Adam's joyful exclamation in verse 23, serve to express two things:

1. A fundamental, essential equality:
    a. "This at last is bone of my bones and flesh of my flesh."
    b. The play on words between 'isch-'ischscha: "She shall be called woman (literally, "female man", 'ischscha), because she was taken out of man ('isch)."
2. The elementary urge of the sexes toward one another, which is

---

Genesis 3:16–19, in which woman is represented as mother, and man, as tiller of the fields, of the outside world. Cf. on this André Feuillet, *Jésus et sa mère d'après les récits lucaniens de l'enfance et d'après Saint Jean. Le rôle de la Vierge Marie dans l'histoire du salut et la place de la femme dans l'Église* (Paris, 1974), p. 206; André Feuillet, "La dignité et le rôle de la femme d'après quelques textes pauliniennes: comparaison avec l'Ancien Testament", *New Testament Studies* 21 (1975): 165. The point of the name giving lies in the direction of cognitive description, of abstraction; cf. Marie de Merode, " 'Une aide qui lui corresponde'. L'exégèse de Gen 2,18–24 dans les écrits de l'Ancien Testament, du judaisme et du Nouveau Testament", *Revue théologique de Louvain* 8 (1977): 333.

[20] Gen 2:4b–25.

[21] Gen 2:18. Cf. Hubert Junker, *Genesis*, Echter-Bibel (Würzburg, 1949), p. 16.

[22] Claus Westermann, *Genesis (1–11)*, BK I,1 (Neukirchen and Vluyn, 1974), p. 309.

[23] C. J. Vos, *Woman in Old Testament Worship* (Delft, 1968), p. 16.

[24] Rad, *Mose*, p. 57.

[25] Gen 2:19–22.

manifested more clearly in verse 24: "Therefore a man leaves his father and his mother and cleaves to his wife, and they become one flesh."[26]

This verse also makes evident the etiological nature of the account, which, according to Gerhard von Rad, starts out from the reality of the far-reaching associatedness of man and woman, and attempts to ground this in God's act of creation.[27]

4. GENESIS 3:16 AND THE PROBLEM OF THE SUBORDINATION OF WOMEN

Strictly considered, the Yahwist account of the fall of man, in Genesis 3, may not belong to the doctrine of creation, but it is closely connected with the statements about the creation of man that precede it.

Genesis 3:16 describes the consequences of sin for the woman: "Your desire shall be for your husband, and he shall rule over you." The rule of man over woman appears here as a punishment that ensues from man's sinful disposition. Woman does not, however, need to accept male oppression as a condition of nature or even of creation but rather may defend herself against it, just as man may take measures to deal with the thorns and thistles that have been put in the fields to punish him.

Still, it would be a case of reading modern liberal ideas into the biblical text if one were to assume that, for the Yahwist, any and every sort of subordination of women to men is a consequence of sin.[28] A certain order of succession can already be found in Genesis 2:18–25. There, woman is created after man and receives her name from man.[29] In the account of creation in the priestly text, too, man is mentioned before woman.[30]

[26] Cf. Henricus Renckens, *Urgeschichte und Heilsgeschichte. Israels Schau in die Vergangenheit nach Gen 1–3* [Primal history and sacred history. Israel's look into the past according to Gen 1–3], 3rd ed. (Mainz, 1964), p. 204.

[27] Von Rad, *Mose*, p. 59. Etiology, however, provides an interpretative perspective not only for facts of the present, but also, precisely with respect to primal history, for statements referring to the past (cf. pp. 198f. above). Whether the creation of Eve "out of" Adam is also an instance of this is better left open here, because it would require an extensive inquiry of its own. This would go far beyond an exegesis of Genesis 2, would have to take into account Tradition as well as the New Testament context and would even have to draw on data from the natural sciences (such as the fact that the hereditary factors of woman can, theoretically, be formed out of those of man, but not vice versa; cf. pp. 181f. above). Cf. DS, 3514.

[28] Thus, among others, Uta Ranke-Heinemann, "Eheliche Partnerschaft" [Partnership in marriage], in Schmaus and Gössmann, *Frau*, pp. 73f.

[29] Gen 2:13.

[30] Gen 1:27. *If* one is inclined to read modern liberalism into the biblical texts, one would

For the Yahwist, however, subordination does not at all imply an inferiority of woman in comparison to man. As we saw earlier, the biblical author clearly stresses the basic sameness in kind, and equality of worth, of the sexes. "In this estimation of the significance of woman, or of being human as an associatedness of man and woman, Genesis 2 is unique among the myths from the whole of the Near East that deal with the creation of man."[31] Since, however, man and woman mutually supplement and depend on one another ("a helper fit for him"), there is also a difference between them, on the basis of which reciprocal exchange first becomes possible. This exchange takes place, by virtue of the specific natures of the sexes, according to a certain lawfulness or orderedness, which appears, for the Yahwist, as a subordination of woman to man. "In Genesis 2:18, what is referred to is the correspondence relationship, the mutuality of being companions; but that does not exclude a relationship of subordination; it simply could not be said, in 2:18, that man was created as a helper for woman."[32]

---

do well to consider Frank Crüsemann, who (for Genesis 2) postulates "a clearly androcentric view of the world": "In the language of domination is expressed abolition of domination, in sexist images, . . . freedom and equality": " 'er aber soll dein Herr sein'. Gen 3,16. Die Frau in der patriarchalischen Welt des Alten Testaments" ["and he shall rule over you", Gen 3:16. Women in the patriarchal world of the Old Testament], in Frank Crüsemann and Hartwig Thyen, *Als Mann und Frau geschaffen. Exegetische Studien zur Rolle der Frau* [As man and woman created. Exegetical studies on the role of women], Kennzeichen 2 (Gelnhausen and Berlin, 1978), p. 60. Do not the ideals of Marxism and the French Revolution serve here as the "filter" for the text?

[31] Westermann, *Genesis*, p. 316.

[32] Westermann, *Genesis*, p. 357. Cf. Renckens, *Urgeschichte*, pp. 200, 254, and Evelyn and Frank Stagg, *Woman in the World of Jesus* (Philadelphia, 1978), pp. 17f. Against Merode, "Aide", p. 331, who identifies subordination with inferiority and then assumes that subordination first arose with the *fall*. From Genesis 3:16, the rabbis were only able to read subordination of women into Genesis 2:18–24 (Merode, "Aide", pp. 349f.) because it was already present there, and ultimately grounded from there as the starting point (cf. Merode, "Aide", p. 350).

The same confusion is found in Walter Vogels, " 'It is not Good that the "Mensch" Should Be Alone: I Will Make Him/Her a Helper Fit for Him/Her' (Gen 2,18)", *Église et théologie* 9 (1978): 17. This author sets, in a dialectical way, old and feminist exegesis against each other (inferiority vs. superiority of women) in order, finally, to postulate equality as a golden mean: W. Vogels, "Mensch", p. 35.

Any exegesis is also illegitimate that plays off Genesis 1:27 (equality) and Genesis 2:18 (difference) against each other; for example, Stagg, *Woman*, pp. 18f. Both texts correspond to each other and are seen, especially in the final editing of biblical primal history, *together*.

We will meet with a similar selection in the case of the Pauline letters as well, where some like to play off 1 Corinthians 11:3, 7–8 against Galatians 3:28 and 1 Corinthians 11:11; cf. pp. 345ff. below. The one-sidedness increases further when *Genesis 1:27 and Galatians 3:28* are presented as a common motto, as in Daly, *Kirche*, p. 196; Parvey, *Ordination*, p. 30; Gerta Scharffenorth, "Die Gemeinschaft von Männern und Frauen in der Kirche. Bericht über die europäische Konsultation des Ökumenischen Rates der Kirchen Bad Segeberg, 20./23. Juni

It is only after the fall that such an arrangement can degenerate into oppression: "What is given at the start in accordance with creation, and is fully in order as such, acquires through sin a fatal list, or, so to speak, an unpleasant aftertaste."[33]

Whether, or to what extent, the notion of a subordination of women is still binding today will be clarified, at the conclusion of this study, in connection with the Pauline Letters. The only thing that remains to be kept firmly in mind is that, contrary to a widespread conception, subordination does not mean the same as inferiority or oppression.

5. CONCLUSION

In the accounts of creation according to the priestly text and the Yahwist's, the associatedness of men and women appears as the fundamental social fact in man's existence. This associatedness is based on an essential equality yet presupposes a certain difference, which is also reflected in a difference in the characteristic activities of the sexes (compare the differing punishments for sin in Genesis 3:16–19).

Now, it would be rather strange if these deep-rooted and God-willed differences between men and women were to be restricted to the order of creation. Rather, they must also, in some way or other, enter into the realization of the order of redemption, which, of course, presupposes created mankind. Granting all this, a restriction of Christian priestly office to men would not appear as simply absurd from the start.[34]

1980" [The community of men and women in the Church. Report on the European consultation of the World Council of Churches, Bad Segeberg, June 20–23, 1980], Ökumenische Rundschau 30 (1981): 93.

[33] Heinrich Baltensweiler, Die Ehe im Neuen Testament [Marriage in the New Testament] (Zurich, 1967), p. 20.

[34] Thus thinks the Anglican theologian Mascall (Women Priests? p. 12): "It would be very strange if the differentiation of function on the level of nature was not paralleled by a not less marked difference of function on the level of grace."

PART TWO

The Question of Women in the Priesthood
Against the Background of
The Order of Redemption

CHAPTER ONE

Preparatory Aspects of the Old Testament

1. DESCRIPTION OF THE PROBLEM

The special priesthood of the New Covenant is the effective representation of the ministry of Christ.[1] This ministry is something radically new, but it did not just suddenly descend from the heavens like a UFO from outer space; rather, many preparations for it can be found in the history of the people of Israel. Especially notable are the roles played by priest, prophet and king, which Christ not only brings to an end in a unique way but also brings to fulfillment.[2] Hence, it makes sense to take at least cursory account of what the Old Testament has to say about the position of women with respect to those roles, so that the order of the New Covenant is brought more clearly to light.

2. THE SOCIAL POSITION OF WOMEN IN ISRAEL

Before examining the religious position of women in the world of the Old Testament, I would like to look briefly at its larger social context.

What immediately attracts the modern observer's attention are the patriarchal conditions that largely determine the situation of the Israelite woman. This woman calls her husband "master":[3] "Thus she refers to him as a slave does to his master or a subject to his king."[4] The elohistic

[1] Cf. pp. 256ff. below.

[2] On prophethood, cf. Mt 13:57 par; on kingship, Mt 21:5 par; Jn 10:11, 18:37; on priesthood, Mt 26:28 par; Heb 8:1–2, 9:26.

[3] Gen 18:12; Ex 21:22; Dt 24:4; 2 Sam 11:26; Prov 31:11; and others.

[4] Roland de Vaux, *Das Alte Testament und seine Lebensordnungen I* [The Old Testament and its social institutions I] 2nd ed. (Freiburg, Basel and Vienna, 1964), p. 75.

version of the Ten Commandments even includes the wife under the category of property, along with manservant, maidservant, ox and ass.[5]

Polygamous customs necessarily lead to a devaluation of women,[6] as does the practice governing divorce. The husband can send his wife away without further ado "if . . . she finds no favor in his eyes because he has found some indecency in her".[7] A later controversy between the rabbinical schools of Hillel and Schammai, in which earlier differences of opinion are reflected, focuses on the interpretation of the notion of indecency. The stricter Schammai limits this to evidence of unchastity, whereas Hillel cites as a reason for divorce "also if she has burnt his meal". Rabbi Akiba even lists "also if he finds someone else who is more beautiful than she".[8]

All of these differences are, in fact, "very important legally, but were usually not so significant in the real-life context".[9] Polygamy, for instance, is a difficult matter from the purely economic viewpoint alone and is by no means the norm.[10] Also, a wife cannot be sold like a slave.[11] She has de facto control over property and the domestic sphere[12] and has, for better or worse, a great influence over her husband.[13]

Her most important task is motherhood,[14] and her limited participation in public affairs is a consequence of her concern for house and family. Children usually take their names from the mother,[15] to whom they must show the same respect as to the father.[16]

---

[5] Ex 20:17; Dt 5:21, however, shows a bit more tact.

[6] Dt 21:15; Gen 29:30.

[7] Dt 24:1.

[8] Billerbeck, *Kommentar I*, p. 313.

[9] Friedrich Nötscher, *Biblische Altertumskunde* [Biblical archaeology], Die Heilige Schrift des Alten Testaments übersetzt und erklärt. Ergänzungsband 3 (Bonn, 1940), p. 82. Cf. also Vos, *Woman*, p. 48: "That the female sex cried in bondage as Israel did in Egypt is nowhere suggested."

[10] Cf. Sir 25:8 and others.

[11] Dt 21:14.

[12] 1 Sam 25:18–19; 2 Sam 4:8f.

[13] Gen 61:5f.; 1 Kings 1:11ff.; 2 Kings 8:18; Jg 3:5–6.

[14] Gen 3:20; 30:1; 1 Sam 1:6–18.

[15] Of the 45 cases of name giving documented in the Old Testament, 5 are by God, 14 by the father and 26 by the mother: Vos, *Woman*, p. 161. In the Orient, names play a large role. They signify the "nature and destiny of the bearer: *nomen est omen*": Nötscher, *Altertumskunde*, p. 71.

[16] Ex 20:12; Dt 5:16; Lev 19:3.

3. THE RELIGIOUS POSITION OF WOMEN

General points

In the theological sense as well, motherhood is the specific calling of women. For being blessed with many children is seen as fulfilling God's promise to Abraham.[17]

Thus, the difference from the position of men in the religious sphere can be explained in large part by maternal duties. Women are therefore not obligated to participate in the three yearly pilgrimages,[18] yet frequently do accompany their husbands on these.[19] During menstruation and childbearing, they are regarded as "unclean",[20] not because these processes are seen as sinful or as the work of demons, but because they entail being excluded from worship. Something similar applies, by the way, in the case of certain processes that can occur in men.[21]

[17] Gen 12:2.

[18] Ex 23:17.

[19] 1 Sam 1–2; cf. Neh 8:2.

[20] Lev 12; 15:25–30.

[21] Lev 15:1–18; cf. Vos, *Woman*, pp. 84f. Not only women but also men (and priests) are accordingly excluded at times from worship. Women, of course, are affected more by this because of their stronger connection with the propagation of the species. The anthropological basis—which is almost totally overlooked in the present-day debate—is the same for both sexes, namely, the strong implicatedness of the soul in the relevant physical processes, which results in a certain indisposition to be wholly involved in worship. Is our inability to understand this fact perhaps conditioned by a modern Manichaean contempt for the body and by the resultant recent outbreak of exaggerated sexual permissiveness? Something similar applies as well, by the way, in the secular sphere, if one takes account, for example, of the behavior of serious athletes before an important game. All of this has nothing whatever to do with an aversion to sex; precisely, the Old Testament discusses sexual matters quite openly.

Prescriptions similar to those in the Old Testament are found among all peoples, if one disregards the situation in most recent times. To be sure, the justified anthropological and religious concerns in this area have often been carried too far; especially since blood was once regarded as embodying the life-force and as "something mysterious, demonical", all sorts of taboos were associated with it (Johannes Döller, *Die Reinheits- und Speisegesetze des Alten Testaments in religionsgeschichtlicher Beleuchtung* [Old Testament laws relating to cleanness and food as seen in the light of the history of religion], Atl. Abhandlungen VII, 2–3 [Münster, 1917], p. 58). In the history of religion, menstrual blood is associated, on the one hand, with magical and healing powers, yet also, on the other hand, with destructive influences (Döller, *Reinheitsgesetze*, p. 10). In popular German superstition, for instance, women "were prohibited even from touching fruits to be cooked or from going out into the garden, since the fruits might then be caused to rot and the plants to die" (Kummer, "Frau" [Woman], in Hanns Bächtold-Stäubli, ed., *Handwörterbuch des deutschen Aberglaubens II* [Dictionary of German superstitions II] [Berlin and Leipzig, 1929/30], p. 1752).

Nevertheless, women belong, in the fullest sense, to the community of the people of God, to a "kingdom of priests".[22] The absence of circumcision can probably be traced back to an exemption from certain functions involved in worship and does not prejudice membership of the people of the Covenant.[23]

The fundamental duties and blessings of the Covenant also apply to women. Together with their husbands, they attend the reading of the law,[24] observe in like manner the Sabbath[25] and take part in festive ceremonies.[26] Accordingly, they incur the same penalties for transgressions of the faith.[27] In the strict regulations against mixed marriage, the great religious importance of women indirectly shows itself.[28]

In comparison to other versions in the history of religion, the prescriptions in the Old Testament are rather mild (Döller, *Reinheitsgesetze*, p. 10). The relevant laws of cleanness were also, in part, retained or revived in the early Church; the Orthodox Church remains relatively strict in this regard even today (Döller, *Reinheitsgesetze*, p. 50; Parvey, *Ordination*, p. 14).

Here, the Latin Church has shown itself to be more open-minded. "*Gregory the Great* was the first to allow new mothers to enter the church as early as the day of the birth" (Döller, *Reinheitsgesetze*, p. 24). After the *Decretum Gratianum*, women were allowed to attend church and to receive Holy Communion even during menstruation (Raming, *Ausschluss*, p. 14, n. 44). Whereas, in the medieval Church, the so-called benediction was seen to a large extent as a purification (Michael Müller, *Grundlagen der katholischen Sexualethik* [Foundations of Catholic sexual ethics] [Regensburg, 1968], p. 85); what came increasingly to the fore later on were the elements of gratitude and blessing, which have been at the heart of the ritual since the *Rituale Romanum* of 1614 (Döller, *Reinheitsgesetze*, p. 25). Birth or *menstruation taboos* can thus hardly have been decisive factors in the exclusion of women from the priesthood, even if they may have had some influence of a third-level or fourth-level sort (contrary to S. H. Pfürtner, *Kirche und Sexualität* [Church and sexuality] [Reinbek, 1972], p. 81; Raming, *Ausschluss*, p. 14; Meer, *Priesturtum*, p. 158; Günter Wagner and Ilse Wiener, "Das Bild der Frau in der biblischen Tradition" [The image of woman in biblical tradition], *US* 35 [1980]: 299). Similar taboos existed, of course, in other religions as well—as in the environment around Israel—and yet women were not excluded in principle from the priesthood because of them. Those who wish to see a hatred of women behind the regulations should be consistent and speak of a hatred of men behind the parallel prescriptions for men. Before unleashing, like a blow below the belt, the accusation of hatred of sexuality (Pfürtner, *Kirche*, pp. 55–90), one ought to investigate the anthropological background, which, despite all religious-historical exaggerations, is certainly not biologically and psychologically unexplained (as held by Pfürtner, *Kirche*, p. 79).

[22] Ex 19:6–8; cf. Dt 29:8–12.

[23] Vos, *Woman*, p. 50.

[24] Dt 31:9–13; Neh 8:2.

[25] Ex 20:10; Dt 5:14.

[26] Dt 12:12.

[27] Dt 17:2, 5; 29:17, 20.

[28] Ex 34:15–16; Neh 13:26–27.

The role of female prophets

That the female sex is by no means regarded as incapable of having a say in religious affairs is shown above all by the female prophets. Huldah, for example, plays an important role in the dissemination of the book of the law that was found in 622 B.C. Without her God-empowered contribution, the five books of Moses (the core of the Old Testament!) would probably not exist as we know them today. The king respectfully asks Huldah for her views on the matter, although such highly significant figures as Jeremiah and (probably) Zephaniah are numbered among her prophetic contemporaries.[29]

Another important personality is Deborah, the "Joan of Arc of the Old Testament".[30] In difficult times, she guides the destiny of Israel and successfully concludes a defensive war.[31] Her song of victory is regarded as one of the pearls of Hebrew poetry.[32]

Miriam, the sister of Moses, also appears as a prophetess[33] and places herself on a level with her brother.[34]

Further evidence of effective activity on the part of female prophets is found in Nehemiah 6:14 (Noadiah), Isaiah 8:3, Ezra 13:17ff. and (as a promise) Joel 2:28.

Hence, it was not unusual to find women in the role of prophet in Israel, and this alone suffices to show that the sweeping thesis about the inferior position of women in Old Testament religion cannot be sustained.

Participation in kingly office

As opposed to kingly and priestly offices, the role of prophet is based on a direct summons from God. The call to prophethood is usually something that applies to a particular person and cannot be passed on by that individual. In this fact, our indisposability over God's gifts is given especially clear expression.

A ministry or "office", by contrast, appears as an institution established by God that maintains itself down through history even without any new charismatic empowerment with respect to the given officeholder.

---

[29] 2 Kings 22:14–20.

[30] Georg Beer, *Die soziale und religiöse Stellung der Frau im israelitischen Altertum* [The social and religious position of women in Israelite antiquity] (Tübingen, 1919), p. 42.

[31] Jg 4:4ff.

[32] Jg 5; cf. Vos, *Woman*, p. 181.

[33] Ex 15:20–21.

[34] Nb 12.

While the activity of female prophets can obviously be taken as unproblematic, women seem to have assumed official directorial functions only in exceptional cases. This is evident, for example, from the undertone in Deborah's remark in Judges 4:9 ("the Lord will sell Sisera into the hand of a woman") and from the fact that a queen takes over the reins of government only when there is no male regent or when he is still too young.[35] The queen mother holds a place of honor next to her son and participates in some (today no longer exactly known) way in the business of government.[36]

It is necessary to bear in mind that the office of king is not a purely worldly matter, for political leadership of the people of God is theologically grounded and goes back to divine disposition.[37] This applies in a special way to the kingship of David.[38] Thus, the office of an Israelite queen is fully comparable to the spiritual leadership responsibilities of a medieval abbess;[39] both sorts of responsibility are given over to women only in exceptional cases, but women are not excluded from them in principle.

Exclusion from the offices of priest and Levite

An exception in the contemporary environment

However, women are totally excluded from the offices of priest and Levite. Even in view of the complicated history of those two institutions,[40] all authoritative commentators agree on this fact.[41]

In the ancient East, priestesses were nothing unusual. They are documented throughout Mesopotamia, where they even acted in the service of male deities.[42] The same is true of Egypt.[43] In the Canaanite environment,

---

[35] 2 Kings 11:1f.

[36] 1 Kings 2:13, 19f.; 15:13; Jer 13:18; 29:2.

[37] 1 Sam 10:1.

[38] 2 Sam 7; Ps 2; 110.

[39] Even more, of course, to those of a medieval Christian queen, which were similarly religiously contexted. Cf. pp. 462–64 below.

[40] On this, see A. H. J. Gunneweg, *Leviten und Priester, Hauptlinien der Traditionsbildung und Geschichte des israelitisch-jüdischen Kultpersonals* [Levites and priests, basic aspects of the formation of tradition and of the history of the Israelite-Jewish religious clergy], FRLANT 89 (Göttingen, 1965), esp. pp. 219–25.

[41] Cf. esp. Vos, *Woman*, pp. 192–97; Vaux, *Testament II*, p. 221; G. B. Gray, *Sacrifice in the Old Testament* (New York, 1971 rpt.), pp. 184–91.

[42] Gray, *Sacrifice*, pp. 186f.; Leopold Sabourin, *Priesthood. A Comparative Study*, Studies in the History of Religions XXV (Leiden, 1973), p. 58; F. M. T. de Liagre Böhl, "Die Religionen der Babylonier und Assyrer",in Franz König, ed., *Christus und die religionen der Erde. Handbuch der Religionsgeschichte II* (Freiburg im Breisgau, 1951), p. 472.

[43] H. L. Jansen, "*Ägyptische Religion*" [Egyptian religion], in Asmussen, *Handbuch I*, p. 415; Leipoldt, *Frau*, p. 16; Bonnet, *Reallexikon*, pp. 607f.

too, whose sociological structure otherwise strongly influenced Israel, there were female priests. This is proven by the excavations at Ugarit[44] and elsewhere in Phoenicia. The same term for priest is found there as in Hebrew, namely, *khn* (*kohen*). Along with this, the Phoenician language, which is most closely related to the Hebrew, also contains a feminine form, *khnt*, which signifies not only the wife of a priest but also a priestess.[45] In Hebrew, however, the feminine form of *khn* is lacking.

Furthermore, in the Miniamin inscriptions from Sinai, there is a feminine counterpart, *lw'h*, to the word *lw'*, which is probably related to the Hebrew *lwj* (*levi*).[46] Here, too, there is no feminine form in Hebrew. Yet it was the Levites who performed all the services in the temple. Only from the earliest times is there evidence of (non-Levite) female service at the entrance to the tent of meeting.[47]

Possible reasons for this exclusion

In the Israelite clergy, then, in opposition to the wider environment of that day, there are no women. How is this fact to be explained?

First, we might examine the range of duties of both Levites and priests.

An official priest[48] is responsible for mediating the decisions of God,[49] for deciding on what is clean and unclean[50] and for determining, in questionable cases, between admission and nonadmission to the assembly of the Lord.[51]

He also holds the official *teaching post*, in that he promulgates God's regulations, the Torah.[52] In this, the priest receives support from the Levites.[53] The charism of the prophet is necessary especially whenever the officially appointed teachers of Israel fail in their duties.[54]

The most important function of the priest is to conduct the public worship of God, at the center of which is the sacrificial offering.

Decisive for the relationship to God is the self-surrender to him that takes place in the heart[55] and that is given particularly clear expression

---

[44] L. H. Muntingh, "The Social and Legal Status of a Free Ugaritic Female", *JNES* 26 (1967): 106.

[45] Gray, *Sacrifice*, p. 184.

[46] Vaux, *Testament II*, p. 221; Gray, *Sacrifice*, p. 186.

[47] Ex 38:8; 1 Sam 2:22.

[48] That there is also a "general priesthood" in Israel has already been suggested: cf. p. 211 above.

[49] 1 Sam 28:6.

[50] Lev 13:15.

[51] Dt 23:2ff.

[52] Hos 4:6; Micah 3:11; Jer 18:18.

[53] Gunneweg, *Leviten*, p. 225.

[54] Jer 26:4; 7:9; Hos 4:2; Zeph 3:4; Malachi 1:6–2:9.

[55] Ps 51:17; Micah 6:8.

through *sacrificial worship*.[56] This glorification of Yahweh, the (inwardly and palpably understood) sacrifice, forms the sole end of the Israelite religion, toward which all of life must be directed.[57]

The tension between a sacrifice that is other than man and man's inner disposition, however, is not resolved until the sacrifice of the New Covenant, in which Christ, with his own blood, offers himself up to the Father.[58] The commemoration of this sacrifice in the Eucharist is at the center of the service of New Testament priests,[59] making them similar to their Old Testament models.

Now, the priests are responsible for carrying out this surrender to God officially and publicly, as leaders and representatives of the whole community. Not every male can become a priest, but only the descendants of Aaron from the tribe of Levi, who have been appointed to that role by God.[60] "As distinct from the office of prophet, the *election* to the *offices of Levite and priest* is linked to biological lineage."[61] This sort of priestly succession served to illustrate to Israel "that it was not by virtue of its own merits that its closeness to Yahweh . . . came about".[62] For, among the Israelites, a priest is not only a representative of the people but also God's delegate, who, as such, is set apart from the people. This form of representation is distinguished from the more political leadership role of a king by its formal ties to religious worship.

The priesthood maintains itself even at times when prophets and kings are lacking. Why does precisely this central office within Israelite religion remain restricted to males?[63]

1. Practical reasons: the priesthood is an occupation through which the father of a family must provide for his family; the slaying of larger animals is obviously regarded as an unfeminine task; women are too much taken up with the demands of motherhood; menstruation involves a relatively long lasting state of uncleanness (seven days per month), as does the period after the birth of a child.

2. Sociological reason: the patriarchal nature of the society.

Since the points just cited are applicable to the Canaanite environment as well, in which priestesses do occur, the decisive factor must have been:

---

[56] Ps 51:16, 19; Malachi 1:11.

[57] Cf. Gerhard von Rad, *Theologie des Alten Testaments I* [Theology of the Old Testament I], 7th ed. (Munich, 1978), pp. 254f.

[58] Heb 9:12.

[59] Cf. pp. 263ff., 332f. below.

[60] This precedence of the Aaronites within the Levites characterized at least the latter stages of development; cf. Gunneweg, *Leviten*, pp. 222f.

[61] J. Schildenberger, "Die Religion des Alten Testaments" [The religion of the Old Testament], in F. König, *Religionsgeschichte III*, p. 499.

[62] Schildenberger, "Religion", p. 499.

[63] On the following listing, cf. Vos, *Woman*, pp. 192–97.

3. Religious reasons: in Canaan, namely, a fertility cult was dominant in which sexual intercourse with temple prostitutes played a large role.[64] In Judaism, however, sexuality is not deified but is a relationship between created beings. Since the Canaanite female clergy was made up largely of prostitutes, eliminating female office was an important measure against the fertility religion.[65]

Naturally, these facts are not sufficient in themselves to prove that there was an internal necessity for the exclusion of women from Old Testament priestly office. Still, they could have been a means used by Divine Providence to prepare the way for the exclusion from New Testament priestly office. Whether or not this fact is an *essential* component of revelation will have to be investigated on the basis of the *New* Testament.

[64] Cf. the remarks on *Hieros Gamos*: p. 149 above.
[65] Vos, *Woman*, p. 194.

CHAPTER TWO

"Sexual" Traits in the Christian Image of God

I. GENERAL PREFATORY REMARKS

First of all, this should be stressed: in total contrast to the fertility cult that was dominant in the religious environment, Israel attributed absolutely no sexual traits to God. "Yahweh stood . . . beyond the polarity of the sexual, and this meant that Israel was prevented from regarding the sexual as a sacred mystery. It had no place in worship, because it was a phenomenon restricted to created beings."[1]

At the same time, Israel and (later on) the Church were not averse to speaking of God in images. It was clearly understood that such images had the character of analogies.[2] Analogies and symbols, however, mean a great deal for the effectiveness of revelation.[3] Every created thing reflects, in some way or another, the essence of the Creator and Redeemer. This is true in particular of man, the "image of God", whose being is made up, in part, of sexually differentiated corporeality.[4] Now, the specific natures of masculine and feminine are too deeply rooted to be explicable in terms of sociocultural conditioning. According to the biblical accounts of creation, they appear as nothing less than the fundamental interpersonal reality. Therefore, it is rash to explain biblical symbols as simply the mere expressions of a patriarchal society and to deny them any sort of significance for our image of God, so that this can then be reconstructed according to personal taste.[5]

---

[1] Von Rad, *Theologie I*, pp. 40f.

[2] Ex 20:4, Hos 11:9.

[3] Cf. pp. 121ff. above.

[4] Gen 1:27; 2:18–24; cf. p. 204 above.

[5] A. E. Carr, "The Church in Process: Engendering the future", in Gardiner, *Expanded Vision*, p. 82: "We in the Church strive to purify our religious language of the implications of patriarchal dominance, to find new words for God"; Russell, *Als Mann*. Similarly: G. H.

The basic structure behind the following investigations is provided by the doctrine of the Holy Trinity, with the Father being treated first, then the Son and finally the Holy Spirit. To this is linked the Old Testament preparation for the Mystery and its fulfillment in the New Covenant, as represented in Scripture, Tradition and the teachings of the Church. In all this, the central role will be played by the figure of Jesus Christ as image of the Father and emissary origin of the Holy Spirit, a role in which Christ's divine and human nature are joined in harmonious unity.

2. GOD AS FATHER

Old Testament preparation for the father image

The secondary significance of "father" as a form of address

In the ancient Orient, "father" was a widespread form of address for the Deity. There were divine forefathers of tribes, peoples and families, and kings often appear as representatives of a father god. In such cases, father

1. expresses a very naturalistically understood *relationship* between the divine and the human worlds, and
2. contains the components of *authority* and compassionate *benevolence*.[6]

In Israel, by contrast, the father image of God plays a comparatively narrow role: "The use of the biological concept, God as a father, gives most substantial emphasis to relationship with the Divinity as a generative blood relationship and thus reduces the feeling of distance between the created and the Creator."[7]

Jeremiah opposes those "who say to a tree, 'You are my father', and to a stone, 'You gave me birth' ".[8]

The image of father leads us, "according to its *root meaning* . . . , out of the sphere of a willed grounding [of being] and into that of a naturalistic one".[9] The father image certainly plays an important role in central

---

Tavard, "Sexist Language in Theology?" in W. J. Burghardt, ed., *Woman. New Dimensions* (New York, 1977), pp. 124–48.

[6] Joachim Jeremias, *Abba. Studien zur neutestamentlichen Theologie und Zeitgeschichte* [Abba. Studies in New Testament theology and cultural history] (Göttingen, 1966), p. 15.

[7] Schrenk, "πατήρ . . .", *ThW* V, p. 966.

[8] Jer 2:27.

[9] Johannes Hempel, *Gott und Mensch im Alten Testament. Studie zur Geschichte der Frömmig-*

passages of the Old Testament, as will be seen in more detail shortly, but there "assimilation [to it] of the creation idea has long since been accomplished".[10]

God is not connected with the world through physical procreation but rather has *created* all of nature in a sovereign way.[11] The people of Israel and their kings are God's sons not in the naturalistic sense but by virtue of having been adopted as such through an act of *historical choice*.[12]

To be sure, the concept of father, as such, is expressive of a certain power and transcendence; but because that concept is understood in a naturalistic way in the pagan world, it has been pushed more strongly into the background for the sake of God's supramundane status. Characteristic of transcendence are God's powerful *superiority to creation*, as grounded in an act of free determination, and his *intervention in history*. Therefore, the title of father does *not* belong "among the *characteristic* expressions of Israelite piety".[13]

God's transcendence as the center point of Old Testament theology

The first of Israel's names for God, which appears as early as the time of the patriarchs, is *"El"*.[14] As a generic term for a divinity, this word referred above all to the highest lord of the Canaanite pantheon, to El, the "father of gods and men".[15]

However, El came to play an increasingly limited role in piety, while his more vital son, the fertility god Baal, acquired greater significance: "Baal is the 'near', and El the 'far', god."[16] Because of his greater distance from the world, which is given expression in terms of creation (although this is understood as demiurgic), he appears as already anticipatory of a transcendent image of God.

In Israel, therefore, it was not Baal but El that was redefined as a result of revelation. The word probably derives from the root *'wl*, which

---

keit [God and man in the Old Testament. Study in the history of piety], 2nd ed. (Stuttgart, 1936), p. 171.

[10] Hempel, *Frömmigkeit*, p. 177.

[11] Gen 1; Is 45:12.

[12] Ex 4:22; 2 Sam 7:14.

[13] Hempel, *Frömmigkeit*, p. 172; cf. Lothar Perlitt, "Der Vater im Alten Testament" [The Father in the Old Testament], in Hubertus Tellenbach, ed., *Das Vaterbild in Mythos und Geschichte*. Ägypten, Griechenland, Altes Testament, Neues Testament [The father image in myth and history. Egypt, Greece, Old Testament, New Testament] (Stuttgart, 1976), p. 99.

[14] Gen 24:12; 46:1, 3, and others.

[15] Eliade, *Geschichte*, p. 145.

[16] W. H. Schmidt, *Alttestamentlicher Glaube in seiner Geschichte* [Old Testament belief in historical context], 2nd ed. (Neukirchen and Vluyn, 1975), p. 138.

roughly means "being strong, being foremost".[17] This attribute of *power* is also expressed in the predicates that are added to El: *El Elyon* = "the highest"[18] and *El Shaddai* = "the powerful, almighty";[19] the latter designation is probably associated with the notion of a majestic mountain range.[20] Precisely here, being almighty appears not "as one attribute of God's . . . among many", but is "experienced as being the one that makes God godly".[21]

The idea of transcendence shows itself most clearly, however, in the plural, *Elohim*, which is particularly characteristic of Israel. Elohim means " 'God as such', 'essence of everything godly', 'the only one that is at all' "; "*'Ihym* is thus the essence of all power and powers."[22] The word touches closely on the proper name for God, Yahweh, with which it is often linked in addressing him and which it can even replace altogether in the elohistic part of the psalter.[23]

As a result of the revelation to Moses, God as *Yahweh* comes to eclipse all other predicates. Its use is therefore grounded in *history* as effected by God.[24] The interpretation in the Bible traces the name (YHWH) back to the root *hyh* (or *hwh*), which means "to be there, to exist". Being is probably used here in a causative sense: "being effective".[25]

God's effective power is also mirrored in the personal cast of the name: "*I am who I am!*"[26] Through his absolute being-as-I, which is expressed in the words *ani hu* = "I am", God is the Lord of history, who has led his people, "with a mighty hand",[27] out of the slave house of Egypt.[28] This fundamental historical miracle implies an everlasting power to effect all things: "I, I am the Lord, and besides me there is no savior."[29]

Yahweh is linked time and again with "Zebaoth" (Sabaoth): *"Lord of hosts"*. This is accompanied by associations of a mighty field army,[30] of a

[17] Paul van Imschoot and Herbert Haag, "El", in Haag, *Bibellexikon*, p. 374.

[18] Gen 14:19–20; cf. H. J. Kraus, *Theologie der Psalmen* [Theology of the Psalms], BK XV 3 (Neukirchen and Vluyn, 1979), p. 27.

[19] Herbert Haag, "Schaddai", in Haag, *Bibellexikon*, p. 1530.

[20] Cf. Jerusalem Bible on Gen 17:1.

[21] Schmaus, *Glaube II*, p. 15.

[22] Kraus, *Theologie*, p. 24.

[23] Kraus, *Theologie*, p. 24.

[24] Ex 3:13–16.

[25] The difficult detailed problems surrounding the interpretation of God's name cannot be gone into here; cf. on this the brief outline by Paul van Imschoot and Herbert Haag, "Yahweh", in Haag, *Bibellexikon*, pp. 796–98.

[26] Ex 3:14.

[27] Dt 4:34; 5:15; cf. Ex 3:19.

[28] Ex 20:2.

[29] Is 43:11.

[30] 1 Sam 17:45.

heavenly host of angels endowed with superhuman power[31] and, not least, by the vision of a starry heaven that extends infinitely above and beyond the little world of men.[32]

Heaven, in the Old Testament, is *the* absolute symbol of God. God created heaven and earth[33] and is their Lord; heaven and earth, however, are not both equally emblematic of him, but only heaven, which appears as his "place of residence". From an infinite height, so to speak, God looks down at mankind,[34] which is as much as nothing before him: "Behold, the nations are like a drop from a bucket, and are accounted as the dust on the scales; behold, he takes up the isles like fine dust. . . . All the nations are as nothing before him; they are accounted by him as less than nothing and emptiness."[35]

It is unusually significant that the heaven symbol comes to the fore here. For, in the Canaanite religion, there were deities that were connected with heaven *and* earth. To be sure, God is also Lord over earth, but, as opposed to heaven, earth is not his symbol. Heaven is so closely associated with God that it can be treated as equivalent to the name of God.[36] Yahweh is the "God of heaven".[37]

Given this thought context for the divine name Yahweh, it is no wonder that the Septuagint translates that name as "*Kyrios*": "the Lord". This quite reasonable transposition is already suggested by the Hebrew titles for God; Baal = "owner" (rare) and Adon(ai) = "commander"; later on, whenever the tetragrammaton occurs, the synagogue almost always reads Adonai.

Ludwig Köhler therefore formulates the *sententia communis* of Old Testament exegesis as follows: "That God is the commanding Lord—this is the one, fundamental tenet behind the theology of the Old Testament."[38]

The same idea is attested to by the title *King*: "Who is the King of glory? The Lord, strong and mighty, the Lord, mighty in battle!"[39]

God's rulership appears as a demand with respect to man, who is held responsible before God: "Say among the nations, 'The Lord reigns! . . . He will judge the peoples with equity.' "[40]

---

[31] Ps 103:21; 148:2.

[32] Cf. Ps 8:3–4 with Is 40:26 and Jer 33:22.

[33] Gen 14:19; Ps 121:2.

[34] Ps 33:13–14; 104:3, 13.

[35] Is 40:15, 17.

[36] Dan 4:23; Ps 73:9; 1 Macc 3:18. In the context of a tendency to use God's name only indirectly, Matthew changes the notion of the Kingdom of God to the Kingdom of heaven.

[37] Ezra 7:12, 21.

[38] Ludwig Köhler, *Theologie des Alten Testaments* [Theology of the Old Testament], 4th ed. (Tübingen, 1966), p. 12; Kraus, *Theologie*, p. 35.

[39] Ps 24:8.

[40] Ps 96:10; [cited in the original German version of this book as:] translated according to

The highest expression of Yahweh's transcendence is his *holiness*,[41] a predicate that is attributed—by contrast with other religions—in an absolute sense to God alone.[42] Already in the Old Testament, holiness, similarly to almightiness, is "not just one characteristic of God's among others. Rather, it is the one that enables God to appear as God."[43]

The word probably stems from "to isolate, to separate off", and means that which is elevated above the world, the "uncreated and totally inaccessible majesty (of God), by force of which everything else (the created) stands opposed to him as absolutely unholy".[44]

Moral injunction is not identical with holiness, but is always bound up with it: "the Lord of hosts is exalted in justice, and the Holy God shows himself holy in righteousness."[45]

Holiness is "just the negative expression of a perfect inner power and plenitude . . . which brings man to his knees", makes him "tremble" and "summons him to the religious act of respect and submission".[46]

The Old Testament father symbol
as a reflection of transcendence

The majestic, transcendent cast of the Old Testament image of God is also reflected in the father symbol. Both of the two elements that are constitutive of any father image, *power* (authority) and *benevolence*,[47] occur here as well and are closely intertwined with each other. The concept father, or its correlate son always makes its appearance in an act of historical choice, with reference to either Israel[48] or the king.[49] At the same time, it serves as

Alfons Deissler, *Die Psalmen* [The Psalms], 2nd ed. (Düsseldorf, 1977), p. 377: cf. Kraus, *Theologie*, p. 35.

[41] Johann Auer, *Gott—der Eine und Dreieine* [God—One and Triune], KKD II (Regensburg, 1978), p. 146.

[42] Cf. esp. Is 6:3; Paul van Imschoot and Herbert Haag, "Heilig" [Holy], in Haag, *Bibellexikon*, p. 687.

[43] Michael Schmaus, *Katholische Dogmatik I* [Catholic dogmatics I], 6th ed. (Munich, 1960), p. 565.

[44] Imschoot and Haag, "Heilig", p. 687.

[45] Is 5:16; similarly, Ezek 28:22, 25. Cf. also Imschoot and Haag, "Heilig", p. 688.

[46] Scheffczyk, *Gott*, p. 94; cf. Leo Scheffczyk, "Die Heiligkeit Gottes: Ziel und Form christlichen Seins" [The holiness of God: end and form of Christian existence], in Leo Scheffczyk, *Glaube als Lebensinspiration. Gesammelte Schriften zur Theologie* [Faith as inspiration for life. Collected theological writings] Sammlung Horizonte, Neue Folge 18 (Einsiedeln, 1980), pp. 153–68.

[47] Cf. Leeuw, *Phänomenologie*, p. 199; Antonie Wlosok, "Vater und Vatervorstellungen in der römischen Kultur" [Father and father images in Roman culture], in Hubertus Tellenbach, ed., *Das Vaterbild im Abendland I* [The father image in the Western world I] (Stuttgart, 1978), p. 52.

[48] Ex 4:22; Dt 1:31; Jer 31:9.

[49] 2 Sam 7:14; Ps 2:7.

an (admittedly demythologized) image of divine creative activity.[50] Precisely the prophets, who repeatedly make strong attacks on pagan religiosity, are especially bold in applying the purified symbol to God:

> When Israel was a child, I loved him, and out of Egypt I called my son. The more I called them, the more they went from me; they kept sacrificing to the Baals and burning incense to idols. Yet it was I who taught Ephraim to walk; I took them up in my arms; but they did not know that I healed them. I led them with cords of compassion, with the bands of love, and I became to them as one who eases the yoke on their jaws, and I bent down to them and fed them. . . . My heart recoils within me; my compassion grows warm and tender.[51]

Benevolence and mercifulness come together here. However, God's love is voluntary and powerful, a free one and no mere infatuation. In Hosea, where God's paternal qualities are perhaps described more feelingly than anywhere else, the following occurs several verses later: "They shall go after the Lord; he will roar like a lion; yes, he will roar, and his sons shall come trembling from the west."[52]

Mercifulness is seen together with righteousness: "The Lord has an indictment against Judah and will punish Jacob according to his deeds." To the ungrateful, "I will be . . . like a lion; like a leopard I will lurk beside the way."[53]

In Third Isaiah, God's mercifulness is directly linked to his creative power, which—like the potter with his clay—has Israel at its free disposal: "The yearning of your heart and your compassion are withheld from me. For you are our Father. . . . O Lord, you are our Father; we are the clay, and you are our potter; we are all the work of your hand."[54]

Similarly in Jeremiah: "Behold, like the clay in the potter's hand, so are you in my hand, O house of Israel."[55] I "am a father to Israel, and Ephraim is my firstborn".[56]

The accent in the father image is on authority. That is already evident from the fact that "strict reserve regarding the expression of feeling [is] far more characteristic of the *relationship of son to father* than of the attitude of father toward son".[57] In the Psalms, therefore, there are just two instances of address in which God is referred to as Father; the first is only a simile,

---

[50] Dt 32:6; Malachi 2:10.
[51] Hos 11:1–4, 8. Cf. Jer 31:9; Is 63:15; 64:7; Malachi 1:6; 2:10.
[52] Hos 11:10.
[53] Hos 12:3; 13:7.
[54] Is 63:15–16; 64:8. Cf. Is 29:16; 45:9.
[55] Jer 18:6.
[56] Jer 31:9.
[57] Schrenk, πατήρ, p. 970.

and the second is not a genuine predication because it relates to children without parents:[58] "As a father pities his children, so the Lord pities those who fear him."[59] "Father of the fatherless . . . is God in his holy habitation."[60]

Mercy is linked here, as well, to the *mysterium tremendum* (fear of God) and to supramundane holiness. The one direct instance of address as Father is in reference to the king, who, by contrast with the people, stands in an especially strongly emphasized relationship to God:[61] "He shall cry to me, 'You are my Father, my God and the Rock of my salvation.' "[62]

God's benevolence is thus always linked together with his omnipotence. In this, the two qualities are by no means competitors, since the greater the benevolence, the stronger the omnipotence through which it is effected. "For as his majesty is, so also is his mercy."[63] The intensity of the benevolence is grounded in its infinite buttress, in immeasurable divine power. Apart from the effective power that underlies it, paternal love would be incomprehensible.

Transcendence as the inner ground of immanence: "the mother symbol inheres in the father symbol"

The foregoing observations can be applied analogically to the relation between righteousness and mercifulness, but also, in general, to the relation immanence-transcendence.

Israel's (and the world's) state of being sustained is expressed in a particularly effective way through comparisons drawn from *shepherding*: "He will feed his flock like a shepherd; he will gather the lambs in his arms; he will carry them in his bosom and gently lead those that are with young."[64]

Arm and hand, in Semitic thought, are "seen so much as a unity that they are often regarded as interchangeable";[65] in the passage just cited, this connection leads, as mediated by the terms in question, to the following statement: "Who has measured the waters in the hollow of his hand and marked off the heavens with a span, enclosed the dust of the earth in a measure and weighed the mountains in scales and the hills in a balance?"[66]

---

[58] Kraus, *Theologie*, p. 35.

[59] Ps 103:13.

[60] Ps 68:5.

[61] 2 Sam 7:14.

[62] Ps 89:26.

[63] Sir 2:18.

[64] Is 40:11; cf. Jer 31:10; Ezek 34:12.

[65] Arie van den Born and Herbert Haag, "Hand", in Haag, *Bibellexikon*, p. 661.

[66] Is 40:12.

Thus, the *"hand"* of God confers security and protection precisely by virtue of the fact that it is possessed of infinite power; it is not a tender, feminine hand, but rather, a forceful, masculine one.[67]

Effective power, however, is surely an inherent aspect of the image of a shepherd, for the good shepherd is not the rather silly daydreamer that our contemporaries imagine him to be, but rather—as has been observed with a touch of humor—the "good cowboy", who protects his drove and guides it through all dangers: "It is a *forceful*, and not a sentimental, image!"[68]

In feminist theology and the immanence religions outlined earlier, the *earth* is seen as symbolic of the maternal primal ground that serves to confer security. Interestingly enough, however, this typically feminine image is not found in Israel, although God's sustaining and protecting immanence is quite intensely experienced: "If I ascend to heaven, you are there! If I make my bed in Sheol, you are there! . . . For you formed my inward parts; you knit me together in my mother's womb."[69] "On you was I cast from my birth, and since my mother bore me you have been my God."[70]

Instead of the earth, we encounter again and again a related, but at the same time distinctly different, symbol: the *rock*. "My God, my rock, in whom I take refuge"—thus reads one of the oldest songs of thanksgiving,[71] and the image recurs in numerous other Psalms. In parallel with this, there often occurs the image of the *fortress*, which no attack, by even the most powerful of enemies, can conquer.[72] More clearly than is the case with the image of the earth, security appears, in this case, as consequent on an immeasurable strength; transcendence is, in a sense, the pillar on which immanence rests.

I have chosen only a few, although definitely central and typical, symbols here in order to illustrate concretely the relation between transcendence and immanence in the Old Testament image of God; the list could be expanded at will. Over and over again, it becomes evident that divine immanence presupposes transcendence and, as "power-charged"

---

[67] What is involved here is a virtually classical biblical symbol. The same associations that appear in Isaiah 40 crop up again, in the New Testament, in John 10:28–29, where the "hand" occurs with reference to the Son and the Father: "no one shall snatch them out of my hand . . . and no one is able to snatch them out of the Father's hand". In the Old Testament, cf. Dt 33:3; Is 51:16; Song 3:1, and elsewhere.

[68] Hempel, *Frömmigkeit*, p. 181.

[69] Ps 139:8, 13.

[70] Ps 22:10.

[71] Ps 18:2; cf. 2 Sam 22.

[72] Ps 18:2, 71:3, and elsewhere.

immanence, is delineated through symbols of a masculine nature: father, shepherd, protecting hand and so forth.

If, in the earlier sections on phenomenology of religion, I have characterized women as representative of divine immanence and men as representative of transcendence, it is not therefore permissible to draw the conclusion that the representations of transcendence and of immanence can be divided up *pari cum pari*. Also, this is not just a matter of more strongly accentuating transcendence, which would be symbolically connected with men, who would then be able to represent immanence only in a secondary way. Rather, as is evident precisely from the example of the Old Testament, immanence is a component part of transcendence and, as such, presupposes its existence. Accordingly, the Old Testament does *not* place the *father and the mother symbolisms* for God *next to each other, but* slots them, as it were, *into one another*: the "mother symbol [inheres] in the father symbol".[73]

A "patriarchal image of God" in the Old Testament?[74]

Thus, it is obvious that the Old Testament image of God presents itself as decidedly masculine. God, therefore, is also always designated as he and not as she.[75] Under the sway of a very strongly developed social-historical mode of thought, people generally like to trace this fact back to the patriarchal society of those times. In fact, many of the images in question were surely partly conditioned by patriarchal influences. The Israelite king, in particular, appears as an absolute monarch, who is often able to decide over the life and death of his subjects;[76] so-called modern man, however, is—as people say—accustomed to democratic ways (or, as the case may be, regards them as ideals).

As well, the power of the father appears greater than it is among us; "servant" and "son" are at times interchangeable terms.[77] Therefore, Haye van der Meer indicates that a revision of the symbolism is needed: "The male is no longer as much the type model of Christ as was once the case. That role has been taken over by the community. Large and small landholders were actually heads. Workers in factories or offices today are

---

[73] Leese, *Mutter*, p. 35.

[74] Cf. pp. 183f. above.

[75] This is so disturbing to female feminist theologians that they replace the term, in their own translations of the Bible, with "he/she" or "he and she". Cf. esp. Russell, "Sprachveränderung", p. 74.

[76] Cf. Hempel, *Frömmigkeit*, p. 179.

[77] 2 Kings 16:7, for example; cf. Schrenk, πατήρ, pp. 970f.

numbers. And the state is no longer ruled by a prince but by a majority of election ballots."[78]

In feminist theology, moreover, even more radically, the father image of God is seen as an ideological "superstructure of a system of male domination".[79]

That criticism would seem to have overlooked the basic assumptions of hermeneutics. For the symbol is always bound up from the start with a specific idea, and its content is an unerring component of Holy Scripture as inspired by the Holy Spirit. The Second Vatican Council designated as a permanent and central Church doctrine the fact that "everything asserted by the inspired authors or hagiographers is to be taken as having been asserted by the Holy Spirit".[80]

In interpreting the symbol, the most that we can do, if the case so requires, is to transpose its imaged garb but not its content. Thus, for example, it might be possible, in the way done above, to turn the "good shepherd" into the "good cowboy" in order to elucidate God's powerfully protective aspect.[81]

Those who are unsympathetic to "father" or "king" would be obliged to look for alternative symbols, although these could not then be such as to point us toward an antiauthoritarian, maternal energy source of all being but would have to give clear and primary emphasis to the notion of omnipotence. Still, the images cited would appear, today as much as ever, to be indispensable—even that of king, in the name of which a special celebration was held in the Church as recently as 1925 (when actual worldly kings had largely disappeared from the scene). In arranging this, Pius XI was not intending to revive monarchy as a political system, but the μοναρχία of God. It is probably all but impossible to imagine the all-powerful, universal God in terms of a symbol such as, for example, the popularly elected president of a country. That God should be required to adapt to democratic conventions is hair-raising nonsense even from a purely philosophical perspective, not to mention from the standpoint of a theology of revelation.[82]

In ancient Israel, people already knew quite well how to distinguish

---

[78] Meer, *Priesturtum*, p. 138.

[79] Ruether, *Frauen*, p. 12.

[80] Dei Verbum 11, in Rahner-Vorgrimler, *Konzilskompendium*, pp. 373f.; *AAS* 58 (1966): 823.

[81] Whether or not *this* particular translation is especially felicitous need not be gone into here.

[82] Kurt Marti, however, makes a "theodemocracy" out of "Thy kingdom come" (Mt 6:10): "Thy democracy come"! Kurt Marti, *Zärtlichkeit und Schmerz. Notizen* [Tenderness and pain. Notes], 4th ed. (Darmstadt and Neuwied, 1980), p. 119.

between a symbol and its symbolic content. King Yahweh was kept well elevated above the secular king, who was seen as but a pale representative of divine power; thus symbol-intensifying titles were used such as "King of glory" and "Lord of hosts".[83]

The questionable nature of the theses under scrutiny here can be demonstrated more clearly through the figure of the father than through the image of a king. For, in the course of the over one thousand years of Israelite history, the role of father seems to have undergone social transformations that were at least as profound as those that occurred during the last two hundred years in Europe and North America. Between the patriarch Abraham, who was head of an entire clan, and a peasant or farmhand of the seventh century, for instance, there was a gap involving considerable differences. In the time of Solomon, the power of the state (and not only of the king as an individual) was very much greater than is the case in Western countries today, and yet it occurred to no one then to regard the community as a symbol of God. Precisely in that day, "with the increasing independence of the individual person vis-à-vis his living group and thus vis-à-vis his family", the transition from larger to smaller families had the "effect of narrowing the headship and sovereignty of the 'father' ".[84]

The critique of the divine father image would seem to skip over not only the theological, but also even the anthropological fundamentals. For, with respect to the human father figure, there is a bipolarity of authority and benevolence, of transcendence and immanence, in which the forceful traits take precedence. Even at the level of the basic biological and psychological questions, as covered in some detail above, his functions are characteristic and nonexchangeable. The social roles are played out within a preexisting framework that has never disappeared, even under a matriarchate. Personal paternal authority, which is not to be confused with paternalism, will never be totally replaced by a society consisting of brothers.[85] If the father is liquidated, authority is quickly transferred to the all-powerful Moloch of the state: "Big Brother is watching you" (George Orwell).[86]

The modern (?) crisis of authority thus serves, in a sense, as the forestructure for feminist theology. Theology presupposes anthropology:

---

[83] For example, Ps 24:7; 103:21.

[84] Hempel, *Frömmigkeit*, p. 171.

[85] Cf. p. 337, n. 105 below.

[86] Scheffczyk, "Wesen", p. 53: when fatherhood and power are discredited, it can be "recognized that this only serves to deprive certifiable, individual power of its legitimacy in favor of anonymous powers and forces".

if the philosophical foundations are unsound, the roof of the doctrine of revelation cannot be built on them: *Gratia supponit naturam*.[87]

"God is also mother"?

What is at issue

The figure of the divine Father, as we meet with it in the Old Testament, is not balanced out by the figure of a divine mother, since the father, and masculine images, predominate. There are, to be sure, traces of maternal symbolism, and this has led some contemporary theologians to ask whether those characteristics ought not to be given new emphasis.[88] Occasionally, the suggestion is also made that there are two traditions in

[87] That this Scholastic axiom does not involve "split-level thinking", but rather, along with the ontological difference, implies an intimate interwovenness of both regions should have been made clear by the example of my relevant comments.

[88] Besides feminist theology in the strict sense, see (among others): Protestantism (or Anglicanism): Barnhouse, "Examination"; Ernst Benz, "Ist der Heilige Geist weiblich? Logos—Sophia—Heiliger Geist" [Is the Holy Spirit female? Logos—Sophia—Holy Spirit], *Antaios* 7 (1966); 452–75; Kurt Lüthi, *Gottes neue Eva. Wandlungen des Weiblichen* [God's new Eve. Transformations of the feminine] (Stuttgart, 1978); Kurt Lüthi, "Was bedeutet die zunehmende Bewusstwerdung der Frau für die Theologie und die Erneuerung der Kirche?" [What significance does women's increasing consciousness have for theology and the renewal of the Church?], *US* 35 (1980): 344–51; Marti, *Zärtlichkeit*; F. K. Mayr, "Trinitätstheologie und theologische Anthropologie" [Trinitarian theology and theological anthropology], *ZThK* 68 (1971): 427–77; F. K. Mayr, "Patriarchalisches Gottesverständnis? Historische Erwägungen zur Trinitätslehre" [Patriarchal understanding of God? Historical reflections on the doctrine of the Trinity], *ThQ* 152 (1972): 224–55; Schipflinger, "Aspekt"; Schrey, "Gott"; Paul Tillich, *Systematische Theologie III* [Systematic theology III] (Stuttgart, 1966), pp. 333–37.

On the Catholic side: Wolfgang Beinert, "Unsere Liebe Frau und die Frauen. Ein mariologischer Beitrag zur theologischen Anthropologie" [Our Lady and women. A mariological contribution to theological anthropology], *Die Frau in Kirche und Gesellschaft: Lebendiges Zeugnis* 35 (3/1980): 29f., 41, 43f., 99 (discussion of Greeley); K. E. Borresen, "Männlich-Weiblich: eine Theologiekritik" [Masculine-feminine: a critique of theology], *US* 35 (1980): 325–34; Barbara Gerl, "Frau und Theologie: Anzeichen eines neuen Bewusstseins?" [Women and theology: signs of a new consciousness?], *US* 35 (1980): 291–95; Greeley, *Maria*; G.-K. Kaltenbrunner, "Ist der Heilige Geist weiblich?" [Is the Holy Spirit female?], *US* 32 (1977): 273–79; Walter Kasper, "Die Stellung der Frau als Problem der theologischen Anthropologie" [The position of women as a problem of theological anthropology], *Die Frau in Kirche und Gesellschaft: Lebendiges Zeugnis* 35 (3/1980): 8; Ursula King, "Geschlechtliche Differenzierung und christliche Anthropologie. Auf der Suche nach einer integralen Spiritualität" [Sexual differentiation and Christian anthropology. In search of an integral spirituality], *US* 35 (1980): 335–43; Heribert Mühlen, "Der Heilige Geist und Maria" [The Holy Spirit and Mary], *Catholica* 29 (1975): 147–51; P. Schmidt, *Vater*; Eulogia Wurz, "Das Mütterliche in Gott" [The motherly in God], *US* 32 (1977): 261–72.

the Old Testament, one supposedly being patriarchal, and the other supposedly breaking away from that context. To revelation belong, then, only the "nonpatriarchal aspects of Tradition", in which the notion of the motherhood of God is contained.[89]

Isaiah 49:14–15

There are two passages in the Old Testament in which God is compared to a mother;[90] the better-known one reads: "But Zion said, 'The Lord has forsaken me; my Lord has forgotten me.' Can a woman forget her nursing child, that she should have no compassion on the son of her womb? Even these may forget, yet I will not forget you."[91]

This passage is concerned with God's pledge to lead his people out of exile in Babylon. His promise is couched in terms of infinite love: "For a brief moment I forsook you, but with great compassion I will gather you. In overflowing wrath for a moment I hid my face from you, but with everlasting love I will have compassion on you, says the Lord, your Redeemer."[92]

This caring benevolence can therefore be rightly compared to the love "of a mother . . . regarding whom it is impossible to imagine how she could abandon her children, who are so much a part of her".[93] The loving care of a mother is the most intimate kind of love known to man.[94]

However, this passage from Isaiah cannot be taken as justifying the

---

[89] G. H. Tavard, *Woman in Christian Tradition* (Notre Dame, 1973), p. 17; Elisabeth Schüssler Fiorenza, "Interpretation patriarchalischer Traditionen" [Interpretation of patriarchal traditions], in Russell, *Als Mann*, p. 51; Hanson, "Metaphors", pp. 316ff.

[90] Is 66:13; 49:14–15.

[91] Is 49:14–15.

[92] Is 54:7–8.

[93] Bouyer, *Woman in the Church*, p. 30.

[94] In order to give expression to this caring aspect of God, *Pope John Paul I*, in an address for the Angelus on September 10, 1978, cited our Isaiah passage and stated, with a view to concern for peace: "We are the object of God's everlasting love. . . . He is our Father; still more, he is also a mother to us" (*Botschafter des Evangeliums. Ansprachen Johannes Paul I.* [Messenger of the gospel. Addresses of John Paul I] [Paderborn, 1978], p. 51). This form of words is a paraphrase of the biblical text that is quite familiar to Catholic Tradition, and only a certain feminist oversensitivity could seize on it as something of significance for the feminist cause. The Pope did not call here for a *pari cum pari* between addressing God as Father and as mother, and he most certainly did not maintain that God is more mother than Father. After the comparison to a mother, this is what he concludes: just as children have a right to maternal love, so we, too, have a "right to be loved by the *Lord*" (ibid., emphasis mine).

assumption that God can be addressed as a mother. Jesus and Paul, in the New Testament, are compared to a mother in a much clearer way,[95] yet their maleness cannot be called into question. Admittedly, the titles "Mother Jesus" and "Mother Paul" crop up occasionally later on as forms of address, but they have no centrally definitive relative worth. In Second Isaiah, the situation is similar. Naturally, God is not a man, but it is no coincidence that he appears, symbolically, as primarily endowed with masculine traits. The mother image is thus a merely indirect sort. God is *not expressly* compared to a mother, and the relevant symbolic gap is specifically emphasized: "Even these may forget, yet I will not forget you."

The mother image in the cited passage has to be seen in the context of the predominant masculine references. At the end of the section, God is abundantly described as the "Mighty One of Jacob", who will dispossess the king of Babylon of his spoils.[96] Just one verse after the cited passage, it is said: "Behold I have graven you on the palms of my hands; your walls are continually before me"[97]; and a bit later: "Behold, I will lift up my hand to the nations, and raise my signal to the peoples."[98]

As an expression of mercy, we thus find here the symbol of the protective and powerful paternal hand.[99]

It is especially necessary, however, to pay attention to the *"basic axis"* of the sexual symbolism in Second Isaiah. It consists in the fact that God is described as the husband of Israel, of "daughter Zion": "For your Maker is your husband. . . . For the Lord has called you like a wife forsaken and grieved in spirit, like a wife of youth when she is cast off."[100]

The context here becomes fully clear when, in the introduction to the mother image, the (female) daughter Zion appears as the speaker and, a few verses later, is described as the bride of God.[101] The mother symbol thus has to be integrated into, and subordinated to, the basic axis: husband/(father)–bride/(daughter).

[95] Cf. pp. 271f. below.
[96] Is 49:26.
[97] Is 49:16.
[98] Is 49:22.
[99] Cf. p. 224 above.
[100] Is 54:5–6.
[101] Is 49:18.

Israel as "daughter" and "son": a relativization of the sexual symbolism?

But—in all of this, may we not have biologized the image of God in an unacceptable way? For, in the Old Testament, and particularly in Second Isaiah, it is quite noticeable that "Israel is referred to both as masculine and as feminine: Israel is made to appear now as daughter, now as son and also as bride. The images are always changing; one alone does not itself express matters with any great stringency."[102] Consequently, according to Schoonenberg, we must not sexualize the Old Testament image of God, but must rather personalize it.[103]

This objection, however, does not do justice to the nature of the symbolism. The concepts son and daughter, or bride, as descriptions of Israel, are not simply interchangeable, but possess in each case their own particular meaning. The feminine predicates bride and daughter Zion are used for Israel as a whole only insofar as it is required to show submissive openness to God's active will.

On the other hand, the concept son, since the time of kings, refers in a particularly concentrated way to the king, who, as a single figure, re-presents the Kingdom of God before the people.[104] The traditions of Zion and David are closely connected in later times, but even at the level of their symbolisms, they are not identical.[105]

The songs of the Lord's servant in Second Isaiah apply the title to a particular figure who, as son, is supposed to mediate God's glad tidings to the nations.[106] The Lord's servant is not only—like the daughter Zion—a personification of Israel, but also stands out from the people

1. as the one who "makes himself an offering [for the many] for sin"[107] and
2. as the representative of God before his people.[108]

In the son, then, the two fundamental strands of priestly representation

---

[102] Meer, *Priesturtum*, p. 164. Similarly, Thierry Maertens, *La promotion de la femme dans la Bible. Ses applications au mariage et au ministère* (Paris, 1967), p. 116. For this author there is no difference at all between the expressive content of masculine and feminine symbolisms: Maertens, *Promotion*, pp. 114, 211, 214.

[103] Meer, *Priesturtum*, p. 166.

[104] 2 Sam 14:17; Is 9:5; 1 Chron 28:5.

[105] Cf. Rad, *Theologie II*, pp. 303f.

[106] Is 42:6; 49:6.

[107] Is 53:10.

[108] Is 42:6; 49:5–6; 53:6, 8, 12.

are prefigured[109] that we will meet with again in Christ;[110] the concept of daughter, or bride, does not have this stamp.

That the biological symbols are closely tied to their personal expressive content is shown as well by the following considerations:

1. The corresponding concept to son (= Israel) in the Old Testament image of God is never mother, or father and mother,[111] but only father.
2. The images of bride for Israel and bridegroom for God, which remain to be discussed, are not interchangeable.

Isaiah 66:13

The second, above-named passage comes from the third part of the Book of Isaiah. In contrast to the passage from Second Isaiah, what we have here is an extended simile, in which God is referred to as mother—the only analogy of that sort, by the way, in the entire Old Testament.[112] The background to these statements is no longer exile but the threatened situation of the people following the return from Babylon. In an apocalyptic poem, Israel is urged to have courage. The daughter Zion appears here, in an unprecedented way, as mother of the people:

> That you may suck and be satisfied with her consoling breasts; that you may drink deeply with delight from the abundance of her glory. For thus says the Lord: . . . and you shall suck; you shall be carried on her hips and dandled on her knees.[113]

Here the mother symbol is thus clearly applied to Israel; immediately after that come the statements in question: "As one whom his mother comforts, so I will comfort you; you shall be comforted in Jerusalem."[114]

The application of the mother symbol to God here is obviously not a totally independent occurrence but is derived from the maternal characteristics of the daughter *Zion*. The primary subject of the expression mother, in the given context, is not God but a human reality that is sustained through divine activity. Thus it is also said that the comfort comes to Israel through Jerusalem = Zion.[115] The mother thus appears as

[109] Cf. pp. 190f. above.
[110] Cf. pp. 263ff. below.
[111] Also not in Ps 27:10.
[112] Hempel, *Frömmigkeit*, p. 185, n. 1.
[113] Is 66:11–12.
[114] Is 66:13.
[115] Or "in" Jerusalem.

a creaturely entity that is permitted, in a certain way, to transmit God's gifts of grace. Zion is a figurative type of the Mother of God and of the Church, similarly to the way in which the son, in Second Isaiah, is interpretable as a prefiguration of Christ.

Thus, it is only through certain roundabout ways that God is here compared to a mother, whereas, in Third Isaiah, the father title is directly applied to God and even—which never occurs with the mother symbol— appears as a form of address for God: "The yearning of your heart and your compassion are withheld from me. For you are our Father."[116]

The *basic axis* of the sexual symbolism here (somewhat differently accentuated than in Second Isaiah) is: father/(husband)–daughter/mother/ (bride).[117]

The "maternal mercy of God"?

As a virtually standard formula within vulgarized Old Testament theology, the claim is made again and again these days that maternal symbolism is implicit in the notion of the "mercifulness" of God: "The connection between our experience of mothers and the image of God is indicated . . . by the Hebrew root word for mercy (*raḥamīm* pl.), which goes back to *reḥäm* (maternal womb). 'Therefore, all the passages that refer in this way to the mercy of God could be translated as "the maternal mercy of God".' "[118]

Based on this maternal mercifulness of God, the conclusion is then sometimes drawn that priestly office must be made representative of this divine trait by being opened up to female membership: "It would seem both logical and theological . . . to expect in the official ministry of the Church a female element to reflect this maternal attribute of God's mercy."[119]

This thesis is correct to the extent that *raḥamīm* (mercy), taken from a purely structural viewpoint, forms the plural of *reḥem*, which does, in fact, mean "maternal womb" or (as *pars pro toto*) "woman".[120]

---

[116] Is 63:15–16; cf. 64:8. This comparison is already anticipated in Isaiah 1:2.

[117] Israel as mother, in addition to Isaiah 66:11ff.: 60:4, 9; 66:7–9; a starting point already in Second Isaiah: 54:1. As bride: 61:10; 62:4–5.

[118] P. Schmidt, *Vater*, p. 132. Schmidt refers to A. Höfer and A. Höfler, *Das Glauben lernen* [Learn to believe] (Donauwörth, 1973), p. 23. Similarly, Wurz, "Mütterliche", p. 262; Katappo, *Free*, p. 66.

[119] Hannon, *Question*, p. 133.

[120] Cf. Wilhelm Gesenius, *Hebräisches und aramäisches Handwörterbuch über das Alte Testament* [Hebrew and Aramaic dictionary of the Old Testament] (Berlin, Göttingen and Heidelberg, 1962 rpt.), p. 755; Ludwig Köhler and Walter Baumgartner, *Lexicon in Veteris*

However, the plural signifies, in a very general sense, not specifically feminine attributes, but all of the soft organs situated in the abdomen or in the inside of the body, especially the intestines. These parts of the body, in a broader sense, appear "as the organic site of the process that occurs in it", namely, "sympathy" and, especially, "mercy".[121]

Such mercy is attributable chiefly to a mother, but is also applied in a characteristic way to a father. In connection with God, it is *only* the father that is identified as the emotional subject of mercy.[122] Mercy appears precisely as a specifically *paternal* quality.

The word signifies, in general, "the 'soft place' in a person's nature".[123] The origin of the concept, therefore, is probably not the already quite specialized word maternal womb. Rather, what appears more as a general term embracing maternal womb and intestines or mercy is the root word *rhm*, which approximately means "to be soft".[124]

Being soft refers by nature more to a mother than to a father. The primally human associations mother–mercifulness and father–justice are therefore not just pure inventions. Nevertheless, regarding the Old Testament image of God, we find only the father referred to by *rhm*. This striking fact requires specific explanation:

> In the Old Testament, *rhm* is always used by the higher of the lower, never by man of God.[125] Four-fifths of the textual occurrences of *rhm pi.*[126] have God as the subject. . . . The texts in Hosea show that, when Yahweh's activity is described in terms of *rhm pi.*, this indicates the introduction (or reintroduction) into the situation of a childlike relationship . . . , which is not just sentimental, but thoroughly real.[127]

However, condescension, as a conscious act, is more strongly associated with a father than with a mother, who remains more closely tied to her child. In the mercy of a *father*, then, "the element of will inherent in this love" is "more strongly marked".[128]

Testamenti Libros (Leiden, 1953), p. 886; Eduard König, *Hebräisches und aramäisches Wörterbuch zum Alten Testament* [Hebrew and Aramaic dictionary of the Old Testament], 6/7th ed. (Wiesbaden, 1969 rpt.), pp. 439f.; Franciscus Zorell, ed., *Lexicon Hebraicum et Aramaicum Veteris Testamenti* (Rome, 1948), p. 767.

[121] E. König, *Wörterbuch*, pp. 439f. Meaningfully expressed, too, in Zorell, *Lexicon*, p. 767: *raḥamīm* = "*viscera, cor, ut sedes affectuum teneriorum, misericordiae, amoris etc.*"

[122] Ps 103:13; Jer 31:19; 42:12; Is 63:15–16.

[123] H. J. Stoebe, "*rhm*", in Ernst Jenni and Claus Westermann, eds., *Theologisches Handwörterbuch zum Alten Testament II* [Theological dictionary of Old Testament II] (Munich and Zurich, 1976), p. 762.

[124] Cf. esp. Köhler and Baumgartner, p. 886.

[125] Stoebe, "*rhm*", 764.

[126] That is, mercy as an active process (author's note).

[127] Stoebe, "*rhm*", p. 766.

[128] Stoebe, "*rhm*", p. 763.

God's love is sovereign and is effected through his omnipotence. This idea comes through, in the linguistic context of mercy, with exceptional clarity. Related in meaning to *rhm* is above all *hnn*,[129] which roughly means "to be gracious".[130] The substantive derived from this, *hen* = "favor, grace", stems from the sphere of courtly usage and refers in particular to the *king*: only the "higher-placed, and not vice versa", can grant a favor.[131]

The concepts gracious and merciful are linked together again and again as a "set liturgical formula. . . . In it, God's being there for man, with respect to its polarity as well as its inherent promise, is represented in terms of the behavior of a lord (king) or a father."[132]

It is notable that the word gracious usually precedes the adjective merciful; by means of putting the image of *king* in first place, the transcendent aspect of the transcendence symbol *father* is further intensified.

In the central formulation, Exodus 33:19, grace and mercifulness are expressive of God's position of absolute power: "I will be gracious to whom I will be gracious and will show mercy on whom I will show mercy."

Accordingly, the exclusiveness of the father symbol should be regarded as deriving "from the decidedly volitional nature of the Israelite religion".[133]

The concept of *rahamīm* thus has anything but a feminist milieu. Rather, precisely in it, transcendence shows itself as the infinite buttress of immanence. The *father* symbol, and not the mother symbol, is the most important expression of *divine* mercifulness.

Deuteronomy 32:18

In the Song of Moses, Deuteronomy 32, a verse occurs that, at least according to many expositors, refers to God not only as father but also as mother: "You were unmindful of the Rock that begot you, and you forgot the God who gave you birth."[134]

The first verb derives from the root *jld* = "to bear" (of a mother), "to sire" (of a father).[135] The second comes from *hwl* or *hjl*, which originally

---

129 Stoebe, "rhm", p. 764.

130 H. J. Stoebe, "hnn", in Jenni and Westermann, *Handwörterbuch I*, p. 587.

131 Stoebe, "hnn", pp. 589f.

132 Stoebe, "hnn", pp. 594f.

133 Bertholet, *Gottheit*, p. 9; cf. Leese, *Mutter*, p. 33.

134 Dt 32:18; translated according to E. Kautsch and A. Bertholet, *Die Heilige Schrift des Alten Testaments I* [The Holy Scripture of the Old Testament I] (Tübingen, 1922), p. 320.

135 Gesenius, *Handwörterbuch*, p. 300.

meant "to twist, to writhe" and later was used especially for a mother's labor pains.[136] This tends to suggest that the first word was applied to God in a paternal sense,[137] and the second, in a maternal one.

The comparisons in this lyrical text must, of course, be understood figuratively, for Deuteronomy argues quite zealously against the pagan nature religions, which took such conceptions literally. The prophet Jeremiah, who probably lived at the time of Deuteronomy, expressly attacks idolators "who say to a tree, 'You are my father', and to a stone, 'You gave me birth' ".[138] In Canaanite cults devoted to local deities, "the worshippers [of the god]" could "receive their being from sacred trees and rocks".[139]

Thus it is no wonder that the Old Testament nowhere else defines God as the father (or mother) of man in the procreative sense. Since Deuteronomy itself shows opposition to the relevant idolatrous cult,[140] many interpreters prefer a neutral form of translation, especially as the verbs in question are often used in the Old Testament in a nonliteral way: "You forget the Rock that brought you into the world, and you are unmindful of God who produced you."[141]

In addition, it must be noted that God is portrayed as the father of Israel in Deuteronomy.[142] In the Song of Moses, that title is linked to the image of the rock, which I earlier discussed as being a masculine symbol.[143] Thus, the anthropological basic axis of the symbolism is not parents-son or mother-son, but rather, father-son.

Birth and bird symbolism

Deuteronomy 32:18 is not the only example that (although in a very restrained and indirect manner) speaks of God as giving birth. In Proverbs 8:24–25, wisdom is "born" of God. But there is no reason for anyone to see typically maternal traits in this, since the word is also used in the

---

[136] S. R. Driver, *Critical and Exegetical Commentary on Deuteronomy*, The International Critical Commentary, 3rd ed. (Edinburgh, 1951 rpt.), p. 364.

[137] Cf. the connection between "rock" and "Father" in Deuteronomy 32:4, 6.

[138] Jer 2:27; cf. 3:9.

[139] W. H. Schmidt, *Glaube*, p. 190; additional documenting references also appear there.

[140] Dt 4:28; cf. 2 Kings 19:18.

[141] Translated according to Henri Cazelles, *Le Deutéronome*, La Sainte Bible, 2nd ed. (Paris, 1958), p. 130. Cf. the earlier Eduard König, *Das Deuteronomium* [Deuteronomy], Kommentar zum Alten Testament II (Leipzig, 1917), p. 209; E. König, *Wörterbuch*, p. 101.

[142] Dt 1:31; cf. Ex 4:22.

[143] Dt 32:4, 6, 14, 30, 31, 37.

nonliteral sense,[144] and the image does not have a very solid effect as such. Therefore, the usual form of translation is "to bring forth".

Psalms 90:2[145] describes the birth-giving power of the *earth*: "Before the mountains were begotten and the earth and the world were brought forth, from everlasting to everlasting you are God."[146]

What is described here is not[147] God's giving birth; rather, the point of the Psalm is simply to emphasize God's eternity and unchangeableness by contrasting it with the transience of nature: "The mountains, elsewhere a symbol of steadfastness . . . and eternity . . . , are here something that has 'come into being', and serve, within their line of development, . . . to bring into view the always existent . . . Creator God."[148]

Consequently, there is also no birth-giving chaos in the Old Testament such as is found in pagan myths but rather the powerful act of creation through God's word.[149]

Johannes Hempel sees connections between the *bird comparisons* in the Old Testament, especially in the Psalms, and feminine symbolism. To him, the decisive factor is the Egyptian Osiris myth, in which Isis and Nephthys shelter the dead god beneath their wings. In the same way, "an attempt is also made to secure protection beneath their feathers for dead men."[150]

No traces of this sort of influence—which, for Hempel, makes the image rather unrespectable—can, however, be found in the Old Testament. Especially in the eschatology, in contrast to the Egyptian example, it plays no role at all. Nevertheless, to female (and male) feminist theologians, the feminine connotations of the image can seem quite sympathetic: just as a mother bird protects its young, so God, too, grants maternal security to his faithful. The protecting "feathers" of God play a large role especially in the psalter: "Keep me as the apple of your eye; hide me in the shadow of your wings."[151]

According to Alfons Deissler, the bird image has a dual source of origin: (1) the temple cult and (2) the eagle image.[152]

---

[144] Prov 25:23.

[145] Cf. Job 38:8.

[146] Ps 354; translated according to Deissler, *Psalmen*.

[147] Thus say Driver, *Commentary*, p. 364, and Gesenius, *Handwörterbuch*, p. 227.

[148] Deissler, *Psalmen*, p. 356; similarly H. J. Kraus, *Psalmen II* [Psalms II] BK XV, 2, 5th ed. (Neukirchen and Vluyn, 1978), p. 798.

[149] Gen 1; Ps 33:6-9; 148:5. Cf. Johannes Nelis, "Schöpfung" [Creation], in Haag, *Bibellexikon*, pp. 1546-51.

[150] Hempel, *Frömmigkeit*, p. 184.

[151] Ps 17:8; cf. 91:4 and many others.

[152] Deissler, *Psalmen*, p. 225.

It is notable that most of the Psalms in which this symbol is used also contain some reference to security within the protection of the powerful temple walls. In fact, the temple served as a place of asylum for those seeking help,[153] and in the holy of holies there was a symbol that evoked pious trust in a special way, namely, the cherubic wings that were placed above the holy Ark and that offered it protection.[154] According to the description in Ezekiel, what was involved here were powerful beings in which human faces were combined with the qualities of the strongest animals of the Near East: bull [ox], lion, eagle.[155] Feminine associations were surely not linked to these figures.[156]

The second source of origin for the bird symbol occurs in the description of Exodus: "You have seen what I did to the Egyptians and how I bore you on eagles' wings and brought you to myself."[157]

God "encircled him; he cared for him; he kept him as the apple of his eye. Like an eagle that stirs up its nest, that flutters over its young, spreading out its wings, catching them, bearing them on its pinions."[158]

If what we have here is maternal symbolism, then it manifests itself rather paradoxically in the image of an eagle, which is a typically masculine symbol. The eagle builds its nest on rocky heights and is thus especially close to heaven, which makes it emblematic of transcendence;[159] like a lightning bolt, it can strike down suddenly from above.[160] Along with the bull and lion,[161] the eagle is regarded as the strongest of animal creatures, whose youthful power, according to Oriental belief, is constantly self-renewing: "Even youths shall faint and be weary, and young men shall fall exhausted; but they who wait for the Lord shall renew their strength; they shall mount up with wings like eagles; they shall run and not be weary; they shall walk and not faint."[162]

The bird comparisons, then, are a virtual showcase example of paternal symbolism, in which benevolence is also always power charged.

[153] Cf. Kraus, *Theologie*, p. 36.

[154] Cf. Deissler, *Psalmen*, p. 225.

[155] Cf. Ezek 1:4ff. On this, see Arie van den Born, "Kerub" [Cherub], in Haag, *Bibellexikon*, pp. 936–40.

[156] Cf. by contrast, as an exemplary instance of a feminist exegesis, and in this case Cabalist as well, the comments by Patai, *Goddess*, pp. 101ff.

[157] Ex 19:4.

[158] Dt 32:11.

[159] Obad 3–4; Jer 49:16 and others.

[160] Job 9:26.

[161] For God: Amos 1:2; 3:6, 8; Hos 13:7f.; Is 31:4f. and elsewhere. The bull symbol is missing because of its association with the Baal cult.

[162] Is 40:30–31; cf. Jer 49:22; Ezek 17:3; Ps 103:5 and others.

Conclusion

Regarding the application of maternal symbolism to the Old Testament image of God, two things are evident:

1. God combines in himself every kind of creaturely value and does so in the most perfect way.
2. Nevertheless, the maternal symbolism has no independent value, but is, so to speak, a component part of the father symbol. Precisely where feminine images occur, they are always found in some context that ties immanence into transcendence and confirms the priority of the latter.

The treatment of several important feminine components of Israelite religiosity, whose implications extend as far as to the image of God (especially "Lady Wisdom"), has been kept for later.[163] There as well, I will be able to show the same thing that has been exemplarily demonstrated on the basis of the most frequently cited references for the axiom "God is also mother": *Masculinity is inherently characteristic of the biblical image of God.*

The Father of Jesus Christ as the fulfillment of the Old Testament image of God

The use of Father as a form of address for God was not able to gain prominence until the revelation of the New Covenant. Christ is the only one who can speak the title Father in its full sense, because he is the Son of God as begotten under the aspect of eternity. The Christian, who is aware of this divine filiation, recognizes at the same time that his own status of being a child does not derive from God in a naturalistically *necessary* way but has resulted from having been freely and lovingly *determined* as an adoptive relationship. In the Gospels, Christ never includes himself along with his apostles under a common form of Father address, but rather, distinguishes between "my Father" and "your Father".[164]

The essential aspects of the Old Testament image of God were not changed by Jesus, but were brought to fulfillment in a consummate way. "The God of creation and promise is the God of redemption and fulfillment, and vice versa."[165] The prophecy of Jesus gives "previously unheard-

[163] Cf. pp. 279–81 below.
[164] Cf. Jeremias, *Abba*, p. 54.
[165] Schmaus, *Glaube II*, p. 23.

of force to the idea that God is absolute benevolence":[166] "Are not two sparrows sold for a penny? And not one of them will fall to the ground without your Father's will. But even the hairs of your head are all numbered."[167]

God's *benevolence* manifests itself especially in the infinite love that he reserves for sinners, in his *mercifulness*. "Jesus' parable of the prodigal son speaks to us in an incomparable way of God's fatherhood."[168] God's benevolence here appears all but scandalous to human understanding: "But while he [the prodigal son] was yet at a distance, his father saw him and had compassion, and ran and embraced him and kissed him. . . . 'Bring quickly the best robe, and put it on him; and put a ring on his hand, and shoes on his feet; and bring the fatted calf and kill it, and let us eat and make merry; for this my son was dead, and is alive again; he was lost, and is found.' "[169]

In the second century A.D., this benevolent attitude on the part of the heavenly Father so impressed the heretic *Marcion* that he was led to play off the thundering and lightning flashing, the just God of the Old Testament against Jesus Christ's God, who had supposedly put aside such traits and become nothing but pure benevolence. From this perspective, any talk of the damnation of many people ought not to appear in the New Testament.

Early on, Tertullian poured his acrid irony over this false doctrine, which is questionable even from a purely intellectual viewpoint: "If you call him [God] the Lord, yet also claim that he need not be feared, that is simply nonsense; for the name Lord designates someone in a position of fear-instilling power. . . . Obviously, he is then also not your Father, for a father properly occasions both love because of his protective behavior . . . and fear because of his power."[170]

In the New Testament, in the same way as in the Old Testament, it is true that: "The fear of the Lord is the beginning of knowledge."[171]

It is not until man becomes conscious of his own minuteness in the face of divine immensity that he can rightly appreciate and humbly worship God's condescending love. Therefore, the above-quoted passage with the sparrow comparison is immediately preceded by: "And do not fear those

[166] Josef Schmid, *Das Evangelium nach Matthäus* [The gospel according to Matthew], RNT 1, 5th ed. (Regensburg, 1965), p. 126.

[167] Mt 10:29–30.

[168] Günther Bornkamm, *Jesus von Nazareth* [Jesus of Nazareth], 10th ed. (Stuttgart, 1975), p. 111.

[169] Lk 15:20, 22–24.

[170] *Adversus Marcionem* I,27:3; cf. also II,13:5; Wlosok, "Vater", p. 52; CCL I, pp. 471, 490f. Marcionist ways of thinking had precedents in pagan philosophical systems that similarly postulated a good God who could not punish anyone; cf. Wlosok, "Vater", p. 49.

[171] Cf., among others, Prov 1:7; Philemon 2:12; 1 Pet 1:17.

who kill the body but cannot kill the soul; rather fear him who can destroy both soul and body in hell."[172]

And in the Sermon on the Mount, which likewise gives bold emphasis to God's paternal benevolence, these words occur and are just as shocking in another way: "Enter by the narrow gate; for the gate is wide and the way is easy, that leads to destruction, and those who enter by it are many. For the gate is narrow and the way is hard, that leads to life, and those who find it are few."[173]

Thus, the tidings of joy become, for those who reject them, tidings of threat.

This antithetical tension is grounded in the fact that Jesus bore our sins *for us* and, with that act, makes an everlasting atonement *in relation to* his *Father*.[174] *Justice* and mercifulness are so closely linked to one another that doing away with the justice would amount to making the love of sinners empty and worthless.

The justice is, so to speak, the pillar on which the mercifulness rests, and the same image applies to the relationship between transcendence and immanence. The newer form of address for God, "Abba", "dear Father", drawn from the language of young children, inspires enormous trust but also demands an obedience that is grounded in God's transcendence:[175] "Abba, Father, all things are possible to you; remove this cup from me; yet not what I will, but what you will."[176]

The merciful and immanence-grounding Father is, at the same time, the "Lord of heaven and earth".[177] Heaven is his throne, and earth, his footstool.[178] He is Lord over earth, too, but his symbol is *heaven*, the absolute symbolic image of transcendence. Father and heaven belong closely together, as is especially evident from the Lord's Prayer: "Our Father—in the heavens".[179]

The form of address "Our Father" is expressive of childlike trust, along with which, of course, the trancendence of God is also included as a background element. This transcendence aspect of the Father title is intensified by the addition of "in the heavens", so that transcendence itself is, as it were, further transcended.

[172] Mt 10:28.
[173] Mt 7:13–14.
[174] Cf. pp. 263ff. below.
[175] Cf. Jeremias, *Abba*, p. 64.
[176] Mk 14:36.
[177] Mt 11:25.
[178] Mt 5:34–35.
[179] Mt 6:9, my translation. This belonging together is found not only in Matthew but—as a glance at any concordance can quickly confirm—in the whole New Testament. Heaven is *the* symbol of God and is at times expressly linked to the Father, as in John 6:32, 38.

The combination Father-heaven corresponds exactly to the association Father-omnipotence, so that the opening of the Apostles' Creed is in complete harmony with the New Testament image of God: *"Credo in Deum, patrem omnipotentem."*

To pray, by contrast, to a "mother in the earth" would be to enter into an unholy alliance with pantheistic and polytheistic immanence religions.

Thus, the heavenly Father of Jesus Christ is none other than the Lord of hosts from the Old Testament. In principle, therefore, my remarks on the Old Testament image of God apply, in their entirety, to the New Testament as well.

God as Father: relic of a patriarchal society?[180]

What has been said in the New Testament remains valid for the whole of the New Covenant until the Day of Judgment. The figure of father, in its differences from that of mother, is so anthropologically central that any loosening-up exercises with the symbolism of the image of God must also necessarily destroy its content.

The essential content of the father image has nothing to do with the patriarchal society that is usually presumed to have existed in antiquity. My excurses in the area of religious studies have already touched on Gnosticism and the most varying sorts of influential philosophical currents, in which God was quite unabashedly addressed as mother. As a rule, those involved were not polytheists, but "enlightened" people who held to a quite spiritually oriented image of God. Particularly Jupiter, the Roman *pater omnipotens*, was often addressed as father and mother. Hence, the title mother was not necessarily tied to a mother goddess.

Now, Christianity was so zealous in its adoption of philosophical ideas from the pagan world that many modern theologians accuse it of a falsifying "Hellenization". This so-called Hellenization, however, was not carried out in the sense of an indiscriminate *aggiornamento* to the world, but was exceedingly selective. Some conceptions were incorporated from Stoicism; still others were rejected. Very many neoplatonic ideas were taken over, while specific contents were set aside, and so on. Regarding mother as a form of address for God, it would have been easily possible—more so than it is today, when philosophical studies are not regarded as an indispensable part of general education—to invoke the fact that God combines within himself all the perfections of creation in their highest form. And yet this philosophically obvious and convenient path of

[180] Cf. pp. 183f., 225–28 above.

accommodation was not taken; rather, a sharp polemic was carried out against it. The Gnostic loosening-up exercises crop up regularly under the rubric "heresy". Moreover, Gnosticism was by no means a tiny sect, but rather, a world religion,[181] and its "Christian" offshoots were perhaps quantitatively stronger than was Catholic Christianity.[182]

The key to the vehement rejection of a mother title for God is probably the almost metaphysically necessary affiliation between that title and pantheistic monism.

Augustine's critical commentary on the Stoic Varro has been noted earlier here.[183] In another context, the Church Father writes with commitment against the notion of a divine mother, saying that the pagans are "born of earth, and so earth is their mother. But, according to true theology, the earth is the work of God."

As an introduction to those remarks, Augustine had established that pagan scholars assume God to be identical with nature.[184]

God as father and mother: examples from antiquity and the Middle Ages

Clement of Alexandria and the problems surrounding John 1:18

Nevertheless, the axiom "God is also mother" has a certain prehistory in Christian antiquity. In the extensive work of Clement of Alexandria (died c. 215), the "first Christian scholar",[185] the mother title occurs in one (and only one) passage: "Look to the mysteries of love, and then you will see the lap [or bosom] of the Father, whom the only-begotten God alone proclaimed. But God, too, is himself love, and out of love he allowed himself to be seen by us. And what was inexpressible in his nature became Father, while what was compassionate toward us became Mother. And as a consequence of his love the Father took on the nature of a woman, and the clear proof of this is the Son, whom he begot out of himself, and the fruit that was born of love is love."[186]

The unbroken thread that runs through this short passage is the concept

---

[181] Quispel, *Gnosis*.

[182] Cf. p. 404 below.

[183] Cf. p. 166 above.

[184] *De civitate Dei*, VI,8: BKV I, pp. 318f.; CCL 47, pp. 176f.

[185] Berthold Altaner and Alfred Stuiber, *Patrologie*, 8th ed. (Freiburg, Basel and Vienna, 1978), p. 191.

[186] "Quis dives salvetur?" 37, 1–2: BKV 2, Series VIII, pp. 268ff.; GCS 17, pp. 183ff.

of love. In the human sphere, however, we tend especially to associate tender love that comes from the heart with the mother, who has a symbolic significance here similar to that in Isaiah 49:15. While the comparison remains very tentative there, it is explicitly drawn here and is referred to the inner-trinitarian generation of the Son from the Father. The Father's giving birth (characterized at the same time as a begetting) points toward John 1:18: "No one has ever seen God; the only[-begotten] Son (ὁ μονογενής 'υιός), who is in the bosom (εἰς τὸν χόλπον) of the Father, he has made him known."

The predicate only[-begotten] (literally, "uniquely descendant") serves to express the uniqueness of the divine filiation. The verb that underlies it, γεννᾶν, can mean "to beget" as well as "to give birth to", and also, in a general sense, "to bring forth". The accent here is not on the coming forth from the Father but on the majestic status of Jesus. μονογενής is translated as only[-begotten] because this word "is often used in the Bible of an only child, who is therefore loved above all else".[187]

The symbolic meaning to give birth to hardly seems suggested here. Rather, because of its link to the Father title, γεννᾶν is rendered as to beget in the doctrine of the Trinity. This image was more strongly expressive in antiquity—when sometimes only the father was seen as the active principle in procreation[188]—than it is today. But even today (as always), the father appears as the more powerfully effective part of the procreative process, as the one from whom the initiative proceeds. Also, in the inner-trinitarian processes and the resultant sending of Son and Spirit into the world, it is the Divine Father who shows himself as the creative-effective impetus.

The point of the passage from Clement does not, however, turn primarily on the only[-begotten] but on the little word lap (in German, Schoss). The basic meaning of κόλπος is bosom, breast (not in the specifically female sense), in which there are connotations of the experience of security: "Even apart from any suggestion of the image of dining in common on the same seat, being at the breast signifies the most intimate social communion."[189]

In an extended sense, κόλπος can also mean lap: "Abraham's lap" (translated as "Abraham's bosom" in the RSV Bible).[190] Analogously to that, one could also read lap (Schoss) of the Father, but in John 1:18, the meaning breast (Brust, translated in the RSV Bible as bosom) seems more likely. The preposition εἰς means in general "directedness toward the

[187] Alfred Wikenhauser, Das Evangelium nach Johannes, RNT 4 (Regensburg, 1961), p. 48.

[188] See below, pp. 458–60.

[189] Walter Bauer, Griechisch-deutsches Wörterbuch zu den Schriften des Neuen Testaments und der übrigen urchristlichen Literatur, 5th ed. (Berlin, 1971), p. 874.

[190] Lk 16:22.

inside of something or toward immediate nearness to it".[191] As an indication of directedness ("toward", "to" or "at"), εἰς probably suggests breast more than lap, for which the particle ἐν would have been available.[192] Also conceivable would be the meaning bag, swell (*Bausch*), of the "folds made by the clothing beneath the breast and above the waistband".[193]

In any case, κόλπος points to the Son's immanence in the Father, to his being kept secure within the threefold divine Life. Insofar as the Father—who contrasts with the Son in being his originator yet not having become man—remains, so to speak, in concealment, "beneath the veil". One might even speak, in a paradoxical way, of the Father as a "feminine principle in the Triad",[194] though only, of course, in a highly figurative sense, for the Father, *as* Father, realizes himself precisely through being the active, eternal originator with respect to both Son and Spirit.

In the Latin Church, this secondary way of speaking about the Father's lap seems to have been connected with two passages from the Psalms. In Psalms 109:3 Vulgate, God says to the Israelite king: "*Ex utero ante luciferum genui te.*" *Uterus* ("womb, lap"), which refers in the original Hebrew text to the king's mother, is asserted here of God. In the New Testament, this (most cited!) psalm is interpreted messianically, with a view to the filiation of Jesus.[195]

More striking is a passage from Second Isaiah, which even speaks of God's "maternal womb": "*Audite me domus Jacob, et omne residuum domus Israel, qui portamini a meo utero, qui gestamini a mea vulva.*"[196]

In the original text, of course, not God but the mother of God's servant is the subject of the relevant notions. Still, the mistaken translations at least show that those who made them were anything but "woman-haters"; however, no feminist theology seems to have been developed on the basis of the passages in question. But to return to Clement: behind the cited

---

[191] Bauer, *Wörterbuch*, pp. 451f.

[192] Cf., for instance, Jn 14:2: "In [ἐν] my Father's house are many rooms"; cf. Bauer, *Wörterbuch*, pp. 511f.

[193] Bauer, *Wörterbuch*, p. 874.

[194] Thus V. A. Demant, "Why the Christian Priesthood Is Male", in *Women*, p. 102: "a feminine principle in the triad".

[195] Cf. Deissler, *Psalmen*, pp. 442f. This is never done, however, with reference to the verse cited here. As an indication of Jesus' eternal origins Psalm 2:7 is more often preferred: "You are my son; today I have begotten you." Cf. Acts 13:33; Heb 5:5. The early Church interpreted Psalm 109:3 again and again in terms of the *uterus cordis*, for instance, Hippolytus: "The *Logos*, which the Father gives birth to from his heart": Commentary on the Song of Songs, 17:1; Hugo Rahner, *Symbole der Kirche. Die Ekklesiologie der Väter* [Symbols of the Church. Ecclesiology of the Fathers] (Salzburg, 1964), p. 17, n. 17; other documentation, pp. 16f.

[196] Is 49:1; André Cabassut, "Une dévotion médiévale peu connue. La dévotion à 'Jésus notre mère' ", *Revue d'ascétique et de mystique* 25 (1949): 237.

passage, there are probably not only Christian but also Gnostic influences. For this Church Father had made excerpts from a large number of Gnostic texts (admittedly, quite critically), including in particular those from Valentinianism. The Father (as the third Principle) is regarded there—similarly to here—as unutterable (for Clement, "inexpressible")[197] and—otherwise than here—as male–female.[198] The feminine fourth Principle, the truth,[199] is regarded as mother of all things and is found even in baptismal formulae.[200] Christ arises out of a divine mother (Sophia), who has separated herself from the paternal pleroma.[201] Clement himself critically dismisses a Valentinian commentary on John 1:18 that is similar to his own statements: "The *Logos* that was 'in the beginning'—that is, in the only-begotten, namely, *Nous* and Truth—he makes known as Christ."[202]

Christ seems here to arise, intradivinely, from a father (*Nous*) *and* a mother (Truth).[203] Of course, Clement does not initiate an ecumenical dialogue with the Valentinian claims, but rejects them. Nevertheless, the opposing position seems to have exerted a certain aftereffect. In view of the extent of the Church Father's writings, however, this sort of influence is minimal. Whereas the divine mother plays a central role for the Valentinians, she is, for Clement, demythologized in the direction of the Father and is shifted, as well, wholly to the periphery.

The hymns of Synesius of Cyrene

Much more clearly than Clement, Synesius of Cyrene (c. 370–414) refers to God again and again as mother in his hymns. For instance, one central passage reads:

> But you are the root
> of things past, present and future.
> You are father; you are mother.
> You are man, and you are woman.
> You are word and silence:
> The fertile nature of natures.[204]

At the start of this text, God is called the "root"—a feminine symbol.[205] This image crops up repeatedly, as does that of the maternal wellspring.

---

[197] Andresen, *Gnosis I*, p. 254.
[198] Andresen, *Gnosis I*, pp. 164f., 256.
[199] Probably the second as well, "silence" (!).
[200] Andresen, *Gnosis I*, pp. 283f.; cf. p. 163 above.
[201] Andresen, *Gnosis I*, pp. 165f., 255.
[202] *Excerpta ex Theodoto* 6:3, in Andresen, *Gnosis I*, p. 288; GCS 17, p. 107.
[203] Cf. p. 163 above.
[204] Hymn II: PG 66, p. 1593.
[205] Cf. p. 139 above.

"He speaks of supraterrestrial births, of the divine primal essence's streaming itself forth."[206] He also uses the symbol of the ocean depths (Βοθός)—in relation to God the Father.[207] God gives birth to the world and is identical with it, similarly to the shining forth of the sun, "the One . . . , in so doing", remains "unmoved in itself and undiminished".[208] The Father appears as the nature of natures and as mother nature.[209]

These same symbols have already come up in my discussion of Neoplatonism, and in fact, Synesius is a Plotinus disciple of the first water.[210] To be sure, he was pressed into the office of bishop, but he never really became, in his heart of hearts, a Christian.[211] He never got beyond the pantheistic doctrine of emanation, which appears again and again in the above-cited symbols. He was especially troubled by the notions of the soul's creation in time (!), the resurrection of the body and the impermanence of the world.[212] Especially in his hymns, in which God appears as both father and mother, he propounds a quite eccentric doctrine of the Trinity. It "is no longer purely Neoplatonic and not yet purely Christian, but a peculiar mixture of both".[213] Supernatural and natural are intermixed for him:[214] "secularized God—deified world".[215]

Firmicus Maternus

"God is also mother" for the Sicilian rhetorician Firmicus Maternus (mid fourth century). In his astrological work—which, however, *ante*dates his conversion to Christianity[216]—he writes: "You are, in like manner, father and mother of everything; you are father and son, bound together by a single bond of necessity."[217] "And you orbits of the everlasting stars: you moon, as the mother of human bodies, and you, too, ruler of all stars, . . . O peerless sun, [you] all above all things."[218]

Here, the mother appears to be symbolized by the moon, and the father,

---

[206] Georg Grützmacher. *Synesios von Kyrene. Ein Charakterbild aus dem Untergang des Hellenismus* [Synesios of Cyrene. A character portrait from the decline of Hellenism] (Leipzig, 1913), p. 105.

[207] Hymn II: PG 66, p. 1596.

[208] Grützmacher, *Synesios*, p. 106; cf. Hymn III: PG 66, p. 1596.

[209] Hymn III: PG 66, p. 1598.

[210] Grützmacher, *Synesios*, p. 103.

[211] Altaner and Stuiber, *Patrologie*, p. 282.

[212] Ivánka, *Plato*, p. 473, n. 1.

[213] Grützmacher, *Synesios*, p. 110.

[214] Ivánka, *Plato*, p. 473.

[215] Ivánka, *Plato*, p. 89.

[216] Altaner and Stuiber, *Patrologie*, p. 360.

[217] Matheseos Libri V, praefatio 3, in W. Kroll and F. Skutsch, eds., *Iulii Firmici Materni Matheseos Libri VIII* II (Stuttgart, 1968), p. 2.

[218] Matheseos Libri V, praefatio 5, in Kroll and Skutsch, *Matheseos II*, p. 3.

by the sun. This impression is confirmed when his astrological work is examined in more detail:[219] father = Saturn = sun; mother = Luna = moon.

In view of this juxtapositioning, it is necessary to take account of Christian tradition. Whereas, for Firmicus, *sun and moon* are both allocated to the divine sphere, the *early Church* recognizes a decided polarization of two symbols: "Just as sun and moon are two great luminaries in heaven's firmament, so, for us, are Christ and the Church."[220] "These luminaries, sun and moon, are bearers of a great mystery. The sun, namely, is the image of God, the moon, the image of man."[221]

Thus, the Church regards the moon as symbolic of receptive and cooperative *creaturely* being: it is the "heavenly body with the femininely soft and maternally fecund light, which receives the masculine and powerful rays of the sun and passes them on, lovingly softened, down to the earth".[222]

When, however, the moon appears along with the sun as symbolic of the divine, as for Firmicus, the warning bell sounds: pantheism. We know that the (monistic) Stoics designated Zeus as likewise sun and moon, in order to give expression to the identity of God and world.[223] Therefore, Konrat Ziegler correspondingly observes that the astrological work of the rhetorician is "a rather washed-out monotheism".[224]

Meister Eckhart

In the Christian Middle Ages, we meet with God as mother in the works of Meister Eckhart. "In the sayings by him that have come down to us, the following occurs by way of a prelude: 'Meister Eckhart says God is not only a Father of all good things; he is also a mother of all things. And he is mother of all things because, just as a creature receives its being from him, so he also stands by it and sustains it in its being. For if God did not stand by, and in, the creature once it comes into being, so it would, of necessity, just as soon fall out of being.' "[225]

These words, at first sight quite appealing, take on a particular significance when seen against their philosophical background in Eckhart's

---

[219] Cf., among others, Matheseos Libri II, 19:13, in Kroll and Skutsch, *Matheseos I*, p. 65; Matheseos Libri VII, 9:1, in Kroll and Skutsch, *Matheseos II*, p. 232.

[220] Thus Origen, *Gen. hom.*, 1:7: translated [in original German text] from H. Rahner, *Symbole*, p. 107; GCS 29, p. 8.

[221] Theophilus of Antioch, *Ad Autolycum*, II,15, in H. Rahner, *Symbole*, p. 92; PGG, p. 1077.

[222] H. Rahner, *Symbole*, p. 99.

[223] Cf. p. 166 above.

[224] Konrat Ziegler, ed. *Iuli Firmici Materni de errore profanum religionum*, Das Wort der Antike III (Munich, 1953), p. 8.

[225] Leese, *Mutter*, p. 36.

mysticism. Eckhart was probably no pantheist, but he emphasized God's immanence so strongly that Creator and creature, so to speak, flowed together.[226] Several pantheistic tenets of his were, therefore, condemned by the Church.[227] Eckhart's special outlook is occasionally compared to the monistic mysticism of the Orient, and especially to Lao-tzu.[228]

Conclusion

The biblical image of the Father is the most important symbol of Christian belief in God. The interplay of transcendence and immanence, of power and goodness, of justice and mercifulness, was anticipated in a variety of ways in the Old Testament, and the Divine Son who became man has revealed to us all of these qualities in their total fullness: "Our Father, who art in heaven."

In a certain respect, the father symbol is even more significant than the symbolic images for the two other Divine Persons, since, for Christians, the decisive relationship to God is constituted *in* the Holy Spirit *through* Christ and *toward* the Father. This basic structure, which is variously indicated in the New Testament,[229] is reflected in the Church's central act of self-consummation, the celebration of the Eucharist, whose midpoint is formed by the high prayer: "Through him, with him and in him, in the unity of the Holy Spirit, all glory and honor is yours, Almighty Father, for ever and ever. Amen."

3. CHRIST'S MALENESS: A SITUATIONALLY CONDITIONED
   COINCIDENCE OR AN ESSENTIAL ASPECT OF REVELATION?

Approach to the question: Christ's maleness against the background of priestly representation

Jesus Christ is *the* representative of God; "he reflects the glory of God and bears the very stamp of his nature" from all eternity.[230] "He who has seen

---

[226] Auer, *Gott*, pp. 219f.

[227] Cf. DS, pp. 950–80.

[228] K. O. Schmidt, *Lao-Tse*, p. 14; cf. pp. 151f. above. Other Western intellectual streams that designate God as mother are usually influenced by Neoplatonism, Gnosticism and Cabala; as a rule, they are centered on an androgynous image of *Jesus* or they regard the Holy *Spirit* as feminine. More on this will be said later.

[229] Especially Ephesians 2:18.

[230] Heb 1:3; cf. Col 1:15; Philemon 2:6; 1 Cor 8:6.

me has seen the Father."[231] "I and the Father are One."[232] "No one knows the Son except the Father, and no one knows the Father except the Son and any one to whom the Son chooses to reveal him."[233]

It is not only in his divinity but also in his human nature that Christ is a likeness and a representative of his Father: "For in him the whole fullness of deity dwells bodily."[234] At the same time, he stands before his Father as the decisive representative of mankind, who, through Cross and Resurrection, wishes to bring the gift of divine life to the world. Given this dual representation,[235] does Christ's maleness have any special meaning? Might his divine filiation and the redemptive task that is grounded in it have a sexual cast?

Christ's maleness: an unbiblical accentuation?

Certainly God's becoming *man* is the fundamental precondition for our redemption, which Christ effected representatively for women as well as for men. In Christ as the head, the new mankind is united into a supernatural body[236] in which even sexual differences have no divisive significance[237] and every believer is to be transfigured into a "new Christ".[238]

Nevertheless, it is not an indifferent matter whether God's becoming man occurs in the form of a male or of a female. All of God's decisions, even if they appear as a mystery to us, are full of wisdom. God does not "play dice", except according to the assumptions of Ockham's nominalism.[239] So it is surely not due to sheer caprice that Christ appeared at a time when the whole Mediterranean region was under the centralized political control of Rome and when the Greek language was spoken everywhere. These factors, together with the equally widespread Jewish diaspora, formed an important precondition for the wide-ranging proclamation of the gospel.

Sexual differentiation is a much more deeply rooted aspect of human existence than are political and cultural superimpositions of the sort just mentioned. After the resurrection of the body, to be sure, the physical

[231] Jn 14:9.
[232] Jn 10:30.
[233] Mt 11:27; cf. Lk 10:22.
[234] Col 2:9.
[235] Of God with respect to man and of man before God; cf. pp. 190f. above.
[236] Col 1:18; Rom 12:5; 1 Cor 12:13.
[237] 1 Cor 11:11; Gal 3:28.
[238] Gal 3:27; Col 3:10–11.
[239] Cf. pp. 74f. above.

functions become spiritualized, so that the sensual reproductive urge ceases,[240] but the particular sexual identity that was bestowed by the Creator does not, as such, change.[241]

In 2 Corinthians 11:2, where the community appears with feminine traits, the exalted Lord, also, is not described as a purely spiritual neuter but as a husband.

Resurrection spiritualizes man's biological nature, but because the physical is an essential part of man's nature, it is not abolished in favor of an angelic sort of being. To those who would like to anticipate a supposedly sexless eschaton, claiming support from Galatians 3:28,[242] the following maxim applies: *"Qui veut faire l'ange, fait la bête."*[243]

Already in the second century, the Gnostic sects, with their aversion to the body, found man's general sexual differentiation—which goes far beyond the purely sexual in the narrow sense—so disturbing that they set up an androgynous ideal.[244] Along with Plato,[245] Origen holds to the sphere ideal, assuming that man will be resurrected as a male-female being in the form of a sphere.[246] There is a sharp polemic by Saint Jerome against this theory,[247] and it was banned by the Church during the Origenist controversy:[248] "Just as God created two sexes, so he will reinstate them both."[249]

Regarding the *maleness* of Jesus, the New Testament makes no explicit

---

[240] 1 Cor 15:35–50; Mk 12:25 par.

[241] *Erklärung*, Nr. 5, p. 17; *AAS* 69 (1977): 112. Cf. as well the appearances of the resurrected: Jn 20:27; (1 Jn 1:1); Lk 24:39.

[242] Cf. pp. 345f. below.

[243] Against Meer, *Priesturtum*, pp. 175, 189, 196. Moreover, even if the sexual stamp would disappear in the eschaton, it would nevertheless possess, in the interim, a signlike meaning through its reference to the Christ-Church mystery; this symbolic connection remains applicable to the sacrament of priestly ordination even if the latter—like all sacraments—becomes superfluous in the eschaton.

[244] Cf. pp. 160f. above and pp. 404ff. below.

[245] Cf. p. 160 above.

[246] *De oratione*, 31:3; *BKV* 48, p. 140; *GCS* 3, p. 397.

[247] Esp. 108:23f.: *BKV* 15, pp. 137f.; *PL* 22, p. 901: "If women are not resurrected as women, and men, as men, then there will not be any resurrection of the dead at all. For each sex has sexual members, and the body as a whole is made up of its members." On Matthew 22:29f.: "The Lord promises us not the nature, but the life and blessedness of the angels." It is unimaginable how Meer, *Priesturtum*, p. 98, could overlook this central passage and bring in an (only seemingly) contrary passage from Jerome in which the concepts soul and body are used in a merely allegorical context.

[248] DS 407.

[249] Augustine, *De civitate Dei*, 22:17; J. M. Nielen, *Ich glaube an die Auferstehung des Fleisches. Väterzeugnisse aus den ersten christlichen Jahrhunderten* [I believe in the resurrection of the body. Patriarchal testimonies from the early Christian centuries] (Freiburg im Breisgau, 1941), p. 94; CCL 48, p. 836. In Augustine there is also a detailed supporting argument that Saint Thomas later developed more deeply: STh Suppl q 83 a 1 ad 1; q 81 a 1.

statement. The reason for this is obviously not, however, to represent it as meaningless. On the contrary, I will be able to show in detail that the masculinity of the incarnate Son of God is most intimately and inseparably linked to his redemptive work. This basic tenet seemed so self-evident to the early Church and to later Christian generations that there was absolutely no need to make it a formal object of reflective thought. Many truths of faith were never put into words until such time as their validity was first contested.

The image of marriage as a central symbol

Basic meaning

The most central symbol from anthropology is that of marriage. In the human sphere, the matrimonial union of husband and wife is more intimate than the love between parents and children: "Therefore a man leaves his father and his mother and cleaves to his wife, and they become one flesh."[250]

The image of marriage thus seems, from the very start, to be the one most suitable to representing God's self-disclosure in relation to mankind. In the New Testament, therefore, the symbol is used not in reference to the Father, but to the Son, in whom God's concern for the world appeared in bodily form.[251]

The marriage symbol in the New Testament

The way for this symbolic image was prepared by the words of Jesus himself, who speaks of the bridegroom: "Can the wedding guests fast while the bridegroom is with them?"[252] "The Kingdom of heaven may be compared to a king who gave a marriage feast for his son and sent his servants to call those who were invited to the marriage feast."[253] "Then the Kingdom of heaven shall be compared to ten maidens who took their lamps and went to meet the bridegroom."[254]

The sacred community is compared here not to the bride but to the wedding guests (or to the maidens). But the identification "bridegroom = Jesus"/"bride = the people" would not yet have been appropriate prior to the events of Easter. For the image—as we will see in more detail

[250] Gen 2:24; cf. Mk 10:7 par.
[251] Col 2:9; Jn 1:14.
[252] Mk 2:19.
[253] Mt 22:2–3.
[254] Mt 25:1.

shortly—had already been extensively developed by the prophets and refers strictly to the behavior of *God* toward Israel. Jesus, however, initially only hinted at his Messiahship and divinity in his public utterances, and that same reservation is evident in his cautious use of the title bridegroom, which at first served only as a counterconcept to wedding guests.

It was also not necessary that, after Easter, Jesus should have expressly said something like: "My divine love for you, the new Israel, resembles the devotion of a bridegroom to his bride." Rather, that sort of interpretation follows implicitly from the internal dynamics of the image itself, which was prefigured in the Old Testament. The Gospel of the favorite apostle, *John*, serves as a prelude here.

John the Baptist says of Christ: "I am not the Christ, but I have been sent before him. He who has the bride is the bridegroom; the friend of the bridegroom, who stands and hears him, rejoices greatly at the bridegroom's voice."[255]

Jesus' first miracle was accomplished at a wedding,[256] and, in the background symbolism of the evangelist's account of this, the marriage image could quite well be suggested.

What is only hinted at in the Gospel of John is brought out more fully in the Apocalypse.[257] The "Lamb of God, who takes away the sin of the world",[258] now appears as the bridegroom of the Church: "Come, I will show you the bride, the wife of the Lamb. . . . And I saw the holy city, the new Jerusalem, coming down out of heaven from God, prepared as a bride adorned for her husband."[259]

The eschatological bride who descends from heaven appears, in so doing, in one perspective with the militant Church of this eon: "The Spirit and the bride say, 'Come'. And let him who hears say, 'Come [Lord Jesus]'."[260]

At its clearest, however, the marriage image occurs in the *Pauline texts*: "I betrothed you to Christ to present you as a pure bride to her one husband."[261]

---

[255] Jn 3:28–29.

[256] Jn 2:1–12.

[257] Like André Feuillet, I proceed here from the assumption that the fourth Gospel and the Apocalypse were by the same author; cf. Feuillet, *Jésus*, p. 36, and its references to additional material. "Critical" minds may well refuse to accept this assumption; still, the significance of the marriage image in the Apocalypse, which is the important thing here, is not thereby diminished.

[258] Jn 1:29.

[259] Rev 21:2, 9.

[260] Rev 22:17; cf. Rev 19:7, 9; 12:17; 14:1; 7:14. The counterimage to the bride of the Lamb is the whore Babylon: Rev 14:8; 17:1f.; 18:2–3.

[261] 2 Cor 11:2.

Be subject to one another out of reverence for Christ. Wives, be subject to your husbands, as to the Lord. For the husband is the head of the wife as Christ is the head of the Church, his Body, and is himself its Savior. As the Church is subject to Christ, so let wives also be subject in everything to their husbands.

Husbands, love your wives, as Christ loved the Church and gave himself up for her, that he might sanctify her, having cleansed her by the washing of water with the Word, that he might present the Church to himself in splendor, without spot or wrinkle or any such thing, that she might be holy and without blemish. Even so husbands should love their wives as their own bodies. He who loves his wife loves himself. For no man ever hates his own flesh, but nourishes and cherishes it, as Christ does the Church, because we are members of his Body. "For this reason a man shall leave his father and mother and be joined to his wife, and the two shall become one flesh." This mystery is a profound one, and I am saying that it refers to Christ and the Church; however, let each one of you love his wife as himself, and let the wife see that she respects her husband.[262]

The Old Testament horizon of understanding

The marriage symbol assumes its full significance only if we take into consideration its Old Testament background. The prophet Hosea takes the firmest of stands against sexualized Canaanite idolatry and defends the prohibition of images.[263] Certainly no biologized notion of God can be expected from him.[264] But precisely Hosea is the first to represent, in an exceedingly bold and previously unheard-of manner, God's relation to the people in terms of the image of marriage. According to the biblical text, this representation was not invented by the prophet himself but goes back to revelation by God, in which something unbelievable is demanded of its mediator: "Go, take to yourself a wife of harlotry and have children of harlotry, for the land commits great harlotry by forsaking the Lord."[265]

Israel as whore, of course, is only the counterimage to the ideal of the last days, when the bride will be faithful to her husband: "And I will betroth you to me in righteousness and in justice, in steadfast love and in mercy."[266]

In the writings of succeeding prophets of Israel, the image takes on an equally central significance. It can be found in the different levels of the

---

[262] Eph 5:21–33. More will be said about this passage in connection with the theme subordination of women: see pp. 351ff. below.

[263] Hos 2:8, 13, 4:10, 13–14; 6:10; 11:1; 13:2 and others.

[264] Cf. Alfons Deissler, "Die Typologie der Frau in der Prophetenliteratur Israels" [The typology of women in the prophet literature of Israel], *US* 35 (1980): 317.

[265] Hos 1:2; cf. especially 2:2ff.

[266] Hos 2:19.

Book of Isaiah,[267] in Jeremiah[268] and in Ezekiel.[269] In all these texts, marriage appears as a *symbol of the Covenant* between God and the people of Israel. It is, anthropologically, the most central symbolic image for designating the most central event in Old Testament sacred history, which continues under the New Covenant. Through it, the divine couple of Canaanite nature religion[270] is reinterpreted in the light of revelation. Masculine and feminine symbolisms *no longer* operate *at the level of the divine* but are transferred, with a new kind of tension, to the *relationship God–man*. As a result, the human and feminine are taken seriously as an independent factor: "The typology of woman in the prophets turns most centrally on the conception of Israel as 'bride' or 'spouse' of Yahweh."[271]

If, in this connection, woman represents *the* symbol of the ideal Israel, then her value is elevated in an unsurpassable way: "Her humanity, as shared with, and equally ranked to, that of the male is the presupposition, as well as the implication, of the whole typology of woman."[272]

The *Song of Songs* was obviously included in the Bible not primarily because of its description of *human* love, but for the sake of its most deeply searching depiction of the mutual love between *God* and Israel.[273] The bride's love here appears as faithful devotion: "Set me as a seal on your heart, as a seal on your arm. For love is strong as death; jealousy is cruel as the grave. Its flashes are flashes of fire, a most vehement flame. [Even] many waters cannot quench love; neither can floods drown it."[274]

Psalm 45, too, was already read from a similar point of view in Judaism. Since it originally referred to the royal court, it is interpreted in terms of a wedding between the Messiah King and Israel: "In many-colored robes she is led to the king, with her virgin companions, her escort, in her train."[275]

---

[267] Is 1:21–26; 5:1ff.; 54:6–7; 62:4–5 and elsewhere.

[268] Jer 2:2; 3:1, 6–12; 31:22.

[269] Ezek 16; 23.

[270] Cf. p. 149 above.

[271] Deissler, "Typologie", p. 324. Strictly considered, therefore, it would be a reversion to pantheistic paganism if, like Grelot, *Couple*, p. 118, we were to regard as the quintessence of all this: "Result: The human couple as an image of *God*" (emphasis mine).

[272] Deissler, "Typologie", p. 324. From this follow quite concrete consequences for the question of the position of women in marriage: Malachi 2:14; Prov 2:17; against Maertens, *Promotion*, pp. 121f.

[273] Cf. Riedel, *Auslegung*, pp. 2–5; Grelot, *Couple*, pp. 75–84; Joseph Heuschen, "Hohes-lied" [Song of Songs], in Haag, *Bibellexikon*, pp. 753–56.

[274] Song 8:6–7.

[275] Ps 45:14–15.

How the symbol was received

The centrality of position that the marriage metaphor occupies in the Old Testament is retained in the New Testament and in Church Tradition.[276] In the Middle Ages—to cite just one example—the Song of Songs was among the books that were commented on most enthusiastically.[277]

The Roman declaration on women in the priesthood thus goes to the heart of the symbolism of the sexes when it interprets the mystery of Christ and his Church in terms of the images of bridegroom and bride.[278] In this, intellectual content is closely linked to expressive form, for the symbols are not interchangeable.

The analogy, in the cited texts, points to the fact that God and Israel, or the Church, are not placed on the same level, but rather every relationship between them originates with God. Given that God grounds the natural and supernatural being of the Church, our thought is led beyond the image of marriage. The ascendant position of the husband was more clearly developed in ancient Israel than it is in modern societies, but nevertheless the symbol retains its enduring value. On the basis of men's physical structure, they incline more strongly toward externally directed activity, whereas women behave more receptively. In the marriage relationship, too, the husband normally tends to assume the leadership role.[279] This does not mean any oppression of the wife involving some presumption of inferiority on her part. Rather, it is much more a matter, insofar as external expression is concerned, of a primacy in the bestowal of love: "Husbands, love your wives, as Christ loved the Church."[280]

The masculine cast of Christ's redemptive work

He taught them as one who had authority (Mark 1:22)

The significance of the symbolism of the sexes is not restricted to the marriage image. This image, rather, is but a concentrated expression of something that is reflected in Christ's entire redemptive work, namely,

---

[276] Cf. especially Riedel, *Auslegung*.

[277] P. Holstein, " 'Place et rôle de la féminité dans le mystère du salut par l'incarnation"; Marie et la question féminine. Pour un dialogue entre théologie et sciences humaines", *Études Mariales* 30/31 (1973–74): 20.

[278] *Erklärung*, Nr. 5, pp. 15f.; *AAS* 69 (1977): 110f.

[279] What was said earlier about eccentricity and centrality with respect to the sexes must be presupposed here.

[280] Eph 5:25; cf. pp. 351ff. below.

his *masculine* human nature. Drawing on the classical doctrine of the three offices,[281] I would like to illustrate this thesis in some detail.

At the center of Jesus' public activity is his preaching. The most familiar designation for Jesus in the Gospel according to Mark is Teacher (διδάσκαλε);[282] in John, too, "the frequent use of 'Rabbi' recalls . . . Mark and the usage original to him".[283] The Gospel according to Matthew gives preeminence to the title *Kyrios*, but precisely in and through his great discourses, Jesus appears, to a special extent, as a teacher.[284]

Now, teaching in a large public forum seems to be something for which men tend to be better suited than women, whereas women seem to be generally more effective in smaller groups and with children. Even in the field of teaching, man and woman complete one another. What we see here is only a difference in emphasis in the participation in the teaching of Christ.

As opposed to men, women have the advantage that their capacity for abstraction is bound up, in an integral way, with intuition and "feeling"; their thinking is more strongly concrete, and is oriented more toward persons than things. Along with this goes the disadvantage that they sometimes confuse the personal and the factual.

Men, by contrast, tend to separate the personal and the factual to a greater degree: And this means they are more likely to be suited to communicating the message of God in its objective content. Their thinking pushes also more strongly into new intellectual territory, whereas women incline more toward appropriating existing possessions and developing and preserving these from within.[285]

His role as teacher thus has an accentuated connection with Jesus as a

---

[281] The offices of teacher, king and priest; cf. Schmaus, *KD II*, 2, pp. 353–57, 487–509.

[282] Friedrich Normann, *Christos didaskalos. Die Vorstellung von Christus als Lehrer in der urchristlichen Literatur des ersten und zweiten Jahrhunderts* [Christos didaskalos. The conception of Christ as teacher in early Christian literature of the first and second centuries], Münstersche Beiträge zur Theologie 32 (Münster, 1967), p. 5.

[283] Normann, *Didaskalos*, p. 54.

[284] Mt 23:8; cf. Normann, *Didaskalos*, pp. 23ff.

[285] Cf. p. 92 above. I am aware that these remarks cause offense, as other authors have already had to experience: Joseph Mausbach, *Die Stellung der Frau im Menschheitsleben. Eine Anwendung katholischer Grundsätze auf die Frauenfrage* [The position of women in the life of mankind. An application of Catholic principles to the question of women], Apologetische Tagesfragen 5, 4th–7th ed. (Mönchengladbach, 1906), pp. 59–63; Robert and Alice Scherer, "Wesen der Frau", p. 9; Ellen Sommer-von Seckendorf, "Das Frauenstudium" [Females as university students], in Scherer, *Frau*, pp. 144–48; Sullerot, *Wirklichkeit*, pp. 527–29 and others. I therefore must ask that the special merits of men be seen together with those of women; the inexchangeable role of Mary, as a counterbalance to these comments, will be dealt with later on.

male. Christ well understands how, in word and deed, to direct his audience's attention wholly toward his heavenly Father; again and again, it is said that, especially after a miracle, the crowds praise *God*.[286]

Objectivity is combined with the newness of this teaching, which breaks through all conventions and has its base in Jesus' powerful authority: "You have heard that it was said to the men of old, . . . But I say to you. . . ."[287]

The teaching thus appears as an expression of Jesus' *power*, which corresponds to his masculine expansivity: "And they were astonished at his teaching, for he taught them as one who has authority, and not as the scribes."[288]

"It is unthinkable that such a comment could be made in connection with a female savior figure."[289]

"Some . . . wanted to arrest him, but no one laid hands on him. . . . 'Why did you not bring him?' . . . 'No man ever spoke like this man!' "[290]

Through his words, Jesus forces people to make a decision. In the prophecy of Simeon, the leading theme of Jesus' activity, the demand for faith, can already be glimpsed: "Behold, this child is set for the fall and rising of many in Israel, and for a sign that is spoken against".[291]

The demand for obedience in faith is given symbolic expression in the image of the sword, a typically masculine attribute: "Do not think that I have come to bring peace on earth; I have not come to bring peace, but a sword."[292]

Even the disciples run up against the stumbling block (σκάνδαλον) of faith: "This is a hard saying; who can listen to it?"[293]

Jesus' words are ultimately grounded in the fact that they originate as the self-testimony of the Father. Jesus appears as identical with what he preaches: he *is* the *Word of God*.

The prologue to the Gospel according to John, which acknowledges Christ as *Logos*, was anticipated in the Old Testament. The evangelist could also have chosen the feminine concept of wisdom, but that of word seems preferable by virtue of its masculine connotations:

> For as the rain and the snow come down from heaven, and return not thither
> but water the earth, making it bring forth and sprout, giving seed to the

---

[286] Cf., among others, Mt 9:8; Mk 2:12; Lk 7:16; 19:36.
[287] Mt 5:21–22.
[288] Mk 1:22; cf. also esp. Mt 7:28–29.
[289] Scheffczyk, "Wesen", p. 53.
[290] Jn 7:44–46.
[291] Lk 2:34.
[292] Mt 10:34; cf. Is 49:2; Rev 1:16; 19:15; Eph 6:17; Heb 4:12.
[293] Jn 6:60.

sower and bread to the eater, so shall my word be that goes forth from my mouth; it shall not return to me empty, but it shall accomplish that which I purpose, and prosper in the thing for which I sent it.[294]

Is not my word like fire, says the Lord, and like a hammer which breaks the rock in pieces?[295]

For while gentle silence enveloped all things, and night in its swift course was now half gone, your all-powerful Word leaped from heaven, from the royal throne, into the midst of the land that was doomed, a stern warrior carrying the sharp sword of your authentic command.[296]

Already at the inner-trinitarian level, the creative power of the divine Word reveals itself as established, in that together with the Father it brings forth, in a single act, the Holy Spirit. This trinitarian connection is continued in the sending of the Spirit after Easter[297] and in its contribution to the life of the Church.[298]

Jesus' acts of power as accompaniments to the Word

The Word, in the cited contexts, is always a dynamic concept: it effects what it proclaims.[299] The power of the *Word* is carried on in Jesus' acts of power (δυνάμεις). The miracles are *the* sign in which historical revelation manifests itself. At the same time, as *factum pro sensibus*, they serve to certify the Word[300] and to proclaim the omnipotence of God: "But when Simon Peter saw it, he fell down at Jesus' knees, saying, 'Depart from me, for I am a sinful man, O Lord.' "[301]

"What is this? A new teaching! With authority he commands even the unclean spirits, and they obey him."[302]

Thomas: "My Lord and my God!"[303]

The miracles are no mere ornament to the redemptive work but are

---

[294] Is 55:10–11.

[295] Jer 23:29.

[296] Wis 18:14–16.

[297] Jn 15:26; 20:22; Lk 24:49; Acts 1:8.

[298] 1 Pet 1:23; Col 1:25–27.

[299] Cf. Leo Scheffczyk, "Die Heilsbedeutung des Wortes in der Kirche", in Leo Scheffczyk, *Schwerpunkte des Glaubens. Gesammelte Schriften zur Theologie* [Crucial points of religious belief. Collected writings on theology], Sammlung Horizonte, Neue Folge 11 (Einsiedeln, 1977), pp. 327–48, esp. p. 352; Leo Scheffczyk, *Von der Heilsmacht des Wortes* [On the saving power of the Word] (Munich, 1966).

[300] Mt 11:2–6; Jn 2:11; 3:2; 6:14; Acts 1:3 and elsewhere. The last cited passage speaks of "proofs"; cf. DS, 3033, 3539.

[301] Lk 5:8.

[302] Mk 1:27.

[303] Jn 20:28.

grounded in Jesus' majesty. They appear as "emanations of his own nature. . . . In the fullness of his power, he reveals, as a man, the power and goodness of God."[304]

Not only the power, but also the graciousness: "In any case, it can only be due to Jesus' boundless goodness and friendliness that his mysterious power struck those around him not as something frightful, but as something inviting."[305]

At one point, this merciful benevolence even leads to a glimmer of maternal traits in Jesus: "O Jerusalem, Jerusalem, killing the prophets and stoning those who are sent to you! How often would I have gathered your children together as a hen gathers her brood under her wings, and you would not!"[306]

Jesus is gentle and lowly in heart: "For my yoke is easy, and my burden is light."[307] But Christ does not appear here—as in some depictions by the Nazarenes—as a sweet and weakly kitsch figure.[308] His goodness arises from no lukewarm humanitarian daydreaming,[309] but is conscious and power charged. The one who uttered the saying about being struck on the cheek[310] is also the one who carried out the cleansing of the temple.[311] Those in Nazareth wanted to throw him to his death: "But passing through the midst of them he went away."[312]

Thus Jesus' benevolence can be understood only through his omnipotence. It is the attitude of the servant of God who, *despite* his power, does not break the bruised reed or quench the dimly burning wick.[313] Jesus' human nature, moreover, is both the image and the instrument of his divinity; Christ's corporeality is inextricably bound up with his divine filiation and with the redemptive work that springs from this. What was said earlier here about the relation between transcendence and immanence in the Old Testament image of God is analogically applicable as well to the Lord's masculinely stamped human nature.

---

[304] Georg Bichlmair, *Der Mann Jesus* [Jesus the man], 4th ed. (Vienna, 1948), p. 91.
[305] Bichlmair, *Jesus*, p. 90.
[306] Mt 23:37; cf. Lk 13:34.
[307] Mt 11:29–30.
[308] Bichlmair, *Jesus*, p. 14.
[309] Bichlmair, *Jesus*, p. 157.
[310] Mt 5:39.
[311] Mt 21:12ff. par; especially palpable: Jn 2:14–16.
[312] Lk 4:30.
[313] Is 42:3.

Christ as King and Lord

The power that is reflected in Jesus' words and deeds and that forms the inner ground of the possibility of his goodness appears especially in his position as Lord. "Jesus Christ is the Lord"—this is the central tenet of the New Testament, as is the corresponding conception in the Old Testament.[314] He who proclaims the kingly rule of God (ἡ βασιλεία τοῦ θεοῦ)[315] is himself "King of kings and Lord of lords".[316] As the Good Shepherd,[317] he simultaneously embodies the benevolence *and* the sovereignty of God. His kingly rule does not aim at forcing belief; therefore, it conceals itself in the garb of humility. But the one who enters Jerusalem, not in splendor and magnificence but mounted on an ass,[318] will appear again, at the end of the day, as mighty, "seated at the right hand of Power, and coming on the clouds of heaven".[319]

Jesus' kingly office also manifests itself in the fact that he not only makes promises, but goes further, and presents himself as a lawgiver: "All authority in heaven and on earth has been given to me. Go therefore and make disciples of all nations . . . , teaching them to observe all that I have commanded you."[320]

As lawgiver, he is also judge: "Before him will be gathered all the nations, and he will separate them one from another as a shepherd separates the sheep from the goats."[321] "And cast the worthless servant into the outer darkness; there men will weep and gnash their teeth."[322]

Now, bearers of authority are more often men than women. On this point, the sociological findings, based on biology, speak in exceedingly clear terms.[323] Advocates of the ordination of women like to contest this fact but often enough tend to confirm it in an indirect way. Time and again, we hear from them the slogan that office does not imply ruling but serving,[324] but in this it is presupposed that women have a greater facility for subordination, for serving.

Jesus' authority cannot, however, be played off against being a servant,[325]

[314] Cf. p. 220 above.
[315] Mk 1:14.
[316] Rev 19:16; cf. Lk 1:32–33; Jn 18:7.
[317] Jn 10:11; cf. Mt 18:12–14; Lk 15:3–7.
[318] Mt 21:5 par.
[319] Mt 26:64.
[320] Mt 28:18–20; cf., among others, Jn 15:10 and DS 1571.
[321] Mt 25:32.
[322] Mt 25:30.
[323] Cf. pp. 104ff. above.
[324] For instance, R. R. Ruether, "Ordination: What Is the Problem?" in Gardiner, *Expanded Vision*, p. 34.
[325] Mk 10:42–45.

for the latter is supported from within by immeasurable power: "If I, then, your Lord and Teacher, have washed your feet, you also ought to wash one another's feet."[326]

The sacrifice on the Cross as pivotal in the matter of sexual symbolism

Introduction

Jesus' kingly position is regarded by some authors as the real reason that the Son of God became man in the form of a male: "The authority with which he was to bring God's revelation to the world and establish the Church was congruent with a more specifically male characteristic. A man seems more capable of commanding, of directing."[327]

I think that this observation is correct, but, in my opinion, it does not yet go to the heart of the matter. Jesus' position of power is most completely realized in that which forms the high point of his activity and influence, namely, in the sacrifice at Calvary, where he said whoever "would be great among you must be your servant, and whoever would be first among you must be slave of all. For the Son of Man also came not to be served but to serve, and to give his life as a ransom for many."[328]

If Jesus' masculinity is of central significance, *then* this must also be reflected in the Crucifixion. With respect to the image of God, I have already shown that there is a specifically masculine dialectic between transcendence and immanence, power and benevolence and righteousness and mercifulness,[329] and, as well, a relevant cast to the offices of king and teacher. Can this support of immanence by transcendence also be found with respect to the sacrifice on the Cross?

Power as the enduring starting point for renunciation

The Philippians hymn contains a concise summary of the entire Christian message of salvation: the Son of God "emptied himself, taking the form of a servant, being born in the likeness of men". He "humbled himself and became obedient unto death, even death on a cross".[330]

The humbling of Jesus can only be understood, however, when its

---

[326] Jn 13:14.

[327] Jean Galot, *Mission et ministère de la femme* (Paris, 1973), p. 197.

[328] Mk 10:43–45.

[329] Cf. pp. 175–85, 217–25 above.

[330] Phil 2:7–8.

enduring starting point is kept in view, namely, infinite divine power. Only then does the amazed prayer become possible, "that at the name of Jesus every knee should bow, in heaven and on earth and under the earth, and every tongue confess that Jesus Christ is Lord, to the glory of God the Father."[331]

For Jesus, the Cross was no blind fate but a conscious act: "For this reason the Father loves me, because I lay down my life, that I may take it again. No one takes it from me, but I lay it down of my own accord."[332]

Thus we can already state that the crucified love is sustained through divine power. This observation can, however, be more precisely broken down.

Crucifixion and dual priestly representation

Representation of God with respect to man. In the Cross, the two basic strands of priestly representation are manifest: the submission of man to God and the mediation of God's grace to man.[333]

The second of these points of view is almost exclusively stressed in recent literature, as much in the conservative sort as in the progressive, although of course from differing directions. Hanna Wolff categorizes decisiveness and authority as masculine practical values, but he says that the Cross evidences God's *grace*, which bestows itself in motherly love on the sinner: "Jesus allows feminine ontological values to dominate in the image of God!" The decisive attitude of God is one of "sheltering and preserving, caring and nurturing, helping and healing".[334]

Louis Bouyer, too, gives particular emphasis to God's devotion to man in Christ. It is Christ's task to represent God's *gift*,[335] but precisely in that, a typically masculine dynamics reveals itself: the "passing on of the purely divine creative initiative".[336]

Jesus' submission produces a new creation; it engenders the life of grace. The Son of God thus stands, precisely in his loving devotion to man, also as powerfully *separate* from man, in that he effects the "offering of sacrifice for sins"[337] and the descent of the Holy Spirit.[338]

[331] Phil 2:10–11.
[332] Jn 10:17–18; cf. Mk 10:45; Mt 26:42, 53.
[333] Cf. pp. 190f. above.
[334] Hanna Wolff, *Jesus der Mann. Die Gestalt Jesu in tiefenpsychologischer Sicht* [Jesus the man. The figure of Jesus in psychoanalytic perspective], 2nd ed. (Stuttgart, 1976), pp. 121f.
[335] Bouyer, *Woman in the Church*, p. 73.
[336] Bouyer, *Woman in the Church*, p. 34, cf. p. 57.
[337] Heb 5:3.
[338] Acts 2:33.

Now, grace is a heightening of the immanence of God in the world: "For by one Spirit we were all baptized into one body."[339] However, this immanence, appropriated to the Holy Spirit, nevertheless comes about through the Father and the Son, who send the Paraclete.[340] In this is shown, in a special way, that the givers are not identical with the gift of grace but rather are separate from it. They direct themselves, to a certain extent, outward; this eccentricity has its symbol in Jesus' masculine human nature. Christ does not mediate grace in the way that life, in the immanence religions, constantly flows forth from the wellspring of being—a feminine image—but rather, in a free and sovereign way: people "are justified by his grace as a gift, through the redemption which is in Christ Jesus".[341]

The concepts gift and grace presuppose the powerful personality of the giver. At the same time, they demand the personal response of the recipient, since redemption does not follow automatically; necessary as well is "faith working through love".[342] Since man is accordingly called to answer for himself, refusal of grace brings judgment on him: "And they will go away into eternal punishment, but the righteous into eternal life."[343]

Representation of man with respect to God. Thus, in the representation of God's grace through Christ, authoritative power and a call to decision are always included. Here, too, immanence is made possible through transcendence.

This idea shows itself even more clearly in the first basic priestly structure, the devotion of man to God. As the representative of the community, the officeholder goes beyond his own sphere in moving outward to stand before God's countenance;[344] public worship is marked by the eccentricity of the male. The aim of devotion is the adoration of God, who towers infinitely above the human and secular realms.

The official, publicly and palpably performed self-surrender of man to God is therefore the characteristic element of the sacrifice: the *sacrifice*, in the narrow sense, is "an external religious observance in which a perceptible gift is offered to God by a legitimized servant in recognition of God's absolute, supreme sovereignty and, since the fall, in reconciliation with God".[345]

Both of the basic priestly structures can be illustrated by the image of

---

[339] 1 Cor 12:13.
[340] Jn 14:26; 16:7.
[341] Rom 3:24.
[342] Gal 5:6.
[343] Mt 25:46.
[344] Cf. p. 190 above.
[345] Ludwig Ott, *Grundriss der katholischen Dogmatik* [Outline of Catholic dogmatics], 9th ed. (Freiburg, Basel and Vienna, 1978), pp. 221f. Cf. Diekamp and Jüssen, *Dogmatik II*, pp. 314ff.; Michael Schmaus, *Der Glaube der Kirche. Handbuch katholischer Dogmatik 2* [The Church's Faith. Handbook of Catholic dogmatics 2] (Munich, 1970), pp. 363f.

the Cross. The horizontal beam symbolizes the *turning toward* sinful mankind of the *God* who became man: Christ spreads out his arms to rescue the lost ones. In this, we see the (power-charged) immanence of God, which grounds the life of grace of the new creation.

However, the horizontal beam would be left, so to speak, hanging in the air if it were not supported by the vertical. Christ's love of man is made possible by a love of the Father that totally ignores personal will and transcends itself: "Father, if you are willing, remove this cup from me; nevertheless not my will, but yours, be done."[346]

The primary purpose of the sacrifice is not to bless man but to glorify the Father. The Son became man in order to atone, as representative of the many, for the sins of mankind. This representative atonement appears in the New Testament as the real aim of Jesus' activity. The "for us" and "for many" in the accounts of the Last Supper should be interpreted as "for our benefit" and "in our stead".[347] "God put forward [Christ] as an expiation by his blood, to be received by faith. This was to show God's righteousness".[348]

Whereas Jesus' love appears, with respect to sinners, as mercifulness, it takes on, with respect to his turning toward God, the aspects of *righteousness*: "I glorified you on earth, having accomplished the work which you gave me to do."[349]

Just as Jesus' love of God goes infinitely beyond his love of man while simultaneously sustaining it inwardly, so, too, is the situation regarding the relationship between righteousness and mercifulness. Anyone who eliminates the expiatory nature of Jesus' suffering also nullifies his love of sinners, his mercifulness. Without love of the Father, Jesus would never have interceded on behalf of man. Righteousness and mercifulness are thus not in competition but rather mutually illuminating by virtue of their inner connectedness. Without the "vertical" of transcendence, to speak in images, the "horizontal" of immanence would fall to the ground and be consigned to oblivion.[350]

---

[346] Lk 22:42.

[347] Mk 14:22–25 par.; cf. Mk 10:45 par.

[348] Rom 3:25; cf. Heb 2:17; 1 Jn 2:2; 4:10 and elsewhere. For more detailed information about the representative atonement, cf. Bernhard Wenisch, "Erlösung durch das Kreuz" [Redemption through the Cross], in Hans Pfeil, ed., *Unwandelbares im Wandel der Zeit II* [The unchangeable in the changes of the times II] (Aschaffenburg, 1977), pp. 242–60; Diekamp and Jüssen, *Dogmatik II*, pp. 324–35; Schmaus, *Glaube IV*, 1, pp. 276–80.

[349] Jn 17:4. These words must be taken together with the Son's "hour", in which the "Lamb of God" takes away the sins of the world: 17:1; 1:29; 19:36.

[350] On the connection between righteousness and mercifulness, cf. Leo Scheffczyk, "Gottes Liebe oder Gottes Gerechtigkeit? Von einer falschen Alternative im Gottesverständnis" [God's love or God's justice? On a false alternative in the understanding of God], in Scheffczyk, *Glaube*, pp. 169–77.

This relationship between transcendence and immanence corresponds, in turn, to typically masculine symbolism. Conversely, a horizontal that, so to speak, lies on the ground—that is, mere immanence without any transcendence both making it possible and going beyond it—tends to be linked to feminine values. According to Hanna Wolff, God is no "unbearable patriarchal monster . . . who has to sacrifice his own Son's blood . . . in order to be able to permit 'grace' to reign once again".[351] The doctrine of representative atonement, whose foundations are laid in the New Testament, and which the words just quoted are intended to caricature, is supposedly "the typical sort of reconciliation theory for the patriarchate of the mind. In it, reconciliation itself becomes but a legal act."[352] As a result, for Wolff, the "feminine scale of values . . . is definitive in Jesus' conception of love or for the image of God. . . . God no longer [seeks] any expiation at all for his wounded majesty."[353]

From this perspective, one could quite consistently postulate God's becoming man as a *female*. The name Jesus has here "undergone a change of key . . . from major . . . to minor".[354] However, if God became man as a male, what follows is a doctrine of God and redemption that differs from the one advocated by Wolff.

One might still raise the objection that the second basic strand in priesthood is more significant than the first. For, in the Christian religion, what ultimately matters is not what *we* give to God, but rather, the grace that we *receive from him*.

Certainly God's turning toward man presupposes the response of his creatures, but the latter is, at the same time, evoked through the former. All creaturely activities have their ultimate end in the glorification of God.[355] What is decisive about the sacrifice on the Cross, however, is that Jesus' human nature does not surrender itself alone to God but in indissoluble personal union with the Divinity. The human element in Christ merges with the direction of the Son's life, the loving turning back toward the Divine Father.

In the life of the Trinity, the mutual turning toward one another of the Father and the Son gives rise to the Holy Spirit, the bond of love. Something similar is characteristic as well of sacred history. The primary element in Jesus' sacred work is the sacrifice at Calvary, but what *follows* from that surrender is the Resurrection and the descent of the Holy Spirit. These factors are so intimately related to one another that death and

---

[351] Wolff, *Jesus*, p. 36.

[352] Wolff, *Jesus*, p. 36.

[353] Wolff, *Jesus*, p. 124.

[354] Bichlmair, *Jesus*, p. 24.

[355] Is 43:7; Ps 19:2; 150; Rom 11:36; Heb 2:10 and elsewhere. Cf. Diekamp and Jüssen, *Dogmatik II*, pp. 15–19; Schmaus, *Glaube III*, pp. 110–17.

Resurrection, in John, appear, as it were, in one perspective: "[being] lifted up".[356] Logical primacy, however, rests with the element of sacrifice, which, by its very definition, is related to the glorification of God. The image of God and sacred history are both concentrated in the figure of the *Logos* become human; the soul of Jesus Christ's activity, however, is the sacrifice.

Conclusion

According to the foregoing, all of Christ's tasks are inseparably bound up with his masculinely stamped human nature: "Its richness and . . . beauty . . . are first [seen] in total fullness—as far as this is possible at all—when we also bring into view its typically masculine aspects. They are present, and are more numerous than we might at first suppose."[357]

In view of the preceding considerations, which should be seen together with what was said regarding the theology of creation, I would like to align myself with the following assessment by Louis Bouyer: "At the risk of provoking storms of righteous indignation, I shall state quite frankly: it would have been monstrous if the Son of God had appeared as a woman."[358]

This thought cannot, however, be taken in isolation within the Catholic Faith, since the Son of God "could . . . only have been born among us, as one of us, of a woman",[359] of Mary, who is "full of grace"[360] and, in her *Fiat*, representative of all mankind. But this must be left for discussion in a later section.[361]

Excursus: "Our mother Jesus"

The androgynous image of Christ

Gnostic influences

Jesus Christ, through his human nature, represented not only men in relation to God but also women. Just as the mother symbol is, in a sense, enclosed within the father symbol, so Jesus, too, embodies "feminine" values such as kindness and mildness. To be sure, human nature is

[356] Jn 12:32 and elsewhere.
[357] Bichlmair, *Jesus*, p. 5.
[358] Bouyer, *Woman in the Church*, p. 72.
[359] Bouyer, *Woman in the Church*, p. 72.
[360] Lk 1:28.
[361] Cf. pp. 297ff. below.

differently formed in men and in women, but it nevertheless provides a common basis for mutual encounter. Christ is thus an example not only for men but for both sexes.

This state of affairs has, at times, led to Christ's being seen as "androgynous". Such a notion seems to have its origin in ancient gnosis,[362] where it was linked to relevant misinterpretations of the biblical accounts of creation. Mediated by way of Cabala,[363] the notion found its way particularly to the Protestant mystic Jacob Boehme (died 1624). For him, primal man was a "masculine virgin", who did not split up into the two sexes until after the Fall. After the Resurrection, Christ reinstated this "original androgynous image" in his own person; this male-female transformation is a mark of the eschaton.[364]

Boehme attributes androgynous traits not only to Christ but also—as is less well-known—to God himself.[365] Because of his pantheistic inclinations and androgynous speculations, he was banned from speaking and writing by the church authorities.[366]

Boehme's theories had a significant effect on, among others, many currents of feeling-oriented Pietism[367] and on the German and Russian Freemasons' lodges.[368] This influence was also behind Romanticism[369] and, not lastly, pantheistic-toned German Idealism, which, according to Benz, can be characterized, in a certain sense, as a "Boehme philosophy".[370]

By way of detour through Freemasonry, the androgynous image of Jesus found acceptance especially in Russia, particularly by Soloviev, Berdyaev and Bulgakov.[371] Cabalist notions, too, experienced a revival of influence here.[372] The Russian Orthodox church took these ideas so seriously that, in 1922, at a time of revolutionary external upheaval, she

[362] Cf. pp. 158ff. above.

[363] Cf. pp. 168ff. above. The Cabalist influence here would appear certain: Benz, *Kabbala*, p. 58, n. 2.

[364] Benz, *Adam*, pp. 20, 72.

[365] Leese, *Mutter*, pp. 37f.: the point of religion is to reach the "eternal mother". Mankind should live as children of one mother, "like the branches on a tree, which all draw sap from one root". The mother is the "depths of God", the "heart of God".

[366] Benz, *Adam*, p. 52.

[367] Benz, *Adam*, p. 22.

[368] Benz, *Adam*, pp. 23, 138, 175f. A good survey of Boehme's significant historical influence can be found in W. Schulze, who exposes the Gnostic-theosophical character of this intellectual current in detail and rejects it from the standpoint of Christian belief in creation.

[369] In Germany and France: Benz, *Adam*, pp. 22f. Some oversweet depictions of Christ by the Nazarenes and the "bloody pictures of suffering in Pietism" would not, therefore, have come about merely by chance; cf. Bichlmair, *Jesus*, p. 14.

[370] Benz, *Adam*, p. 23.

[371] Benz, *Adam*, pp. 23f.

[372] Tavard, *Woman*, pp. 159, 163.

condemned Bulgakov's theories and excommunicated their originator.[373] The ban applied not only to his doctrine of an androgynous Christ but also to his sophiology, which, under the influence of Palamism[374] and Cabala, regarded God as androgynous and characterized him equally as "Father" and as "Mother".[375]

A certain continuing influence of these theories seems to be found, too, in Paul Evdokimov, who, although not describing God as androgynous, does describe Christ as such. The polarity of the sexes is thus represented for him not in the figures of Jesus and Mary (at least not in the first instance), but in Mary and John the Baptist: "The pair man–woman ascends as far as to the archetypal pair Virgin–John the Baptist, after which point all separation into man and woman is overcome in Christ, the unification of the masculine and the feminine."[376]

Evdokimov's thought here is strongly influenced by C. G. Jung[377] and several texts from the early Church that are Gnostic in origin.[378] Mediated by Origen and Gregory of Nyssa, the influence of the Platonic sphere ideal continues to be felt.[379]

A certain contradiction in Evdokimov can be seen in the fact that, on the one hand, a male–female image is assumed as the ideal in view; yet, on the other hand, Jesus is replaced by John the Baptist as the male ideal. Such an exchange seems superfluous when the Baptist, too, is transformed into an androgyne, just as, of course, is Mary.

Sympathies for Jacob Boehme's androgynous image of Christ can be found in Protestant theologians such as Ernst Benz,[380] Hanna Wolff,[381] Kurt Lüthi,[382] and Kurt Marti.[383] The "androgynous ideal" in feminist theology has already been mentioned.[384] A relevant work by a Catholic theologian was placed, in its day, on the index.[385]

The Gnostic character of the Christ androgyne comes out especially

---

[373] Benz, Adam, pp. 23f.; Benz, "Geist", p. 460; cf. Tavard, Woman, p. 163.

[374] On this, see Ivánka, Plato, p. 445; Tavard, Woman, p. 158.

[375] Tavard, Woman, pp. 158–70.

[376] Evdokimov, Frau, p. 255.

[377] Evdokimov, Frau, p. 152; cf. pp. 128ff. above.

[378] The Gospel of the Egyptian and a passage dependent on this from 2 Clement: Evdokimov, Frau, pp. 31, 163; cf. on this p. 405, n. 5 below.

[379] Evdokimov, Frau, p. 305, n. 19; cf. p. 251 above.

[380] Benz, "Geist", pp. 473f.

[381] Wolff, Jesus, pp. 47, 53. The influence of C. G. Jung is evident there; cf. Wolff, Jesus, p. 70.

[382] Lüthi, Eva; Lüthi, "Frau", pp. 194–97, 203.

[383] Marti, Zärtlichkeit.

[384] Cf. pp. 65f. above.

[385] Georg Koepgen, Gnosis der Christentums [The gnosis of Christianity], 2nd ed. (1939): "Only in him [Christ] do we find this combination of masculine and feminine in seamless unity", in Wolff, Jesus, p. 58.

clearly in the work of Otfried Eberz. In his opinion, there existed an original, androgynously minded Judaism, which was only later suppressed: "Between the Absolute [of the primal Hebrew gynecocracy] that was called 'Yahweh', however, and the *personal* God of Moses that was called Yahweh there is nothing in common but the name. . . . Rather, Yahweh as the Absolute that was thought of noumenally as *androgynous* was . . . supplanted . . . by the new, *ego-delimited* . . . Yahweh."[386]

Neoplatonism

Running through almost the entire history of ideas, a further source of the androgynous image of Jesus is Neoplatonism. The androgynous, with its accent on feminine values, still remains hidden in Plotinus but forces its way occasionally up out of the underground and into the light of day, as (regarding the image of God) in Porphyry and Synesius of Cyrene.[387] In the early Middle Ages, Scotus Erigena characterized (the resurrected) Christ as androgynous.[388] His Neoplatonically oriented thought succumbed to the danger "that God . . . is seen first of all in terms of his relation to the world; this amounts to placing limits upon God's divinity".[389]

Neoplatonism[390] and similarly inclined Indian philosophy must be included, if partly by way of mediation through Meister Eckhart and Jacob Boehme,[391] among the main sources of German Idealism. In a

---

[386] Otfried Eberz, *Sophia und Logos oder die Philosophie der Wiederherstellung* [Sophia and Logos, or the philosophy of restoration] (Munich, 1967), p. 366; italics mine. These ideas also apply, vice versa, to the "androgyne" Jesus-Mary: Eberz, *Sophia*, p. 368. Eberz describes his own philosophy as "gnosis" (*Sophia*, p. 11); this "knowledge" obviously came to him through Cabala (*Sophia*, p. 366). Cf. Otfried Eberz, *Vom Aufgang und Neidergang des männlichen Zeitalters. Gedanken über das Zweigeschlechterwesen* [On the rise and fall of the male epoch. Thoughts on the two-sexed creature], 3rd ed. (Munich, 1973), p. 128.

[387] Cf. pp. 167, 246f. above.

[388] *Periphyseon*, II, 6–10: PL 122, pp. 532–38. Scotus knows that not his, but the opposing view is generally held: *Periphyseon* II, 14: PL 122, pp. 542f.

[389] Anton Ziegenaus, *Die trinitarische Ausprägung der göttlichen Seinsfülle nach Marius Victorinus* [The trinitarian shaping of divine fullness of being according to Marius Victorinus], Münchener Theologische Studien II, 41 (Munich, 1972), p. 366. Similar views are expressed by Leo Scheffczyk, "Die Grundzüge der Trinitätslehre des Johannes Scotus Erigena. Untersuchung ihrer traditionellen Elemente und ihrer spekulativen Besonderheit" [Foundations of the doctrine of the Trinity in Johannes Scotus Erigena. A study of their traditional aspects and speculative peculiarities], in Johann Auer and Hermann Volk, eds., *Theologie in Geschichte und Gegenwart: (Fs M. Schmaus)* [Theology in past and present (Essays in honor of M. Schmaus)] (Munich, 1957), p. 511; Ivánka, *Plato*, p. 378, n. 3. Hirschberger, *Geschichte I*, p. 402: the relevant theses were condemned in 1225 by Pope Honorius III.

[390] Ziegenaus, *Marius*, p. 367.

[391] Ernst Benz, *Schelling. Werden und Wirken seines Denkens* [Schelling. Development and influence of his thought] (Zurich, 1955), pp. 9f., 12; Benz, *Adam*, pp. 209ff.

special way, all these influences come together in the pantheistic philosophy of Schelling, who, while not himself developing an androgynous image of Christ, nevertheless provided certain starting points for this in his doctrine of wisdom.[392] The Russian philosophers of religion mentioned above, who were most strongly dependent on Schelling's thought,[393] developed those starting points further.

Schelling's philosophy forms a decisive background to Paul Tillich's theology,[394] which clearly reflects the pantheistic aspects of that background source.[395] Tillich attempts to "androgynize" all three "Persons" of the Divinity. The Father is, above all, a maternal "ground of being", and the Spirit "broods" over chaos.[396] Jesus' self-sacrifice "is neither an essential characteristic of the masculine as masculine nor of the feminine as feminine"; therefore it "cancels out the opposition between the sexes".[397]

Certainly, men and women are equally capable of going beyond themselves in the love of God. In the case of Jesus' sacrifice, however, what is involved is not just an internal act but also its external representation. For that, however, masculine eccentricity is essentially constitutive.

It has already been noted that Tillich is probably the most important precursor of feminist theology;[398] if that is true of Tillich, however, then it is also indirectly true of Neoplatonism, Hinduism, Gnosticism and Cabala. All of these thought systems stand out through their leveling of the distinction between God and the world. The androgynous image of Christ is ultimately aimed at neutralizing the sovereignly authoritative traits in Jesus, so that the divine Lord can be recast in the role of maternal ground for a lordship of one's own.

Jesus as "Mother" in the Catholic sphere:
Julian of Norwich

Apart from the obviously heresy-saturated androgynous ideal, the history of the Church contains a kind of worship of maternal traits in the image of Christ that accommodates itself to the framework of the Faith. In the New Testament, Christ is nowhere described as mother, but he himself draws a comparison between himself and a hen that gathers her brood under her wings.[399]

[392] Benz, Adam, p. 212.

[393] Ivánka, Plato, p. 479; Benz, Adam, pp. 269ff.

[394] Lengsfeld, "Symbol", p. 212; Ziegenaus, Marius, p. 368.

[395] Cf. Leo Scheffczyk, Gott-loser Gottesglaube? Die Grenzen des Nichttheismus und ihre Überwindung [Godless belief in God? The limits of nontheism and the overcoming of these] (Regensburg, 1974), pp. 128–53, esp. pp. 145ff.

[396] Cf. pp. 281f. below.

[397] Tillich, Theologie, p. 337.

[398] Cf. p. 70 above.

[399] Mt 23:37; Lk 13:34; cf. p. 260 above. Luke 15:8–10, where God is compared to a

Use of the mother title for Christ crops up for the first time in the apocryphal Acts of Peter (early third century), in which the following words are claimed to have been spoken by the first pope before his martyrdom: "To me you are a father, to me you are a mother; to me you are a brother, a friend, a servant, a supervisor—you are everything, and everything is in you. You are being, and there is nothing other than you."[400]

Admittedly, the Acts of Peter are for the most part Catholic, but the presence of Gnostic influences cannot be overlooked.[401] The concluding sentence of the cited prayer is reminiscent of pantheistic systems.[402] It was probably for this reason that the Latin translator applied his red pencil, striking out the titles "mother" and "brother", which suggested a certain equivalency with the Lord; the remaining names were changed to read: "*auctor et perfector salutis*".[403]

In one of his sermons, John Chrysostom refers incidentally to the "motherliness" of Jesus.[404]

It was not through any direct connection with the New Testament, but indirectly, by way of Pauline theology, that the rise of the worship of Mother Jesus in the Middle Ages came about. Paul characterizes himself, in relation to his communities, as "father",[405] but also as "mother".[406]

In the Middle Ages, there was less inhibition than there is today about applying the title mother to male superiors,[407] and thus it is not surprising that Saint Anselm—perhaps the first to do so—applies, in a prayer to Paul, the mother title to the apostle and also to Jesus:

"*Sed et tu, Jesu, Bone Domine, nonne et tu mater? Annon es mater, qui tanquam gallina quae congregat sub alas pullos suos?*[408] *Vere Domine, et tu mater.*"[409] "But you, Jesus, Good Master, are you not also mother? Yes, you are mother, as the hen who gathers her chicks under her wings."

---

woman seeking a lost coin, seems not to have had any noticeable effect until the advent of feminist theology.

[400] Acts of Peter X, p. 39: translated [in the German edition of this book] from Cabassut, "Dévotion", p. 237.

[401] Altaner and Stuiber, *Patrologie*, p. 134.

[402] Cf. Ramakrishna on the "Divine Mother": "My dear child, nothing exists in the world except me": p. 157 above.

[403] Cabassut, "Dévotion", p. 238.

[404] In Mt hom 76:5: PG 58, p. 700.

[405] 1 Cor 4:15; 1 Th 2:12; Philemon 10.

[406] Gal 4:19; 1 Th 2:7.

[407] Cabassut, "Dévotion", pp. 234–36.

[408] Mt 23:37.

[409] PL 158, pp. 981f. Anselm is perhaps going back here to an Augustinian interpretation of Ps 101:7 (Vg), in which maternal love is attributed to Christ and Paul; cf. Edmund

The mother title is used in connection with the idea that redemption has been effected through a painful birth process, the suffering on the Cross: "*Tu . . . parturiendo mortuus es et moriendo peperisti. . . . Desiderio enim gignendi filios ad vitam, mortuum gustasti et moriens genuisti.*"[410] "In giving birth you died and in dying you gave birth. . . . In the desire of bringing forth sons to life, you tasted death and dying you gave birth."

During the Middle Ages, this idea eventually became quite widespread, above all in the monasteries of England, Germany and France;[411] its influence continued all the way up to modern spirituality.[412] It was further embellished, especially by members of female religious orders, through talk of Christ as a child at the mother's breast.[413]

Both of these strands within Tradition—the painful "birth" in suffering and the "nursing" of creaturely thirst through the flowing of divine grace—can be found at their most pronounced in the English mystic Julian of Norwich (fifteenth century). Especially in Anglo-Saxon literature, her "Revelations", which were ignored by her contemporaries, have recently become a much-cited source, invoked, in fact, for the purpose of supporting the axiom "God is also Mother".[414]

At first sight, that sort of interpretation actually seems to suggest itself: "As truly as God is our Father, so truly is God our Mother."[415]

Under close scrutiny, however, it emerges that nowhere is the Father or the Holy Spirit described as "mother", but only Christ, as eternal wisdom (!) in his human reality. Jesus is "Mother" primarily through his suffering and the altar sacrament: The Father "wanted the second person to become our Mother, our brother and our savior. From this it follows that as truly as God is our Father, so truly is God our Mother. Our Father wills, our Mother works, and our Lord the Holy Spirit confirms."[416] In "accepting our nature he [our Mother Jesus] gave us life, and in his blessed dying on the Cross he bore us to endless life. And since that time . . . he feeds and fosters us."[417] "The mother can give her child to suck of her milk, but our

---

Colledge and James Walsh, *Julian of Norwich, Showings*. Translated from the critical text with an introduction by Edmund Colledge and James Walsh. Preface by Jean Leclercq (New York, 1978), p. 87.

[410] PL 158, pp. 981f. This is probably based on John 16:21.

[411] Cabassut, "Dévotion", pp. 239f.

[412] Cf., for example, J. B. Chautard, *Innerlichkeit* [Inwardness], 6th ed. (Schlierbach, 1947), p. 14.

[413] Especially Mechtild von Hackeborn: Cabassut, "Dévotion", p. 241.

[414] For example, Jean Leclercq, in *Julian*, p. 8; Colledge and Walsh, in *Julian*, p. 25.

[415] Long text, p. 59, in *Julian*, p. 295.

[416] Long text, p. 59, in *Julian*, p. 296.

[417] Long text, p. 63, in *Julian*, p. 304.

precious Mother Jesus can feed us with himself, . . . with the blessed sacrament." "The mother can lay her child tenderly to her breast, but our tender Mother Jesus can lead us easily into his beloved breast through his sweet open side."[418]

In some places, Julian seems to suggest that Christ's "motherhood" is constituted in a special way through the mediation of the Church and Mary:[419] "It is . . . good . . . to be fastened and united to our mother Holy Church, who is Christ Jesus. For the flood of mercy which is his own dear blood and precious water is plentiful to make us fair and clean."[420] "We can . . . go to Holy Church, into our Mother's breast, that is to say into our own soul, where our Lord dwells."[421] "So our Lady is our mother, in whom we are all enclosed and born of her in Christ . . . ; and our savior is our true Mother, in whom we are endlessly born and out of whom we shall never come."[422]

Jesus' "motherliness" thus fits in quite well with classical [Catholic] conceptions. Moreover, in Julian, the Lord's "feminine" traits are not placed *pari cum pari* alongside of the masculine ones, but rather are integrated with and subordinated to them. Thus the pronounced "mother" statements are also found only in chapters 52 to 63 of the "long text", while they are still absent from the first version of the "Showings".[423] Jesus' immanence in the soul is linked by the mystic to powerful transcendence: "In the midst of this city [= soul] sits our Lord Jesus, true God and true man, a handsome person and tall, honorable, the greatest Lord. And I saw him splendidly clad in honors. He sits erect there in the soul, in peace and rest, and he rules and he guards heaven and earth and everything that is."[424]

In Christ, God has become a tiny child: "The little thing that was created beneath our Lady, the Holy Mary, God made to appear to me as small as a hazelnut."

This image does not, however, stand in isolation, but in an infinite tension: the world, too, appears as a "hazelnut" in God's hand. Thus the immanence of the Incarnation is to be seen together with the transcendence of the world's Ruler.[425]

---

[418] Long text, p. 60, in *Julian*, p. 298.

[419] Cf. what was said about Isaiah 66:13 on pp. 232f. above.

[420] Long text, p. 61, in *Julian*, pp. 301f.

[421] Long text, p. 62, in *Julian*, p. 303.

[422] Long text, p. 57, in *Julian*, p. 313.

[423] Moreover, there is a lack of any reference to Jesus' "motherliness" in the table of contents written by Julian herself: "It seems . . . that when Julian composed the summaries of the revelations for chapter 1 of the long text, she had not yet received the most important of the insights which it now expounds" (for Colledge and Walsh): *Julian*, p. 25.

[424] Short text, p. 22, in *Julian*, pp. 87f.

[425] Short text, p. 4, in *Lady Julian of Norwich, Offenbarungen von göttlicher Liebe*. In der

In Julian, we find the clearest statement in the whole of Western intellectual history on the "motherliness" of Jesus, but in a thoroughly ecclesial context. This English mystic can surely not be aligned with the interests of feminist theology. Anyone who thinks that Julian's writings support the thesis "God is also Mother" (in the sense of a *"pari cum pari"*) might well ponder the concluding words of her "Revelations":

> I pray almighty God that this book may not come except into the hands of those who wish to be his faithful lovers, and those who will submit themselves to the faith of Holy Church. . . . And beware that you do not accept one thing which is according to your pleasure and liking, and reject another, for that is the disposition of heretics. But accept it all together, and understand it truly.[426]

The significance of devotion to the Heart of Jesus

While the history of Julian's influence remained up to most recent times confined to her cloister cell, which was sealed off from the surrounding world,[427] similar sorts of ideas were accorded authentic reception by the Church. Devotion to the heart of Jesus is "devotion to Christ's love in and through the symbol of his Heart".[428] Its biblical origins lie in the Gospel according to John: "If any one thirst, let him come to me and drink. He who believes in me, as the scripture has said, 'Out of his heart shall flow rivers of living water.' "[429] One "of the soldiers pierced his side with a spear, and at once there came out blood and water".[430]

Drawing upon these passages in order to characterize Christ as an "incarnation of the suppressed 'Great Mother' "[431] is certainly taking things too far.[432] But it is nevertheless clear that the symbol "heart", in terms of which these passages were later interpreted, represents, in a special way, a feminine attribute. It signifies the quality of wholeness, life as seen from its center.[433] An important promoter of devotion to the heart

---

ursprünglichen Fassung zum ersten Mal übersetzt und eingeleitet von Elisabeth Strakosch [Julian of Norwich, Revelations of Divine Love, in the original version as translated for the first time, with introduction, by Elisabeth Strakosch] (Einsiedeln, 1960), pp. 35f.

[426] *Julian*, p. 343.

[427] Julian was a "recluse", that is, she had herself walled up within the side cell of a church.

[428] Friedrich Schwendimann, *Herz-Jesu-Vehrung heute?* [Devotion to the Heart of Jesus today?] (Regensburg, 1974), p. 7.

[429] Jn 7:37–38.

[430] Jn 19:34; cf. on this Schwendimann, *Herz*, pp. 94f.

[431] Kaltenbrunner, "Geist", p. 174.

[432] Wurz, "Mütterliche", pp. 270f., interprets κοιλία as "maternal womb" and claims: "To drink from a person—that can be done only from a mother."

[433] Cf. pp. 56, 187f. above.

of Jesus was Saint John Eudes, whose interest in the matter derived from reflection on the mystery of the heart of Mary.[434]

The heart of Jesus is not, of course, a feminine symbol, but an expression of the total integration of the feminine components into his masculine human nature. It is no sentimental image but is bound up with his consciously assumed expiatory suffering, which consumes itself, in thoroughly masculine passionate ardor, for the salvation of sinners. The revelations to Margaret Mary Alacoque came during an age of rationalism and Jansenism, when the life of feeling, which finds its echo in the heart, struck the true Gnostic as all but subhuman.[435] The present age is certainly exposed to similar dangers, as is the Church. Theophora Schneider calls attention to a typical product of masculine rationalism. In Luke 2:19 it is said: "But Mary kept all these things, pondering them in her heart." This became, in the first version of the German common translation: "and thought long about them".[436]

Precisely female feminist theologians have recently set themselves against modern clerical rationalism of a "progressive" bent.[437] The cure for that, however, ought not to be sought in an androgynous image of Jesus, but, more probably, in devotion to the heart of Jesus (and supplementary devotion to the heart of Mary),[438] which is of great significance not only for spirituality but also for dogmatics.[439] After all, it was not past times, but precisely our twentieth century that has been consecrated to the heart of Jesus.[440] Could it perhaps be that feminist theology was able to penetrate the Church's sphere only because this oft-repeated appeal failed to meet with sufficient response and was made light of as tasteless sentimentality?

---

[434] Schwendimann, *Herz*, p. 102.

[435] Cf. the analogous reception given by Protestant Pietism to John 7: H. Rahner, *Symbole*, p. 234.

[436] Schneider, "Kirche", p. 209.

[437] Halkes, *Söhne*, pp. 95, 114.

[438] Cf. pp. 307f. below.

[439] Cf. on this the thoroughgoing study by Schwendimann.

[440] Schwendimann, *Herz*, p. 13: "Leo XIII regarded the dedication of the world as the most significant act of his pontificate." All modern Popes have been enthusiastic supporters of devotion to the Heart of Jesus; cf. Schwendimann, *Herz*, pp. 15–25.

4. THE HOLY SPIRIT: "HYPOSTATIZED MOTHERLINESS"?

Introduction

While the masculine character of Father and Son appears quite unequivocal and necessary, the situation regarding the symbolism of the Holy Spirit is somewhat different. Since all external activity, directed upon the created realm, is common to the three Divine Persons,[441] what was said in general about the image of God also applies, in principle, to the Pneuma. Nevertheless, we can attribute (or appropriate) to the Divine Persons specific qualities that approximately reflect the innertrinitarian processes.

The Spirit of God in the Old Testament, the "*ruach* Yahweh", is feminine according to linguistic usage. In the Greek New Testament, the feminine *ruach* becomes the neuter *pneuma*, and is then fully masculinized in Latin to *spiritus*. Catharina Halkes sees in this a suppression of feminine values and calls for a revitalization of the "forgotten" female references in the Third Divine Person: A "feminist theology" must be a "primarily pneumatological theology".[442] Does this mean that speaking in a new way, about the "Holy Spiritess", is perhaps the need of the moment?[443]

"*Lady* Ruach"?

The basic meaning of *ruach* is "breath, wind, spirit".[444] In the background is the human experience of breathing, in which life manifests itself. This *ruach* also means the principle of life, which acts from within, out of the depths of man. Feminine associations are, therefore, conceivable in the way that they seem to be represented in the mandala symbol of mysticism and in the Indian equivalence between brahman and atman.[445]

Of course, the meaning breath of life expands, precisely with respect to the Spirit of God, into more masculine references. *Ruach* also means the wind, especially the storm wind, which, suddenly and unexpectedly, takes powerful hold of a man and drives him into action.[446] The Spirit

---

[441] DS 800, pp. 1330f.

[442] Halkes, "Theologie", p. 297.

[443] Thus suggests Marti, *Zärtlichkeit*, p. 109.

[444] Gesenius, *Handwörterbuch*, p. 478.

[445] Cf. p. 153 above.

[446] Cf., for instance, the original descriptions in Judges 13:25; 14:6; 3:10; 1 Samuel 10:10; 11:6.

can, therefore, as a creative force, be taken as paralleling the "Word".[447]
As opposed to flesh, Spirit signifies the superhuman dynamics of God.[448]

The Greek *pneuma* is almost identical with *ruach*: "breeze, puff, wind, breath, soul, spirit" and so forth.[449] During the feast of Pentecost, according to what the apostle's account reports, "suddenly a sound came from heaven like the rush of a mighty wind, and it filled all the house. . . . And they were all filled with the Holy Spirit."[450] "The wind [πνεῦμα] blows where it wills, and you hear the sound of it, but you do not know whence it comes or whither it goes; so it is with every one who is born of the Spirit" [πνεῦμα].[451]

This wind arises from Christ's "breath": he "breathed on them, and said . . . 'Receive the Holy Spirit'."[452]

Feminine (breath) and masculine (wind) references thus balance each other out. The fact that *ruach* is treated as a feminine substantive seems to be of no great significance, since *all* Hebrew nouns are either masculine or feminine; the neuter is nonexistent. To be sure, grammatical gender is, to a certain degree, an "extension of the natural to each and every object".[453] But this "theory is unqualifiedly correct only for the original foundations, not for the individual cases, of the . . . language. In countless instances, the gender of a word is simply dependent upon its form, partly through conceptual analogy with some other word."[454]

Had the neuter existed in Hebrew, then it would have served as probably the most suitable category for the noun. For *ruach*, in the Old Testament, does not yet signify any Divine Person but rather an impersonal force of God's. The influence of this meaning continues on into the New Testament: *pneuma* is neuter. There, however, the Spirit appears as a Person;[455] since personality is usually grammatically bound up with sex differentiation,[456] *pneuma* is sometimes linked, in the Gospel according to John, not to a neuter but to a masculine pronoun.[457] In this usage, the masculine *spiritus* is already foreshadowed.

[447] Ps 33:6; perhaps, too, Gen 1.
[448] Is 31:3; cf. 40:6–8.
[449] Bauer, *Wörterbuch*, pp. 1338ff.
[450] Acts 2:2, 4.
[451] Jn 3:8.
[452] Jn 20:22.
[453] Jakob Grimm, *Deutsche Grammatik* [German grammar], 1890, in Bertholet, *Gottheit*, p. 6.
[454] Jakob Wackernagel, *Vorlesungen über die Syntax* [Lectures on syntax], 1924, in Bertholet, *Gottheit*, p. 7.
[455] Cf. among others Mt 28:19; Jn 14:26; 16:13; Acts 20:28.
[456] Bertholet, *Gottheit*, pp. 4f.; cf. p. 179 above.
[457] ἐκεῖνος: Jn 16:8, 13f.

Old Testament wisdom as archetype of the Holy Spirit

Whereas *ruach*, in the Old Testament, is not expressly invested with female attributes, the situation is different regarding "wisdom" (*chokma*). If the word *ruach* had, in fact, implied specifically feminine associations, a sidestep over to the—in many respects similar—concept of *chokma* would probably not have been necessary.

In the Old Testament, wisdom appears quite clearly as a kind of hypostatized force of God's that possesses feminine traits. She is God's companion[458] and "sits by" his throne.[459] In relation to mankind, she appears as "bride"[460] and "mother".[461] *Chokma* occasionally occurs as a synonym for *ruach*;[462] thus the Church Fathers have interpreted wisdom in relation not only to Christ but also to the Pneuma.[463]

Quite similarly to the Indian shaktis,[464] wisdom embodies God in his *connection with the world*, in his immanence. From its very origins, theological wisdom speculation in Israel aims at investigating the nature of God's activity in the cosmos.[465] All the regions of the world offer themselves to the wonder-struck gaze of the devout wise man: "For from the greatness and beauty of created things comes a corresponding perception of their Creator."[466]

God's immanence is described, quite descriptively, as a *"dwelling in"*: wisdom will not "dwell in a body enslaved to sin".[467] "Among all these [peoples] I sought a resting place; I sought in whose territory I might lodge. Then the Creator of all things gave me a commandment . . . : 'Make your dwelling in Jacob, and in Israel receive your inheritance.' . . . In the beloved city . . . he gave me a resting place, and in Jerusalem was my domain. So I took root in an honored people."[468] In a complete way, the spirit of wisdom shall rest upon the Messiah.[469]

Already in Exodus, God's immanence in the people of Israel is intimated

---

[458] Wis 8:3.

[459] Wis 9:4.

[460] Wis 8:2, 9.

[461] Sir 15:2.

[462] Wis 1:4–6; 7:7, 22; 9:17.

[463] Yves Congar, *Der Heilige Geist* [The Holy Spirit]. (Freiburg im Breisgau, 1982), pp. 27, 426.

[464] Cf. p. 154 above. See also the texts reprinted in Schipflinger, "Aspekt", pp. 282f.

[465] Rad, *Theologie I*, p. 463.

[466] Wis 13:5.

[467] Wis 1:4.

[468] Sir 24:7–8, 11–12.

[469] Is 11:2.

by the cloud that covers the tent of meeting.[470] The same occurrence is repeated at Solomon's consecration of the temple: the cloud filled "the house of the Lord, so that the priests could not stand to minister . . . ; for the glory of the Lord filled the house of the Lord. Then Solomon said, '. . . I have built you an exalted house, a place for you to dwell in for ever.' "[471]

In rabbinical Judaism, the "dwelling" of the cloud, or of wisdom, in Israel leads to the notion of God's shekina; which quite clearly allows the Lord's immanence to be represented through feminine traits. When Rabbi Joseph hears his mother approaching, he is reminded of God's presence: "I must rise at the approach of shekina."[472] The Talmud often treats the concepts shekina and Holy Spirit as synonymous.[473]

Wisdom not only appears as an aspect of God but also stands as something separate and distinct from him. We see it in the role of mediatrix between God and Israel, and it is emblematic of the perfect response of creation to the activity of its Lord: "When he marked out the foundations of the earth, then I was beside him, like a master workman; and I was daily his delight, rejoicing before him always, rejoicing in his inhabited world and delighting in the sons of men."[474] "In the holy tabernacle I ministered before him, and so I was established in Zion."[475]

Worldly features seem to be suggested by the comparison, on equal terms, with the Torah in the Book of Jesus Sirach, while, at the same time, a mediatory element is also suggested.[476] Similarly to the way in which wisdom was transmuted into shekina, the Torah is later hypostatized as a preexistent being by the rabbis; the "law", too, appears as a female mediatory figure.[477]

To a certain extent, then, "wisdom" is left hanging in the air. On the one hand, it is allied with God, as something distinct from the created realm; on the other hand, it appears as a principle that, so to speak, effects the world's response to God from within, and itself exhibits worldly features.

Without doubt, the most important New Testament fulfillment of "wisdom" is the figure of Christ, with whom it is expressly associated.[478]

---

[470] Ex 40:34–38.

[471] 1 Kings 8:10–13.

[472] Translated (in the original German version of this book) from Raphael Loewe, *The Position of Women in Judaism* (London, 1966), p. 31.

[473] Patai, *Goddess*, p. 148.

[474] Prov 8:30–31.

[475] Sir 24:10.

[476] Sir 24:23.

[477] Loewe, *Women*, p. 28.

[478] Cf. especially Mt 11:19 par; Lk 11:49; 1 Cor 1:24–30. Wisdom 7:26 is taken up in John 1:9; 2 Corinthians 4:4; Colossians 1:15; Hebrews 1:3.

This means that the feminine aspects of wisdom are practically eradicated. To a certain extent, however, they can be attributed both to the Holy Spirit, who—as I will elaborate upon later—embodies God's "immanence", and, to a still greater extent, to the figure of Mary.[479]

Water symbolism

A key part in the problem of whether there is a sexual cast to the Spirit is played by water symbolism, which, in certain contexts, is expressive of feminine values.[480]

Time and again the Bible describes the Holy Spirit in terms of the symbolic image of life-giving water, which, in the New Testament, effects a new "birth" through baptism: "Unless one is born of water and the Spirit, he cannot enter the kingdom of God."[481]

"Baptism" and "Spirit" are intimately related: you "have received the spirit of sonship. When we cry, 'Abba! Father!' "[482]

Already in the New Testament, the Holy Spirit is associated with bridal-maternal reception into the Church,[483] and this is later formulated especially clearly in the texts for the sacrament of baptism by water: "May this water here, prepared for the re-birth of man, be fructified by the Holy Spirit through the mysterious infusion of his divine breath . . . and may a heavenly people arise from the immaculate womb of the divine font, born as new creatures. And . . . may grace bear them, in common infancy, as if their mother."[484]

The sacrament of baptism by water is also related to the opening verses of the Bible, which describe the Holy Spirit as "moving over" the waters: "In the beginning God created the heavens and the earth. The earth was without form and void, and darkness was upon the face of the deep; and the Spirit of God was moving over the face of the waters."[485]

The images used here overlap with ancient Oriental creation myths, in which the world is held to have arisen from an undifferentiated primordial state, from chaos (tohuvabohu). The word abyss (t^{e}hom) is reminiscent of the female sea monster Tiamat, against whom—in the Babylonian epic Enuma elish—the demiurge Marduk does battle, and out of whose body the earth

---

[479] Cf. pp. 316f. below.
[480] Cf. p. 141 above.
[481] Jn 3:5.
[482] Rom 8:15; cf. Gal 4:6; Mk 1:8 par.
[483] Rev 22:17; cf. Lk 1:35.
[484] Das vollständige Römische Messbuch [The complete Roman missal], ed. by the Benediktinern der Erzabtei Beuron (abridged: Schott) (Freiburg im Breisgau, 1963), p. 417.
[485] Gen 1:1–2.

is formed. Thus, feminine associations are linked with the waters of the primordial ocean not only psychologically but perhaps even historically.

Now, "*ruach* Yahweh" is set up as an opposite to these feminine images. On the basis of Syrian linguistic usage,[486] some earlier expositors have translated the verb associated with the Spirit as "to brood", which would be linked to connotations of a mother bird. This was even seen as evidence for biblical acceptance of the myth of the cosmic egg.[487]

However, such a notion was by no means admitted into the Old Testament, as is apparent from the central significance of the Genesis verses. More appropriate is the translation "to move over" (German: *schweben* = "to hover, float, hang suspended"), which has a literal parallel in Deuteronomy: God leads his people like an eagle "that stirs up its nest, that flutters over its young".[488]

Furthermore, what is involved here is not the image of a bird but of the wind: "God's storm-wind was moving over the surface of the waters."[489] According to Claus Westermann, the cosmic-egg hypothesis that is linked to the translation "to brood" has been "generally rejected".[490]

Consequently, creation is no emanation from the depths, but rather a process from above, as is suggested even by the relevant preposition (*al* = "upon, over"). In contrast to the case in pagan myths, creation is not "born" out of God but is *established* through his powerful Word: "And God said, 'Let there be light'; and there was light."[491]

The same idea is expressed by the verb (*bara*) used in Genesis 1:1, which "[mediates] a conception of the absolute effortlessness of divine creation. The short enunciation of Yahweh's will suffices to call the world into being. But if the world is a product of the creative Word, it is, on the other hand, sharply distinguished ontologically from God himself; it is neither an effusion (emanation) nor a mythically understandable self-representation of the divine nature and its powers."[492] Particularly in the merely negative concept of night (as absence of light), we can probably see an allusion to the "creation ex nihilo".[493]

---

[486] Cf. pp. 292f. below.

[487] Cf. pp. 137f. above.

[488] Dt 32:11. Involved here is the only parallel to the verb form *rhf pi*; cf. Glesenius, p. 756.

[489] According to the translation by Westermann, *Genesis*, p. 141; cf. Rad, *Mose*, p. 27. In interpreting the term *rhf*, which appears only three times in the Old Testament, we must rely on Ugaritic parallels: "The Ugaritic cognate describes a form of motion as opposed to a state of suspension or rest": E. A. Speiser, *Genesis*, The Anchor Bible (Garden City, 1964), p. 5.

[490] Westermann, *Genesis*, p. 148.

[491] Gen 1:3.

[492] Rad, *Theologie I*, p. 156.

[493] This, to be sure, is first formulated conceptually in 2 Maccabees 7:28. Cf. Rad, *Theologie I*, p. 156; Rad, *Mose*, p. 31; Westermann, *Genesis*, pp. 150ff.

The Spirit's connections with the wellspring waters of baptism and with the primal ocean in creation may well suggest feminine images, but these are balanced out, in a paradoxical way, by masculine symbolism. The rebirth occurs not through the earthly forces of creation, which, as it were, bring forth a wellspring from themselves,[494] but rather, "from above": "Unless one is *born from above*, he cannot see the kingdom of God."[495]

However, what comes down from above, particularly rain, is almost always seen in the psychology of religion as masculine, as is, in the Old Testament, particularly the Word of God.[496] But the Spirit, too, does not flow up out of the depths of man's unconscious; instead, he is "poured out" from above: "I will pour my Spirit upon your descendants, and my blessing on your offspring. They shall spring up like grass amid waters, like willows by flowing streams."[497]

This linguistic context gives expression to the idea that the Holy Spirit does not send himself, but is *sent*. As something sent, he embodies the gracious immanence of God that inheres, so to speak, like life-giving water in created things. Feminine associations can, then, become attached to this, especially if the Spirit not only arises from a "wellspring",[498] but is even himself a "wellspring" of grace: the "water that I shall give him will become in him a spring of water welling up to eternal life".[499]

God's immanence is linked here with man's immanence: you "shall be like a watered garden, like a spring of water, whose waters fail not".[500] In respect of their life-giving sustenance of Israel and nature, both God himself, in the Old Testament, and Christ, in the New Testament, can evoke associations of wellspring symbolism: "For with you is the fountain of life; in your light do we see light."[501] "They have forsaken me, the fountain of living waters, and hewed out cisterns for themselves . . . that can hold no water."[502]

That the feminine associations of wellspring are so lacking in prominence

---

[494] Cf. pp. 138f. above.

[495] Jn 3:3; cf. James 1:17–18; 1 Pet 1:23.

[496] Is 55:10–11.

[497] Is 44:3–4; cf., among others, Joel 3:1–2; Acts 2:17; Rom 5:5; Titus 3:5. Apropos the verb ἐκχέειν: everything "that comes from above [is] connected with this verb": Bauer, *Wörterbuch*, p. 490.

[498] As in Jn 7:38; 19:34.

[499] Jn 4:14; cf., too, the Church hymns to the Holy Spirit: *"fons vivus, ignis, caritas et spiritalis unctio"*. *"Lava, quod est sordidum, riga, quod est aridum, sana, quod est saucium."* From *"Veni Creator Spiritus"* and *"Veni Sancte Spiritus"*, whose symbolism is, of course, richer in content and encompasses more than just "feminine" aspects.

[500] Is 58:11; cf. Ps 1:3, and many others.

[501] Ps 36:9; cf. 42:2–3.

[502] Jer 2:13; cf. 17:13. Christ as "wellspring": Jn 4:10, 13f.; 7:38; 1 Cor 10:4.

is perhaps due to the fact that the wellspring expands into a mighty stream, fertilizing the earth and thus appearing as masculine: "To the thirsty I [Christ] will give [to drink] from the fountain of the water of life without payment."[503] "Then he showed me the river of the water of life . . . , flowing from the throne of God and of the Lamb."[504]

The symbolic image of the dove

Associations even more feminine than those surrounding the image of water are found in the symbol of the dove,[505] which the rabbis had already applied to Genesis 1:2.[506] Particularly emphasized are the bird's quick flight[507] and its softness.[508] It is *the* symbol for the young bride.[509] "Spirit" and "Bride" (as a symbol of the Church) are linked with each other in the Apocalypse.[510]

In the early Church, the eucharistic dove had a significance similar to that of the tabernacle today; as image of the Holy Spirit—which descended on Christ in the Jordan and brought about his Incarnation as well as effecting the transubstantiation of the eucharistic offering—the dove, cast in precious metal, harbors the sacred Host, which is present in the church to be worshipped.[511]

It is well to take this liturgical reference into consideration when the Fathers designate both Mary and the Church as "Dove", and thereby draw closer, in a special way, to the activity of the Holy Spirit.[512]

The Holy Spirit and God's immanence

God's immanence in the baptized is attributed by the New Testament, in a preeminent way, to the Holy Spirit. The course of the Christian's life unfolds *in* the Spirit *through* the mediation of Christ *toward* the Father.[513]

---

[503] Rev 21:6.

[504] Rev 22:1; cf. Ezek 47:1–12; Ps 46:5; Gen 2:10.

[505] Mk 1:10 par.

[506] Hendrik Frehen, "Taube" [Dove], in Haag, *Bibellexikon*, p. 1712.

[507] Ps 55:7.

[508] Mt 10:16.

[509] Song 2:14; 6:9; cf. 4:1; 2:12.

[510] Rev 22:17.

[511] This fact, previously given little attention in liturgical studies, has been emphasized recently by Gottfried Melzer, *Die Aufbewahrung der Eucharistie seit frühchristlicher Zeit* [The preservation of the Eucharist since early Christian times] (Sillian, 1975), esp. pp. 22f., 55f.

[512] Julius Tyciak, *Mariengeheimnisse* [Marian mysteries] (Regensburg, 1940), pp. 40, 43.

[513] Eph 2:18.

"But you are not in the flesh, you are in the Spirit, if in fact the Spirit of God dwells in you."[514] This dwelling in of the Spirit turns the body of the Christian into "God's temple": "Do you not know that you are God's temple and that God's spirit dwells in you?"[515]

In the Old Testament, this notion of dwelling in is linked to that of the cloud, as suggestive of God's presence[516] as well as of (feminine) wisdom.

According to the New Testament, God's gracious immanence pervades the innermost part of the baptized, the "heart": "God's love has been poured into our hearts through the Holy Spirit which has been given to us."[517]

With this, the promise to Ezekiel is fulfilled: "A new heart I will give you, and a new spirit I will put within you; and I will take out of your flesh the heart of stone and give you a heart of flesh . . . , and cause you to walk in my statutes and be careful to observe my ordinances."[518]

The divine immanence of grace in the world has its ultimate ground in the mystery of God itself. It is because he is the innermost, the "heart" of God, that the Holy Spirit dwells in the heart of the Christian: "God has revealed [the foregoing] to us through the Spirit. For the Spirit searches everything, even the depths of God. For what person knows a man's thoughts except the spirit of the man which is in him? So also no one comprehends the thoughts of God except the Spirit of God."[519]

It was not until the New Covenant that this mystery of God was able to be revealed in its fullness. In a certain sense, the Holy Spirit can even be characterized as the hypostatized mysteriousness of God, in which the mystery becomes manifest *as* a mystery. Immediately preceding the just-cited passage, it is said: "What no eye has seen, nor ear heard, nor the heart of man conceived, what God has prepared for those who love him."[520] The "mystery of Christ"[521] is revealed by the Holy Spirit.[522]

God's immanence in nature and grace is thus attributed, in a special way, to the Holy Spirit, because he is himself the intradivine immanence in person. As I have shown earlier,[523] however, immanence can be brought into relation with feminine symbolism, especially when transcendence does not appear as an inner constituent. For, at the inner-

[514] Rom 8:9.
[515] 1 Cor 3:16; cf. 6:19; Rom 8:11; Eph 2:22; 2 Tim 1:14; James 4:5 and elsewhere.
[516] Ex 40:34–38; 1 Kings 8:10–13.
[517] Rom 5:5; cf., among others, 2 Cor 1:22; Eph 3:16–17; Gal 4:6.
[518] Ezek 36:26–27.
[519] 1 Cor 2:10–11.
[520] 1 Cor 2:9.
[521] 1 Cor 3:7; Col 1:27; 4:3.
[522] Jn 16:13; Acts 2:4.
[523] Cf. pp. 119f., 141f. above.

trinitarian level, the Holy Spirit is, to be sure, referred to its origins, to the Father and the Son, and thus to something transcendent to it; yet, *as* Spirit, it embodies the innermost aspect of the Divinity, its "immanence".

That the Holy Spirit is bound up in a special way with God's "heart" seems to be suggested particularly in the fourth Gospel: one "of the soldiers pierced his side with a spear, and at once there came out blood and water".[524]

As *the* intradivine mystery, the Holy Spirit is simultaneously the completion of inner-trinitarian life. The movement of the Father's life brings forth the Son as its perfect image, and the reciprocal love between Father and Son attains such fullness that it becomes itself a Person: the Holy Spirit, the "Person in two Persons",[525] in whom archetype and image are interfused with one another. The divine "circular movement" is closed in and through personal love.

As the completion of the life in God, it is to the Holy Spirit "that the last mystery of the world is left: its marriage" to the incarnated Son of God.[526] Only after the rising of Jesus is the Spirit poured upon the disciples,[527] which is intended to stir all of creation and to evoke the prayer: "Abba! Father!"[528] "Come, Lord Jesus!"[529]

The Holy Spirit as a "relational being"

As the one that constitutes the "innermost" aspect of the Trinity, the Holy Spirit is, at the same time, the connecting link between Father and Son. Of course, the Son, too, is a bond between the First and Third Divine Persons, insofar as he mediates the divinity of the Father to the Spirit. But whereas the Son is first engendered and then mediates,[530] the Spirit is identical with his mediatory function.

Therefore, the Holy Spirit appears, even with respect to his healing role, not so much as a Person vis-à-vis the blessed, but more as "a mediation that mediates itself".[531] He hardly shows himself in his

---

[524] Jn 19:34; cf. 7:38–39; 4:10, 13f.

[525] Heribert Mühlen, *Der Heilige Geist als Person* [The Holy Spirit as person], 2nd ed., Münstersche Beiträge zur Theologie, 26 (Münster, 1966), p. 168.

[526] Rudolf Graber, *Maria im Gottgeheimnis der Schöpfung. Ein Beitrag zum Wesen des Christentums* [Mary in the divine mystery of creation. A contribution on the essence of Christianity], 2nd ed. (Regensburg, 1949), p. 101.

[527] Jn 20:22; Acts 2.

[528] Rom 8:15.

[529] Rev 22:20; cf. 22:17.

[530] What is involved here is naturally not a series of events in time, but the material-logical order of the inner-trinitarian processes of emergence.

[531] Heribert Mühlen, "Das Christusereignis als Tat des Heiligen Geistes" [The Christ event as a deed of the Holy Spirit], in *MySal* III, 2, pp. 514–43.

independent nature, and the New Testament characterizes him less as giver than as gift. The Holy Spirit is *the* gift of God absolutely.[532]

Liturgical prayer is directed only in exceptional instances to the Spirit; rather, he tends to remain in the background because his mediation points the Christian's existence toward the Father: God has "sent the Spirit of his Son into our hearts, crying, 'Abba! Father!' "[533]

In themselves, the Divine Persons are, of course, substantial relationships. Still, to the Holy Spirit we can attribute, in a special way, a mode of being that, although sustained by personal identity, is exhaustively constituted in and through relationality. Within the Trinity he is identical with "being a bond", and as intradivine relationality he is also effective in the baptized. Through this, the Christian is brought into the process of trinitarian life but also, simultaneously, is linked to all the members of the mystical Body of Christ: "For by one Spirit we were all baptized into one body . . . and all were made to drink of one Spirit."[534] Be eager "to maintain the unity of the Spirit in the bond of peace. There is one body and one Spirit."[535]

Now, "relationality" is characteristic to a greater degree of women than of men.[536] Women are more strongly bound up with their "near world", especially in taking care of home and children. Their personality makes them particularly suited to devoting themselves wholly to human relationships and to exerting a formative influence on these from within. Their being as persons is as little canceled out by this as is the Holy Spirit's: from this perspective, "relational being" would no longer be a term of abuse[537] but—properly understood—a title of honor.

A "priority" of the Holy Spirit in the image of God?

In today's world, the Holy Spirit's relational and "bonding" character wins him special sympathy. The striving for "one" world, the longing for "communal experience" and "brotherliness" link up with the ecumenical movement, which feels itself to be especially indebted to the Spirit's amalgamating dynamics. The "storm" of the Pneuma at the Pentecost unleashed a movement that can break through petrified structures, so that what results is a special nearness to the notion of change that is valued on almost all sides.

[532] Lk 11:13; Acts 2:38; 10:45; Jn 3:34; Rom 8:23; 1 Th 4:8.
[533] Gal 4:6.
[534] 1 Cor 12:13.
[535] Eph 4:3–4.
[536] Cf. pp. 120, 178 above.
[537] As in Halkes, *Söhne*, p. 23.

Feminist theology is, therefore, according to Catharina Halkes, pre-dominantly pneumatological theology: "More so than to the Father and the Son, female feminist theologians have access to God the Spirit, who embodies the relational (the referential) and the dynamic, and who lights the sparks in what takes place between human beings" [especially, here, in the experience of "sisterhood"]. "Fire and storm, the Dove and the Comforter awaken experiences of God in us more readily than do the images of the Father and the Logos. To them we are indebted for vitality and new life."[538] "God is seen not as the all-controlling Father . . . , but as the Holy Spirit, creation's ground of being."[539]

It is noteworthy that these sentences extend preference, as it were, to the Spirit as opposed to the figure of the Son and, above all, the Father, whose authority and transcendence instill a certain discomfort in feminist theologians. Moreover, while there is much talk of the Spirit's implications for group dynamics, there is absolutely none about his holiness.[540] But this sort of selection (αἵρεσις) is not legitimate, for the task of the Spirit consists precisely in directing the Christian toward the *Father*. His authenticity evidences itself in the prayer that begins not with "*Veni Sancte Spiritus*" but with "Abba! Father!"[541]

The dynamics of the Spirit is not aimed at the introduction of change in the nature of the Church, that is, a new revelation,[542] but at "remembrance" of the Lord's religious message: he "will teach you all things, and bring to your remembrance all that I have said to you".[543] The Spirit will guide the disciples "into all the truth",[544] but its essential structures are already preindicated: "Guard the truth that has been entrusted to you by the Holy Spirit who dwells within us."[545]

Whoever separates the dynamics of the Holy Spirit from the un-changeability of God and his revelation runs the danger of mistaking his own thinking and the often very short-winded dynamics of the spirit of the times for the Spirit of God. Whoever centers the relationality of the Pneuma on sisterhood or brotherhood without directing it, through prayer and sacrifice, toward the heavenly Father has basically put the

---

[538] Halkes, *Söhne*, pp. 42f.

[539] Ruether, *Frauen*, p. 97.

[540] As also elsewhere; cf. Leo Scheffczyk, "Die Heiligkeit Gottes: Ziel und Form christlichen Seins" [The holiness of God: end and form of Christian being], in Scheffczyk, *Glaube*, p. 153.

[541] Gal 4:6; Rom 8:15, 26.

[542] Cf. pp. 68f. above.

[543] Jn 14:26.

[544] Jn 16:13.

[545] 2 Tim 1:14; cf. 4:2–5; 1 Tim 6:20–21.

"spirit of the world" in God's place. The Holy Spirit cannot be surgically removed from the Trinity and the total structure of revelation.

The Holy Spirit as "the divinely receiving"

The essential, the proprium of the Holy Spirit is defined by his position in the process of trinitarian life. The Son arises from the Father; the Spirit, from the Father and Son: his essence is passive breath. Whereas the Father only engenders, while the Son at first receives the Divine Nature and then passes it on in conjunction with the Father (active breath), the Holy Spirit is constituted only by receiving.

In a certain sense, we can, therefore, "designate" him "as the feminine principle in the divinity. . . . He is, in fact, the divinely receiving."[546]

Thus, Matthias Joseph Scheeben, the Catholic dogmatic theologian who, in modern times, has probably provided the most searching theological elaboration of the relation between the sexes,[547] interprets the Holy Spirit as having a "bridelike" or "maidenly" character.[548] For him, this comparison, taken from the corporeal sphere, is more telling than analogies from the intellectual sphere. For he holds that the Augustinian triad of memory, intellect and will represents "strictly considered, only the appropriata, and not the propria of the Divine Persons".[549]

Although not absolutely necessary logically, this idea is developed even further by Scheeben: "In any case, the analogical comparison must first be established on the basis of productions through and in, or with, nature."[550] He distinguishes a double basis in man for analogical comparison with the Trinity: one is held by man in common with the angels, and it is realized "*in his mind* through the act of knowledge and love"; the other "is realized in the *lower part of his nature* through the production of a son by means of

---

[546] Thus says, following M. J. Scheeben, Julius Tyciak, who is strongly influenced by the spirituality of the Eastern Church: Tyciak, *Mariengeheimnisse*, p. 41.

[547] H. U. von Balthasar, *Herrlichkeit. Eine theologische Ästhetik*, I (Einsiedeln, 1961), p. 108. English edition: *The Glory of the Lord. A Theological Aesthetic, I* (San Francisco: Ignatius Press, 1982), p. 116.

[548] M. J. Scheeben, *Die Mysterien des Christentums* [The mysteries of Christianity], Deutsche Klassiker der katholischen Theologie aus neuerer Zeit, I, ed. by Henrich Getzeny (Mainz, 1925), pp. 167–75; M. J. Scheeben, *Handbuch der katholischen Dogmatik, III/IV* [Handbook of Catholic dogmatics, III/IV], Gesammelte Schriften V, ed. by W. Breuning and F. Lakner, 3rd ed. (Freiburg, Basel, and Vienna, 1961), no. 440–45, pp. 188–91.

[549] Scheeben, *Handbuch III/IV*, no. 372, p. 153.

[550] Scheeben, *Handbuch III/IV*, no. 372, p. 153.

procreation and that of a wife, as the companion who binds together father and son, out of the man's side".[551]

Accordingly, "the production of the man, which follows directly from God alone", appears as "an analog of eternal procreation", and "the production of the woman, in which the man plays a mediating part, as an analog of eternal procession".[552]

Presupposed here is a combination of Genesis 1:27 and 2:22, where it is assumed that Eve originated "out of" Adam. Scheeben links this idea to the *"emanation of the Holy Spirit* from the *divinity of Christ"*,[553] which is carried over into the descent in time. Blood and water, which flow from Jesus' side on the Cross, he regards as emblematic of both the eternal emanation and the temporal sending of the Spirit.[554]

He finds a similar symbol, for the origination of the first woman out of the first man, in the biblical story of the "forming" of Adam's "rib" so as to produce "Eve".[555] This parallelism between the old and the new Adam was already pointed out by the Church Father Methodius, who characterized the Holy Spirit as *"costa Verbi"*, or "rib of the Word".[556]

The relation Christ-Spirit corresponds to the relation husband-wife, but also to the relation Christ-Church. Not only the Holy Spirit but also the Church arose from Christ: "The element of divine life that constitutes the Church as bride is taken from the side of the new Adam as he lies deep in the sleep of love."[557]

Spirit and Church are closely linked together: the grace of the Holy Spirit is built into the Church, which is, "so to speak, expanded", "just as Adam's rib becomes Eve's body".[558]

It should be noted that Scheeben does not take the biblical images—including the accounts of creation—as naïve but as revealed expressions of an underlying deeper meaning. The origination of Eve "out of" Adam is the salient point here. This range of problems cannot be discussed in detail here,[559] nor can Scheeben's doctrine of man as an image of God, which would require some "filigree work" in order to refine it systematically and exegetically.[560]

---

[551] Scheeben, *Handbuch III/IV*, no. 373, p. 154.

[552] Scheeben, *Handbuch III/IV*, no. 375, p. 155.

[553] Scheeben, *Handbuch III/IV*, no. 443, p. 189.

[554] Scheeben, *Mysterien*, p. 171.

[555] Scheeben, *Mysterien*, p. 170; Scheeben, *Handbuch III/IV*, no. 440–45, pp. 188–91.

[556] Methodius, *Conviv. Virg. or.* 3:8, in Scheeben, *Mysterien*, p. 171; PG 18, p. 73.

[557] Scheeben, *Mysterien*, p. 170.

[558] Scheeben, *Handbuch III/IV*, no. 443, p. 190.

[559] Cf. on this p. 202, n. 27, above.

[560] From a systematic viewpoint, for example, I would interpret the "double basis in man for analogical comparison with the Trinity" in the sense given it by Saint Thomas. What first

Nevertheless, taking the Holy Spirit as the divinely receiving would be a way of explaining the symbolic representation of God through woman in the most pertinent way. Relationality and immanence are certainly significant connections as well, but the receptivity of woman corresponds particularly with what makes the Holy Spirit, in inner-trinitarian terms, the Holy Spirit: passive breath.

The Holy Spirit: Mother Jesus and our Mother?

Woman is, in a certain respect, an image of the Holy Spirit. However, the feminine traits of the Spirit do not give cause for speaking of the Third Divine Person as a woman or even as a mother, for the mother title leads to such grave misunderstandings that the Church consciously avoids it here.

Scheeben's observation that the "mother, with respect to her participation . . . in man's nature, . . . appears as a binding element between father and son, as does the Holy Spirit with respect to the Divinity",[561] already shows the "brokenness" of the relevant symbolism.

Michael Schmaus objects that, in the analogy of the family for the Trinity, it is not really the Spirit but the Son who should be designated as mother, for the mother, together with the father, passes on to the child the human nature that it receives. In terms of the family symbol, passive breath should be aligned not with the Spirit but with the Son.[562]

---

makes man an *imago Dei* is not his corporeality but his spirituality. For the "doctor angelicus", *imago* implies the highest possible degree of imaged correspondence: (1) a similarity (*similitudo*) that (2) is grounded in the origin (*origo*) of the corresponding image out of the original image and that (3) represents a specification of the original image; however, this cannot here be grounded in corporeality. Cf. Franz Dander, "Gottes Bild und Gleichnis in der Schöpfung nach der Lehre des hl. Thomas von Aquin" [God's image and emblem in creation according to the doctrine of Saint Thomas Aquinas], in *ZkTh* 53 (1929), 1–40, 203–46, esp. 5ff. with reference to Expos. in 2 Cor 4, lect. 2 (the second part of the essay has recently been reprinted in Scheffczyk, *Mensch*, pp. 206–59); cf. Diekamp and Jüssen, *Dogmatik II*, pp. 100–103. Still, corporeality may well also represent an "emblem" of God, but *per modum vestigii*: not the "form" of God (divine nature) but a "trace" (an effect) is then represented (cf. Dander, "Bild", p. 9).

To be sure, Scheeben speaks not of an emblem of God (of the divine nature) but of a symbol of the Trinity. Here, the *vestigium* of sexually stamped corporeality seems to correspond, in fact, to the *proprium* of especially the Holy Spirit.

561 M. J. Scheeben, *Handbuch der katholischen Dogmatik II* [Handbook of Catholic dogmatics, II], Gesammelte Schriften IV, ed. by Michael Schmaus, 3rd ed. (Freiburg, 1948), no. 1019, p. 431.

562 Michael Schmaus, in Scheeben, *Handbuch II*, p. 431, n. 6. See STh, q 93 a 6 ad 2, where Saint Thomas treats a similar question in connection with Augustine, De Trinitate 12:6.

Thus the notion of a "divine family" as symbolic of the Trinity appears more than questionable. If the First Divine Person is to represent the father, and the Third, the mother, then the Son has to be regarded as produced in part by the Holy Spirit, which is theological nonsense.[563] Moreover, this would involve attributing bodily processes to God, and the concrete associations of these would call into question the Creator's spiritual nature.

This problem had already cropped up on a large scale in the "Christian" Gnosticism of antiquity. I have already cited the hymns in the Acts of Thomas, which, among other things, invoke the Holy Spirit in eucharistic epicleses as "mother".[564] These songs originated in Syria, where the cult of the Great Mother played a large role from time immemorial. The *"Dea Syria"*, recorded in Lucian,[565] determines religiosity there to an extent far surpassing that of all other figures, similar to the worship of the mother of the gods, Cybele, in Asia Minor. Since the word for spirit in Syrian—as in the related Hebrew—is feminine, the mother title is often transferred there to the Third Divine Person, a practice obviously following on from pagan religiosity. The Gospel of Philippus, which probably originated in second-century Syria[566] and is related to Valentinian Gnosticism, uses the following argument against the notion that the Spirit

---

[563] Also caught up in this aporia is the philosopher of religion F. K. Mayr, who wants to supplement the supposedly one-sidedly "paternally" oriented doctrine of the Trinity with the Holy Spirit, the intradivine "maternity", as part of a "family" (Mayr, "Gottesverständnis", pp. 249ff.): "The proper analogy for the presence of the Holy Spirit in his relation to the other divine Persons and to the community of the faithful (. . .) could well be *maternitas"*(Mayr, *Anthropologie*, p. 471).

It is hard to see just how Mayr can attempt to resolve the "illogicality" that results from this (Mayr, *Anthropologie*, p. 473) through distinguishing between sociological and biological maternality (Mayr, "Anthropologie", pp. 473f.); for biology, precisely here, is the elementary presupposition for sociology. It is also nonsensical to play off a "sociological" against a "metaphysical" theology of the Trinity (Mayr, "Gottesverständnis", p. 242; Mayr, "Anthropologie", pp. 472, 474), especially when in doing so one uses metaphysical concepts such as "existential ontology" (Mayr, "Anthropologie", p. 474).

The theory that starting from "a masculinely-femininely constituted mankind" is "the only hermeneutic principle" of the theology of the Trinity rests on a misinterpretation of Genesis 1:27 that has been generally rejected in Old Testament exegesis today (Mayr, "Anthropologie", p. 429) and that was advocated in a similar way by Karl Barth (cf. p. 199 above). Also ignored is the fact that, already on biblical evidence, it is not any human group, but the (naturally socially contexted) individual person that is first characterized as an "image of God" (cf. pp. 199f. above).

F. K. Mayr is the "guarantor" for the Catholic dogmatist Heribert Mühlen, who in his lectures presents pneumatology as the point of access to "God's maternality"; cf. also Mühlen, "Maria", pp. 147–51.

[564] Cf. p. 164 above.

[565] H. W. Attridge and R. A. Oden, eds., *The Syrian Goddess (De Dea Syria)*, Society of Biblical Literature. Texts and Translations 9. Graeco-Roman Series I (Missoula, 1976).

[566] Andresen, *Gnosis II*, p. 94.

had any effect on Mary: "Some say: 'Mary was impregnated by the Holy Spirit.' They are in error. . . . When was a woman ever impregnated by a woman?"[567]

In the Syrian language, the Holy Spirit is not called "Comforter", but "Comfortress",[568] and the liturgy of the Didascalics (third century) characterizes the deaconess as an "image of the Holy Spirit".[569] The Church Father Aphraates (fourth century), in an interpretation of Genesis 2:24, even expressly calls the Spirit a mother: "That means: Man, as long as he has not led home the Bride, loves and worships God, his Father, and the Holy Spirit, his Mother; and he has no other love."[570]

To my knowledge, and in contrast to the Gnostic sects, there is in Aphraates no invocation, or even address, directed to the Holy Spirit as mother. For Catholic Syrians, the mother title refers not to the Holy Spirit but to Mary.

Characteristic, too, is the Gospel of the Hebrews, which probably originated in Egypt (second century) and belongs, theologically, "to a strongly mythological-gnostic Judaeo-Christianity":[571] "At once my mother, the Holy Spirit, grasped me by one of my hairs and carried me off to the great Mount Thabor."[572]

In the baptismal story, the Holy Spirit seems to replace the heavenly Father: when "the Lord had climbed up out of the water, the entire source of the Holy Spirit descended and rested upon him and spoke to him: My Son . . . you are my rest, you are my first-born Son."[573]

In the Coptic Letter of Jacob (Egypt, second century), whose Gnostic coloring is somewhat paler,[574] the "Holy spirit" speaks "like the hypostatized divine Wisdom in Jewish wisdom-literature".[575]

The way for these speculations had already been prepared by Philo Judaeus of Alexandria: "To the Logos was apportioned a divine . . . pair of parents, God himself as father . . . and Sophia as mother." "The divine Logos issues forth like a stream from the well-spring [!] of Sophia."[576]

Sophia does not derive from the Logos, but vice versa. To Bishop

[567] Philippus-Evangelium, Saying 17, in Andresen, Gnosis II, p. 98.

[568] Evdokimov, Frau, p. 242.

[569] Didascalia Apostolorum, 2, 26, 6, in F. X. Funk, ed., Didascalia et Constitutiones Apostolorum I/II (Paderborn, 1906), pp. 104, 7–8.

[570] De virginitate et sanctitate, demonstratio 18:10: PS I, 1, p. 839. Additional information and literature on the Syrian theology in Congar, The Holy Spirit, 426f.

[571] Philipp Vielhauer, Geschichte der urchristlichen Literatur [History of early Christian literature] (Berlin and New York, 1975), p. 661.

[572] Philipp Vielhauer, "Judenchristliche Evangelien" [Judaeo-Christian Gospels], in Hennecke and Schneemelcher, Apokryphen I, p. 108.

[573] Vielhauer, "Evangelien", p. 107.

[574] Altaner and Stuiber, Patrologie, p. 130.

[575] Vielhauer, "Evangelien", p. 106.

[576] Benz, "Geist", p. 461f.

Theophilus of Antioch (late second century), Wisdom appears as the heavenly spouse of God, with whom he begets the Logos.[577]

After the second century, the "divine families of the mystery religions and the Gnostic sects" then disappeared completely from the Church's theology.[578] Apart from Meister Eckhart and Jacob Boehme, it was not until the aforementioned Russian thinkers[579] that a certain reissue of sophiological speculation appeared again.

According to Bulgakov,[580] God discloses himself from the standpoint of eternity as Wisdom, which, in turn, represents itself in the two hypostases of Son and Spirit. The Son is an archetype of men, and the Spirit, as "daughter of God", serves as the archetype of women.[581] Paul Evdokimov sees things quite similarly: "The Virgin [Mary] is the locus of the presence of the Holy Spirit, and the Child, the locus of the presence of the Logos. Both together transfer the mysterious countenance of the Father into the human realm."[582]

For Bulgakov, the Holy Spirit is "hypostatized maternality".[583]

Here, masculine and feminine appear, in like measure, as symbols of the divine. The alignment of women with representation of the created realm, and of men with representation of God, thereby recedes into the background.

Similarly to the case in Gnosticism, "Son" and "Daughter" appear as emanations of an androgynous "Father". That a Daughter is found alongside the Son probably has some connection with the Orthodox doctrine of the Trinity. As a rule, the "filioque" is rejected there, that is, the Spirit does not arise from the Son, too, but *only* from the Father. Accordingly, succession for both Son and Spirit consists equally, and in fact exclusively, in having originated out of the Father. Thus there is *no* inner-trinitarian difference between Son and Spirit;[584] but since, in view of the New Testament, the existence of two Sons can hardly be assumed, another solution is found: alongside the Son there stands a Daughter.

The application of the concept maternality to the Holy Spirit appears rather awkward, too. Whose Mother is the Holy Spirit within the Trinity?

Evdokimov attempts to get around this difficulty by distinguishing the

---

[577] Benz, "Geist", p. 460.

[578] Benz, "Geist", p. 467.

[579] Benz, "Geist", p. 456; cf. p. 268 above.

[580] Cf. pp. 268f. above.

[581] Sergej Bulgakov, *Le Paraclet* (Paris, 1946); cf. Tavard, *Woman*, pp. 164–66.

[582] Evdokimov, *Frau*, p. 22.

[583] Evdokimov, *Frau*, p. 242. "The Holy Spirit . . . is image and expression of hypostatized maternality": Evdokimov, *Frau*, p. 243.

[584] At least given strictly logical thought; here, too, of course, there is the phenomenon of fortunate inconsistency.

trinitarian role of the Holy Spirit from his function in revelation: "The Holy Spirit . . . gives him [the Son], in a certain sense, existence and life, that is, at the level of life, of evangelization, of revelation."[585] Thus, according to him, the Credo contains the expression "incarnate out of the Holy Spirit and the Virgin Mary".[586]

However, this interpretation is not correct, for the Nicene Creed speaks not of the "birth" but of the Incarnation of Jesus: σαρκωθέντα ἐκ πνευματος ἁγίου καί μαρίας. Furthermore, ἐκ (not the same as "ex") is not to be understood in the sense of "out of". Therefore, the Latins translate: "incarnatus est *de* Spiritu Sancto *ex* Maria Virgine".[587]

This translation is confirmed by a glance at the New Testament. Giving birth to Jesus is attributed only to Mary,[588] not to the Holy Spirit. The Spirit *effects* Jesus' conception,[589] but Mary, and not the Spirit, is the "Mother of the Lord".[590] Jesus is not born of a *Divine* Person, but has a *human* Mother.

The trinitarian processes of emergence and the effects of revelation cannot be separated from one another, for the Trinity as immanent and the Trinity as related to sacred history form a unity.[591] Being a mother does not primarily mean receiving a germ of life; rather, it means acting together with the father toward production of a child. Jesus owes his human nature wholly to his Mother, just as his divinity stems wholly from his Father. In accordance with his identity as passive breath, the Spirit could be characterized as the sustaining principle behind the receptivity that becomes productive in the human maternality. In my opinion, however, formal application of the mother title would tend to conceal Jesus' true human descent and to encourage a certain Docetism.

An acceptable interpretation of the relations between the Holy Spirit and the human mother, and especially Mary, would seem to be provided by M. J. Scheeben, who can thereby do justice to the previously mentioned criticism by Schmaus. Scheeben explains that, on the one hand, the human family is emblematic of the Trinity, but, on the other hand, any strict parallel in terms of "mother-Spirit" moves on thin ice:

> In the human context, the Son appears as the third Person and his origin as the second; in God, the Son is the second Person and his origin the first. But why? Just as duality holds sway in all created things, a separation between

---

[585] Evdokimov, *Frau*, p. 242.
[586] Evdokimov, *Frau*, p. 243.
[587] DS 150. The same situation arises regarding the Symbolum Apostolicum: DS 10f., 30.
[588] Mt 1:23; Lk 1:31; 2:7; Gal 4:4; Rev 12:5.
[589] Lk 1:35; Mt 1:18, 20.
[590] Lk 1:43.
[591] Cf. on this Scheffczyk, *Gott*, 112–23; Schmaus, *Glaube II*, pp. 76f.

act and potency, so man's nature, too, is split into two principles, one predominantly active, the male, and one predominantly passive, the female. Propagation, as the highest act of nature as such, is therefore here, too, necessarily a product of the conjoined parts of the species. In God, by contrast, in whom there is no separation between act and potency and who is the purest and most perfect nature, propagation, as the most natural and principal act of nature, must issue directly and exclusively from the first Person. And just as, in man, it is the *ultimum in executione* because it presupposes, in its realization, the separation of the sexes, but is simultaneously the *primum in intentione* because the separation of the sexes occurs only for its sake; so, in God, it must be, in absolutely every respect, the first production. Thus it is precisely because propagation in God is true propagation that it must originate from one Person and not from two.[592]

Conclusion

Thus we find in the Holy Spirit certain characteristics that can link up with feminine symbolism, such as immanence, relationality and above all his identity as receptive. To be sure, it is only with utmost caution that feminine references can be associated with the Spirit, as is evident particularly from the discussion of the mother title. Also, it should be noted that the Holy Spirit himself is almost never represented; his function is much more one of guiding man toward Christ and the Father. Not the Spirit but the Logos is the image of the Father. The ultimate reason for this lies in the fact that the Pneuma arises not from the cognitive side of the Father, in which—as indicated by the image of propagation—an imaging tendency is inherent,[593] but from the reciprocal love between Father and Son, that is, from a process of mental-spiritual conation. Cognition represents; love binds together. Of course, the Holy Spirit possesses the same divine nature as that of Father and Son and in this respect is their image, but not in respect of his personal uniqueness, in which the force of active breath possessed by the first two Divine Persons is lacking.

Thus, in contrast to a *repraesentatio Christi*, we will hardly encounter an explicit *repraesentatio Spiritus Sancti*. Nevertheless, it can be assumed that there is a certain closeness to the feminine nature in the Holy Spirit's way of functioning. Using the example of the figure of Mary, I hope to be able to show that woman should be, in a specific way, *vas spirituale*, a "vessel of the Holy Spirit".

[592] Scheeben, *Mysterien*, pp. 168f.
[593] Cf. Schmaus, KD I, pp. 604–6.

CHAPTER THREE

Mary: Archetype and Mother of the Church

I. INTRODUCTION

"Mary figured profoundly in the history of salvation and in a certain way unites and mirrors within herself the central truths of the Faith."[1]

This sentence from the Second Vatican Council may serve to introduce the following exposition. The figure of Mary is like a mirror from which all the truths of Faith of the Catholic Church "are reflected out into the world".[2] It was no coincidence that the Church, at the last Council, brought her description of her self-understanding to a culmination in Mariology. With the introduction of the new title for Mary, "Mother of the Church", Paul VI initiated impulses that are still far from being exhausted.

Nevertheless, for many contemporaries, the figure of Mary has become caught up in crisis. In particular, most of today's women are no longer able to recognize Mary as their ideal image: "The mirror has become clouded, or rather: it has taken on the appearance of an unquiet surface of water, in which only distorted images appear, misshapen or broken."[3]

In my opinion, however, this crisis is not one of the "mirror", but of the observer. The last Council and the Apostolic Exhortation, *Marialis cultus*, by Paul VI, may help us to rediscover, with reference to present times, how the Church has seen Mary's essential traits throughout all epochs of Church history.

Like the Holy Spirit, Mary is, in a special way, a "relational being". The

---

[1] *Lumen gentium*, 65, in Rahner and Vorgrimler, *Konzilskompendium*, p. 194; *AAS* 57 (1965): 64.

[2] Leo Scheffczyk, *Neue Impulse zur Marienverehrung* [New stimuli toward Marian devotion] (St. Ottilien, 1974), p. 17.

[3] Translated (in the original German edition of this book) from René Laurentin, "Marie et l'anthropologie chrétienne de la femme", in *NRTh* 89 (1967): 485.

eighth chapter of *Lumen gentium* bears the heading: "The Blessed Virginal Mother of God in the Mystery of Christ and the Church". This means that Mary is wholly referred to Christ (and, along with that, to the Triune God), and appears in that connection as archetype and Mother of the Church.[4] Mary is not only an object that demonstrates of what the Church consists but also an independent personality: She is archetype *and* mother. But her person finds its realization in this association with the Church, which I regard as Mary's decisive relationship within sacred reality; it is no coincidence that the Council's mariological pronouncements form the conclusion of the Church's decree. As I will show in more detail, it is from this fundamental determination that the trinitarian and christo-logical orientation of the Mother of God arises. Mary does not, in the first instance, stand on the side of God, but, as *Mother* of God, on the side of *man*.

Through this orientation toward ecclesiology[5] and against the back-ground of philosophical and theological anthropology, important con-sequences follow not only for the understanding of the Christian in general but also for the position of women. If the masculinity of Christ is essential to his redemptive work, then so, too, is the femininity of Mary to representation of the Church which opens herself to that work.

2. MARY AS A REPRESENTATIVE OF MANKIND

The receptivity of Mary as Virgin[6]

The obedience of faith

According to the Protestant historian of dogmatics W. Delius, the infancy narrative given in the Gospel according to Luke is a concentrated biblical

---

[4] The express concern of *"Marialis cultus"* is the trinitarian, christological and ecclesio-logical relation; cf. especially nos. 25–28 and 16:22: *AAS* 66 (1974): 113–68; in German: Scheffczyk, *Impulse*, pp. 123–200.

[5] The explicit working out of the relationship between Mariology and ecclesiology is one of the central themes of twentieth-century theology. On this, cf. G. Philips, "Marie et l'Église. Un thème théologique renouvelé", in D'Hubert du Manoir (ed.), *Maria. Études sur la Sainte Vierge VII* (Paris, 1964), 363–419; this contains copious references to relevant literature. See, too, Schmaus, *KD V*, pp. 270–320.

The newest study of theology of office and of Mariology as the two central structural elements of ecclesiology is: Leo Scheffczyk, "Petrus und Maria: Hindernisse oder Helfer auf dem Wege zur Einheit?" [Peter and Mary: Hindrances or helpers on the way to unity?], *Catholica* 34 (1980): 62–75.

[6] On the conceptual opposition "reception-cooperation", see p. 118 above.

point in which the significance of Mary is exemplarily reflected: "With the hand of a master, Luke has sketched a picture of Mary here that contains almost all of the essential aspects of devotion to Mary in its centuries-long development."[7]

The statements about Christ here are bound up, according to the "law of overarching parallelism",[8] with the preparatory events surrounding John the Baptist. Mary, too, participates in this parallelism. While the man and office bearer Zechariah doubts the angel's promise,[9] the virgin from Nazareth shows herself as a believer who readily places herself at the disposal of God's activity: "Behold, I am the handmaid of the Lord; let it be to me according to your word."[10]

Mary is therefore called blessed by Elizabeth as the one who had *believed*.[11] Her corporeal motherhood is not to be seen in isolation but as embedded in a personal readiness for receptivity: the Blessed Virgin bore in faith the Jesus whom she had received in faith.[12] It is probably for this reason that the Magnificat draws a connection with Abraham,[13] the first believer in sacred history.[14]

The Church Fathers even see an antithetical parallel with the beginning of man's history, with the Fall. Faith is always related to obedience,[15] to subordination. Women, because of their biological constitution, possess in principle a greater readiness for this than do men. At the same time, the personal commitments of women are more strongly embedded in a comprehensive attitude ("centrality"): "Seen in cosmic perspective, men stand at the forefront of power, women encamp in their depths."[16]

The Old Testament scholar Theodor Schwegler interprets against this background the Yahwist's account of the Fall, according to which not Adam but Eve is the first to be seduced: women carry out "everything that they do with much greater intellectual commitment than men. The prospect of dragging the whole of visible creation into a fall away from God was much greater for the devil when he succeeded in getting woman on his side."[17]

---

[7] W. Delius, *Geschichte der Marienverehrung* [History of Marian devotion] (Munich, 1963), p. 26; Scheffczyk, *Impulse*, pp. 23f.

[8] Josef Ernst, *Das Evangelium nach Lukas (RNT)* [The Gospel according to Luke (RSV)] (Regensburg, 1977), p. 56.

[9] Lk 1:18, 20.

[10] Lk 1:38.

[11] Lk 1:45.

[12] Cf. Augustine, Sermo 215:4: PL 38, p. 1074.

[13] Lk 1:55.

[14] Cf. Gen 12:3; 15:6.

[15] Rom 1:5; 5:19; 16:29 and elsewhere.

[16] Fort, *Frau*, p. 20; cf. pp. 93f., 187f. above.

[17] Theodor Schwegler, *Die biblische Urgeschichte* [Biblical primordial history], 2nd ed. (Munich, 1962), p. 122.

From this perspective, the story of the Fall is not a product of misogyny but rather more the opposite. The power of women is also reflected in the Old Testament warnings against mixed marriage, which were based on a very high estimation of the religious influence of a wife over her husband.[18] In a midrash on Genesis, it is said: "Once upon a time it happened that a pious man was married to a pious woman. But they produced no children. Then they said: We are useless before God. They separated from one another. He went out and took a godless wife, who made him godless. She went out and took a godless husband, and made him righteous. Thus you see how everything depends on the woman."[19]

The influence of women can lead mankind into emancipation against God, but can also anchor the obedience of faith in the deepest levels of human existence: "Eve . . . received into her womb the word of the serpent and bore disobedience and death. Mary, on the other hand, received faith and joy. . . . Thus, by means of this [Virgin], the one came into this world . . . through whom God . . . tramples . . . the serpent and its kind."[20]

Irenaeus was the first to formulate expressly the law of reversal (*recirculatio*) of sacred history: "Just as that one [Eve] became the cause of death for herself and the whole human race, so Mary became . . . the cause of salvation for herself and the whole human race. . . . In Mary, the direction begun by Eve experiences its reversal." What "Eve had knotted up through disobedience [was] untied again through Mary's obedience; for what the Virgin Eve had bound fast through her unbelief was set free again by the Virgin Mary through her belief."[21]

Thus the way for the obedience of the "new Adam"[22] is prepared by the "new Eve". In this, the significance of Mary extends far beyond that of her predecessor. Nowhere in the New Testament does Jesus appear as believer, because he does not first have to endorse his revelation but proclaims it himself as one who sees.[23] In contrast, the Mother of God is, by virtue of her belief, the first and exemplary Christian: "In Mary, the Church already has physical existence, before it is organized in Peter."[24]

---

[18] Ex 34:15–16; Neh 13:26–27.

[19] O. Schneider, *Macht*, p. 204.

[20] Justinus, *Dialogus cum Trypho*, 100:4–6: PG 6, pp. 709f.

[21] Irenaeus, *Adversus haereses*, 3:22: PG 7, pp. 958–60.

[22] Rom 5; 1 Cor 15:22.

[23] Jn 3:11, 31–32; 8:38; cf. Mt 11:27; 26:34 and many others. On the whole problem, see Bertrand de Margerie: "Les sept yeux de l'Agneau. Reprise du dossier sur la science humaine de Jésus avant Pâques" [The seven eyes of the Lamb. Resumption of the treatise on the human knowledge of Christ before Easter], Divus Thomas, 86 (1983): 3–54.

[24] H. U. von Balthasar, "Epilog: Die marianische Prägung der Kirche" [Epilog: The Marian stamp of the Church], in Wolfgang Beinert (ed.), *Maria heute ehren* [Devotion to Mary today], 2nd ed. (Freiburg, Basel, and Vienna, 1977), p. 276.

Humility

Along with faith, the humility of the Mother of Jesus appears as a second main strand in the mariological statements by Luke. According to the definition by Saint Bernard, humility means the "low estimation of oneself as a result of true self-knowledge"; according to the Church's ascetic tradition, this attitude is the foundation and root of all virtues.[25] Objectively considered, such an evaluation is fully justified, since humility means the self-knowledge of the created being who acknowledges his own createdness. Because man is like a "grain of sand" before God, he develops a readiness to bow down before the Lord's greatness and to allow God to be God. This attitude then gives rise to humility in the etymological sense of the German word *Demut*, the *Dienmut* or *Mut zum Dienen* (readiness to serve).

Humility is mirrored in Mary's response that gives permission for God to act as he will with her: "Behold, I am the handmaid of the Lord; let it be to me according to your word."[26] The Magnificat elaborates this motif: God "has regarded the low estate of his handmaiden".[27]

The expression ταπείνωσις corresponds to the Hebrew word for "misery, suffering, servitude"[28] and designates the attitude of poverty that we find variously described in the Psalms. What is meant there is not initially a state of economic need but rather the state of complete, trustful subjectedness to God. God's activity, not human possibilities, is decisive: "Blessed are the poor in spirit, for theirs is the kingdom of heaven."[29]

The "lowliness" = "humility" of Mary[30] shines forth in such bright splendor in the Magnificat because it is accompanied by the appearance of the negative foil to this attitude, the haughtiness of the (male) potentate: "He has shown strength with his arm, he has scattered the proud in the imagination of their hearts, he has put down the mighty from their thrones, and exalted those of low degree" (ταπεινούς).[31]

Readers knowledgeable about Scripture will see in these words associations with the Old Testament.[32] The powerful foreign rulers and their downfall[33]

---

[25] Mausbach and Ermecke, *Theologie II*, pp. 292–97.

[26] Lk 1:38.

[27] Lk 1:48.

[28] Rudolf Schnackenburg, "Das Magnificat, seine Spiritualität und Theologie" [The Magnificat: Its spirituality and theology]; *Schriften zum Neuen Testament* [Writings on the New Testament] (Munich, 1971), p. 205.

[29] Mt 5:3.

[30] Heinz Schürmann, *Das Lukasevangelium I* [The Gospel according to Luke, I], HThK III (Freiburg, Basel, and Vienna, 1969), p. 74.

[31] Lk 1:51–52.

[32] Esp. Judith 13:18–19; Jg 5:24–26.

[33] Cf. also Is 14:2.

should be understood as typifying the rule of Satan that is conquered by Jesus, if we take account of the macrocontext that applies for Luke.[34] In the Magnificat, then, the power of the devil appears as already overcome in principle—overcome through the incarnation of the Kyrios in Mary.

Thus, Christian tradition sees in the Mother of God the new Eve, whose offspring tramples the serpent's head.[35] As "father of lies",[36] Satan is equally the ultimate generator of all false doctrines.[37] The antithesis, however, to Satanic haughtiness is Marian humility; the Mother of God is regarded by the Church Fathers as "scepter of orthodoxy" and as "destroyer of all heresies".[38]

The virginity of the Mother of God as a material symbol

In considering the figure of Mary, particularly given her attitudes of faith and humility, we can observe two basic structures:

1. The powerful activity of God that effects the conception of the Messiah and scatters the "potentates".
2. The receptive openness and readiness for devotion of the Mother of the Lord.

Both of these ideas are concentrated into the bodily material symbol of Mary's virginity:[39]

> The significance of Mary's virginal conception points, on the one hand, to the creative-divine factor, in which the absolutely God-effected and gracious new beginning of salvation, "from above" and without the assistance of natural necessities, is to become recognizable as a sovereign determination of God's. . . . On the other hand, however, this sign points . . . to the complete readiness and openness of Mary, who knew no other partner and object of her devotion than God himself.[40]

God appears here not as "a depth of being that, so to speak, runs beneath everything in some unknown way or other", but as "he who acts".[41] The undivided devotion of Mary, as a response to that action, is to be

[34] Lk 10:18; 4:6.

[35] Gen 3:15.

[36] Jn 8:44; cf. Gen 3:4–5.

[37] Rev 12:17; 13:5; 2:24; 3:9.

[38] Scheffczyk, Impulse, p. 18.

[39] The concept of "material symbol" is used here, as by Karl Rahner, to indicate the anchoring of the symbolic image in the bodily sphere.

[40] Leo Scheffczyk, Marianische Hochfeste, dogmatische Grundlagen (1. Januar) [Marian celebrations: Dogmatic foundations (1 January)], in Beinert, Maria, p. 120.

[41] Joseph Ratzinger, Die Tochter Zion. Betrachtungen über den Marienglauben der Kirche Kriterien 44 (Einsiedeln, 1977), p. 59. English edition: Daughter Zion. Meditations on the Church's Marian Belief (San Francisco: Ignatius Press, 1983), p. 61.

understood not only intellectually-spiritually but as embedded, in a special way, in the whole person, right down to the bodily aspects. "When the biological is removed from humanity, humanity itself is denied."[42]

Virginity has been accorded a special esteem in many cultures; one might think, for example, of the Roman vestals. But not until Christianity, in the time after Mary, did it become a generally recognized and lived value. The Virgin does not stand inside of the chain of human generations, "but rather, she closes generation". "From that standpoint, she demands belief in an ultimate value of the person in itself"; she "signifies figuratively the religious emphasis and affirmation of the value of the person in its ultimate immediate relation to God alone".[43]

The idea that the Virgin is elevated above matrimonial subordination has recently been an inspiration to feminist theology, too: "The woman that is described as a virgin is not defined exclusively through her relation to men." The "symbol of virgin" is "a message of *independence*", of feminine "autonomy".[44] Mary was "not obedient to a man".[45]

With this, of course, an unbalanced alternative is set up. For the freedom of the Christian realizes itself precisely in obedience: "The more a man is responsible to God, the more God can, if he wishes, bring him, in his independence, into the light."[46] Mary's life together with Joseph was, correctly seen, by all means a marriage, and her maternal authority regarding Jesus has to give way: "Do whatever he tells you."[47] Mary's life is played out, in contrast to the activity of her Son, in total concealment. But precisely for that reason, God is able to elevate her that much more later on: "For behold, henceforth all generations will call me blessed."[48]

Virginity does not imply having "autonomy" before God but rather readiness for receptivity. With this, a true revolution has occurred vis-à-vis old and new paganism. The significance of a virgin is so strong in Church antiquity that the term is even applied to men.[49] For, indeed, "if . . . the spiritual is inseparable . . . anywhere in man . . . from the physical-bodily,

---

[42] Joseph Cardinal Ratzinger, "Erwägungen zur Stellung von Mariologie und Marien-frömmigkeit im Ganzen von Glaube und Theologie" [Considerations on the position of Mariology and Marian piety within the totality of faith and theology], in Joseph Cardinal Ratzinger and H. U. von Balthasar, *Maria–Kirche im Ursprung* [Mary—the Church in its origin] (Freiburg, Basel, and Vienna, 1980), p. 33; cf. Ratzinger, *Zion*, pp. 51ff.

[43] Fort, *Frau*, p. 38.

[44] Daly, *Vater*, p. 104.

[45] P. G. Washbourn, in Halkes, *Söhne*, p. 108.

[46] H. U. von Balthasar, "Maria in der kirchlichen Lehre und Frömmigkeit" [Mary in Church doctrine and piety], in Ratzinger and Balthasar, *Maria*, p. 44.

[47] Jn 2:5; cf. Lk 2:48–50; Mk 3:31–35.

[48] Lk 1:48.

[49] Cf. Graber, *Maria*, pp. 69–77; see even Rev 14:4.

then it is so here."[50] What is crucial is no longer the activity of *man*, but the efficacy of *God*: "The passive-receiving of the feminine, in which ancient philosophy saw the purely negative, appears in the Christian order of grace as the positive-deciding."[51]

Aristotle sees the soul mainly as the formal principle of the body, as something actively effective. This view is certainly correct, but one-sided. For, in relation to *God*, the soul is receptive, feminine.

The Christian mystics have occupied themselves again and again with the Song of Songs; in so doing, they never saw themselves as the bridegroom, but only in the role of the bride.[52] For mystical experience too, then, woman seems to have the greater receptivity; Teresa of Avila was declared a Doctor of the Church by Paul VI not primarily because of any abstract pedagogical expositions but because of empathic descriptions of her own experience.[53] In the course of her life, John of the Cross was but her companion: "The male's business is to clarify the waters of the well-spring, which he seems incapable of bringing to flow himself."[54]

In her receptiveness, Mary is thus, in special measure, *the representative of creation as creation*. At the same time, especially in her affirmative response to the angel's Annunciation, she represents *mankind*. Here, however, unlike the case regarding her Son, it is not a matter of an official and public representation, but of the representation of the "daughter Zion", whose bridal-receptive disposition takes on personal qualities in Mary. According to Saint Thomas, the Annunciation by the angel was necessary "so that the existence of a marriage, to a certain degree spiritual in nature, between the Son of God and the race of mankind would be demonstrated: and therefore, through the Annunciation, the acceptance by the Virgin *in place of the entire race of mankind* was expected".[55]

---

[50] Bouyer, *Woman in the Church*, p. 61.

[51] Fort, *Frau*, p. 14.

[52] This tradition has links extending back as far as Origen's commentary on the Song of Songs; cf. Riedel, *Auslegung*, pp. 52–68, 113.

[53] Cf. Feuillet, *Jésus*, p. 229.

[54] Bouyer, *Woman in the Church*, p. 70, cf. p. 68.

[55] STh III, q 30 a 1; translation (in the original German edition of this book) and emphases by me. This idea plays an outstanding role in the whole history of theology: Carl Feckes, ed., *Die heilsgeschichtliche Stellvertretung der Menschheit durch Maria* [The redemptive historical representation of mankind by Mary] (Paderborn, 1954). The cited Thomas quote crops up again and again, in a central position, in the doctrinal pronouncements of modern Popes: Karl Schwerdt, "Die heilsgeschichtliche Stellvertretung der Menschheit durch Maria nach der päpstlichen Lehrverkündigung in den letzten hundert Jahren" [The redemptive historical representation of mankind by Mary according to papal doctrinal pronouncements of the last hundred years], in Feckes, *Menschheit*, pp. 1–25. For a systematic evaluation, see H. M. Köster, "Die Stellvertretung der Menschheit durch Maria. Ein Systemversuch" [The representation of mankind by Mary. A systematic approach], in Feckes, *Menschheit*, pp.

The representation of mankind through Mary, according to Saint Thomas, is thus precisely not to be identified with the task of Jesus.[56] Rather, it is that: "In Mary, the universe is returned to its ontological position as the receiving and, with that, the feminine; now the mysterious wedding of heaven and earth, of God and creature, can take place, whose blessed fruit is the Son of the Most High and, at the same time, of Mary."[57]

Thus the virginal conception of Jesus implies a priority of woman in the representation of creation and of mankind before God. Like probably no other scholar of divinity in recent times, the Protestant theologian Karl Barth has brought this incomparable value into the light. Already from the viewpoint of God, the role of the male is relativized through the activity of the Holy Spirit. Added to this, moreover, is the birth by the Virgin:

> Once again, and now from the viewpoint of mankind, the male is here excluded. . . . To that which is to begin here, mankind, with its actions and its initiative, is to contribute nothing. Mankind is not simply excluded: for the Virgin is involved. But the male, as the specific bearer of human action and history, with his responsibility for leadership of the human race, must now step, as the powerless figure of Joseph, into the background. That is *the* Christian answer to the question of women: here, woman stands absolutely in the foreground, and indeed, the *virgo*, the Virgin Mary. God did not choose mankind in its pride and defiance, but in its weakness and humility, not mankind in its historical role, but mankind in the weakness of its nature, as this is represented by woman.[58]

The cooperation of Mary as Mother

In his subsequent comments, to be sure, Karl Barth stresses the activity of God so strongly that Mary appears as more or less passive. On the basis of his strongly delineated, reformation doctrine of grace, he is unable to recognize any sort of coefficacy on the part of Mary; any merit of mankind's, under the inspiration of Christ's redemptive work, is excluded: God acts *alone*.

In opposition to this, the Second Vatican Council and the whole of

---

323–59; Otto Semmelroth, "Die Stellvertretungsrolle Mariens im Lichte der Ekklesiologie" [Mary's representative role in the light of ecclesiology], Feckes, *Menschheit*, pp. 360–67.

[56] Against Meer, *Priesturtum*, p. 186.

[57] Graber, *Maria*, p. 21.

[58] Karl Barth, *Dogmatik im Grundriss* [Outline of dogmatics], 3rd ed. (Zurich, 1947), p. 116; this is just as clearly stated in Barth, *KD I*, 2, pp. 211f.

Church Tradition stress "that Mary was not simply passively used by God, but helped, in free faith and obedience, to effect the salvation of man".[59]

Receptivity and cooperation can thus not be separated but are, so to speak, the two sides of one medallion. The "uniqueness of the mediation of the Redeemer does not preclude differentiated participation of the created realm in the unique source of the cooperation, but grounds it".[60] The theme of cooperation is not just one building block of Mariology among others, but its basic structure: "Expressed concisely, the Marian dogma means the doctrine of the co-operation of the created being in redemption." Mary is "the cosmos' power of surrender in the form of bridal woman".[61]

Whereas Mary's receptivity combines above all with the concept of virgin, the theme of cooperation links up with the *mother* title. Even at the purely human level, women realize themselves especially in (bodily or psychologically understood) motherhood. The father, too, is certainly an indispensable personality for the raising of a child but, owing to his occupational duties and "eccentricity", he is at all times more strongly engaged in the world outside the household, while the mother occupies herself more as "minister of the interior" in her "centrality". A woman is more strongly determined by being a mother than is a man by the task of fatherhood.[62]

Anthropology is, so to speak, raised to infinity by theology, for the highest, and highest conceivable, title of honor for Mary is "Mother of God". That God is brought forth from creation, here concretely from a woman, is an event that surpasses all understanding. The myths of origin in the history of religion, according to which the divine brings itself forth from the ocean, a cosmic egg or the earth, find here—now freed of all pantheistic-immanentistic dross—their unexpected fulfillment. The Incarnation of God is, in itself, a free act of love but even more so the taking on of flesh from a woman. Christ could also have appeared on this earth as a grown man, but he wanted to derive, down to the smallest fibers of his corporeality, from the created realm and to be formed in Mary's womb.

Because Mary gave birth not only to a man but to the Son of God who was personally bound up with mankind, she possesses, in the words of

[59] *Lumen gentium*, 56, in Rahner and Vorgrimler, *Konzilskompendium*, p. 189; *AAS* 57 (1965): 60.

[60] *Lumen gentium*, 62, in Rahner and Vorgrimler, *Konzilskompendium*, p. 193; *AAS* 57 (1965): 63.

[61] Fort, *Frau*, p. 15.

[62] Cf. p. 189, n. 357 above.

Saint Thomas, a virtually infinite worth,[63] which is already hinted at in the Gospel according to Luke. Christ appears there as Kyrios[64]—a name that is regarded in the Septuagint as absolutely *the* designation for God. Only the "mother of the Lord",[65] whose Kingdom endures forever,[66] can say of herself: "Henceforth all generations will call me blessed."[67] In this way, the Mother of Jesus participates in her Son's high majesty. The cooperation of the Mother of God appears at first in the Incarnation. Mary shows not blind but rather conscious obedience: she "considered in her mind what sort of greeting this might be". "How shall this be, since I have no husband?"[68]

Another passage stresses Mary's feminine internalization of God's word, namely, through intuitive sensing and meditative pondering: "But Mary kept all these things, pondering them in her heart."[69]

In the central biblical symbol of the heart, special expression is given to the total surrender of the person, which takes hold of all the intellectual-spiritual and affective powers: "Blessed are the pure in heart, for they shall see God."[70] Now, as emblematic of the midpoint of man (centrality!), the heart image is attributed by preference to women,[71] and the Indian mystic Ramakrishna once stated (independently of Christian influence): "All women are manifestations of the Divine Mother. But her greatest manifestation is in the heart of the pure virgin."[72] In 1942, Pius XII entrusted the world to the Immaculate Heart of Mary, thereby providing, as a feminine pendant to devotion to the heart of Jesus, new impulses toward a comprehensive theology and piety.[73]

"In Jesus' public life, his mother appears expressly at the beginning, at the marriage at Cana in Galilee, where, acting on sympathetic feeling, she occasions, through her intercession, the beginning of the signalling of Jesus as the Messiah."[74] Hans Urs von Balthasar points out the typically

[63] STh I, q 25 a 6 ad 4: *"quamdam dignitatem infinitam ex bono infinito, quod est Deus"*.

[64] Lk 1:43; 2:11.

[65] Lk 1:43.

[66] Lk 1:33.

[67] Lk 1:48; cf. 1:28, 42 and the relevant commentaries on Luke (Ernst, Schürmann) regarding these passages.

[68] Lk 1:29, 34.

[69] Lk 2:19; cf. 2:51.

[70] Mt 5:8.

[71] Cf. pp. 56, 187f., 275f. above.

[72] *Botschaft*, p. 195.

[73] On this, cf. the notes by Leo Scheffczyk, *Gedenktage Mariens, dogmatische Grundlagen (Unbeflecktes Herz Mariä)* [Marian commemorative days, dogmatic foundations (Immaculate Heart of Mary)], in Beinert, *Maria*, pp. 218–20.

[74] *Lumen gentium*, 58, in Rahner and Vorgrimler, *Konzilskompendium*, p. 190; *AAS* 57 (1965): 61. Cf. Jn 2:1–11.

feminine anthropological background: "It was already shown how greatly her womanly experience begins with the *tactus*—sensing by touching—and then unfolds from it only to return to it, to the point of developing a spiritual perception and sense of touch for all that pertains to her Son."[75]

Mary's cooperation, already in her life on earth, is thus related to her Son's activity in a specifically feminine way. Jesus' redemptive work, which is inextricably bound up with his masculine human nature, reaches its culmination on the Cross.[76] Consequently, we can anticipate that Mary's role, which is linked to her femininity, also reaches its peak at Calvary. The Mother of God, as the absolutely "favored one",[77] marred by no stain of sin,[78] corresponded in a complete way to God's will. According to *Marialis cultus*, she gave "full of love, her assent to the surrender and offering up of the sacrifice that she had given birth to . . . , that she, too, offered up to the eternal Father".[79]

This cosacrifice by Mary presents no competition to the unique sacrifice of Christ, no more than the masculine and feminine modes of action can be measured off against each other. Mary's activity consists, as in the Incarnation, "in a *bestowal of consent*, which presupposes her faith and her love".[80] "Mary is not a mediator *like* Christ, but *under* Christ, *in* him and *through* him." Her merit is grounded in "the willed grace of God, who *integrates* the work of the redeemed creatures in the redemptive event". This integration follows from the intimate connection between receiving and cooperating: "Men take an active part in the redemptive event to the extent that they have been previously redeemed by Christ."[81]

Mary is thus no priestess in the fullest sense, for her sacrificial love adds nothing new to Christ's work. The Church, therefore, occasionally had to show resistance to contrary tendencies within popular piety. "In the year 1916, the Holy See published an edict in which it was stated: 'The image of the Blessed Virgin Mary dressed in priestly robes is to be rejected.' "[82]

Mary's surrender is not identical with Jesus' sacrifice, which is made present through the service of the official priest. To attribute to Mary the title priestess, in the sense of the special priesthood, would therefore be

---

[75] Balthasar, *Glory of the Lord* I, p. 362.

[76] *Marialis cultus*, 20, in Scheffczyk, *Impulse*, p. 147; *AAS* 66 (1974): 131f.

[77] Lk 1:28.

[78] DS, 2803.

[79] *Marialis cultus*, 20, in Scheffczyk, *Impulse*, p. 147; *AAS* 66 (1974): 132. Similarly, *Lumen gentium*, 58, in Rahner and Vorgrimler, *Konzilskompendium*, p. 190; *AAS* 57 (1965): 61.

[80] René Laurentin, *Kurzer Traktat der mairanischen Theologie* [Short treatise on Marian theology] (Regensburg, 1959), p. 169; emphases mine.

[81] Laurentin, *Traktat*, p. 172.

[82] Meer, *Priesturtum*, p. 122; cf. DS, 3632.

atrocious. Rather, Mary's priestly tasks remain wholly—if in the highest conceivable degree—within the framework of what we designate as the "common priesthood": "In all these respects, her surrender completes the sacrifice of the Cross, just as the surrender of the faithful completes the sacrifice of the Mass."[83]

3. MARY: MOTHER, OR MOTHERLINESS, OF GOD?

Everything created is an emblem of God. Therefore, classical theology already saw, in the tender care of the Mother of the Lord, a symbol of divine activity: Mary "is like a gracious revelation of certain inexpressible ultimates in the essence of God that are too delicate and too tender to be grasped other than through the mirror of a mother".[84]

Andrew Greeley, in parallel with feminist theology,[85] claims that this aspect has so far not been given sufficient consideration: "The thesis of this book is: Mary reveals to us the tender, kindly, caring, protective, 'feminine' dimension of God." "When I say: Mary is the *great mystery*, the *image of God*, then I give her an even greater title than 'Theotokos'."[86]

This last comment, of course, makes one stop and listen. Is a higher title than "Mother of God" at all possible for a created person? But Greeley is

---

[83] Laurentin, *Traktat*, p. 170. The remarks by Wolfgang Beinert that suggest a "priesthood of women" on the basis of the "priesthood of Mary" (Wolfgang Beinert, "Unsere Liebe Frau und die Frauen. Ein mariologischer Beitrag zur theologischen Anthropologie" [Our Lady and women. A mariological contribution to theological anthropology], in *Frau in Kirche*, p. 19, n. 12) are more than questionable, especially as they claim support from René Laurentin. His standard work (René Laurentin, *Marie, l'Église et le sacerdoce I/II* [Paris, 1952/1953]) advocates precisely the opposite thesis (cf. especially Laurentin, *Sacerdoce II*, pp. 69–79). Regarding a role for Mary approaching that of the official priesthood, Laurentin comes to the conclusion: "Marie est essentiellement mère, et ce qu'il y a de sacerdotal en elle est un aspect de sa maternité." "Il s'agit moins d'un *sacerdoce* maternel que d'une *maternité* sacerdotale." "Du point de vue marial, le bilan de ce travail . . . est . . . essentiellement négatif": Laurentin, *Sacerdoce II*, pp. 200f.

[84] Karl Adam, *Das Wesen des Katholizismus* [The essence of Catholicism], 8th ed. (Düsseldorf, 1936), p. 144; and similar statements by Graber, *Maria*, p. 38; Cabassut, "Dévotion", p. 234; M.-J. Nicolas, "La doctrine mariale et la théologie chrétienne de la femme": D'Hubert du Manoir (ed.), *Maria. Études sur la Sainte Vierge VII* (Paris, 1964), p. 356; Feuillet, *Jésus*, p. 219.

[85] Cf. Halkes, *Söhne*, p. 117; Ruether, *Mary*; Joan Arnold, "Maria—Gottesmutterschaft und Frau" [Mary—God's motherliness and woman], in *Conc* 12 (1976): 24–29; Elisabeth Schüssler Fiorenza, "Feminist Theology as a Critical Theology of Liberation", in Burghardt, *Woman*, pp. 44ff.

[86] Greeley, *Maria*, p. 24.

not concerned with Mary as an element of creation, not even, in fact, with Mary herself, but with God: "This is not a book about Mary in the traditional sense. It is, rather, *about God*, who reveals himself in Mary."[87]

The special fact about Mary is therefore not being the Mother of God, but rather, evidencing the motherliness of God. From this perspective, the figure of Mary in its own inherent significance is unimportant or even superfluous, for her function is only to represent something different from her.[88] According to Greeley, "Mary stands [from the viewpoint of the social sciences] in the great tradition of female deities"[89] who represent a general human conviction that should be positively evaluated: "In God . . . *feminine and masculine traits* are combined *in equal degrees*."[90] Accordingly, that the Church in antiquity did not apply the mother title to God himself must be traced back to a missing *aggiornamento*, a lack that can, however, be made good in present times: "The . . . Romans were, theologically, in precisely the right position with their formula '*Sive Deus, sive Dea*'. . . . There is absolutely no . . . reason why we cannot address God as a woman."[91]

Mary is thus, in principle, replaceable: "The present-day emancipation-movement could certainly step out under the name of any other female deity. But I think that Mary stands closest to our culture."[92] To our culture—but how are missionaries to proceed, for instance, in India?

If Mary's decisive role consists in being a symbol of God, it must be asked whether the worth of the blessed human being is not thereby underestimated. "The invocation of Mary does not mean the invocation of a goddess, but rather, it is a matter of calling upon human readiness and devotion—and thus, of insight into the mystery of the co-operation" of the created being.[93] Anyone who wants to give Mary a greater title than "Mother of God" runs the risk of blotting out the God-supported dignity of man in the exclusive efficacy of God. In an author who otherwise stresses the emancipation and experience of man,[94] this tendency would not seem totally without contradiction.

[87] Greeley, *Maria*, p. 9.

[88] Feminist theology takes a more radical position here: "Mary becomes the dutifully domesticated symbol of that which she is *not*": Katappo, *Free*, p. 73. Or Ida Raming, "Von der Freiheit des Evangeliums zur versteinerten Männerkirche. Zur Entstehung und Entwicklung der Männerherrschaft in der Kirche" [From the freedom of the Gospel to the petrified Church of men. On the origin and development of male domination in the Church], in *Conc* 16 (1980): 230: "Mariology . . . is a compensatory phenomenon within the otherwise patriarchally-stamped Church."

[89] Greeley, *Maria*, p. 18.

[90] Greeley, *Maria*, p. 147.

[91] Greeley, *Maria*, p. 75.

[92] Greeley, *Maria*, p. 145.

[93] Fort, *Frau*, p. 15.

[94] Greeley, *Maria*, pp. 33, 59, 145.

The postulate "God is also Mother" can probably be traced back especially to Protestant influences, and in particular to Paul Tillich: "The increasing symbolic power of the image of the Holy Virgin . . . presents Protestantism with a difficult problem. In the struggle of the Reformation against all human mediators between God and man, this symbol was abolished, and, with that process of purification, the feminine element in everything of ultimate concern to us was largely eliminated. The spirit of Judaism, with its exclusively masculine symbolism, established itself within the Reformation."[95]

The (wide-ranging) elimination of the figure of Mary from Protestantism is, according to Tillich's statements, traceable back to the rejection of any human mediation of grace. The reformational axioms *"solus Deus"*, *"solus Christus"* and *"sola gratia"* have forced the creaturely components of religion into the background, or even blotted them out. Mary is here the "showcase example".

It would therefore be logically appropriate to subject the *"solus Deus"* notion to critical examination. This step is not, however, taken by Tillich, for he regards Mary as a poetic symbol not deserving of worship.[96] The dignity of the created being is not renewed, but rather, God is invested with symbols of immanence: maternal ground and depths of being. Immanence symbols, however, are simultaneously emblematic of the cooperation of the created realm, which is nevertheless not brought into this theology.

The transference of the mother symbol to God in an equal (?) mixture with the father image ultimately comes down to a leveling out of the difference between creation and Creator: "secularized God—deified world".[97] The divinity of God and also the independent worth of created beings are called into question here.

Tillich's theology is to be understood as a dialectical reversal of dialectical theology, which wanted to exclude any cooperation on the part of created beings and, to a certain extent, attempted to think in terms of a divine transcendence apart from immanence. However, the pendulum then seems to have swung to the opposite extreme, now moving only in the direction of immanence.

The figure of Mary, by contrast, concretizes *the Catholic "et-et"*,[98] according to which God and created beings, sustained by divine activity, work harmoniously together in nature and grace. God's actions are decisive and all-effective, but not solely effective. Mary is not, in the first instance, the symbol of God's "motherliness" but the human *Mother* of God.

---

[95] Tillich, *Theologie*, p. 336.
[96] Tillich, *Theologie*, p. 336.
[97] Cf. pp. 167, 271 above.
[98] On this, Scheffczyk, *Glaubenswelt*, pp. 57–60, 67–78.

If, by the way, Mary were to reveal, in the first instance, not creaturely but divine values, then the same sort of transference would also have to apply to the Church, whose archetype is the Mother of God. Greeley, then, actually also seems to suggest that the daughter Zion, as archetype of the Church, is identical with God. He sketches the "picture of the romantic love story between Yahweh and the daughter Zion",[99] and claims: "Whether God is the *passionate daredevil* or the *tender seducer*—the message is the same in both cases: God has a divine desire for us, he urges us toward unification with him."[100]

To see the Church, in her believing, receptive attitude, as an image of God is, however, as inappropriate as to see God as an image of the Church. Creaturely and divine values should be brought together with one another but not confused. Otherwise, the Church and Mary, as recipient of God's grace, would be idolized into an absolute, and the Lord's sovereignty demeaned: "passionate daredevil".

4. MARY: AN EXEMPLARY IMAGE OF THE CHRISTIAN WOMAN?

Haye van der Meer, like many other authors, raises the question: "Would it not be better to consider Mary as the prototype of created beings in general, that is, of women and men, and not as the prototype of women alone?"[101]

It is certainly correct that believing readiness to receive and creaturely cooperation are not exclusive qualities of Mary, but apply, as ideal demands, to every Christian. On the other hand, the Mother of God, as *the* personal symbol of creation, realized these attitudes in the most exemplary way possible. Not the male apostles but the "Queen of Apostles"[102] is seen at the very focal point of the worship of saints. Mary's womanliness is a bodily precondition that sustains and symbolizes, in a special way, her decisive personal devotion. God made his Incarnation dependent not on the assent of a man or a neuter but on the humble affirmation of a *woman*.

Mary's life is embedded in concrete temporal-historical circumstances, and thus cannot, in its factual, earthly form, simply be mechanically copied. Paul VI therefore states that Mary is exemplary not "because of

---

[99] Greeley, *Maria*, p. 102.
[100] Greeley, *Maria*, p. 181.
[101] Meer, *Priesturtum*, p. 189.
[102] Lauretan Litany.

the sociological-cultural context" of her existence but rather "because, within her concrete life-circumstances, she rendered obedience, unconditionally and conscientiously, to the will of God".[103]

With these words, Paul VI did not intend—as is confirmed by numerous addresses[104]—to call for an equivalence between the sexes or even to propagate a bizarre "masculinization" of the Mother of God, but rather to provide some guidelines for "the *woman* of today".[105] Mary's womanliness, which finds special expression in receptivity and humility, is a self-evident presupposition for the Pope.[106] Explicitly stressed is the "maternal mission", which "extended itself" beyond Christ "and assumed, on Mount Calvary, universal dimensions".[107]

Nevertheless, the historical situation of Jesus and Mary would seem to be of high significance as well. God did not reveal himself in just any epoch, but in the "fullness of time".[108] Now, precisely in Jewish society of the pivotal age, the *specific* characteristics of the sexes had developed extraordinarily sharp contours. Christ proclaims the gospel because, as a male, he is oriented in a characteristic way through his outward-thrusting eccentricity toward the public sphere. Mary, by contrast, remains largely in concealment; as "hearer of the Word",[109] she withdraws completely behind her Son. The accents of masculine and feminine activity have certainly shifted somewhat today, but, on the basis of physical structure alone, men are (not exclusively, but more strongly) oriented "outward", and women, "inward".[110]

Gertrud von le Fort and Oda Schneider, two thoroughly self-assured women, therefore detect a deep, redemptive-historical meaning in the biblical situation:

> Fallen nature harbors a tendency to rebellion. . . . Since, now, the attitude of service must be required with particularly strong necessity of women, . . . it was thus obviously better to keep them bowed down for a while still, both by nature and also according to the constitution of their freedom in the supernatural.[111]

> Therefore those times, too, that force a woman back out of public life are not at all detrimental to her metaphysical significance; in fact, it is likely that

---

[103] *Marialis cultus*, 35, in Scheffczyk, *Impulse*, pp. 165f.; *AAS* 66 (1974): 148.
[104] For example, the words on the "Year of Women": *AAS* 67 (1975): 265.
[105] *Marialis cultus*, 37, in Scheffczyk, *Impulse*, p. 165; *AAS* 66 (1974): 148. Emphasis mine.
[106] On this, Scheffczyk, *Impulse*, pp. 93ff.
[107] *Marialis cultus*, 37, in Scheffczyk, *Impulse*, p. 166; *AAS* 66 (1974): 149.
[108] Gal 4:4.
[109] Cf. Lk 2:19, 51.
[110] Cf. pp. 95f., 119–20 above.
[111] O. Schneider, *Priestertum*, p. 15.

precisely such times—although probably most often without realizing it—cast the immense weight of the feminine onto the world's weighing scales.[112]

Mary is thus not only an ideal model for the Christian in general but also for the Christian *woman* in particular. According to Pope John Paul II "the nature of woman contains a special bond to the mother of the Savior."[113] In the history of the Church, Marian devotion has not oppressed women but rather has allowed them to appear in their highest dignity. This applies as much to the evaluation of virgins as to the positions of wife and mother. In the Mother of God, women find an exemplary model who can be surpassed by no masculine figure.

5. THE TRINITARIAN REFERENCES OF MARY AS ARCHETYPE OF THE CHURCH

That Mary represents a personal and effective symbolic image of the Church is confirmed by an examination of the relation of the mother of Jesus to God.

Mary's decisive association is with her Son; everything Marian derives its value solely through Christology and is, at the same time, the necessary counterpoint to that. The title "Mother of God" serves as the highest possible distinction for Mary, but being a mother implies bringing forth a child (here, the Son of God).

Motherhood is thus *the* specific fact about Mary. This high title cannot, however, be isolated, for Mary's maternal cooperation in the redemptive work occurs only by virtue of the fact that she is redeemed in advance from any stain of sin. Mary is, therefore, subordinated to her Son. Her motherhood presupposes the Immaculate Conception, which reflects itself, as receptivity, in the bodily virginity that is bound up with a readiness of the soul. This virginity maintains itself even through motherhood, since the Son "did not diminish her virginal intactness, but rather, hallowed it".[114] Mary is mother *and* ever Virgin (*semper virgo*); her maternal cooperation is related, as an enduring constitutive element, to her virginal receptive capacity.

---

[112] Fort, *Frau*, p. 19.

[113] Encyclical *Redemptoris Mater*, 46: *AAS* 79 (1987): 424. For more on this, see pp. 460f. below.

[114] *Lumen gentium*, 57, in Rahner and Vorgrimler, *Konzilskompendium*, p. 190; *AAS* 57 (1965): 61.

Cooperation and reception are combined in the material symbol of bride, the specific symbolic image for the Church.[115] Like the Church, so its archetype too is aligned with the incarnate Logos. That the designation "bride" for Mary is bound up above all with the Holy Spirit becomes evident only in later Church history.[116]

The situation that was prepared for in writings of the early Church Fathers is represented most clearly in the European Middle Ages: "Among the bridal designations that are used for Mary, 'Bride of Christ' becomes increasingly prominent, especially as Mary is recognized more clearly and distinctly as Christ's helper in his redemptive work, as a mediatrix of grace."[117]

This mediatory role presupposes the state of having received, of being redeemed (as seen in the perspective of Ephesians 5): "I am your sister, . . . your mother, . . . bride, too, since I became hallowed through grace."[118]

Especially in commentaries on the Song of Songs, Mary, the Church, and man's soul before God are seen as mutually aligned: "Bride to him [Christ] is the Church, the individual soul, and Mary, who is called his bride in a unique sense."[119]

Along with the titles of bride and mother, which represent Mary more strongly as standing *over against* the Son, there also occurs a type of thought—admittedly more rare—in which Mary is placed alongside of Christ, as his equal image. After all, every Christian is an "other Christ" (*alter Christus*)[120] and is thus modeled upon the trinitarian sonship. In this line of thought, M. J. Scheeben, like some of the Church Fathers, even characterizes Mary as "*agna Dei*".[121]

As a child of God, Mary also stands in a special relation to the Father, the originator of the trinitarian sonship. The daughter title is, therefore, the most frequent designation that links Mary to the First Divine Person.[122] With this, the Old Testament archetype "daughter Zion" receives its fulfillment.

---

[115] Cf. pp. 252–56 above. The following remarks have points in common with the exposition by Leo Scheffczyk, "Der trinitarische Bezug des Mariengeheimnisses" [The trinitarian reference of the Marian mystery], in *Catholica* 29 (1975): 120–31.

[116] K. Wittkemper, "Braut" [Bride], in Konrad Algermissen et al. (eds.), *Lexikon der Marienkunde I* [Encyclopedia of Marian studies, I] (Regensburg, 1967), p. 908.

[117] K. Wittkemper, "Braut", p. 900.

[118] Ephraem, In Nat. Domini, Sermo 11, in K. Wittkemper, "Braut", p. 899.

[119] Thus says the Carthusian theologian Dionysius, Proem. in Cant. Cant.: K. Wittkemper, "Braut", p. 901.

[120] Cf., for example, Rom 8:29; Col 3:11.

[121] K. Wittkemper, "Dreifaltigkeit" [Trinity], in Algermissen, *Marienkunde I*, p. 1446.

[122] Cf. K. Wittkemper, "Dreifaltigkeit", p. 1447; Scheffczyk, "Mariengeheimnis", pp. 126f.

The Father's state of being the eternal origin has a temporal analogy in Mary: just as the divinity of the Son derives from the Father, so mankind derives from the Mother.

The most appropriate relational link to the Holy Spirit would seem to define itself by way of the biblical symbols of "temple", "dwelling place" and "sanctuary". In this, the Spirit, as God's immanence, makes Mary his effective instrument in a special way. His identity as the "divinely receiving"[123] combines with Mary's readiness to receive, permeating this in a perfect way and thereby enabling the sending of the Son into time. The relationality of the Spirit, in his "power that overcomes all 'opposition' and that presses wholly toward communication and 'ensoulment' ",[124] corresponds to the particular womanly nature of the Mother of God, who lives totally for her relationship to her Son and expands herself, at the Cross, into universal motherhood.[125] Her act of internalization, undergoing the redemptive event from her very heart, finds its counterpart in the immanence of the Third Divine Person, the "heart" of the Triune God.

This state of affairs is perhaps intimated at the beginning of the Acts of the Apostles. While Peter assumes the role of "head" of the Church and proclaims the gospel at the Pentecost, Mary appears earlier as the "heart" of those who plead in prayer for the descent of the Holy Spirit.[126]

According to Luke's understanding, the Pentecostal event was, to a certain extent, already anticipated in the conceiving of Jesus;[127] the mention of Mary refers back to the story of his childhood. In the Holy Spirit, Mary appears as the "heart" of the Church and is associated with the fulfillment of salvation; at least this is the interpretation contained in early Church art: "All the ancient icons of Pentecost show Mary in the midst of the apostles, at the center from which the Spirit radiates."[128]

Mary's task can thus be described, in an outstanding way, by the words of the "little" Thérèse, who rejects a priesthood for women precisely because, as a woman, she possesses an inexchangeable worth: "*My vocation is love!* . . . Yes, I have found my place in the Church, and that place you, my God, have bestowed upon me . . . in the heart of the Church, my

[123] Cf. pp. 289–91 above.

[124] Scheffczyk, "Mariengeheimnis", pp. 126f.

[125] Cf. Jn 19:26.

[126] Acts 1:14; cf. the explication by Louis Bouyer, *Le Thrône de la Sagesse. Essai sur la signification du culte marial* (Paris, 1957), pp. 253f.

[127] Lk 1:35. Cf. the references to the activity of the Spirit in Luke 1:41 and 2:25f.; Feuillet, *Jésus*, pp. 18ff.

[128] Bouyer, *Sagesse*, p. 254.

Mother, I will be *love* . . . and thus I will be everything . . . thus my dream will become reality!"[129]

Mary can, therefore, be characterized as "the most perfect human personal image of the Holy Spirit",[130] although here, of course, the qualifications noted earlier must be kept in mind.[131] Precisely in her particular feminine nature, Mary is the "chalice of devotion" (*vas spirituale*), wholly open toward what is "on high", which presents itself as a personal, effective instrument of the Holy Spirit.

Mary does not replace the Holy Spirit,[132] but mediates him through her intercession. The title "bride of the Holy Spirit", which has meanwhile become classical in popular piety, is justified to the extent that it represents Mary as the Third Divine Person's cooperator. This attribution is nevertheless subject to misunderstanding, because the counterconcept is bridegroom (which, however, is significantly avoided in this context); the Spirit is not the Father of Jesus, since, in his activity, "the essence of procreation is not realized in any way". Therefore, more recent Mariology is inclined to avoid the title in question altogether.[133]

In my opinion, the most appropriate account of the relations between the Marian mystery and the Trinity can be found in the theology of the High Middle Ages,[134] which is expressed in the mariological statements by Vatican II: Mary has had "conferred upon her the highest charge and dignity, which is to be the *mother of the Son of God* and therefore the preferentially loved *daughter of the Father* and the *temple of the Holy Spirit*".[135]

---

[129] Therese vom Kinde Jesu [Thérèse of the Child Jesus], *Selbstbiographische Schriften* [Autobiographical writings], 8th ed. (Einsiedeln, 1978), pp. 200f.

[130] Scheffczyk, "Mariengeheimnis", p. 128.

[131] Cf. pp. 290f. above.

[132] Heribert Mühlen makes this accusation against classical theology, which often describes the communication of grace as a three-staged process: God-Christ-Mary (Mühlen, "Maria", p. 151), Mary's mediatory role is perhaps enunciated most clearly, in modern times, by Grignion de Montfort. This Church teacher from the eighteenth century, sanctified by Pius XII, emphasizes more than almost any other theologian the mediation of grace by Mary but also, at the same time, its trinitarian reference. Her association with the Holy Spirit is most clearly brought out as one in which Mary does not replace the Third Divine Person but is his "bride". Cf. Ludwig Maria Grignion von Montfort, *Das Goldene Buch der vollkommenen Hingabe an Jesus durch Maria* [The golden book of consummate devotion to Jesus through Mary], 21st ed. (Freiburg [Switzerland], 1975), for example, pp. 47ff., 147ff.

[133] K. Wittkemper, "Braut" [Bride], pp. 908f.

[134] Cf. K. Wittkemper, "Dreifaltigkeit", p. 1445.

[135] *Lumen gentium*, 53, *AAS* 57 (1965): 58. Emphases mine.

6. THE RECIPROCAL INTERPENETRATION OF MARIOLOGY AND ECCLESIOLOGY

Mary as the "Church in its origin"

In her virginal motherhood, which simultaneously embodies reception and cooperation, Mary is the "Church in its origin".[136] However, "Mariology can never be reduced to principles for ecclesiology", for, in theology, "the person" is not "to be traced back to the principles, but the principles back to the person".[137] According to Ratzinger, a doctrine of the Church that is not Mariology-centered runs the risk of sinking to the level of purely sociological thought and of forgetting the mystery. However, the Church is not initially "an organization, but the organism of Christ".[138]

The relationship Mary-Church is already intimated in the infancy narrative in the Gospel according to Luke. In the Magnificat, Mary takes her place in the redemptive-historical situation of Israel: "He has helped his servant Israel, in remembrance of his mercy, as he spoke to our fathers, to Abraham and to his posterity for ever." "And his mercy is on those who fear him from generation to generation . . . he has put down the mighty from their thrones."[139]

Mary speaks here as a representative of her people, but her independent accent does not, for that, get lost. Even on the basis of linguistic structure, the individual and the collective parts of the Magnificat[140] are closely linked to one another. The beginning of the second part ("power" and ἐποίησεν) (Luke 2:51) picks up again a theme from the first (2:49) and simultaneously forms an antithesis to the preceding verse (2:50): power-mercy. The "lowliness" of Mary (ταπείνωσις) corresponds to "those of low degree" (ταπεινούς), who are contrasted with the "mighty" (2:52).[141]

The structural linkage corresponds to the material content of the song. The singer appears not as a mere type of the people, but has a uniquely individual cast that shatters the Jewish background: "*my* Savior", "he

---

[136] Ratzinger and Balthasar, *Maria*.
[137] Ratzinger, "Erwägungen", p. 25.
[138] Ratzinger, "Erwägungen", pp. 23f.
[139] Lk 1:50, 52, 54–55.
[140] Verses 46–50, 51–55.
[141] Further references are given in Jacques Dupont, "Le Magnificat comme discours sur Dieu", in *NRTh* 102 (1980): 321–43, especially 328–32.

who is mighty has done great things for *me*" and, above all, "henceforth all generations will call *me* blessed".[142]

Mary's personal distinctness and her orientation toward the people appear in the song as two poles between which the exposition moves and neither of which can be abolished at the expense of the other. Scheeben later formulates this state of affairs by saying that Mariology and ecclesiology exist in perichoresis, that is, in reciprocal interpenetration.[143]

The Church appears, in the image of Mary, as having feminine traits, while all of Mariology was predesigned as ecclesiology already in patristic times: "The *Virgo Ecclesia*, the *Mater Ecclesia*, the *Ecclesia immaculata*, the *Ecclesia assumpta*—everything that was later to become Mariology was initially conceived as ecclesiology."[144]

Being the Church does not initially mean representing Christ—that, in the specific sense, is the task of the office bearer[145]—but rather, representing the bride as receptively and cooperatively opposed to the bridegroom. Anyone who reduces ecclesiology to Christology thereby negates the independent efficacy of the creaturely and the human.[146]

Through Mary, "the Church" is "to be called feminine in its entire core",[147] which can hardly surprise anyone in view of the anthropological background.[148] "This femininity of the Church is all-embracing, whereas the official service-role that is performed by the apostles and their male successors is merely a function within this all-embracing dimension."[149] While all the adult members of the Church, including the saints, are

---

[142] Cf. on this Schürmann, *Lukasevangelium*, pp. 73f., and especially Dupont, "Magnificat", who shows in detail that verse 48 cannot be detached from its context as a supposed later interpolation. The Magnificat obviously forms a unity that presented itself to Luke as such and that is traceable to the Mother of God in its general sense or even literally; among others, Schnackenburg, "Magnificat", p. 201, and Schürmann, *Lukasevangelium*, p. 78, endorse the first alternative, while the second possibility is presented especially by: Paul Gaechter, *Maria im Erdenleben. Neutestamentliche Marienstudien* [Mary in earthly life. New Testament Marian studies] (Innsbruck, Vienna, and Munich, 1953), pp. 133–37; J. G. Machen, *The Virgin Birth of Christ* (New York and London, 1930), p. 97. Raymond Brown's theories about a post-Easterly Christian origin of the song do not do justice to the Magnificat's Old Testament-Jewish coloring: R. E. Brown, *The Birth of the Messiah: A Commentary on the Infancy Narratives*, 2nd ed. (New York, 1979), p. 363.

[143] M. J. Scheeben, *Handbuch der Dogmatik* [Handbook of dogmatics], vol. 2, Gessamelte Schriften VI, 2, ed. by Carl Feckes, 2nd ed. (Freiburg im Breisgau, 1954), no. 1819, p. 488.

[144] Ratzinger, "Erwägungen", p. 27.

[145] Cf. pp. 330ff., 335ff. below.

[146] Cf. Ratzinger's censure of "Christomonism", in "Erwägungen", p. 24.

[147] H. U. von Balthasar, "Maria in der kirchlichen Lehre und Frömmigkeit" [Mary in Church doctrine and piety], in Ratzinger and Balthasar, *Maria*, p. 59.

[148] Cf. pp. 252ff. above.

[149] Balthasar, "Frömmigkeit", p. 59.

sinfully fallen, Mary alone, in the sense of the Pauline marriage metaphor,[150] is to be described as "*Immaculata*". Not only the purity of faith effected by Christ and the upholding of the means to grace prevent the "Church of sinners" from becoming the "sinful Church"; for the Mother of God is not just a "symbol" but the "deepest origin and unflawed core" of the Church.[151]

In opposition to a misconceived response to Vatican II, Balthasar[152] and Ratzinger[153] lay stress on the primacy of the feminine traits in the image of the Church. "Paul gave expression to the *differentia specifica* of the New Testament Church, as contrasted with the 'wandering people of God' of the Old Testament, through the concept 'body of Christ' ",[154] in which the mysterious and grace-borne participation in the life of God—only *promised* in the Old Testament[155]—comes to fulfillment. "In elucidating the essence [of the Church] . . . nothing nobler and more excellent, nothing more divine, can be found than that expression in which she is characterized as the 'mystical body of Jesus Christ'."[156]

The term *body of Christ* should be understood against the background of Genesis 2:24: "They [man and wife] became one flesh."[157] Christ is the "head" of the Church, but, at the same time, he realizes himself in her as his "fullness".[158]

The image of the body should be seen, from the viewpoint of its origin, together with the central symbol of bride.[159] Without woman, redemptive history is but a torso, for it was in Mary that the Church gave its assent to the Incarnation, and it is in the Marian-stamped mystical body of Christ that Jesus' redemptive act completes itself.

Christ is a *male*: "As male, however, *out of* woman (the sacred community of the Old Covenant, whose apex is Mary) and, again, fruitful *in* woman (in the same sacred community, which *becomes in Mary the Church*)".[160] In

---

[150] Eph 5:27.

[151] H. U. von Balthasar, "Das marianische Prinzip" [The Marian principle], in *Klarstellungen. Zur Prüfung der Geister*, Kriterien 45 (Einsiedeln, 1978), p. 69. English edition: *Elucidations* (London: SPCK, 1971).

[152] H. U. von Balthasar, "Die umgreifende Mütterlichkeit der Kirche" [The all-embracing motherliness of the Church], in *Der antirömische Affekt* (Freiburg im Breisgau, 1974), p. 156. English edition: *The Office of Peter and the Structure of the Church* (San Francisco: Ignatius Press, 1986), p. 183.

[153] Ratzinger, "Erwägungen", pp. 23f.

[154] Ratzinger, "Erwägungen", p. 23.

[155] Ezek 36:26–28; Jer 31:33 and elsewhere.

[156] Pius XII, *Mystici corporis*, no. 402; cf. *Lumen gentium*, 7, AAS 57 (1965): 9–11.

[157] Ratzinger, "Erwägungen", p. 24.

[158] Cf. Eph 4:13 with 4:16; 5:29.

[159] Gen 2:24; Eph 5:31f.

[160] H. U. von Balthasar, "Maria-Kirche-Amt" [Mary-church-office], in *Kleine Fibel für*

Mary, the Church and at the same time everything feminine are personally polarized.[161]

The Mother of God and the motherliness of the Church

This personal polarization is also applicable with respect to Mary's motherhood. If "Mother" is the highest title for Mary, then, in an analogical
sense, so it is too for the Church; her prototype, the daughter Zion,
appears already in the Old Testament as the "mother" of the children of
Israel,[162] and Paul speaks of the "Jerusalem above" as "our mother".[163]

The images of bride and mother merge, in fact, into one another within
Pauline theology,[164] and in the Revelation of John the bridal mother
appears in threefold perspective: "The commentators are right to see in
the loudly crying *woman of the Apocalypse*, in the first instance, the Old
Testament sacred community, which, however, really brings forth its
Redeemer in the person of Mary, and from then on becomes the New
Testament Church, since the woman goes on to have further children
who 'bear testimony to Jesus'."[165]

Wisdom in the Old Testament, too, insofar as it embodies the
creaturely response to God's call,[166] is, as bride and mother, a type
of Mary and the Church. Precisely wisdom's feminine traits leave a
"remainder behind that could never be completely integrated into Christology".[167] Therefore the liturgy of the Church, in East and West, has read
the texts on wisdom[168] as implicitly related to Mary.[169]

Since the earliest period of Church history, the mother has been the
central image for the Church's mediatory function. Body of Christ

---

verunsicherte Laien, Kriterien 55 (Einsiedeln, 1980), p. 72. English edition: *A Short Primer for Unsettled Laymen* (San Francisco: Ignatius Press, 1985), p. 91.

[161] H. U. von Balthasar, *Sponsa Verbi* (Einsiedeln, 1961), p. 160.

[162] Cf. especially Is 66:8–13; Lk 19:44.

[163] Gal 4:25–27. The question of whether, in the infancy narrative in Luke, there are
express linkages of Mary to the "daughter Zion" is controversial; there is, for instance, a
positive position taken by René Laurentin, *Struktur und Theologie der lukanischen Kind-
heitsgeschichte* [Structure and theology of the infancy narrative in Luke] (Stuttgart, 1967),
especially pp. 91ff., while other authors are more reserved: Schürmann, *Lukasevangelium*,
pp. 64f., n. 161; Schnackenburg, "Magnificat", pp. 214ff.

[164] 2 Cor 11:2; Gal 4:26; Eph 5:27.

[165] Balthasar, *Sponsa Verbi*, p. 70; a detailed exegetical argument for this thesis occurs,
among other places, in Feuillet, *Jésus*, pp. 30–46.

[166] Cf. p. 280 above.

[167] Ratzinger, *Daughter Zion*, p. 26.

[168] Especially Sir 24 and Prov 8.

[169] Bouyer, *Sagesse*, pp. 39–50, 76f.

implies the binding together in grace of the Church members; the title
mother refers to the Church as contrasted with the individual. In the
baptismal wellspring, she brings her children forth into new life and
accompanies them at all times with her loving care.[170] The "heart" of the
believer and the "maternal womb of the Church" are the "staging place
for divine birth" and thus symbolic of receptive cooperation: "The
birth-giver that bears the masculine Logos in the hearts of the faithful is
our mother, the Church."[171] The heart serves, at the same time, as "the
mysterious resting place of wisdom", which releases from itself the
λόγος.[172]

In all this, the mother title is not initially a cipher for the activity of the
hierarchy, but signifies, "so to speak, a continuation of Mary's care",[173]
and comprehends the entire religious community. Just as the devotion of
the Mother of God is wholly "permeated with human experience, all the
way down to the most hidden depths of the bodily, of the womblike",[174]
so the Church, too, must receive into herself the life germ of grace and
allow it to grow.

The Church does not, in the first instance, represent herself—according
to Ratzinger[175]—in the "masculine, activist-sociological approach of the
'Populus Dei' (people of God)", but rather—if we consider her cooperative,
mediatory role—in the image of the virginal Mother. "Wherever the
mystery of the Marian nature of the Church is overshadowed or
abandoned, there Christianity necessarily becomes mono-sexual (homosexual), that is, totally masculine."[176] "Without Mariology, Christianity
threatens to become inhuman . . . and people will desert such a Church in
droves."[177]

Mary as Mother of the Church

Mary is not only the archetype of "Mother Church" but also "Mother of
the Church". Through this, the independent significance of the bearer of
God—which is not exhausted in being an abstract type—is expressed in an
outstanding way. In this connection, the Second Vatican Council cites

[170] Cf. Lumen gentium, 64, AAS 57 (1965): 64.
[171] Methodius of Philippi, Symposion 8:11, in H. Rahner, Symbole, pp. 13f.; PG 18, p.
153.
[172] H. Rahner, Symbole, pp. 14ff.
[173] Marialis cultus, 28, in Scheffczyk, Impulse, p. 156; AAS 66 (1974): 140.
[174] Balthasar, Glory of the Lord I, p. 342.
[175] Ratzinger, "Erwägungen", p. 23.
[176] Balthasar, "Marianisches Prinzip", p. 69.
[177] Balthasar, "Marianisches Prinzip", p. 72.

Saint Augustine: Mary is not only the mother of Christ, but "even the mother of the members [of Christ], . . . for she co-operated in love so that the faithful would be born in the Church who are the members of this head".[178]

The Mother of God cooperates at all times "toward reinstatement of the supernatural life of the soul. Therefore she is, in the order of grace, a mother to us."[179]

The way for the new title "Mother of the Church" was prepared, in some ways, by Louis de Montfort,[180] whom Pius XII named as a doctor of the Church in 1947: "A mother obviously does not bring the head into the world without the members, nor the members without the head; otherwise there would result a monstrosity of nature. And it is also true in the order of grace that the head and the members must be born of the same mother." "All true children of God have God as their Father and Mary as their Mother."[181]

Factually considered, of course, the name "Mother of the Church" is not new: "In the image of the cloak of grace, for instance, the archetype of the Church and the whole Church, as alive in that archetype's sphere, flow into one another."[182] Hans Urs von Balthasar illustrates the relation between Mary and the Church in the "image of successive but common-centered circular waves. . . : Among all the other circles, Mary is the largest, whose radius extends through all the remaining ones and includes them in itself; she is, in other words, co-extensive with the Church, insofar as she is the Church of the Holy, 'Bride without blemish or wrinkle'."[183]

---

[178] Augustine, De sancta virginitate 6: Lumen gentium, 53, AAS 57 (1965): 59. The title "Mother of the Church", which crops up for the first time in a commentary on Revelation from the eleventh or twelfth century, has, from the start, been linked again and again with this image: Mary is "Mother of the Church because she gave birth to the head of the Church": Walter Dürig, Maria, Mutter der Kirche. Zur Geschichte und Theologie des neuen liturgischen Marientitels [Mary, Mother of the Church. On the history and theology of the new liturgical Mary-title] (St. Ottilien, 1979), p. 13; PL, 17, p. 960.

[179] Lumen gentium, 61, to be compared with 62, p. 192; AAS 57 (1965): 63.

[180] Not the title as such, but its content.

[181] Montfort, Hingabe, pp. 57, 55; cf. 257 and many others. These statements can, of course, in isolation, lead to misunderstandings. The Council's moderator, Julius Cardinal Döpfner, nevertheless thinks that Grignion's ideas correspond to the doctrine of Vatican II: cf. Hubert Pauels, Maria Mittlerin al Gnaden nach den lehramtlichen Verlautbarungen von Leo XIII, Pius X, Pius XII und Paul VI [Mary, Mediatrix of All Graces according to the doctrinal proclamations of Leo XIII, Pius X, Pius XII and Paul VI], 2nd ed. (Stein am Rhein, 1976), p. 61; similarly, Rudolf Graber in his foreword to Montfort, Hingabe, p. vii.

[182] H. U. von Balthasar, "Frauenpriestertum?" ["Women Priests?"], in Neue Klarstellungen, Kriterien 49 (Einsiedeln, 1979), p. 113. English edition: New Elucidations (San Francisco: Ignatius Press, 1986), p. 194.

[183] Balthasar, "Epilog", p. 275; cf. Eph 5:27.

Thus, the Church is Marian in her basic structure and therefore exhibits, in contrast to Christ and his official representatives, typically feminine traits. The official functions, which culminate in the special priesthood,[184] must be seen within this more comprehensive framework. For, as members of the Church, the office bearers are, in the first instance, receptively and cooperatively active like all other believers. In their specific representation of Christ, they are also distinct from and in contrast to the Church, but only as "intermediaries" and "instruments". They represent the Lord, from whom they themselves are different. Mary, by contrast, does not only represent the Church but is herself the "Church in its origin".

In an analogical way, therefore, women, too, are representatives *and* embodiments of the Church. As opposed to men and the male priesthood, they symbolize a reality with which they are themselves identical.[185] This indicative of identity of women and the Church is, of course, also an imperative, which takes its direction in a special way from the example of Mary: "Become what you are!"

The only reason that the Church is endowed with male office is "so that she . . . does not forget her primary womanliness". That office must "represent the self-giving Lord of the Church", "but within her feminine receptivity". "The Church is first of all—and this primacy is an enduring one—feminine, before she receives her supplementary masculine side in the form of ecclesiastical office."[186] To be sure, in "office", the male (more precisely, some males) is "head" of the female (and not only of the female), but, at the same time, he is dependent on the Marian as the "sheltering hearth and exemplary realization" of being a Christian.[187] For the Christian existence of the office bearer, the "Marian principle" is "the more comprehensive and all-embracing"; "everything in it that is majestic, authoritative, hierarchical [must] be lived out and permeated by the spirit and by the attitude of the Marian Fiat".[188]

A "desire for ecclesiastical office in a woman [can] arise only from a misconception of her proper position of worth within the Church (*as Church*) . . . , a misconception that levels down the mystery of the sexes

---

[184] Cf. pp. 330ff., 335f. below.
[185] Cf. pp. 189f. above.
[186] Balthasar, "Epilog", p. 276.
[187] Balthasar, "Welches Gewicht", p. 57.
[188] Scheffczyk, "Maria", pp. 71f.

instead of living it out in its open and consummate tension and fruit-fulness".[189] Leo Scheffczyk therefore remarks that the figure of Mary is given, "in consequence of a correct instinct, no [attention] at all" by the advocates of a female priesthood.[190]

From this perspective, attempts by women to enter the official priest-hood would be explicable by assuming that the critical Marian dimension of the Church had not been sufficiently internalized. At the same time, a certain overvaluation of the masculine element in the Church may be suspected, and perhaps even a hidden clericalism.[191] For the clergy does not constitute the essence of the Church (*as* Church), but is only its necessary accident. In any case, as the relevant sociological data show quite clearly,[192] women will never be able to play a role equivalent to that of men even if admitted to the clergy. The specific worth of woman becomes all the more clearly apparent when the priesthood is prohibited to her.

In order to conclude what has been said here, two characteristics of the figure of Mary may be emphasized:

1. It is precisely in her specific feminine nature that Mary is archetype and Mother of the Church. The worth of the created being, in cooperation and reception, is realized here in a way that can be surpassed by no male.
2. That Mary was not a priest in the official sense, like the apostles, is due to her central position in the redemptive process.

These two ideas have been given what is probably their most deeply probing intuitive expression by a *woman*, namely, the writer, theologian and philosopher Gertrud von le Fort, whose observations are worthy of remembrance. In Mary,

> Catholic dogmatics [has] made the most powerful statements . . . that have ever been made about woman. Compared to those statements, all other attempts at metaphysical elucidation of the feminine fade away as mere echoes of theology or as devoid of religious content and meaning.[193]
>
> The Church was not able to entrust the priesthood to women, since she would thereby have destroyed the proper significance of women in the Church—she would have destroyed a part of her own essence, that part whose symbolic representation was entrusted to women.[194]

---

[189] Balthasar, "Epilog", p. 276.

[190] Scheffczyk, "Wesen", p. 40.

[191] On this, see the pertinent expositions by Oda Schneider, one of the [female] pioneers of the Catholic lay apostolate: O. Schneider, *Priestertum*, p. 27.

[192] Cf. pp. 104–6 above.

[193] Fort, *Frau*, p. 13.

[194] Fort, *Frau*, p. 133.

CHAPTER FOUR

The Behavior of Christ

1. THE MOST IMPORTANT POINT OF DEPARTURE: THE SUMMONING OF THE TWELVE APOSTLES

The origin of the office that is mediated through consecration to the priesthood lies in the actions of Jesus. Here the selection of the twelve disciples seems especially significant, since, as commissioned by their Lord, they form the nucleus of a particularly prominent sort of service, which unfolds in its total fullness after Easter.[1] As is well known, this group of twelve consists only of males.[2] In what follows here, I will inquire into whether this restriction is based in the contemporary situation of the people of Israel or whether it goes beyond that contextual framework.

2. CHRIST'S POSITION REGARDING WOMEN WITHIN THE FRAMEWORK OF HIS TIMES

The Jewish environment

Women were regarded as incapable of bearing witness, which means that a female "apostle" would have met with consternation among the Jews.[3] They remained excluded from the essential religious tasks of men as well.

[1] Josef Finkenzeller, *Von der Botschaft Jesu zur Kirche Christi. Zweifel-Fragen-Probleme-Antworten* [From the message of Jesus to the Church of Christ. Doubts-questions-problems-answers] (Munich, 1974), p. 100: "The proper theological approach to ecclesiastical office is by way of apostolic office."

[2] Mk 3:13–19 par.

[3] Billerbeck, *Kommentar III*, p. 559; cf. already Dt 19:15, 17.

This tendency, which was originally explicable in part because of their maternal duties, had become considerably stronger over the course of time. Whereas both sexes had equal rights of entry to the temple in Shiloh[4] and the two older temples in Jerusalem, women were allowed only as far as the forecourt of the Herodian temple. In the synagogue, their assigned place was the gallery or an outer chamber.[5] Contrary to relevant Old Testament texts,[6] the rabbis no longer regarded the female sex as belonging to the community.[7]

According to Rabbi Jehuda (second century A.D.), Jews should recite the following prayer every day: "Praised [be God], that he did not create me as a goy [Gentile]! Praised, that he did not create me as a woman! Praised, that he did not create me as an ignorant person!"[8]

In later times, this prayer of praise was included as a daily morning prayer in numerous Jewish prayer books.[9] Its gratitude was related particularly to the fact that men knew the Law, but women did not. Instructing the female sex in the Torah was not considered obligatory and was even seen, in part, as improper. Rabbi Eliezer wrote (around 90 A.D.): "He who teaches his daughter the Torah is like one who teaches her dissoluteness. . . . May the words of the Torah be burnt before anyone delivers them up to women."[10] Women are often "placed on a level with slaves and children in respect of fulfillment of certain commandments. This, more than anything else, attests to the inferior position occupied by women, as compared with men, in respect of the Law."[11]

Conversing with a woman, even with one's wife, was frowned upon: "For any unnecessary talk that occurs between a man and his wife, the man will be called to answer at the hour of death."[12]

When, around 110 A.D., a Galilean rabbi wanted to ask a woman (the spouse of a professional colleague) for directions, the following exchange ensued: "Which of these roads will take me to Lydda?" She replied, "Foolish Galilean, has it not been stated by the scholars: 'He shall not converse at length with a woman'? You should have said: 'Which way to Lydda?' "[13]

---

[4] 1 Sam 1.
[5] Leipoldt, *Frau*, pp. 79f.
[6] Ex 19:6–8; Dt 29:8–12 and elsewhere.
[7] Leipoldt, *Frau*, p. 82.
[8] Billerbeck, *Kommentar III*, p. 661; cf. Leipoldt, *Frau*, pp. 85f.
[9] Cf. Loewe, *Women*, p. 43.
[10] Billerbeck, *Kommentar III*, p. 469; cf. Dt 11:19, which speaks of "sons". [Trans.: RSV: "children".]
[11] Billerbeck, *Kommentar III*, p. 559.
[12] Babylonian Talmud, in Leipoldt, *Frau*, p. 90.
[13] Billerbeck, *Kommentar II*, p. 438.

When guests came, the wife did not share in the meal,[14] and even "for the wife to serve at the table was considered unacceptable".[15]

In view of this situation, Haye van der Meer draws the conclusion that "Jesus and the apostles were not able to include any women as witnesses to the Resurrection in the apostolic group: at that time, the witness of women would never have been taken seriously."[16]

What is new in Christ's attitude

As opposed to all this, it must be stressed that, in many things, Jesus showed no respect for his religious and sociocultural surroundings. The Sabbath commandment, for instance, or the prescriptions about "clean" and "unclean", were, because of their Mosaic origin, at least as deep rooted as the determinations on the position of women, which were formed in part only after the period of exile. Nevertheless, on the basis of his Messianic claim, Jesus set himself sovereignly above these, in that way correcting Moses himself.[17]

His gospel, therefore, not only was "not taken seriously" by the Pharisees and scribes but also brought him mortal enemies.[18] To an even greater extent, his divine mission and certain of his claims gave cause for offense.[19] Later on, the message of the Cross was "a stumbling block to Jews and folly to Gentiles".[20]

In his attitude to women, too, Jesus aroused anger. He allows himself to be touched by a female sinner,[21] does not respect the uncleanness of a woman with a flow of blood[22] and takes the part of an adultress.[23]

These facts could still be explained, though with difficulty, as consequences of Jesus' general love for sinners, but that would no longer be possible in the case of the following ones:

During his wanderings, he accepts the accompaniment of women,[24] who stay with him all the way to the Cross.[25] When meals are taken, too,

[14] Cf. already Gen 18:6–10.
[15] Billerbeck, Kommentar I, p. 480; cf. Leipoldt, Frau, pp. 90f.
[16] Meer, Priestertum, p. 19.
[17] Mk 2:23–28; 3:1–6; 7:18–23; cf. also the antitheses in the Sermon on the Mount, Mt 5:21–48.
[18] Mk 2:6.
[19] Jn 5:18; Mk 14:62–64; Jn 6:52, 60, 66; Lk 9:57–62.
[20] 1 Cor 1:23; cf. already the mocking in Mk 15:29–32 par; 15:16–20 par; Lk 23:11.
[21] Lk 7:37ff.
[22] Mk 5:24–34 par.
[23] Jn 8:11.
[24] Lk 8:1–3.
[25] Mk 15:40–41 par.

women are present, and Jesus allows himself to be served by them as a matter of course.[26]

He conducts conversations, some even amounting to teaching, with women, and this is by no means just an instance of "unrabbinical" or "layman's" behavior[27] but causes offense even among "laymen".[28]

Jesus' special capacity for empathy with the world of women is evidenced also by his parables[29] and miracles.[30] Characteristic as well are the many female names that are recorded, in particular, by Luke (in the Gospel and later in the Acts of the Apostles). Given the great significance attached to names in antiquity, this is a striking testimony to the important role of women in the original Church, as grounded in the behavior of Jesus.[31]

In the Old Testament, by contrast, women are not as a rule identified by name, even in the case of so important a personality as the queen of Sheba,[32] and this indicates the lower esteem in which they were held.[33]

Jesus not only stimulated a general attitude of goodwill toward women but also consciously appealed to the divine order of creation. This radical reorientation occurs in relation to the position of women in marriage, with Christ sharpening awareness of the absolute prohibition of divorce and tracing this back to the original will of God.[34] Only those who know the extent of the evils of successive polygamy in the ancient world—including among the Jews—can assess the protection that Christ's commandment brought to the world of women.[35]

In short: Jesus' attitude toward women was, in his times, "revolutionizing";[36] through him, woman is placed "side by side with man, having equal rights as a child of God".[37]

---

[26] Lk 10:38–42; Mk 2:31 par.

[27] Thus claims Krister Stendahl "Auffassung", p. 148.

[28] Jn 4:27; further conversations in Lk 10:39 and Mk 7:24–30.

[29] Mt 13:33 par; Lk 15:8–10; 18:1–8.

[30] Mk 1:29–31 par; 5:25–34 par; 5:35–41 par; Lk 7:12; 13:12.

[31] Lk 8:1–3; 10:38–39; 24:10 par; Mk 15:40–41 par; Acts 1:14; 9:36; 16:1; 16:13–15; 18:18, 26; 21:9; Rom 16:1–15.

[32] 1 Kings 10:1.

[33] Cf. Leipoldt, Frau, p. 72.

[34] Mt 5:31–32; 19:3–9; Mk 10:2–12; Lk 16:18; 1 Cor 7:10–12.

[35] Oepke, "γυνή": ThW I, p. 783: "The really cancerous damage was done, in the Jewish world as in the Hellenic, along with adultery and prostitution, by successive polygamy"; cf. Oepke, pp. 778, 780.

[36] Gärtner, Amt, p. 8.

[37] Oepke, p. 785.

3. THE MEANING BEHIND EXCLUSION OF WOMEN FROM THE OFFICE OF APOSTLE

Representation of Jesus Christ as the essence of apostolic service

The twelve apostles[38] may have had a special significance, as representatives of the new Israel, which was linked to the old people of twelve tribes with its twelve ancestral fathers. Thus Lukas Vischer thinks that the restriction of the group of twelve to male members "may be understood more as a fulfillment of the promises of God to Israel than as a law determinative of the future of the Church".[39]

At best, however, this notion is hinted at in Matthew 19:28 and Luke 22:30, where mention is made of the participation of the Twelve in the Last Judgment. The most clearly prominent aspect of their office lies not in symbolizing the ancestral fathers but "in the total mission that they were charged with by Christ: 'And he appointed twelve, to be with him, and to be sent out to preach.' "[40]

Of course, the eschatological components of apostolic office need not be kept from view. The mission of preaching is directed toward the end times, as is evident particularly from the giving of that mission as found in the Gospel according to Matthew:[41] the task is "to lead the peoples to the blessed lordship of Christ".[42] The same applies with respect to the Eucharist, which "[proclaims] the death of Christ until he comes again".[43] According to the Apocalypse,[44] "the Church" is "stamped by the 'twelve apostles' even in her fulfilled form".[45] An orientation toward the Parousia is required not only of the apostles but of all office bearers. The Twelve, however, have a specific function as "foundation" of the Church,[46] which is thoroughly comparable to the founding of Israel by the twelve ancestral fathers. Now, before one—like Vischer—brushes this connection aside as

---

[38] Cf. Lk 6:13; Mk 6:30.

[39] Lukas Vischer, "Die Ordination der Frau" [The ordination of women], in *Ordination*, p. 13.

[40] Commentary in Declaration 32; cf. Declaration 8, n. 10; *AAS* 69 (1977): 103, n. 10. Mk 3:14.

[41] Mt 28:18–20; cf. Lk 24:47f. with Acts 1:8.

[42] Rudolf Schnackenburg, "Apostolizität: Stand der Forschung" [Apostolicity: The state of research], in *Katholizität und Apostolizität* [Catholicity and Apostolicity], Kerygma und Dogma, Beiheft 2 (Göttingen, 1971), p. 59.

[43] 1 Cor 11:27; cf. Lk 22:16, 18. Similarly, Mt 26:29; Mk 14:25.

[44] Rev 21:14.

[45] Schnackenburg, *Apostolizität*, p. 59.

[46] Rev 21:14; cf. Eph 2:20.

"merely" an aspect of sacred history, one ought to ask whether there is not already an essential structure implicit in the representation of Israel by twelve *males*. After all, the figure of Christ, too, is typologically prefigured in a variety of ways in the Old Testament by, among others, Adam,[47] Jacob (= Israel),[48] Moses[49] and David.[50] Again, even before the Twelve, *Christ* is the "ancestral father" and "foundation" of the Church.[51] Thus, the Incarnation of the Son of God as a man is also prepared for in sacred history, but its theological significance extends—as I have attempted to show earlier—above and beyond the historical moment.

The eschatological reference of the Twelve, as "ancestral fathers" and foundation of the Church, cannot be played off against their missionary task[52] but rather is linked together with it. Representation of Christ takes place through both aspects of the office of the Twelve.

According to Luke 10:1, a group of seventy (or perhaps seventy-two) disciples was sent out for a time, similarly to the way that the Twelve were. Judging by the context of the remaining appointments of disciples and by the practice of the original Church as rooted in Jesus' activity, it is quite improbable that there were female members in that group either.[53]

At the end of the long speech sending forth the disciples, which Luke records as directed to the seventy (seventy-two), and Matthew, to the twelve, the following sentence occurs: "He who receives you receives me, and he who receives me receives him who sent me";[54] and, in the other context: "He who hears you hears me, and he who rejects you rejects me, and he who rejects me rejects him who sent me."[55]

Here, with reference to the missionary sermon, a special office of *representation* is declared: Christ's envoy is like Christ himself.[56]

This notion of representation, as related to Christ, forms the core of the original Christian understanding of office; the central concept "apostle" ("envoy") is its clearest expression. Josef Finkenzeller therefore character-

---

[47] Rom 5:14, 19.

[48] Lk 1:32.

[49] Mt 5:21–48.

[50] Mk 11:10 par.

[51] Cf. Eph 2:15, 21.

[52] Thus, for instance, Fiorenza, "The Twelve", p. 117: "The essential character of the Twelve is eschatological-symbolical and not historical-masculine."

[53] Cf. pp. 394, 398, 406f. below.

[54] Mt 10:40; cf. Jn 13:20.

[55] Lk 10:16.

[56] Behind this idea stands the so-called shaliach institution, according to which the following applies to an envoy invested with special authority by the Jewish central governing body: "The envoy (Hebrew: *shaliach*; Greek: *apostolos*) of another man is like that man himself." Cf. Ernst, *Lk*, p. 336; Schnackenburg, *Apostolizität*, p. 58, n. 17.

izes an apostle as follows: "a representative of Christ who is fully empowered and invested with authority as such".[57]

Although already established before Easter, it is only after Easter that the apostolate develops into its total fullness, in consequence of the sending of the Risen Christ. Two things belong to apostolic office in the narrower sense: one must have seen the Risen Christ and have received a special calling from God.[58]

From these follows the authority for official and public preaching of the gospel[59] and for directing the Church together with the power to bind and to loose.[60] In all these activities, the apostle represents the exalted Lord and, with that, God himself.[61] As "servant of Christ and steward of the mysteries of God",[62] he has "a special mandate for commemorative realization of the redemptive actions of Christ".[63]

The special role of the Eucharist

Now, "the most concentrated and intensive form of this commemorative realization" is, however, "the celebration of the Eucharist",[64] through which Christ's sacrifice radiates its efficacious implications.[65] For the conducting of this, "the position of a director" was "constitutive . . . who spoke and did, in persona Christi, what Jesus had spoken and done at the Last Supper".[66]

---

[57] Josef Finkenzeller, "Zur Diskussion über das kirchliche Amt in der katholischen Theologie" [On the debate about ecclesiastical office in Catholic theology], in Jörg Baur (ed.), Das Amt im ökumenischen Kontex. Eine Studienarbeit des ökumenischen Ausschusses der VELKD [Office in ecumenical context. A study paper by the ecumenical committee of the VELKD] (Wiesbaden, 1980), p. 58.

[58] 1 Cor 9:1; 15:8; Gal 1:1; Rom 1:1; cf. Peter Bläser, "Amt und Eucharistie im Neuen Testament" [Office and Eucharist in the New Testament], in Peter Bläser et al. (eds.), Amt und Eucharistie [Office and Eucharist] (Paderborn, 1973), pp. 13–19.

[59] Mt 28:18–20; 2 Cor 5:20.

[60] Mt 28:20; 2 Cor 5:20.

[61] 2 Cor 5:20; Gal 4:14.

[62] 1 Cor 4:1.

[63] Bläser, Amt, p. 41.

[64] Bläser, Amt, p. 41.

[65] 1 Cor 11:23–26 par.

[66] Bläser, Amt, p. 46. Prof. Bläser refers there especially to Acts 20:11, where Paul assumes the position of authorized "head of the house". Cf. the Lutheran interpreter Johansson (Women, p. 20): "precisely in the cultus, centered in the Lord's Supper, the basic structure of the Church becomes apparent . . . the picture of the household must have stood clearly before the community that celebrated the Lord's Supper, and at every such gathering some person must have acted as head of the family."

To the consummation of this, however, Jesus summoned only the twelve apostles from among the large circle of his followers.[67] That no woman received the apostolic charge is particularly remarkable, for:

1. The Eucharist was made present in a Passover meal, or at least has a clear connection with such.[68] Now, women and children were also admitted to the Paschal feast, and they dined at the table along with everyone else.[69] But even though the most esteemed women among Jesus' company, and the most intimate group of his followers, were in Jerusalem at the relevant time,[70] no one except the Twelve participated in the Last Supper.

2. This fact is even more remarkable given that, with reference to "all the other dining scenes during Jesus' lifetime that are described in the Gospels", we hear nothing "about any similar drawing of boundaries".[71]

3. According to the reports of Matthew[72] and John,[73] women were the first to whom Jesus manifested himself after the Resurrection. He appointed them as witnesses for the disciples, as "apostles to the apostles". This was done contrary to contemporary practice, which recognized no women as witnesses.[74] Nevertheless, Christ did not—as with the Twelve and, later, Saint Paul—confer on them the apostolate.

4. PROVISIONAL RESULT

The facts about Jesus' life that have been cited so far cannot prove with complete certainty that no women should be called to membership of the succession of apostolic office. They can, however, serve as a cautionary warning against any assumption that the example of Christ is irrelevant in this connection.[75] Consequently, if a decision is to be made about whether

[67] Mk 14:17–25; Mt 26:20–29; Lk 22:14–20; cf. DS, 1752.

[68] Mk 14:12, 22 par.

[69] Cf. Gärtner, *Amt*, p. 9.

[70] Mk 15:40f. par; Jn 19:25–27.

[71] Gärtner, *Amt*, p. 10.

[72] Mt 28:9f.

[73] Jn 20:11–18.

[74] Cf. Lk 24:9–11.

[75] According to the Roman declaration, too, "these considerations" provide "no direct evidence". "*Inter insigniores*", however, correctly points out that there are nevertheless "a number of converging facts" that add up to a case against women in the priesthood: Erklärung no. 2, p. 8; *AAS* 69 (1977): 103.

to alter or to retain Church practice as established according to the model of Jesus, the burden of proof would then rest clearly on the "reformers".[76]

5. OBJECTIONS TO ATTACHING LASTING SIGNIFICANCE TO CHRIST'S BEHAVIOR

To conclude this chapter, I would like to comment briefly on some widespread objections to attaching lasting significance to Jesus' behavior.

Objection 1: Jesus called not only no women to apostolic office but also no Gentiles. Nevertheless, in subsequent times, the Church has not restricted herself to Jewish Christians.[77]

Reply: The widening of office is already implicitly contained in Jesus' missionary commandment, which initiates the program of extending the Church to all peoples.[78] Therefore, there was never any controversy about the pros and cons of admitting Gentile Christians to apostolic office but only about the question of observance of certain Jewish customs by new members.[79]

Objection 2: The "transition from the concept of apostle and the Twelve to the concept of priest (and bishop)" is "too simple".[80]

Reply: As bearers of revelation, the apostles certainly possessed a special function as "foundation" of the Church.[81] However, since their office remains necessary until Christ's Second Coming,[82] they transferred it, with laying on of hands and prayer, to their successors.[83] Thus, in respect of centrality of position within the Holy Mass, the task of a "normal and unpretentious parish priest and conductor of the celebration of the Eucharist

---

[76] As opposed to Rahner, who places the burden of proof on the "conservatives" because of Jesus' supposed conformity to the cultural situation of his times: K. Rahner, *Priesturtum*, p. 297. Cf. p. 474 below.

[77] Thus Richardson, "Women", p. 75; cf. Küng and Lohfink, "Keine Ordination", p. 144; Krister Stendahl, in Refoulé, "Problème", p. 86.

[78] Mt 28:19; Lk 24:47; Acts 1:8.

[79] Gal 2:3, 7–9; Acts 15.

[80] Thus K. Rahner, *Priesturtum*, p. 295, with reference to the Roman declaration; cf. J. A. Komonchak, "Theological Questions on the Ordination of Women", in Gardiner, *Expanded Vision*, p. 254.

[81] Eph 2:20.

[82] Mt 28:20; 1 Cor 11:26.

[83] Cf. Acts 14:23; 1 Tim 4:14; 5:22; Titus 1:5; 1 Clement 42:1–3. On the last reference from early [Church] tradition, cf. J. A. Fischer, *Die Apostolischen Väter* [The apostolic Fathers], Schriften des Urchristentums I, 7th ed. (Darmstadt, 1976), pp. 76–79.

in any latter-day community"[84] distinguishes itself in no way from that of Saint Peter or John.[85]

Objection 3: The emphasis on Jesus' masculinity is foreign to the New Testament.[86] It is his humanity that remains decisive.[87]

Reply: The Bible offers no comprehensive "recipe book" for questions raised by later times. In revelation, much is contained only in budlike form and cannot come to blossom until later on, through the assistance of the Holy Spirit.[88] Precisely progressive theologians ought not to reject such new ideas from the very start. Also, I do not mean to emphasize sexual differentiation more than humanity here,[89] but simply to take seriously the fact that "humanity" occurs only as "being a man" or "being a woman".[90] That being, specifically, a man or a woman plays a role in revelation has, however, been explained already.

Objection 4: Since Christ intends, through becoming a man, to bring God's gifts of grace to men and women equally, both sexes must be involved in this priestly task. Therefore, the male office bearer cannot alone represent Christ in the full sense.[91]

Reply: Effective, consummate representation of Christ occurs, in fact, through the totality of God's people.[92] Special priestly office, however, is not a reduced reflection of the general priesthood,[93] or even a democratically legitimized deputation of that,[94] but a service of its own sort. The priest's representation of Christ is realized not only in the "being together with" of the community but also, in a special measure, as a "set over against".[95] It implies the "directive furthering of a redemptive

---

[84] K. Rahner, *Priesturtum*, p. 255.

[85] On the extensive historical questions surrounding apostolic succession, delimitation of the office to the charismata and so forth, cf. the brief survey in Ludwig Ott, *Das Weihesakrament* [The sacrament of consecration], Handbuch der Dogmengeschichte IV, 5 (Freiburg, Basel and Vienna, 1969), especially chaps. 1 and 2 on Holy Scripture and ante-Nicene Fathers.

[86] Thus Komonchak, "Questions", p. 251.

[87] Phil 2:7; Jn 1:14.

[88] Jn 16:12f.

[89] An accusation raised by Küng, "Thesen", p. 129.

[90] Gen 1:27.

[91] Thus Carr, "Church", p. 79; she hopes for "a Fuller Sign in Sacrament" from female priests. Meer, *Priesturtum*, p. 196, asks whether men alone "can really adequately represent the 'fullness of Christ's divinity' "; cf. Meer, *Priesturtum*, p. 167.

[92] 1 Pet 2:9.

[93] Eyden, "Amt", p. 107: Office as "self-realization of the Christian community".

[94] This line is taken by many American authors, for instance, by Gardiner, *Expanded Vision*, pp. 33f., 83, 100, 133; or in *Conc* 12 (1976): 5, 21–23, 71.

[95] *Lutheran* opponents of the ordination of women emphasize this often more strongly than Catholic theologians: Brunner, "Hirtenamt", p. 326; Dietzfelbinger, "Dienst", p. 172; Prenter, *Ordination*, pp. 14–16.

current in life without which there could be no life at the basic level".[96] Through being consecrated, a priest receives the ontological capacity for this, in which the grace of the sacrament effects "an approximation to Christ as mediatory and redemptive head of the Church".[97]

From among the priestly people of God, Christ called comparatively few members to official representation of his redemptive work, and we know that when selecting his apostles he passed over not only women but also the largest part of his male followers. This procedure gives expression to the fact that Christ, and not the Church, is the actual bestower of grace: "You did not choose me, but I chose you".[98]

Objection 5: A priest represents not only Christ but also the Church. "If men can thus fulfill the role of bride within the community, one must ask why women cannot, supposedly, fulfill the role of bridegroom."[99] So far, no one has taken the conception of representation (men as typal of Christ, women as typal of the Church) as a basis for "concluding that the community should consist solely of women".[100]

Reply: "Representation of Christ" and "representation of the Church" cannot be played off against each other in regard to a *priest*. He represents the Church insofar as he first *represents Christ as the head of the Church*.[101]

---

[96] Leo Scheffczyk, "Die Christusrepräsentation als Wesensmoment des Priesteramtes" [Representation of Christ as an essential aspect of the office of priest], in Scheffczyk, *Schwerpunkte*, p. 375.

[97] Scheffczyk, "Christusrepräsentation", p. 383.

[98] Jn 15:16; cf. Erklärung no. 6, p. 19; *AAS* 69 (1977): 114. See also Scheffczyk, "Wesen", p. 52.

[99] Meer, *Priesturtum*, p. 171.

[100] Meer, *Priesturtum*, p. 170; similarly, Komonchak, "Questions", p. 252.

[101] This central idea is clearly stressed by Pius XII and the Second Vatican Council in particular:

"A priest acts in place of the people only because he represents the person of our Lord Jesus insofar as the latter is head of all members and sacrifices himself for them" (*Mediator Dei*, in NR, p. 721; DS, p. 3850).

"A minister of the altar represents the person of Christ as the head who sacrifices in the name of all the members" (*Mediator Dei*, in NR 723; DS 3852).

Through the sacrament of ordination "priests by the anointing of the Holy Spirit are signed with a special character and so are configured to Christ the priest in such a way that they are able to act in the person of Christ the head" (*Presbyterorum ordinis* 2, *AAS* 58 [1966]: 992).

"Priests exercise the function of Christ as Pastor and Head in proportion to their share of authority" (*Presbyterorum ordinis* 6, *AAS* 58 [1966]: 999).

"Exercising, within the limits of the authority which is theirs, the office of Christ, the shepherd and Head, they assemble the family of God . . ." (*Lumen gentium* 28, *AAS* 57 [1965]: 34). Cf. also Erklärung no. 5, pp. 17f., esp. n. 21; *AAS* 69 (1977): 112f.

For additional information, see Scheffczyk, "Christusrepräsentation", pp. 367–86; Leo Scheffczyk, "Das kirchliche Amt im Verständnis der katholischen Theologie" [Ecclesiastical

A priest participates in this way in the dual representation of Christ:[102] the self-surrender of Christ, as the head of *mankind* (or of the Church), in the sacrifice of the Cross[103] is made present in the sacrifice of the Mass, which comes into being only through the actions of a consecrated priest.[104] Through instruction and leadership, too, a priest, as representative of Christ the head, guides man toward God.

In effectively representing *God* vis-à-vis man, a priest also participates in Christ's "headship". It is his task to mediate further God's sovereign claim by preaching revealed truth and leading the Church. That "authority", or "power", and "service" cannot in this context be played off against one another[105] is shown particularly by the administration of the sacraments: the transubstantiation of the eucharistic offerings, the absolution after

---

office as understood in Catholic theology], in Karlheinz Schuh (ed.), *Amt im Widerstreit* [Office in conflict] (Berlin, 1973), pp. 17–25.

[102] Since I have already described the "offices of *Christ*" in some detail (cf. pp. 256–67 above), I need only briefly recapitulate here.

[103] Cf. Eph 1:10; 2:16.

[104] DS 1771; 3850. On the participation of the faithful, whose significance is not hereby diminished, cf. DS 3851–55 and *Presbyterorum ordinis* 2, *AAS* 58 (1966): 992f.

[105] Cf. what was said about Christ on p. 262 above. In the representation of Christ as "head", the office bearer is not "identified" with Christ—as for Raming, *Ausschluss*, p. 212—but rather, participates in his headship. By virtue of baptism, of course, every Christian has some *participation* in the office of Christ; but, by virtue of ordination, an official priest has a sort of participation that goes above and beyond this. The modern debate, to be sure, has been influenced by the fact that Protestantism largely rejects the just-mentioned, binding Church doctrine. Nevertheless, particularly in High Church and traditional Lutheran circles, there is a conception of office that emphasizes precisely the representation of Christ as *head* of the community, and that thus comes close to the Catholic conception. Cf. especially Brunner, "Hirtenamt"; Dietzfelbinger, "Dienst"; Prenter, *Ordination*, Gärtner, *Amt*; Johannsson, *Women*.

That Ida Raming, with reference to Matthew 23:8 ("you are all brethren"), calls into question the special authority of the office bearer—"as members who remain such, they [can] never assume the position of head as opposed to the 'body' "—does not do justice to the *representation* of Christ (Raming, *Ausschluss*, pp. 212f.). The idea of participation applies as well in other areas of life. The earthly father also participates in God's "fatherhood" (Eph 3:15), and he can nevertheless be called "father". If Frau Raming were to be logically consistent, then she would also have to discard her title of doctor, for Matthew 23:10 says: "for you have one teacher ['doctor'], the Christ". (On the theological criticism of the opposition between "hierarchy" and "service", cf. Scheffczyk, "Christusrepräsentation", pp. 370, 374f.; Scheffczyk, "Wesen", p. 53.)

The dogmatic excursus in Raming seems, on the whole, to go wrong by attacking the "questionableness of the traditional conception of office and representation", even though what is at issue is not a traditional opinion, but a constant Church doctrine, which has received especially authoritative expression of late by Pius XII and Vatican II. There is obviously the underlying influence in Raming of a Protestant theologian who cannot but reject the Catholic concept of office on the basis of his background assumptions; cf. the notes in Raming, *Ausschluss*, pp. 202ff.

expiation of sins and the anointing of the sick can be performed only by a priest, but, precisely through a priest's authority, he contributes to strengthening the divine life in man and imparting more intensive form to man's relation with Christ.

This nourishing function, to Christ as head of the body, is described in the New Testament especially in the Letter to the Ephesians,[106] where the symbols "head" and "bridegroom" are virtually merged into one another.[107] Mediation of grace forms the common material content of both these symbols. The head symbol signifies, at the same time, the Christian's orientation toward God (Father), which is tied to mediation,[108] while the symbol of the bridegroom refers primarily to Christ's love for the Church.

Every Christian, of course, stands as a receiver before God and thus fulfills the bridal role. Whenever he passes divine grace on to another, he represents Christ, the "bridegroom", as well. However, this representation of Christ attains a special intensity in the service of a priest. Since the representation of Christ ranks higher than the representation of the Church, which is subordinate to it, there is good sense in not distributing priestly office to all the members of God's people but only to a relatively small part. If this selection remains limited to male candidates, then an added symbolic approximation to Christ takes place.

Objection 6: That God became man in the form of a male may well be of sacred historical significance. But why must the *representative* of Christ be a male? In the secular realm, for example, a woman can represent a male head of state, and do not "profane offices", too, "function at the level of the symbolic"?[109]

Reply: The relationship between Christ and his official representatives is not merely an external legalistic but rather "a sacramental significative one, with the signifier being, however, the whole living person".[110] This imaging relationship has its foundation in the sacrament of ordination to the priesthood, through which, in a way that goes beyond baptism by virtue of its *character indelebilis*, an ontological approximation to Christ is realized.[111] Just as Christ, as mediator of salvation, "can exist in his

---

[106] Eph 4:16; 5:29; cf. Col 2:19.

[107] Eph 5:21–33.

[108] Eph 1:10; 2:16.

[109] Meer, *Priesturtum*, p. 176.

[110] Scheffczyk, "Wesen", p. 53.

[111] *Signum configurativum*: STh III q 63 1 3; cf. Diekamp and Jüssen, *Dogmatik III*, pp. 28ff. Important points on the symbolic character of the *repraesentatio Christi* from the perspectives of dogmatics, history of dogma and history of liturgy can be found in Joseph Pascher, "Die Hierarchie in sakramentaler Symbolik" [Hierarchy in sacramental symbolism], in *Episcopus. Studien über das Bischofsamt. Fs Kardinal Michael von Faulhaber* [Episcopus. Studies on the office

totality only if his masculine identity is included", so things stand too regarding his priestly representative.[112]

Already at the level of philosophy of religion, we can establish that symbolic connections are much more important for the priesthood than for profane occupations;[113] in Christianity, however, we find not only symbols, but effective symbols, that is, sacraments. Similarly to the way that bread and wine were singled out by Christ as redemptive symbols, so, too, were the apostles as fully authorized office bearers.[114]

The efficacy of the sacrament, moreover, depends on the integrity of the symbol. To be sure, we find ourselves living in an age of rationalism, but if the Church were to adapt herself to this temporally conditioned deficiency in symbolic thinking, then "she would be incapable of bringing the world the very thing that it particularly needs today. At the same time, she would clog up the channels of her own life, namely, of grace, which ought to be effectively embodied in a mankind that God has created as a priori suited for that."[115]

---

of bishop. Essays in honor of Cardinal Michael von Faulhaber] (Regensburg, 1949), pp. 278–95.

[112] Scheffczyk, "Wesen", p. 53.

[113] Cf. pp. 193–94 above.

[114] On the religious philosophical significance of the "singling out" of symbols, cf. p. 128 above.

[115] Bouyer, *Woman in the Church*, p. 89.

CHAPTER FIVE

The Testimony of Saint Paul

Jesus' behavior toward women was taken up and continued by the Church. The earliest evidence of this are the letters of Saint Paul.[1]

I. THE SOCIOCULTURAL ENVIRONMENT

If one attributes the exclusion of women from apostolic office to the milieu of the times, then this argument does not apply in a uniform way to the early Church. In the Hellenistic world, from which Saint Paul came, the activity of women in social and religious life was much more extensive than in Palestine.[2]

The social position of women

In Greece and Rome, women's position regarding property rights was equal to that of men. In the middle and upper classes, the same was true in

---

[1] Those letters in the Corpus Paulinum whose Pauline authorship is regarded as contestable by many interpreters (Eph, Col, 2 Th, 1 and 2 Tim, Titus, Heb) will be drawn on here only in a supplementary way.

[2] On what follows, cf. especially: Oepke; Leipoldt, *Frau*; Ludwig Friedländer, *Darstellungen aus der Sittengeschichte Roms I* [Excerpts from the history of manners and morals in Rome, I], 10th ed. (Leipzig, 1922), pp. 267–317; Klaus Thraede, "Frau" [Woman], in RAC VIII (Stuttgart, 1972), pp. 198–269; Klaus Thraede, "Ärger mit der Freiheit. Die Bedeutung von Frauen in Theorie und Praxis der alten Kirche" [Irritation with freedom. The significance of women in the theory and practice of the early Church], in Gerta Scharffenorth and Klaus Thraede, *"Freunde in Christus werden". Die Beziehung von Mann und Frau als Frage an Theologie und Kirche* ["Become friends in Christ." The relation between men and women as a question for theology and the Church], Kennzeichen I (Gelnhausen and Berlin, 1977), pp. 31–182.

respect to occupation. There were, for instance, female goldsmiths, medical doctors (particularly in Asia Minor) and land-estate owners. We hear that in imperial Rome female "bosses" were known in some manual trades and even in shipyards.[3]

In matters of marriage and divorce, both sexes were practically independent. By contrast with Jewish law, women could also dismiss their husbands; hence, on Greek gravestones, the title μόναvδ ροσ (wife of *one* man) was regarded as a special distinction, and in Rome the women reckoned "the years not by consuls but by husbands".[4]

In traditional Greek culture, as influenced by Athens, women still lived "totally, or almost totally, as if in a harem"[5] and remained all but excluded from public affairs. A personal, exclusive love relationship between men and women was not the rule. The remarks of an Athenian from the year 342 B.C. are characteristic: "We have courtesans for purposes of pleasure . . . ; concubines for the daily care of our bodies . . . ; wives so that we can beget suitable children and have faithful custodians of our houses."[6]

Correspondingly, women were often seen, in comparison to men, as inferior beings. According to Plato, for instance, a man who fails in this life is reborn first as a woman, then as an animal.[7]

The restriction of women to the domestic sphere that was particularly widespread in ancient Greece was, however, transformed by a virtual emancipation that took hold in most of the Roman Empire. In the imperial age there were numerous philosophically and artistically educated women, who even wrote books, and a whole succession of well-known poetesses. Regarding the relationship of women to men, many philosophers advocated an emphatic equality ideal. For example, the Stoic Musonius Rufus, a contemporary of Saint Paul, called for sons and daughters to be given the same sort of education, with certain differences to apply only in the area of sports.[8]

Among the Pythagoreans we find female teachers of philosophy, and in the Epicurean school women were even given preference as teachers.[9] Exactly like their male colleagues, many of these female philosophers traveled from place to place and gave full-fledged public sermons. Paul,

[3] Thraede, "Frau", pp. 199, 204, 223; Leipoldt, *Frau*, p. 18; Friedländer, *Darstellungen*, p. 278.

[4] Oepke, pp. 778, 780.

[5] Leipoldt, *Frau*, p. 30; on this, Thraede, "Freiheit", pp. 35–40.

[6] Leipoldt, *Frau*, p. 35.

[7] Leipoldt, *Frau*, p. 57.

[8] Leipoldt, *Frau*, pp. 59f. Cf. already Plato's projected state: Thraede, "Freiheit", pp. 51f.; Joseph Vogt, *Von der Gleichwertigkeit der Geschlechter in der bürgerlichen Gesellschaft der Griechen* [On the equivalence of the sexes in middle-class Greek society], Abhandlungen der geistes- und sozialwissenschaftlichen Klasse 1960, 2 (Wiesbaden, 1960), pp. 27f.

[9] Leipoldt, *Frau*, p. 55; Thraede, "Frau", p. 203.

too, made appearances in a style similar to that of these traveling preachers.[10] If he had chosen female colleagues in office, instead of Timothy, Silas or Barnabas, then that would have been cause for no great offense among the Greeks.

Along with the increasing education of women went a refinement in the tone of social conduct between the sexes. By contrast with earlier times (and with the practices of the Jews), reciprocal address in the forms of "Sir" and " Lady" became generally customary, even among closest relatives and couples in courtship.[11] The behavior of women in public, especially in the cities, became increasingly similar to that of men. Kahrstedt writes of the Roman woman in the imperial age: "Her daily life and her presence at every type of function were distinguished in no way from those of men: visits and receptions; theater and concerts; a thousand social obligations; summer and bathing trips, even without her husband's accompaniment if need be, as far as to Egypt; conferences with the overseer of her own land-estate; discussions with her lawyer about proceedings—all exactly as done by men."[12]

In the area of sport, women took part in hunting, chariot racing, fencing and wrestling.[13] At times, even female gladiators were common,[14] and in some regions there were amazons "who, in part themselves armed, accompanied men into battle".[15]

Thus, in the environment of early Christianity, emancipation was taken even further in some respects than it is today, which means that the widespread characterization of late antiquity as "patriarchal"[16] has to be questioned.[17]

The religious position of women

In the religious sphere, too, the activity of women had a significantly greater scope than was the case in the Jewish milieu. Admittedly, women

[10] Acts 17:17–18. Stoics and Epicureans are explicitly mentioned there.

[11] Leipoldt, Frau, p. 69; Thraede, "Freiheit", p. 85.

[12] U. Kahrstedt, Kulturgeschichte der römischen Kaiserzeit [Cultural history of the Roman imperial age], 2nd ed. (Berlin, 1958), pp. 248f.; Thraede, "Frau", p. 220.

[13] Decimus Junius Juvenalis, Satiren [Satires], Langenscheidtsche Bibliothek sämtlicher griechischen und römischen Klassiker 63, 7th ed. (Berlin, 1930), 6th Satire, verses 219ff., pp. 137f.

[14] Thraede, "Frau", p. 221.

[15] Thraede, "Frau", p. 214.

[16] Thus, among others, Ruether, "Ordination", p. 30; Fiorenza, "Women Apostles", pp. 96f.

[17] This has been done recently especially in the publications by Klaus Thraede: Thraede, "Frau"; Thraede, "Freiheit".

were denied membership of certain cults (for example, those of Hercules and, especially, Mithras),[18] but their role was that much more prominent in others. Even in early times, the vestals exerted a great influence in Rome,[19] and in Greece there were priestesses of Artemis and Demeter, to whose holiest places only women were admitted.[20] Among the twenty-six priests of the most diverse Italian cults known to us by name we find six women.[21] Particularly in the Greek region, they stood in the service not only of female but also of male deities.[22] Priests of both sexes occasionally served in the same sanctuary.[23]

The participation of women in leading positions within the religious sphere was strengthened even further by the powerful rise of the mystery religions. Much more than traditional worship of the gods or drier philosophy, these cults affected "the whole person", "the senses, the understanding and the conscience".[24] "The sensations that these religions aroused, the consolations that they offered, won for them especially the sympathies of women."[25] This accentuation of feeling increased at times to the level of trancelike ecstasy, as in the cults of Cybele and Attis in Asia Minor.[26] In almost all respects women shared equal rights with men and were initiated into all the mysteries. Often, they themselves performed the ceremonies and delivered the relevant preliminary instructions, even in respect of male participants.[27] This sort of activity is documented especially, among others, for the cult of Dionysus,[28] in which all distinctions between men and women, adults and children, freemen and slaves were broken down.[29]

In the case of the Isis cult, which originated in Egypt and was one of the

---

[18] Particularly in the case of the latter, the military background must be taken into account: "Tests of courage" were involved there, and it "was predominantly active members of the military who allowed themselves to be consecrated to Mithras": Karl Prümm, *Religionsgeschichtliches Handbuch für den Raum der altchristlichen Umwelt* [Religious-historical handbook on the area forming the environment of early Christianity] (Rome, 1954), p. 291.

[19] Heiler, *Frau*, pp. 32ff.

[20] Thraede, "Frau", p. 207.

[21] S. K. Heyob, *The Cult of Isis among Women in the Graeco-Roman World* (Leiden, 1975), p. 95, n. 51.

[22] Hardy, "Priestess", pp. 56–62.

[23] Sabourin, *Priesthood*, p. 38.

[24] Franz Cumont, *Die orientalischen Religionen im römischen Heidentum* [Oriental religions in Roman paganism], 6th ed. (Darmstadt, 1972 reprint), p. 41.

[25] Cumont, *Heidentum*, pp. 41f.

[26] Cumont, *Heidentum*, p. 55.

[27] Johannes Leipoldt and Walter Grundmann, *Umwelt des Urchristentums I* [The environment of early Christianity, I], 3rd ed. (Berlin, 1971), p. 107; Thraede, "Frau", p. 207.

[28] Johannes Leipoldt, *Dionysos* [Dionysus], Archiv für ntl. Zeitgeschichte und Kulturkunde, Beiheft 3 (Leipzig, 1931), p. 25, n. 190.

[29] Leipoldt, *Dionysos*, pp. 53–55.

most popular mystery religions,[30] men and women likewise received the highest type of initiation.[31] Women were by no means in the majority,[32] but numerous priestesses were included among the highest ranks.[33] In some proclamations, Isis, the "originator of marriage contracts", is even "praised as a harbinger of equal rights for women".[34] In one famous hymn it is said of her: "You have given women the same power as men."[35]

The relevant directives by Saint Paul on the role of women in divine service are to be found in the First Letter to the Corinthians.[36] The emancipatory practices against which the apostle has to take a stand are obviously connected with his sociocultural environment. Corinth appears as the city of Aphrodite, whose priestesses can be daily observed making their way down from their temple to the city.[37] A whole range of mystery religions flourish there as well, especially those of Dionysus and Isis, which I have just described.[38]

2. THE FUNDAMENTAL ROLE OF WOMEN IN THE PAULINE COMMUNITIES

The active cooperation of women

The role of women in the Pauline communities is extremely significant. In many passages of his letters, the names of women occur[39] who render assistance to the apostles even in the spreading of the Faith.[40] His mention

---

[30] Heyob, *Isis*, p. 36. Contrary to what earlier researchers occasionally assumed, this was not a "cult of the *demimonde*"; against that view, see Heyob, *Isis*, p. 130.

[31] Heyob, *Isis*, pp. 57ff., 100.

[32] Contrary to Leipoldt, *Frau*, p. 49, which is countered by impressive literary and archaeological findings in Heyob, *Isis*, pp. 82f., 129.

[33] Heyob, *Isis*, pp. 82–91, 99. The highest posts, admittedly, were often reserved for men: Heyob, *Isis*, p. 95.

[34] Thraede, "Frau", p. 211.

[35] Oxyrhynchus-Hymn, 214–16: translated [in the German original version of this book] from Heyob, *Isis*, p. 52, where the comment is made: "This seems to be a sort of summation of all her other activities on behalf of women."

[36] 1 Cor 11:2–16; 14:33b–38.

[37] Johansson, *Women*, p. 19.

[38] Hardy, "Priestess", p. 60.

[39] In the list of greetings in Romans 16:1–23, nine times. Cf. 1 Cor 16:19; Col 4:15; Philemon 2.

[40] Acts 18:26; Phil 4:2f.

of the married couple Priscilla and Aquila makes evident the fact that the woman is always named first, which indicates the outstanding degree of respect in which she was held.[41]

In part, Paul is able to take advantage of the lively interest that pagan women showed for Jewish religion.[42] At the prayer house in Philippi, he even encounters only female visitors, and the proselyte Lydia undergoes (as the first woman in Europe!) baptism there. In the Jewish diaspora, women were given the title "synagogue superior" and the even higher distinction "mother of the synagogue", although, to be sure, no official function in divine service was connected with this.[43] In a similar way, Christian women then came to feel themselves responsible for individual domestic communities.[44]

The relation of the sexes to one another in Christ

Galatians 3:28 and 1 Corinthians 12

Nevertheless, Saint Paul's attitude toward women is no mere linear continuation of Jewish proselytism. Like no other, the apostle of the Gentiles emphasized what was new in the Christian religion as opposed to Judaism,[45] and this radical break with the old order of redemption also entails a new appreciation of the position of women.

The apostle's obvious freedom from bias against women with respect to mission and missionary assistance stands out agreeably from the otherwise generally prevalent attitude of the rabbis, with which Paul had surely become familiar in Gamaliel's strict Pharisaic academy and had also practiced.[46]

This new attitude is based on Christ's redemptive work, through which all the baptized have become equally children of God. Between men and women, too, there are thus no differences at all before God: "(26) For in

---

[41] Rom 16:3; 2 Tim 4:19; Acts 18:2, 26. The only exception is 1 Corinthians 16:19, where the church in their house is mentioned.

[42] Acts 13:50; 17:4. Cf. Leipoldt, Frau, p. 157.

[43] Leipoldt, Frau, pp. 98f.; cf. Billerbeck, Kommentar III, pp. 467f.

[44] This is hinted at in 1 Corinthians 1:11; 16:19 and Acts 12:12. It remains unclear whether, in Colossians 4:15, the accusative Νύμφαν derives from the male name Νύμφας or the female Νύμφα. Cf. Bauer, Wörterbuch, p. 1078; Friedrich Blass and Albert Debrunner, Grammatik des neutestamentlichen Griechisch I [Grammar of New Testament Greek, I], 14th ed. (Göttingen, 1976), p. 100; Joachim Gnilka, Der Kolosserbrief [The letter to the Colossians], HThK X, 1 (Freiburg, Basel and Vienna, 1980), p. 244.

[45] Cf., for example, Rom 3:21–28; Gal 2:16.

[46] Acts 22:3; 26:5; Phil 3:5f.; cf. what is said about the behavior of the rabbis on pp. 327f. above.

Christ Jesus you are all sons of God, through faith. (27) For as many of you as were baptized into Christ have put on Christ. (28) There is neither Jew nor Greek, there is neither slave nor free, there is neither male nor female; for you are all one in Christ Jesus."[47]

I have already mentioned earlier a Jewish prayer in which the Israelite praises God for not having created him as a Gentile or a woman or ignorant.[48] A similar prayer is attributed to Socrates, according to which the philosopher is glad to be alive not as an animal but as a human being, not as a woman but as a man and not as a barbarian but as a Greek.[49] As opposed to this contemporary arrogance, Galatians 3:28 appears almost polemical in nature.

The new unity in Christ is effected by the Holy Spirit, who sends his gifts to all the baptized. However, this Holy Spirit does not level out all differences in favor of a common equality. Exactly the reverse is the case.

Parallels to the statement in Galatians 3:28 (neither Jew nor Greek . . .) can be found in Colossians 3:11 and—especially clearly—in 1 Corinthians 12. There, Paul compares the baptism of the Christian to being integrated into a multimembered body whose every member possesses its own special and inexchangeable function: "(13) For by one Spirit we were all baptized into one body—Jews or Greeks, slaves or free—and all were made to drink of one Spirit. (14) For the body does not consist of one member but of many. . . . (17) If the whole body were an eye, where would be the hearing? If the whole body were an ear, where would be the sense of smell? (18) But as it is, God arranged the organs in the body, each one of them, as he chose."[50]

Now, the different gifts of grace are not distributed according to the principle of equality, but rather: "All these are inspired by one and the same Spirit, who apportions to each one individually as he wills."[51] "But each has his own special gift from God, one of one kind and one of another."[52]

Thus, the Spirit of God does not do away with differences but makes possible their fruitful development. Galatians 3:28 does not, therefore, speak simply of "being equal" but rather of "being one" (εἷς ἐστε ἐν Χριστῷ Ἰησοῦ) on the basis of a common Christian piety within the Holy Spirit.

[47] Gal 3:26–28.
[48] Cf. p. 327 above.
[49] Ludwig Hick, *Stellung des heiligen Paulus zur Frau im Rahmen seiner Zeit* [Saint Paul's position on women in the framework of his times] (Cologne, 1957), p. 20.
[50] 1 Cor 12:13f., 17f.; cf. also Rom 12:4–8.
[51] 1 Cor 12:11.
[52] 1 Cor 7:7.

In many respects, the differences between Christians go back to the period before the granting of grace, and are grounded—insofar as they are not distorted by sin and its consequences—in creation. This is the case especially regarding the differences between the sexes, as the First Letter to the Corinthians also attests to eloquently. In chapter 11, Paul writes:

(3) But I want you to understand that the head of every man is Christ, the head of a woman is her husband, and the head of Christ is God. (4) Any man who prays or prophesies with his head covered dishonors his head, (5) but any woman who prays or prophesies with her head unveiled dishonors her head—it is the same as if her head were shaven. (6) For if a woman will not veil herself, then she should cut off her hair; but if it is disgraceful for a woman to be shorn or shaven, let her wear a veil.

(7) For a man ought not to cover his head, since he is the image and glory of God; but the woman is the glory of man. (8) (For man was not made from woman, but woman from man. (9) Neither was man created for woman, but woman for man.) (10) That is why a woman ought to have a veil on her head, because of the angels.[53]

Saint Paul's aim here is to oppose emancipatory practices and to require the wearing of veils by women at the divine service. This requirement corresponds particularly to Jewish conceptions, according to which women should show themselves outside the home only with covered heads.[54] Such veiling serves as an outward expression of their subordination to men, as a sign of the power of the husband.[55]

Paul, too, demands the same sort of subordination.[56] He justifies this by referring to the biblical accounts of creation,[57] according to which only a man is directly "the image and glory of God", whereas a woman is "the glory of man", since she was formed out of man.[58]

Similar ideas can be found in rabbinical explications of Scripture.[59] In

---

[53] 1 Cor 11:3–10.

[54] Billerbeck, *Kommentar III*, p. 427; cf. Hans Conzelmann, *Der erste Brief an die Korinther* [The first letter to the Corinthians], Kritisch-exegetischer Kommentar über das NT V (Göttingen, 1969), pp. 217f.; Stefan Lösch, "Christliche Frauen in Korinth (1 Cor 11:2–16). Ein neuer Lösungsversuch" [Christian women in Corinth (1 Cor 11:2–16). A new attempt at a solution], in *ThQ* 127 (1947): 426ff. Lösch calls attention to the contrast with pagan religious practices.

[55] Billerbeck, *Kommentar III*, p. 435; cf. Lösch, "Korinth", pp. 220–22.

[56] 1 Cor 11:5, 10. This point leads into the household lists, which I will discuss in more detail shortly: Col 3:18f.; Eph 5:21–33.

[57] 1 Cor 11:7–9.

[58] On the interrelation of the concepts δόξα, εἰκών and κεφαλή, cf. Conzelmann, *Brief*, pp. 215; 219, n. 49; 220f.

[59] Billerbeck, *Kommentar III*, p. 435; cf. Jervell, *Imago Dei*, pp. 111f., 292–96; J. B.

view of modern exegesis, however, their method of treating the Bible is thoroughly contestable, so that, given the contemporary Jewish stamp of 1 Corinthians 11, we have to ask: What in all of this is still valid today?

The "prescription on veils" is quite obviously not an essentially necessary component of the *depositum fidei*. Thus, too, Paul does not justify it on the basis of a divine commandment but rather appeals to common knowledge of "nature"[60] and "propriety"[61] and to Church order. However, in many respects, good manners and Church custom are subject to the changes of time.

Nonetheless, Paul's declarations have, above and beyond their changeable aspects, a thoroughly paradigmatic meaning. The covering or uncovering of the head is only an expression of the underlying difference between the sexes. For Paul, this difference has its foundation in creation, and its effects extend all the way to the divine service. Propriety, whose form of expression is changeable but whose objective existence remains constant, ought "to render . . . intuitable the order of creation—in this case, the division into male and female".[62]

Whether the subordination of women is also an aspect of this fundamental division has no crucial relevance to the subject in hand. The decisive thing remains the fact that the activities of men and women are *different in kind*, always falling, despite varying contexts, into the pattern of authority and dependence, headship and subordination.[63] Insofar as men, by virtue of their "eccentric" predispositions, are more inclined than women to seize the initiative, they appear the leader. In my opinion, this is what lies at the core of headship or, as the case may be, subordination.[64]

For Paul, none of this implies any inferiority of women. In 1 Corinthians 11:11f. it is said: "Nevertheless, in the Lord woman is not independent of man nor man of woman; for as woman was made from man, so man is now born of woman. And all things are from God."

The general sense of these statements corresponds fully with Galatians 3:28. Therefore, the headship of men appears not as a mechanism of oppression but as a primacy of service. "Husbands, love your wives, as

---

Schaller, *Gen 1.2 im antiken Judentum* [Gen 1 and 2 in ancient Judaism], dissertation (Göttingen, 1961), which, to be sure, also points out the multiplicity and variability of the relevant "exegeses": "For no other passage from Genesis 1 and 2 have so many interpretations and explanations come down to us as for Genesis 1:26, 27" (Schaller, *Gen 1.2*, p. 135).

[60] 1 Cor 11:14.

[61] 1 Cor 11:13, 6.

[62] Gärtner, *Amt*, p. 14.

[63] Barth, *KD III*, 4, p. 189.

[64] More on this theme is contained in the following excursus.

Christ loved the Church and gave himself up for her."[65] "With this, everything called 'patriarchalism' is turned upside down."[66]

Even when woman is regarded as "the glory of man" and not, directly, as "the image and glory of God",[67] a lesser degree of being-in-the-image-of-God is not thereby asserted of her.[68] Christ, too, is described in the Pauline letters as "image" or "glory" of the Father,[69] yet that in no way diminishes his equality with God.[70] The same applies in the subordinate position of Christ to the Father.[71]

My exposition of the ways that men and women represent God is roughly set out already by Paul. At the level of *representation*, I attributed to men the greater similarity to God because of their "eccentric" predisposition, which is oriented toward mastery.[72]

Now, in the Old Testament, being similar to God is strongly related to man's mastery over nonhuman realities;[73] both sexes take part in this task, but in differing ways. If being the head is allotted to men in the marriage relationship, then so too in a special way is mastery. The head, or the countenance, appears as the bearer of a specific similarity to God.[74] *With respect to being*, however, women are on the same level as men, just as Christ is with God the Father.

Men's special representation of God[75] has to be brought together with women's (more intensive) representation[76] of blessed creation. Already in the Second Letter to the Corinthians and the Letter to the Galatians, women appear as symbolic of the Church or the community[77]—an analogy that is developed further, particularly in the Letter to the Ephesians.

The "angels" in 1 Corinthians 11:10 do not signify demonic beings in relation to which women would prove easier to corrupt than men,

[65] Eph 5:25. The Letter to the Ephesians may, perhaps, be deutero-Pauline, but it was certainly written in the spirit of the apostle: cf. 1 Cor 13; Rom 13:8–10.

[66] Gärtner, *Amt*, p. 24.

[67] 1 Cor 11:7.

[68] Contra Jervell, *Imago Dei*, p. 335.

[69] 2 Cor 4:4; Rom 8:29; Col 1:15; cf. Heb 1:3.

[70] Phil 2:6.

[71] 1 Cor 11:3; 15:28.

[72] Cf. pp. 142f., 175ff. above.

[73] Cf. p. 200 above.

[74] 2 Cor 3:18; 4:4, 6. On this, see Jervell, *Imago Dei*, pp. 299–303.

[75] Regarding representation of Christ, cf. what is said in the following excursus about Ephesians 5.

[76] Cf. pp. 189f., 304f. above.

[77] 2 Cor 11:2; Gal 4:6.

therefore being, in a certain sense, "inferior". Rather they signify, as is common in late Judaism, the guardian angels "as keepers of pious ways".[78]

Around the turn of the century, attempts were already made in liberal Protestant theology to play off against one another Paul's statements on the *equality* and the *subordination* of women.[79] That sort of procedure has its successors even today. Aloys Funk talks of a "break": "The second-rate position of women deriving from the Old Testament is . . . overlaid . . . by an . . . egalitarian order." "Paul justifies . . . the unequal ranking of men and women by means of Jewish arguments, whereas he derives the equal ranking from a specifically Christian way of seeing things."[80]

This thesis is fatally reminiscent of Marcion's approach, in which the (Old Testament) order of creation was played off against the (Christian) order of redemption.[81] The "theory of a break" fails from the start because of the fact that the orders of creation and redemption are not placed alongside one another like two building blocks but are, so to speak, interwoven with each other. The subordination of women vis-à-vis men is compared with the subordination of Christ vis-à-vis the heavenly Father and is thus brought into a christological context. In so doing, Paul links up with the accounts of creation by both the priest *and* the Yahwist in a way that is absent from the rabbis' approach.[82]

The first account of creation gives expression particularly to the equality of the sexes, while the second reflects the differentiation and the subordination of women as well.[83] Both must be seen together: just as Jesus, in his

[78] Billerbeck, *Kommentar III*, p. 438; cf. p. 372 below.

[79] Leopold Zscharnack, for instance, speaks of two opposing impulses: Galatians 3:28; 1 Corinthians 7:14; 11:11 are supposedly specifically Christian, while 1 Corinthians 11:3, 7 evaluate women negatively because they supposedly do not express "the idea of the equality and fraternity of all people": Zscharnack, *Dienst*, pp. 13–16. Gerhard Delling later repudiated the "theory of a break" and simply accused the apostle of "misogyny"; for him, supposedly, woman was "a second-class person": Gerhard Delling, *Paulus' Stellung zu Frau und Ehe* [Paul's position on women and marriage], BWANT 4, 5 (Stuttgart, 1931), pp. 97, 108. A survey, from a Catholic viewpoint, of developments in earlier Protestant exegesis that are still instructive for the present situation is given in Hick, *Isis*, pp. 91–99.

[80] Aloys Funk, "Mann und Frau in den Briefen des heiligen Paulus" [Men and women in the letters of Saint Paul], in *US* 32 (1977): 283. A further possibility would be to declare the "equality assertions" in 1 Corinthians 11 as "authentic" from a literary viewpoint, and everything else as "inauthentic", so that Paul would become the "apostle of equality"; cf. p. 369, n. 219 below.

[81] Cf. p. 391 below. In the Protestant sphere, there are currents whose adherents speak of "expunging" the order of creation; cf. pp. 76f. above.

[82] Conzelmann, *Brief*, p. 219, n. 52, sees a "Jewish midrash" as being behind this: Jervell, *Imago Dei*, p. 296, n. 410, but rightly points out that the existence of such a midrash, which would tie together Genesis 1 and Genesis 2, cannot be proven.

[83] Cf. p. 202f. above.

statement on divorce, refers to both the first and second accounts of creation,[84] so too does Paul.[85] Jesus and Paul are not opposites, but supplement each other. A hierarchical structure like that suggested by the head symbol need not be in conflict with an essential equality.

Excursus on the "hierarchical structure of marriage" in the *household lists* set out in Colossians 3 and Ephesians 5

The theme "subordination of women", which has just been under discussion here, is represented most clearly, in the New Testament, in the so-called household lists,[86] which are set out most plainly in the letters to the Colossians and the Ephesians. There, wives and husbands, children and parents, slaves and freemen are all admonished in turn. As literature, the already-cited[87] exhortation on marriage in the Letter to the Ephesians is dependent on the Letter to the Colossians, which lays down, in concise form, a fundamental principle: "Wives, be subject to your husbands, as is fitting in the Lord. Husbands, love your wives, and do not be harsh with them."[88] We meet with catalogings of ethical duties in popularizations of Stoic philosophy, too.[89] There, however, it is "almost always the male, adult, freeman who is addressed as reader and instructed in how he should behave in relation to women, children, and slaves. That women, children, and slaves might also be able to do what is ethically 'fitting' is hardly taken into account here."[90]

Hellenistic Judaism, however, especially in Philo and Josephus, reverses the emphasis of the Stoic schema: the reciprocity of duties is brought out more sharply, with the sociologically inferior group being mentioned before the more highly positioned one. In connection with the commandment about parents in the Decalogue, the subordination of the weaker party is emphasized more strongly than it was in the pagan environment.[91]

The household list (in Colossians) thus has links with "a form of ethical

---

[84] Mk 10:6–8.

[85] 1 Cor 11:7–8, 12. This reference I owe to Feuillet, "Dignité", p. 190.

[86] On this, cf. the excursus "Die Haustafeln" [The household lists] in Gnilka, *Kol*, pp. 205–16, which gives a survey of the history of research on the household lists and references to relevant specialist literature, among which especially the recent fundamental study by Crouch merits consideration: J. E. Crouch, *The Origin and Intention of the Colossian Haustafel*, FRLANT 109 (Göttingen, 1972).

[87] Cf. p. 254 above.

[88] Col 3:18f.

[89] Crouch, *Haustafel*, pp. 56ff.

[90] Eduard Schweizer, *Der Brief an die Kolosser* [The Letter to the Colossians], EKK (Zurich, 1976), pp. 159f.

[91] Crouch, *Haustafel*, p. 79; Gnilka, *Kol*, p. 213.

instruction that was current in the non-Christian sphere" and cannot "be spoken of as a genuinely Christian creation".[92] The instructions, according to many interpreters, are therefore "not Christian, but social evaluations".[93] The subordination of women is then often seen as a mere reflection of patriarchal historical circumstances, which have been superseded today by the view of marriage as a "partnership".[94] By way of comparison, references are readily made to the subordination of slaves, which no one talks of any more today either.[95]

As will be shown more precisely later, the subordination of women and the corresponding allocation of being the head to men[96] in Church Tradition appear as shorthand expressions under which all the statements on the theme "women in the priesthood" that derive from the orders of creation and redemption can be drawn together. Now, if the subordination of women were to have disappeared just as the subordination of slaves has done, despite having also been defended by appeals to the New Testament household lists, then might not the prohibition of female priests, which was already linked in the New Testament itself to the notion of subordination,[97] collapse in a similar way?[98]

First of all, the argument that the household lists were merely historically conditioned would need to have a question mark appended to it. Early Christianity did not blindly adopt behavioral models from its social environment, but in each particular case considered very precisely "which aspects of general ethics were to be taken over unchanged, given new form, or discarded altogether".[99] The first signs of an independent assessment can be seen already in the Letter to the Colossians, in which the subordination of women is expressly linked to the order of redemption ("in the Lord"), and according to which the behavior of husbands should manifest not passion for power but Christian *love*.[100]

---

[92] Gnilka, *Kol*, p. 214.

[93] Thus already Karl Weidinger, *Die Haustafeln. Ein Stück urchristlicher Paränese* [The household lists. A piece of early Christian paraenesis], UNT 14 (Leipzig, 1928), p. 51.

[94] For instance, Johannes Gründel, *Die Zukunft der christlichen Ehe. Erwartungen–Konflikte –Orientierungshilfen* [The future of Christian marriage. Expectations—conflicts—orientational aids], 2nd ed. (Munich, 1979), pp. 20, 71.

[95] Crouch, *Haustafel*, p. 156.

[96] The latter idea goes back especially to Ephesians 5:23 and 1 Corinthians 11:3.

[97] Cf. on 1 Cor 14:35 and 1 Tim 2:12: p. 396 below.

[98] There are especially substantial hints in this direction in Wijngaards, *Did Christ?* pp. 14–16, 49f.

[99] Schweizer, *Brief*, p. 155; cf. Gnilka, *Kol*, p. 210; Joachim Gnilka, *Der Epheserbrief* [The letter to the Ephesians], HThK X, 2 (Freiburg, Basel and Vienna, 1971), p. 294; Josef Ernst, *Die Briefe an die Philipper, an Philemon, an die Kolosser, an die Epheser* [The letters to the Philippians, Philemon, the Colossians and the Ephesians], RNT (Regensburg, 1974), pp. 380f.

[100] On this, see Gnilka, *Kol*, pp. 217f.

The "Christianization" of existing conditions is developed even further in the Letter to the Ephesians. In the first instance, a respect and readiness to serve on the part of all the members of the community toward one another is the overarching norm, which is characterized as a mutual subordination.[101] Nevertheless, social differentiations remain in existence under that norm. Further, the respective admonitions to husband and wife are more strongly elaborated and are brought into relation with Christ's bondedness in love to the Church. As with any analogy for a spiritual reality, so here, too, the dissimilarity is greater than the similarity. For it is not the husband but Christ who is the wife's redeemer, and the wife is subordinate to the husband not because he *is* her lord, but because he is *like* the Lord.[102] Still, the comparison remains valid: since the husband appears in the image of Christ, the requirement that he "love his wife" contains, "with its allusion to Christ's sacrificial death, an even stronger obligation for self-surrender than does the remark, so offensive to many, about the wife's 'being subject to' [the husband]".[103] Of the husband is demanded "not only a superiority of position, but also a dedication . . . that is directed toward the well-being of his wife".[104]

The most noteworthy thing, however, is that marital instruction and instruction about the Church are closely linked to one another. Marriage becomes an emblem of the relationship Christ-Church, and is assimilated to the redemptive power of that union. We encounter here "the high-point of marital instruction within the New Testament".[105]

The reciprocal relationship of husband and wife, as the most anthropologically central symbol of the Christ-Church relation, is anchored in both the order of creation and the order of redemption, as is shown especially by the quotation from the Yahwist's account of creation.[106] According to the Gospel of Mark, Jesus invoked the same biblical passage in calling for renewal of the marriage tie.[107] The Pauline theology of the Letter to the Ephesians thus accords with Jesus' demand for restoration

---

[101] Eph 5:21; cf. Gal 5:13; Phil 2:3.

[102] Eph 5:26, 22.

[103] Gerhard Friedrich, *Sexualität und Ehe. Rückfragen an das Neue Testament* [Sexuality and marriage. Questions directed back to the New Testament], KBW (Stuttgart, 1977), p. 93. Of interest, too, is the merely formal observation that only four verses are used for admonishing wives, but double that number for appealing to the responsibility of husbands.

[104] Gnilka, *Eph*, p. 277.

[105] Gnilka, *Eph*, p. 279. Here, we are already caught up in a significant historical tradition that reaches back to the prophetic Old Testament theology of the Covenant (cf. pp. 254f. above). An extensive monograph treating this is J. P. Sampley, *"And the Two Shall Become One Flesh." A Study of Traditions in Ephesians 5:21-33*, SNSMS, 16 (Cambridge, 1971); cf. also the excursus *Hieros Gamos* in Gnilka, *Eph*, pp. 290-94.

[106] Gen 2:24 in Eph 5:31.

[107] Mk 10:1; cf. Mt 19:5.

and renewal of the relation between husband and wife that was established at creation.

In this context, as in I Corinthians 11, express reference is made to the subordination of the wife, which not only is not a consequence of the Fall[108] but can be compared with subordination of the Church to the new redemptive order—which has nothing oppressive about it.

It is surely correct that the gospel did not overthrow some misguided social institutions in a revolutionary way, but—as in the case of the mammals—took over "structures that persisted as such externally and changed them from within".[109] This applies particularly to the matter of slavery,[110] but probably also has a degree of relevance to the position of women. Still, even in respect to the slavery question, it is necessary to caution against drawing overhasty conclusions. Abolishing subordination in a particular social sphere by no means leads to conditions of universal equality, for, as we know, things like the relationship employer-employee, or ruler-citizen, have continued in force even after the abolition of slavery. Even on the "new earth" of the coming eon, no abolition of every sort of subordination can be expected. The slag of sin may well be burnt out of the structures of society, and the worldly scale of values turned upside down,[111] but a general equalization of the manifoldly differentiated realities of creation cannot be expected.[112] Ontological and functional differentiation presupposes, however, headship and subordination—assuming that we do not proceed on the basis of the equalization slogans of prereflective (vulgar) Marxism.

The extent to which headship and subordination are to be retained within legitimate attempts at "anticipation of the eschaton" depends on their relative anthropological value. By and large, no one would want to maintain today that children should no longer have to obey their parents because such a relationship is similar to slavery.[113] The reason for this lies in the fact that the relationship of parents and children has deeper anthropological roots than does the relationship of slave and master, which arose, and later disappeared, as a result of external social developments.

---

[108] Not Genesis 3:15, but Genesis 2:24 is cited; cf. pp. 202–4 above.

[109] Ernst, *Kol*, p. 382.

[110] On this, see the pertinent summary in Mausbach and Ermecke, *Theologie III*, pp. 454–56. The reference to a supposed "condemnation" of slavery by Vatican II (Wijngaards, *Did Christ?*, pp. 15f., which claims support from *Gaudium et spes* 29), played off in an exaggerated way against earlier instructional Church statements, ignores the complicated subtleties of the problems involved.

[111] Mk 10:31 par.

[112] Cf. Rev 21:26.

[113] Cf., however—even after the downfall of "antiauthoritarian education"—the remarks of the neo-Marxist Bornemann, *Patriarchat*, p. 9.

Even more central, however, than the relationship of parents and children is the relation of husband and wife,[114] which, in contrast to slavery, is expressly anchored in creation, as are the headship and subordination that go with it.[115]

That the relation of men and women today has become more like a partnership is a (justified) commonplace.[116] Nevertheless, the fact remains, simply on the basis of the difference between men and women, that "the part played by women in marriage takes a different form from that played by men".[117] How this differentiation manifests itself, in a certain way, as headship of the husband and subordination of the wife—even if that terminology is not explicitly used—has been shown earlier here by drawing on philosophical anthropology, as based in biology and sociology.[118] Furthermore, it is not just in recent years that subordination of wives (like the specific responsibility of husbands) has been rejected. In Marxism and liberalism,[119] such views have been promoted for over one hundred years. The liberal branch of Protestant theology—with particular intensity, for instance, around the turn of the century—is well versed in setting up an opposition between equality and subordination.[120] Subsequently, large-scale resistance to this was mounted by dialectical theology,[121] but the Catholic Church has taken a strong stand against

---

[114] The household lists in Colossians and Ephesians are structurally divided according to anthropological intensity: (1) wife-husband, (2) children-parents (or children-fathers), (3) slave-master.

[115] The subordination of women is even terminologically distinguished from the subordination of slaves: Gnilka, *Eph*, p. 289. That marital subordination is totally different from a slave-master relationship was familiar also to pagan antiquity; cf. Gnilka, *Kol*, p. 217; Thraede, "Freiheit", p. 52.

The factors cited here are not taken into consideration in the "slave" excursus in Meer, *Priesturtum*, pp. 101–7. On this, see already Leo Scheffczyk, "Priestertum der Frau oder nicht?" [Priesthood of women or not?], in *CGG* 22 (1970): 341: "Both phenomena [the slave question mentioned by Meer and the tribute question] are not so closely connected with the central mystery of the Church and of two-sexed human existence as is the question of a priesthood of women, in which more essential and more lasting issues come together. Moreover, regarding slavery, it is evident that the Gospel takes a relatively indifferent attitude (for thoroughly legitimate reasons), which cannot at all be said regarding its attitude to female priesthood."

[116] Cf. Gründel, *Zukunft*, p. 21.

[117] Schweizer, *Brief*, p. 164.

[118] Cf. pp. 119f., 114f. above.

[119] Cf. pp. 30–33 above.

[120] For example, Zscharnack, *Dienst*, pp. 15f.

[121] Especially Karl Barth: cf. pp. 75ff. above. Elsewhere, the "orders" of classical Lutheranism are strongly stressed, as with Peter Brunner: he who contests the subordination of women—"he would be a heretic". At issue here is a central point "at which the totality of the Christian message is ultimately placed at risk": Brunner, "Hirtenamt", p. 322.

such oversimplifications from the very start. In particular, the encyclical *Casti connubii* should suggest most clearly to dogmatic and moral theologians that not only "equality in difference" but also "equality in headship and subordination" are, and will remain, a binding component of Church doctrine. That headship and subordination can assume quite varied forms in the course of varying sociocultural epochs is fully recognized in the cited encyclical.[122] It should be added here that the demands for subordination of women by Judaism and, with a new motivation, by Christianity may well have caused offense even in antiquity.[123]

Those who reject the "hierarchical structure of marriage"[124] must, if they are consistent, trim back the symbolism for the Christ-Church relationship: since headship and subordination are to be excised, the sole remaining analogue is the notion of an "indissoluble bond".[125] For the characterization of the Church's subordination vis-à-vis Christ, one would have to try to devise alternative symbols. To my knowledge, such an attempt has not yet been made. Instead, it seems not only that the marital "hierarchy" has been rejected, but also that the subordination vis-à-vis Christ has been pushed into the background. Kurt Lüthi, for instance, regards God's bond with man as "a relationship of mutual fidelity in which the partners in the bond are legitimized through their actions and not through their positions (higher-lower)".[126]

That sort of conclusion does not come about accidentally. For marriage, as the most anthropologically central relation, also possesses the strongest powers of symbolic expressiveness for the religious sphere. If there were to be full equality between husband and wife, the relation of Christ to the Church would also be affected analogically, for the Letter to the Ephesians, in particular, describes both of those relationships as "being inseparably combined. Each illuminates the other. The Church has its image in marriage."[127]

In contrast to the relationship Christ-Church, husband and wife are fully equal in worth; but if every functional difference between them that entails a relation of headship and subordination were to vanish, marriage would lose its power of symbolic expressiveness: for in God's *bond* with man, the *first* "partner" *has priority over* the other as an object of devotion.[128]

---

[122] On this and on the interpretation of Vatican II, cf. pp. 55–60 above.

[123] Cf. Gnilka, *Eph*, p. 278.

[124] Gertrude Reidick, *Die hierarchische Struktur der Ehe* [The hierarchical structure of marriage], Münchener Theologische Studien III, 3 (Munich, 1953).

[125] Freidrich, *Sexualität*, p. 91.

[126] Lüthi, *Eva*, p. 154.

[127] Gnilka, *Eph*, p. 274.

[128] Cf. Barth, *KD III*, 4, p. 182.

Conclusion

For Paul, both men and women are, through the Holy Spirit, children of God.[129] Within this fundamental equality, however, allowances are made for the differences between the sexes[130] that are grounded in creation[131] and that are also expressed within the divine service according to ecclesiastically regulated order.[132]

3. SAINT PAUL'S POSITION ON FEMALE OFFICES

The "deaconesses"

The clearest indication of female cooperation in tasks of an official nature can be found in Romans 16:1f.: "I commend to you our sister Phoebe, a deaconess of the church at Cenchreae [οὖσαν διάκονον τῆς ἐκκλησίας τῆς ἐν Κεγχρεαῖς], that you may receive her in the Lord as befits the saints, and help her in whatever she may require from you, for she has been a helper of many and of myself as well [προστάτις πολλῶν . . . καὶ ἐμοῦ αὐτοῦ]."

In the New Testament, the words διάκονος and διακονία are, to be sure, used in a very general sense,[133] but in this passage διάκονος may well amount to "something like an official title", since the service being discussed is both permanent and recognized by the community.[134]

At any event, the word προστάτις by no means signifies "female superior"[135]—in that case, Paul would subordinate his apostolic office to the service of Phoebe (προστάτις ἐμοῦ, *my* superior)—but denotes more generally the help given to many community members and to Paul.

---

[129] Gal 3:28; 1 Cor 11:11; 12:13.

[130] 1 Cor 11:2–16; 12.

[131] 1 Cor 11:7–9.

[132] 1 Cor 11:2–16. The preceding writings show many similarities with the excellent analysis of S. B. Clark, although there is no direct dependence: Clark 71–87, 166–82.

[133] Adolf Kalsbach, *Die altkirchliche Einrichtung der Diakonissen bis zu ihrem Erlöschen* [The early Church institution of deaconess up to the time of its extinction], Römische Quartalschrift, 22, Supplementheft (Freiburg im Breisgau, 1926), p. 9.

[134] Heinrich Schlier, *Der Römerbrief* [The letter to the Romans], HThK VI (Freiburg, Basel and Vienna, 1977), p. 441.

[135] As in K. H. Schelkle, *Der Geist und die Braut. Die Frau in der Bibel* [The Spirit and the Bride. Woman in the Bible] (Düsseldorf, 1977), p. 160. Lively powers of imagination are also shown by Küng, "Thesen", p. 130: "community superior, Phoebe"; and similarly, J. M. Ford, "Women Leaders in the New Testament", in Swidler, *Women Priests*, p. 132; Elisabeth Schüssler Fiorenza, "Die Rolle der Frau in der urchristlichen Bewegung" [The role of women in the early Christian movement], in *Conc* 12 (1976): 7.

Diaconal activity is, perhaps, part of what is addressed in Philippians 1:1,[136] and is probably also mentioned in 1 Timothy 3:11.[137]

The official designation "apostle" is not applied to women in the New Testament, nor are those of bishop, presbyter, evangelist or teacher.

Excursus: a female "apostle Junia"?

In the list of greetings in the Letter to the Romans, it says: "Greet Andronicus and Junias, my kinsmen and my fellow prisoners; they are [the RSV Bible adds: men] of note among the apostles, and they were in Christ before me."[138]

Andronicus and Junias are numbered among the "apostles" here. Either they had received—as apostles in the narrower sense—the mission themselves after Christ's Resurrection or—which is more likely—they were, in the broader sense, "wandering preachers of the gospel".[139] Being sent out in pairs has its model as early as in the life of Jesus prior to Easter.[140]

To begin with, the accusative Ἰουνιᾶν, from a purely lexicographic viewpoint, can derive as well from the masculine Ἰουνιανός (Junianus) as from the feminine Ἰουνία (Junia). Throughout patristic literature, the feminine "Junia" (sometimes in the variant form "Julia") seems to have been recognized,[141] perhaps because there is no record elsewhere of a masculine "Junias", whereas "Junia" and, above all, "Julia" were known.[142] The Fathers, in particular John Chrysostom, granted the title "apostle" to "Junia", although only in an extended sense, for they do not seem to have attributed any official teaching role to the "lady apostle".[143]

Bernadette Brooten attempts to take up the Church Fathers' text critical

---

[136] διάκονοι; cf. the masculine ending in Phoebe's title in Romans 16:1.

[137] On the basis of early patristic evidence, however, it is questionable whether women were "διάκονοι" in the official sense; cf. on this the "Excursus on Deaconesses": pp. 440f. below.

[138] Rom 16:7.

[139] Schlier, *Römerbrief*, p. 444.

[140] Mk 6:7; Lk 10:1.

[141] Bernadette Brooten, " 'Junia . . . hervorragend unter den Aposteln' (Röm 16, 7)" ["Junia . . . of note among the apostles" (Rom 16:7)], in Moltmann-Wendel, *Frauenbefreiung 2*, pp. 148f.

[142] Friedrich Preisigke, *Namenbuch* [Book of Names] (Heidelberg, 1922), pp. 150f. In this work (based on Egyptian documents), Ἰουνιανός and Ἰουλία crop up, while Ἰουνία is not found *here*; but cf. Brooten, "Junia", p. 151.

[143] Cf. for instance John Chrysostom, *In Epistolam ad Romanos*, hom. 31, 2: PG 60, pp. 669f. In this sense still in M.-J. Lagrange, *Saint Paul. Épître aux Romains*, Études bibliques, 6th ed. (Paris, 1950), p. 366.

work again, but now she places the "apostle Junia" on a level with the apostolate of Paul[144] and claims her for the cause of female priesthood. [145]

Even assuming that "Junias" could be interpreted as feminine, the function of a "lady apostle" need not lie in the area of public preaching. The strict "bans on teaching" in 1 Corinthians 14 and 1 Timothy 2[146] would not be easy to understand given the supposed existence of a female missionary preacher.

Modern exegesis, to be sure, usually comes down on the side of the "abbreviated hypothesis", according to which Ἰουνιᾶς derives from Ἰουνιανός. In addition to the Pauline context, this is supported by the following arguments in particular:

1. "Shortened names . . . exhibiting a great variety of suffixes [have] been widespread in Greek from time immemorial".
2. The New Testament, like Hellenism, "knows almost solely the suffix -ᾶς, and not just in cases where the full name contains the α". [147]
3. Examples of this sort of modification are exceedingly numerous. In Acts, for instance, "Silvanus"[148] becomes "Silas".[149]
4. The way that Ἰουνιᾶν is written is masculine in form. If it were feminine, "it would be written as Ἰουνίαν; cf. P 46 Ἰουλίαν and 16:15 Ἰουλίαν with the variant Ἰουνίαν".[150]

An "apostle Junia" thus seems to fall into the category of a modern myth, which, to be sure, had precedents already in antiquity. [151]

[144] Brooten, "Junia", p. 151.
[145] Of late, other commentators, too, declare in favor of a "lady apostle"; cf. "Biblical Commission Report: Can Women Be Priests?" in Swidler, Women Priests, p. 343: "Junias . . . , with regard to whom one or another raises the question whether it is a man". Küng and Lohfink, "Keine Ordination", p. 145: Junia—"a highly respected female apostle!"
[146] Comments on this are made later below.
[147] Blass and Debrunner, Grammatik, p. 100.
[148] 1 Th 1:1.
[149] Acts 15:40; 18:5. According to Bernadette Brooten, the name Junianus (per analogiam Silvanus) would have had to be lengthened (Brooten, "Junia", p. 150. Additional references are in Blass and Debrunner, Grammatik, p. 100, n. 3, 5; cf. Bauer, Wörterbuch, p. 751; Hans Lietzmann, An die Römer [To the Romans], Handbuch zum NT 8, 5th ed. (Tübingen, 1971), p. 125.
[150] Blass and Debrunner, Grammatik, p. 101, n. 6.
[151] Cf. what is said of Thecla in the "Acts of Paul": pp. 406f. below.

Fundamental community structures

In order to comprehend more exactly the position of women within Pauline community structures, it is necessary to consider the way that office was organized.[152]

Office and charism

In the new communities, the gifts effected by the Holy Spirit play a significant role, as is indicated particularly by chapters 12 to 14 of the First Letter to the Corinthians. Paul stresses that each Christian has "his own special gift from God, one of one kind and one of another".[153] The variety of services in 1 Corinthians 12 are linked to various spiritual gifts,[154] and Paul also grounds his own office in χάρις[155] or in χάρισμα.[156]

These facts, however, by no means imply a purely "charismatic" community structure in the sense that there are no permanent offices traceable to this or that special mission. Like the apostles in Jerusalem,[157] Paul knows himself to be directly charged with his office by the Risen Christ.[158] With respect to his communities he is therefore empowered to act as Christ's representative[159] and to appoint associates who assist in his work. Thus, immediately after the apostle's departure, there is evidence of "superiors" in the newly founded community of Thessalonia,[160] and in the Corinthian community also there are, among others, "apostles", "prophets" and "teachers".[161] These institutions, which were especially prominent there, must be examined more closely next.

Apostles, prophets and teachers

In the apostolate, all the basic sorts of task are obviously bound together in unity, as is shown by the example of Saint Paul and other authorized community founders.[162]

The "prophet" is not an office bearer in the proper sense but rather—

---

[152] For more exact information, cf. Bläser, "Amt", especially pp. 11–33 with the references to other relevant works.

[153] 1 Cor 7:7.

[154] 1 Cor 12:1; 11:28.

[155] 1 Cor 15:16; Rom 12:3; Gal 1:16.

[156] Rom 12:6.

[157] Gal 1:17.

[158] Gal 1:1, 15–16.

[159] Gal 1:8; 2 Cor 5:11, 20.

[160] Cf. 1 Th 5:12 with 3:1–6; cf. Phil 1:1; Acts 14:23; Titus 1:5.

[161] 1 Cor 12:28; cf. Eph 2:20; 4:11.

[162] 1 Cor 3:10–22; 9:9, 1.

similarly to the case in the Old Testament—"God's direct channel".[163] He has no continuous mission, but speaks only when inspiration comes to him.[164] Even when a prophet makes "speeches"[165] and thereby confers "upbuilding and encouragement and consolation",[166] this does not imply any institutionalized teaching office, but is effected anew in each case by the Holy Spirit.

By contrast, the "teachers", the διδάσκαλοι,[167] have an official, long-term mission of spreading the word. Their task is clearly distinguished from the activity of the prophet.[168] It consists initially in fundamental instruction in the Faith, "catechesis".[169] In pursuing it, the διδάσκαλοι take on a role similar to that of the Jewish rabbis. Above all, however, they participate in Christ's teaching office, which the evangelists repeatedly describe as "διδάσκαλος".[170]

The role of teacher in divine service

Besides their function as religious teachers, they are also active in divine service. To be sure, this field of activity is nowhere expressly described in the New Testament, but that is no cause for surprise. The apostolic letters contain nothing on liturgical rites but are writings of an occasional nature in which basic instruction in the Faith and an organized community are already presupposed. In particular, the First Letter to the Corinthians no longer needs to concern itself with the already regulated order but primarily with that area where disorder quickly creeps in, namely, with free "charism": "Precisely that side of divine service in which talents not subject to regulation may find expression is especially liable to the danger . . . of

---

[163] Johansson, *Women*, p. 85. A résumé of "prophet research" is given in Gerhard Dautzenberg, *Urchristliche Prophetie. Ihre Erforschung, ihre Voraussetzungen im Judentum und ihre Struktur im ersten Korintherbrief* [Early Christian prophecy. Its scholarly study, its preconditions in Judaism and its structure in the first letter to the Corinthians]. BWANT 104 (Stuttgart, 1975), pp. 16–27.

[164] 1 Cor 14:29–31; cf. 1 Th 5:20; Acts 11:27f.; 21:9–11.

[165] Acts 15:32.

[166] 1 Cor 14:3.

[167] 1 Cor 12:28; Rom 12:7; cf. Eph 4:11; 2 Tim 1:11; Acts 9:1. Cf. Heinrich Greeven, "Propheten, Lehrer, Vorsteher bei Paulus" [Prophets, teachers and superiors in Paul], in *ZNW* 44 (1952/53): 16–30.

[168] Rom 12:7; 1 Cor 12:28; cf. Eph 4:11. Dautzenberg, *Prophetie*, p. 22, opposes tendencies to "rationalize"—as applies above all to Protestantism—the phenomenon of early Christian prophecy, which in some respects is alien to the present age: "If the prophets have to be characterized, they are lumped together with the apostles and teachers under the category 'preachers' or 'teachers'."

[169] Gal 6:6; 1:12; cf. Phil 4:9 and Rom 16:17; James 3:1 and Heb 6:1–2.

[170] Mk 4:38; 9:17, 20; Mt 10:24; 23:10; Lk 7:40 and others. Cf. Normann, *Didaskalos*, pp. 1–66 and pp. 256ff. above.

falling . . . out of the larger framework."[171] Thus, it would make no sense to take the fact that Paul deals at such length with the free spiritual gifts of grace in 1 Corinthians 14 as implying a purely charismatic cast to community gatherings.

Instead, there are various indications that give us a quite vivid picture of the basic structure of Pauline divine service, including the role of the διδάσκαλοι within that structure.

First of all, there is Acts 20:7–12. As evidenced by the precise, concrete details, what we have here is an eyewitness account reflecting the performance of a celebration of the Eucharist:

> (7) On the first day of the week, when we were gathered together to break bread, Paul talked with them, intending to depart on the morrow; and he prolonged his speech until midnight. (8) There were many lights in the upper chamber where we were gathered. (9) And a young man named Eutychus was sitting in the window. He sank into a deep sleep as Paul talked still longer; and being overcome by sleep, he fell down from the third story and was taken up dead. (10) But Paul went down and bent over him, and embracing him said, "Do not be alarmed, for his life is in him." (11) And when Paul had gone up and had broken bread and eaten, he conversed with them a long while, until daybreak, and so departed.[172]

That Paul alone "had broken bread"[173] indicates the conducting of the Eucharist by an office bearer.[174] Even more important in the present connection, however, is the characterization of Paul's "speech". In verses 7 and 9, this is designated by the verb διαλέγεσθαι, and in verse 11 by ὁμιλεῖν.[175]

As a rule, διαλέγεσθαι conveys the notion of a conversation in the sense of "to confer, to talk about something, to discuss". Our present-day word *dialectic*, which originally meant the art of speech and argument, derives from this.

In connection with Saint Paul's sermonizing, too, διαλέγεσθαι is used in the just-noted sense. This is quite plainly the case in Acts 17:2, 17f. and 24:25f.; compare also 18:4–6; 19:8f.

Things are quite similar regarding ὁμιλεῖν. In the general sense, this word means "to speak, to address". When linked to a personal pronoun, it indicates a conversation,[176] and it occasionally goes together with verbs

---

[171] Gärtner, *Amt*, p. 18.

[172] Acts 20:7–11.

[173] Verse 11.

[174] Cf. p. 332, n. 66 above.

[175] On the following analysis of the words and their meaning, cf. Johansson, *Women*, pp. 58ff.

[176] Acts 24:26; Lk 24:14.

that have only that meaning, as, for instance, in Luke 24:15. There, συζητεῖν is used to mean a conversation or discussion; in other passages, the word expressly signifies disputation between rabbis or teachers, as in Mark 8:11; 12:28 and Acts 6:9. The verb "to speak" (λαλεῖν) also crops up in this connection.[177]

Thus, in the preaching of the word at Pauline community gatherings, there are conversational elements. This observation is confirmed in the light of contemporary parallels. As we know, Paul was educated in Jerusalem at Gamaliel's rabbinical school.[178] Rabbinical instruction did not, however, take the form of a monologuelike lecture but was carried on more as an educative conversation involving reciprocal questions and answers.[179]

The situation is similar regarding Paul's pagan colleagues, the itinerant philosopher teachers. They, too, did not deliver pure monologues, but rather their "diatribes" took the form of a dialogue. The origins of this kind of teaching extend back to the time of Socrates and Plato.[180]

Accordingly, we cannot project our present-day conception of the Sunday sermon back on the preaching of the word in the communities of Saint Paul. Before (and possibly after) the "breaking of bread" in the celebration of the Eucharist, there was a process of actualizing the gospel in which not just one person took part. Along with one element in the style of an address, there were also questions and answers. The officially appointed teachers were surely represented in a prominent position within this educative conversation.

The "ban on speaking" in 1 Corinthians 14

A stumbling block regarding the topic "women and the Church"

Probably no other text on the topic "women and the Church" has fired the passions as much as the apostle's statements in 1 Corinthians 14. In verses 34–35, women are prohibited from "speaking" in the church—a stumbling block for everyone who wishes to advance the cause of female participation in public life: "When *Christ* talks to women, there is a sound of redemption and liberation, and peace is on the way. When *Paul* speaks,

---

[177] Acts 9:29.
[178] Acts 22:3.
[179] Johansson, *Women*, pp. 66f.
[180] "Platonic dialogues"; cf. Johansson, *Women*, p. 67.

an old Mosaic wind blows for the new Christian woman." This was said as early as the twenties by the Catholic suffragette Emanuele Meyer.[181]

Nevertheless, this ban on speaking (whose contents are still to be explained), together with 1 Timothy 2:11–12, constitutes the most penetrating biblical evidence that can be brought against the ordination of women. But here we might allow Paul to speak for himself:

> As in all the churches of the saints, (34) the women should keep silence in the churches. For they are not permitted to speak, but should be subordinate, as even the law says. (35) If there is anything they desire to know, let them ask their husbands at home. For it is shameful for a woman to speak in church. (36) What! Did the word of God originate with you, or are you the only ones it has reached? (37) If anyone thinks that he is a prophet, or spiritual, he should acknowledge that what I am writing to you is a command of the Lord. (38) If anyone does not recognize this, he is not recognized (even by God).[182]

The intensification in recent times of the problems surrounding this issue

Those who are familiar with the *loci classici* of traditional dogmatics will surely have noticed the length of the preceding quotation, which continues beyond the customarily cited verses 34 and 35.[183] It is only as a result of recent exegetical research that the internal cohesiveness of the cited verses has come to light.[184] This discovery has been made possible primarily by the work of Swedish New Testament scholars who have so far had little opportunity to publish in German-speaking and English-speaking countries. Through that work, the seriousness of the problems involved in the issue of whether or not women should be admitted to the priesthood has been intensified to a hardly surpassable degree.

From this newly opened viewpoint, namely, Paul puts forward all of the arguments that he has at his disposal: the apostle enlists support from the general moral code,[185] the customs of the Church,[186] the Old Testa-

---

[181] Peter Ketter, *Christus und die Frauen I* [Christ and women, I], 4th ed. (Stuttgart, 1948), p. 204.

[182] 1 Cor 14:33b–38.

[183] Cf. Meer, *Priesturtum*, pp. 27ff. The Declaration of the Sacred Congregation also argues, with respect to 1 Corinthians 14, with only these two verses: Erklärung Nr, 4, p. 11; *AAS* 69 (1977): 106.

[184] Johansson, *Women*; Gärtner, *Amt*; Dautzenberg, *Prophetie*, pp. 253–73, 291–98; Gerhard Dautzenberg, "Tradition, paulinische Bearbeitung und Redaktion in 1 Kor 14:26–40" [Tradition, Pauline adaptation and editing in 1 Cor 14:26–40], in B. Jendorff and G. Schmalenberg (eds.), *Tradition und Gegenwart* [Tradition and the present], Theologie und Wirklichkeit 5 (Bern and Frankfurt, 1974), pp. 17–29.

[185] Verse 35.

[186] Verse 33b, 36.

ment[187] and, above all, "a command of the Lord".[188] In conclusion, he emphasizes that disobedience to this command would place one's eternal salvation in jeopardy.[189]

The interpolation hypothesis

The text-critical starting point

The ordering of verses 33b–38 that is found in editions of the Bible today does not accord with several variants of the so-called western text, in which verses 34–35 are placed after verse 40. In modern times, this uncertainty in the transmission of the text has led to the assumption—first, it seems, by J. S. Semler—that the verses in question do not belong to the original contents of the First Letter to the Corinthians. They are, supposedly, a marginal note that was added later on—to be sure, by Paul himself—and that could, therefore, have had its position changed from one manuscript copy to another.[190]

Other authors, following Semler, regarded verses 34–35 as a post-Pauline interpolation, "which was supposed to have been based on 1 Timothy 2:11–15 or to have originated in connection with that passage".[191] This suggestion enjoyed great favor, especially in Germany, at the turn of the century,[192] that is, during the heyday of the "old" women's movement, which attained its most important aim, universal suffrage, in 1919. In the course of later years, this hypothesis had largely disappeared again from Protestant exegesis,[193] but cropped up anew in the sixties in the work of Gottfried Fitzer.[194] Fitzer drew upon text-critical, literary-critical, historical and theological arguments, the most important of which may be briefly outlined here:

---

[187] Verse 34.

[188] Verse 37.

[189] Verse 38.

[190] J. S. Semler, *Paraphrasis in primam Pauli ad Corinthios Epistolam* (Halle, 1770), p. 384.

[191] Brunner, "Hirtenamt", p. 314.

[192] Cf. the authors cited by Lietzmann: Hans Lietzmann, *An die Korinther I/II* [To the Corinthians, I/II], Handbuch zum NT 9, 5th ed. (Tübingen, 1969), p. 75; particularly, Johannes Weiss, *Der erste Korintherbrief* [The first letter to the Corinthians], Kritisch-exegetischer Kommentar über das NT V, 9th ed. (Göttingen, 1910).

[193] Brunner, "Hirtenamt", p. 314.

[194] Gottfried Fitzer, *Das Weib schweige in der Gemeinde. Über den unpaulinischen Charakter der mulier-taceat-Verse in 1 Kor 14* [Women should keep silence in the churches. On the un-Pauline nature of the *mulier-taceat* verses in 1 Cor 14], Theologische Existenz heute, Neue Folge 110 (Munich, 1963).

— The sources in which 1 Corinthians 14:34–35 is placed after verse 40 "refer back to original texts from the second century",[195] so they are very old.

— In context, no break in sense is discernible if verses 34–35 are left out. Moreover, a connection to verse 36 is lacking.[196]

— The formula "as the law says" is un-Pauline.[197]

— The verses would be in contradiction with prophetic freedom. For prophecy is "sermon, proclamation of the word of God".[198]

— Verses 34–35 run contrary to 1 Corinthians 11, where Paul presupposes "active service by women in worship, in the pulpit and at the altar".[199]

— Given the charismatic nature of the community, the apostle "would be utterly disinclined to any differentiation into masculine and feminine functions".[200]

— "From the standpoint of what is new", there is no "difference between men and women in the sense of a downgrading or 'subordination' ".[201]

Literary-critical developments

This interpolation hypothesis nevertheless rests on fairly shaky foundations. For, according to more recent studies of the text of the Pauline letters, western variants that do not correspond to P46, B and 1739 are usually erroneous.[202] The number and importance of the other text documentations argue against them.

Hence, these theses have met with considerable opposition in more recent exegesis.[203] Since the appearance of the commentary on Corinthians by Hans Conzelmann, therefore, the text-critical argument has been largely discounted by those biblical scholars who postulate that the ban on

---

[195] Fitzer, *Weib*, p. 7.

[196] Fitzer, *Weib*, p. 10.

[197] Fitzer, *Weib*, p. 12.

[198] Fitzer, *Weib*, p. 12.

[199] Fitzer, *Weib*, p. 15.

[200] Fitzer, *Weib*, p. 16.

[201] Fitzer, *Weib*, p. 34.

[202] B. M. Metzger, "Recent Developments in the Textual Criticism", in *Historical and Literary Studies*, New Testament Tools and Studies VIII (Leiden, 1968), p. 155.

[203] Cf. Alfred Wikenhauser and Josef Schmid, *Einleitung in das Neue Testament* [Introduction to the New Testament], 6th ed. (Freiburg, Basel and Vienna, 1973), p. 429.

speaking is an interpolation. The line of argumentation shifts from text criticism to literary criticism: the *mulier-taceat* passage was introduced into the *Corpus Paulinum* by a later editor. "This directive reflects the bourgeois consolidation of the Church, in this case, at the level of the pastoral letters: One must hold to the general moral code."[204]

Together with the new line of argumentation, there is also an expansion in the scope of the "interpolation". Verse 33b fits in better as an introduction to verses 34–35 than as a conclusion to verses 29–33a. This peculiarity was already sensed by John Chrysostom and by Jerome, both of whom append a verb to 33b: διδάσκω, or *doceo*.[205]

If, however, verse 33b to verses 34–35 is to change position, then so too must verse 36, which expresses a similar idea and rounds off the *mulier-taceat* verses with a reference to the scope of their validity. Since verse 37 speaks of a (single) "command of the Lord", and since verse 38 follows on from this, Conzelmann claims: "this idea fits in better with the interpolation than with Paul and is suggested by it."[206]

In justification of the interpolation hypothesis, Conzelmann basically puts forward two arguments regarding verses 33b–36: "This self-contained passage . . . interrupts the theme of prophecy and disrupts the stylistic flow of the exposition." "In terms of content, it is in contradiction with 11:2ff., where active participation of women in the community is presupposed."[207]

The work of Gerhard Dautzenberg, who has published what is probably the most thorough and comprehensive study of the ban on speaking so far, remains within the framework established by Conzelmann. More clearly than Conzelmann, he arrives at the conclusion that verses 33b to 38 belong together.

What is involved here is an authoritative directive "issued under improper employment of the highest theological qualifications: of the custom in all communities, of the intention of the law, of a command of the Lord, of the apostle as its transmitter".[208]

This assertion is significant to the dogmatic theologian insofar as it refers to the "highest theological qualifications". What if the "inter-

[204] Conzelmann, *Brief*, p. 290.

[205] Cf. C. K. Barrett, *A Commentary on the First Epistle to the Corinthians*, Black's-Harper's NT Commentary (London and New York, 1968), p. 324; F. G. Gutjahr, *Die zwei Briefe an die Korinther* [The two letters to the Corinthians], Die Briefe des hl. Apostels Paulus II, 2nd ed. (Graz and Vienna, 1921), p. 357. Semler, *Paraphrasis*, p. 383, already notes this problem.

[206] Conzelmann, *Brief*, pp. 290f.

[207] Conzelmann, *Brief*, p. 289.

[208] Dautzenberg, "Tradition", p. 28.

polation" should stem from Paul after all? But even if the passage is the product of a later interpolator, the question of its theological significance remains. The interpolation would not necessarily have to represent a distortion of Paul's doctrine but could also be a materially justified supplementation by a student of Paul's.

In his day, Karl Marx found it necessary to turn his teacher Hegel upside-down, whether it be "onto his head" or "onto his feet". Perhaps a similar procedure would be applicable in the case of the interpolation hypothesis as well. For, especially with Dautzenberg, the exegesis seems to be influenced by background assumptions that pose certain problems. Dautzenberg speaks of the "laying-down of a quite specific, patriarchal order for divine service . . . , which, according to the theological qualifications deployed, can permit of no future changes in the light of new experiences".[209]

We are familiar, of course, with very accentuatedly patriarchal statements by Paul in 1 Corinthians 11, the authenticity of which is also accepted by Dautzenberg. Moreover, there is a traditionalism in the understanding of revelation not only in the pastoral letters[210] but also (among other places) in the Letter to the Galatians, whose Pauline origin is not contested by any modern expositor: whoever "should preach to you a gospel contrary to that which we preached to you, let him be accursed".[211] This pronouncement by Paul[212] is certainly not a reference to "an as yet still unconcluded . . . process of divine revelation"[213] or even to the supposition that "the real authority of the community" is not the established Jesus tradition but rather charismatic knowledge and the Spirit.[214] Furthermore, Dautzenberg's remark that the position of the interpolation was "cleverly chosen" by the "interpolator" is rather perplexing.[215]

Thus there is every reason to elucidate the *mulier-taceat* verses, which are a classical biblical source for dogmatics, in somewhat more detail. I hope to be able to show that the interpolation hypothesis has a certain basis in history, even if not in the sense entertained by the originators of this theory.

First, however, I want to put verses 33b–38 into the larger context of

---

[209] Dautzenberg, "Tradition", p. 28.
[210] For instance, 1 Tim 6:20; 2 Tim 1:12–14; 4:3.
[211] Gal 1:8.
[212] Dautzenberg, *Prophetie*, p. 299.
[213] Dautzenberg, "Tradition", p. 28.
[214] For more on this, see p. 386 below.
[215] Dautzenberg, *Prophetie*, p. 271.

the Pauline writings and especially of the First Letter to the Corinthians. After the completion of that procedure alone, the most important objections against the authenticity of the passage may well already have been cleared up.[216]

1 Corinthians 14:33b–38
in context of 1 Corinthians 11–14

The section from 1 Corinthians 11:2 to 14:40 forms a more-or-less self-contained unity. It takes a stand against abuses that have found their way into the community at Corinth and that pertain especially to the way that the performance of divine service is ordered.[217] At the beginning and at the end of the section, the same theme is found, namely, the position of women in divine service.

In 1 Corinthians 11:3–16,[218] Paul deals with the fundamental relation of the sexes to each other and combines his reflections with the practical directive that women are to cover their heads when praying or prophesying. The apostle justifies this requirement through a short interpretation of the biblical accounts of creation, as well as through propriety and what is the custom in the other communities. These statements, which almost no commentator regards as post-Pauline,[219] occur in a contemporary environment that—as is especially clear in Corinth—does not agree with them and even has, in part, a virtually emancipatory coloring.[220]

Paul himself may unwillingly have lent support to the tendencies that were already present in Corinth through statements such as those in Galatians 3:28 ("neither male nor female").[221] It is striking, therefore, that in 1 Corinthians 12:13, a passage whose text parallels Galatians 3:28

---

[216] To the extent that this has not already been accomplished by what was said on "office and charism" and on 1 Corinthians 11.

[217] Only 1 Corinthians 13, the "spiritual song of love", forms something of a digression, but is nevertheless closely linked to the remarks on spiritual gifts.

[218] Cf. pp. 347–51 above.

[219] A recent exception is an essay by W. O. Walker, "1 Corinthians 11:2–16 and Paul's Views Regarding Women", in *JBL* 94 (1975): 94–110. The author sets out to show that talk of "subordination of women" did not arise until after Paul: Paul knows "no male superiority and female subordination in any form" (Walker, "Paul's Views", p. 109). However, Walker's exegetical argumentation does not seem, in general, to have been especially well received even by those of his professional colleagues who are in agreement with him "dogmatically". See, for instance, the essay in the same journal by Jerome Murphy-O'Connor, "The Non-Pauline Character of 1 Corinthians 11:2–16?" in *JBL* 95 (1976): 615–21.

[220] Cf. p. 345 above.

[221] Galatians and 1 Corinthians are very close in terms of their time of composition: Wikenhauser and Schmid, *Einleitung*, pp. 417–19, 432.

almost down to the very wording, the pair of concepts "male-female" is missing.[222] Perhaps Paul did not want to feed any further misunderstandings.

1 Corinthians 14:33b–38 speaks to the same situation. It is there that the theme "women in the community" reaches its high point, with Paul invoking the highest theological qualifications, which he does not draw on for the "prescription on veils".

That Paul did not present the expositions in 1 Corinthians 11 and 14 as an unbroken whole is not at all unusual for him. The theme of the "spiritual gifts"[223] also is interrupted by chapter 13, as are the expositions on food offered to idols.[224]

The pronouncements on divine service occur in the broader framework of a reply by Paul to questions raised in a letter from the Corinthian community. This reply takes up the entire second main part of the letter, which extends from 7:1 to 16:18.[225] The question-and-answer structure is evident particularly in chapter 7, where thoroughly different problems are dealt with from a unified point of view (marriage and celibacy). In the course of this, the transition from one question to another can be quite abrupt without our having to assume (more than) half a dozen interpolations. Thus, precisely in the context of the First Letter to the Corinthians, the (still to be investigated) isolation in content of the ban on speaking[226] is not a pertinent argument for an interpolation, especially as the verses fit in with the leading topic in view, "divine service".

Paul treats the relevant problems in a certain stylistic form, characterized by H. W. Bartsch as "community regulation",[227] which I regard as particularly well developed in chapters 7, 8:2–3, 11:16 and, not least, in 1 Corinthians 14:26–40, the immediate context of our verses. Paul starts off with a fundamental directive regarding the question or problem, and for almost all the individual regulations he deals with eventual objections. Then, there is a conditional clause followed by (what is at least conceptually) an imperative. This counterstroke reads as follows in 1 Corinthians 14:37: "If anyone thinks that he is a prophet [εἴ τις δοκεῖ προφήτης εἶναι], . . . he should acknowledge that. . . ."

Very similar formulations are already met with earlier on: "If anyone

---

[222] Just as in Colossians 3:11; shortly after this mention is made of the subordination of women.

[223] 1 Cor 12, 14.

[224] 1 Cor 8, 10:18ff.

[225] Cf. Wikenhauser and Schmid, *Einleitung*, p. 424.

[226] Dautzenberg, *Prophetie*, p. 255.

[227] H. W. Bartsch, *Die Anfänge urchristlicher Rechtsbildungen. Studien zu den Pastoralbriefen* [The beginnings of early Christian legal structures. Studies on the pastoral letters], Theologische Forschung 34 (Hamburg, 1965), p. 69.

thinks [εἰ δέ τις ἀσχημονεῖν]. . . , let him do. . . ."[228] "If anyone imagines that he knows something [εἴ τις δοκεῖ ἐγνωκέναι τι], he does not yet know. . . ."[229]

Especially clearly in: "If anyone is disposed to be contentious [εἰ δέ τις δοκεῖ φιλόνεικος εἶναι]. . . ."

Among the words cited from 1 Corinthians 8:2, the key word "gnosis", which plays a significant role in the First Letter to the Corinthians, also crops up.[230] With it, Paul obviously takes up the theme of the self-estimation of the "Gnostics", to which, especially in 1 Corinthians 13, he opposes the principle of *love*.[231]

The theme of knowledge is also taken up in 1 Corinthians 14:37–38 and brought into confrontation with the "command of the Lord", for it is only in obedience to Christ that the authenticity of love shows itself: the prophet should "acknowledge" (ἐπιγινωσκέτω) the command. "If anyone does not recognize this, he is not recognized (even by God)" (εἰ δέ τις ἀγνοεῖ, ἀγνοεῖται).

That the *mulier-taceat* verses are neither stylistically nor conceptually isolated is shown especially by a look at their immediate context. As "community regulation", verses 27–38 form a coherent whole, which is framed by its own introduction (verse 26) and by the conclusion of chapter 14 (verses 39–40).[232] The themes "speaking in tongues", "prophets" and "women" are treated in turn.[233] All three regulations center on the same pair of concepts: *"to speak"* (λαλεῖν (five times) and *"to keep silent"* (σιγάτω, σιγάτωσαν) (three times). Speaking is prohibited or regulated.

In verses 33b–38, the concept ἐκκλησία occurs in two different senses: "(local) community" (verse 33b) and "community assembly" (verses 34, 36). The second sense is already found in the formulation (λαλεῖν) ἐν ἐκκλησίᾳ (verse 36) some verses earlier on: (σιγάτω) ἐν ἐκκλησίᾳ (verse 28).[234]

In the sense of "local community", we read in 1 Corinthians 4:17 and 7:17 almost the same formulation that occurs in verse 33b: Ὡς ἐν πάσαις ταῖς ἐκκλησίαις τῶν ἁγίων.[235] καθὼς πανταχοῦ ἐν πάσῃ ἐκκλησίᾳ δισάσκω.[236] οὕτως ἐν ταῖς ἐκκλησίαις πάσαις διατάσσομαι.[237]

---

[228] 1 Cor 7:36; cf. 7:2, 9, 11, 15, 28, 39–40; 14:27, 30.

[229] 1 Cor 8:2.

[230] Especially 1 Cor 8:1–3, 7, 10; cf. the study by Walter Schmithals, *Die Gnosis in Korinth* [Gnosticism in Corinth], FRLANT 66, 3rd ed. (Göttingen, 1969).

[231] 1 Cor 13:2, 8–9, 12; cf. 8:3.

[232] Cf. Dautzenberg, *Prophetie*, p. 253.

[233] Vv. 27–28, 29–33a, 33b–38.

[234] Cf. v. 19: ἐν ἐκκλησίᾳ θέλω . . . λαλῆσαι; similarly, vv. 23, 4, 5.

[235] Verse 33b.   [237] 1 Cor 7:17.

[236] 1 Cor 4:17.

The mention of subordination of women (ὑποτασσέσθωσαν) is prepared for, in the surrounding context, by the subordination of the "spirits of prophets" to the prophets;[238] an exact material correspondence is found in chapter 11:3: the husband is "head" of the wife.

The whole of chapter 14 is concerned with "order" in the general sense: "edification",[239] "order",[240] "decently",[241] "one by one";[242] "For God is not a God of confusion but of peace."[243]

The appeal to the "law" (νόμος) in verse 34 finds a parallel not only in 1 Corinthians 9:9[244] but also in the context of divine service itself.[245] In all three passages, of course, the citing of the νόμος is not the primary but a subordinate justification, and that is especially the case here: "as *even* the law says".

The content of the "ban on speaking" and its relation to 1 Corinthians 11

Thus, the *mulier-taceat* verses not only are not isolated from their immediate and broader contexts in the First Letter to the Corinthians but are virtually intermeshed with them. The hypothetically assumed interpolator must, therefore, have proceeded with quite unbelievable cunning.

Nevertheless, the most important problem still remains unclarified: In 1 Corinthians 14:34–35, Paul prohibits women from "speaking in church", while, in 1 Corinthians 11:4–5, 13, he seems to presuppose their "praying" and "prophesying".

In order to resolve the tension here, there are—besides the interpolation hypothesis—basically three possible solutions.

First possible solution: "The directives in 11:2–16 refer to the behavior of women who pray or prophesy at home or in smaller, more intimate prayer groups, while the ban on speaking in 14:33b–36 applies for the community congregation."[246]

It is, however, to the divine service, as *Sitz im Leben*, that the "prescription on veils" clearly refers. From 1 Corinthians 11:17 onward, this situation is obviously presupposed in the comments on the " Lord's

---

[238] Verse 32: ὑποτάσσεται.

[239] οἰκοδομή: verse 3, 5, 12 and esp. 26.

[240] τάξις: verse 40.

[241] Verse 40.

[242] Verse 31.

[243] Verse 33a.

[244] Cf. p. 381 below.

[245] Verse 21. Against Dautzenberg, *Prophetie*, p. 273, n. 6: "The straightforward appeal to the nomos is quite exceptional and inconceivable for Paul."

[246] Dautzenberg, *Prophetie*, p. 266.

Supper", which are already prepared for immediately prior to chapter 11.[247] The mention of the "angels" in 11:10 also refers to the communal divine service. Judaism, especially in the Qumran writings,[248] had already recognized the presence of the "messengers of God" in the worship ceremony, and early Christian liturgy views heavenly and earthly glorification in one and the same perspective.[249]

More plausible, therefore, appears the *second possible solution*: "In 11:2–16, too, a public communal assembly is presupposed. In this passage—assumedly—Paul wants to criticize the wrong practice of women's participating with their heads uncovered. He only mentions prophesying by women, without sanctioning it. Not until 14:33b–36 does he take up this problem as such, and there he prohibits speaking by women."[250]

Tensions similar to that between 11:5 and 14:34 crop up in other places precisely in the First Letter to the Corinthians. The directives about the food offered to idols, which are also split up between two different parts of the letter, in 8:10 appear to sanction, at least in principle, eating food that has been offered to the gods. In 10:21, however, this apparent concession is rescinded: "You cannot partake of the table of the Lord and the table of demons."

In 6:1ff., Paul presupposes lawsuits occurring between Christians, for which he at first demands Christian arbitrators; only afterward does he characterize legal proceedings as wrong in principle.[251]

In 15:29, the apostle mentions the custom of being baptized on behalf of the dead. This is, however, only an *argumentum ad hominem* here, for whether he sanctions the relevant custom remains more than questionable.

It is therefore often assumed that Paul, in 1 Corinthians 14:34, also forbids prophesying. After all, the entire chapter deals with this theme, which is, moreover, expressly mentioned immediately before.[252] "Therefore, too, there is . . . talk only of a λαλεῖν, and not of a προφητεύειν or διδάσκειν or ἑρμηνεύειν. λαλεῖν is not equivalent to any of those expressions. Rather, it includes in itself all varieties of charismatic speech. What is meant is in no case a different kind of speaking from that in verse 26. The specific nuance of the word, in this passage, lies in its being opposed to silence."[253]

Early Church Tradition does not appear to contradict this thesis.

---

[247] 1 Cor 10:14–22.
[248] Cf. Dautzenberg, *Prophetie*, p. 267, n. 47. Against Conzelmann, *Brief*, p. 223.
[249] This liturgical orientation can be seen particularly in the relevation to John.
[250] Dautzenberg, *Prophetie*, p. 266.
[251] 1 Cor 6:7.
[252] Vv. 29–33a.
[253] Blum, "Amt", p. 150.

Origen, in opposition to the Montanists, very emphatically espouses the view that women may prophesy only outside of the community assembly.[254] By contrast, Irenaeus mentions "men and women who prophesy in the church".[255] Here, *ecclesia* can, of course, also mean "church" in the general sense, for the opponents of the Church Father advocate the thesis that the prophetic spirit should be repudiated altogether.[256] The debate is not centered on a contrast between female prophecy inside the community assembly and such prophecy outside it.

Tertullian accuses Marcion of having no authentic prophetesses around him[257] and stresses that the command to keep silent in 1 Corinthians 14 in no way prohibits women from prophesying.[258] If only we had direct access to those statements, we could make Tertullian the antipode to Origen and perhaps trace this back to the Montanist influences that left their mark on the African theologian.[259]

In his Montanist(!) period, however, Tertullian mentions a woman who regularly receives revelations while in the community assembly. This description is strongly reminiscent of 1 Corinthians 14:6, 26, 30, where there is also talk of ἀποκάλυψις. Tertullian adds to his remarks that the female seer does not communicate her revelations during the divine service but only afterward.[260] Thus, for him, this rule is not at odds with prophetic freedom, which, however, 1 Corinthians 14 curtails. There the gift of prophecy is not exercised "ecstatically" but under regulation; immediately prior to the *mulier-taceat* verses, this is said: "And the spirits of prophets are subject to prophets. For God is not a God of confusion but of peace."[261]

Directly after the "command to keep silent", verse 37 turns to countering the resistance of presumed prophets who oppose such regulation.

This second proffered solution appears thoroughly acceptable. Still, the context of 1 Corinthians 14 points toward yet another possibility. Dautzenberg rightly notes the significance of verse 35: "If verse 35a forbids speech of a questioning sort at divine service, verse 34 would seem to forbid speech of an instructive sort."[262]

---

[254] Cf. pp. 408ff. below.

[255] Irenaeus, *Adversus haereses*, III, 11, 9: BKV 3, 245; PG 7, p. 891.

[256] Irenaeus, *Adversus haereses*, p. 244; PG 7, pp. 890f.

[257] Tertullian, *Adversus Marcionem*, V, 8, 12: CCL 1, p. 688.

[258] Tertullian, *Adversus Marcionem*, V, 8, 11: CCL 1, p. 688.

[259] Altaner and Stuiber, *Patrologie*, p. 154: *Adversus Marcionem* already belongs to Tertullian's Montanist period.

[260] Tertullian, *De anima*, 9, 4: CCL 2, pp. 792f.

[261] 1 Cor 14:32–33a.

[262] Dautzenberg, *Prophetie*, p. 258.

That the question plays a large role in instructive conversation in the early Christian communities has been already noted.[263] The ban on speaking would, accordingly, be a direct ban on teaching.

The *third possible solution* is, therefore: *In 1 Corinthians 11 a different sort of speaking is meant than in 1 Corinthians 14.*

If we interpret this different sort of speaking as "instructing", then, according to Dautzenberg, a contradiction arises between that and the context, which deals with prophecy. Consequently, it is supposedly necessary to dismiss our passage as an interpolation. It stems from another type of divine service, in which the main role is no longer played by prophecy, but rather by the "instructive lecture and, perhaps, the instructive conversation. This probably means that it belongs to the synagogic type. It is not concerned with charismatic experiences and charismatic speaking."[264] In the communities at the time of Paul, it was not instruction but prophecy that occupied "the position . . . held by the law in the divine service of the synagogue".[265]

This thesis does not, however, appear so clear-cut in the context of the First Letter to the Corinthians. In the fourteenth chapter, Paul deals primarily with the misuse of uncontrolled speaking in tongues, to which he opposes prophecy as the preferred form of charismatic speaking. Thus, prophecy obviously did not play the main role in Corinth before then.

On the other hand, it also cannot be assumed that, prior to Paul's intervention, the divine service had consisted solely of ecstatic speaking in tongues. In verse 26 other structures of divine service are suggested: revelation is aligned with prophecy, and both speaking in tongues and interpretation with glossolalia, while the hymn and the lesson, as forms of speaking, do not appear in the two community regulations that follow. Psalm singing is mentioned earlier on,[266] while the διδαχή in verse 26 represents the "sole element that cannot be accounted for in terms of the context".[267]

To be sure, instructing and learning also seem to be connected with prophecy in chapter 14.[268] But prophesying is not an institution that is constantly ready for action; rather, it is dependent on activity of the Spirit that is not at our disposal.[269] Prophetic instruction, in the proper sense,

---

[263] Cf. pp. 363 above.
[264] Dautzenberg, *Prophetie*, p. 261.
[265] Dautzenberg, *Prophetie*, p. 299.
[266] 1 Cor 14:15.
[267] Dautzenberg, *Prophetie*, p. 254.
[268] 1 Cor 14:3, 31.
[269] 1 Cor 14:40.

has thus probably never existed. In διδαχή, the deciding role is to be attributed instead to the "teachers" (διδάσκαλοι); this group had assumed a special position in Corinth.[270]

Thus it would be conceivable, based on verse 26, that the first community regulation refers to glossolalia, the second to prophecy and the third directly to the Didache.

Nevertheless, this solution is still a bit too smooth, since it does not explain why verses 33bff. immediately follow the regulation on prophets. They seem not only to be added on but even to take up the preceding and to develop it further. The prophetic element in divine service does not consist only of monologuelike delivery of revelations; rather, the prophet is "tested", and this can even give rise to discussion: " Let two or three prophets speak, and let the others weigh what is said." "For you can all prophesy . . . , so that all may learn and be encouraged."[271]

This "testing" would have been common in the Pauline communities[272] and is documented in the early Christian sphere, particularly by the Didache.[273]

The aim of the discussion, as distinct from prophecy, is described in verse 31, in part, as "learning" (μανθάνωσιν). The same verb root crops up again in verse 35: "If there is anything they desire to know [μαθεῖν θέλουσιν], let them ask their husbands at home."

The ban on speaking, accordingly, does not apply to prophecy as effected by the Spirit but rather to participation in the discussion of such prophecy. This suggestion was already made in an essay by Reinhold Seeberg, which has been largely overlooked by recent authors:

> I therefore think that Paul, in the passage in question here, forbids women to participate, within the community, in critical discussion of the sayings of the prophets, in the debate that springs up around these. Accordingly, it then makes good sense when, as a substitute for this, he refers to their discussing the questions at home. Seen in this light, however, the passage also instructs us about what was mainly involved in that "weighing" of prophetic speech. It was questions aimed at achieving deeper understanding, or further elucidation and justification, of what was heard.[274]

This position would seem to offer the best resolution of the tensions between 1 Corinthians 11:5 and 14:34. To be sure, Seeberg's insight needs

---

[270] 1 Cor 12:28.

[271] 1 Cor 14:29, 31.

[272] Cf. 1 Th 5:20f.; see also Mt 7:15–23.

[273] Didache 11:9–12, in J.-P. Audet, La Didache. Institution des Apôtres. Études bibliques (Paris, 1958), p. 237.

[274] Reinhold Seeberg, "Über das Reden der Frauen in den apostolischen Gemeinden" [On speaking by women in the apostolic communities], in Aus Religion und Geschichte I [From religion and history, I] (Leipzig, 1906), p. 131.

to be supplemented by noting that the debate ultimately refers back to the service of teachers. The διδάσκαλοι must have already assumed a special role in instructive conversations conducted through question and answer, and this would naturally have been carried over into any instructive discussions of the sayings of prophets. On the part of the community members, participation in this debate is no prophetic task but is similar to the διδαχή, whose counterconcept here is formed by μαθεῖν ("allow to be instructed"). The ban on speaking thus ultimately means a ban on teaching. Through questions,[275] women could easily be drawn into the instructive conversation and may occasionally have felt inclined to act as teachers themselves. This may have been the case especially in Corinth, where the Spirit—or what was taken as that[276]—disregarded existing distinctions and traditions.[277] The self-appointed "pneumatics" are now confronted by Paul, in verse 37, with the "command of the Lord".

Quite probably, this command was familiar to the Corinthians, for Paul does not need to take a direct stand against teaching by women, but only the indirect one forbidding their questioning. Through this questioning, however, Corinthian women began to take possession of the service of teacher.

Hence, 1 Corinthians 14:34 aims at *teaching* by women, while 1 Corinthians 11:5 presupposes their praying and prophesying (γυνὴ προσευχομένη ἤ προφητεύουσα).

In 1 Corinthians 14:27–38, all three kinds of speaking seem to crop up again. The first two present themselves as directly effected by the Spirit and are permitted for women; the third, official instructing, is forbidden for them. Glossolalia and prophecy are distinguished in 1 Corinthians 14 by the fact that the speaker in a tongue speaks to *God*, whereas the prophet speaks to *men*.[278] Speaking to God, however, is the same as praying; thus it says in verse 14: "If I pray in a tongue, my spirit prays." The speaking in tongues documented in 1 Corinthians 14 is thus at least a component of the praying mentioned in 1 Corinthians 11;[279] the identity of "prophecy" in both chapters is self-evident.

Thus Dautzenberg's central argument, which ascribes 1 Corinthians 14:33b–38 to another type of community than that of Pauline Corinth, appears unsound. The significance of instruction and of discussions occurring after prophetic utterance has obviously been underestimated.

[275] 1 Cor 14:35a.
[276] 1 Cor 14:37a.
[277] Cf. 1 Cor 11:2–34.
[278] 1 Cor 14:2f.
[279] In 14:15, a distinction is drawn between a praying τω πνεύματι (= speaking in tongues) and a praying with the mind—τω νοΐ—which expresses itself (verse 16) in "thanksgiving" and the "Amen".

Furthermore, if the interpolation is ascribed to a community model of synagogic Jewish stamp, and the context to one of a more charismatic sort,[280] several internal contradictions result:

—The "charismatic" appearance of the prophets is not typically Corinthian, but has a "Judaeo-Christian character",[281] just as does the instructive conversation.[282] So not only the hypothetical interpolator,[283] but also Paul himself, behaves in a "Judaeo-Christian" way.

—On the one hand, mirrored in the "interpolation", according to Conzelmann, is the "bourgeois consolidation of the Church", which binds itself to a pregiven order and "the general moral code".[284] Dautzenberg himself characterizes this consolidation as "prescription of a . . . patriarchal order of divine service" in order to set it in opposition to a "tradition of freedom in divine service".[285] On the other hand, verses 39–40, which are accepted as authentic by Conzelmann, give "a concluding formulation of the leading point of view" (in 1 Corinthians 14), which has "here expressed [itself], in correspondence with the context, in practical-bourgeois terms": "decency", "order".[286] Dautzenberg refers descriptively to the "framing of the community regulations in 14:26c and 40 through the two principles that determine, in a similar but never so consciously expressed way, the Jewish way of thinking about divine service".[287]

—1 Corinthians 14:33b–38 amounts to an "interpolation stemming from the time when the Pauline letters were collated"[288] and prohibits "instructive speaking".[289] Conzelmann holds that this time corresponds "roughly . . . to the stage of the pastoral letters".[290] But why does the interpolation forbid questioning only, and not instructing? A ban on teaching, allied to 1 Timothy 2:12, would have been much more clearly formulizable. Precisely the *differences* in orientation and linguistic form between the two bans on speaking—in 1 Corinthians 14 and 1 Timothy 2—testify against any intervention by an interpolator.

---

[280] This sort of division is suggested especially in Dautzenberg, *Prophetie*, pp. 261–63, 299f.; Dautzenberg, "Tradition", p. 27.

[281] Dautzenberg, *Prophetie*, p. 299.

[282] Dautzenberg, *Prophetie*, p. 261.

[283] Dautzenberg, *Prophetie*, p. 273.

[284] Conzelmann, *Brief*, p. 290; the emphasis here and in what follows is my own.

[285] Dautzenberg, "Tradition", pp. 27f. Cf. also Barrett, *Commentary*, p. 332: "good order was thought more important than the freedom of the Spirit".

[286] Dautzenberg, *Prophetie*, p. 291.

[287] Dautzenberg, *Prophetie*, p. 291.

[288] Dautzenberg, *Prophetie*, p. 271.

[289] Dautzenberg, *Prophetie*, p. 258.

[290] Conzelmann, *Brief*, p. 290; cf. Dautzenberg, *Prophetie*, p. 272. Most clearly, in modern times, in Fitzer, *Weib*, p. 37: 1 Tim 2 is "the place . . . from which the *mulier-taceat* words were formulated and interpolated into the Pauline text".

Moreover, it should not be hastily assumed that there is an interpolation in the *Corpus Paulinum*. All the cited instances are contested.[291] The First Letter to the Corinthians—if we ignore for the moment the offensive *mulier-taceat* passage—is, as a rule, *not* subjected to literary-critical exercises.[292]

These comments are not intended to detract from the scholarly value of Gerhard Dautzenberg's thorough exegetical study. Nevertheless, in the present connection, might it not perhaps be that preconception has become so productive that what should not be cannot be?

In older works of Protestant origin, the view is sometimes taken that Paul means only to oppose solely any "disturbance of the divine service through *nonspiritual* speaking and questioning".[293] For edification of the community, however, speech by everyone is supposedly allowed.

If by "speaking" Paul meant nothing but disturbances, he could certainly have expressed himself more clearly.[294] Furthermore, in the New Testament, the Greek word λαλεῖν never means "to chatter, to interrupt" or anything similar but quite often refers to official preaching of the gospel if it occurs in certain turns of expression, for example, λαλεῖν τὰ ῥήματα, λαλεῖν τὸν λόγον. Also, λαλεῖν ἐν ἐκκλησίᾳ may well belong in this context, especially since it occurs twice in close succession,[295] virtually as a *terminus technicus*.[296]

Furthermore, Paul would not regale us with the weightiest theological arguments if what he wanted was only to protect the peace of the divine service from the talkativeness of women.[297]

Some authors regard 1 Corinthians 14:34–35 as an interpolation because these verses supposedly contradict other passages in which Paul mentions the cooperation of women in missionary work, such as Philippians 4:2f. and Romans 16:12.[298] It is even reported of Priscilla that, together with her husband, she instructed the cultured Jew Apollos in the Faith and brought about his conversion.[299]

However, there is nothing contradictory in this. In 1 Corinthians 14 it is not instruction by women as such that is forbidden but rather official and

---

[291] Cf. the relevant discussions in Wikenhauser and Schmid, *Einleitung*, on the "authenticity" and "uniformity" of the individual letters.

[292] Cf. Wikenhauser and Schmid, *Einleitung*, pp. 429ff.

[293] This is still found in H.-D. Wendland, *Die Briefe an die Korinther* [The letters to the Corinthians], NTD 7, 2nd ed. (Göttingen, 1954), p. 117.

[294] For example, ταράσσειν.

[295] 1 Cor 14:34a, 35b.

[296] Johansson, *Women*, pp. 52ff.

[297] Cf. p. 385 below.

[298] Thraede, "Frau", p. 232; Schelkle, *Geist*, p. 162.

[299] Acts 18:26.

public instructive activity such as occurs especially in the liturgy, in the "community assembly".[300]

In the *mulier-taceat* verses themselves, a distinction between domestic discussion and instructive conversation at divine service is already intimated: "let them ask their husbands at home" (ἐν οἴκῳ ... ἐπερωτάτωσαν) "to speak in church" (λαλεῖν ἐν ἐκκλησίᾳ).[301]

An additional weighty argument for the assumption that Paul ultimately means teaching when he refers to speaking in the church are the statements in 1 Timothy 2, a close parallel to the First Letter to the Corinthians. Verses 9–10 resemble 1 Corinthians 11:2–12, and verses 11–15 are strongly reminiscent of 1 Corinthians 14:33b–38. In verses 11–12, it says: "Let a woman learn in silence with all submissiveness. I permit no woman to teach or to have authority over men; she is to keep silent."

In the given context, teaching means official instruction, especially during the divine service. It is therefore highly probable that λαλεῖν ἐν ἐκκλησίᾳ tends to have the same sense. Whether or not the First Letter to Timothy was written by Paul himself is of little importance here. The author is, in any case, closely connected with the intellectual world and the communities of Saint Paul. Consequently, 1 Timothy 2 forms an authentic interpretation of 1 Corinthians 14 by the New Testament itself.[302]

In 1 Timothy 2:12 the ban on teaching appears as a directive of the apostle, while in 1 Corinthians 14:37 it appears, above and beyond that, as a "command of the Lord". But it cannot be excluded here that 1 Timothy, too, alludes to a command of Jesus. This tacit assumption is also found in other statements by the apostle.[303]

Conclusion: the ban on speaking in 1 Corinthians 14 is a ban on teaching that is directed against the participation of women in official teaching activities during the divine service.

The manner of argumentation

The justification of the ban on speaking in 1 Corinthians 14:33b–38 corresponds to the apostle's manner of argumentation elsewhere. A clear example of the ordering of the arguments occurs in 1 Corinthians 9:1–14. Paul demonstrates that he is entitled to financial support from the community and that he has quite freely renounced his right to such support.

---

[300] The verb κοπιᾶν, which is pointed to by Thraede, "Frau", p. 232, and Schelkle, *Geist*, p. 162, is not restricted to "missionary preaching" but means any sort of "labor in the Lord"; it applies also to whole communities and not only to their office bearers: 1 Th 1:3; 1 Cor 15:58; cf. Greeven, "Propheten", pp. 32–34.

[301] 1 Cor 14:35. The difference between "private" and "public" teaching shows itself more clearly in the pastoral letters; cf. p. 403 below.

[302] On the significance of 1 Tim 2, cf. pp. 397ff. below.

[303] For example, Gal 5:14; Rom 13:9; 1 Th 5:2, 6, 15.

This important parallel is clearly stressed by the Swedish commentator Johansson, whereas Dautzenberg overlooks it. He also deals with verses 33b–36 and 37–38 in separate places, and it is only through analysis of verse 37 ("command of the Lord") that he comes to the conclusion that verses 37–38 are connected with the ban on speaking.[304] In my opinion, however, the typically Pauline ordering of the argumentational steps in 1 Corinthians 9:1–14 constitutes the most important basis for demonstrating that the authenticity and especially the *interconnectedness* of verses 33b–38 are matters of certainty.

Paul justifies his right in the following way:

1. The *practice of the Church* (verses 5–6).
2. The *general moral code* (verses 7–8a, 12a).
3. The *argument from Scripture*: the law (verses 8b–11, 13; cf. Deuteronomy 25:4; the same citation in 1 Timothy 5:18).

Thus, explicit reference to Old Testament law (νόμος; "For it is written in the law of Moses") is not at all unfamiliar to the apostle (cf. also 1 Corinthians 14:21).

4. A *command of the Lord* (verse 14; "In the same way, the Lord commanded that . . .").

This reference to the Jesus tradition forms the high point of the chain of argument. In the present case, we know of a parallel tradition in the synoptic Gospels, namely, in Matthew,[305] in Luke[306] and, indirectly suggested, in Mark.[307]

First Corinthians 14:33b–38 argues in exactly the same manner:

1. The *practice of the Church* (verses 33b, 36).

A similar reference to Church custom appears in 1 Corinthians 11:16. Compare 1 Corinthians 7:17.

2. The *argument from Scripture*: "As even the law [ὁ νόμος] says" (verse 34).

"The demand for women to be subordinate . . . does not literally occur among the provisions of Sinaitic law."[308] Thus, either what is meant is the whole tenor of the law, including its traditional elaboration, or Paul is alluding to Genesis 3:16.[309]

[304] Cf. Dautzenberg, *Prophetie*, pp. 291–97.
[305] Mt 10:10.
[306] Lk 10:7.
[307] Mk 6:8–9.
[308] Peter Bläser, *Das Gesetz bei Paulus* [The law in Paul's writings], Ntl. Abhandlungen XIX, 1–2 (Münster, 1941), p. 36.
[309] Cf. Blaser, *Gesetz*, p. 36; see also pp. 202f. above.

Other Old Testament provisions, which are, to be sure, all brought into a New Testament context, can be found in Romans 12:19f.; 1 Corinthians 9:9 (= 1 Timothy 5:18); 2 Corinthians 6:16–18; 10:17; Ephesians 4:25f.; 6:2f.[310]

Of course, Paul, the onetime rabbinical student, intersperses allusions to Old Testament texts even much more frequently. In 1 Corinthians 11:7–9 there is a clear reference to Genesis 1–2, which, like 1 Corinthians 14:34, throws into relief the subordination of women (cf. 1 Corinthians 11:3, 5, 10).[311]

The demand for subordination is closely interwoven with the interpretation of the accounts of creation as we find it in 1 Corinthians 11. If I have begun this book with considerations about the theology of creation, that procedure has a prominent predecessor in Saint Paul.

3. The *general moral code*: "It is shameful for a woman to speak in church" (verse 35). 1 Corinthians 11:6, 13–15 also refer to "shamefulness".

4. "*A command of the Lord*" (κυρίου ἐστὶν ἐντολή) (verse 37).[312]

Apart from the reversal of points 2 and 3, the only difference from the argumentation in 1 Corinthians 9 consists in the fact that the command of Jesus mentioned there is known from the synoptic tradition, whereas that is not true for 1 Corinthians 14:37.

The thesis has often been advocated that Paul is referring, with the phrase "command of the Lord", to his own authority or to the custom of the communities. Karl Maly thinks, for instance: "By authority of his apostolic office, all that he prescribes is a command that comes from the Lord."[313]

However, Paul distinguishes very precisely between his own directives, Church custom and the Old Testament, on the one hand, and the commands of Jesus on the other. This separation manifests itself especially clearly in 1 Corinthians 7. There he cites support from a command of Christ only for the prohibition of divorce, while keeping his own authoritative directives separate from that in the clearest of ways: "To the married I give charge, not I but the Lord. . . . To the rest I say, not the Lord. . . . Now concerning the unmarried, I have no command of the Lord [ἐπιταγὴν κυρίου οὐκ ἔχω], but I give my opinion. . . . And I think that I have the Spirit of God."[314]

---

[310] Bläser, *Gesetz*, p. 229.

[311] Cf. pp. 347ff. above.

[312] The word ἐντολή is missing in a part of the variants of the western text, which reverse vv. 34–35. Cf. the comments on the interpolation hypothesis (pp. 366f. above) and the discussion by Dautzenberg, *Prophetie*, p. 292.

[313] Karl Maly, *Mündige Gemeinde. Untersuchungen zur pastoralen Führung des Apostels Paulus im 1. Korintherbrief* [The community comes of age. Inquiries into the pastoral leadership of the apostle Paul in the first letter to the Corinthians], Stuttgarter biblische Monographien 2, KBW (Stuttgart, 1967), p. 226. Similarly, Werner de Boor, *Der erste Brief des Paulus an die Korinther* [The first letter of Paul to the Corinthians], Wuppertaler Studienbibel (Wuppertal, 1968), p. 249: Paul's directives correspond to the "mind of Christ" (1 Cor 2:16). Conzelmann, *Brief*, p. 290: "One adheres to the general moral code."

[314] 1 Cor 7:10, 12, 25, 40.

In the matter of food offered to idols, Paul argues by citing reasons implied by the principles of "knowledge" (γνῶσις) and "love".[315] In doing so, he certainly also speaks, as an apostle, "in the name of the Lord Jesus", as, for instance, in the judgment on transgression in 1 Corinthians 5:4. Nevertheless, Paul does not cite support from a directive of Jesus.

Thus the apostle cannot, by virtue of authority of office or appeals to the Holy Spirit, just invent a "command of the Lord". In 1 Corinthians 11:2–16 what is at issue is a thoroughly important matter, but Paul does not cite support from a command of Jesus. He refers only to the Old Testament and social custom and is obviously aware that those arguments will not be found convincing by everyone. Therefore, he finally breaks the discussion off with a reference to Church prescription. He does not mention any punishment for those who disobey.

Things are quite different in 1 Corinthians 14:38. There it says: "If any one does not recognize this, he is not recognized (even by God)."

This "recognition" refers to the Last Judgment, in which man's eternal salvation or eternal damnation is decided: "Not every one who says to me, ' Lord, Lord', shall enter the Kingdom of heaven, but he who does the will of my Father. . . . On that day many will say to me, ' Lord, Lord, did we not prophesy in your name. . . ?' And then I will declare to them, 'I never knew you; depart from me, you evildoers.' "[316]

According to Dautzenberg, 1 Corinthians 14:38 does not refer to divine judgment but amounts instead to a "canonical threat": the interpolator (or even Paul) threatens the pneumatics "with withdrawal or restriction of their influence on the community".[317] This notion supposedly stems from a later period "in which the communities and individual Christians began to secure and protect themselves against false doctrines by reciprocal 'recognition' and 'nonrecognition' ".[318] In any case, verses 37–38, like the rest of the First Letter to the Corinthians, contain an "authoritarian image of Paul", and furthermore: "The rudeness of the two verses is hardly compatible with the conciliatory closing, 14:39–40."[319]

References to judgment are not something rare for Paul, but rather, as it were, an "unbroken thread" in his letters. Deliverance "from the wrath to come" is a basic concern of the gospel.[320] This theme manifests itself with special clarity precisely in the First Letter to the Corinthians: anyone who "eats and drinks without discerning the body eats and drinks judgment

[315] 1 Cor 8–10; cf. Rom 14.
[316] Mt 7:21–23; emphases mine. Cf. Mt 25:12, 30, 41; 2 Cor 5:10. On the positive effects of "knowledge" through God, cf. 1 Cor 13:12.
[317] Dautzenberg, *Prophetie*, pp. 255f.
[318] Dautzenberg, *Prophetie*, p. 298.
[319] Dautzenberg, "Tradition", p. 25.
[320] 1 Th 1:10; 5:3.

upon himself".[321] "If any one has no love for the Lord, let him be accursed."[322]

When Paul uses judgment as a threat, it is never a case of merely canonical questions but always one of contexts central to the gospel, as in Galatians 1:9: "As we have said before, so now I say again, If any one is preaching to you a gospel contrary to that which you received, let him be accursed."

In 1 Corinthians 15:2—that is, shortly after the ban on speaking—Paul makes salvation under judgment dependent on obedience to the word of God as "I preached [it] to you . . . —unless you believed in vain."

This "word" refers to "traditions" not invented by Paul himself but received by him as already formed.[323] It is not the word of men but the word of God;[324] only for that reason can it bring men before judgment.[325]

This sort of reference to the Jesus-tradition occurs in the *mulier-taceat* passage itself: "What! Did the word of God [ὁ λόγος τοῦ θεοῦ] originate with you, or are you the only ones it has reached?"[326]

The "command of the Lord" obviously stems from received tradition. Only for that reason is the threat of judgment appropriate. This state of affairs is formulated, in words similar to those in 1 Corinthians 14, in Galatians 5:10: he who "is troubling you will bear his judgment, whoever he is".

The Letter to the Galatians is also a showcase example of how "candy and the stick" follow closely on each other in the often impulsive statements of Saint Paul. On the one hand the apostle threatens with anathema[327] and cries out, "O foolish Galatians! Who has bewitched you. . . ?"[328] On the other hand, in the same letter, there is found one of the gentlest comments on the relation of the pastor to his community: "My little children, with whom I am again in travail until Christ be formed in you!"[329]

At the end of the First Letter to the Corinthians, it says: "Greet one another with a holy kiss." And in just the second sentence after that: "If any one . . . , let him be accursed."[330]

Just two verses after the conciliatory closing of chapter 14, there is talk of judgment; why not already one verse before?

[321] 1 Cor 11:29; cf. verses 31–32, 34.
[322] 1 Cor 16:22; additional references: 1 Cor 1:8; 3:12–15; 4:4f.; 5:5, 13; 6:2, 9f.; 9:22, 24–27; 10:11–12, 33.
[323] 1 Cor 15:3; cf. 11:2, 23.
[324] 1 Th 2:13.
[325] 1 Th 2:16.
[326] 1 Cor 14:36.
[327] Gal 1:8f.
[328] Gal 3:1.
[329] Gal 4:19.
[330] 1 Cor 16:20, 22.

This shocking threat has, of course, been cause for offense from earliest times, with the result that some manuscripts have transformed the harsh ἀγνοεῖται into the harmless ἀγνοείτω: "If any one does not recognize this, then he does not want to recognize", that is, "then he should just leave the matter there".

Johannes Weiss already characterized this kind of reading as "a vulgar enfeeblement".[331]

With Paul, the judgment sanction is never applied to comparatively harmless problems such as that of preventing disturbances during divine service, with which the other directives in 1 Corinthians 14 are concerned. After all, it would hardly fit the picture if, for example, Paul were to threaten with eternal punishment in hell for violation of the following directives: "If any speak in a tongue, let there be only two or at most three, and each in turn. . . . If a revelation is made to another sitting by, let the first be silent."[332]

Hence, 1 Corinthians 14:38 is defending not merely disciplinary norms of the just-named kind but rather an especially important matter: a "command of the Lord".

The "command of the Lord" and the Jesus-tradition

As a rule, the concept ἐντολή refers, in the New Testament, not to a body of regulations but to a single commandment. ἐντολή is the most frequent designation for the individual norms of Old Testament law.[333] The foundations for this linguistic usage were already laid in the Septuagint, through which the concept developed into a technical term of "solemn religious character".[334] The verb belonging to it stands, "in by far the greatest number of cases", "for divine commanding and directing: Genesis 2:16".[335]

"Regarding the concept ἐντολή as used by Paul, we find . . . that this, for him, is the concrete Mosaic νόμος, yet, at the same time, the characteristic attribute of the law as such: its commanding nature."[336]

In this connection, the New Testament also designates Jesus' pre-scriptions as ἐντολάς.[337] A material parallel to ἐντολή that is used by Paul occurs in 1 Corinthians 7:25.[338] The comprehensively general concept law of Christ also occurs in his writings.[339]

---

[331] J. Weiss, *Korintherbrief*, p. 343.

[332] 1 Cor 14:27, 30.

[333] Cf., among others, Mt 5:19; Mk 10:19 par; 12:28, 31 par; Rom 13:9.

[334] Schrenk, "ἐντέλλομαι, ἐντολή": *ThW II* (Stuttgart, 1935), pp. 542f.

[335] Schrenk, "ἐντέλλομαι, ἐντολή", p. 541.

[336] Schrenk, "ἐντέλλομαι, ἐντολή", p. 548; cf. Rom 7:8ff.

[337] Jn 13:34; 14:15, 21; 15:10, 12; cf. Mt 28:20.

[338] "Command of the Lord" (ἐπιταγήν κυρίου); cf. p. 382 above.

[339] Gal 6:2; cf. Rom 8:2.

With respect to Christ, the concepts command and law attain a new level.[340] This does not mean, however, that their interpretation is left to arbitrary determination by the community members. Jesus gave life not only to hazy basic principles such as love but also to thoroughly concrete individual directives.[341] These cannot be played off against the Spirit, as 1 Corinthians 14:37 shows: "If any one thinks that he is a prophet, or spiritual, he should acknowledge that what I am writing to you is a command of the Lord."

After all this, we can say with certainty: the word ἐντολή refers to the individual rule that immediately precedes it, the ban on speaking. This is also indicated by the linkage to the statement in verse 38 (threat of judgment) and by the described position as high point in a chain of argumentation.

The directives of Jesus constitute the weightiest component of the traditions, the παραδόσεις. It is to these traditions that Paul, at the beginning of the section on divine service,[342] expressly refers.[343] Among them belongs, in particular, the Eucharist: "For I received from the Lord what I also delivered to you" (παρέδωκα).[344] An additional important piece of tradition is found in 1 Corinthians 15:3–8.

Only in a few passages, which stand out in particular because of this, does Paul cite support directly from the words of Jesus.[345] Allusions to the Jesus-tradition are, of course, much more frequent.[346]

"Word" and "command", too, as used by Paul, are probably to be understood as coincident concepts: The command is the demanding character of the gospel. This idea never occurs explicitly in Paul but may be presumed self-evident in view of the evangelical tradition, especially in Matthew and John, and of wider, early Church Tradition. In the Gospel according to Matthew, Christ appears, so to speak, as a new Moses; "his

---

[340] According to the classical interpretation: "lex Spiritus, lex amoris, lex libertatis, lex gratiae, lex aeterna"; cf. on this Mausbach and Ermecke, *Theologie I*, p. 124.

[341] For example, Mk 10:11f.; 22:19; 1 Cor 11:24. Regarding Pauline theology, one might consult: Wolfgang Schrage, *Die konkreten Einzelgebote in der paulinischen Paränese. Ein Beitrag zur neutestamentlichen Ethik* [The concrete individual commands in the Pauline *paraenesis*. A contribution to New Testament ethics] (Gütersloh, 1961), esp. pp. 9ff., 249, 270f.; the quintessence of this work is that love concretizes itself fully in obligatory individual commands.

[342] 1 Cor 11:2–14, 40.

[343] 1 Cor 11:2.

[344] 1 Cor 11:23ff.

[345] 1 Cor 7:10–12; 9:14; 11:23–25; 14:37; 1 Th 4:15.

[346] Alfred Resch numbers them at 1206, which, to be sure, is probably exaggerated: Alfred Resch, *Der Paulinismus und die Logia Jesu in ihrem gegenseitigen Verhältnis untersucht* [Paulinism and the *logia* of Jesus examined in their mutual relationship], TU 12 (Leipzig, 1904); on this, see W. D. Davies, *Paul and Rabbinic Judaism, Some Rabbinic Elements in Pauline Theology* (London, 1955), p. 137.

'teaching' is simultaneously a 'command', the following of which vouch-safes the authentic fulfillment of the old law".[347] The "pneumatic" Gospel according to John takes as parallel διδαχή, ἐντολαί, λόγοι and ῥήματα; obeying the commands is identical with preserving the words.[348]

In the *Corpus Paulinum*, Christ is seen as the originator of a body of religious knowledge that must be passed on in exact detail and that is to be preserved through those who serve as teachers.[349] Even by the Church Father Clement of Alexandria, the Church is seen virtually as a school or lecture hall whose traditions go all the way back to the apostles, and whose mode of transmission is reminiscent of rabbinical mnemonic techniques: "Those teachers, however, who preserved intact the true tradition, as it stems directly from the holy apostles Peter and James, John and Paul, by ensuring that a son always received it from his father, came, by the help of God, to us as well, in order . . . to sow [in us] those apostolic seeds."[350]

Oral gospel tradition also contained quite specific directives for its preachers, as the example of 1 Corinthians 9:14 shows. Paul does not quote there but passes on only the content of the relevant directive; the same probably applies for 1 Corinthians 7:10–12. The "traditions" were already known in Corinth and were also largely followed.[351] Accordingly, in 1 Corinthians 14:37, a mere reminder of the "command of the Lord" was sufficient to recall the relevant instruction by Jesus to the minds of the Corinthians.

Some authors advocate the hypothesis that Paul had received the "command of the Lord" in a dream or vision.[352] There are, however, three arguments against this:

1. In the First Letter to the Corinthians, Paul refers to established Tradition that he himself has received.[353]
2. Verse 36 presupposes the validity of the command for the Church as a whole, including those communities that were not founded by Paul.
3. This command is not a new regulation, but something already in effect. This is indicated in verse 34 especially by the expression "they are not permitted" (οὐ . . . ἐπιτρέπεται).[354]

---

[347] Normann, *Didaskalos*, p. 39; cf. especially Mt 5:17–20 and 28:18–20.

[348] Jn 8:31, 51; 14:21, 23; 17:6 and others; cf. Normann, *Didaskalos*, pp. 62f.

[349] Cf. p. 360 above.

[350] Clemens Alexandrinus, *Stromata*, I, 11, 3, in Normann, *Didaskalos*, pp. 175f., also gives additional documentation: GCS 15, p. 9.

[351] 1 Cor 11:2.

[352] Cf. the particulars given by Dautzenberg, *Prophetie*, p. 294.

[353] 1 Cor 11:2, 23; 15:3.

[354] Cf. Conzelmann, *Brief*, p. 290, n. 53, and J. Weiss, *Korintherbrief*, p. 342. Schrage, *Einzelgebote*, p. 242, points out "that Paul, despite being conscious of admonishing as an

Thus, everything suggests that the command came from the mouth of Jesus himself. "Precisely according to 1 Corinthians 7, a dissolution of the boundaries between a somehow justified apostolic determination and an *entolē kyriou* is hardly imaginable."[355] However, Dautzenberg rejects the historical explanation without any real argument: That Paul "could have been acquainted with" a command of Jesus "on the regulation of matters concerning divine service is extremely improbable".[356]

Paul's knowledge of the sayings of Jesus goes beyond the material in the synoptic Gospels, as is shown by 1 Thessalonians 4:15.[357] The New Testament, after all, is not a handbook on dogmatics or a complete, protocol-like compilation of things said by the Lord. Many surviving texts are rather incidental in nature, as, for example, that on baptism in Romans 6 or the description of the Lord's Supper in 1 Corinthians 11, which we owe only to the relevant Corinthian abuses.

In the early Church, too, there were special regulations on office by no means all of which must have been written down. In the first letter of Clement, it says:

> Our apostles, too, knew from our Lord, Jesus Christ, that contention would surround the office of bishop. For this reason, then, having received precise instructions in advance, they instituted the arrangements cited above, and, in so doing, directed that, after their deaths, other tried and tested men should take over their service.[358]

The directives on office are to be seen in context of the entire apostolic mission:

> The apostles received the Joyous Tidings for us from the Lord, Jesus Christ; Jesus, the Christ, was sent by God. Christ thus comes from God, and the apostles come from Christ; both these things happened as they did, in beautiful order, according to God's will. Thus they received commissions, were instilled with certainty through the Resurrection of our Lord, Jesus

---

apostle with the commission and authority of the Lord, did not appeal to inspirations and revelations from on high—the only word from on high that has come down to us in 2 Corinthians 12:9 is, characteristically, not a moral directive but a particularized word of consolation—in order then to present them as words of the Lord, but that he also identifies words of the Lord as such".

[355] Dautzenberg, *Prophetie*, p. 296.

[356] Dautzenberg, "Tradition", p. 26; cf. Dautzenberg, *Prophetie*, p. 296.

[357] Which does not, of course, mean that the apostle was acquainted with the full extent of the synoptic tradition. In his statements on celibacy in 1 Corinthians 7, for instance, he does not cite support from Matthew 19:12.

[358] 1 Clem 44:1–2: Fischer, *Väter*, p. 81.

Christ, and were made fast in faith through the word of God. . . . Thus they went about preaching in city and country, and appointed their immediate successors, after prior testing in spirit, to office as bishops and deacons for future generations of believers.[359]

The author of this letter, Pope Clement, thus claims here "that the appointment of ecclesiastical superiors by the apostles, as well as the regulations by the apostles on future succession of community leadership, were also based on certain provisions made by Jesus".[360]

According to the testimony of Irenaeus, Clement is the third successor to Saint Peter. He had "also seen the blessed apostles and associated with them . . . and still [had] the apostles' preaching in his ears and their tradition before his eyes—and not he alone; for at that time there were still many alive who had undergone instruction by the apostles".[361]

This postapostolic reference is confirmed by the statements in the New Testament. According to the reports of all four of the Gospels, the apostles had still received directives from Jesus even after Easter (up until the Ascension).[362] Included in these were all matters necessary to the founding of the Church, especially those pertaining to baptism[363] and office.[364]

It is quite readily conceivable that Christ may have explained to the Twelve, in concise terms, why it was precisely they whom he summoned to the apostolate and not one of his female followers. That a specific directive for the future went along with this may be taken as certain in view of 1 Corinthians 14:37.

In Corinth Paul was exposed to severe attacks on his person and office.[365] If he had claimed support from a nonexistent command of Jesus, then sooner or later he would have been convicted of untruth.[366]

The factuality of this command also comes to expression in unbroken Church Tradition, which repeatedly cites the ban on teaching by women and, despite all opposition, saw the will of the Lord behind the ban on the ordination of women.[367] Thus Origen,[368] during the controversy with

---

[359] 1 Clem 42:1–4: Fischer, *Väter*, pp. 77, 79.

[360] Fischer, *Väter*, p. 81, n. 254.

[361] Irenaeus, *Adversus haereses*, III, 3, 3: Fischer, *Väter*, p. 17; PG, 7, pp. 849f.

[362] Mt 28:16–20; Mk 16:9–20; Lk 24:44–49; cf. Acts 1:2f.; Jn 20:22f.; 21:15–23.

[363] Mt 28:20; Acts 1:5.

[364] Jn 20:22f.; 21:15–23.

[365] 1 Cor 1:12; 4:3; 2 Cor 10–12.

[366] To be sure, Paul had founded the community in Corinth, but its members later used other sources to supplement their information about the Faith. In 1 Corinthians 1:12, Apollos and Petrus are mentioned in particular.

[367] See below.

[368] About 185–253/4: Altaner and Stuiber, *Patrologie*, p. 197.

the Montanists, also spoke expressly of a "command" (ἐντολή) with respect to 1 Corinthians 14.[369]

4. THE INFLUENCE OF MARCION: THE KERNEL OF TRUTH IN THE INTERPOLATION HYPOTHESIS

Down through time, the opponents of the ordination of women have always placed primary emphasis upon two facts: the example of Christ and the enduring Tradition of the Church.

Something new, however—if we ignore Origen and the relatively little documented earliest period of the Church—is the appeal to an explicit command of Jesus Christ that is found in early Church Tradition and documented by Paul. It was Swedish commentators who recently reminded us of the existence of this command, and also—if unintentionally—the German New Testament scholar Dautzenberg.

Are we not, perhaps, reading too much into the text here? After all, it is remarkable that awareness of an expressly mentioned "command of the Lord" should, so to speak, lie slumbering in obscurity for almost eighteen hundred years.

Still, there is a credible explanation for this. The advocates of the ordination of women, who would like to remove Saint Paul's relevant statements from the New Testament because they are a later, "Judaic" or "proto-Catholic" interpolation, unwittingly provide us with a starting point.

They often refer to variants of the western text in which verses 34–35 of 1 Corinthians 14 are placed after verse 40.[370] Given this transposition, the directive on women's keeping silent no longer appears as a command of the Lord but is justified only through Old Testament law and propriety.

Perhaps, as well, the cited verses were initially left out but were put back in again later, although in the wrong place.

This sort of textual intervention leads us to suspect that 1 Corinthians 14:34f. must already have caused offense very early on. Now, in the early Church there was a man who exerted a great influence on the textual history of the New Testament. Among the things we know about him is

---

[369] The relevant, otherwise little-known fragment by Origen was published in the *Journal of Theological Studies* 10 (1909), 41f.; cf. p. 410 below.

[370] D, F, G, a, b, vg^ms, Ambst, in Eberhard Nestle and Kurt Aland, *Novum Testamentum Graece*, 26th ed. (Stuttgart, 1979), p. 466.

the fact that he was on a war footing precisely with Paul's prescriptions on the position of women. The man in question is Marcion, a popularly effective heretic from the second century.

The cited variants of the western text refer back to documents from this period.[371] The Marcion edition of the New Testament proved especially influential, leaving traces that have endured to the present. There are "roughly one hundred passages with respect to which the Marcion text—as against the other main editions—accords with the western text".[372] Many textual peculiarities are certainly to be understood as tendentious Marcionist revisions.[373]

These changes have their basis in Marcion's teachings. According to him, there is an unbridgeable gap between the law and the gospel. He repudiates the Old Testament with its wrathful and righteous Creator-God, and recognizes only the order of redemption, in which, through Christ, the previously unknown God of mercifulness and love presents himself to us.

Allusions to creation and to Old Testament law are therefore suspect to Marcion. Among the four Gospels, he gives preference to that of Luke, although in an expurgated version, and the Pauline text, too, is "thoroughly cleansed of 'interpolations' ": "According to Marcion, it is impossible that Paul could have taught the sorts of thing that are stated in his extant writings; instead, those writings have been corrupted by numerous Judaic insertions and deletions. Ten of his letters, all still preserved except for the pastoral writings, were recognized by Marcion as belonging to the apostle, although they had to undergo a thorough clean-up before they could pass as such."[374]

Through Tertullian, we learn that Marcion was particularly offended precisely by the apostle's statements on women. In the writing called *Adversus Marcionem*, Tertullian brings the accusation against his opponent that the women in Marcion's community were failing to observe the discipline enjoined by Paul. What was meant here is that women should wear veils and keep silent at community congregations. Marcion had claimed that the Holy Spirit bestows his various gifts on each one, without taking notice of preexisting differences.[375]

---

[371] Fitzer, *Weib*, p. 7.

[372] Adolf von Harnack, *Marcion: Das Evangelium vom fremden Gott. Eine Monographie zur Grundlegung der katholischen Kirche* [Marcion: The gospel of the alien God. A monograph on the foundation of the Catholic Church] (Leipzig, 1921), p. 128.

[373] Harnack, *Marcion*, p. 129.

[374] H. J. Vogels, *Handbuch der neutestamentlichen Textkritik* [Handbook of New Testament text criticism], 2nd ed. (Bonn, 1955), p. 140.

[375] On Marcion, cf. also pp. 404f. below.

In opposition to this, Tertullian appeals explicitly to 1 Corinthians 12, according to which the one Body of Christ consists of different members with differing gifts. The Redeemer cannot, he says, be played off against the Creator. Furthermore, unequivocal prescriptions on the position of women in the Church are found in Paul's writings.[376]

On the basis of the evidence of Tertullian, it is more than probable that the passage 1 Corinthians 14:33bff. struck Marcion as suspect, and that he found himself forced to make a minor intervention.

Just prior to that, the "Jewish" expression θεὸς had already been eliminated, and in verse 34 Marcion transformed "they . . . should be subordinate" into "they . . . are subordinate".[377] Codices D and G, like the Old Latin translations, place verses 34–35 after verse 40; this transposition probably has its basis in the activities of Marcion. In particular, the Codex Cantabrigiensis (D), as "center point of the Vetus Latina",[378] is "virtually infected by Tatian".[379] Tatian and the Old Syrian translation are, in turn, clearly dependent upon Marcion.

The Syrian, Tatian, probably bequeathed to his countrymen, along with the Diatessaron—that well-known harmonization of the Gospels— the Marcion edition of the Pauline letters. In the so-called *Apostolos*, the Letter to the Galatians was placed "at the head, because everything else needs to be seen in the light of what is recounted there".[380] The same thing applies in the case of the most ancient canon of the Syrian church, which forms an important component of the western text.[381] It is noteworthy that Marcion singled out precisely the Gospel according to Luke, which mentions particularly many women, and that the Letter to the Galatians is taken, so to speak, as the "hermeneutic principle" for an understanding of Paul. As we know, it is there that the (frequently misunderstood) statement occurs: "There is . . . neither male nor female; for you are all one in Christ Jesus."[382]

Marcion's indirect effect on those Catholic circles that place particular

[376] CCL 1, pp. 685–88.

[377] Cf. the apparatus for the Nestle text (Nestle and Aland, *Testamentum*) and Harnack, *Marcion*, pp. 90f.

[378] H. J. Vogels, *Textkritik*, p. 149.

[379] A view already taken by von Soden in H. J. Vogels, *Textkritik*, p. 147.

[380] H. J. Vogels, "Der Einfluss Marcions und Tatians auf Text und Kanon des Neuen Testamentes" [The influence of Marcion and Tatian on the text and canon of the New Testament], in *Synoptische Studien. Festschrift: Alfred Wikenhauser* [Synoptic studies. Essays in honor of Alfred Wikenhauser] (Munich, 1953), p. 284.

[381] H. J. Vogels, *Textkritik*, pp. 284f.

[382] Gal 3:28. Galatians 3:27–4:1, however, was omitted by Marcion, probably because of its reference to Old Testament promises: Ernest Evans, *Tertullian. Adversus Marcionem*, 2nd vol., Oxford Early Christian Texts (Oxford, 1972), p. 645.

emphasis on their orthodoxy is plainly odd. "We possess, in numerous Latin biblical manuscripts, prologues to the Pauline letters that . . . are undoubtedly of Marcionist origin."[383] In particular, the so-called Ambrosiaster, who places 1 Corinthians 14:34–35 after verse 40, repeatedly argued against Marcion and his adherents without having the slightest notion of "how much his understanding of Paul had been influenced by the Marcionist prologues".[384]

Hans von Campenhausen characterizes Marcion's text edition as a great danger that almost deprived the Church of authentic access to her origins: "On the philological level his text [is] . . . the corruption of an ancient tradition; if it had prevailed, it would have forever prevented the Church from knowing her origins."[385]

If, therefore, someone has been consciously dabbling at the text of 1 Corinthians 14:33b–38, then it was not the Church, as many today like to claim without too much examination, but obviously Marcion. In the ecclesiastical milieu—which the representatives of the interpolation hypothesis usually see as the origin of the "intervention"—especially during the period of the pastoral letters, we find an instinctive aversion to any altering of revelation: " Guard the truth that has been entrusted to you by the Holy Spirit, who dwells within us."[386]

Marcion and other nonecclesiastical expositors behave, however, as anything but guardians: "Marcion and those who stem from him have been bold enough to excise parts of the Scriptures. Some repudiate them altogether, others recognize nothing as authentic except what they themselves have mutilated."[387]

According to Tertullian, "Every discerning person finds it just as unbelievable that we who are the first and original beginners should have applied the falsifying stylus to Scripture as that they who are the later and of hostile disposition should *not* have done that. The one corrupts the texts (Marcion), the other, the explanation of the meaning (Valentin)." In this, Marcion is regarded as the worse, for he made use not only of the "stylus" but also of the "knife", thus committing "murder upon Holy Scripture".[388]

Hence, it is quite well possible that a heretic from the second century has deprived Christians up to the present of a weighty argument against

---

[383] H. J. Vogels, *Textkritik*, p. 142.

[384] H. J. Vogels, "Einfluss", p. 287, n. 24a.

[385] Hans von Campenhausen, "Marcion et les origines du canon néotestamentaire", in *Revue d'histoire et de philosophie religieuses*, 46 (1966): 220.

[386] 2 Tim 1:14; similarly, 1 Tim 6:20; 2 Tim 4:1–5, 7 and elsewhere.

[387] Irenaeus, *Adversus haereses*, III, 12, 12: BKV 3, 258f.; PG 7, p. 906.

[388] Tertullian, *De praescriptione haereticorum* 38: BKV 24, 348; CCL 1, pp. 218f.

women in the priesthood, namely, of clear awareness of the "command of the Lord".

5. THE DOGMATIC VALUE OF 1 CORINTHIANS 14:33b–38

The Roman declaration on women in the priesthood comments as follows on the Gospel Tradition: "In order to understand the ultimate meaning of the mission of Jesus and that of Scripture, purely historical exposition of the texts cannot be sufficient."[389]

This remark applies as well to our Pauline passage. No matter how much the historical-critical studies of a biblical text might tend to suggest a particular conclusion, the fact remains that an isolated philology cannot of itself engender any dogmatic certainty. The deciding thing is much more how the relevant question is reflected in the religious Tradition of the Church and how it is interpreted there. As I see it, the specific, and certainly necessary, inquiry into the "command of the Lord" can be reduced to two fundamental problems:

1. Is there, in the early Church, an *exclusion* of women from tasks of the kind involved in priestly office?
2. If so, how is that exclusion *justified*?

Any appeal to the will of Jesus would correspond materially to the "command of the Lord".

From a theoretical viewpoint, these questions could be cleared up even apart from any exposition of 1 Corinthians 14. Someone like the Frenchman Jean Galot arrives at a very decided rejection of priesthood for women although, along with Conzelmann, he regards the *mulier-taceat* verses as an interpolation.[390] Nevertheless, I believe that our Pauline passage already answers both questions in an exemplary way.

First Corinthians 14 does not deal with the office of priest but rather imparts a *ban on teaching* by women. It is aimed at official and public activity as διδάσκαλος, while teaching activity outside of this office (ἐν οἴκῳ) seems thoroughly appropriate for women in the Pauline community.

If, however, official teaching is forbidden, then this applies even more strongly to the role of community superior and, especially, to that of apostle, both of which include teaching functions. As experts in knowledge

---

[389] Erklärung no. 2, p. 8; *AAS* 69 (1977): 103.
[390] Galot; cf. especially pp. 51, 111f.

of the Christian message, the διδάσκαλοι in Corinth were perhaps also capable of serving in leadership positions that had an episcopal character and culminated in the celebration of the Eucharist. The First Letter to Timothy may—even if its composition should be set at a later date—be related to the situation in Corinth, assuming that it associates the group of presbyters or bishops in a special way with teaching.[391]

We meet with a similar group of problems throughout the entire history of the Church. The issue of a female priesthood is seldom dealt with directly but usually by way of its "foreground"[392] or its functional aspects, especially teaching and leadership. It is in tasks of a teaching nature, apparently, that most of the encroachments by female activity are possible, so that, in the relevant statements, we find the ban on teaching recurring in first place.

The deciding thing is how this ban on teaching is justified. If the really crucial point of view were that of a patriarchal social structure, then the biblical and patristic documents would lose their significance for present times. However, Paul's style of argumentation already took a more differentiated form.

The apostle argues:

1. In terms of the kinds of knowledge that are already open to us at the level of natural reason. In verse 35, he makes use of the concept of propriety, which appears already, in a similar form, in the "prescription on veils": "Does not nature itself teach you that. . . ."[393]

These purely human considerations are grounded in biological and social structures. To the extent that the social framework and perceptions of propriety should change, new viewpoints have to be considered. The prescription on veils in 1 Corinthians 11 could, therefore, be dropped in modern times. Yet the fundamental appeal to heed the natural order remains.

2. For Paul, the natural order presents itself as the order of creation and can appear, in certain of its basic aspects, as an obligatory component of revelation: in 1 Corinthians 14:34 (and elsewhere), the subordination of women is grounded in the law. Even if there is a reference to the Fall implied in this,[394] it is, in any case, connected with the preordained creation of man: in 1 Corinthians 11:7–10, Paul derives the subordination from the biblical accounts of creation.[395] Even if—which is not necessary[396]

---

[391] 1 Tim 5:17; cf. already 1 Th 5:12.
[392] Ministering, for example.
[393] 1 Cor 11:14.
[394] Gen 3:16; cf. 1 Tim 2:14.
[395] Cf. 1 Tim 2:13.
[396] Cf. pp. 350f. above.

—we reject the apostle's exposition as outmoded "rabbinism", the basic reference back to creation nevertheless remains. In the documents on the office of teaching, too, what is initially important is not the individual arguments that are given for a precept[397] but the statement itself. Here, this statement is: the difference between men and women is grounded in creation: women are subordinate to men.

3. The order of creation also leaves its mark on the Tradition of the Church,[398] which, in this case, cites support expressly from the will of Jesus.[399]

4. In the Pauline context, the command of the Lord not only appears as a positive statute, but is also linked to the order of redemption: just as Christ, by virtue of his redemptive work, is the "head" of man, so, in an analogical way, man is the "head" of woman.[400] The subordination of Christ to the Father[401] appears here as a model for subordination, as determined by creation, in the human sphere. Equality and difference are not opposite for Paul but, rather, complementary quantities.[402] Subordination is thus no merely canonical directive but a shorthand term for basic structures of the orders of creation and redemption.

The four strands of argumentation listed above may be reduced to two basic points of reference:

1. The *order of creation* as the revealed interpretation of the natural order.

2. The *order of redemption*, which brings creation to fulfillment and is the ultimate reference of the will of Jesus. *If* there is a command of the Lord pertaining to our question, *then* it exists not for the sake of the command itself but as a safeguard for effective delineation of the economy of redemption. To keep insisting on the command in an isolated way, without elucidating its internal principles, would be nominalistic positivism. If we anchor the will of Jesus in the order of redemption, then investigation of the symbolical representative character of man and woman is an irrevocable postulate of theology. Sacred history, nature and the supernatural must, then, be linked up with one another in an appropriate way. Here, study of the *depositum fidei* by means of historical method comes together with the *ratio theologica* of speculative thought.

---

[397] These can change, as is shown especially by the doctrine of original sin in connection with Romans 5:12.

[398] 1 Cor 14:33a, 36.

[399] 1 Cor 14:37.

[400] 1 Cor 11:3.

[401] 1 Cor 11:3; 15:28.

[402] Cf. what was said about 1 Corinthians 12 and 11 in pp. 345ff. above.

6. THE BAN ON TEACHING IN 1 TIMOTHY 2

Along with 1 Corinthians 14:34–35, 1 Timothy 2:12 is seen, in traditional dogmatics, as the most important *locus classicus* from the Bible for justifying the exclusion of women from the priesthood. We cannot, of course, be satisfied with the mere citation of the texts but most pose the questions with a view to their context and dogmatic weight. First Corinthians 14 and 1 Timothy 2 are to be viewed together but are nevertheless rooted in different situations. It is precisely through this that their common meaning becomes evident.[403]

First Corinthians 14 is directed against enthusiasts; the pastoral letters, by contrast, take a stand against heretics. From these contexts, as different in each case, one cannot draw overhasty conclusions about differences in the character of divine service. In the First Letter to the Corinthians, prophecy is dealt with, yet the service of the διδάσκολος is presupposed.[404] The pastoral writings emphasize, from given thematic standpoints, the "sound doctrine",[405] but prophetic activity seems to be thoroughly in evidence.[406] Common prayer for men and women is known to 1 Timothy just as to 1 Corinthians, and in both of these such prayer is regulated in a special way.[407] In both letters, we find the ban on teaching by women: 1 Corinthians 14 mentions it indirectly, and 1 Timothy 2, directly.

Even if Paul should happen not to be the author of the pastoral letters,[408] these writings would not, therefore, become second-class texts. No more than within the New Testament can a "canon in the canon" be set up within the *Corpus Paulinum*: even if we assume that the "real" Paul had never spoken of subordination or a ban on teaching regarding women, the

---

[403] Important comments on 1 Timothy 2 have already been made earlier: cf. p. 380 above. The following discussion supplements what has been said there.

[404] Cf. pp. 375f. above.

[405] 1 Tim 1:10 and elsewhere.

[406] 1 Tim 1:18; 4:14.

[407] 1 Tim 2:8–10; 1 Cor 11:4–5.

[408] This theory seems to have almost become a commonplace in German, including Catholic, exegesis; cf., for instance, the commentary by Norbert Brox, *Die Pastoralbriefe* [The pastoral letters], RNT 7, 2 (Regensburg, 1969); Wikenhauser and Schmid, *Einleitung*, pp. 515ff. One cannot, however, speak of a general exegetical consensus; weighty objections are found in C. Spicq, *Les épîtres pastorales I*, Études bibliques, 4th ed. (Paris, 1969), and especially clearly of late in non-Catholic commentators: Bo Reicke, "Chronologie der Pastoralbriefe" [Chronology of the pastoral letters], in *ThLZ* 101 (1976): 81–94; Gottfried Holtz, *Die Pastoralbriefe* [The pastoral letters], Theologischer Handkommentar zum NT XIII, 2nd ed. (Berlin, 1972); J. A. T. Robinson, *Redating the New Testament* (London, 1976), pp. 67ff.

"Deutero-Paulines" have, in any case, spoken of such[409] and are just as inspired as all the other texts in the Bible.

I am here opposing those theories that assume the existence of a progressive "falling away" from the will of Jesus in the early Church. Earlier, Jesus and Paul were often played off against one another,[410] whereas there is an attempt today to oppose Jesus and the "real" Paul to "proto-Catholic" epigones.

Supposedly, Paul was acquainted with female community leaders and had raised no barriers to official activity by women; but in later times, under the influence of the contemporary environment (!), antifemale tendencies had come to the fore again and had then driven women out of their positions. The pastoral letters are an outgrowth of this attitude. Only in Gnosticism and Montanism[411] was genuine Paulinism retained.[412]

This sort of theory of a falling away is immediately improbable for the reason that the pastoral letters have as their aim precisely *not* adapting to the sociocultural environment; rather—with reference to Paul—they are very strongly tied to Tradition, wanting not to push anything old aside but rather to adhere consciously to such: "*Guard* the truth that has been entrusted to you."[413] New doctrines are proclaimed by the heretics.[414]

Our passage, 1 Timothy 2:9ff., by the way, is typically Pauline, even if it may not have been written by Paul personally. This applies to precisely those "offensive" statements that follow the ban on teaching: "(13) For Adam was formed first, then Eve; (14) and Adam was not deceived, but the woman was deceived and became a transgressor. (15) Yet woman will be saved through bearing children, if she continues in faith and love and holiness, with modesty."[415]

That Adam was created first, and that, therefore, special authority is

---

[409] Col 3:18; Eph 5:21ff.; 1 Tim 2:11–12.

[410] For example, Emanuele Meyer: Ketter, *Christus II*, p. 204; Zscharnack, *Dienst*, pp. 15f.

[411] Cf. on this pp. 404ff. below.

[412] In connection with Thraede, these ideas are advocated particularly by Elisabeth Schüssler Fiorenza, in (among other places) "Women Apostles", Gardiner, pp. 94–102: "Jesus called women to full leadership and the Spirit empowered them as apostles, prophets and leaders in the early Church" (p. 98). "Whereas in Paul's time leadership roles were still diversified and based on charismatic authority, the process of institutionalization set in gradually toward the end of the first century" (p. 97). The active women "were as heretics eliminated from mainstream Christianity" (p. 98) under the influence of "Judaism and Hellenism" (p. 97). *Now* "we want to recover the full apostolicity . . . of the Church" (p. 99). The same conception is advocated also by, among others, Ida Raming, "Männerkirche", pp. 230–35.

[413] 2 Tim 1:14 and elsewhere.

[414] 1 Tim 4:3; 2 Tim 2:18; 4:3–4.

[415] 1 Tim 2:13–15.

due to men as opposed to women,[416] is mentioned by Paul in 1 Corinthians 11:3, 8, 12. Concerning this idea, we encounter the same interpretation of the biblical accounts of creation in the rabbis, with whose methods the apostle was, of course, familiar. Whether all this means that Paul presents men as being "worthier" than women[417] may be left open here. Even if it is factually the case—this is seen particularly in patristic and medieval commentaries on Paul—that man, by virtue of his originality of creation, should be accorded along with his authority a certain superiority, these ideas are not necessarily linked logically: Christ originated out of the Father and is subordinate to him[418] but is not inferior to him, because he possesses the same divine nature.[419] An authentic, freely willed subordination can occur only between beings that stand at the same ontological level.

Even if a certain superiority of men were asserted in 1 Timothy 2:13, that would not necessarily be an anti-Christian statement. Without detriment to the equality in worth of being a person, on the natural plane (which is not identical with the situation before God) there can be "valuable" and "less valuable" people and life situations, similarly to the way that silver possesses a value that is considerable in itself yet still exceeded by that of gold. In the Christian sphere, marriage is good, but celibacy for the sake of the Kingdom of heaven is better;[420] matrimonial love does not therefore become inferior.

Earlier I put forward the postulate that men and women are of equal value not only in their being as persons but in all other attributes as well;[421] demonstrating this in individual cases can be rather more difficult than our contemporaries imagine. Our postulate may well appear as the consequence of a fundamental equality in worth of men and women that has every probability in its favor; nevertheless, it is not logically necessary, which means that we should not be too quick to make a devil of "rabbinical" influences in the past.

First Timothy 2:14 presupposes a stronger susceptibility in women to being led astray, which hinders them from taking on a leadership role vis-à-vis men. What is meant is the seduction by the "serpent";[422] that Adam was not led astray in this way does not mean that he might not have

---

[416] 1 Tim 2:13.

[417] As obviously applies for the rabbis: Billerbeck, III, pp. 645f.; to be compared with Billerbeck, *Kommentar III*, pp. 256f. and 626.

[418] Cf. 1 Cor 11:3; 15:28.

[419] Cf. pp. 349f. above.

[420] Mt 19:12; 1 Cor 7:38; DS 1810.

[421] Cf. pp. 114f. above.

[422] Gen 3:12f.

sinned. Therefore, 1 Timothy 2:14 need not contradict Romans 5:12, where Adam's sinning is seen as crucial, since the context of the statement is different in each case.[423] The notion that women have the stronger susceptibility to temptation also occurs in Paul's writings in 2 Corinthians 11:3.[424]

First Corinthians 14 and 1 Timothy 2 are addressed to differing situations and are also differently formulated; nevertheless, we meet with common stylistic and conceptual elements: use of the unusual verb ἐπιτρέπειν ("to permit"),[425] "subordination",[426] "keeping silent"[427] and, not least, "learning".[428] The last-named characteristic distinguishes the Pauline letters clearly from Jewish rabbinism. For whereas the study of the Torah by women is taboo there,[429] here women are expressly invited to learn about Christ's message.

The statement in 1 Timothy 2:15 that women will be saved "through bearing children" strikes some commentators[430] as especially un-Pauline (or "sub-Pauline"). However, it does not represent a "backslide into Judaism", for "there is no Jewish parallel [to this notion]".[431] Bearing children does not, as such, seem an actual means to salvation but rather, in the sense of raising children and domestic activity,[432] a locus of trial and proof; the deciding factors are "faith", "love" and "holiness".[433] We can probably see in this a polemical gibe against heretics who oppose marriage.[434] Marriage is the normal and good situation for women,[435] which does not mean that the ideal of continence is therefore to be abandoned.[436]

The ban on teaching should be seen as an antithesis to the heresy in

---

[423] Cf. Spicq, *Pastorales*, p. 381; as against Brox, *Pastoralbriefe*, p. 135.

[424] No devaluing of women needs to be connected with this. Cf. pp. 254–55, 299f. above.

[425] Cf. p. 387 above. What is involved here is a slightly modified rabbinical technical term, which refers to a pregiven command; cf. S. Aalen, "A Rabbinic Formula in 1 Cor 14:34", in F. L. Cross (ed.), *Studia evangelica II*, TU 87 (Berlin, 1964), pp. 513–25, esp. 513f., 552.

[426] 1 Cor 14:34; 1 Tim 2:11–14.

[427] 1 Cor 14:34: σιγάτωσαν; here ἡσυχία: vv. 11, 12.

[428] μανθάνειν: 1 Cor 14:31, 35; 1 Tim 2:11; 2 Tim 3:6.

[429] Cf. p. 327 above.

[430] As already to Friedrich Schleiermacher, *Über den sogenannten ersten Brief des Paulos an den Timotheos* [On the so-called first letter of Paul to Timothy] (Berlin, 1807), pp. 185–87; today, for instance, Brox, *Pastoralbriefe*, p. 138.

[431] Holtz, *Pastoralbriefe*, p. 71.

[432] 1 Tim 5:10.

[433] 1 Tim 2:15. For an extensive justification of this statement cf. Spicq, *Pastorales*, pp. 382ff.

[434] 1 Tim 4:3.

[435] Cf. 1 Tim 5:10, 11.

[436] 1 Tim 3:2, 12; 5:9; Titus 1:6; cf. 1 Cor 7:38–40.

which the Gnostic systems of the second century were already announcing themselves. Two traits are characteristic of the heretics:

1. A repudiation of marriage and an exaggerated abstention from food;[437] this attitude is obviously based on a spiritualism that takes a hostile attitude to the realm of the body.
2. The claim that resurrection has already taken place:[438] resurrection applies "only to the spirit, and not to the body, which belongs instead to the material, God-extraneous cosmos".[439]

Between "gnosis" and teaching by women there is a direct connection:

> Whereas the ecclesiastical ban is amply grounded in the difference between men and women . . . , the Gnostic attaches no value to such differences. For him, man's sexual differentiation lies on the merely physical—that is, on the totally irrelevant—plane; hence, no distinctions can be derived from it, which means that women may, without further ado, be permitted to take on the activities of men, such as teaching in the congregation.[440]

The attitude of the Gnostics to teaching office for women is grounded in the context of the times. The First Letter to Timothy refers to the situation in Ephesus, the economic, political and religious center of Asia Minor.[441] In that region the social position of women was especially well developed. Professional activity by women in the Roman Empire was probably most widespread there—for instance, the large number of female physicians in Asia Minor is well known[442]—and in politics, too, women were thoroughly involved in leadership: "The full observation of civil rights is found at its most developed in the Asia Minor of the imperial age."[443]

Ephesus was also a center of philosophy. Particularly in the schools of the Stoics, Epicureans and Pythagoreans, female philosophers were known to teach, probably appearing publicly in the same way as did Paul, who chose a lecture hall in Ephesus as a place of work.[444]

In the religious sphere, female leadership was even more widespread: the Phrygian cult of Cybele, in which the god mother played the central role, had made its way to Ephesus,[445] along with its priestesses and

---

[437] 1 Tim 4:3.

[438] 2 Tim 2:18.

[439] E. Haenchen, "Gnosis und Neues Testament" [Gnosis and the New Testament] (Berlin, 1973), pp. 325–39.

[440] Brox, *Pastoralbriefe*, p. 133.

[441] 1 Tim 1:3; 3:14; Acts 20:30 along with 1 Tim 1:20; 2 Tim 1:15–18; 2:17; 4:14, 19.

[442] Thraede, "Frau", p. 204.

[443] Thraede, "Frau", p. 198.

[444] Acts 19:9; cf. pp. 341f. above.

[445] Dieter Knibbe, "Ephesos—nicht nur die Stadt der Artemis" [Ephesus—not only the city of Artemis], in Sencer Sahin et al. (eds.), *Studien zur Religion und Kultur Kleinasiens II. Fs*

priests. Also known were the priestesses of Demeter[446] and of the mystery cult of Isis, which had made equal rights for women its platform.[447] Leading positions were held by women in the cult of Dionysus, too, in whose worship ceremonies all members had equal rights, playing out their parts in colorful intermixture;[448] in Ephesus, this cult was especially "ecstatic". Tradition has it that Bishop Timothy, the addressee of our letter, was killed by Dionysian zealots when he took a public stand against their orgies.[449] Most characteristic of Ephesus, however, is the cult of Artemis.[450] In it, priestesses took priority.[451]

Thus, the sociocultural environment in Ephesus was anything but hostile to priesthood for women; instead, this question was very much in the air.[452]

It should not be said that Christian community services cannot be compared at all with pagan customs. Precisely official teaching by women was something quite familiar in the schools of philosophy, and it was organized in a way similar to that found in Christian communities.[453] Despite all the differences, there are also certainly some parallels to the pagan priesthood: Timothy was not only a teacher of the community, but also a director of worship ceremonies.[454] In particular, the "mystery priests, seen from a phenomenological viewpoint, take on a certain closeness to the idea of the Christian sacramental priesthood".[455]

It is probable that in the metropolis Ephesus, women from higher social levels had also embraced Christianity; the social structure of the communities was probably "more elevated" than it was in Corinth.[456] Educated ladies must have shown a special zeal for learning, which, to be sure, could also be guided in false directions; we hear of women "swayed by various impulses, who will listen to anybody and can never arrive at a knowledge of the truth".[457] Along with this, learning may occasionally have translated itself into a desire to teach.

F. K. Dörner [Studies on the religion and culture of Asia Minor. Essays in honor of F. K. Dörner] (Leiden, 1978), pp. 490f. Cf. pp. 145, 161 above.

[446] Knibbe, "Ephesos", pp. 496f.

[447] Knibbe, "Ephesos", pp. 500f.; Holtz, Pastoralbriefe, p. 68; cf. pp. 343f. above.

[448] Cf. p. 344 above.

[449] Cf. on this Knibbe, "Ephesos", p. 495.

[450] Cf. Acts 19:23ff.

[451] Prümm, Handbuch, p. 634.

[452] Holtz, Pastoralbriefe, p. 68.

[453] Cf. p. 363 above.

[454] Cf. on this Spicq, Pastorales, pp. 356, 361.

[455] Prümm, Handbuch, p. 226.

[456] Acts 18:19; 1 Tim 2:9; 6:17–19 among others; on this see Spicq, Pastorales, pp. 423–25.

[457] 2 Tim 3:6f.

Experts on the sociocultural environment of the pastoral letters draw the conclusion that the demand for subordination and the ban on teaching by women were decidedly anachronistic,[458] for the contemporaries were used to a liberal state of affairs. The attitude of the early Church is therefore often attributed to the influence of the synagogue, where—even in Asia Minor—similar restrictions on female activity were found.[459]

In fact, the parallels with Judaism are quite close, all the way down to the rabbinic exposition in 1 Timothy 2. On the other hand, clear differences from Judaism are also prominent: learning is not only not prohibited for women but rather made a duty, as is teaching at the private level: older women are "teachers in what is good" (καλοδιδάσκαλους), and the instructing of Apollos by Priscilla and Aquila is also certainly well known.[460]

The clearest difference from Judaism probably lies, however, in the more extensive field of activity in community life. The pastoral letters not only declare a decided "No" on official teaching by women, but also, at the same time, throw open new possibilities: there are women who devote themselves, most likely within the institutional framework, to welfare matters,[461] and widows constitute a class of their own,[462] which also seems to have functioned in a specific way.[463] It is in the pastoral letters (!) that those New Testament texts are found that deal most extensively with matters close to women and offer practical help for Christian living.[464]

---

[458] Spicq, Pastorales, p. 386; cf. Thraede, "Freiheit", pp. 115–25 (on the household lists).

[459] Meer, Priesturtum, pp. 50ff.; K. Rahner, "Priesturtum", p. 298 and elsewhere.

[460] Acts 18:26; 2 Tim 4:19.

[461] 1 Tim 3:11. Cf. on this Kalsbach, Diakonissen, pp. 10–14; Roger Gryson, Le ministère des femmes dans l'Église ancienne, Recherches et synthèses, section d'histoire, IV (Gembloux, 1972), pp. 29–31; cf. p. 441 below.

[462] 1 Tim 5:9.

[463] 1 Tim 5:10; cf. also Titus 2:3–5.

[464] On the topic "woman" in the pastoral letters, cf.: 1 Tim 2:9–15; 3:11; 5:2, 3–16; 2 Tim 1:5; 3:6–7, 14; 4:19, 21; Titus 2:3–5. See also Spicq's excursus "La femme chrétienne et ses vertus", in Spicq, Pastorales, pp. 385–425.

CHAPTER SIX

The Period of the Church Fathers

I. THE STRUGGLE OF THE CHURCH IN THE SECOND CENTURY—A PRELUDE TO THE MODERN CONTROVERSY

Tertullian and Irenaeus on Gnostics and Marcionites

In the views that he holds, Marcion[1] is no isolated thinker but a child of his times. The ancient society within which the early Church developed cannot at all be categorized indiscriminately under the rubric "patriarchalism". Instead, powerful "emancipatory" currents held sway[2] and threatened to force their way into the Church as well. In those days, Catholic Christians did not adapt to the sociocultural situation but, for the most part, "swam against the stream".

The Church had to struggle particularly hard against the Gnosticism of the second century.[3] "The volume of heretical Christian-Gnostic literature exceeded that of orthodox writing."[4]

The Gnostics often perceived the difference between men and women, which is rooted in material being, as something disturbing and attempted to do away with it. As justification, they frequently appealed to the new order of redemption, which supposedly liberated Christians from all inequalities with one another. In this sense, the apocryphal Gospel of Thomas puts the following words into Christ's mouth: "If you . . . make the masculine and the feminine into but one thing, so that the masculine is not masculine and the feminine is not feminine . . . , then you will enter the kingdom." "Behold, I will educate her [Mary] in such a way as to make her masculine, so that she will also become a living spirit equal to

---

[1] Cf. pp. 390–94 above.
[2] Cf. pp. 340–44 above.
[3] Cf. pp. 158–65 above.
[4] Lortz, *Geschichte I*, p. 85.

you men. For a woman who makes herself a man will enter the kingdom of heaven."[5]

This attitude naturally also had an effect on the structuring of ecclesiastical order. Tertullian tells of a blurring of the distinction between clergy and laity as well as of generally widespread participation by women in official functions:

> And so, then, one person is bishop today, and another tomorrow; today someone is deacon, and tomorrow, lector; today priest, and tomorrow, layman. . . . In fact, although they hold divergent opinions, there is also no difference between them when they join forces in common opposition to the one truth. All are conceited, all promise knowledge. The catechumens are already fully accomplished before they have received any instruction. And even the heretical women—how cheeky and presumptuous they are! They know all about how to teach, to debate, to perform exorcisms, to promise cures, perhaps also even to baptize.[6]

By heretics, Tertullian refers primarily to the adherents of Marcion, Apelles and Valentinus.[7] Tertullian appears to know nothing more precise about baptism by women, but Epiphanius confirms this supposition in relation to the Marcionites.[8] An example of activity in worship ceremonies is provided, from Valentinian Gnosticism, by Irenaeus.[9]

[5] Ernst Haenchen, *Die Botschaft des Thomas-Evangeliums* [The message of the Gospel of Thomas]. Theologische Bibliothek Töpelmann 6 (Berlin, 1961), Spruch 22, 114, pp. 19, 33; cf. also Jervell, *Imago Dei*, pp. 161–63. A similar "saying of the Lord" can be found in the Gnostic Gospel of the Egyptian. Salome asks when death no longer has any power, and Jesus answers: "When you trample the cloak of shame underfoot, and when the two become one and the masculine bound up with the feminine becomes neither masculine nor feminine": Clement of Alexandria, Stromata III, 13 92; GCS 15, p. 238. In Clement, this quotation is used by Iulius Africanus, the founder of Docetism. The same passage from the Gospel of the Egyptian crops up in the so-called 2nd Letter of Clement: Wilhelm Schneemelcher, "Ägypter-Evangelium" [Gospel of the Egyptian], in Hennecke and Schneemelcher, *Apokryphen I*, p. 111. Cf. what was said above on the "androgynous utopia" of the Gnostics: pp. 160–61 above. Still more drastic statements characterize childbearing as the work of Satan; cf. among others Irenaeus, *Adversus haereses*, I, 24, 2; PG 7, p. 675; Clement of Alexandria, Stromata III, 9, 67; GCS 15, p. 226.

[6] Tertullian, *De praescriptione haereticorum*, 41; CCL 1, p. 221.

[7] Tertullian, *De praescriptione haereticorum*, 30: "We list precisely those named because, as falsifiers of truth, they are the most prominent and have the most followers." The three names form the "unbroken thread" of the whole polemic. Apelles is an earlier adherent of Marcion (CCL 1, pp. 210f.). On the "feminist theology" of Valentinian Gnosticism, cf. pp. 162f. above.

[8] Epiphanius, *Adversus haereses* 42, 4: PG 41, p. 700. The source of this information is probably the (lost) "Syntagma" by Hippolytus from the second century: R. A. Lipsius, *Zur Quellenkritik des Epiphanios* [On criticism of Epiphanius' sources] (Vienna, 1865), p. 205; on the "Syntagma", cf. also Altaner and Stuiber, *Patrologie*, pp. 316, 158.

[9] Cf. p. 408 below.

Some Gnostic writings seem to suggest that the sectarians tried to play Jesus' teaching off against the practice of the Catholic Church. The contemporary situation was read back into the life of Christ, and the attacks were directed against Peter. Thus, in the *Pistis Sophia*, Mary Magdalen complains: "My Lord, my mind is always knowledgeable, so that I could stand up at any time and . . . discourse . . . on the unraveling of the words, but I am afraid of Peter because he threatens me and despises our sex."

To this, Jesus replies: "Anyone who is filled with the spirit [πνεῦμα] of light, for the purpose of discourse and to discourse on the unraveling of things that I say—no one will be able to prevent him."[10]

The situation is similar in the "Gospel according to Mary", where Levi defends Mary against Peter: "Now I see how zealously you oppose the woman, as if she were the adversary. But if the Redeemer has made her worthy, who then are you, that you reject her?"[11]

The "active" women of the gospel, especially Mary Magdalen, Martha and Salome, are given great prominence by the Gnostics and are seen in an "emancipatory" light. According to the Acts of Philip,[12] Mariamne appears as the sister of the apostle and is obviously sent out to preach together with her brother.[13]

The apocryphal *Acta Pauli et Theclae* report the following dialogue: "Thecla . . . said to Paul, 'I am going to Iconium.' But Paul said, 'Go there and teach the word of God.' "[14]

Some (female) champions of the ordination of women therefore maintain that, in the earliest Church, women had at times held public teaching office and that this was only later suppressed.[15] Regarding this thesis, however, one should take into account, among other things, Tertullian's statements on the background of the "Acts of Thecla". These, he says, are

[10] *Pistis Sophia*, 72, in Carl Schmidt (ed.), *Die Pistis Sophia. Die beiden Bücher des Jeû. Unbekanntes altgnostisches Werk* [The *Pistis Sophia*. The two books of Jeû. An unknown ancient Gnostic work], edited by W. Till, Koptisch-gnostische Schriften I: GCS 45, p. 13, 3rd ed. (Berlin, 1959), p. 104.

[11] H.-C. Puech, "Gnostische Evangelien und verwandte Dokumente" [Gnostic gospels and related documents], in Hennecke and Schneemelcher, *Apokryphen I*, p. 254.

[12] Originating from around 500, they still reflect in some ways a milieu that existed already in the second century: R. A. Lipsius and M. Bonnet, *Acta apostolorum apocrypha II, 2*, reprint (Hildesheim, 1959), p. 82; Cf. Gryson, *Ministère*, p. 39.

[13] *Acta Philippi*, 94f., in Lipsius and Bonnet, *II, 2*, pp. 36f. Additional information on the role of women in the heterodox sects of the second century can be found in Gryson, *Ministère*, pp. 39f., and Zscharnack, *Dienst*, pp. 160–62.

[14] *Acta Pauli et Theclae*, 41, in Wilhelm Michaelis, *Die apokryphen Schriften zum Neuen Testament* [The apocryphal writings on the New Testament] (Bremen, 1956), p. 305.

[15] Thus already in Lydia Stöcker, *Die Frau in der alten Kirche* [Woman in the Early Church], (Tübingen, 1907), pp. 11–16; cf. Fiorenza, "Women Apostles", pp. 94–102.

the work of a presbyter from the province of Asia, who was suspended from office because of his all-too-creative imagination, particularly regarding the activities of Thecla.[16]

In connection with this, Tertullian describes the apostle Paul's negative position on public teaching (and baptizing) by women.[17] In the writing De virginibus velandis, it is then put especially tersely: "It is forbidden for a woman to speak in church; she is also not allowed to teach, to baptize, to sacrifice or to presume to the rank of male office, not to mention priestly service."[18]

This position is not a private opinion or the manifestation of a moody "hatred of women"[19] but rather a concrete expression of the recognized liturgy. Pierre de Labriolle writes on this:

> It [the passage] relies on the prevailing discipline, and its reasoning is dependent upon this being authoritative, without adding anything beyond that. So we have here in precise detail the prohibitions regarding women in the Church's worship, or, in other words, the practical applications the Church made from Paul's general precept.[20]

The text from De virginibus velandis carries even more weight because it stems already from Tertullian's Montanist period;[21] it was, of course, precisely the Montanists who were accused of granting women too many liberties.[22] In contrast to the Catholic Church in North Africa, the Montanist group there included widows among the clergy (ordo), which means all the Church officials.[23] In seeking reconciliation, penitents threw themselves down in the middle of the church before the presbyters and the widows, who held a place of honor in the congregation;[24] the above-mentioned ban applied, however, to the widows (viduatus) as well.[25]

---

[16] Tertullian, De baptismo 17: CCL 1, p. 291.

[17] The occasion for the Church Father's indignation was the propaganda of a woman from the sect of the Cainites; cf. De baptismo, 1, 3: CCL 1, p. 277; 17, 4: CCL 1, pp. 291f. See also the commentary in Gryson, Ministère, p. 42.

[18] Christoph Stücklin, Tertullian: De virginibus velandis. Übersetzung, Einleitung, Kommentar. Ein Beitrag zur altkirchlichen Frauenfrage [Tertullian: De virginibus velandis. Translation, introduction, commentary. A contribution to the question of women in the early Church], Europäische Hochschulschriften XXIII, 26 (Bern and Frankfurt, 1974), chap. 9, 1, p. 45.

[19] Cf. on this pp. 428f. below. Against J. K. Coyle, "The Fathers on Women and Women's Ordination", in Église et théologie 9 (1978): 68; against Meer, Priesturtum, p. 70.

[20] Pierre de Labriolle, La crise montaniste (Paris, 1913), p. 318.

[21] Altaner and Stuiber, Patrologie, p. 158.

[22] Cf. on this pp. 408ff. below.

[23] Cf., among others, Tertullian, De exhortatione castitatis 13, 4: CCL 2, p. 1035; De monogamia 11, 1: CCL 2, p. 1244.

[24] Tertullian, De pudicitia 13, 7: CCL 2, p. 1304; De virginibus velandis 9, 2f.: CCL 2, p. 1219.

[25] On the relevant texts, cf. Gryson, Ministère, pp. 45-49.

Irenaeus (second century) tells of women who, on the advice of a Valentinian sorcerer named Marcus, felt themselves driven to celebrating the Eucharist by the Holy Spirit.[26] This incident took place in Asia Minor.[27] The anger of the Church Fathers was directed primarily at the sorcery of Marcus, but condemnation of celebration of the Eucharist by women is obviously presupposed.[28]

The controversy with Montanism[29]

The Montanists are also well-known, an enthusiastic movement that placed great emphasis on the unrestrained "exhalations of the Holy Spirit" and granted women more extensive participation in the liturgy than did the Church. The Montanist movement cannot be taken as evidence of female activity at the time of Paul.[30] Rather, consideration must be given to the contemporary environment, about which Franz Cumont writes: "The bent for passionate ecstasy was an endemic disease in Phrygia from time immemorial. Even under the Antonines, Montanist prophets that sprang up in this country attempted to introduce it into Church practice, and the dervishes perpetuated it under Moslem rule."[31]

But even the Montanists seem to have generally respected the ban on ordination of women.[32] Not until Epiphanius (fourth century) were there reports of female clergy in an offshoot of the sect. There, women were active as bishops and presbyters, and their ordination was justified on the basis of Galatians 3:28. The difference between the sexes was held to play no role, for, in Christ Jesus, there is neither male nor female.[33]

This is the same argument that serves today as a password in almost all writings favoring ordination of women. Since his opponents claim support

[26] Irenaeus, *Adversus haereses* I, 13; PG 7, pp. 577ff.

[27] Cf. Coyle, "Fathers", p. 66.

[28] Against Coyle, "Fathers", p. 66, who thinks that this text says nothing against ordination of women because it does not mention that.

[29] I include Epiphanius and Firmilian, too, under the rubric "second century" here because the occurrences described by them reflect a milieu that has its roots in Phrygian Montanism or even—in the case of Epiphanius—elaborates sources from the foundational period of the sect. The existence of Montanism in Asia Minor is documented all the way up into the eighth century: Wilhelm Schepelern, *Der Montanismus und die phrygischen Kulte. Eine religionsgeschichtliche Untersuchung* [Montanism and Phrygian cults. A study in the history of religion] (Tübingen, 1929), p. 33.

[30] Thus F. E. Vokes, "Montanism and the Ministry", in SP IX (TU 94) (Berlin, 1966): 306f.

[31] Cumont, *Heidentum*, p. 47.

[32] Labriolle, *Crise*, p. 510.

[33] Epiphanius, *Adversus haereses* 49, 2: PG 41, p. 881.

from Paul, Epiphanius can easily counter with the relevant statements by the apostle. He combines 1 Corinthians 14:34 with 1 Timothy 2:12 and makes reference to the Pauline statements on the order of creation in 1 Corinthians 11:8: the Montanists "ignore the word of the apostle: 'Women are not permitted to speak or to have authority over men.' And similarly: 'For man was not made from woman, but woman from man.' "[34]

Since the Montanist group claimed support—in addition to citing the example of Old and New Testament prophetesses[35]—from Eve, who had eaten from the tree of knowledge,[36] Epiphanius, drawing on Paul, can counter sarcastically: "Adam was not deceived, but first Eve was deceived and became a transgressor."[37] Like several other early Church authors, the Church Father also cites the Yahwist's account of the Fall: "Your desire shall be for your husband, and he shall rule over you."[38]

Thus, the deciding argument for the refusal of female priesthood is the appeal to the directives of Saint Paul, which is supplemented elsewhere[39] by additional important considerations.

The female priesthood of the "Quintillians" seems to be connected with a theology that—perhaps linked in turn to Galatians 3:28—regards Christ as androgynous. Epiphanius records the following vision had by the prophetess Priscilla at the time of the founding of Montanism: "*In the form of a woman*—so she said—Christ came to me in radiant garb, inspired me with wisdom and pronounced this place [the Phrygian village Pepuza] holy; it was there that the Heavenly Jerusalem would descend."[40]

It is also necessary to consider the sociocultural context of Montanism. Phrygia, as we know, is in Asia Minor, where participation by women in public activities was especially well developed.[41] In Phrygian paganism, the god mother Cybele was the center point of worship, and this could have had a subconscious effect on Priscilla's vision, in which Christ appears as a woman. If we can believe Jerome, Montanus—the founder of the sect—had earlier been a priest of Cybele.[42]

In the Montanist groups that had priestesses, seven virgins often played a role in the gatherings, bringing those present "to tears" in order to arouse feelings of repentance. "The women themselves overflow with

---

[34] Epiphanius, *Adversus haereses* 49, 3: PG 41, p. 881.

[35] Miriam and the daughters of Philip: Epiphanius, *Adversus haereses* 49, 2: PG 41, p. 881.

[36] This idea crops up again recently in the "post-Christian" writings by Mary Daly: e.g., *Beyond God the Father*, p. 67.

[37] Cf. 1 Tim 2:14.

[38] Epiphanius, *Adversus haereses* 49, 3: PG 41, p. 881.

[39] Cf. pp. 416–18 below.

[40] Epiphanius, *Adversus haereses* 49, 1: PG 41, p. 880.

[41] Cf. pp. 401–3 above.

[42] Jerome, *Epistula* 41, 4: BKV; CSEL 54, p. 314.

tears and bemoan, with appropriate gestures, the life of mankind."[43] This behavior is strongly reminiscent of the pagan Phrygian festival of spring, at which a group of women "lamented the fate of Attis [son of Cybele]".[44] Montanism is certainly no pagan religion, but the influence of the social environment is unmistakable. The Church had set itself more strongly apart from this.

To the controversy with Montanism belongs, as well, a commentary by Origen on 1 Corinthians 14:34–35, which has fortunately come down to us in a catena.[45] The Alexandrian theologian is here attacking Montanists, among whom, after the example of the prophetesses Priscilla and Maximilla, women make speeches at community gatherings. To that practice, he opposes the ban on speaking from 1 Corinthians 14:34, describing it as a "command".[46] A bit later, he also cites the ban on teaching from 1 Timothy 2:12.

His opponents, similarly to the group mentioned by Epiphanius, refer for support to the daughters of Philip,[47] to Anna[48] and to the Old Testament prophetesses, namely, Miriam,[49] Deborah[50] and Huldah.[51] Origen counters that all these women would never have spoken in public in the presence of men. Acts mentions nothing about prophesying by the daughters of Philip in the congregation, nor is that reported of Anna. Miriam only directed the singing of a group of women. In contrast to Jeremiah and Isaiah, we hear of no address to the people by Deborah. Huldah, likewise, did not address the people; rather, it was necessary to go to her home to hear her.

Origen does not reject any and every sort of female teaching,[52] but only public-official teaching, through which women assume superiority over men.[53]

[43] Epiphanius, *Adversus haereses* 49, 2: PG 41, p. 881.

[44] Schepelern, *Kulte*, p. 127.

[45] *Journal of Theological Studies* 10 (1909): 41f.; cf. the translation and commentary in Gryson, *Ministère*, pp. 56–58.

[46] Αἱ γυναῖκες ὑμῶν ἐν ταῖς ἐκκλησίαις σιγάτωσαν. ταύτης δὲ τῆς ἐντολῆς οὐκ ἦσαν οἱ τῶν γυναικῶν μαθηταί, οἱ μαθητευθέντες Πρισκίλλη καὶ Μαξιμίλλη, οὐ Χριστοῦ τοῦ ἀνδρὸς τῆς νύμφης. Whether the ἐντολή του κυρίου is consciously aimed at here is, however, not clearly recognizable.

[47] Acts 21:9.

[48] Lk 2:36.

[49] Ex 15:20f.

[50] Jg 4:1.

[51] 2 Kings 22:14–20.

[52] He cites here, among others, Titus 2:3–4; cf. p. 403 above.

[53] We encounter a similar argumentation in the Homilies of Isaiah: hom in Is. 6, 3: GCS 33, p. 273. The behavior of the Montanists that the Alexandrian had before his eyes need not be in contradiction with the practice attested to by Tertullian (cf. on this pp. 374f. above).

The testimony of the bishop Firmilian of Caesarea is also perhaps directed against a Montanist prophetess. In a letter to Cyprian of Carthage, he supports his colleague in the controversy about baptism by heretics. What was at issue is the defense of the thesis that only a bearer of the spirit can mediate the Holy Spirit in baptism, that is, not a heretic and certainly not someone possessed.

Firmilian describes the activities of a possessed woman who had been unmasked by an exorcist:

> Through the deceptions and illusions of the demon, this woman had previously set about deluding believers in a variety of ways. Among the means by which she had deluded many was daring to pretend that, through proper invocation, she consecrated bread and performed the Eucharist. She offered up the sacrifice to the Lord in a liturgical act that corresponded to the usual rites, and she baptized many, all the while misusing the customary and legitimate wording of the question. She carried all these things out in such a manner that nothing seemed to deviate from the norms of the Church.[54]

The tenor of this statement is that someone possessed cannot validly baptize. The accusation of being possessed could, however, also have been directed against the Montanists. That their prophets were "inspired" was not doubted; in question was only the source: Is the mover the Spirit of God, or a demon?[55] If, however, a demon "baptizes", the baptism is naturally invalid. Since the prophetess came from Cappadocia and was accused of being possessed, the influence of Montanism may well have been in the background here.[56]

Firmilian speaks primarily against the validity of baptism by demons, but rejection of baptism by a woman is presupposed in the same statement: "What are we, then, to say of a baptism in which a worthless demon baptizes through a woman?"[57]

The North African Montanist group does not seem to have been exactly comprehensively informed about the doctrines of its fellow believers in Asia Minor, as is shown particularly clearly by the central example of eschatology (cf. on this Schepelern, *Kulte*, pp. 31f.).

[54] *Inter epistulas Cypriani* 75, 10: CSEL 3, pp. 817f.

[55] Schepelern, *Kulte*, p. 11.

[56] Cf. Schepelern, *Kulte*, p. 13.

[57] "Quo nequissimus daemon per mulierem baptizauit?" (*Inter epistulas Cypriani* 75, 11: CSEL 3, p. 818). The alternative postulated here by Coyle, "Fathers", p. 72, is thus only apparent: "The woman's activities are thus repudiated, not because she is a woman, but because she is a heretic." Coyle attempts to call into question all patristic references against priesthood for women by saying that the *ordination* of women is nowhere *directly* condemned: Coyle, "Fathers", pp. 98f. Coyle here ignores the elementary basic principle of logic that a statement about a part—for example, the ban on teaching—can signify by inclusion a statement about the whole (= priesthood). Furthermore, priesthood for women is also certainly, at times, described *explicitly* as "heresy": cf. pp. 417f. below.

Hippolytus on widows

Indirect evidence from the second century—this time from Rome—is also provided by the "Apostolic Tradition" of Hippolytus:

> When a widow is accepted into the widowhood [καθίστασθαι], then she is not ordained [χειροτονεῖν], but appointed as such through the title ["widow"]. . . . One should not lay hands upon her, for she does not offer up the sacrifice [προσφορά] and performs no liturgical service [λειτουργία]. Ordination [χειροτονία] takes place, namely, for the clergy [κλῆρος] with a view to liturgical service. A widow, however, is appointed for prayer, which is the task of everyone.[58]

The function of a widow[59] is thus set apart from the service of the clergy, which is decidedly grounded in the capacity to offer up the eucharistic sacrifice. That a widow is excluded from this task because of her *femaleness* is not explicitly stated yet is still suggested; a later revision of the *Traditio apostolica* then supplements the cited passage as follows: for widows, too, "the prescriptions of the apostle are valid. They are not allowed to be ordained, but rather, one should pray over them; for ordination is for men."[60] Regarding contemporary Rome, moreover, the influence of the Pauline letters must be taken into account,[61] and the description of the *regula fidei* probably corresponds materially to the statements made by Tertullian. Along with Tertullian and Irenaeus, Hippolytus, too, takes a similar stand against the activities of mainly Gnostic sectarians.[62]

The literary documents from the earliest period of Church history are, to be sure, relatively scanty, but, precisely in their partly indirect character, they point quite clearly to the fact that refusal of female priesthood was regarded as a matter of course by the Catholic Church. Imaginative interpretations of archaeological findings in Rome, such as crop up of late here and there, must therefore have a question mark placed after them.[63]

---

[58] Hippolytus, *Traditio apostolica* 10, in Bernard Botte, *La tradition apostolique de Saint Hippolyte*, Liturgiewissenschaftliche Quellen und Forschungen 39 (Münster, 1963), p. 31.

[59] Deaconesses in Rome are not documented until later: cf. p. 440 below.

[60] *Canones Hippolyti* 9: *Patrologia orientalis* 31, p. 363; translated [in the German original of this book] from Gryson, *Ministère*, p. 88. The text originated in Egypt between 336 and 340.

[61] 1 Cor 14:34–35; 1 Tim 2:12.

[62] Especially in the *Refutatio omnium haeresium* and in the (lost) *Syntagma*; cf. Altaner and Stuiber, *Patrologie*, pp. 165, 168.

[63] For instance, Joan Morris claims to be able to recognize a female celebrant and concelebrants in a eucharistic ceremony depicted on a fresco in the Priscilla catacomb, and she interprets the inscription *episcopa Theodora* in the Roman St. Praxedis church as referring to a "female bishop": Joan Morris, *Against Nature and God. The History of Women with Clerical Ordination and the Jurisdiction of Bishops* (London and Oxford, 1973), pp. 7f., 4f. Similarly, Dorothy Irvin: cf. *CGG* 32 (1980): 119: "Were women in priestly and episcopal office in the

2. PATRISTIC TESTIMONIES FROM THE THIRD TO EIGHTH CENTURIES

The Eastern Church

Didascalia and Apostolic Constitutions

The Didascalia, which reflect the Syrian liturgy in the first half of the third century,[64] also regulate, among other things, the tasks of women in the community. The institution of deaconess is introduced here as something new,[65] but at the same time women are strictly prohibited from holding teaching office and performing baptism. With respect to teaching activity, there had obviously been some encroachments on clerical functions by the widows, and baptism by women also seems to have occurred: "Now, as far as women are concerned, we advise against baptizing, or allowing oneself to be baptized, by a woman, for that is a transgression of the command and very dangerous for her who baptizes and him who is baptized."[66] "It is not in order to teach that you women, and especially you widows, are appointed, but in order to pray and to petition God the Lord."[67]

To conclude from this ban that it put an end not only to specific encroachments but to generally widespread teaching and baptizing by women[68] would probably not do justice to the historical facts. The existence of a "solid hierarchy" in the Syrian metropolis Antioch for one

---

early Church?" Among other things, it is necessary to note that, in the early Church, the wives of bishops and presbyters were often addressed as *episcopa* and *presbytera*, in a way similar to something that occurs today in the German Protestant sphere: "Frau Pastor". Such titles are not isolated instances—the "evidence" of Morris' and Irvin's research could be significantly increased—but rather, are documented by the hundreds; cf. Adolf Kalsbach, "Diakonisse" [Deaconesses], in *RAC* II (Stuttgart, 1957), p. 916.

[64] Altaner and Stuiber, *Patrologie*, pp. 84f.

[65] Cf. p. 441 below.

[66] *Didaskalia* III, 9, 1 (arranged by F. X. Funk), in Hans Achelis and Johannes Flemming (eds.), *Die syrische Didaskalia* [The Syrian Didascalia], TU, Neue Folge X, 2 (Leipzig, 1904), p. 81.

[67] *Didaskalia* III, 6, 1–2, in Achelis and Flemming, *Didaskalia*, p. 77.

[68] As Raming obviously does, *Ausschluss*, pp. 27f., in connection with the commentary by Achelis (1904): "The ban on baptizing (as well as the ban on teaching) is directed . . . against the widows. Previously, they had obviously administered baptism by virtue of their nature as charismatics." "In place of the charismatically stamped institution of the widowhood, which was limited to silent prayer and also perhaps to caring for the sick, the Didascalia introduces the office of female deacon as a flexible agency under the bishop's control and occupying a fixed position within the Church hierarchy."

and a half centuries previously is authenticated (letters of Ignatius), and that precisely widows should have been, as it were, clerical "office bearers" is more than improbable for Syria. Widows appear, together with orphans, precisely as *objects* of ecclesiastical caritas and lead a life of prayer in "reciprocation";[69] their "charismatic" functions are restricted to prayerful intercession and blessing at the bedsides of the sick.[70]

The justification for the ban on teaching by widows is their lack of theological knowledge, which gives the pagans occasion for laughter and mockery of the gospel, "especially" if it "is presented" to them "through discourse by a woman". The latter argument here, then, is one of (historically conditioned) propriety. An ignorance of doctrine is shared by widows with the laity, who are also called on to exercise reserve. This does not, however, seem to be the crucial reason, for as we know all clergymen were themselves laymen prior to their consecration. In the case of deaconesses, knowledge of doctrine is presupposed, for they are expressly charged with the instruction of women after baptism.[71] Theological ignorance on the part of women is thus probably not so self-evident as van der Meer assumes.[72] The fundamental ban on teaching, and especially on baptizing, nevertheless holds for deaconesses, too.[73]

Does all this mean that the crucial reason is propriety? That assumption would suggest itself if the justification finished here. Yet the argumentation goes further still. For the ban on baptizing as well as for that on teaching, the decisive factor is an appeal to the behavior of Jesus:

> For if it were permissible to be baptized by a woman, then our Lord and Master would have been baptized by his mother, Mary; yet he was, however, baptized by John.[74]

> For it is not to teach that you women . . . are appointed. . . . For he, God the Lord, Jesus Christ our Teacher, sent us, the Twelve, out to teach the (chosen) people and the pagans. But there were female disciples among us:

[69] Cf. Gryson, *Ministère*, pp. 72–75.

[70] There is no indication that "caring for the sick" was also a task of the widows, even if such service may occasionally have been undertaken. Prior to the Didascalia, female community charity was probably carried out in a spontaneously motivated way: cf. p. 441 below.

[71] *Didaskalia* III, 12, 2; in F. X. Funk, *Didascalia I*, pp. 208f.

[72] Meer, *Priesturtum*, p. 67.

[73] Cf. Gryson, *Ministère*, pp. 77f., and pp. 441f. below.

[74] *Didaskalia* III, 9, 2; in Achelis and Flemming, *Didaskalia*, p. 81. Even regarding the ban on baptizing, it is thus anything but plainly clear that the ban was issued merely "on grounds of decency" since "the baptismal candidate" was, "after all, totally naked" (Meer, *Priesturtum*, p. 67). Female baptismal candidates were also naked, but the preparatory anointing was carried out by deaconesses.

Mary of Magdala, Mary the daughter of Jacob and the other Mary; he did not, however, send them out with us to teach the people. For, if it had been necessary that women should teach, then our Teacher would have directed them to instruct along with us.[75]

Hence, among the three arguments of the Didascalia (education, propriety, example of Jesus), the third, namely, the *behavior of Jesus*, is obviously seen as the most important and ultimately grounds the decision. Although the Syrian liturgy does not cite here the relevant statements by Paul, a materially similar structure of argumentation is found there.

That contemporary influences were the decisive factor behind the bans on baptizing and teaching thus remains questionable. Priestesses were also known to Syrian paganism,[76] and Marcionist communities have been documented all the way up to the sixth century.[77] At the end of the second century, Marcionism was seen as *the* great danger to the Syrian Church.[78] Therefore, Roger Gryson makes the following judgment about the bishop who wrote the Didascalia:

If he denies women the right to teach and to baptize, it is above all because he does not see in the Gospel that Christ conferred these ministries upon women, even though there were women among his followers.[79]

An explicit reference to the pagan example is found in the Apostolic Constitutions from the fourth century, which revise and expand the liturgy of the Didascalia: "If, in the foregoing, we do not allow women to teach, how can anyone agree that they—in contempt of their nature—should assume the office of priest? For it is ignorant heathen ungodliness that leads to the ordination of priestesses for female deities, but not the command of Christ."[80]

The mention of female deities is already an initial explicit, if restrained, reference to the anchoring of the argumentation in the image of God, which fundamentally distinguishes Christians and pagans from each other. There were, of course, also priestesses for male deities in antiquity. In any case, the pagan priesthood was understood as analogous to the Christian, but its practice of consecrating women to liturgical service was not adopted. Significant here again, too, is the reference to the example of Jesus.

---

[75] *Didaskalia* III, 6, 2, in Achelis and Flemming, *Didaskalia*, p. 77.

[76] Cf. Attridge and Oden, *Goddess*.

[77] Altaner and Stuiber, *Patrologie*, p. 106.

[78] On this, see E. C. Blackman, *Marcion and His Influence* (London, 1948), pp. 3f.

[79] Gryson, *Ministère*, p. 74.

[80] *Constitutiones Apostolorum* III, 9, 3, in F. X. Funk, *Didascalia I*, p. 201.

Epiphanius

Bishop Ephiphanius of Salamis (fourth century) is the patristic witness who takes the most detailed position on our topic. Whereas he confronts the priestesses among the Montanists with the authority of Paul,[81] he refers, with respect to the Collyridian women, to sacred history. The following had come to the Church Father's attention:

> It is reported that certain women there in Arabia [that is, in the region east of Palestine] have introduced this absurd teaching from Thracia: how they offer up a sacrifice of bread rolls [κολλυρίδα] in the name of the Ever Virginal [that is, of Mary] and hold their meetings in that very name, and how they undertake something that far exceeds proper measure in the name of the Holy Virgin. In an unlawful and blasphemous ceremony, they ordain women, through whom they offer up the sacrifice in the name of Mary. This means that the entire proceeding is godless and sacrilegious, a perversion of the message of the Holy Spirit; in fact, the whole thing is diabolical and a teaching of the impure spirit.[82]

The controversy with the Collyridian women is intended to demonstrate primarily that Mary is not a divinity but a created being. She is, to be sure, deserving of the highest veneration, but not of adoration[83] and certainly not sacrifices. The Collyridian women have obviously transferred the pagan cult of a goddess to Mary.[84]

In principle, the rejection of the adoration of Mary would be enough, but, in the same context, Epiphanius also mounts a strong attack on female priesthood. The Church Father looks first at the sacred history of the Old Covenant and then concludes: "Nowhere did a woman serve as priestess."[85]

The Old Covenant is fulfilled in the New, where there are also no female priests. This fact is grounded in the will of God. That the exclusion from priestly office is not based on any inferiority of women is evident from the example of Mary:

> If women were to be charged by God with entering the priesthood [ἱερατεύειν] or with assuming ecclesiastical office [κανονικόν τι ἐργάζεσται ἐν Ἐκκλησία], then in the New Covenant it would have devolved upon no one more than Mary to fulfill a priestly function. She was invested with so great an honor as to be allowed to provide a dwelling in her womb for the

---

[81] Cf. p. 409 above.

[82] Epiphanius, *Adversus haereses* 78, 13: PG 42, p. 736.

[83] Epiphanius, *Adversus haereses* 79, 7: PG 42, p. 752.

[84] Something similar is found in the Old Testament, where cakes are sacrificed to the "queen of heaven", Astarte: Jer 7:18; 44:19; cf. on this Meer, *Priesturtum*, p. 64.

[85] Epiphanius, *Adversus haereses* 79, 2: PG 42, p. 744.

heavenly God and King of all things, the Son of God. . . . But he did not find this [the conferring of priesthood] good. Not even baptizing was entrusted to her; otherwise, Christ could better have been baptized by her than by John.[86]

When Epiphanius storms against the witlessness of the Collyridian women, he caricatures feminine folly and fickleness: "For the female sex is easily misled, weak and without much sense."[87] "Every heresy is a bad woman, but even more so this heresy of women." One should honor Eve, but not follow her.[88] "May we therefore be on our guard, servants of God! Let us array ourselves in the sensibleness of men, so that we dispel this madness of women."[89]

To modern sensibilities, these remarks seem to overstep the bounds of propriety. But it would be utterly wrong to accuse the Church Father of hatred of women because of them and to claim that this was the cause of his rejection of priesthood for women. What we find here is not a theoretical treatise on women but a polemical attack on *bad* women, who have made themselves successors of Eve. That there are also, however, holy women, who follow in the footsteps of Mary, must have been something that Epiphanius knew quite well. It is hardly conceivable that he would have said of Mary that she was "easily misled, weak and without much sense".

The "misogynous" remarks therefore only explain why women have fallen prey to false doctrine but not why they are excluded from priesthood. When the ordination of women is under discussion, the Church Father does not use negative foils that make the female sex appear deficient in means but rather a positive background for justification of his thesis, namely, the superiority of Mary. For Epiphanius, women can appear as an outstanding example of wickedness but also as a model of all-surpassing holiness. Priesthood for women does not, therefore, depend on their holiness or unholiness but on the will of Christ.

This will shows itself, for Epiphanius, not in the position of Mary but in the selection of the apostles, whose priestly service is perpetuated in the Church:

From this bishop [the brother of the Lord, James in Jerusalem] and the just-named apostles, the successions of bishops and presbyters in the house of God have been established. Never was a woman called to these. . . . According to the evidence of Scripture, there were, to be sure, the four

---

[86] Epiphanius, *Adversus haereses* 79, 3: PG 42, p. 744.

[87] Epiphanius, *Adversus haereses* 79, 1: PG 42, p. 741.

[88] Epiphanius, *Adversus haereses* 79, 8: PG 42, pp. 752f.

[89] Epiphanius, *Adversus haereses* 79, 2: PG 42, p. 741.

daughters of the evangelist Philip, who engaged in prophecy, but they were not priestesses.

The ecclesiastical office of deaconess (διακονισσῶν τάγμα!) is "not conferred for priestly service or functions of that sort, but rather, for the preservation of the dignity of the female sex when baptism is administered or when care for sickness and infirmity is required."[90]

Thus we see that Epiphanius anchors the exclusion of women from the sacramental priesthood in the will of Jesus, which corresponds to the divine plan for salvation. Female priesthood is therefore not described as a mere infringement of disciplinary order, but is represented as a heresy. Accordingly, the ecclesiastical practice of not ordaining women as priests appears as an obligatory component of sacred Tradition and must therefore remain closed to all contrary influences from the sociohistorical environment (Montanists and the Collyridian women).

The reception of Epiphanius' statements by Augustine and John Damascene

The characterization of official priesthood for women as a heresy met with general acceptance in patristic tradition. This is shown in particular by two authors—Augustine and John Damascene—who, like Epiphanius, drew up whole catalogues of heresies, integrating into these the information of the Bishop of Salamis.

The Quintillians "give women predominance (*principatus*) so that these, too, can be honored with the priesthood (*sacerdotium*) among them. They say, namely, that Christ revealed himself at . . . Pepuza to Quintilla and Priscilla in the form of a woman."[91] "But they confer upon women the office of superior and priest" (ἄρχειν καὶ ἱερατεύειν).[92]

It should be noted that Augustine, as the high point of the Latin Fathers, had an important influence on later Church history, and that John Damascene, so to speak, set the final seal on the Greek Fathers. Both authors expressly categorize female priesthood under the rubric "heresy", that is, it contradicts the binding Faith of the Church. In this connection, the subordination of women, who are to be denied "leadership" (in the sacred official sphere), is made indirectly apparent.[93]

John Chrysostom

The question of female priesthood is also alluded to by John Chrysostom, a contemporary of Epiphanius. In his writing on the priesthood, he deals

---

[90] Epiphanius, *Adversus haereses* 79, 3: PG 42, p. 744. On deaconesses, cf. pp. 440f. below.

[91] Augustine, *De haeresibus* I, 17: PL 42, p. 31.

[92] John Damascene, *De haeresibus* 49: PG 94, p. 708.

[93] Cf. pp. 432f. below.

at one point with the calling of Peter as exemplary for the priestly calling in general. For the Christian life, things such as fasting, vigils or caring for the afflicted and orphans are decisive.

In his calling of Peter, however, Christ had left all that aside, saying instead: "Tend my sheep!"

> For the tasks that I just listed could readily be performed by many of the subordinates, too, not only men, but women as well. If, however, it is a matter of being entrusted with direction of a church and with the care of so many souls, then, first of all, the entire female sex must step back from so great a task, but also the majority of males. . . . For . . . , great as the difference is between rational man and the irrational creatures, the shepherd towers just as high over the flock entrusted to him, not to say even higher. After all, the goods involved here are much greater.[94]

John Chrysostom thus points out the lesser capacity of the female sex for leadership duties. Naturally, this argument alone can hardly be decisive for strict exclusion of every woman from the official priesthood. For the Church Father was quite familiar with secular rule by women, even in the Christian imperial house.[95]

The deciding factor in the argumentation is thus obviously provided by the example of Christ, who had called no woman to the office of apostle. That women tend to have a lesser capacity for leadership is an important argument of propriety but cannot—taken on its own—justify an absolute ban on priesthood for women.

Following on from Paul, Chrysostom more than once quite emphatically confirmed the ban on public teaching by women, but, at the same time, using the example of the instructing of Apollos by Priscilla,[96] illustrated the possibility of nonofficial teaching.[97] Theologically educated women were among his best acquaintances.[98] What is decisive for the ban on teaching is the authority of Saint Paul, not the possible spiritual incapability of a woman. The statements by the apostle to the Gentiles and the reference to the behavior of Jesus are thus, for Chrysostom, the deciding arguments against priesthood for women.

The Apostolic Church Order

The otherwise almost never cited "Apostolic Church Order" is quite interesting for our topic. In it are reflected the ecclesiastical structures and perceptions of a small provincial community in fourth-century Egypt.

---

[94] John Chrysostom, *De sacerdotio* 2, 2; PG 48, p. 633.
[95] Cf. pp. 432f. below.
[96] Acts 18:24–26.
[97] Cf. the relevant passages in Gryson, *Ministère*, pp. 135ff.
[98] Cf. p. 434 below.

The conversations of the twelve apostles, as they discuss the directives of Jesus, serve as its literary device.

One of these conversations documents the fact that there had been a discussion in the community about the topic "priesthood for women":

> Andrew says, "Brothers, it would be useful to institute an office for women." Peter says, "We have already made preparations for that. But regarding the sacrifice of the Body and Blood, we need to express ourselves more precisely."
>
> John says, "You have forgotten something, brothers: When our Master asked for the bread and the cup and blessed them with the words: 'This is my body and my blood', he did not allow the women to join us [for the consecration]."
>
> Martha says, "That was only because of Mary, since he saw her smiling."
> Mary says, "That was not because I had laughed. For, before then, he had said to us, as he taught, that the weak will be saved by the strong" [that is, woman by man].
>
> Cephas says, "Undoubtedly you will recall that it is not appropriate for women to pray while standing, but rather, while sitting on the ground."[99]

To pray while standing is characteristic of office bearers who are offering up the sacrifice. The special priesthood is thus not appropriate for women. The advocates of the ordination of women, drawn in the image of the "activistic" Martha,[100] obviously regard the nonadmission of women to priestly service as an accident of history, which no longer has any validity for the current pastoral situation. In opposition to that position, two arguments are put forward:

1. The *will of Jesus*, which was expressed particularly in his behavior at the Last Supper.
2. The *order of redemption*, which is illustrated through an (apocryphal) statement by Jesus: "The weak will be saved by the strong." This logion is put into the mouth of Mary, whose "listening contemplative" attitude is preferred in the gospel to the "activism" of her sister. The offering up of the sacrifice mediates saving grace and strengthens the Christian for eternal life; this strengthening tends, however, to be symbolized more by men than by women—which probably explains the antithesis "strong-weak".[101]

---

[99] *Apostolische Kirchenordnung* 24, 1–28, 1 [Apostolic Church order 24:1–28:1]. Theodor Schermann (ed.), *Die allgemeine Kirchenordnung des zweiten Jahrhunderts* [The general Church order of the second century], Studien zur Geschichte und Kultur des Altertums, 3. Ergänzungsband, 1. Tel (Paderborn, 1914), pp. 31–33.

[100] Cf. Lk 10:38–42.

[101] Cf. Gryson, *Ministère*, pp. 84f.

This argument is materially identical to the modern reference, as anticipated by Bonaventure,[102] to the central symbol of marriage: Christ is the "bridegroom" through whom the "bride" (the Church) is rescued. Christ is the (dominant) "head", and the Church, the "body".[103] "Being weak" is then a synonym for "readiness to receive".

The Apostolic Church Order does not, to be sure, rest content with simply saying no to female priesthood. Rather, women are directed toward specific sorts of tasks that are especially suited to their nature. In this case, the institution of the "widows" is established, who are to devote themselves to prayer and community care. These widows appear as a female pendant to the presbyters and enjoy an elevated status. There is, then, a female office but no female office of priest: the celebration of the Eucharist, as the central aspect of priestly service, is denied to women by the will of Christ.

The Church in the West

The peculiarity of the evidence

The attitude of the Eastern Church to our question is manifest also in its position on deaconesses and on liturgical service by women. This indirect evidence against women in the priesthood is much more extensive than the few direct statements.[104]

The same structure of Tradition is also found in the Western Church. In the early period, among the surviving sources, female priesthood is condemned directly only by Tertullian and Augustine.[105] However, there were numerous "oversteppings of the bounds" of female activity in the liturgy and the area of official teaching, some selected examples of which I would like to present here. Again, this evidence is of an indirect sort.

The commentaries on Paul by Ambrosiaster

The fourth-century commentaries on Paul that have been attributed to Ambrose (or Augustine), now called "Ambrosiaster", had an important influence during the Middle Ages. These texts are repeatedly cited as a showcase example of the undervaluing of women that supposedly lay

[102] Cf. p. 452f. below.

[103] Eph 5:21ff.

[104] One might compare the ample collection of texts in Gryson, *Ministère*, and, further on here, the excursus on the "female diaconate", pp. 440–43.

[105] Cf. pp. 406–7, 418 above.

behind the ban on ordination of women. Ida Raming, for instance, finds there "the statement about an inferiority of woman as something already given at creation, in consequence of which her likeness to God is expressly denied, thereby rendering the extent of the disdain especially visible".[106]

In fact, more clearly than in all other texts of the Fathers, subordination of women forms the unbroken thread of the relevant expositions, and this is, of course, particularly offensive to modern liberalism. Ambrosiaster identifies the "authority" of men so closely with likeness to God that, in the order of creation, he denies the latter quality to women. It should be noted here that the more modern notion of likeness to God, as prepared by Augustine and Thomas,[107] had not yet been introduced; with respect to material content, however, the differences are not all that great.

Those who accuse Ambrosiaster of disdaining women must also add to that a disdain for Christ: "Just as the Son comes the Father, so, too, woman comes from man, in order that the authority of a single principle be preserved."[108]

Woman does not reflect the image of God for the reason that the first man was created as a single being, from which the others arise, and embodied, so to speak, the sovereignty of God as his representative.[109] "Although man and woman are of the same essence, man should, nevertheless, as head of woman, have authority (over her), which is to say that he is greater not in respect of his essence, but in respect of his being the origin and his understanding."[110]

Apart from this, the texts of Ambrosiaster are a paraphrase of the relevant passages from Saint Paul. Now, regarding 1 Timothy 3:11, we find a remark that is related to ordination of women:

> Since the apostle speaks about women after the deacons, the Cataphrygians seize the favorable opportunity for heresy and maintain with vain insolence that deaconesses must be consecrated, too; and this, even though they know that the apostles chose seven men as deacons. Are we to suppose that no suitable woman could be found at that time, when we nevertheless read that holy women were present along with the twelve apostles?

Paul, however, "commands that women should keep silence in the churches".[111]

---

[106] Raming, *Ausschluss*, p. 54; similarly, Meer, *Priesturtum*, p. 72.
[107] Cf. pp. 451ff., 460 below.
[108] *Liber questionum Veteris et Novi Testamenti* 21: CSEL 50, p. 48.
[109] Cf. *Liber quaestionum Veteris et Novi Testamenti* 45: CSEL pp. 50, 82f.
[110] Commentary on 1 Cor 11: CSEL 81, 2, p. 121.
[111] Commentary on 1 Tim 3: CSEL 81, 3, p. 268.

Ambrosiaster was obviously not informed about the practice of the Eastern Church, which at that time already ordained deaconesses and numbered them among the clergy. What he condemns, namely, equivalence between deacons and deaconesses, did not exist there.[112] Ambrosiaster seems, however, to have presupposed such a blurring of spheres of duty among the Montanists (= Cataphrygians); insofar as he makes reference to the ban on speaking and to the authority of the apostles who would have been able to act otherwise, this evidence against sacramental deaconship for women is simultaneously a testimony for exclusion of women from sacramental priesthood.

The occasion for the statements against deaconesses and in favor of the ban on teaching was probably provided by a certain revival of Montanism, which, under the name "Priscillianism", was condemned by the Councils of Saragossa (380) and Nîmes (391 or 396). Saragossa reiterates the Pauline ban on teaching, and Nîmes opposes the *ministerium leviticum* of women, that is, a female diaconate that has been made equivalent to the male one.[113] We find similar bans occurring repeatedly, at later periods, in Gaul.[114]

Bans in the wider liturgical setting of the priesthood

In 494, Pope Gelasius issued the following ban: "As we have noted with vexation, contempt for divine truths has reached such a level that even women, it is reported, serve at holy altars; and everything that is entrusted exclusively to the service of men is performed by the sex that has no right to do so."[115]

In the East, the Council of Laodicea had already prohibited women from entering the sanctuary.[116] In the West, relevant bans are encountered from the fourth century onward, particularly in Gaul—not because the practices in question were tolerated by the Church in other regions but because repeated "oversteppings of bounds" occurred here well into the early Middle Ages. As late as in a communication by several bishops to Louis the Pious, for instance, it is said:

> We have tried in every possible way to prevent unallowed access to the altar by women. Since we . . . have found that, in some provinces, contrary to divine law and canonical directive, women enter the sanctuary, handle consecrated vessels without fear, pass clerical vestments to the priests

---

[112] Cf. pp. 440–44 below.

[113] Cf. the texts and the commentary in Gryson, *Ministère*, pp. 162–64.

[114] Cf. Gryson, *Ministère*, pp. 164ff.

[115] *Gelasius* I, *Epistola* IX, 26: PL 59, p. 55.

[116] Between 347 and 381: cf. Raming, *Ausschluss*, p. 16, n. 53; Gryson, *Ministère*, p. 94.

and—something even more monstrous, improper and unseemly than all that—distribute the Body and Blood of the Lord to the people and do other inherently indecent things, we have attempted to prevent it so that such liberties do not continue to be taken. . . . It is most astonishing that this practice, which is forbidden in the Christian religion, could have crept in from somewhere; . . . undoubtedly, it took hold through the carelessness and negligence of some bishops.[117]

This passage may serve as representative of many other bans that we meet with well into most recent times. Precisely what is prohibited or allowed is, to a certain extent, varied: entering the sanctuary or removing the altar cloths, for example, were not always and everywhere forbidden. To my knowledge, there was complete constancy regarding the bans on ministering and especially—apart from some exceptional arrangements made primarily in present times—on "female ministers of Communion". It is not necessary to deal with the relevant points of canonical law in more detail here. They are of dogmatic importance for the following reason.

The primary task of a priest consists in offering up the sacrifice at Mass.[118] All other activities are, in one way or another, related to that yet are not restricted to the power of consecration. Particularly regarding the sacrificial celebration itself, priestly service is bound up with a specific range of things—liturgical ceremonies, vestments and so forth—extending beyond what is theoretically the only necessary thing: the pronouncing of the words of consecration. Now, distribution of Communion is normally the task of the priest who has consecrated the offering; although a lay service, ministering is also, in a certain way, both referred to and derived from the priestly activity. In my opinion, preservation of this sphere of priesthood, through which the bounds of the holy are made sensibly perceptible, is the real reason behind the issuing of the relevant bans. Because they persist, precisely in their variability, throughout history, the regulations of canonical law thus possess a not inconsiderable dogmatic significance. "Motives of respectability" or concerns about celibacy[119] may have played a certain role here, but they are not the real reason, which lies in the ban on women in the priesthood.[120]

If we reject *priesthood* for women, then we should be logically consistent and not treat women, for purposes of the liturgy, as "imperfect men":

[117] Mansi, 14, p. 565.

[118] DS 1739; 1764; *Presbyterorum ordinis* 6, p. 566; *AAS* 58 (1966): 996; *Lumen gentium* 28, p. 158; *AAS* 57 (1965): 33 and elsewhere.

[119] Meer, *Priesturtum*, pp. 119f. Raming, *Ausschluss*, p. 14, refers also to the Old Testament prescriptions on cleanliness; on this, see pp. 209f., n. 21 above.

[120] Against Raming, *Ausschluss*, p. 132.

Precisely because of the equality in worth of the sexes, however, it is . . . necessary to exclude women from office entirely, and not to grant them certain lower positions, such as ministering or swinging the censer at divine service. It should not, after all, be the case within the Church hierarchy that every level up to the highest is open to men, and only the lower levels, by contrast, to women.[121]

3. THE DOGMATIC VALUE OF THE PATRISTIC TESTIMONY

The problem

Whenever the Church Fathers have occasion to speak, directly or indirectly, about "women in the priesthood", they reject it clearly and unanimously. Now, is this rejection a component of sacred Tradition, which is binding on us at all times and even still today?

Authors who speak out in favor of female priesthood give a negative answer to this question. As justification, they cite first of all the temporally conditioned conception of woman that is supposedly responsible, in the end, for the ban on ordination of women. Ida Raming, in particular, puts forward the following causal chain: disdain for women—inferior legal position—exclusion from priesthood.[122] Kari Borresen speaks of a male-centered outlook in patristic theology ("androcentrism") and postulates, too, that a low evaluation of women led to their nonadmission to the priesthood.[123] Haye van der Meer puts forward the thesis that "their [the Fathers'] rejection of priesthood for women arose from an (at least) remarkable conception of woman, which entitles us to ask whether they were not actually speaking about a totally different subject".[124] Ancient woman may well have been excluded from the priesthood because of her

---

[121] O. Schneider, *Priesturtum*, p. 40.

[122] Raming, *Ausschluss*, esp. pp. 162, 222. The statements there apply initially to the canonical writings of the Middle Ages, which are still to be discussed here, but refer equally to the testimony of the Fathers that is the basis of those writings.

[123] K. E. Borresen, *Subordination et équivalence. Nature et rôle de la femme d'après Augustin et Thomas d'Aquin* (Oslo and Paris, 1968); K. E. Borresen, "Die anthropologischen Grundlagen der Beziehungen zwischen Mann und Frau in der klassischen Theologie" [The anthropological bases of the relation between man and woman in classical theology], *Conc* 12 (1976): 10–17; Borresen, "Männlich-Weiblich", pp. 325–34. Augustine (and, for the Middle Ages, Thomas) are treated as "showcase examples" here.

[124] Meer, *Priesturtum*, p. 86.

subordination and deficient education, but modern woman is a completely different being.[125]

On the logical linkage of the predicates "inferiority of women" and "exclusion from priesthood"

I will have more to say about the claim that the Fathers had a disdainful conception of women. But let us assume for the moment—purely hypothetically—that it is true. Would, then, an inferiority of women be a logically necessary reason for exclusion from priesthood?

Such a conclusion is extremely questionable. There are priestesses even in places where, as women, they are decidedly disadvantaged.[126] Priestesses were familiar enough in antiquity, particularly, among others, in the mystery religions that had some things in common with Christianity; yet there was by no means necessarily an equality of women with men in the background. The vestal virgins, for instance, were subordinate to the *Pontifex maximus*, who could punish his charges for transgressions.[127] In the Isis cult, there were priestesses, although the higher posts were usually filled by men.[128] We find female philosophers who teach even in places where there is by no means general acceptance of the intellectual equality of women.[129] The Gnostics advocate a philosophy hostile to the body that is, in particular, also directed against women: bearing children is often regarded as the work of Satan.[130] Nevertheless, we find among them women who assume teaching office.[131]

Hence, a low evaluation of women by no means necessarily speaks against female office bearers. On the contrary: among the Gnostics, disdain of the female nature was even a condition for admission to official duties. On the other hand, a high estimation of women is not at all correlated with priestly office. Among the Teutons, for instance, the

---

[125] This is the tenor of the entire third chapter: Meer, *Priesturtum*, pp. 60–110, esp. 86–90, 107.

[126] For example, in Mexico, Japan and Greece: Bertholet, "Priesturtum", pp. 44f.

[127] "If a vestal was found guilty of having allowed the sacred flame to go out, she was only given a sound thrashing by *Pontifex maximus*." As a consequence of sexual misbehavior, she was buried alive (Dacre Balsdon, *Die Frau in der römischen Antike* [Woman in Roman antiquity], Munich, 1979, p. 265).

[128] Heyob, *Isis*, pp. 88f.

[129] According to Plato's social utopia in the *Republic*, which was known everywhere in antiquity, women should have access to all occupations: "In all things, however, woman is weaker than man" (Plato, *Politeia*, 455E: Thraede, "Freiheit", p. 52).

[130] Cf. p. 405, n. 5 above.

[131] Cf. pp. 405f. above.

religious mantic capacities of the female sex were held in high regard, but women seem to have been official priestesses only in exceptional cases.[132]

Nevertheless, I would like to take a position on the theories mentioned above by dealing with two central questions: (1) Was androcentrism or disdain of women a predominant influence at the time of the Church Fathers? (2) Were women regarded as incapable of official leadership duties and of acquiring theological education?

The Church Fathers as "androcentrists" or "woman haters"?[133]

In antiquity, to a large degree, *males* were seen as the measure of being human. Of course, there was certainly also the notion that the two sexes were to be viewed as complementary versions of the one essence, "human being". The "androgynous utopia"[134] shows that not only the male appears as valuable.

A certain androcentric vision can also occasionally be found in the Church Fathers and can become apparent even in their "equality proclamations": "Therefore women, too, as well as men, should practice philosophy, even if men are superior to them and have primacy in all things, except when they have grown soft."[135]

Augustine is even of the opinion: "[I can] not discover what sort of help

[132] Cf. Bertholet, "Priesturtum", p. 49, with F.-X. Arnold, *Mann und Frau*, p. 80.

[133] In the framework of this book, it is nowhere near possible to collate and evaluate the rich variety of statements by the Church Fathers. Instead, I must content myself with some basic remarks and selected examples in "telegram style".

There is still no comprehensive scholarly monograph on the topic "woman in patristic writings". Since the "pluralism of opinion" in the secondary literature is quite large, it is advisable to consult the most important sources directly; cf. on this especially: France Quéré-Jaulmes, *La femme. Les grands textes des Pères de l'Église* (Paris, 1968) (List of sources: pp. 321f.); Wilhelm Schamoni, *Heilige Frauen des Altertums* [Holy women of antiquity] (Düsseldorf, 1963); M. M. Fiasconaro, *Le donne del Vangelo nel pensiero dei Padri e scrittori ecclesiastici* (Palermo, 1965) (Bibliography, pp. 13–20).

From the secondary literature, I would like to call attention particularly to: J. P. Broudéhoux, *Mariage et famille chez Clément d'Alexandrie* (Paris, 1970); Rösler, *Frauenfrage*; Joseph Mausbach, *Altchristliche und moderne Gedanken über Frauenberuf* [Early Christian and modern ideas on female vocation], Apologetische Tagesfragen VI, 4th–7th ed. (Mönchengladbach, 1910); Joseph Mausbach, *Die Ethik des heiligen Augustinus I* [The ethics of Saint Augustine, I], 2nd ed. (Freiburg im Breisgau, 1929), pp. 324f., n. 2 (= Exkurs über die Frau bei Augustinus); Borresen, *Subordination*; Borresen, "Grundlagen"; D. S. Bailey, *Mann und Frau im christlichen Denken* [Man and woman in Christian thought] (Stuttgart, 1963); Tavard, *Woman*; Theophora Schneider, "Das Bild der Frau in der Väterzeit" [The image of woman in the patristic period], in *Gloria Dei* 8 (1953): 193–212.

[134] Cf. pp. 158–60 above.

[135] Clement of Alexandria, *Stromata* IV, 62, 4; GCS 15, p. 277.

to man it might be that woman was created for, if one leaves aside childbearing."[136]

Statements of this sort are not, of course, put forward as "contents of Faith". Alternative judgments are also found,[137] for instance:

> It is a mark of Divine Providence and wisdom that one [sex] is able to undertake great things, yet is incapable of smaller things, so that the function of women is necessary. For, if God had made man capable of fulfilling both sorts of function, then the female sex would be contemptible. . . . Thus, he did not give the two functions to one sex alone, in order to avoid humiliation of the other as useless, but also not to both sexes equally, in order that men and women might not—being placed on the same level—compete and quarrel.[138]

The Christian equality of women with men with respect to marital fidelity was, in antiquity, a true revolution. Through the virginal life, woman is accorded an independent worth that was unknown, in this form, to paganism and Judaism.[139] Virginity and martyrdom are regarded by Christianity as the preeminent embodiments of holiness. Therefore, there is no assumption that women are morally inferior, as is evident simply from the veneration of numerous female saints. "In virtue, women are often enough the instructors of men; while the latter wander about like jackdaws in dust and smoke, the former soar like eagles into higher spheres."[140]

"Hostility to marriage"[141] or contempt for the body are characteristic of the Gnostics but not of the Catholic Church, which resisted tendencies of that kind. To even such a rigorist as Tertullian, physical beauty appears "not exclusively as a danger, but as an estimable gift from God, as an image of inner beauty".[142]

Already in nineteenth-century liberal anti-Church polemics, Tertullian

---

[136] Augustine, De Genesi ad litteram IX, 3: PL 34, p. 395.

[137] In part, among the same Church Fathers; cf. for instance Clement of Alexandria, Stromata IV, 60, 1: BKV, 2nd series, 19, 46; GCS 15, p. 275.

[138] John Chrysostom, Homilia quales ducendae sint uxores: Montfaucon (ed.): PG 57, pp. 230ff.

[139] Cf. pp. 303f. above.

[140] John Chrysostom, In epistulam ad Ephesios, hom. 13, 4: Mausbach, p. 29; PG 62, p. 99.

[141] Non-Catholic scholars often equate the higher evaluation of celibacy with a contempt for marriage; this is already countered by DS 1810. Bailey, for instance, describes preference for the celibate life as "asceticism" and detects this—rightly—already in Paul (Bailey, Mann und Frau, p. 20). Since a relevant statement by Jesus—Matthew 19:12—is also known to have come down to us, Bailey finds himself forced into a rather divided assertion: "Jesus' teaching on marriage, however, is almost completely free of asceticism" (Bailey, Mann und Frau, p. 18; my emphasis).

[142] Mausbach, Frauenberuf, p. 9; cf. Tertullian, De cultu feminarum II, 2, 6: CCL 1, p. 355.

served as a showpiece for illustration of the "Church Fathers' contempt for women".[143] The quote most frequently used has always been the opening of the book on the "Adornment of Women", where we read:

> And you do not want to hear that you are an Eve? The sentence that God hung over your sex still lives on in the world; hence, your guilt must still live on as well. It was you who let the devil in. . . , it was also you who misled the one whom the devil could not come near. . . . Because of your guilt . . . the Son of God also had to die, and yet it still occurs to you . . . to adorn yourselves?[144]

In citing Tertullian, the following has to be taken into account:

— The excessive zeal against female adornment is part of an ethical rigorism that ultimately led Tertullian out of the "lax" Catholic Church and into Montanism.

— Regarding the African lawyer, "[we] must not forget how often he lets rhetoric run away from him".[145]

The latter point forbids any isolating of the just-cited quote such as occurs in more recent presentations. The relevant writing has two parts. The first book censures female love of finery. But in the second Tertullian seems "to regret this impetuosity; he tries to placate the insulted women, referring to them as his collaborators in service and sisters,[146] holy women, blessed ones, priestesses of modesty, daughters of wisdom; physical beauty appears . . . as an image of inner beauty".[147]

What applies in the case of Tertullian holds similarly true of Jerome, who is next in frequency as an object of relevant attacks,[148] although this Church Father contributed more than any other to the high standing and education of women.[149]

The most comprehensive statements about women, which also exerted particular influence on the Western Church,[150] are found in the writings

---

[143] About which Joseph Mausbach was already content to remark: "The Church Fathers' 'contempt for women' has almost become part of the stock contents of modern cultural history and polemics. Usually, however, the familiarity with the Fathers' writings is in inverse proportion to the certainty and indignation with which one sits in judgment over them" (Mausbach, *Frauenberuf*, p. 6).

[144] Tertullian, *De cultu feminarum* I, 1, 1–2; CCL 1, p. 343.

[145] Mausbach, *Frauenberuf*, p. 8.

[146] Even immediately prior to the "gates-of-the-devil citation", the address is worded: "*sorores dilectissimae*" (Tertullian, *De cultu feminarum* I, i, i: CCL 1, p. 343).

[147] Mausbach, *Frauenberuf*, p. 9; cf. Tertullian, *De cultu feminarum* II, 2: CCL 1, pp. 352ff.

[148] Again, cf. on this already Mausbach, *Frauenberuf*, p. 10.

[149] Cf. pp. 433f. below.

[150] Cf. Tavard, *Woman*, p. 102; M.-L. Portmann, *Die Darstellung der Frau in der Geschichtsschreibung des früheren Mittelalters* [The representation of woman in the historical writing of the earlier Middle Ages], Basler Beiträge zur Geschichtswissenschaft 69 (Basel and Stuttgart, 1958), p. 15.

of Ambrose, who stresses, among other things, that what God had made was called "very good" only *after* the creation of woman.[151] "Without woman, then, man receives no praise; it is in woman that he is praised!"[152]

Like Tertullian, Irenaeus and Justin[153] before him, he observes: "Just as sin began with woman, so, too, the good had its beginning with a woman."[154]

The *patristic typology of the sexes* seems to be determined by two basic analogies:

1. The feminine is seen as the weaker, closely bound up with the senses, while the masculine appears, by contrast, as the bearer of effective spiritual and moral force. Gerontius, for instance, writes in the "Life of Saint Melania": "Who would be capable of graphically describing the masculinely robust moral life of this saint?"[155]

Origen allegorizes Exodus 33:17[156] in the following way: "Our behavior is either masculine or feminine." Now, since the feminine is explained on analogy with the bodily or the (in the Bible negatively qualified) "fleshly", it then follows: "What appears before the eyes of the Creator is masculine, not feminine. For God does not deign to look at the feminine and fleshly."[157]

This allegorization may be traced back in part to Origen's spiritualism, which undervalues bodily things.[158] In my opinion, however, to infer a contempt for women from this exegesis[159] is to take things too far. For Origen recognizes yet another sort of typology:

2. The feminine appears as the exemplary realization of man's relation to God. In particular, the soul and the Church are represented in terms of feminine symbolism.

Origen shares the responsibility for this development to a special degree. His interpretation of the Song of Songs,[160] which encompasses ten

---

[151] Cf. Gen 1.

[152] Cf. Ambrose, *De paradiso* 18, 22: PL 14, pp. 314f.

[153] Cf. p. 300 above.

[154] Ambrose, *In Lucam* II, 28: PL 15, p. 1643.

[155] Gerontius, *Vita sanctae Melaniae, praefatio*; *Vie de Sainte Melanie. Texte grec, introduction, traduction et notes par Dr. Denys Gorce*, Sources chrétiennes 90 (Paris, 1962), p. 126.

[156] "Three times in the year shall all your males appear before the Lord God, the God of Israel."

[157] Origen, *Selecta in Exodum*: PG 12, p. 296.

[158] Specific theses within the Origenist intellectual position were condemned by the Church in the sixth century: DS 403ff., esp. 407. Augustine rejects Origen's typology but uses a similar one, in which he "sees woman in terms of practical reason, oriented toward the temporal, and man in terms of speculative reason, oriented toward the eternal" (Mausbach, *Augustinus I*, p. 324, n. 2).

[159] Like, obviously, Meer, *Priesturtum*, p. 81.

[160] Cf. on this pp. 255, 304 above.

volumes and twenty thousand lines, presents the relation "bridegroom-bride" to us in a threefold aspect: Yahweh-Israel, *Christ-Church*, Word of God–soul.[161]

Jerome preserved for us two small parts of this work, about which he writes in his foreword to Pope Damasus I: "If Origen rises above everyone else with his other books, too, then with the Song of Songs [commentary] he has outdone even himself."[162]

The work was not intended for a scholarly or mystical "ivory tower": "Origen compiled them [the sermons] in everyday language for the 'children' who still partake of 'mother's milk'."[163] The feminine symbolism for Church does not lead to a split between empirical and metaempirical femininity,[164] but rather, the symbol also exerts its power in concrete, everyday life: husbands are enjoined to love their wives, as Christ loved the Church.[165]

Already in the early Christian period, "virginality", "brideliness" and "motherliness" of the Church appear as living symbols that are deeply rooted in religious consciousness. To an increasing extent the Church becomes, as it were, personally polarized through the figure of Mary, whose degree of esteem reaches a particular culminating point in the High Middle Ages.[166] Virgin, bride and mother are repeatedly seen together with the Church in one and the same perspective, as, for instance, by Augustine: "You saw, my God . . . , with what fervor . . . I . . . longed . . . for baptism from the pious love of my mother and of the mother of us all, your Church."[167]

The Gnostics and Marcionites, with their hostility to the body, do not seem to have shown very much sympathy for the motherliness, or even the brideliness, of the Church. While the Gnostics associated the entire symbolism of the sexes with the divine realm, the Marcionites regarded especially the marriage metaphor as a sexualization of the relation to God. An Old Syrian writing from the third century takes a stand against this: for the heretics, the relation bride-bridegroom is an impure one, "but our

---

[161] On the latter relation, cf. p. 304 above. In this connection, Ambrose gave the following formulation to masculine and feminine symbolism: *in relation to the body*, the soul is *"masculine"*, but *in relation to God*, *"feminine"*; cf. Tavard, *Woman*, p. 105.

[162] Origène, *Homélies sur le Cantique des Cantiques. Introduction, traduction et notes de Dom O. Rousseau*, Sources chrétiennes 37 (Paris, p. 58).

[163] Origène, *Homélies*.

[164] This is a frequent accusation, as, for instance, in R. R. Ruether, "Misogynism and Virginal Feminism in the Fathers of the Church": Ruether, *Sexism*, p. 179. Cf. on this pp. 460f. below.

[165] Origène, *Homélies*, p. 80; cf. Eph 5:25.

[166] Cf. p. 462 below. On the "motherliness" of the Church, see pp. 321–22 above.

[167] Augustine, *Confessiones* I, 11, in Augustine: PL 32, p. 669.

Lord drew a comparison between his path and that imagery, for John says, 'He who has the bride is the bridegroom.' "

Ephesians 5:25ff. is then cited as a central passage, and the Old Testament preparation of the way by the prophets (Isaiah, Jeremiah, Ezekiel) is reviewed at length. The résumé, then, is: "According to these words of the prophets, our new Scripture (= New Testament) has confirmed that the Church really is comparable to a bride, and Christ, to a bridegroom."[168]

Subordination and deficient education as justifications for exclusion from the priesthood?

Against the backdrop just outlined, it would seem to be idle to speak of a "hostility to women" in the Fathers. But the second question still remains: Were the women of the early Church (as opposed to the modern) perhaps still not ready to assume an office like that of priesthood?

The argument based on subordination of women plays an important role in the patristic expositions. This subordination was more strongly developed than it is today, so that, for instance, Jerome (like Paul) regards it as unnatural for women to speak at a gathering of men.[169] The religious-clerical and the secular realms were not, however, placed on the same level here, for the Church Fathers were aware that women could also be suitable for leadership tasks in the profane sphere.

Although Roman law excluded women from public office,[170] actual practice, particularly in the Imperial Age, was much more liberal.[171] Secular law, therefore, especially during the early period of Christianity, enters into the picture as only a secondary influence at best. Furthermore, its exceptions went so far that women could be empresses, ruling the entire Roman Empire.[172] Mammaea, for instance, the mother of Alexander

---

[168] Joseph Schäfers, *Eine altsyrische antimarkionitische Erklärung von Parabeln des Herrn und zwei andere altsyrische Abhandlungen zu Texten des Evangeliums. Mit Beiträgen zu Tatians Diatessaron und Marcions Neuem Testament* [An early Syrian anti-Marcionite explanation of parables of the Lord and two other early Syrian treatises on texts of the Gospel. With contributions on Tatian's Diatessaron and Marcion's New Testament], Ntl. Abhandlungen VI, 1–2 (Münster, 1917), pp. 60, 64. Marcion had rejected any symbolic comparison; therefore the Catholic opponent explains at length the parables of Jesus from the Gospel according to Luke that Marcion had not accounted for (Schäfers, *Parabeln*, pp. 200f.). Marcion had not, to be sure, been fully consistent in terms of his thesis; cf. Blackman, *Marcion*, p. 1.

[169] Jerome, *In epistolam I ad Corinthios* XIV: PL 30, p. 762.

[170] Raming, *Ausschluss*, p. 67.

[171] Cf. pp. 340ff. above.

[172] 200–235 A.D.: cf. Balsdon, *Frau*, p. 174; Theodor Birt, *Frauen der Antike* [Women of antiquity] (Leipzig, 1932), p. 208.

Severus, was "energetic, decisive and boundlessly diligent, calculating and managerial as an important financier and head of all offices, who could easily have run a major department store with a hundred branches or a dozen oil combines".[173]

In the Christian ruling houses, this political influence was not diminished, and was especially well known in the eastern Roman Empire. The empresses Irene and Theodora ruled alone for a long period and played a crucial role in the iconoclastic controversy. Ambrose is able to encourage independent action among the widows by referring to the example of Deborah: "A widow leads peoples, commands armies, appoints generals, makes campaign plans, holds victory celebrations." "You need no support . . . for the house, for you could climb even the summit of public power."[174]

"The disdain for Negroes because of their cultural backwardness and deficient education" is, for Ida Raming, "a classical parallel case" to that of undervaluation of women.[175] This was also supposedly the reason for refusal of priesthood to women. For education, as we know, is the prerequisite for official teaching.

However, theologically educated—indeed, even highly educated—women were well known to the Church Fathers. Such women also received recognition and encouragement from them. Origen's lectures in Alexandria, for instance, were particularly well attended by women. It was there that Clement had encouraged women to pursue philosophy in the same way that men do,[176] by which he meant the *true* philosophy, namely, the teachings of Christianity.[177] Gerontius (fourth century) praised the life of Saint Melania: "At Constantinople, from early in the morning until late at night", she "instructed those who came to her in the divine sciences, 'because she bore in her heart the Holy Pneuma', and thus she was able to benefit all her visitors by her 'God-inspired teaching' ".[178]

Gregory of Nyssa received his basic religious instruction from his sister, Macrina, to whom he remained grateful for this throughout his life. We have from him the deeply probing "Conversations with Macrina on the Soul and Resurrection".[179] At that period, a circle of cultured women

[173] Birt, *Frauen*, p. 213. Mammaea had also occupied herself with Origen's theological lectures and was well known to him (Balsdon, *Frau*, p. 182).

[174] Ambrose, *De viduis* 44, 52: PL 16, pp. 248, 250.

[175] Raming, *Ausschluss*, p. 61, n. 255.

[176] Cf. p. 427 above.

[177] At that time, the expression "theology" was still avoided so as not to arouse any associations with the myths of polytheism.

[178] Gerontius, *Vita sanctae Melaniae*, paraphrased from T. Schneider, "Frau", p. 208; cf. Melanie.

[179] Cf. on this Altaner and Stuiber, *Patrologie*, p. 304.

who had gathered around Theodosia, the sister of the bishop of Iconia, rose to prominence. Chrysostom had close ties to this group, as is evidenced by his various letters to the women.[180] Gregory of Nazianzus composed a eulogy to Olympias, a highly educated and holy woman from this circle who was active as a deaconess.[181]

Most of all, it is the group of women around Jerome that comes to notice here. As the most important interpreter of his time, this Church Father dedicated his voluminous biblical commentaries to educated women, and these books were also read (and understood) by those women. He even conducted proper study courses on the Bible for women and taught them the Hebrew language. Regarding the education of a girl, he recommends: "The daughter should always have the works of Cyprian in her hands, and she may read without fear the works of Athanasius and Hilary."[182]

Marcella, who took a public stand against the Origenists in Rome, proved significant for the history of the Church: "As soon as she . . . noticed how the Faith praised by the mouths of the apostles suffered shipwreck among so many, with even priests and several monks . . . endorsing the heretical doctrine, and how the good-naturedness of the Pope was continually . . . mocked, she protested publicly; for she had a mind to please God rather than men." Along with Marcella, other theologically educated women took part in the controversy, and not without success: "She was the first inducement to condemnation of the heretics."[183]

The educated women around Jerome were not an isolated exception but already had many companions in their own day. Jerome's pedagogical concepts became *the* model, especially for the education of women in convents during the Middle Ages;[184] the Fathers did not suppress—like Rabbinism and later Islam—the intellectual and spiritual capacities of women but rather encouraged them in a variety of ways.

In any case, it is fairly questionable to present women's lack of education or their subordination in the profane sphere as the *decisive* factors that led to their being excluded from the priesthood. These things were certainly involved in a secondary way, but they alone cannot account for the fact that the ban on ordination of women was found generally and everywhere throughout the period of the Church Fathers.

---

[180] Tavard, *Woman*, p. 89.

[181] Tavard, *Woman*, p. 90.

[182] Jerome, *Epistula* 107, 12: CSEL 55, p. 303.

[183] Jerome, *Epistula* 127, 9–10: CSEL 56, pp. 152f.; cf. A. E. Finkley, *Women in the Roman Aristocracy as Christian Monastics* (Ann Arbor, 1987).

[184] Heinrich Finke, *Die Frau im Mittelalter* [Woman in the Middle Ages] (Kempten and Munich, 1913), pp. 26–29; for more on the Middle Ages, cf. pp. 465–66 below.

The will of Christ as the crucial reference point of the patristic testimony

Neither an androcentric vision nor the subordination or deficient education of women in ancient society can explain the strict exclusion from priestly office. Therefore, Klaus Thraede sees, regarding the early period of the Church (and much more so for today), a "dilemma between official theology and society"[185] and a "contradiction" between the education of women and their allotted duties.[186] Now, he would like to see this contradiction eliminated but must, at the same time, admit that the early Church found itself in a situation similar to that of the modern one. Who is surprised, however, that the Church responds to the same inquiry with the same answer, namely, a yes to the special nature of women and a no to priesthood?

To characterize the Fathers as "simply conservative and more tied to their times than the heretics were" is also not acceptable.[187] The greater tie to their times, as I have shown earlier, was found among the heretics; this means that only the accusation of conservatism (worthless in terms of material content) would remain. Karl Rahner, the teacher of van der Meer, elaborates this charge by referring to Jewish influences: the "structure of a Hellenistic community [was] considerably co-determined . . . by early, Judaic Christianity".[188] Van der Meer himself writes that the Fathers "passed on, almost unthinkingly, certain Old Testament *and rabbinist* conceptions of woman".[189]

Judaism was, in fact, more conservative than its liberal pagan environment. The subordination of women was—with reference to biblical revelation—emphatically stressed, and female rabbis or synagogue wardens are something unknown.

However, Christianity found itself in a different sort of situation, as I have already suggested in connection with Saint Paul.[190] The subordination was also defended through reference to the order of redemption, and the sociological conditions were much more favorable for integration of women into the office of presiding than they were in Judaism. While the Jewish woman remained restricted to caring for her husband and children, the Christian woman enjoyed the possibility of life as a virgin, which opened up a new sort of community service, primarily that of charity. Widows and virgins, as opposed to already "tied" married women, were

---

[185] Thraede, "Freiheit", p. 142.
[186] Thraede, "Freiheit", p. 146.
[187] Against Meer, *Priesturtum*, p. 73.
[188] K. Rahner, "Priesturtum", p. 298.
[189] Meer, *Priesturtum*, p. 90.
[190] Cf. pp. 347ff., 403 above.

potential priestesses, but that opportunity was expressly closed off.[191] Furthermore, theological education of women was not regarded—as it was by the rabbis—as improper but was approved and encouraged. A relation of mutuality existed, then, not primarily with Judaism *as* Judaism, but mainly with the revelation of the Old Covenant, which was its foundation and was fulfilled in the New Covenant.

The exclusion of women from the priesthood is also no mere defensive reaction to heresy, in the sense, for instance, that everything new introduced by the heretics would have met with rejection on general principle.[192] The Church Fathers did not direct sweeping accusations of heresy at anything and everything but, rather, specified *particular* deviations from the rule of Faith and always rebutted them in detail. In the present connection, especially 1 Corinthians 14 and 1 Timothy 2 were seen as "stalwart" contratheses. Without consciousness of ecclesiastical Tradition, which was regarded as binding, it would have been difficult to condemn the relevant practices of the heretics.

This reference to Scripture and Tradition also explains only the unanimous rejection of female priesthood. For, regarding private expressions of opinion about the virtues and vices of the female sex, van der Meer observes rather pointedly, but with some justification: "No accord about women."[193] If the decisive factor for our question had been that of antipathy or sympathy regarding public activity by women, then we would have met with quite differing sorts of approach in the early Church. At the level of the secular world, there were already, of course, differing conceptions of female activity: "The early Church extended from the first century to the sixth, from Clement of Rome to Gregory the Great, from Ireland to Egypt and from North Africa to the shores of the Black Sea. We have to ask ourselves whether the conception of woman was subject to deviation from one particular epoch or place to another. Simply to say that the early Church had a certain understanding of woman, and that this was why it barred women from entering the priesthood, is at least precipitous." The differing legal spheres alone, with each having its own "level of liberality",[194] are evidence against the "milieu theory".[195]

The exclusion of women from the priesthood is justified mainly through two lines of argumentation:

---

[191] Namely Tertullian and the Didascalia; cf. pp. 407, 413ff. above.

[192] Carolyn Osiek, "The Church Fathers and the Ministry of Women", in Swidler, *Women Priests*, p. 78: "anything connected with the heretical sect must be wrong".

[193] Meer, *Priesturtum*, p. 75.

[194] Roman law, customary law in Egypt, in Asia Minor and so on.

[195] Translated [in the German original of this book] from Gryson, *Ministère*, p. 16.

1. The statements of the apostle *Paul* (1 Corinthians 14, 1 Timothy 2; 1 Corinthians 11).
2. The *behavior of Jesus*, who called no woman to apostolic service although he could also have acted differently.

At the same time, the Pauline passages are drawn on as interpretative of what the Lord had intended. Even if *formal* consciousness of the "command of the Lord" in 1 Corinthians 14:37 was lacking, the appeal to the will of Jesus was *materially* decisive. Only for that reason could the contrary practice of the Gnostics and Montanists be characterized as heresy rather than as just an anthropological blunder.

All other reasons are integrated into, and subordinated to, these two central strands of argumentation. Whether or not androcentric conceptions also found their way into them is unimportant for justification of the thesis "nonordination of women". In earlier times, for instance, people formed notions of heaven that were bound up with the ancient conception of the universe; to my knowledge, however, no modern theologian worth taking seriously has so far hit on the idea that God and heaven do not, therefore, exist. Georg May thus passes the following pertinent judgment on Ida Raming's argumentation: "She nowhere conclusively shows that a conventional view of woman or inadequate justification of a norm barring women from the priesthood engendered the norm itself. Everywhere, rather, precisely the reverse state of affairs presents itself: Those involved knew themselves to be bound by the word and example of the Lord, and searched, as well, for a justification. This was drawn from varied sources, including, among others, contemporary views and attitudes."[196]

In addition, as I see it, there is also the significance of the symbolism of the sexes, which has its ground in Jesus' activity. The Church is viewed, very concretely, through the symbols of "virgin", "bride" and "mother", thus being understood as "feminine" and, conjointly, the ideal model of woman. In turn, the Church more and more appears as prefigured in Mary, who is ultimately regarded by an Ambrose as *typus Ecclesiae*.[197] Epiphanius was the first to have expressly justified exclusion of women from the priesthood by using the example of Mary. Now, since Christ and the Church (or Mary) are the "crystallization points" around which the life of the early Christians moved, the symbolism of the sexes certainly entered, in a subsurface but still significant way, into our question. To my

---

[196] Georg May, "Priesturtum der Frau? Kritische Erwägungen zu einem jüngst erschienenen Buch" [Priesthood for women? Critical reflections on a recently published book], in *TThZ* 83 (1974): 181.

[197] Cf. on this Schmaus, *KD V*, p. 306; Philips, "Marie", p. 375.

knowledge, this complex of ideas had still not been explicitly articulated at that time, but, as we know, symbolic structures reach far deeper than "surface ratio". As various parallel examples show,[198] many idea complexes can be implicitly contained in sacred Tradition that are not brought to the light of explicit formulation until a later stage in the development of reflective thought: "When the Spirit of truth comes, he will guide you into all the truth."[199]

4. EXCURSUS: WOMAN AS A MINISTER OF BAPTISM

We also encounter the historical unfolding of sacred truth in the context of the question of administration of baptism. The Church Fathers often condemn baptism by a woman just as strictly, and sometimes even more emphatically, than official teaching. Whether they had sanctioned such baptism for urgent cases remains unclear. Only since the early Middle Ages has there arisen general conviction that baptism by a woman is valid.[200] Might there be, therefore, a similar development regarding the question of the validity of ordination of women to the priesthood?

It is necessary to note first here that baptism and ordination to priesthood differ in relative positional value. Baptism alone is absolutely necessary for the supernatural salvation of the individual, whereas the exclusive duties of a priest strengthen the life of grace (Eucharist) or restore it (sacrament of penance). Baptism must also be quickly dispensable even in cases where death may be imminent: hence the widely available element of water[201] and the possibility of administration by laymen and even by the unbaptized.[202] Christ is the actual minister of baptism, while the human baptizer is only the "transmitter".[203]

The symbolic underpinnings of the sacrament are not thereby annulled.

[198] For instance, the dogmatizations of the *Immaculata Conceptio* or the *Assumptio Mariae*.

[199] Jn 16:13.

[200] A first express affirmation of this thesis—always with a view to baptism in urgent cases—can be found in Isidore of Seville (cf. Raming, *Ausschluss*, p. 29, n. 117); through the statements of Pope Urban II (1094), it became a component of theology and canon law (Raming, *Ausschluss*, p. 25; cf. also Johann Auer, *Die Sakramente der Kirche* [The sacraments of the Church], KKD VII [Regensburg, 1972], p. 72).

[201] STh III q 67 a 3.

[202] STh III q 67 a 3 a 5.

[203] "In generatione spirituali neuter operatur in virtute propria, sed instrumentaliter tantum per virtutem Christi" (STh III q 67 a 4 a 3). "Christus est, qui principaliter baptizat" (STh III q 67 a 4).

In normal cases, therefore, a priest, as Christ's official representative, should administer baptism. For that reason, the patristic testimonies against baptism by a woman are also testimonies against female priesthood. If, in urgent cases, a layman must step in to replace a priest (or deacon), then a man is, at least in principle, preferable to a woman, because he symbolizes to a greater degree the special nature of Christ as "head" of the Church.[204] Baptism by a woman should not, therefore, be the rule but an exception. In this connection, Saint Thomas draws a comparison between solemn baptism and official teaching:

> Although it is not permitted for women to teach *publicly* [*publice*], they may nevertheless instruct someone through *private* teaching or admonition. In the same way, it is not permitted that they baptize publicly or *solemnly* [*solemniter*], but notwithstanding that, they may baptize if necessity demands [*in necessitatis articulo*].[205]

The *Doctor Angelicus* does not in every case require of a minister of baptism the symbolic attribute of being the head that he regards as a condition of validity for the receiver (and minister) of ordination.[206] There is no contradiction in this, since ordination is intended only for a limited circle of office bearers, whereas baptism is received by all Christians and forms the basis of their being Christian. Through the sacramental *character indelebilis*, a priest is assimilated to Christ as *head* of the Church in a more intensive way than is a layman.[207] This representation of Christ realizes itself most concentratedly, however, in the Eucharist, the entrance to participation in which is formed by baptism.[208] Thus, administration of baptism requires a "lesser" sort of representation of Christ than does the celebration of the Eucharist, for which, as the central aspect of his service, a priest is ordained.[209] Furthermore, a woman administers baptism only

[204] Cf. STh III q 67 a 4, where Thomas refers to 1 Cor 11:3.

[205] STh III q 67 a 4 a 1. Emphases by me. This statement corresponds to CIC (1917) can. 742 §2: "Si tamen adsit sacerdos, diacono praeferatur, diaconus subdiacono, clericus laico et vir feminae, nisi pudoris gratia deceat feminam potius quam virum baptizare, vel nisi femina noverit melius formam et modum baptizandi." The distinction between "solemn baptism" (that is, official ecclesiastical) and "urgent baptism" already occurs materially in Tertullian (cf. Auer, *Sakramente*, pp. 68f.).

[206] Cf. pp. 447f. below.

[207] Cf. pp. 336f. above and pp. 447–54 below.

[208] Cf. STh III q 67 a 2.

[209] "This . . . is the outstanding and unique thing about it (the Holy Eucharist): that the remaining sacraments possess their sanctifying power only if they are employed, but in the Eucharist the originator of sanctity is present before it is employed" (Council of Trent, Doctrinal Decree on the Holy Eucharist, Chap. 5: cf. DS 1639). The special intensity of the representation of Christ is therefore already manifest in the words of consecration at the sacrifice of the Mass, which serve to ground not only a mediation of grace but also a

in urgent cases, whereas the service of a priest is *officially* regulated. Finally, from the special necessity of baptism for redemption, as mentioned above, it follows that baptism must, in cases of emergency, be administrable by anyone.[210]

5. EXCURSUS ON DEACONESSES

The problem of deaconesses does not, as such, fall within the scope of this book.[211] Since, however, more recent debate often aims at the office of female deacon as a step toward the priesthood,[212] some concise comments of a basic sort may be allowed here.[213]

A female office with the title "deacon" or "deaconess" as *terminus technicus* is documented only since the third century. The three relevant records prior to the Syrian Didascalia[214] more likely refer to services of a welfare-diaconal nature than to a permanent office with the title of deacon.

---

transubstantiation of the eucharistic elements: "This is *my* Body." "This is *my* Blood"; on this, see STh III q 78 a 1.

[210] DS 802.

[211] Cf. p. 25 above.

[212] Cf. p. 62 above.

[213] Precisely here, an exact assessment of the historical evidence is indispensable to any debate in the area of systematic theology. The most thorough works are those of Kalsbach, *Diakonissen* (summarized in Kalsbach, "Diakonisse") and Gryson, *Ministère*. Regarded as a specialist for relevant questions in the area of the Eastern Church is Evangelos Theodorou, who gives a résumé in: Evangelos Theodorou, "Das Amt der Diakoninnen in der kirchlichen Tradition" [The office of female deacon in Church Tradition], in *US* 33 (1978): 162–72. The work begun by Theodorou is taken further by, in particular, Cipriano Vagaggini, "L'ordinazione delle diaconesse nella tradizione greca e bizantina", in *Orientalia Christiana Periodica* 40 (1974): 145–89.

Extensive references to relevant literature are given by Gryson and Vagganini. A continuing source of information about questions of the female diaconate is the *Zeitschrift des Internationalen Diakonatszentrum* (IDZ), *Diakonia XP*. Informative about directions of the current debate is, for instance, Ilse Schüllner, "Überblick und Perspektiven. Zum Stand der Entwicklung des Diakonats der Frau" [Survey and perspectives. On the state of developments regarding the female diaconate], *Diakonia XP* 13 (1978): 23–40. The best monograph is certainly A.-G. Martimort, *Deaconesses: An Historical Study* (San Francisco: Ignatius Press, 1986).

The three verdicts by the Würzburg Synod on the "female diaconate" (Peter Hünermann, Herbert Vorgrimler, Yves Congar) are reproduced in: *Amtliche Mitteilungen der Gesamten Synode der Bistümer in der BRD* 7 (1973): 23–28; for a summary and critical discussion, see Bardo Weiss, "Zum Diakonat der Frau" [On the female diaconate], in *TThZ* 84 (1975): 14–27.

[214] Rom 16:1; the "women" in 1 Tim 3:11; the "ministrae" in Pliny: cf. Gryson, *Ministère*, pp. 22, 30f., 39; Kalsbach, *Diakonissen*, pp. 9ff.

The letters of Ignatius and Polycarp, which reflect the situation of the communities founded by Paul around the year 100, give no evidence of female deacons but seem to concede a special role to the group of widows.[215] In Egypt, especially during the fourth century, we know that some of the widows engaged in specific duties of service, but there is no record of a female "deacon".[216] In the Latin West, "deaconesses" were not known until after the fourth century, as an innovation from the East that never quite gained full acceptance.[217]

An institutionalized female office that would correspond to the male diaconate was only anticipated in a preparatory way, as a station in life, by the group of widows, and it was not introduced until the third century, when the growing communities needed a proper office for female services that had previously been carried out in a more "familiar" way.[218] In the Syrian Didascalia (middle of the third century), which mentions the female deacon for the first time (ἡ διάκονος), this office is seen as an innovation that requires separate justification.[219] The introduction of female deacons is presented as a recommendation, not as a strict order. As opposed to the male deacon, the "right hand" of the bishop, the female pendant has duties that are essentially limited to two things:

1. Anointing of the female body before baptism, which could hardly be done by men for reasons of decency. Anointing of the head and baptism itself could be performed only by a bishop or a priest, or possibly also, a (male) deacon.

2. Care of sick women and visits to female living quarters.[220] The female diaconate is thus tied to baptism of adults and to the strong separation between the worlds of male and female in the Orient. Since more liberal circumstances prevailed in the West, the office of deaconess could be dispensed with there. The appearance of deaconesses thus presupposes patriarchal conditions; their disappearance is not evidence of patriarchalism but more probably of its opposite.[221]

The Apostolic Constitutions (end of the fourth century), which develop the lines laid down in the Didascalia, preserve for us a consecrational prayer for "deaconesses",[222] which comes immediately after the prayer

[215] Gryson, *Ministère*, pp. 34–38; Kalsbach, *Diakonissen*, pp. 16–19.

[216] Gryson, *Ministère*, pp. 61f., 85.

[217] Gryson, *Ministère*, p. 151.

[218] Kalsbach, *Diakonissen*, pp. 104f.

[219] Gryson, *Ministère*, pp. 75ff., 173; Martimort, *Deaconesses*, pp. 35–45.

[220] *Didaskalia* III, 12, 7; 13, 1, in F. X. Funk, *Didascalia I*, 208, 8; 214, 3.

[221] Against Küng, *Thesen*, p. 131, according to which the female diaconate "was first abolished in the Western Church and then disappeared from the Eastern Church".

[222] διακόνισσα. This title crops up here for the first time after the Can. 19 of the Council of Nicaea: Gryson, *Ministère*, pp. 77, 104.

for deacons. The two prayers, to be sure, are different in content; cited as exemplary models for deaconesses are the Old Testament prophetesses, Mary the Mother of God, and the women who served at the entrance to the tent of meeting.[223] The male and female diaconates are expressly distinguished: "A deaconess does not bless and performs none of the duties carried out by a priest or a deacon; she is only a doorkeeper and assists the priests in administering baptism for the sake of decency."[224]

The Council of Nicaea (325) expressly describes the deaconesses as laity,[225] whereas Chalcedon (431) later numbers them among the clergy. As probably already in the Apostolic Constitutions, there followed consecration with laying on of hands (χειροτονία) and prayer.[226] Equal inclusion among Church officers ensued under Justinian (535). If the individual levels of consecration are named, then deaconesses come after deacons; if, however, Justinian makes use of the collective term "cleric", then he regularly gives additional special mention to deaconesses, which indicates their special position.[227] Epiphanius (end of the fourth century) had already numbered deaconesses among the "clergy" (τὸ ἐκκλησιαστικὸν τάγμα),[228] but he explicitly sets them apart from the priestly hierarchy (ἡ ἱερωσύνη), which extends from bishop down to subdeacon.[229]

The Byzantine consecration of deaconesses has "morphological parity with the cheirotonies of the higher clergy" and is integrated into the ritual of the Mass.[230] A deaconess receives, as does a deacon, the stola but puts it on underneath the veil. During the consecration the chalice is handed to her, but she receives no authorization to distribute its contents. Preaching, baptizing and any performance of priestly duties are most strictly forbidden her.[231]

The most extensive duties known for deaconesses are those allotted to diaconal abbesses among the Syrian Monophysites of the fifth century. If no male clergyman is present, these nuns are allowed to distribute Communion to their sisters as well as children up to the age of four and to read the Epistle and Gospel at divine services attended solely by females.

---

[223] Ex 38:8; 1 Sam 2:22. The deaconesses were responsible for showing women to their places in the church: Constitutiones Apostolorum VIII, 20, 1–2, in F. X. Funk, Didascalia II, 524, 13–23.

[224] Constitutiones Apostolorum VIII, 28, 6, in F. X. Funk, Didascalia II, 530, 22–25.

[225] Martimort, Deaconesses, pp. 101–4.

[226] Can. 15: Gryson, Ministère, p. 109; Martimort, Deaconesses, p. 108.

[227] Kalsbach, Diakonissen, p. 67; Gryson, Ministère, p. 123; Martimort, Deaconesses, p. 110.

[228] Numbered among these, if one so desires, are all "employees of the Church" down to doorkeeper and gravedigger.

[229] Gryson, Ministère, p. 134; Martimort, Deaconesses, pp. 112f.

[230] Theodorou, "Diakoninnen", pp. 167f.; Martimort, Deaconesses, pp. 148–56.

[231] Theodorou, "Diakoninnen", p. 169.

However: "Again and again we observe an anxious carefulness on the part of the lawgivers to keep the deaconesses away from the altar", at which only a male deacon is suitable to serve.[232]

The possibility of dispensing Communion is granted also by the Monophysite *Testamentum* (fifth century), but only in a narrowly restricted, exceptional sort of case: during the Easter period for pregnant women who are not able to attend church.[233]

Thus, it is most highly negligent when Haye van der Meer writes, without further comment, as follows on deaconesses: "Much [was] permitted them: reading the Epistle and Gospel, placing incense, distributing Communion, wearing the stola."[234] Rather, there was always a clear line of separation drawn between the male and the female diaconates;[235] in particular, deaconesses were always kept away from preaching, distributing Communion and serving at the altar. The reason for this probably lies in the fact that the just-mentioned male diaconal tasks are oriented toward priestly office, but those of a deaconess are not.[236] From the beginning, there was present in the Church "a sensitive feeling for the fact . . . that the special nature of woman, in its best and highest capacity, does not fulfill itself in the pulpit before the community, on the speaker's platform at national assemblies but, for one part, in the work and duties of the home, and then in the service of loving care in the community".[237]

For both deacons and deaconesses, consecration is performed through laying on of hands and prayer, but the respective prayers are always clearly distinguished. In its explicit form, the distinction between sacramental and sacrament may well have originated with Scholasticism, but if we consider the embryonic stage of the relevant material content, then ordination of deaconesses does not seem to point in the direction of sacrament. In summarizing the results of a liturgical conference, Andreas Heinz is thus right when he observes: "There was agreement that . . . no firm basis . . . for a . . . female diaconate" can be "derived" "from history".[238] Martimort says even about the Byzantine deaconess:

> However solemn may have been the ritual by which she was initiated into her ministry, however much it may have resembled the ritual for the

[232] Kalsbach, *Diakonissen*, p. 58.
[233] Gryson, *Ministère*, p. 119.; Martimort, *Deaconesses*, pp. 138–43.
[234] Meer, *Priesturtum*, p. 109.
[235] Kalsbach, *Diakonissen*, p. 109.
[236] Galot, *Mission*, p. 61: the orders of deaconesses and widows "are profoundly different from what they are in the masculine hierarchy. They are not aligned with the sacerdotal ministry."
[237] Kalsbach, *Diakonissen*, p. 97.
[238] Heinz, "Liturgischen Dienste", p. 130.

ordination of a deacon, the conclusion nevertheless must be that a deaconess in the Byzantine rite was in no wise a female deacon. She exercised a totally different ministry from that of the deacons.[239]

To reinstate the diaconate of the early Church would be an anachronism (visits to female living quarters and assistance at baptism . . .).[240] On the other hand, to establish a female diaconate equivalent to the male diaconate would be a step in the direction of priesthood for women. *If* a female diaconate should be created, then these two fundamental difficulties would require consideration.

---

[239] Martimort, *Deaconesses*, p. 156.

[240] Also instructive are the developments in the Anglican church, where the office of deaconess, which was introduced in 1920, has encountered certain difficulties. Cf. on this, already in 1939, Paula Schäfer, "Das Diakonissenamt in der anglikanischen Kirche" [The office of deaconess in the Anglican church], in *Eine heilige Kirche* 21 (1939): 79.

CHAPTER SEVEN

The Middle Ages

1. PREFATORY NOTE

Like no other period in Church history, the Middle Ages attempted to bring about a synthesis of the spiritual and the worldly, of the order of redemption and the order of creation. The Church was presented with unique opportunities for shaping society according to the teachings of Christ. The historically developed "model" of the Middle Ages can certainly not be thoughtlessly imitated, but in many respects it remains paradigmatic. In particular, the great theologians of the High Middle Ages (Thomas, Bonaventure, Scotus, among others) formulated patterns of argumentation, including some relevant to our question here, whose structures remain guiding standards for "translation" into the present situation. High Scholasticism was, after all, the first thoroughgoing attempt to comprehend the whole of sacred Tradition systematically and to bind it together with natural reason as illumined by faith.

2. THE TESTIMONY OF THE CANONISTS

Initially, the field of canonical studies was concerned with questions relevant to our theme. The starting point for studies in canon law is Gratian's *Decretum*—written around 1140—in which relevant legal regulations that were already in force were compiled. Involved here were bans intended to protect the wider setting of the priesthood[1] and to exclude

---

[1] Cf. pp. 423–25 above. Withheld from women in particular are: the touching of consecrated vessels and cloths as well as altar incense; distribution of Communion to the sick; cf. Raming, *Ausschluss*, pp. 7f.

women from partial aspects of priestly duty, from baptizing and teaching.[2] These regulations had their origin in the Pauline ban on teaching by women,[3] which came down to Gratian by way of the Didascalia, the Apostolic Constitutions, the *Statuta Ecclesiae antiqua* and the pseudo-Isidorean Decretals, and ultimately influenced the relevant canon of the present-day statute book: "Sacram ordinationem valide recipit solus vir baptizatus".[4]

The fact that "falsifications" occur within the chain of Tradition[5] does not affect our topic, since the relevant documents already reflect the legally ordered situation of the Church. The same, or similar, regulations are found in earlier texts that have not been "falsified".[6] Regarding the canonists, it appears quite problematic to allege that a personally colored conception of an inferiority of women was the reason behind the legal norms.[7] What is at issue here, namely, is not the motivation behind a law that has to be newly comprehended but reflection on a norm that already exists and is regarded as binding. Since the lawgiver knows himself "to be bound by higher law, the justification does not give an account of the lawgivers' motives; rather, it sould be seen as an attempt to discover the *ratio* behind a pregiven *lex*. That errors can slip in during the course of such an attempt is self-evident."[8]

In fact, misogynous remarks do occur, in which women are reproached with deficient education and moral "softness",[9] but we also find statements to the contrary that—as distinct from certain private remarks—are of an official nature. Again and again, the text of a "Council of Carthage" is cited,[10] in which the ban on teaching is introduced as follows: "No matter whether a woman is also educated and holy, she is nevertheless not allowed. . . .[11]

The existence of women who are not objects of "misogyny" is thus presupposed.

---

[2] Raming, *Ausschluss*, pp. 7f.

[3] 1 Cor 14; 1 Tim 2.

[4] CIC can. 1024.

[5] As says Raming, *Ausschluss*, pp. 9, 76 and elsewhere, with reference to the pseudo-Isidorean Decretals.

[6] For example, the letter of Gelasius I cited above: cf. p. 423.

[7] But thus runs the argumentation by Raming, *Ausschluss*.

[8] Georg May, "Zu der Frage der Weihefähigkeit der Frau" [On the question of women's capacity for ordination], in *Zeitschrift der Savigny-Stiftung für Rechtsgeschichte* 91 (Kanonistische Abteilung LX) (1974): 387.

[9] Cf. pp. 456f. below.

[10] In fact, it stems from the *Statuta Ecclesiae antiqua* of the priest Gennadius of Marseilles (about 480): Raming, *Ausschluss*, pp. 19f.

[11] Raming, *Ausschluss*, p. 19.

Since the time of Innocent III, every canonist has included his "ban on preaching and hearing confession" for "emancipated" abbesses,[12] which is argued on the basis of the position of Mary: "No matter whether the most blessed Virgin Mary stands higher, and is also more illustrious, than all the apostles together, it was still not to her, but to them, that the Lord entrusted the keys to the Kingdom of heaven."[13]

It is significant that all the canonists who occupy themselves with the question of the validity of the sacrament of orders regard any ordination of women[14] as ineffective. This thesis would not seem to stem solely from the juridical subordination of women to men, for male slaves—who are subordinated legally in a much stronger way—receive quite readily the *character indelebilis*. Ordination of slaves is illicit yet valid, while ordination of women appears as illicit *and* invalid.

No author is known among the canonists who would have regarded ordination of a woman as valid. Only John the Teuton reports the opinion of "others" who view baptism as the sole condition for validity.[15] These opponents, not identified by name, may have taken early Church attestations about *presbyterae* and *diaconissae* too literally.[16] In any case, their opinion "was not accepted, but was clearly rejected as erroneous".[17]

3. GREAT THEOLOGIANS OF HIGH SCHOLASTICISM

Thomas Aquinas

The Scholastic theologians deal with the question of whether a woman could receive the sacrament of orders from a primarily dogmatic viewpoint. The relevant quaestio crops up almost everywhere in the *Commentaries on the Summa Sententiarum*,[18] although Peter Lombard himself does not mention the topic.[19] Partial aspects of the question are addressed when the

---

[12] Cf. Raming, *Ausschluss*, pp. 121f.

[13] Innocent III, *Decretale Nova quaedam* (1210), in Meer, *Priesturtum*, p. 149.

[14] This applies also for the—in present-day terminology—sacramental diaconate.

[15] Raming, *Ausschluss*, p. 115.

[16] Cf. F. Gillmann, "Weibliche Kleriker nach dem Urteil der Frühscholastik" [Female clerics according to the judgment of early Scholasticism], in *Archiv für katholisches Kirchenrecht* 93 (1913): 251.

[17] May, "Weihefähigkeit", p. 391; against Raming, *Ausschluss*, p. 115.

[18] IV Sent d 25.

[19] G. H. Tavard, "The Scholastic Doctrine", in Swidler, *Women Priests*, p. 100. This link to the structure of the Commentary on the Sentences precludes the assumption that the

ban on official teaching by women or the position of abbess ("power of jurisdiction") are discussed.

The passage that is most important in terms of continuing historical influence is found in Saint Thomas.[20] The question of whether being of the female sex poses an obstacle to receiving the sacrament of orders is first answered affirmatively with two arguments:

1. First Timothy 2:12: "I permit no woman to teach in church or to have authority over men."

Thomas thus cites support from the Pauline ban on teaching, and in so doing brings together 1 Timothy 2 and 1 Corinthians 14.[21]

2. Tonsure is necessary for a cleric but is inappropriate for women, according to 1 Corinthians 11 ("prescription on veils").

This idea, at first sight rather odd from a modern point of view, becomes understandable if we consider its background. First Corinthians 11, namely, speaks of the order of creation, according to which the "head" of a woman is her husband. There is thus an allusion to the subordination of women, the significance of which is then presented in more detail by what follows.

Their subordination is an obstacle for women to valid reception of ordination. This fact results not only from a merely external "juridical" precept (*necessitas praecepti*) but from the special nature of the sacrament itself (*necessitas sacramenti*):[22]

> Since every sacrament is a sign, not only the thing (or grace) [*res*] is necessary to what is undertaken in the sacrament, but also the signification of the thing [*significatio rei*]. Thus, in the case of extreme unction, it is necessary that the recipient be ailing, so that it becomes clear that he is in need of salvation. Now, as an eminence of position [*eminentia gradus*] cannot be signified in the female sex, since the state of subjection [*status subiectionis*]

Scholastics regarded this more as a canonical problem than as a theological one. Certainly the theologians were conscious of the situation in canon law, yet their mode of argument was not primarily "canonical" but—as will be seen shortly—"dogmatic"; against Tavard, "Scholastic Doctrine", p. 99. A balanced treatment of the subject can be found in J. H. Martin, "The Injustice of Not Ordaining Women: A Problem for Medieval Theologians" ThS 48 (1987): 303–16.

[20] IV Sent d 25 q 2 a 1 = STh *Suppl* q 39 a 1. Similar arguments are evident in the treatment of the ban on teaching and baptizing: STh II II q 177 a 2; III q 67 a 4. Important as well is the rejection of jurisdictional "power of the keys" for abbesses: STh Suppl q 19 a 3 ad 4.

[21] The *in Ecclesia* is taken from 1 Corinthians 14; otherwise, this passage can replace 1 Timothy 2: STh Suppl q 19 a 3 ob 4. Regarding the ban on teaching, both passages are in accord: STh II II q 177 a 2.

[22] On the terminology, cf. Diekamp and Jüssen, *Dogmatik III*, pp. 83f.

is inherent in that sex, it cannot, therefore, receive the sacrament of ordination.[23]

Thus, the "subordination" of women and the "authority" of men are not just legal categories but belong, in this context, to the realm of the sacramental. The sex-specific characteristics do not remain in the realm of mere biology but appear as *symbol* bearers and thus form a natural precondition for reception of the sacrament of ordination. The citing of I Corinthians 11 already alludes to this sacramental symbolical relation, as becomes clearer in another passage: "Because . . . the head of a woman is her husband and the head of a man is Christ, as is said in I Corinthians 11, a woman should not, therefore, baptize if enough men are available."[24]

The man's symbolic quality of "being the head" is here related to the sacramental realm. Consequently, there is also no contradiction when Thomas expressly states that, in the worldly sphere [*in temporalibus*], a woman can quite well function as ruler, but not in priestly spiritual matters [*in sacerdotalibus*].[25]

Regarding the nonordination of women, Thomas replies to various objections that are not dissimilar to certain modern ways of arguing:

1. Not only the priest mediates between God and mankind, but also the *prophet*, whose office is even more important. Now, since women have also been prophetesses, why, then, can they not become priestesses?

"Prophecy is not a sacrament, but a gift from God. For that reason, the signification of the thing (grace) is not required, but only the thing itself. And because women do not differ, in respect of the thing, from men in matters concerning the soul—for, regarding the soul, a woman is sometimes better than many men—they can therefore receive the gift of prophecy and other such things, but not the sacrament of ordination."[26]

2. For ordination, an *eminence of position* is required. That is also found, however, in the office of superior, in martyrdom and in membership of religious orders, and women, too, are included in all of these. If there are abbesses and if a Deborah appeared in the Old Testament, why are there no priestesses?

[23] STh Suppl q 39 a 1.
[24] STh III q 67 a 4. Cf. on this pp. 439f. above.
[25] STh Suppl q 39 a 1 ad 2/3. Meer, *Priesturtum*, p. 133, overlooks this sacramental dimension when he accuses Thomas of a contradiction: the Church doctor should also have refused women leadership office in the worldly sphere, for "he does not go on to explain in what . . . the difference between profane and priestly jurisdiction consists."
[26] STh Suppl q 39 a 1 ad 1.

Thomas replies that, in the spiritual area, abbesses are, "as it were", superiors "by delegation", "due to the dangers posed by men and women living together".[27] Deborah, on the other hand, undertook direction only of secular concerns, not priestly ones.[28]

3. In response to the objection that the power of ordination is based in the *soul*, which has *no sexual nature*, Thomas refers to the importance of the physically based quality of "signification" (*significatio*).[29]

Saint Thomas' *symbolism of the sexes* must be understood against a wider background that is closely related to the biblical evidence: in his numerous statements on marriage, the Church Doctor cites no passage as often as Ephesians 5:32:[30] "('For this reason a man shall leave his father and mother and be joined to his wife, and the two shall become one flesh.') This mystery is a profound one, and I am saying that it refers to Christ and the church."

Drawing on an idea of Saint Augustine, Thomas deals with two questions:

1. "Did Christ have to assume a sexual nature?"
2. "Did Christ have to assume his fleshly nature from both sexes?"[31]

Regarding the first point, it is said, among other things, that Christ is the *head* of the Church and that it was therefore appropriate that he become man as a *male*. Galatians 3:28 means that men and women equally are admitted into the mystical Body of the Church but not that the differences between the sexes are annulled.

God's becoming man implies, however, not only a priority of the male but, in another respect, a primacy of the female, for the male was not permitted to contribute anything to the bringing forth of Christ's human

---

[27] In another passage, Thomas says that not the *power of the keys* itself (*potestas clavium*) accrues to women but only a certain participation in that (*aliquis usus clavium*). As justification, the subordination of women is cited (*status subiectionis*), which is grounded in revelation (1 Tim 2) and can also be known by natural reason (Aristotle). Cf. STh Suppl q 19 a 3 ad 4.

[28] STh Suppl q 39 a 1 ad 2/3.

[29] Cf. above. Bonaventure, as we will soon see, speaks even more clearly on this, but wholly in the same sense as does his friend.

[30] G. M. Manser, *Die Frauenfrage nach Thomas von Aquin* [The question of women according to Thomas Aquinas] (Olten, 1919), pp. 13f.

[31] III Sent d 12 q 3 a 1/2: *S. Thomae Aquinatis Opera Omnia I* (Stuttgart and Bad Cannstatt, 1980), pp. 302f.: "Utrum Christus debuerit aliquem sexum accipere" / "Utrum debuerit Christus carnem assumere ab utroque sexu."

nature: "Christ came in order to save both sexes, but he himself became a man. Consequently, he had to assume his fleshly nature from woman."[32]

For Thomas, the nonordination of women is thus ultimately grounded in the Incarnation, even if this relation is not expressly brought out: Christ became man as a male because he represents "being the head" of the Church in a sensibly perceptible way as well; only a male can receive the sacrament of orders because he is "head" of the female. Both of these ideas can be tied to one another through the priestly representation of Christ, which is grounded in its sacramental character and completes itself most fully in the sacrifice of the Mass: "A priest bears the image of Christ, in whose person and power he pronounces the words of consecration."[33]

The pendants to Christology are ecclesiology and Mariology, as Thomas already also intimates: the Annunciation to Mary occurred so that "the existence of, so to speak, a spiritual marriage between the Son of God and human nature might become manifest; and therefore, in the Annunciation, the assent of the Virgin on behalf of the entire human race was expected."[34]

Thomas did not yet apply the above-noted ways of thinking to the question of the ordination of women, but they are a logical consequence of the sacramentally embedded "headship" of the male recipient of ordination to the priesthood. The expression *status subiectionis*,[35] which is usually seen today merely as a negative term of provocation, shows itself in this context to be a *concise formula for basic structures of the orders of creation and redemption*.

Bonaventure

Bonaventure stresses the symbol argument based on the representation of Christ much more clearly than does his friend Thomas.[36] At first, he inquires into the *legal* side of the problem, which is unequivocal: women are prohibited from touching sacred vessels and cloths as well as altar incense; consequently, they *may* not become priests. Then, however, like

[32] Cf. also STh III q 31 a 4 ad 1, where Thomas cites Augustine (*De agone christiano* 11): "Nolite vos ipsos contemnere viri: Filius Dei virum suscepit. Nolite vos ipsas contemnere foeminae: Filius Dei natus ex foemina est."

[33] STh III q 83 a 1 ad 3.

[34] STh III q 30 a 1.

[35] Cf. on this pp. 458, 460 below.

[36] IV Sent d 25 a 2 q 1: *Doctoris Seraphici S. Bonaventurae Opera Omnia IV* (Quaracchi, 1889), pp. 649-51. Unless otherwise indicated, all the following is from this quaestio; emphases are mine.

Thomas, Bonaventure poses the fundamental, *theological* question: *Can women receive ordination as priests?*

After disposing of several misunderstandings about deaconesses and the term *presbytera*, he observes that never in the Church was a woman admitted to sacred orders. "And according to the sounder and wiser opinion of the doctors", this fact is significant not only legally (*de jure*), but in principle (*de facto*): women are incapable of receiving the sacrament of orders.

The reason for this thesis "arises not from institution by the Church, but from the fact that the sacrament of orders is not appropriate for women. In this sacrament, namely, *the person* who is consecrated *signifies Christ as Mediator*; and since the Mediator belonged only to the male sex and can be signified only by the male sex, the capacity for receiving ordination is therefore appropriate only for men, who alone can *represent* [Christ] *by nature* and can bear the sign of the [ordained] character conformably with its reception."

Here, the argumentation derived from Christ's Incarnation is explicitly brought to bear on our question for the first time. "Christ as Mediator" means, at the same time, "Christ as *Head*". The Son of God became man as a *male* for the reason that he is "the Head of the whole Church"; according to Saint Paul, namely, the husband is the "head" of a woman. to have become man as a female would, therefore, have been "a perversion of the order of things" (*perversio ordinis*).[37] Because, however, women are not to be excluded from the work of redemption, God therefore assumed fleshly nature solely from a woman.[38]

Signification of Christ as Mediator implies *representation of Christ as Head*, which becomes clear particularly in the office of leadership. To the objection that Deborah's judicial activity in the Old Testament was a priestly mandate, Bonaventure replies that Deborah had merely a temporal mandate and not a spiritual one.[39] "It is, to be sure, quite permissible for women to govern in the temporal (secular) realm, but not to have *spiritual rule*, which is a *sign* (*signum*). For the one who rules *bears the image of Christ the Head* (*gerit typum capitis Christi*); since, however, a woman cannot be head of a man, she cannot, therefore, be ordained."

This idea is supplemented by additional biblical symbolism. As far as I know, Bonaventure was the first to make explicit use of the image of marriage in connection with our topic: "The remaining ordinations are

[37] III Sent d 12 a 3 q 1: *Bonaventurae* III, p. 269.

[38] III Sent d 12 a 3 q 2: *Bonaventurae* III, pp. 271–73.

[39] On abbesses, the same argumentation is found as in Thomas: they are appointed "because of the danger of living together with men (as abbots); therefore they cannot bind and loose in the proper manner."

preparatory for the office of bishop, if someone has proven himself in them. A *bishop*, however, is the *bridegroom* of the Church. Consequently, a woman cannot attain to the office of bishop, but only a man. Otherwise, he would not be bridegroom of the Church. Thus, only men can be admitted to the preparatory ordinations as well."

The historical source of this image is obviously Ephesians 5, where *Christ* is depicted as "bridegroom" of the Church. If a bishop is "bridegroom", too, then it is as the *representative* of Christ.

Priestly symbolization of the "head" of the Church is grounded in the order of creation. There, the man takes on a task of ruling that allows him to appear, in a special way, as "image of God" (*imago Dei*). This idea had already been explained earlier: "The difference between the sexes results, of course, from the body, and, on the basis of sexual differentiation, the representation of ruling or of originating is greater [in men] because man is the head of woman. . . . In *this* respect, the likeness of God is present in a higher way in the masculine sex than in the feminine. This refers not to the *being* of the likeness, but to something additional to that."[40]

The primacy of men regarding the *representation* of God in his sovereign dignity thus in no way affects the fundamental equality between them and women, who, from the standpoint of their *being*, are just as much in the likeness of God.[41]

In my expositions concerning the representation of God by men and by women, I set out materially the same position; I hope that, in so doing, I may be able to revitalize, through various clarifying additions, an important idea that, in connection with Genesis 1–2 and 1 Corinthians 11, is found already in patristic literature.[42]

For Bonaventure, the male's position as "head" thus plays an important role in the orders of creation and redemption, and provides—as for Thomas—the deciding argument in justification of the nonordination of women. We find in this the internal demonstration of the positive, external directive in 1 Timothy 2:12 (or 1 Corinthians 14:34), which the *Doctor Seraphicus* cites as a "foundation" of the quaestio: "I permit no woman to teach in the congregation (*in ecclesia*) or to have authority over men."

The remaining arguments resemble very strongly those put forward by Thomas. An interesting variation, to be sure, is that reference is made to

---

[40] II Sent d 16 a 2: *Bonaventurae* II, p. 403.

[41] This idea occurs in a quite similar way in Saint Thomas; cf. p. 460 below.

[42] Especially clearly in Augustine: insofar as woman "is man's 'helper' and differs from him sexually, [she is] not an image of God. . . . [She] *possesses* the spiritual dignity of being in the likeness of God, but . . . 'does not symbolize this *through her physical sex*' ": Mausbach, *Augustinus*, p. 324, n. 2. See also what was said on Ambrosiaster: pp. 422f. above.

the special nature of priestly grace: "There is no greater perfection than monastic life and no greater strength than endurance of martyrdom. Women, however, are admitted to religious orders and to martyrdom: consequently, they must also be given access to the sacrament of orders."

To this objection is opposed:

> The perfection of monastic life and of martyrdom concerns sanctifying grace (*gratia gratum faciens*), and a woman can receive that just as well as a man. There is also, however, a sort of perfection that refers to the salvation of others (*qui concernit aliquid gratis datum*) and falls only to the one sex. . . . For it concerns not only the inner, but also the outer. This, however, is the case with the perfection of the sacrament of orders, in which a (spiritual) power is conferred that . . . is little suited to women."

Hence, if Bonaventure denies women the capacity for receiving ordination, then this is not because he regards them as second-rate Christians. The *priestly redemptive authority* that he introduces here as *"gratia gratis data"*[43] is not granted for purposes of personal elevation, but for those of service to others.

As with Thomas, the following objection arises: The *sacrament of orders* applies not to the body but to the *soul*, in which there is no sexual differentiation. Hence, women can also receive priestly ordination.[44]

Bonaventure replies:

> The sacrament of orders . . . applies not to the soul as such, but to the soul insofar as it is bound up with the body. Through this manner of *signification*, which consists in a *visible* sign, [the sacrament of orders] also relates to the body. It has regard, simultaneously, to its [own] *practice* and to its use. Since, however, neither the *signification* of the sacrament of orders nor its *administration* is appropriate for women . . . , therefore. . . .

Duns Scotus

Duns Scotus, the *Doctor Subtilis*, introduces a new element into the Scholastic debate. He grounds exclusion of women from ordination not

---

[43] This concept also includes the charisms which are as little denied of women as of—in modern usage—the "lay apostolate". The same terminology occurs in Thomas; cf. on this Diekamp and Jüssen, *Dogmatik II*, pp. 423f.

[44] The same objection crops up again in a petition to Vatican II that cites support from Saint Thomas (!): "the sacramental quality is located in the faculty of knowledge, and this is present in the same way in women as it is in men, namely, as an inherent faculty of immaterial reason". Consequently, through refusal of priestly ordination, a woman is "hindered . . . from being active in accordance with the capacities of her soul" (Heinzelmann, *Schweigen*, pp. 36f.). Raming, *Ausschluss*, p. 214, adopts a more bellicose formulation, censuring the classical understanding of office for "lack of spirituality and an overemphasis on the sexual".

only on the basis of symbolic representation, the Pauline statements and the *will* of Christ but postulates an explicit *command* of the Lord. Because the nonordination of women is determined by Christ, more is at issue than merely a question of propriety or a mere command of the *Church*. Rather, at the basis is a fundamental state of affairs that ultimately derives from a directive of Jesus. Otherwise, exclusion of women would be immoral:

> I do not believe, namely, that any office useful for salvation has been withheld from any person through institution by the Church or prescription of the apostles, and much less still from an entire existing sex. If, then, the apostles or the Church cannot justly withhold from a person any office useful for salvation unless Christ, as their head, has so determined, and much less still from the entire female sex, therefore Christ alone first prescribed this, he who instituted the sacrament.[45]

For using this sort of argumentation, Scotus has recently been accused of "voluntarism".[46] The charge may well be rightly applicable to some passages from Scotus' theology, but it is inappropriate in the present context. It is correct that Scotus has here developed a special sense for the necessity of Jesus' directive; the command is not, however, perceived as an *arbitrary* decree, but is bound up with reasons of congruence: women are less suited to teaching and, above all, they are subordinate to men. The office bearer must, however, signify a position of superiority; in this— admittedly more reservedly than in Bonaventure and Thomas—the symbolic sacramental plane is addressed. Because of the natural sub- ordination of the female sex, a bishop who wanted to ordain a woman would "not only act wrongly, by offending against the command of Christ, but also effect nothing, and the woman would receive nothing". Thus, the command of revelation serves to protect a structure that is already grounded in the order of creation.

Although Scotus is not acquainted with the "command of the Lord" in 1 Corinthians 14:37, he seems almost to have sensed it intuitively. Regarding 1 Timothy 2, namely, he provides the following supplementation: "Not only I [the apostle Paul], but the Lord does not permit it" (official teaching).

All regulations that exclude women from partial duties or from the wider setting of the priesthood are, for Scotus, concrete applications of the command of Christ: "What is taken, in addition, from the decrees [= canon law] or from the prescriptions of Paul in order to exclude

---

[45] Ox IV Sent d 25 q 2: *Joannis Duns Scoti Opera 24* (Paris, 1894), pp. 369f. All that follows is taken from this *quaestio*.

[46] Francine Cardman, "Non-Conclusive Arguments: Therefore: Non-Conclusion?" in Swidler, *Women Priests*, p. 93.

women from receiving orders—all these are but particular supplements to, or rather expressions [*expressiones*] of, Christ's command on this matter."

The exclusion from the sacrament of orders has nothing to do with an inferiority of women, as the reference to Mary that was already made by Innocent III[47] shows: "The Mother of Christ . . . was the worthiest and holiest, but still no [ordained] authority was conferred upon her."

Scotus dismisses two objections to his thesis. One pertains, as was the case in Thomas and Bonaventure, to the question of deaconesses and the term *presbytera*; the other—the first—could derive as well from an *auctor modernus*: "In Galatians 3[:28] it is written: In Christ Jesus there is neither male nor female, neither slave nor free; therefore neither sex nor condition in life seems to be an obstacle to reception of ordination."

Against this, Scotus calls attention to the biblical context: "With respect to salvation and eternal life, no distinction is made between male and female, slave and free.[48] Nevertheless, there is a distinction between them regarding office and priority of rank in the Church, because here, as noted, men are given preference over women."

4. ON THE TOPIC: "WOMEN IN THE MIDDLE AGES"

"Feminine weakness"

On the question of whether a "disdain" for women may have caused their exclusion from the priesthood, the answer that emerges is basically the same as it was for the patristic period.[49] Nevertheless, it is helpful to look more closely at the topic "woman in the Middle Ages" because the complex of relevant problems seems to stand out even more clearly there.

Ida Raming calls attention to several unpleasant assertions by medieval authors that do not, in fact, show a very high estimation of women. Aegidius Bellamera (fourteenth century), for instance, explains the more lenient treatment of women by the courts in terms of their "weakness", "instability" and "naturally lesser solidity of character and capacity of

---

[47] Cf. p. 447 above.

[48] Like Thomas and Bonaventure, Scotus remarks that the subordination of women, by contrast with that of slaves, is naturally determined: *naturalem subiectionem*. The Scholastics do not place subordination of women on the same level with the subjectedness of slaves; cf. pp. 459f. below.

[49] Cf. pp. 427–32 above.

judgment".[50] A certain basis for this assertion is already found in the "etymology" of Ambrose as adopted by Gratian, according to which *vir* ("man") and *mulier* ("woman") designate not individual persons but qualities: the one term derives from *virtus animi* ("moral force, perfection"), the other, from *mollitus mentis*, that is, from "weakness" and "softness of character".[51]

Feminine weakness and fragility are a stock formula in most medieval literature, a fact that indicates that the female nature was often seen not as an equally valuable complement to the male but as something inferior.[52] Roswitha von Gandersheim, the first German poetess, introduces one of her books with the comment that science far surpasses her feminine mentality.[53]

"Warning about women"

Censure of bad women is repeated in a way similar to that found in the Fathers. When citing the relevant assertions, however, one ought to note their pendant, the praise of *good* women.[54] "Know that no reasonable man reproaches the female sex as such, for he knows that it has been well created by God. Therefore, when there are warnings about women in Scripture, the word woman is almost always accompanied by a modifier indicating badness."[55]

If, therefore, the remark possibly crops up in some of the canonists, with reference to Plato, that women's earlier physical maturity makes them comparable to weeds, which also, of course, grow more quickly,[56] then this rudeness is not necessarily typical of the mentality of the Middle Ages.

The monastic warnings against familiarity with women betray a general devaluation of women just as little as, conversely, the pertinent counsels to nuns provide evidence of a "hatred of men".[57]

[50] Raming, *Ausschluss*, p. 151.

[51] Raming, *Ausschluss*, p. 48. On the structure of this typology, cf. pp. 430f. above.

[52] Matthäus Bernards, *Speculum Virginum. Geistigkeit und Seelenleben der Frau im Hochmittelalter* [Speculum Virginum. Spirituality and psychology of woman in the high Middle Ages], Forschungen zur Volkskunde 36/38 (Cologne and Graz, 1955), p. 214; Portmann, *Darstellung*, p. 59.

[53] Portmann, *Darstellung*, p. 67.

[54] An extensive survey of the problems involved here can be found in Rösler, *Frauenfrage*, pp. 293ff.; cf. also Frances Gies and Joseph Gies, *Women in the Middle Ages* (New York, 1978), pp. 38f.

[55] Johannes Rider, Formicarius 3, c 4, in Rösler, *Frauenfrage*, p. 300.

[56] Raming, *Ausschluss*, p. 149, n. 102; p. 151.

[57] Bernards, *Geistigkeit*, p. 172; cf. also Mausbach, *Frauenberuf*, p. 38.

On "androcentrism": the example of Saint Thomas

Thomas takes over from Aristotle the notion that, in a certain respect, woman is an "imperfect man": "The seed of the father would, in itself, be predisposed toward production of a child completely similar to him, and thus a child of male sex. That a girl is conceived as a result of a weakness in the active force of the seed, a sort of indisposition of matter or also the consequence of the influence of negative external factors such as the sultry midday winds."[58]

In this way, women appear not only as subordinate to men but also as inferior. Both notions are combined in the talk of the *status subiectionis* of women, of their "state of subjection".[59] There is also in Thomas a recurrence of Augustine's opinion that, for every other sort of work besides propagation of the species, a man can be better assisted by another man than by a woman.[60]

The accusation of "androcentrism"[61] thus applies with some justification to Saint Thomas. It is necessary, of course, to draw certain distinctions. The just-cited statement on the significance of women to the reproductive process does not imply a devaluation of the personal relationship between husband and wife. Already in the article that comes next, we read that—by contrast with the case of the animals—"in the case of mankind, the male and the female are bound together not only for the sake of the need to reproduce, but also for the sake of domestic life, in which certain sorts of task are appropriate to the husband, and others to the wife."[62] Matrimonial love is regarded by the Church doctor not as a necessary evil but as the greatest and most intense friendship conceivable between human beings.[63]

The idea that the father plays the most important role in the reproductive process came to Thomas by way of his teacher Albert, from Aristotle. However, Aristotle's statements underwent revision in a crucial respect: Albert had already amended the expression "truncated" man (*femina quasi*

[58] STh I q 92 a 1 ad 1.
[59] On this combination, cf. p. 451 above.
[60] STh I q 92 a 1.
[61] Borresen, *Subordination*, pp. 250–53; Borresen, "Grundlagen".
[62] STh I q 92 a 2.
[63] ScG III 123: *maxima amicitia*; on this, see Manser, *Frauenfrage*, pp. 13f. It is therefore all but absurd to claim, with Meer, *Priesturtum*, p. 135, that Thomas has no understanding "of other sorts of tasks for women that are not directly connected with the conception of children". Pertinent information on "woman in Thomas Aquinas", along with extensive bibliographical material, can be found in Alfons Hufnagel, "Die Bewertung der Frau bei Thomas von Aquin" [Evaluation of woman in Thomas Aquinas], in *ThQ* 156 (1976): 133–47.

mancus), which Aristotle occasionally uses as a designation for woman, to "imperfect" or "incomplete" man (*mas occasionatus*).[64] But even this "imperfect" is placed in a new context, so that any devaluation of women almost disappears:

> With respect to particular nature [*natura particularis*], woman is something defective and contingent, for the active force in the man's seed is directed toward production of something completely similar to him. . . . With respect to universal nature [*natura universalis*], however, woman is by no means something contingent, but is oriented through the purposiveness of nature toward the work of propagation: The purposiveness of universal nature, however, is dependent upon God, the originator of universal nature, and therefore . . . he created not only man, but also woman.[65]

Thus, the nature of woman is, in itself, complete and good and originates in Divine Providence,[66] a fact that ought to blunt the point of Aristotle's phrase *mas occasionatus*.[67] In a certain respect, moreover, not only woman but also man is something incomplete, namely, in relation to human nature, which God wanted to see realized in *both* sexes.[68]

Finally, it should be noted that the adoption of Aristotelian biology reflects the private convictions of Saint Thomas. Even in antiquity, especially in the Hippocratic school of medicine and in Galen, there was an alternative theory, which assumed the existence not only of male but also of female seed.[69] By way of Avicenna, the anti-Aristotelian hypothesis survived into the Middle Ages,[70] where it recurred in Bonaventure and probably also already in Albert,[71] before beginning, since the eighteenth century, its triumphal march in modern times. In its ancient and medieval formulations, it, too, attributes a certain primacy to the male seed in the imparting of form,[72] but nevertheless does so in a more moderate way than does the Aristotelian theory.[73]

The subordination of women and biological theories of reproduction are thus two different sorts of subject matter.[74] Also important is the fact

[64] Sebastian Killermann, "Die somatische Anthropologie bei Albertus Magnus" [Somatic anthropology in Albert the Great], in *Angelicum* 21 (Seria Albertina) (1944): p. 229.

[65] STh q 92 a 1 ad 1.

[66] II Sent d 20 q 2 a 1 ad 3: Thomae I: *per providentiam divinam*.

[67] Cf. Hufnagel, "Bewertung", p. 141.

[68] Cf. STh I q 93 a 4 ad 2 with Hufnagel, "Bewertung", pp. 137, 141.

[69] Lesky, *Nachwirken*, pp. 24, 178–80.

[70] Lesky, *Nachwirken*, p. 24.

[71] Killermann, "Anthropologie", p. 255; K. E. Borresen, *Anthropologie médiévale et théologie mariale* (Oslo, Bergen and Tromso, 1971), p. 89.

[72] Lesky, *Nachwirken*, p. 180.

[73] In another way, modern biology, too, holds to a certain "priority" without calling into question the equal value of the contribution of each parent: cf. p. 189 above.

[74] Cf. pp. 112–13 above.

that in the Middle Ages subordination of women was not placed on the same level as that of slaves but was given its own sort of justification. On this, Saint Thomas cites the following popular interpretation of the story of creation: "Woman should not be the master of man: therefore, she was not formed out of his head. She should also not be disdained by man and slavishly subject to him: therefore, she was not formed out of his feet", but out of his side.[75] Thomas' contemporary, the preacher Berthold von Regensburg, adds: "God took her from your heart, and thus she should be close to you."[76]

Hence, woman is not the "slave" (serva) of man but his "companion" (socia).[77] Insofar as she is derived from man and is subordinate to him, she is emblematic of the relation of the Church to Christ.[78]

On the question of woman's being in the likeness of God, Thomas expresses a position similar to Bonaventure's:[79] man's specific quality of being an imago is something secondary[80] and does not operate at the level of his essential—woman is just as much an imago Dei as is man—but at the level of symbolic representation, that is, of a vestigium.[81]

The high estimation of women in chivalry, bride mysticism and Marian devotion

High estimation of women did not decline in the Middle Ages, but rather increased. One specific form in which this esteem was expressed is chivalry, in which the knights chose noble women as their "ladies". The

---

[75] STh I q 92 a 3.

[76] Rösler, Frauenfrage, p. 267. The cited interpretation of the story of creation goes back to Augustine (especially De civitate Dei XII, 27: PL 41, p. 376) and is found in the Commentary on the Sentences by Peter Lombard, the most important theological textbook of the Middle Ages: II Sent d 18 c 1: Petri Lombardi Libri IV Sententiarum. Liber I. et II., Ad Claras Aquas (prope Florentiam), 2nd ed., 1916, p. 388; its core is formulated as follows: "mulier . . . viro nec domina nec ancilla parabatur, sed socia". A similar text also occurs in the Talmud; cf. W. Vogels, "Mensch", p. 25.

[77] Cf. ScG III 124.

[78] STh I q 92 a 2 and 3. This reference to the relation Christ-Church, which was already widespread in the patristic period, is enough in itself to preclude playing "equality in value" and "subordination" of women off against each other; not only the "equality in value" but also the "subordination" are grounded in the orders of creation and redemption. Against René Metz, "Recherches sur la condition de la femme selon Gratian", Studia Gratiana 12 (1967): 395; Borresen, Subordination, p. 255.

[79] Cf. p. 453 above.

[80] STh I q 93 a 4 ad 1: aliquid secundarium.

[81] STh I q 93 a 6.

distribution of roles here followed the principle: *"woman* as beautiful and good, *man* as to be educated", because the woman was regarded as an "exemplary representation of virtue" and culture.[82] Horst Wenzel discerns in the Middle High German literature on chivalry two basic characteristics, *"the elevation of women and the moral refinement of men"*.[83] This attitude is surely tied to the conditions of the times, but it is grounded in a degree of respect for women that can otherwise be found (even in modern times) only rarely. Schopenhauer cynically characterizes the "veneration of women" as the "fullest blossoming of Christian-Germanic stupidity", at which the Greeks would have laughed and which even today is mocked by Asia.[84]

The esteem for women was not influential solely in aristocratic circles but had its concrete effects on every marriage, because the Church took a position against divorce. Didactic poetry in the early Middle Ages, to cite but one example, not only praises the celibate life but portrays, from the natural and supernatural standpoints, a "transfiguration of marriage".[85]

Also significant are medieval bride mysticism and Marian devotion,[86] which were furthered, in particular, by Bernard of Clairvaux.[87]

Saint Hildegard, as a contemporary, explicitly put into words that an entire epoch's image of woman was elevated by this.[88] The misogynous statements of the Middle Ages[89] stem largely from authors other than the

[82] Horst Wenzel, *Frauendienst und Gottesdienst. Studien zur Minne-Ideologie* [Service to women and service to God. Studies in the ideology of knight service], Philologische Studien und Quellen 74 (Berlin, 1974), pp. 201, 82.

[83] Wenzel, *Minne-Ideologie*, p. 15.

[84] Lersch, *Wesen*, p. 14.

[85] Wenzel, *Minne-Ideologie*, p. 83.

[86] Cf. on this the survey by Marianus Müller, "Maria. Ihre geistige Gestalt und Persönlichkeit in der Theologie des Mittelalters" [Mary. Her spiritual character and personality in the theology of the Middle Ages], in Paul Sträter (ed.), *Katholische Marienkunde I* [Catholic Marian Studies I], (Paderborn, 1947), pp. 268–316.

[87] Vergil Redlich, "Bernhard von Clairvaux und das Frauenbild des Mittelalters" [Bernard of Clairvaux and the image of woman in the Middle Ages], in *Gloria Dei* 8 (1953): 212–20.

[88] Redlich, "Bernhard", p. 220. That the devotion to Mary remained "largely without effect on the evaluation of women in the social sphere" (Küng, "Thesen", p. 129) can thus not be very well maintained; nor that Mary is "the only exception" to the "contempt for women" (Gertrud Heinzelmann, "Zur kirchlichen Stellung der Frau" [On the position of women in the Church], in Heinzelmann, *Schweigen*, p. 11; cf. Daly, *Kirche*, p. 60; Ruether, *Mary*, p. 33).

[89] A relevant selection is given by August Wulff, who notes that statements of this sort are found in all cultures and literatures (August Wulff, *Die frauenfeindlichen Dichtungen in den romanischen Literaturen des Mittelalters bis zum Ende des XIII. Jahrhunderts* [Misogynous poetry in the Romanic literatures of the Middle Ages up to the end of the thirteenth century], Romanistische Arbeiten IV [Halle, 1914], pp. 1ff.). Devotion to Mary and the poetry of the troubadors were a powerful counterweight to this in the Middle Ages (Wulff, *Dichtungen*, p. 1).

authors of the "positive" ones[90] and, as opposed to those, were granted no official or semiofficial recognition.

Prophetesses

The most influential women in the history of the Church are to be found in the "dark" (?) Middle Ages. To the powerful influence of the prophetic figure of Hildegard there is "no parallel in the whole of world history":[91] "Never before had a prophet commanded so high a degree of respect as she."[92] By "popes and princes, [she was] asked for advice, beseeched for her support, and this in terms of humility as were not employed even vis-à-vis the most powerful".[93]

Without Catherine of Siena, the stay of the Popes in Avignon would not have been ended so soon: "To my knowledge, no man has yet dared to speak to a wearer of the tiara as radically and openly as she spoke to Pope Gregory XI in Avignon."[94]

It would be wrong, however, to number the medieval prophetesses among the forerunners of the emancipation of women or to play them off against the Pauline ban on teaching.[95] What is involved here is *not* the activity of quasi-clerical office bearers but of women whom God himself has directly charged with exposing the failures of the "official Church": "The almighty God permitted that to happen in order to show what he is able to effect through a creature that has, of itself, nothing to boast about."[96] "Just as I once sent to the Jews and to pagan peoples men who, although inept, were equipped with my wisdom, so today I will send women, who are ignorant and frail by nature, but whom I will provide with divine wisdom, so that they can teach the high and mighty a lesson that will shame them."[97]

[90] Wulff, *Dichtungen*, pp. 81, 166f., 177.

[91] Gisbert Kranz, *Herausgefordert von ihrer Zeit. 6 Frauenleben* [Challenged by their times. The lives of six women] (Regensburg, 1976), p. 33.

[92] Ignaz Döllinger, in Kranz, *Herausgefordert*, p. 33.

[93] Finke, *Frau*, p. 81.

[94] Walter Nigg, in Walter Nigg and H. N. Loose, *Katharina von Siena* [Catherine of Siena] (Freiburg, Basel and Vienna, 1980), p. 8. The list of prophetic women of the Middle Ages could be extended further: Birgitta, Joan of Arc. . . . I have here selected only two especially significant examples.

[95] Walter Nigg says: "Catherine of Siena brushed the Pauline statement aside with particular magnificence" (Nigg and Loose, *Katharina*, p. 8).

[96] Hildegard to Abbot Philipp Park, in Kranz, *Herausgefordert*, p. 17.

[97] Christ in the visionary call to Catherine of Siena: Adrian Schenker, *Das Leben der heiligen Katharina von Siena (Legenda maior des Raimund von Capua)* [The life of Saint Catherine of Siena (Legenda maior by Raymond of Capua)] (Düsseldorf, 1965), p. 99.

Female rulers

Especially during the early Middle Ages, worldly rule by women was nothing unusual or offensive. A Queen Theodelinde, who, as her husband's representative, administers the Lombard kingdom and collaborates with the Pope in suppressing Arianism;[98] a Duchess Matilda, who, under armor, leads troops for Gregory VII against the German emperor;[99] an Adelaide and a Theophano, who govern the gigantic "Holy Roman Empire" for eight years without male "trusteeship"; and various others —all these found a recognized place in the Middle Ages. Saint Thomas, for example, as one who uses the "subordination" argument in rejecting priesthood for women, writes a friendly letter to the duchess of Brabant in which he says nothing to suggest that women without male partners are incapable of governing.[100] In the tenth and eleventh centuries, numerous biographies document for us how highly queens and empresses are respected.[101] As a rule, the female sovereign is "only" a participant in the government of the male sovereign,[102] but in that she assumes a non-exchangeable role and serves as the model for description of Mary as "Queen of Heaven".[103] In the fact of those female sovereigns who govern alone, however, it is apparent that the assumption about a natural lack of capacity for leadership office on the part of women could not be decisive for nonadmission to the sacrament of orders. Rather, the decisive things here are that the authority of the male office bearer is sacramentally embedded in the representation of Christ and that guidance was taken from the statements of Paul as well as the behavior of Jesus.

---

[98] Peter Stockmeier, "Theodelinde, Königin der Langobarden" [Theodelinde, queen of the Lombards], in Georg Schwaiger (ed.), *Bavaria Sancta. Zeugen des christlichen Glaubens in Bayern III* [Bavaria Sancta. Testaments of Christian belief in Bavaria III] (Regensburg, 1973), pp. 9–20.

[99] Gies and Gies, *Women*, p. 23.

[100] Hufnagel, "Bewertung", p. 136.

[101] Thilo Vogelsang, *Die Frau als Herrscherin im hohen Mittelalter. Studien zur 'consors regni'-Formel* [Women as rulers in the high Middle Ages. Studies in the *consors-regni* concept], Göttinger Bausteine zur Geschichtswissenschaft 7 (Göttingen, Frankfurt and Berlin, 1954), p. 22.

[102] The *consors-regni* concept goes back to the Old Testament: Vogelsang, *Herrscherin*, p. 3.

[103] Vogelsang, *Herrscherin*, pp. 38f.; "from a letter by Alcuin we can see that he had turned to the Queen after having been asked to intercede with Charlemagne" (Vogelsang, *Herrscherin*, p. 13).

On the "jurisdiction" of abbesses

The very office of queen, like that of king, is clothed in sacred significance.[104] This religious reference is even clearer in the case of the medieval abbesses, whose powers in many cases are of the same order as those of a bishop. The abbess of a community of choir nuns, for instance, administers the community property and awards benefices and spiritual offices, and the members of the community are obliged to swear an oath of obedience to her.[105] The women even participate at imperial diets and synods.[106] The Church not only tolerated the spiritual power of these women but even defended it against rebellious clergymen.[107] To what extent we speak here of "spiritual jurisdiction" in the proper sense is debatable.[108] At any event, it is clear that the powers of an abbess are never simply equivalent to those of an abbot or bishop.[109] The "power of the keys", in the proper sense, is always denied to abbesses. In a letter from Innocent III to the bishop of Burgos, we can recognize the great influence of women and, at the same time, its limitations: "The abbesses are openly blessing . . . their own nuns, . . . hearing . . . confession from them, and are presuming, in addition, when reading the gospel, to proclaim it publicly as well."

In forbidding such practices, the Pope makes reference to the will of Jesus: "No matter whether the most blessed Virgin Mary stands higher . . . than all the apostles together, it was still not to her, but to them, that the Lord entrusted the keys to the Kingdom of heaven."[110]

---

[104] In the Pontificale Romanum there are consecrations for a coreigning and a reigning queen; cf. Meer, *Priesturtum*, pp. 141f.

[105] Raming, *Ausschluss*, p. 127. On the canonesses, cf. K. H. Schäfer, *Die Kanonissenstifter im deutschen Mittelalter. Ihre Entwicklung und innere Einrichtung im Zusammenhang mit dem altchristlichen Sanktimonialentum* [Canoness foundations in the German Middle Ages. Their development and internal structure in connection with early Christian sanctimonialism], Kirchenrechtliche Abhandlungen 43/44 (Stuttgart, 1907); K. H. Schäfer, "Kanonissen und Diakonissen" [Canonesses and deaconesses], in *Römische Quartalschrift* 24 (1910): 49–80.

[106] Morris, *Jurisdiction*, p. 60.

[107] For example, Pope Honorius III in 1212; cf. Meer, *Priesturtum*, p. 143.

[108] Meer, *Priesturtum*, p. 142, declares that "the abbesses had spiritual jurisdiction". The canonists, however, regularly deny this thesis. Even Ida Raming expresses herself more cautiously than van der Meer: Raming, *Ausschluss*, p. 126, n. 23.

[109] In the just-mentioned decretal of Honorius III, for instance, the abbess herself is not allowed to excommunicate, but this must be done in her place by a neighboring abbot: Raming, *Ausschluss*, pp. 126f.

[110] Innocent III, Decratal Nova quaedam (1210); Meer, *Priesturtum*, p. 155. For additional material, I refer to Meer, *Priesturtum*, pp. 142–58. Extensive discussion of this can be forgone here, since one thing is very clear: the "jurisdiction" or "quasi-jurisdiction" of abbesses was always kept separate from priestly clerical powers. The CIC probably applies to the situation in the Middle Ages as well when it states that *iurisdictio* (as a technical term in the present-day sense) was held only by clerics (CIC can. 29).

The education of women

"Almost no other epoch has given women of distinction so many opportunities for unhampered measurement of their powers of mind against those of men as did the Middle Ages."[111] The early Middle Ages was familiar, especially under the influence of Jerome and Ambrose, with an ideal image of woman containing, among other things, "study in depth of the Holy Scriptures and the works of the Church Fathers".[112] In particular, high theological standards were often attained in convents. Lioba, the sister of Saint Boniface, was most completely educated in the worldly and spiritual sciences. She knew the Bible almost by heart, and, besides that, "she studied . . . the Church Fathers, the councils and the whole of canon law".[113] She passed her wealth of knowledge on to numerous female students, and princes and bishops sought her out from afar because—according to her biographer—she "was very well versed in Scripture and prudent in her advice".[114] Lioba was, moreover, by no means an eccentric blue stocking but, rather, a real woman.[115]

Writing from Abbess Hilda's English homeland, Bede (eighth century) was able to report that under her "five bishops were produced from her school at Whitby abbey".[116] John Scotus Erigena, the most important theologian of the early Middle Ages, was "discovered" by the cultured Queen Hermentrud.[117]

Such cultivation was not, however, restricted to communities of nuns: "The cultural-historical representations of the Middle Ages all agree that women of noble lineage received a better formal education than did the men, who were to be trained for military careers."[118]

The clergy, the members of religious orders and women were the educated classes of the Middle Ages. Primarily involved here were the ranks of the nobility, but not exclusively: the popular preacher Berthold von Regensburg (thirteenth century) presupposed that his female audience had read the Holy Scriptures.[119]

In academic professions, too, women are documented, namely, female doctors, pharmacists and teachers.[120] Women appear at various times as

[111] Rösler, *Frauenfrage*, p. 286.

[112] Portmann, *Darstellung*, p. 142.

[113] Sommer-von Seckendorff, "Frauenstudium", pp. 147f.

[114] Portmann, *Darstellung*, p. 60.

[115] Cf. Sommer-von Seckendorff, "Frauenstudium", p. 145.

[116] Sommer-von Seckendorff, "Frauenstudium", p. 145.

[117] Finke, *Frau*, p. 33.

[118] Wenzel, *Minne-Ideologie*, p. 82. Determinative here, along with the convents, were the schools of the canonesses: K. H. Schäfer, *Kanonissenstifter*, pp. 115, 178f.

[119] Rösler, *Frauenfrage*, p. 279.

[120] Luise Hess, *Die deutschen Frauenberufe des Mittelalters* [Occupations for women in the

members of guilds and take on specifically female tasks that nevertheless involve considerable responsibility, such as the directorship of hospitals.[121] Admittedly, retrogressive trends also occurred, especially during the late Middle Ages; Christine de Pisan and Jean Gerson, the spiritual chancellor of the University of Paris, defended (successfully) female scholarship against "public opinion".[122] To the decline of education of women in the modern age, a not insignificant contribution was made later on by the German Reformation.[123]

Thus, the position of womankind in the Middle Ages cannot at all be compared with that of uneducated Blacks in the United States,[124] for, in the convent situation, women enjoyed almost as much educational freedom as did men, while among the laity they even had—at least for a long period—an educational advantage. Accordingly, that a deficiency in the intellectual attainments of women could have functioned as the *deciding* argument would appear doubtful.

If, then, Master Gratian excludes women from the sacrament of orders even when they are holy and *educated*,[125] then that is certainly more than a rhetorical flourish. To be sure, women were generally not admitted to the universities, which arose in the high Middle Ages. But something that was still unthinkable in German universities at the start of the twentieth century was already known to Gratian in twelfth-century Bologna: female professors.[126] "At a time . . . when Kant was still claiming that a woman needs to know nothing more of the universe than is necessary 'to make looking at the heavens on a beautiful evening a moving experience' and to comprehend that there are still other worlds where still more 'beautiful creatures can be found', Benedict XIV and other Popes were installing female professors at universities, such as Agnesi for philosophy and mathematics and Bassi for philosophy and physics at Bologna."[127]

German Middle Ages], Beiträge zur Volkstumsforschung 6 (Munich, 1940), pp. 122f., 127.

[121] Hess, *Frauenberufe*, pp. 58ff., 90ff., 109.

[122] Finke, *Frau*, pp. 41–44.

[123] Sommer-von Seckendorff, "Frauenstudium", pp. 147f.

[124] Against Raming, *Ausschluss*, p. 61, n. 255.

[125] Cf. p. 445–46 above.

[126] Documented in Italy in Bologna and elsewhere between the twelfth and the eighteenth centuries: Mausbach, *Frau*, p. 61.

[127] Mausbach, *Frau*, p. 71. Nevertheless, precisely the Middle Ages provide outstanding evidence of the differentiation between the spiritual gifts of men and those of women. In the early Middle Ages, one of the outstanding tasks of women was "to guard what has come down from intellectual-spiritual Tradition with careful hands and to pass it on to future generations" (Sommer-von Seckendorff, "Frauenstudium", p. 145). "*In the 12th and, above all, the 13th centuries*, as science became more independent and more creative, leadership passed, quite naturally and more and more exclusively, to the masculine sphere" (Sommer-von Seckendorff, "Frauenstudium", p. 145). "Cultured women . . . had no reason to complain . . . that they were suppressed. However, there is not a single work by a woman

5. CONCLUSION AND OUTLOOK

That the sociological conditions of the Middle Ages are not sufficient to account for a strict exclusion of women from the priesthood is demonstrated for us, in particular, by the behavior of certain sects. I have already pointed out elsewhere that (1) female preachers were known among the Waldensians and Catharists, and (2) in both these groups women celebrated the Eucharist, which was understood by the Waldensians as the sacrifice of the Mass in the full Catholic sense.[128]

This sort of practice must have been quite familiar to Saint Thomas, for his order had a particular mandate for opposing heretics.[129] That women had not reached the highest levels of the heretic hierarchy is of little importance here; in ecclesiastical office, too, after all, there are various levels. In the Middle Ages, however, women were admitted neither to the office of bishop nor to that of priest, nor even to the (sacramentally understood) diaconate. What holds true for the patristic Church is valid as well for the medieval Church: women were not admitted to ordination *even though* the conditions of the times would have been favorable.

Accordingly, the reason for that behavior can lie only in a norm that has binding *priority* over the conditions of the times: the will of Christ. Scholastic thought sees this will at work in the very fact that God became man as a *male* and links it, by way of the symbols "head" and "bridegroom", to the orders of creation and redemption. Thomas understands the male priest's characteristic of being the *"head"* symbolically-sacramentally, Bonaventure concentrates on the representation of Christ and Scotus adds to this the explicit "command of Christ". All three great theologians regard women, for reasons of principle, as *incapable* of receiving ordination. All the canonists known to us by name express a similar position: ordination of a woman would be invalid.

The fundamental arguments from the theology and canon law of the

---

that is at all comparable to the speculative and theoretical achievements of Scholasticism" (Rösler, *Frauenfrage*, p. 286).

This does not imply an "inferiority" of women, for their intellectual-spiritual strengths are manifest in other areas: "In the field of practical mysticism, the works of Saint Hildegard, Gertrude, Mechtilde and Catherine of Siena have become immortal" (Rösler, *Frauenfrage*, p.286). Cf. P. Dinselbacher, D. R. Banz, ed. *Frauenmystik im Mittelalter* [Mysticism of Women in the Middle Ages] (Ostfildern, 1985). Catherine of Siena and Teresa of Avila, who were named as "doctors of the Church" by Pope Paul VI, are not speculative philosophers or theologians but mystics. "Official", "abstract" teaching and the handing on of "intuitive experience" complement each other—in the individual person, but also in the duality of the sexes (cf. pp. 92f. above).

[128] Cf. p. 106 above.

[129] Hufnagel, "Bewertung", p. 135.

Middle Ages were passed on to later periods more or less unchanged. Nevertheless, a study of the subsequent history of theology would not be lacking in interest.

Certain "androcentric statements", such as Aristotle's theory of reproduction, have, in fact, disappeared since the eighteenth century; thus there was no difficulty in distinguishing them quite well from the fundamental theological statements. It is, therefore, not quite appropriate for advocates of the ordination of women to attack the "androcentrism" of high medieval Aristotelianism instead of dealing more closely with the modern opponents of female priesthood.

Not enough studies have yet been done on the theology of the sixteenth, seventeenth, eighteenth and nineteenth centuries, whose sociocultural context was structured differently from that of the Middle Ages. The theme "equality of women" in science and art, for instance, was already discussed very fully.[130] In the nineteenth century—similarly to today— "equality slogans" were much in vogue, and the example of various Protestant groups with female pastors was also already known. J. P. Migne (1864) makes reference to contemporary Protestantism[131] and observes of the argumentation of the advocates of ordination of women: "Their primary foundation is the authority of Saint Paul, who says in Galatians 3[:28]. . . ."

But this thesis had, he says, already been "destroyed" by Epiphanius. The appeal to the Holy Spirit, who calls all Christians to be office bearers, was already familiar to Saint Thomas.[132] Migne describes the nonordination of women as de fide and the opposite as haeresis.[133]

Within the framework of the present study, however, I would like to bring things to a certain conclusion with the treatment of medieval theology. For it was not until more recent times that the topic "women in the priesthood?" was given more far-reaching scholarly scientific consideration, when the "emancipation of women" forced itself, not only in ideal typical models like that in Plato's Republic but also through the social situation, more massively than ever before on the consciousness of the Church. Preoccupation with this question today is probably more intensive, but the structures of argumentation are already contained, if often only germinally, in the history of theology. The evidence of Tradition is therefore indispensable.

---

[130] Mausbach, Frau, p. 61.
[131] J. P. Migne, Theologiae cursus completus 24 (Paris, 1864), p. 822.
[132] Migne, Theologiae, pp. 826f., 829.
[133] Migne, Theologiae, pp. 825f.

CHAPTER EIGHT

A Historically Conditioned Undervaluation of Women as the Reason for Their Exclusion from Priesthood?

Discussions about "priesthood for women" usually begin with a reference to the supposed fact that we find ourselves today in a completely new situation, which calls into question the Church's traditional position. Earlier women were regarded as inferior beings, whereas today, as a result of social and scientific progress, the equality of the sexes is recognized. All the positions taken by the Church in the past had presupposed the inferiority of women, and this prejudice was the real reason behind the exclusion from priesthood.[1]

I have already given repeated consideration to this thesis.[2] I have established that it was not because of a presumed inferiority of women that the Church regarded their ordination to the priesthood as impossible but because of a high esteem for the uniqueness of the specifically female nature, along with what was indicated by the behavior of Jesus. Marian devotion alone is enough to show that an undervaluation of women cannot have been decisive in the matter of their exclusion from priesthood. For ages, in the Litany of Loreto, the Church has praised Mary as "Queen of the Apostles"; that she was not herself an apostle, however, has its basis in the will of Christ.

Even if we assume that the Church's past was characterized by a devaluation of women, then that would still not have been a decisive reason for prohibiting the ordination of women. The Gnostics and Marcionites even admitted women to official duties precisely because they disdained the female nature as such. This Gnostic androcentrism seems to have found various successors in the modern age. Simone de Beauvoir's

---

[1] Cf. Meer, *Priesturtum*, esp. pp. 87–90; Raming, *Ausschluss*, p. 222.
[2] Cf. pp. 183f., 225–28, 340ff., 401f., 435–38, 465f. and elsewhere above.

view of women is totally male-centered: the good for woman lies in making herself as similar as possible to man.[3] Also, the androgynous ideal held by the most varied sorts of thinker, not the least being those within feminist theology, is grounded, as I see it, in a flight from the feminine:[4] the psychic wholeness of the human individual consists in developing masculine and feminine structures in one and the same way (*pari cum pari*).[5] The necessary, specifically masculine or feminine accentuation is deemed to be something indifferent, and this would have to lead, logically, to the demise of human communication, because the tension-charged polarity of the sexes is left to fall by the wayside.

The question ought, therefore, to be asked whether it may not be in modern feminism that we find the most radical contempt for women in world history. Those women who would like to discard or to androgynize their female nature[6] just turn, in often poorly concealed hatred, against themselves and the will of the Creator, while the wealth of the feminine (and of the masculine) remains hidden from them. They thus align themselves—perhaps unintentionally, but particularly effectively—with the infamous woman haters of our epoch. The most misogynous pro-nouncements known to us stem not from antiquity or the Middle Ages but from the "enlightened" nineteenth and twentieth centuries, from Kant, Schopenhauer, Virchow and Nietzsche up to Esther Vilar.[7] In 1908, for instance, the book *On the Physiological Feeble-mindedness of Women* by P. J. Möbius appeared in its ninth edition, and, around the turn of the

---

[3] Cf. pp. 33ff. above.

[4] Regarding this expression, cf. the book by the American psychiatrist Karl Stern, , *Die Flucht vor dem Weib. Zur Pathologie des Zeitgeistes* [The flight from woman. On the pathology of the spirit of the times] (Salzburg, 1968).

[5] Cf. pp. 65f. above.

[6] Cf. pp. 35–39, 42 above.

[7] Some samplings:

Schopenhauer: woman is "in every respect the backward second sex". The "veneration of women" is the "highest blossoming of Christian-Germanic stupidity".

Disraeli: "Every woman should marry—and no man."

Nietzsche: "Woman is God's second mistake" (cited from Buytendijk, *Frau*, pp. 63–66).

Esther *Vilar*: "Men are strong, intelligent, imaginative; women weak, stupid, and unimaginative." Men make the mistake of "measuring woman by standards that place man and animal on the same level. That is probably not necessary, for she would not have the slightest chance in the species *homo sapiens*." Women live "a bestial—that is, animal-like, lower—existence". Their motherhood consists of mere "rules for brooding" (Esther Vilar, *Der dressierte Mann* [The well-trained man], 6th ed. [Munich, 1976], pp. 10, 16, 27). The only difference between, on the one hand, feminists such as Simone de Beauvoir and Kate Millet and, on the other, Esther Vilar seems to be that the former hide their inferiority complex behind radical emancipation slogans, while Vilar openly admits, in a cynical way, to the supposed inferiority of women.

century, a similar work by Otto Weininger went through twenty-five editions and was translated into almost every European language.[8]

Otherwise, testimonies favoring both a low evaluation and a high estimation of women run through the whole of human history without any recognizable sign of essential historical progress.[9] The present-day situation, too, is not as new as many contemporaries like to suppose. For instance, the social position of women in the second century A.D., as outlined earlier here, is in many respects a veritable showcase of "modern" conditions.

It does not, therefore, seem presumptuous to put forward a twofold thesis: the demand for female priesthood, which was provoked historically by certain forms of the emancipation movement, ultimately stems— whether consciously or unconsciously—from a Gnostic-like contempt for women: only "a woman who makes herself a man will enter the Kingdom of heaven".[10]

Nonordination of women is grounded, however, in a high estimation of the specifically female nature.

[8] Cf. Kampmann, *Grundlagen I*, pp. 79f., 89ff. Both these books have just recently been reprinted.

[9] Cf. V. A. Demant, "Why the Christian Priesthood is Male", in *Women*, p. 104.

[10] Cf. pp. 404f. above.

CHAPTER NINE

The Result of This Work and Its Degree of Theological Certainty

1. ARGUMENTS OF PROPRIETY FROM RATIO THEOLOGICA

At the end of this work, the task that still remains is to formulate the result and to establish its degree of theological certainty.

I began by inquiring into the implications of the order of creation for the possibility of female priesthood, starting out with the human sciences and ranging all the way up to philosophical theology. Already at that level of inquiry, the outstanding significance of the symbolism of the sexes became recognizable, which, on the one hand, allocates priestly representation to men and, on the other, allows women to appear as the preferred representatives of creatureliness before God.

This basic structure of the order of creation receives the highest fulfillment conceivable in the order of redemption: the Son of God became man as a *male* in order to illustrate the representation of the heavenly Father vis-à-vis man and the "official" representation of mankind before God. In this, Christ is the archetypal image of the official priest, who, by virtue of his ordination, represents, in a special way, both the Son of God who became man and his redemptive work.

Nevertheless, the order of redemption by no means eliminates the feminine element from the fundamental symbolic structures of creation. For the Son of God desired to assume his human nature from a woman, and indeed, *only* from a woman. The receptive and cooperative attitude of Mary embodies the ideal image of the Christian in the most complete way and provides, at the same time, a criterion for the sort of effective activity that is specific to women. The response of Mary expands itself, so to speak, out into the Church, whose basic structure is Marian in character.

The relations Christ-Mary and Christ-Church are the points on which the Christian symbolism of the sexes turns.

2. THE SIGNIFICANCE OF THE ARGUMENT FROM PRESCRIPT

The order of creation already provides important *arguments of propriety against* women in the priesthood, and the force of these is confirmed and strengthened through the order of redemption. The ultimately *crucial* factor for our question is, however, the will of Jesus, which made itself known in the revelation of the New Covenant. The behavior of Christ, as represented in the Gospels, already suggests the assumption that women are to be excluded from the priesthood in principle and not just on grounds of particular sociohistorical conditions.

In any case, this consideration suffices to give faithfulness to the will of Jesus absolute priority over any changing of Church practice. Accordingly, the *burden of proof* rests not on the side of Tradition but on the side of those who want to change the behavior of the Church. If it is not known with absolute certainty whether the behavior of Jesus is binding or not, then there is but one possibility, namely, to remain with Tradition. Any change of practice would have to result from authentic religious insight and be based on an ability to refute decisively all opposing arguments.[1] A mere adaptation to existing social structures or a catchword appeal to Galatians 3:28 ("in Christ there is neither male nor female"), especially from the perspective of modern equality slogans, would not do justice to the standards of faith.

For Catholic dogmatic theology the aforementioned priority of Tradition is a matter of course. What is involved here is the so-called argument from prescript, which is found already in Tertullian and substantially states: "Supposing that a doctrine or an institution could, according to its nature, stem purely from Church Tradition, it is, nevertheless, to be traced back to the apostles if it is recognized in the whole of the Church and there is nothing known of its having been introduced by Church instrumentalities."[2]

---

[1] Cf. Auer, *Sakramente*, p. 365; F. X. Remberger, "Priestertum der Frau?" [Priesthood for women?], in *Theologie der Gegenwart* 6 (1966): 135.

[2] Diekamp and Jüssen, *Dogmatik I*, p. 64. Against Karl Rahner, according to whom "the burden of proof rests with the [Roman] declaration [on female priesthood] and not with its opponents" (K. Rahner, "Priesturtum", p. 297; cf. already Meer, *Priesturtum*, p. 129). In Rahner's case, was the "progressive" consciousness of the times perhaps more dominant than the methodology of dogmatics?

Regarding our question, however, I will go even beyond the conclusiveness of the argument from prescript, because (1) Church Tradition has already reacted in a binding way to the opposing thesis, and (2) according to the testimony of Saint Paul, Jesus himself issued a ban pertinent to "priesthood for women".

First, some comments on the second point.

3. A COMMAND OF THE LORD: STILL VALID TODAY?

Some years ago, the Bible Commission of the Swedish Lutheran Church extensively examined the biblical foundations relevant to the topic "ordination of women". On the basis of the ample existing New Testament studies, it was necessary to acknowledge that 1 Corinthians 14 takes a clear position on the question and does so, moreover, in connection with a "command of the Lord".

However, it was nevertheless thought permissible to disregard that command. Paul and Jesus had "derived" the directive "from the rabbinical conception of woman", and that attitude of mind had been left behind today. In view of the completely changed social circumstances, continued adherence to 1 Corinthians 14 would even contradict "central biblical intentions" such as were given expression particularly in Galatians 3:28.[3]

Many theological authors advocate a position similar to this. Karl Rahner, for instance, expressed the opinion that Christ could not possibly set up a law for the whole of Church history because, after all, he lived only in imminent expectation (*Naherwartung*).[4] J. A. Komonchak even calls Jesus' messianic consciousness into question with a view to making possible the ordination of women.[5]

These conceptions have to be measured against the authentic Tradition

[3] Cf. Danell, "Bibelkommission". The same situation had arisen already at the end of the 1950s. *All* interpreters, even the proponents of the ordination of women, were aware of the command of Jesus—otherwise than was thus far the case in Anglo-Saxon, French and German biblical scholarship. Regarding the interpretation of to precisely what the "command" referred, there were several differences of opinion, which did not, however, prove crucial. *Decisive* was the question about whether a directive by Jesus was at all binding. Many theologians did not feel themselves bound by such. Particularly the principle of "justification", which was held to transcend all individual norms, was played off against the "command of the Lord". Cf. especially the account of the discussion as given by Refoulé, "Problème".

[4] K. Rahner, "Priesturtum", p. 295; cf. A. Gyllenkrok, in Refoulé, "Problème", p. 92. Against the position already in DS 3462, 3500.

[5] Komonchak, "Questions", p. 254; see also Alcalà, "Frauenemanzipation", p. 285.

of the Church. The earliest and most outstanding expression of this is the New Testament. What, then, does the biblical testimony tell us about the validity of the directive of Jesus?

Christ speaks with the authority of the "Son of Man" who lives in the immediate presence of God and will later judge the world.[6] By virtue of this title, Jesus claims the sorts of power that accrue only to God.[7] He places himself above Moses[8] and acts in the knowledge that he proclaims the ultimate will of God.[9]

His demands are condensed into the twofold command of love,[10] but without invalidating the particular commands that are related to that: "Think not that I have come to abolish the law and the prophets; I have come not to abolish them but to fulfill them. For truly, I say to you, till heaven and earth pass away, not an iota, not a dot, will pass from the law until all is accomplished. Whoever then relaxes one of the least of these commandments and teaches men so, shall be called least in the Kingdom of heaven; but he who does them and teaches them shall be called great in the Kingdom of heaven."[11]

Jesus' knowledge is not of the merely human sort, but is supported by God's supernatural knowledge, in which Christ's divine nature is grounded: "All things have been delivered to me by my Father; and no one knows the Son except the Father, and no one knows the Father except the Son and any one to whom the Son chooses to reveal him."[12]

This self-awareness manifested itself especially clearly after Jesus' Resurrection. Unless one wishes to deprive this basic religious fact of its reality, then it must be admitted that, after Easter, Christ spoke with his disciples and that, at least by that time, there can be no talk of Jesus' living in "immediate expectation". Decisive directives by Christ concerning baptism and office were given, however, according to the testimony of the Gospels, at the time immediately following the Resurrection.[13]

The revelation of Jesus is determinative not only for a certain epoch, but for the entire history of mankind: "Heaven and earth will pass away, but my words will not pass away."[14] "Go therefore and make disciples of all nations . . . , teaching them to observe all that I have commanded you."[15]

[6] Cf. Dan 7ff.
[7] Mk 2:10; Lk 5:24; Mk 2:28.
[8] Mk 7:15; 10:1–12; Mt 5:21–48.
[9] Mk 1:15.
[10] Mk 12:28–31.
[11] Mt 5:17–19.
[12] Mt 11:27. Cf. Lk 10:22; Jn 1:18 and elsewhere.
[13] Cf. p. 389 above.
[14] Mk 13:31.
[15] Mt 28:19f.

Even the Holy Spirit will not change the directives of Jesus but "will teach you all things and bring to your remembrance all that I have said to you".[16]

According to Saint Paul, it is not the following of Old Testament law but responsiveness to Jesus' representative sacrifice for man's sins that is the basis for salvation. It is precisely the apostle of the Gentiles who gave abundantly clear emphasis to the relativity of the "law".

It would be a sign of modern relativism, however, to conclude from this that, for Paul, any and every particular norm can be played off against the command of "love". For the apostles, the "law" found not only its end but also its fulfillment (τέλος) in Christ,[17] which means that every directive of the Lord is absolutely binding.[18]

To the early Church, it was thus self-evident that the law from the hand of Jesus was also binding on the new religious community. It is not Christ who has to conform to the Church but rather the Church to Christ. Obedience to a command of the Lord is not dependent on ever-changing sociocultural circumstances, but is obligatory until the Day of Judgment. Any compromise with the spirit of the times imposes a grave responsibility: "If any one thinks that he is a prophet, or spiritual, he should acknowledge that what I am writing to you is a command of the Lord. If any one does not recognize this, he is not recognized [even by God]."[19]

4. THE VALUE OF TRADITION AS EVIDENCE

If my interpretation of 1 Corinthians 14 is correct, then it is not difficult to formulate the result: by force of divine law, only a baptized male can validly receive consecration to priesthood.

First Corinthians 14:37–38 has the same structure as a conciliar or papal anathema: "If any one says that . . . , he is under a ban."

If we encounter such a formula in which an *article of faith* is defended through an anathema, then we find the highest dogmatic classification: *de fide definita*.

---

[16] Jn 14:26.

[17] Rom 10:4; cf. Mt 5:17.

[18] 1 Cor 7:10–12; 14:37f. Schrage, *Einzelgebote*, p. 249: "A saying of the Lord has, for Paul and his communities, an ultimate, unquestionable authority, and is therefore strictly binding." See also p. 386 above.

[19] 1 Cor 14:37–38.

This formal characteristic is not, however, reflected in 1 Corinthians 14, because:

1. the awareness of the "command of the Lord" is, at least up until now, merely the result of a "private" exegesis;
2. the "office of priest" is affected only indirectly, by way of the "ban on teaching", and
3. no ecclesiastical definition by a Pope or council is involved.

A dogma is something that not only must be contained in revelation but also must have received the *propositio Ecclesiae*, that is, proposal by the Church: "With divine and Catholic faith, therefore, everything is to be believed that is contained in the written or transmitted word of God and is proposed by the Church in solemn declaration or through ordinary and universal teaching office, for belief as revealed by God."[20]

It is thus not possible, using the historical-critical method, to discover a truth of faith that would have been forgotten by the Church for eighteen hundred years. My interpretation of 1 Corinthians 14 can, therefore, only provide a clarifying reference to a sacred Tradition that has been alive in the Church down through the ages. Whether nonordination of women is a truth of revelation can be determined through historical cross-sectioning of any epoch in Church history, although it must be noted that progress can occur from "implicitly" given to "explicit" or "more explicit" religious knowledge.[21] What the exegesis of 1 Corinthians 14 may contribute to our question is, above all, clarification of the theological qualification of such a religious fact: the "command of the Lord", as a truth of revelation (the quality of certainty of the statement), is defended at the level of theological *science* (the degree of certainty),[22] which means that our thesis would be a *sententia fidei proxima*, and its opposite, a *sententia haeresi proxima*.

This qualification is elevated still further if the thesis is declared a truth of revelation through the *universal teaching office* of the Church: *sententia de fide*; the opposite thesis: *haeresis*. If the revelatory character of the doctrine is still not proclaimed with full clarity, yet is nevertheless suggested, it is customary to speak of a *sententia fidei proxima*.

---

[20] Cf. DS 3011.

[21] Citation of the Pauline ban on teaching and of theologically understood subordination—explicit reference to the will and behavior of Christ—linkage to the Incarnation and the Christ-Church relation.

[22] On the terminology, cf. Albert Lang, *Fundamentaltheologie II* [Fundamental theology II], 4th ed. (Munich, 1968), p. 260; Diekamp and Jüssen, *Dogmatik I*, pp. 74f.; Schmaus, *KD I*, pp. 167–69.

In fact, ordination of women has been rejected in the Church with remarkable unanimity throughout two thousand years. This testimony is all the more impressive when—above all during the early period in Church history—it stands in contrast to existing "emancipatory" trends. If women are ordained among the heretics, or even if they only take on official teaching or baptismal duties, then such behavior is branded not only as a breach of Church discipline, but as *heresy*. This occurs explicitly in Tertullian, Epiphanius, Augustine and John of Damascus. In addition, Epiphanius, the Didascalia, the Apostolic Constitutions and the Apostolic Liturgy make formal appeal to the will of Jesus, and this at least comes close to characterizing the opposite thesis as heresy. Hence, in the Fathers, nonordination of women was obviously regarded as a secure "truth of *faith*", that is, in modern terms, as a *veritas de fide* or at least a *veritas fidei proxima*.

This attitude persisted into later times. The canonists of the Middle Ages regard sacramental ordination of women as invalid, which, although still not a strict proof, is nevertheless a clear indication of the fact that canon law aims at protecting a tradition of *faith*. All Scholastic theologians known to us by name who dealt with the problem were, in fact, of the view that women not only *may* not receive the sacrament of ordination but, as a matter of principle, never can receive such a sacrament. The ban on ordination of women is seen as belonging not to canon law but to divine law.

Only in John the Teuton[23] and Bonaventure[24] do we encounter a certain insecurity, which—as the commentators of *Inter insigniores* are probably right to assume—was occasioned by the problem of the ordination of deaconesses.[25] Precisely regarding this aspect of the larger problem, it is remarkable that, "up into modern times, the theologians and canonists who treated this problem were almost unanimously of the view that such exclusion [of women from the sacrament of orders] was absolute and traceable back to God himself".[26] The theological qualification of this statement extends from *sententia communis*[27] up to *sententia de fide*.[28]

The Congregation for the Doctrine of the Faith, with the sanction of the Pope, has decreed: "In fidelity to the example of her Lord, the Church

[23] The reference to "others".

[24] The characterization of our thesis as the "sounder and wiser opinion of the doctors" (*secundum saniorem opinionem et prudentiorem doctorum*).

[25] *Erklärung*, p. 30.

[26] *Erklärung*, p. 29.

[27] Cf., for instance, Joseph Pohle and Josef Gummersbach, *Lehrbuch der Dogmatik III* [Textbook of dogmatics III], 9th ed. (Paderborn, 1960), p. 581.

[28] On this, cf. *Erklärung*, p. 30; Meer, *Priesturtum*, p. 126.

does not regard herself as having the right to admit women to ordination as priests."[29]

This sentence is certainly not expressly characterized as *de fide credenda et tenenda*;[30] still, determination of such a qualification is not, as a rule, the task of a doctrinal document but is a matter for theology.

5. CONCLUSION

For the qualification of my thesis—by way of summary of what was said above—three criteria would appear particularly important:

1. The "command of the Lord" in 1 Corinthians 14, which is linked to an "anathema".
2. The Tradition of the Church, in which the opposing thesis is generally rejected as heresy.
3. The theological and canonical assumption that sacramental ordination of a woman is invalid in principle.

To this must be added the significance of *ratio theologica*: official priesthood for women would obscure the spiritual nature of the relationship Christ-Church and endanger the Christian image of God. The polarity of the sexes, in its symbolic effectiveness, is so deeply anchored in man's being that disavowing it in connection with our question would be likely to lead, in the longer term, to devastating consequences.

At the least, accordingly, the qualification *fidei proxima* would seem to be appropriate: *only a baptized male can validly receive ordination to priesthood. Sententia fidei proxima.*

[29] *Erklärung*, p. 5; *AAS* 67 (1977): 100.
[30] As remarked by Hünermann, "Erklärung", p. 207.

CONCLUDING NOTE

"Incline my heart to thy testimonies, and not to gain!"[1] In this rather provocative form, Barbara Albrecht began a treatise on the theme "priesthood for women".[2] On the basis of current theological research, Mrs. Albrecht arrives at the same result that I have come to: official priesthood for women is contradictory to binding Church doctrine and to the nature of woman. In the first instance, this "negative" statement needs, for once, to be most clearly stressed; otherwise, all too many theologically educated women of goodwill are in danger of expending themselves on false goals and, like Don Quixote, jousting with windmills. Not only with respect to Church politics but also theologically this undertaking has no prospects. The earlier-described tactic of attempting to win official priesthood "piece by piece"[3] ought, therefore, to be abandoned.

The need of the hour is not an "emancipatory war" between the sexes in the Church but rather a *cooperation* between men and women that takes its orientation from the orders of creation and redemption. Here, it is precisely women who have an irreplaceable role to play that is far too neglected in the current social and ecclesiastical situation. By contrast, a "masculinization" (Simone de Beauvoir) or the "androgynous utopia" (feminist theology) are equally but a flight from the feminine, which becomes all the more bizarre the more it is championed by women. The ultimate goal of any debate about priesthood for women should be to bring out the greatness and beauty of the respective callings of men and women in the Church. I hope that I have provided some stimuli to such discussion. General theological reflection must, of course, be carried over into pastoral practice. Determinative for both, in my opinion, are the figures of *Jesus* and *Mary*, in which, respectively, the basic structures of masculine and feminine activity are predelineated. The ultimate purpose of the differentiation of the sexes is to point beyond itself to the relations God-creation and Christ-Church. Now, since Mary is the archetypal

---

[1] Ps 119:36.
[2] Albrecht, *Frau*, p. 7.
[3] Cf. pp. 61–62 above.

481

image of the Church, the "self-understanding of the Church must renew its orientation toward Mary, the Church must find its way back to its Marian character. There can hardly be anything more urgent, to the service of the Church in the world as well, than this."[4]

In reception and cooperation, Mary is the exemplary image of the Christian that cannot be surpassed by any man. Precisely because she is, in this way, "Queen of the Apostles", it would be inappropriate for her to assume the apostles' role of official representation of Christ.

In the figure of Mary, it is quite clearly manifest that the clergy do not constitute the real essence of the Church but only represent Christ's redemptive work within a more comprehensive whole that is Marian in character. An official priest has no claim to a higher kind of Christian being but bears a specific sort of responsibility. This is related to, and supported by, the priesthood of all believers, which is reflected especially clearly in the tasks that fall to women. The revitalization of monastic life, the lay apostolate and, not least, the quite manifold forms of present-day charitable work offer countless, and far from exhausted, opportunities for female commitment, without which the world and the Church would collapse in ruin. Especially in an age marked by the "masculine" belief in the "manipulatability" of all things and a rationalism that is tearing itself away from the roots of life, we are confronted with the great task of discovering once again the value of woman. This is not only to the benefit of women themselves but also in the interest of the health and "wholeness" of the Church and the world. The No to priesthood for women and the Yes to the worth of women are, to a certain extent, two sides of the same coin. What is determinative for men and women in the Church is not the "confusion between what pertains to oneself and to others"[5] but the quest for one's own proper path to sanctity. The official hierarchy ought not to be confused, with respect to bearing the impress of grace, with the "hiearchy before God". It is not the office bearers who are the great figures of the Church, but the saints.[6]

---

[4] Albrecht, *Frau*, p. 37.
[5] Barth, *KD III*, 4, p. 172.
[6] Cf. *Erklärung* no. 6, p. 20; *AAS* 69 (1977): 115.

ABBREVIATIONS

AAS	*Acta Apostolicae Sedis*
Billerbeck	H. L. Strack and Paul Billerbeck. *Kommentar zum Neuen Testament aus Talmud und Mirdrasch I–IV.* Munich, 1922–1928
BK	*Biblischer Kommentar*
BKV	*Bibliothek der Kirchenväter.* Kempten and Munich, 1911–
BWANT	*Beiträge zur Wissenschaft vom Alten und Neuen Testament*
CIC	*Codex Iuris Canonici.* Rome, 1976
CCL	*Corpus Christianorum*, series latina. Turnhout, 1953–
CGG	*Christ in der Gegenwart*
Conc	*Concilium*
CSEL	*Corpus scriptorum ecclesiasticorum latinorum.* Vienna, 1866–
Diss	Dissertation
DS	Henricus Denzinger and Alfonsus Schönmetzer. *Enchiridion Symbolorum, Definitionum et Declarationum de rebus fidei et morum*, 36th ed. Barcelona, Freiburg im Breisgau, and Rome, 1976
EKK	*Evangelisch-katholischer Kommentar zum Neuen Testament*
EvTh	*Evangelische Theologie*
FRLANT	*Forschungen zur Religion und Literatur des Alten und Neuen Testaments*
Fs	Festschrift
HK	Herder correspondence
HThK	*Herders Theologischer Kommentar zum Neuen Testament*

JBL	*Journal of Biblical Literature*
JEcSt	*Journal of Ecumenical Studies*
JNES	*Journal of Near Eastern Studies*
KD	Karl Barth. *Kirchliche Dogmatik*
KBW	*Katholisches Bibelwerk*
KKD	*Kleine Katholische Dogmatik*
LJ	*Liturgisches Jahrbuch*
LThK	*Lexikon für Theologie und Kirche.* Ed. J. Höfer and K. Rahner, 2nd Edition. Freiburg im Breisgau, 1957–
Mansi	J. D. Mansi. *Sacrorum Conciliorum nova et amplissima collectio.* Florence and Venice 1757–
MThZ	*Münchener Theologische Zeitschrift*
MySal	*Mysterium Salutis. Grundriss heilsgeschichtlicher Dogmatik.* Ed. J. Feiner and M. Löhrer. Einsiedeln, Zürich, and Cologne, 1965–
NR	Josef Neuner and Heinrich Roos, *Der Glaube der Kirche in den Urkunden der Lehverkündigung,* 9th edition. Regensburg, 1971
NRTh	*Nouvelle Revue Théologique*
ÖAKR	*Österreichisches Archiv für Kirchenrecht*
par	parallel(s)
PG	*Patrologia Graeca,* ed. J. P. Migne. Paris, 1857–
PL	*Patrologia Latina,* ed. J. P. Migne. Paris, 1844–
PS	*Patrologia Syriaca,* ed. R. Graffin. Paris, 1894–
QD	Quaestiones Disputate
RAC	*Reallexikon für Antike und Christentum.* Ed. T. Klauser. Stuttgart, 1941–
RGG	*Die Religion in Geschichte und Gegenwart. Handwörterbuch für Theologie und Religionswissenschaft.* Ed. K. Galling. Tübingen, 1956–

RNT	*Regensburger Neues Testament*
ScG	Thomas Aquinas. *Summa contra Gentiles*. Rome, 1924
SNSMS	Society for New Testament Studies Monograph Series
SP	*Studia Patristica*
STh	Thomas Aquinas. *Summa Theologica*. Rome, 1925
ThLZ	*Theologische Literaturzeitung*
ThPQ	*Theologisch-praktische Quartalschrift*
ThSt	*Theological Studies*
ThQ	*Theologische Quartalschrift*
ThW	*Theologisches Wörterbuch zum Neuen Testament*. Ed. G. Kittel. Stuttgart, 1933–
TThZ	*Trierer Theologische Zeitschrift*
TU	*Texte und Untersuchungen zur Geschichte der altchristlichen Literatur*
UNT	*Untersuchungen zum Neuen Testament*
US	*Una Sancta*
VELKD	*Vereinigte Evangelisch-Lutherische Kirche in Deutschland*
Vg	Vulgate
WMANT	*Wissenschaftliche Monographien zum Alten und Neuen Testament*
ZkTh	*Zeitschrift für katholische Theologie*
ZNW	*Zeitschrift für die neutestamentliche Wissenschaft*
ZThK	*Zeitschrift für Theologie und Kirche*

INDEX